THE INTER-AMERICAN SYSTEM
OF HUMAN RIGHTS

The Inter-American System of Human Rights

Edited by

DAVID J. HARRIS

and

STEPHEN LIVINGSTONE

CLARENDON PRESS · OXFORD
1998

Oxford University Press, Great Clarendon Street, Oxford OX2 6DP

Oxford   New York
Athens   Auckland   Bangkok   Bogota   Bombay
Buenos Aires   Calcutta   Cape Town   Dar es Salaam
Delhi   Florence   Hong Kong   Istanbul   Karachi
Kuala Lumpur   Madras   Madrid   Melbourne
Mexico City   Nairobi   Paris   Singapore
Taipei   Tokyo   Toronto   Warsaw

and associated companies in
Berlin   Ibadan

Oxford is a trade mark of Oxford University Press

Published in the United States
by Oxford University Press Inc., New York

A catalogue record for this book is available from the British Library

Library of Congress Cataloging in Publication Data
The inter-American system of human rights / [edited by] David J. Harris
and Stephen Livingstone.
p.   cm.
Includes bibliographical references (p. 441)
1. Human rights—America.   I. Harris, D. J. (David John)
II. Livingstone, Stephen, 1961–   ).
KDZ574.I576   1998
341.4´81—dc21   97–45971
ISBN   0–19–826552–2

Typeset by Vera A. Keep, Cheltenham
Printed in Great Britain
on acid-free paper by
Bookcraft Ltd., Midsomer Norton, Somerset

Preface

In the 1970s and 1980s central and latin America was synonymous with some of the world's worst human rights violations. Much of the region was in a state of civil war or under the rule of brutal military dictatorships. Incommunicado detentions, torture and extra judicial killings were frequent. A new phenomenon among human rights violation, the 'disappeared person', emerged in this region in this period. In the past decade, with the transition to democratic rule in much of the region, new challenges have arisen. Peace agreements or transition arrangements have raised the issue of what human rights guarantees are required and how they should be given effect to, the legacy of amnesties for human rights violations have posed the question of what should be done about such violations committed by past regimes and the claims of indigenous peoples have become ever more difficult to ignore.

At the centre of all of these issues has been the inter-American human rights system, represented primarily by the Inter-American Commission and Court of Human Rights. In the first half of the 1980s this system, which was established and funded by the region's states, struggled to fashion a response to the wave of gross human rights violations which swept across the continent. However since the Commission's path breaking country report on Argentina in 1979 and the Court's recognition and condemnation of the phenomenon of disappearances in the *Velasquez Rodriguez* case in 1988 it has played an increasingly prominent role. Rulings on issues such as fundamental guarantees in states of emergency and the validity of amnesty laws passed by previous regimes have set precedents for human rights lawyers throughout the world. The system's innovative mechanisms such as the country report have excited the interest of human rights lawyers well beyond the Americas, as has the rule by which a petitioner's factual assertions are accepted as true in the absence of contradiction by the state.

As human rights lawyers in Europe we are aware of some of these developments but not of their detail. Perhaps too struck by the rapid development of our own regional human rights system in the past twenty years and the lack of material (particularly English language material) on the inter-American system, we felt that lawyers in this part of the world had failed to pay as much attention as they should have to such an important and developing regional system. To this end the Human Rights Law Centre at the University of Nottingham organized a conference on the inter-American system in London in November 1995. The conference was exceptionally well attended. Testimony both to the interest in the topic among human rights lawyers in the UK and to the excellence of our speakers, which included three of the contributors to this book: Antônio Cançado Trindade, Tom Farer and José Miguel Vivanco. One of the things which emerged most clearly from the conference was that the inter-American system had an experience of much more severe human rights violations than that of the European but with Europe now having to confront gross human rights violations, notably in former Yugoslavia and Turkey, the American experience may have increasing resonance.

Encouraged by the interest shown at the London conference we felt there would be interest in a collection of essays analysing the inter-American system. We have been exceedingly fortunate to receive a positive response from many of the leading commentators on the system. Their contributions all display comprehensive detail allied to critical analysis. The story they tell, as to how the system has evolved and how it has responded to particular problems, is not always a positive one but it is one that is full of interest and pointers as to how this most significant of regional systems may continue to develop.

In the preparation of this book we have incurred a number of debts of gratitude. All the contributors produced their essays in excellent time and were very tolerant of our requests and suggestions. First among equals must be Verónica Gómez, who in addition to providing her own chapter, was a mine of information and of helpful contacts both in relation to the London conference and this collection. The financial support of the Human Rights Policy Department of the United Kingdom Foreign and Commonwealth Office made the initial conference possible and Philip Astley the former head of the Department is especially to be thanked for his support of it. Myfanwy Milton and Nancy Higginbotham at OUP were most helpful editor and copy editor respectively. While at Nottingham Jan Goodman and Maureen Welch-Dolynskyj provided sterling assistance both for the conference and book parts of this enterprise.

DAVID HARRIS
STEPHEN LIVINGSTONE

Table of Contents

List of Contributors

Lisa L. Bhansali is a consultant on justice sector reform projects with the Inter-American Development Bank, and with the Open Society Institute

Christina M. Cerna is Senior Specialist in Human Rights at the Inter-American Commission on Human Rights of the Organization of American States

Matthew Craven is Senior Lecturer in Law at the School of Oriental and African Studies, University of London

Scott Davidson is Associate Professor of Law in the Faculty of Law, University of Canterbury, New Zealand

Tom Farer is Dean of the Graduate School of International Studies, University of Denver, and past President of the Inter-American Commission on Human Rights (1976–83)

Joan Fitzpatrick is Professor of Law and Foundation Scholar, University of Washington

Verónica Gómez is a Research Student at the University of Nottingham

Hurst Hannum is Professor of International Law, The Fletcher School of Law and Diplomacy, Tufts University

David Harris is Professor of Public International Law at the University of Nottingham

Ellen Lutz is a Research Fellow at the Fletcher School of Law and Diplomacy, and teaches International Human Rights Law at Tufts University

Cecelia Medina is Professor of International Public Law and International Human Rights Law at the University of Diego Potales, Santiago, Chile, a member of the United Nations Human Rights Committee and is currently Robert F. Kennedy Visiting Professor at Harvard Law School

Dinah Shelton is Professor of Law, Notre Dame Law School

Antônio Augusto Cançado Trindade is Judge and Vice President of the Inter-American Court of Human Rights and Professor of International Law at the University of Brasilia and at the Rio-Branco Institute

José Miguel Vivanco is the Executive Director of Human Rights Watch/Americas

Table of International Instruments

AMERICAN CONVENTION ON HUMAN RIGHTS

Article

VIENNA CONVENTION ON THE LAW OF TREATIES

Article

INTERNATIONAL COVENANT ON CIVIL AND POLITICAL RIGHTS

Article

EUROPEAN CONVENTION ON HUMAN RIGHTS

Article

Table of Cases

Provisional Measures

Advisory Opinions

EUROPEAN COURT OF HUMAN RIGHTS

Note on Abbreviations

IACHR Annual Report   Annual Report of the Inter-American Commission on Human Rights
I/A Court H.R.   Inter-American Court of Human Rights
I/A Court H.R. Annual Report   Annual Report of the Inter-American Court of Human Rights
HRLJ   Human Rights Law Journal
IHRR   International Human Rights Reports
Eur. Ct. H.R.   European Court of Human Rights

At Appendix IX of this book we give a full list of Annual and Country Reports of the Inter-American Commission of Human Rights up to 1 August 1997. All of these documents can be found in documents published by the OAS with the citation OEA Ser/L. . . . The citation starts with the abbreviation of the OAS in Spanish (Organizacion de los Estados Americanos) followed by L, which indicates legal series, followed by roman numerals V/II (for Commission documents) or V/III (for Court documents) and then the document number. Hence the 1991 Commission Annual Report is OEA/L/V/II.81, doc 6 rev 1 (1992) and the 1996 Court Annual Report is OEA/Ser.L/V/III.35 (1997).

The decisions of the Court are published by the Secretariat of the Court in its official series with Series A referring to Advisory Opinions, Series B to principal documents of advisory opinions, Series C to decisions and judgments in contentious cases and series D to principal documents of these decisions. A full list of these decisions to 1 August 1997 is also given at Appendix IX of this book.

1

Regional Protection of Human Rights: The Inter-American Achievement

DAVID HARRIS[1]

The substantive guarantee of the inter-American system for the protection of human rights is found in the American Declaration of the Rights and Duties of Man 1948[2] and the American Convention on Human Rights 1969.[3] The supervisory institutions are the Inter-American Commission on Human Rights and the American Court of Human Rights. The system is a creature of the OAS, whose 1948 Statute contains references to human rights and whose political organs play a part in the operation of the system.

The inter-American system differs in many ways from the other well established regional system for the protection of human rights, namely that under the European Convention on Human Rights, and it may serve to highlight some of the key characteristics of the inter-American system by identifying the differences at the outset. The inter-American system is more complex than that of the European Convention in that it is based upon two overlapping instruments, namely the American Declaration on the Rights and Duties of Man and the American Convention, with the jurisdiction of the Inter-American Commission on Human Rights over states depending upon whether they are parties to the Convention or not and the Court having jurisdiction in contentious cases only over Convention parties.[4] It also has

---

[1] I would like to thank Veronica Gomez, a research student in the Department of Law, University of Nottingham, for reading this Chapter in draft form. Her comments on the draft and our many conversations on the inter-American system have been invaluable.

[2] For the text, see Appendix II.

[3] For the text, see Appendix III. See also the Additional Protocol to the Convention on Economic, Social and Cultural Rights 1988 (the San Salvador Protocol), OASTS 69, and the Protocol to the Convention to Abolish the Death Penalty 1990, OASTS 73: texts in Appendix III. Other human rights treaties in the inter-American system are the Inter-American Convention to Prevent and Punish Torture 1985, OASTS 67; the Inter-American Convention on Forced Disappearance of Persons 1994, 3 IHRR 226 (1996); the Inter-American Convention on the Prevention, Punishment and Eradication of Violence against Women 1994, 3 IHRR 232 (1996). For status information on the Convention and these other treaties, see Appendix VIII, below. On the draft Declaration on the Rights of Indigenous Peoples, see Hannum, 334, below.

[4] Whereas there is a political obligation of Council of Europe membership to ratify the European Convention upon becoming a Council member, there is no such obligation within the OAS and ten of its 35 member states are not American Convention parties: see p. 6, below.

more than one dimension in that the Inter-American Commission not only hears petitions but also conducts *in loco* visits, leading to the adoption of country reports on the human rights situation in OAS member states.[5] This second, very important dimension to the Inter-American Commission's work has no counterpart in the European system.

Another crucial difference is the political context within which the two systems operate. Whereas the European system has during its forty year history generally regulated democracies with independent judiciaries and governments that observe the rule of law,[6] the history of much of the Americas since 1960 has been radically different,[7] with military dictatorships, the violent repression of political opposition and of terrorism and intimidated judiciaries for a while being the order of the day in a number of countries. The result is that human rights issues in the Americas have often concerned gross, as opposed to ordinary, violations of human rights. They have been much more to do with the forced disappearance, killing, torture and arbitrary detention of political opponents and terrorists than with particular issues concerning, for example, the right to a fair trial or freedom of expression that are the stock in trade of the European Commission and Court.[8] This difference is apparent both in the country reports of the Inter-American Commission and in its decisions on individual petitions. A remarkable feature of the Commission's annual reports has been the long sequences of cases of forced disappearances on the street and extra-judicial killings by state agents in which the Commission, in the absence of any government response, finds a breach of the right to life on the basis of the petitioner's credible allegations.[9]

Other less dramatic differences between the two systems are that the right of individual petition in the inter-American system is compulsory upon ratification of the American Convention, whereas this will only be achieved in Europe when Protocol 11 to the European Convention enters into force;[10] and that, in contrast with Europe, the right of states to bring petitions against other

---

[5] On this aspect of the Commission's work, see Medina, Chap. 4, below. The Commission also has a role in the development of human rights standards.

[6] The only ECHR findings of torture or arbitrary killings are the *Greek Case*, 12 Y.B.E.C.H.R. 1 (1970); *McCann et al.* v. *UK.*, 21 E.H.R.R. 97 (1996) and recent Turkish cases, e.g. *Aksoy* v. *Turkey*, 23 E.H.R.R. 553 (1997).

[7] See the graphic account by Farer, Chap. 2, below.

[8] To put the matter in context it should be noted that increasingly there are ordinary human rights cases being decided by the Inter-American Commission. See, for example, Report 24/92, Cases 9884 et al (Argentina), IACHR Annual Report 1992–3, 74 (right of criminal appeal) and Report 12/96, Case 11.245 (Argentina), IACHR Annual Report 1995, 33 (detention on remand). The *Baby Boy* and *Juvenile Death Penalty* cases are other well known earlier examples: see Davidson, 216 and 223, below.

[9] See, e.g., the many cases concerning Guatemala and Peru in IACHR Annual Report 1990–1, 105ff.

[10] This will be in 1998. Note also that, whereas petitions may only be brought under the ECHR by the victim, in the inter-American system they may be brought by any individual: see Cerna, 78, below.

states has not been used within the inter-American system, where the tradition of non-intervention is particularly strong and the Inter-American Commission has a power to make country reports.[11]

As to the enforcing bodies within the two systems, both the Inter-American and the European Commission and Court are at present part-time bodies, but the new European Court of Human Rights, which will come into being under Protocol 11, will be a permanent, full-time body. The bodies are noticeably different in size, with the Inter-American Commission and Court having only seven members each, whereas the European Commission and Court both have over thirty.[12] Another difference in practice is the less frequent use in the inter-American system of the friendly settlement procedure, which results partly from the fact that gross human right violations do not lend themselves easily to mediation or conciliation. There are also less favourable arrangements than those in Europe for the representation of the petitioner before the Inter-American Court[13] and the absence of any power on the petitioner's part to seize the Court. Each of these last two differences may, like some others, be in part a consequence of the different temporal stages in the history of the inter-American and European systems, with the European Court being two decades or so ahead.

A final difference exists at the stage of enforcing final decisions and judgments. The inter-American system provides no counterpart to the supervisory role of the Committee of Ministers of the Council of Europe.[14] Related to this is the fact that the outcome of proceedings in the inter-American system is not necessarily a legally binding decision.[15] The judgments of the Inter-American Court are legally binding upon the parties.[16] But very few cases as yet go on to the Court, and the conclusions and recommendations of the Commission, which are the end result in the great majority of cases that are completed on the merits, are not legally binding.[17] Although there would not appear to have been any comprehensive study of the

[11] On this and the other points concerning the Commission in this paragraph, see Cerna, Chap. 3, below.

[12] The number depends on the number of European Convention parties and of Council of Europe members. The European bodies often sit in smaller chambers, but the ECHR arrangements result in a larger pool of manpower and local knowledge. Provision is made in both Courts for an ad hoc judge where a state party to a case lacks a national judge.

[13] The 'victim' has standing only at the reparations stage of a case under Art. 23, Rules of the Court, as revised with effect from 1997.

[14] See Gomez, 191, below.

[15] All European Convention cases result in Court judgments or decisions of the Committee of Ministers that are legally binding. Under Protocol 11, all cases will result in binding Court judgments.

[16] Art. 68, Convention.

[17] In the *Cabellero Delgado and Santana* case, I/A Court H.R. (1995), para. 67 (1996), 17 *HRLJ* 24, 3 IHRR 548 (1996) the Court stated that the Commission's recommendations in Art. 50 and 51 reports were, in accordance with the ordinary meaning of the term, not binding, and it can be supposed that the same is true of the Commission's conclusions

record of states in responding to the recommendations of the Commission, such indications as there are suggest that they have not been followed in the many cases of gross violations by military regimes.

One further introductory comment that may be made about the inter-American system is that it applies to the whole of a region that has a certain dislocation within it, between the United States and Canada and the rest. As one reads the annual reports of the Commission and the judgments of the Court, one has the sense that the system is essentially a Latin American one, with the United States and, more recently, Canada making an occasional appearance.[18]

THE AMERICAN DECLARATION OF THE RIGHTS AND DUTIES OF MAN

The American Declaration of the Rights and Duties of Man shares a common background with the Universal Declaration of Human Rights, which it pre-dates by some months. Both instruments were a response to the events of the Second World War and give meaning to the references to human rights in the constitutional instruments of the international organisations concerned, namely the OAS and the UN. The two instruments are comparable also in containing extensive guarantees of both civil and political rights and economic, social and cultural rights.

Like the Universal Declaration, the American Declaration was not intended to be legally binding. Although it still does not have direct legal effect, the Declaration has come to be indirectly legally binding by virtue of the human rights obligations in the OAS Charter[19], which incorporate the substance of the American Declaration.[20]

The human rights obligations in the OAS Charter, which is a treaty, derive

in its reports under those articles as to whether a breach has occurred. For a different view as to Art. 51 recommendations, see Cerna, 105, below, and Vivanco and Bhansali, 433, below. The Commission's decisions under the American Declaration procedure are also not legally binding.

[18] A small number of individual petitions have been brought under the Declaration against the US and, in a few cases, Canada (neither are bound by the Convention) and the Commission has made *in loco* visits to the US: see n. 105, below, and Cerna 88, below (individual petition case). But otherwise, outside of the political organs, and despite the active participation of US nationals on the Commission and the Court, the impression is very much one of Latin American concerns and priorities. The English speaking states of the Carribbean also do not seem fully integrated within the system, although there have been a significant number of death row and other petitions coming from them and their nationals have been Commission and Court members.

[19] Another possibility would be that it has come to state rules of regional customary international law in the way that, to some extent, the Universal Declaration has at the universal level, but this would not appear to have happened.

[20] See Craven, below, 291.

from Articles 3 and 16 of the Charter.[21] Article 3 states, somewhat awk-wardly: 'The American states reaffirm the following principles: . . . (l) The American states proclaim the fundamental rights of the individual without distinction as to race, nationality, creed or sex'. This reads more like a statement of principle in the light of which other Charter provisions might be interpreted, than as a provision that itself imposes a binding legal obligation concerning human rights. More concretely, Article 17 provides:

Each State has the right to develop its cultural, political and economic life freely and naturally. In this free development, the State shall respect the rights of the individual and the principles of universal morality.

Although the wording here, with the obligation being tucked away at the end, is also not what one might expect in a text intended to do something as important as impose a legal obligation concerning human rights, it can certainly be understood as setting a legal limit to state sovereignty.

As to the human rights or 'rights of the individual' referred to in the Charter text, in Advisory Opinion No 10,[22] the Inter-American Court of Human Rights stated that 'the Declaration is the text that defines the human rights referred to in Charter.' In reaching this conclusion, the Court relied primarily upon an amendment to the OAS Charter, which resulted in its present Article 106, and on the revised Statute of the Commission. The new Article 106[23] established the Inter-American Commission on Human Rights as a principal organ of the OAS whose 'principal function is to promote the observance and protection of human rights . . .' Article 1 (2) of the revised Statute of the Commission[24] provided that for the purpose of the present Statute, 'human rights are to be understood to be: a) the rights set forth in the American Convention on Human Rights, in relation to the States Parties thereto, b) the rights set forth in the American Declaration of the Rights and Duties of Man, in relation to the other member states.' In the Court's view, it followed from these and other OAS texts[25] that 'by means of an authoritative interpretation, the member states of the Organization have

---

[21] Other texts that mention human rights are the preamble, para. 4, and Arts. 45, 49, and 145 of the Charter, as amended. None of these add to the argument in favour of binding legal obligations. The preamble is only a preamble and Arts. 45 and 49 require states to 'dedicate' or 'exert' their 'effort' to further human rights. Art. 145 simply refers to the Commission's mandate to promote 'human rights'.

[22] I/A Court H.R. Series A No.10, para. 45 (1989), 11 *HRLJ* 118.

[23] The new text results from an amendment made by the 1967 Protocol of Buenos Aires. For the Commission's constitutional standing before that, see, 66, below.

[24] The 1979 revision was needed because the original Statute had to be amended to take into account the entry into force of the American Convention on Human Rights in that year. The amendment to the Statute was approved by the OAS member states in the General Assembly.

[25] See especially the General Assembly resolutions cited by the Court, Advisory Opinion No. 10, I/A Court H.R. Series A No. 10, para. 42 (1989).

signaled their agreement that the Declaration contains and defines the fundamental rights referred to in the Charter.'[26]

The above interpretation is followed by the Commission, which is the body seized with the task of monitoring compliance with the human rights obligations in the Charter. In that capacity, it applies the rights in the Declaration as an indirectly binding legal text.[27] The Court can also be understood as taking the view that the Declaration is legally binding in this indirect way, although its language in the relevant advisory opinion is equivocal.[28] However, not all states share this opinion. The United States argues that, although the Commission has jurisdiction under the Charter to monitor US compliance with the Declaration, the obligations being monitored are not legal ones.[29]

The question of the legal effect of the Declaration is important for the reason that, although the intention was that all OAS member states[30] would ratify the Convention, they have not yet done so. Ten are missing, namely, the United States, Canada, Cuba and a number of English speaking states from the Caribbean and the surrounding area.[31] For the missing states, the only general[32] regional human rights obligations of a legal kind that exist are those that emanate from the American Declaration, through the medium of the OAS Charter.

It may be argued that the American Declaration remains an important source of obligations for parties to the Convention also. The point here is that the Declaration protects rights that are not found in the Convention. To

---

[26] Id., para. 43. Cf Advisory Opinion No. 5, I/A Court H.R. Series A No. 5, para. 44 (1985), 7 *HRLJ* 74

[27] See *Roach and Pinkerton* cases (the *Juvenile Death Penalty* cases): Resolution 3/87, Case 9647 (United States), IACHR Annual Report 1986–7, 147, at 165, 8 *HRLJ* 345. There the Commission stated: 'As a consequence of Articles 3j, 16, 51e, 112 and 150 of the Charter, the provisions of other instruments of the OAS on human rights (identified as the Declaration and the Commission's Statute and Regulations) acquired binding force.' Cf. the *Baby Boy* case: Resolution 23/81, Case 2141 (United States), IACHR Annual Report 1980–1, 25, 38, 2 *HRLJ* 110. Whereas Art. 20, Commission Statute empowers the Commission, when considering petitions, to 'pay particular attention to the observance of the rights referred to in Articles I, II, III, IV, XVIII, XXV, and XXVI of the Declaration', the Commission understands that this does not exclude it from considering breaches of other Declaration rights: see Craven, 295, below.

[28] Advisory Opinion No. 13, I/A Court H.R. Series A No. 13, paras. 42, 45 (1993), 14 *HRLJ* 252. The Court cites OAS General Assembly resolutions that refer to the Declaration as a 'source of "international obligations" ', without adding the word 'legal'.

[29] See the US argument in *Roach and Pinkerton*, loc. cit. at n. 27 above, 259. A wide range of views on this issue were expressed by states in the pleadings leading to Advisory Opinion No. 13, loc. cit.. in the preceding note.

[30] The 35 member states are the 25 Convention parties listed in Appendix VIII and the 10 non-parties listed on this page.

[31] These are, Antigua and Barbuda, the Bahamas, Belize, Guyana, St Kitts and Nevis, St Lucia and St Vincent and the Grenadines.

[32] Apart from the Declaration and the Convention, there are the specific OAS human rights treaties listed in n. 3 above. The UN Covenants and other UN human rights treaties may apply.

the extent that this is so, the Declaration may be seen as imposing, through the Charter, additional legal obligations upon parties to the American Convention. This is particularly significant in respect of economic, social and cultural rights.[33] The Declaration contains a long list of such rights,[34] as well as of civil and political rights, and does not in any way differentiate between the two groupings of rights. In contrast, the Convention protects only civil and political rights fully, with just a very generally worded obligation, in a single article, to 'adopt measures . . . with a view to achieving progressively . . . the full realization of the rights implicit in the economic, social, education, scientific, and cultural standards set forth in' the OAS Charter.[35] The question is whether the Convention totally replaces the obligations that Convention parties have under the Declaration and the Charter in respect of rights that are not protected in the Convention, thereby, surprisingly, releasing them from the obligations in respect of economic, social and cultural rights that they previously had.

The process of supplementing a non-binding declaration by a binding treaty on the same subject is a familiar one in international human rights law. The inter-American situation is more complicated in that it is also a matter of superimposing the treaty obligations in the Convention upon those concerning human rights in the OAS Charter. It is submitted that the Charter human rights obligations, which incorporate the substance of the Declaration, continue to apply fully to Convention parties. There are several reasons for considering that the two sets of treaty obligations co-exist: neither the coverage of the human rights obligations nor, as yet, the con–tracting parties are the same, and, as a constitutional instrument of an international organisation, the Charter is of a different order from the Convention. This view is supported by Article 29(d) of the Convention, which states that no provision in the Convention shall be interpreted as 'excluding or limiting the effect that the American Declaration . . . may have.' One of these effects is to give meaning to the term 'human rights' in the OAS Charter, which remains binding upon all OAS member states. In Advisory Opinion No 10, the Court stated:[36]

---

[33] See Craven, 306, below.

[34] It lists the rights to health, education, the benefits of culture, work and fair remunera-tion, rest and leisure, social security, and property as well as the hybrid rights of association, the family, and mothers and children.

[35] Art. 26, Convention. See Craven, 298, below.

[36] I/A Court H.R. Series A No. 10, para. 46 (1989), 11 *HRLJ* 118. Art. 29(b), Conven-tion may also be relied upon. In Advisory Opinion No 5, I/A Court H.R. Series A No. 5, para. 52 (1985), 7 *HRLJ* 74, the Court concluded that Art. 29(b) meant that, as a matter of interpretation of the Convention, 'if in the same situation both the American Conven-tion and another international treaty are applicable, the rule most favourable to the individual must prevail.' The OAS Charter, with its Declaration based human rights obli-gations, would qualify as 'another international treaty' for this purpose.

For the states parties to the Convention, the specific source of their obligations with respect to the protection of human rights is, in principle, the Convention itself. It must be remembered, however, that, given the provisions of Article 29 (d), these states cannot escape the obligations under the Declaration, notwithstanding the fact that the Convention is the governing instrument for the states parties thereto.

However, there remains the problem of the competence of the Commission, which is governed by the terms of its revised Statute, to monitor compliance with the Declaration. Article 1(2) of the revised Statute, which is quoted above and which is state practice (having been approved by members states in the OAS General Assembly[37]), is clear enough: the Commission applies the Convention to its contracting parties and the American Declaration to non-Convention party states. The Commission has acted on this basis in its practice. For example, in Cases 9777 and 9718 (Argentina),[38] the Commission ruled that the guarantee of the right to work in the American Declaration could not be applied as against Argentina, which was a Convention party, because the Convention did not incorporate the rights in the Declaration and because the Commission's Statute, Article 19, only authorised it to apply the Convention *vis à vis* Convention parties. The first of these arguments ignores the more obvious consequence of Article 29, Convention. As to the second argument, Article 29 and the object and purpose of the Convention, which is to protect human rights, may also be called in aid. The 1979 amendment to the Commission's Statute (see above) was not concerned with the position of Convention parties; instead it was intended to ensure that the Commission retained its monitoring powers over non-Convention parties once the Convention had entered into force.[39] It cannot have been the intention that, by a sidewind, Convention parties should have their human rights treaty obligations under the Charter reduced and the Commission should lose its powers to monitor compliance with them.

A separate question concerning the Declaration is the extent of the human rights commitments that it contains. The Declaration is very generally phrased and limitations have to be implied. Thus it cannot have been intended that the statement of the 'right to life' (no further definition in Article 1) was an absolute one; there must, for example, be the limitation that is usually found in national and international human rights law that permits the taking of life in self defence.[40] There is also no derogation clause

---

[37] Art. 39, Convention provides that the Commission prepares its Statute, which it submits to the Assembly for approval.

[38] Report on Cases 9777 and 9718 (Argentina), IACHR Annual Report 1987–8, 31, at 75. See also Resolution 74/90, Case 9850 (Argentina), IACHR Annual Report 1990–1, 41, at 71, where the Commission applied the Declaration to the facts of the case, which concerned civil rights, for the period before Argentina became a Convention party, and the Convention for the period thereafter.   [39] See Farer, 41, below.

[40] Articles 28–38 provide a basis for such limitations. For limitations in the case of abortion, see the *Baby Boy* case, discussed by Davidson, 216, below.

under the Declaration or the OAS Charter for situations of public emergency, which, again, national and international human rights law guarantees generally contain,[41] and no power to make reservations (but some treaties lack this also).[42] With regard to the economic, social and cultural rights that are guaranteed in the Declaration, the difficulty is that the obligations that states are prepared to accept in respect of them are commonly couched in terms of 'progressive' implementation only and made subject to 'available resources.'[43] To the extent that this is the case, they may not be very meaningfully enforced by petition under the Declaration. Whether such limitations concerning economic, social and cultural rights are to be read the American Declaration has not been determined by the Commission or the Court.

THE AMERICAN CONVENTION ON HUMAN RIGHTS

Interpretation of the Convention

The American Convention on Human Rights is a treaty and must be interpreted by reference to the rules of international law on treaty interpretation, which are found in the Vienna Convention on the Law of Treaties 1969.[44] The Convention must as a result be interpreted 'in good faith in accordance with the ordinary meaning to be given to the terms of the treaty in their context and in the light of its object and purpose' (Article 31, Vienna Convention). Where the authentic language texts disagree, the interpretation that is most consistent with the object and purpose of the Convention must be followed (Article 33(4), Vienna Convention).[45] The 'object and

[41] The Inter-American Commission has applied Art. 27, Convention on derogations in emergencies to non-Convention parties under the Declaration, although there is no mechanism for giving notice: see J. Oráa, *Human Rights in States of Emergency in International Law* (Oxford, 1992) 26.

[42] In the *Baby Boy* case, the Commission noted that the US, which would have made a reservation concerning abortion had it ratified the Convention, was not able to do so under the Declaration.

[43] See, e.g., Art. 2(1), International Covenant on Economic, Social and Cultural Rights.

[44] See Advisory Opinion No. 2, I/A Court H.R. Series A No. 2, para. 19 (1982), 3 *HRLJ* 353 and Resolution 16/88, Case 10.109 (Argentina), IACHR Annual Report 1987–8, 102, at 108. The Vienna Convention also applies to the OAS Charter, which incorporates the terms of the American Declaration.

[45] *Neira Alegría* case, Court Order, I/A Court H.R. Annual Report 1992, 62, 13 *HRLJ* 407. There is no provision in the Convention identifying its authentic language texts and the *travaux préparatoires* do not help. However, the OAS has four official languages— Spanish, English, Portuguese and French—and the texts in these languages can be taken as authentic. The text was drafted in Spanish. The English and Portuguese texts are translations of the Spanish; the French text is a translation of the English. In practice, the Court uses the Spanish and English texts. It relies on the Spanish text in a case of doubt. The author thanks Dinah Shelton for this information.

purpose' of the Convention has been identified as being to protect human rights.[46] Accordingly, in a case of ambiguity or uncertainty as to the meaning of the Convention, the interpretation must be adopted that best protects human rights, within the limits of the clear meaning of its text. As a general guide to interpretation, the Inter-American Court has also made use of the paragraph in the Convention preamble by which the signatory states reaffirm 'their intention to consolidate in this hemisphere, within the framework of democratic institutions, a system of personal liberty and social justice based on respect for the essential rights of man.'[47] Recourse may be had to the *travaux préparatoires* in order to resolve any ambiguity or to confirm the meaning of the text (Article 32, Vienna Convention).[48]

The Commission and the Court have developed a number of principles and rules that they use when interpreting the Convention. When applying a non-absolute guarantee, the Court has had recourse to the principle of proportionality. In Advisory Opinion No 5, when interpreting the formula in Article 13(3) by which a restriction on freedom of expression is permissible as being 'necessary' for certain public interest purposes (protection of morals, etc), the Court stated that 'the restriction must be proportionate and closely tailored to the accomplishment of the legitimate governmental objective necessitating it.'[49] In a different factual context, in the *Neira Alegría* Case,[50] when considering whether the taking of life by blowing up a prison building where rioting prisoners were detained was 'arbitrary' in the sense of Article 4, Convention, the Court held that it was, being a 'disproportionate' use of force. Elsewhere, the Commission has stated that limitations upon rights must be interpreted restrictively.[51]

Interestingly, when spelling out its proportionality test in Advisory Opinion No 5, the Court did not introduce the 'margin of appreciation' concept that is a well recognised doctrine in the interpretation of the European Convention on Human Rights.[52] In accordance with that doctrine, a state is

---

[46] See, e.g., Advisory Opinion No. 2, I/A Court H.R. Series A No. 2, para. 29 (1982), 3 *HRLJ* 353 and Report 5/96, Case 10.970 (Peru), IACHR Annual Report 1995, 157, at 173.

[47] Advisory Opinion No. 5, I/A Court H.R. Series A No.5, para. 41 (1985), 7 *HRLJ* 74.

[48] Art. 32, Vienna Convention on the Law of Treaties. See the *Baby Boy* case, Resolution 23/81, Case 2141 (US), IACHR Annual Report 1980–1, 41, 2 *HRLJ* 110, and the *Neira Alegría* case, I/A Court Annual Report 1992, 62, 13 *HRLJ* 407.

[49] I/A Court H.R. Series A No.5, para. 46 (1985), 7 *HRLJ* 74.

[50] I/A Court H.R. Series C No. 20, para. 76, 16 *HRLJ* 403; 3 IHRR 362 (1996).

[51] Report 5/96, Case 10.970 (Peru), IACHR Annual Report 1995, 157, at 170.

[52] See D. Harris, M. O'Boyle and C. Warbrick, *The Law of the European Convention on Human Rights* (London, 1995) 12. No margin of appreciation doctrine is applied under the International Covenant on Civil and Political Rights either, largely for fear of state abuse. In Advisory Opinion No 5, I/A Court H.R. Series A No.5, para. 60 (1986), 7 *HRLJ* 74, and in the Commission report on the *Schmidt* case, Resolution 17/84, Case 9178 (Costa Rica), IACHR Annual Report 1984/5, 51, at 66, 6 *HRLJ* 211 on the same facts, both the Court and the Commission noted that a number of American states had licensing laws comparable to that in question. In such a situation, the Strasbourg institutions will sometimes apply a margin of appreciation in favour of the state concerned.

allowed a certain measure of discretion when it takes legislative, judicial and executive action in the area of a Convention right.[53]

The Inter-American Court does adopt a similar approach to the European Court in that it recognises that the American Convention is not a treaty that establishes bilateral relations between states in the way that, for example, a treaty of friendship does. Instead the contracting parties have agreed to establish an objective legal regime for the protection of human rights, with the ramifications that this entails for its interpretation.[54]

Another principle of interpretation that has been established is that the terms in the Convention do not refer back to national law but have their own autonomous Convention meaning. Most significantly, the term 'law' has been interpreted in this way.[55] In interpreting the term 'compensation' in Article 63(1), Convention, the Court gave it the meaning that it has in public international law, which excluded the possibility of punitive damages in a common law sense, which had been argued for.[56]

There have been few signs that the Commission or the Court are overtly following national law standards common to the Americas.[57] To the contrary, it is noticeable that the Court has stated that a 'certain tendency to integrate the regional and universal system for the protection of human rights can be perceived in the Convention'.[58] In accordance with such an approach, both the Court and the Commission have referred to, and generally followed, the jurisprudence of the European Court and Commission of Human Rights where appropriate.[59]

---

[53] The doctrine is not used in the European system in a context such as that of the *Neira Alegría* case concerning the right to life: see *McCann* v *UK*, E.Ct.H.R. Rep. A 324 (1995).

[54] Advisory Opinion No. 2, I/A Court H.R. Series A No. 2, para. 29 (1982), 3 *HRLJ* 153.

[55] Advisory Opinion No. 6, I/A Court H.R. Series A No.6, para. 20 (1986), 7 *HRLJ* 231. The Convention meaning may, however, vary from one article to another: ibid., and Advisory Opinion No. 7, I/A Court H.R. Series A No.7, para. 27 (1986), 7 *HRLJ* 238. The term 'recourse' in Art. 25 also has an autonomous meaning: Report 5/96, Case 10.970/96 (Peru), IACHR Annual Report 1995, 157, at 191.

[56] *Velasquez* case, Compensatory Damages, I/A Court H.R. Series C No..7, para. 38 (1989), 11 *HRLJ* 127.

[57] The Commission has referred to a norm prohibiting the execution of children that is 'accepted by all the states of the inter-American system': *Roach and Pinkerton*, Resolution 3/87, Case 9647 (United States), IACHR Annual Report 1986–7, 147, at 170, 8 *HRLJ* 345. It has also referred to 'hemispheric discourse' and 'continental solidarity' concerning political rights: Resolution 1/90, Cases 9768 et al (Mexico), IACHR Annual Report 1989–90, 98, at 107, 108. The Court has applied the 'principle of legality' as a principle found in almost all of American constitutions (and elsewhere in the democratic world): Advisory Opinion No. 6, I/A Court H.R. Series A No. 6, para. 23 (1986), 7 *HRLJ* 231.

[58] Advisory Opinion No 1, I/A Court H.R. Series A No. 1, para. 41 (1982), 3 *HRLJ* 140. The Court referred to Art. 29, Convention in particular.

[59] See, e.g., *Velasquez* case, Interpretation, I/A Court H.R. Series C No. 9, para. 26 (1990), 12 *HRLJ* 14, and Report 1/96. Case 10.970 (Peru), IACHR Annual Report 1995, 157, at 188. The Commission also refers to the text of the International Covenant on Civil and Political Rights, upon which much of the Convention text is based: see, e.g., Resolution 12/85, Case 7615 (Brazil), IACHR Annual Report 1984–5, 24, at 31.

This contrasts with the approach of the European Commission and Court which tend to set their standards quite openly by reference to the law in the great majority of European states.[60] Moreover, on matters touching upon public morality (for example, obscenity, blasphemy), where values vary from one European state or group of European states to another, the tendency of the European Court has been to permit particular states a measure of discretion through the use of the 'margin of appreciation' doctrine. The European system has also had to accommodate the differences between common and civil law judicial systems, generally allowing each to operate in their own ways provided that justice can be seen to be done overall.[61]

Given that most of the cases that reach the Inter-American Commission and Court involve gross violations of basic human rights upon which all legal systems and societies would agree, there has yet been little occasion for the application of specifically American standards or for cultural relativism otherwise to become an issue. Nor has the question whether a change in social values has been sufficiently generally acknowledged throughout the region for the Commission or the Court, applying a dynamic approach to interpretation, to recognise a new social standard arisen in practice.[62] It may be anticipated that, as the American system evolves, with the number and percentage of ordinary, as opposed to gross, human rights violations increasing, these kinds of issues will arise for the Inter-American Commission and Court. Certainly, there are varying conceptions of morality and honour and kinds of legal systems in different parts of South and North America.

The Commission and the Court have adopted the 'fourth instance' rule, by which they do not act as a court of appeal from national courts on the interpretation and application of national law. Instead, the function of the Commission and the Court is to look for breaches of the Convention, either of the right to a fair trial in the way that the national court has functioned or of other Convention rights in the decision that the national court has taken.[63]

---

[60] D. Harris, M. O'Boyle and C. Warbrick, *The Law of the European Convention on Human Rights* (London, 1995), 9.

[61] Generally, i.e., not in the particular context of the administration of justice, the Inter-American Court has recognised the need to take account of the civil or common law traditions of states: Advisory Opinion No. 6, I/A Court H.R. Series A No. 6, para. 20 (1986), 7 *HRLJ* 231.

[62] The European Court has had to tackle this question in connection, for example, with homosexuality and transsexualism: see D. Harris, M. O'Boyle and C. Warbrick, *The Law of the European Convention on Human Rights* (London, 1995), Chap. 9. The Commission has referred to 'modern procedural law', Report 27/92, Case 10.957 (Mexico), IACHR Annual Report 1992–3, 108, and the 'modern doctrine' on the rights of the accused, Report 1/96, Case 10.559 (Peru), IACHR Annual Report 1995, 196, but not so as to indicate the application of a dynamic approach.

[63] Resolution 29/88, Case 9260 (Jamaica), IACHR Annual Report 1987–8, 154, at 161. See also the *Marzioni* case, discussed by Vivanco and Bhansali, 430, below.

Although there is no rule of binding precedent, both the Commission and the Court refer to and generally follow their own earlier decisions.[64] The Commission follows the jurisprudence of the Court, both on the interpretation of the Convention[65] and on its enforcement machinery.[66]

The Rights Protected

The Convention contains a full and detailed guarantee of civil and political rights. While the American Convention has its own very distinctive character, it echoes in some respects the terms of the substantive guarantee of the International Covenant on Civil and Political Rights 1966, which had been adopted three years earlier. But the American Convention differs from the Covenant in some particulars. For example, it contains guarantees of the rights to reply (Article 14) and to property (Article 21), which the Covenant lacks. The American Convention guarantee is also, in these and in other respects, more elaborate and advanced, at least in its text,[67] than the 1950 European Convention on Human Rights and its Protocols. For example, it contains a fuller guarantee of the right to participate in government (Article 23) and a guarantee of the right to equal protection (Article 24). Much, of course, turns on interpretation and the meaning of many of the provisions of the American Convention has still be be established by the Commission and the Court.

The Basic Obligations accepted by Contracting Parties

The basic or 'general'[68] obligations of contracting parties to the Convention are set out in Articles 1 and 2. These provisions are to be read in conjunction with the later guarantees of particular rights.[69] Article 1 (1) reads:

[64] See, e.g., Report No. 27/92, Case 10.957 (Mexico), IACHR Annual Report 1992–3, 108 and the *Neira Alegría* case, I/A Court H.R. Series C No. 20, paras 82–84 (1995), 16 *HRLJ* 403; 3 IHRR 362 (1996).

[65] E.g., the Commission refers often to the Court's pronouncements in the *Velasquez* case on the duty to prevent, investigate and punish breaches of the the right to life: see, e.g., Report No. 28/92, Cases 10.147 et al (Argentina), IACHR Annual Report 1992–3, 49, 13 *HRLJ* 336.

[66] See, e.g., Report No 19/92, Case 10.865 (US), IACHR Annual Report 1992–3, 142, at 151 (following the Court's view of domestic remedies). See, however, Cerna, 105, below, who argues that it is for the Commission, not the Court, to rule on the competence of the Commission.

[67] The European Convention guarantee has been developed by interpretation. For an early, textual comparison between the American and European Conventions, see Frowein, 1 *HRLJ* 44. One difference between the two texts to the disadvantage of the American Convention is the absence of a guarantee of criminal legal aid (contrast Art. 8, American Convention with Art. 6(3)(c), European Convention).

[68] The title of Chapter I of the Convention is 'General Obligations.'

[69] They are not to be used independently of a Convention provision guaranteeing a

The states parties to this Convention undertake to respect the rights and freedoms recognised herein and to ensure to all persons subject to their jurisdiction the free and full exercise of those rights and freedoms, without any discrimination for reasons of race, color, sex, language, religion, political or other opinion, national or social origin, economic status, birth or any other social condition.

Obligation to Respect and Ensure

The first part of this sentence requires parties to 'respect' and 'ensure' the Convention rights. This wording was interpreted by the Inter-American Court in the *Velasquez* case[70] in the context of forced disappearances. As to the duty to 'respect', the Court stated that '(w)henever a state organ, official or public entity violates one of these rights, this constitutes a failure of the duty to respect the rights and freedoms set forth in the Convention'. This was so whether or not the act in question was *intra vires*: 'any violation of rights recognized by the Convention carried out by an act of public authority or by persons who use their position of authority is imputable to the state', thereby giving rise to state liability under the Convention.[71]

As to the duty to 'ensure' human rights, the 'state has a legal duty to take reasonable steps to prevent human rights violations and to use the means at its disposal to carry out a serious investigation of violations committed within its jurisdiction, to identify those responsible, to dispose the appropriate punishment and to ensure the victim adequate compensation.'[72] This duty exists in respect of violations by both public and private actors. Private acts or acts by persons whose identity is unknown can give rise to state responsibility under the Convention where the state shows a 'lack of due diligence to prevent the violation or to respond to it as required by the Convention'.[73] In the case of public actors, the state will be directly liable for their acts that fail to 'respect' human rights and will be under the same duty as exists in respect of private actors to prevent a violation of human rights by a public actor or to bring him to justice. The mere failure to prevent or

particular right: *Neira Alegría* case, I/A Court H.R. Series C No. 20, para. 85 (1995), 16 *HRLJ* 403; 3 IHRR 362 (1996).

[70] I/A Court H.R. Series C No. 4, para. 170 (1988), 9 *HRLJ* 212. See also Trindade, 405, below.

[71] Id., para. 172. The state is also in breach of its Art. 1(2) obligation where a violation by a private actor occurs 'with the support or the acquiescence of the government': id., para. 173.

[72] Id., para. 174. The Court also stated, id, para. 167, that the duty to 'ensure' 'implies the duty of the states parties to organise the governmental apparatus and, in general, all the structures through which public power is exercised, so that they are capable of juridically ensuring the free and full enjoyment of human rights.' Cf. Advisory Opinion No. 11, I/A Court H.R. Series A No.11, para. 23 (1990), 12 *HRLJ* 20.

[73] I/A Court H.R. Series A No. 4, para. 172 (1988), 9 *HRLJ* 212.

punish an offender is not in itself a breach of the duty to ensure; the obligation is to take reasonable and serious steps.[74]

The Court's language in the *Velasquez* case interpreting Article 1(1) is in some respects tailored to the situation of forced disappearances that was present on the facts. The language of 'respect' and 'ensure', which is found in other human rights treaties[75], imposes negative and positive duties in other contexts also.[76] Thus the duty to 'respect' freedom of expression will be infringed by censorship of the press that cannot be justified in the public interest under the terms of Article 13, American Convention even though the censorship is authorised by national law. The positive obligation to 'ensure' human rights may involve the putting of laws or institutions in place to secure the enjoyment of human rights. This may require the taking of steps to ensure, for example, that persons who have been the subject of inaccurate statements in the press have a right of reply (Article 14, Convention).[77]

Obligation not to Discriminate

The final part of Article 1(1), American Convention requires parties to guarantee the rights and freedoms in the Convention 'without any discrimination for reasons of race, color, sex, language, religion, political or other opinion, national or social origin, economic status, birth, or any other social condition.' This comprehensive wording is, in effect, read into each of the Convention articles that guarantees a right. The result is that they each contain an additional obligation by which a party must not discriminate on a ground contained in Article 1(1) when acting in the subject area of the right concerned. This parasitic provision is supplemented by the free-standing 'equality before the law' guarantee in Article 24, Convention which prohibits discrimination on similar grounds by legislation or other state action in any subject area. Article 24, therefore, concerns discriminatory legislation or decisions in the context of econonic, social and cultural rights (for example, social security law) as well as in the area of the civil and political rights in the Convention.[78]

---

[74] Id., paras. 175, 177 Cf. *Caballero Delgado and Santana* case, I/A Court H.R. Series C No. 21, para. 58 (1995), 17 *HRLJ* 24, 3 IHRR 548 (1996).

[75] See, e.g., Art. 2 (1), International Covenant on Civil and Political Rights.

[76] The Commission has drawn a distinction between positive and negative obligations in the context of rape: Report 5/96, Case 10.970 (Peru), IACHR Annual Report 1995, 188 (rape by soldiers a breach of a negative obligation). See also on positive and negative obligations, Resolution 1/90, Cases 9768 et al (Mexico), IACHR Annual Report 1989–90, 98, at 116–18.

[77] Advisory Opinion No. 7, I/A Court H.R. Series A No. 7 para. 28 (1986), 7 *HRLJ* 238.

[78] Cf the position under the International Covenant on Civil and Political Rights: see Harris and Joseph, (eds), *The International Covenant on Civil and Political Rights and United Kingdom Law* (Oxford, 1995), 4 and Chap. 17. On Art. 24, see Davidson, 284, below.

Scope of the Convention ratione personae *and* loci

The American Convention extends *ratione personae* to 'all persons', the term 'person' being limited by Article 1(2) to 'every human being'. The Convention thus does not extend to other legal persons such as companies or trades unions, although injuries to individuals that result from action taken against such legal persons may be subject to the Convention guarantee as affecting, for example, their right to property, to organise or to exercise freedom of religion. 'All' persons are protected regardless of their nationality or lack of it. *Ratione loci*, the Convention applies to any person who is subject to the 'jurisdiction' of a contracting party. 'Jurisdiction' here refers to a state acting publicly against an individual, whether this occurs on its territory or elsewhere. It includes, for example, the situation where a consulate or a soldier abroad infringes a person's right to freedom of movement or to life respectively.

Whether Self-Executing

Where the exercise of the rights and freedoms recognized in the Convention 'is not already ensured by legislative or other provisions', the contracting parties undertake in Article 2 'to adopt, in accordance with their constitutional processes and the provisions of this Convention, such legislative or other measures as may be necessary to give effect to those rights or freedoms'. Apart from reinforcing the obligation that a state party to the Convention would have in any case under the international law of treaties to ensure that its law and administrative practice is in line with its treaty obligations,[79] the wording of Article 2 is relevant to the question whether the Convention, or any part of it, is self-executing, so that it may be the basis for a claim in a national court by an individual whose rights are allegedly infringed. Although this is ultimately a matter for national courts to decide in accordance with their own constitutions, the wording of Article 2 clearly supports the view that the Convention was not intended to be self-executing and that further national steps were to be taken to incorporate its provisions into national law.[80] However, it remains open for a national court to decide otherwise in the light of the wording and intention of Article 2 and the particular Convention article concerned and of its own constitution.[81]

---

[79] Advisory Opinion No. 7, I/A Court H.R. Series A No.7, para. 29 (1986), 7 *HRLJ* 238.

[80] For an account of the drafting and the mixed intentions of the drafting states, see Buergenthal, in Meron, (ed.), *Human Rights in International Law* (Oxford, 1984), 442–5.The Commission has expressed the view that Art. 8(2), Convention is not self-executing: Report 24/92, Cases 9328 et al (Costa Rica), IACHR Annual Report 1992–3, 74.

[81] In practice, the national courts of a number of states have relied upon the Convention in their decisions. The most well known example concerns Argentina, whose Constitution, Art. 75 (22), provides that human rights treaties ratified by Argentina have 'constitutional hierarchy', so that they prevail over other law. See, e.g., Ekmekdjian c Sofovich, La Ley 1992 C, 540.

Derogation in time of Public Emergency

Article 27 (1) of the Convention provides that '(i)n time of war, public danger, or other public emergency that threatens the independence or security of a state party', the state concerned may 'take measures derogating from its obligations under' the Convention 'to the extent and for the period of time strictly required by the exigencies of the situation', provided that the measures are 'not inconsistent with its other obligations under international law and do not involve discrimination on the ground of race, color, sex, language, religion, or social origin.'[82] However, Article 27(2) provides that no derogation is permitted from certain listed rights. It also provides that derogation is not permitted from 'the judicial guarantees essential for the protection of such rights.'[83] Article 27(3) requires any derogating state 'immediately' to inform the other states parties through the Secretary General of the OAS of the provisions suspended, the reasons for their suspension and the date of the termination of the suspension.

Article 27 is similar to derogation provisions in other human rights treaties, such as Article 4, International Covenant on Civil and Political Rights (ICCPR). It allows states less freedom to derogate than some other human rights treaties in that it has a non-discrimination clause in Article 27(1) and has a longer list of non-derogable rights and guarantees than most. Although many of the cases that arise under the individual petition procedure concern gross violations involving non-derogable rights, other rights may be concerned in these or other cases in respect of which Article 27 may provide a shield.[84]

A number of parties to the Convention have declared national states of emergency since its entry into force. In not all such cases has the state sent a notice of derogation to the OAS. Oráa refers to several cases in which, remarkably, the state concerned notified the United Nations that it was derogating from its obligations under the ICCPR but did not send any comparable notice to the Secretary General of the OAS under the

[82] On Art. 27 and human rights in states of emergency generally, see Fitzpatrick, Chap. 12, below. On non-Convention parties and emergencies under the American Declaration, see above, 9.

[83] See Advisory Opinions Nos. 8 and 9, I/A Court H.R. Series A Nos 8. and 9 (1987), 9 *HRLJ* 94, 204. The effective suspension of habeas corpus in a state of emergency was a breach of Art. 27 (2) in the *Neira Alegría* case: I/A Court H.R. Series C No. 20, para. 77, (1995), 16 *HRLJ* 403, 3 IHRR 362 (1996)

[84] See, e.g., Report No 1/96, Case 10.559 (Peru), IACHR Annual Report 1995, 136, in which the Commission found Peru liable under the Convention for killings, torture, rape and arbitrary detention on the part of its soldiers. Whereas most of the rights involved were non-derogable, Art. 27 might have benefited Peru in respect of the arbitrary detentions (Art. 7, Convention) had it declared a state of emergency.

Convention.[85] The Inter-American Commission has, on occasion, found that the situation did not justify a state of emergency or that the measures were not strictly required.[86]

The Federal Clause

Article 28 (1) provides that where a contracting party is a federal state, so that some matters are within the jurisdiction of units (states, provinces, etc) within the federal state and not the federal government, the latter, which will have ratified the Convention for the state, is obliged to 'implement all of the provisions of the Convention over whose subject matter it exercises legislative and judicial jurisdiction'. As far as matters that are within the exclusive jurisdiction of units within the federal state are concerned, their acts will not engage the responsibility of the federal state under the Convention and the only obligation of the federal state is 'to immediately take suitable measures, in accordance its constitution and its laws, to the end that the competent authorities of the constituent units may adopt appropriate provisions for the fulfillment of this Convention.' This limitation upon the liability of a federal state under the American Convention is not found in the International Covenant on Civil and Political Rights, which, like most modern treaties, extends to all parts of federal states without any limitations or exceptions (Article 50, ICCPR). Article 28 was inserted at the suggestion of the United States[87] and would exclude from the scope of the Convention, to which the United States is not yet a party, matters in the area of a state's law that were not within the scope of the federal United States constitution. Since, however, most matters regulated by state law in the United States that fall within the American Convention also raise issues under the Bill of Rights in the US Constitution and so fall within Article 28(1) of the American Convention, not Article 28(2),[88] the Article 28 exception is of limited significance.

[85] *Human Rights in States of Emergency in International Law* (Oxford, 1992), 83. The states were Bolivia (1985, 1986), Ecuador (1986), Colombia (1980), El Salvador (1983, 1984, 1985), Panama (1987). Notices of derogation that are sent to the OAS are not officially published. See Grossman, 'A Framework for the Examination of States of Emergency under the American Convention on Human Rights' 1 *Am.U J Int'l. L and Policy* 35, 55 (1986), who argues that they should be published, possibly in the Commission's Annual Reports. There is no Convention obligation to publish a notice of derogation nationally.

[86] See the examples of Bolivia and Chile given by Oráa, op cit, 23, 26.

[87] See Buergenthal, in Meron, (ed.), *Human Rights in International Law* (Oxford, 1984), 446–7, for a full discussion.

[88] Thus the *Baby Boy* case, the *Juvenile Death Penalty* cases and the *Celestine* case, as to which see Davidson, 216, 223, and 225, below, would not have been excluded from the Commission's jurisdiction under Art. 28. There is no 'federal clause' limitation in the American Declaration under which they were considered. The Commission has found Mexico liable under the Convention in respect of the units within its federation in the context of elections: Final Report on Cases 9768, 9780 and 9828 (Mexico), IACHR Annual Report 1989–90, 99, at 120 and Report No. 8/91, Case No. 10.180 (Mexico), IACHR Annual Report 1990–1, 237, at 248.

THE INTER-AMERICAN COMMISSION ON HUMAN RIGHTS

The Inter-American Commission on Human Rights was established by a resolution of the General Assembly of the OAS and began functioning in 1960.[89] It is now provided for by the American Convention on Human Rights, which contains the rules concerning its organisation and functioning. These are supplemented, and to some extent duplicated, by the Commission's Statute, which has been approved by the General Assembly of the OAS.[90]

The Commission is composed of seven members, who sit as independent experts. The members are nominated by OAS member states and elected by the OAS General Assembly, which takes into account the need to have an equitable representation of the legal systems and geographic areas of the region.[91] As with other such bodies, the members almost always have a legal background. Members often have diplomatic or political experience also, which has been justified by reference to the need for the Commission to discuss and negotiate with governments when conducting *in loco* visits.[92]

The Commission is a part-time body that is permitted to meet in session for just eight weeks a year.[93] These meetings are held in Washington DC, at the headquarters of the OAS, where the Commission's permanent secretariat is based. Given the Commission's part-time character and the great volume of its work, it is not surprising that the Commission's secretariat, headed by an Executive Secretary, whose role is an important one, plays a large, discretionary part in the Commission's work. In particular, decisions rejecting individual petitions as not being *prima facie* admissible are in the hands of the Secretariat, not the members of the Commission,[94] as is the task of communicating with governments to obtain their observations on petitions that are deemed by the Secretariat to be *prima facie* admissible.

The Commission is distinguishable from most other comparable bodies in the international human rights world by the multiplicity of functions that it

[89] On the Commission generally, see Cerna, Chap. 3, below.
[90] For the text of the Statute, see Appendix IV. For the Commission's Regulations, which were adopted by the Commission, see Appendix V.
[91] The only state that has always had a national member is the US. On the background and independence of Commission members, see Cerna, 70, below; Gomez, 207, below; and Vivanco and Bhansali, 424, below.
[92] See Cerna, 70, below.
[93] Commission members may also be deputed to make *in loco* visits to states in the preparation of country reports.
[94] The Commission can take the final decision as to admissibility in the case of petitions that have been declared *prima facie* admissible, but it has no role in the reverse situation. However, the Secretariat has tended to be generous in finding petitions *prima facie* admissible and a petition that is turned away for non-exhaustion of local remedies can be re-submitted once they have been exhausted.

has.[95] In practice, it has established as its two main tasks the preparation of country reports on the general state of human rights in a country, normally following an *in loco* visit,[96] and the examination of individual petitions.[97] It also participates in the drafting of treaties and other documents[98] and prepares thematic reports on the protection of human rights in the region.[99]

In the first fifteen or so years of its history, the Commission made *in loco* visits and country reports the central part of its work, not the examination of individual petitions.[100] Faced with gross violations of human rights by military regimes that would be unlikely to respond to rulings against them of the European kind,[101] the Commission prioritised the need to establish and publicise what was happening and to seek change by negotiation, and possibly by pressure through the General Assembly of the OAS, rather than through adverse ruling in petition cases. Consequently, the Commission focused on visiting states and talking with governments and on the publication of country reports and their presentation to the General Assembly for debate. The Commission's work in this regard parallels that of the UN Commission on Human Rights.[102] On occasions, the Inter-American Commission's reports have acted as a catalyst or had some other beneficial effect. A vivid example was the 1980 report that brought home to people in Argentina the record of their military government on disappeared persons in the late 1970s.[103] Such effect as the Commission's reports have achieved has not been with the backing of the General Assembly of the OAS. Apart from a short period in the late 1970s when pressure from the Carter

[95] See Cerna, 66, below. The African Commission on Human and Peoples' Rights also has a wide remit and has recently been undertaking visits to states.

[96] Such visits depend upon the consent of the state concerned. States usually give their consent and in some cases have taken the initiative to request a visit. But the seven Commission reports on Cuba were prepared without a visit in the absence of consent and other states have also refused consent: see Farer, 50, below.

[97] The Commission is also empowered to examine inter-state communications, but none have been lodged.

[98] For example, it played a large part in the drafting of American Convention on Human Rights and it has recently contributed to the draft Declaration on the Rights of Indigenous Populations. As to the latter, see Hannum, 334, below.

[99] These reports may be printed in the Commission's Annual Reports. See, for example, the 'Report on the Compatibility of "Desecato" Laws with the American Convention on Human Rights', IACHR Annual Report 1994, 197.

[100] The power to examine individual petitions was granted in 1965: see Cerna, 76, below.

[101] See Farer, 33, below.

[102] Some of the UN Commission reports have been on American states, e.g., Bolivia, Chile, Cuba, El Salvador, Guatemala and Nicaragua: see Tolley, *The UN Commission on Human Rights*, (Boulder, 1987), 118. The UN Commission's special rapporteurs or working groups on particular themes have also reported on American states: see, e.g., the Inter-American Commission's reliance on the UN Special Rapporteur against Torture's report on Peru in Report 5/96, Case 10.970 (Peru), IACHR Annual Report 1995, 157, at 179.

[103] On the Argentine report, which was widely circulated in Argentina, see Farer, 52–9, below, who gives the 1978 report on Nicaragua as another example of an influential report.

Government in Washington led the Assembly to discuss the Commission's reports and generally support its work, the non-interventionalist tradition within the OAS has led other states largely to ignore the evidence presented to them, with such criticism as has been mounted in the Assembly being addressed against the Commission by the state that it has dared to attack, rather than by other states against the delinquent state.[104]

While *in loco* visits and country reports remain an important and necessary part of the Commission's work,[105] the consideration of individual petitions has come to play an increasing role in its activities in recent years. This has been prompted by the entry into force of the American Convention in 1979, which introduced the possibility of cases being referred to the Inter-American Court for a final, legally binding decision, and the return to democracy and law and order in South and Central American states since then, which has reduced the number of instances of gross violations of human rights for which *in loco* visits are particularly appropriate.[106]

A consequence of the increased attention given to individual petitions is that there are now calls for reform of the Commission's working methods to achieve a more depoliticised approach in its examination of individual petitions, one that consistently follows acceptable legal procedures.[107] The catalogue of criticisms of the Commission's procedures at the admissibility and later stages that emerges from the following chapters is a long one.[108] Criticisms include the absence of a formal admissibility stage, attempts by states to influence cases prior to the registration of a petition, inconsistencies in the treatment of cases according to their political significance for states, acts such as the closure, as an administrative measure, of 5000 Argentine cases without a final decision on the merits,[109] the haphazard nature of the decision to conduct oral hearings[110] and the failure to develop an extensive jurisprudence interpreting the Convention.

Some improvements can be effected simply by a change in Commission practice, and recently there have been encouraging signs and developments.

---

[104] See Gomez, 196, below. The Assembly is composed of government delegations, not a cross-section of national parliamentarians.

[105] In 1996, the Commission made an *in loco* visit to Mexico, which will lead to the preparation of a country report. The Commission also visited prisons in the US to examine the conditions of detention of the Marielitos (Cuban prisoners) and in Venezuela (general prison conditions). The latter was the first ever Commission visit to Venezuela. In the same year, visits were made to the Dominican Republic, to investigate the circumstances of an individual petition, and to Argentina to promote a friendly settlement.

[106] The large scale problems now are those that result from the reaction of governments to terrorism, as in Peru and Colombia, and from the fragile hold on democracy and the rule of law that some governments still have.

[107] See Gomez, 210, below; Trindade, 411, below; and Vivanco and Bhansali, 424, below.

[108] See Trindade, 411, below; and Vivanco and Bhansali, 422–35, below.

[109] See Cerna, 100, below.

[110] See Cerna, 97, below.

In other respects, the part-time character of the Commission and the limited size and resources of its Secretariat present difficulties that can only be overcome by the allocation of greater funds.[111]

Unfortunately, states are not at present well motivated to add to the funding of an institution that may criticise them. Whereas the need is for states to be convinced by the argument that they should put themselves at risk in the interest of the protection of human rights in the region at large, some currently are more concerned to contain the sources of criticism and to have the Commission discount their human rights obligations in recognition of the problems of terrorism that they face.[112]

But the record of the Commission as a whole has much to commend it. Quite apart from its invaluable contribution to the protection of human rights in the Americas through its country reports, its approach to the problem of tackling situations involving gross human rights violations within a petition system has been inventive and human-rights minded. It has interpreted the 'denial of justice' exceptions to the domestic remedies rule in a broad way that recognises the reality of the situation that exists where judges find it difficult to be independent.[113] It has also been determined to ensure that petitions are not stymied by a lack of government cooperation. Its Rule 42 procedure, by which a credible petition may be assumed to be accurate in its presentation of the facts when it is not challenged by the government, has been accepted by states and has solved a difficult problem.[114] More recently, the Commission has resisted strong pressure from some states to rewrite the Convention to move the focus of attention from states to terrorist acts. While acknowledging that a terrorist group's actions may themselves be 'serious violations of human rights', the Commission has insisted that a state 'in its efforts to defeat terrorist subversion, was not entitled to use methods that violated international commitments.'[115] Another issue of great current concern with which the Commission has been faced is that of the conformity with the Convention of the various kinds of amnesty laws that states have adopted. In the leading cases concerning Argentina and Uruguay, the Commission found breaches of the Convention, as a human rights body must.[116]

---

[111] Another question is whether a body that has the diplomatic and political role that the Commission exercises in connection with *in loco* visits can be expected at the same time to undertake the quasi-judicial function that the examination of individual petitions involves.

[112] See Gomez, 199, below.

[113] See Cerna, 85, below.

[114] See Cerna, 87, below.

[115] Report 1/96. Case 10.559 (Peru), IACHR Annual Report 1995, 136. One difficulty that may arise in this connection is that of establishing whether the killings or other acts complained of, often occurring in remote areas, were committed by terrorists or by the army: see Report 6/91, Case 10.400 (Guatemala), IACHR Annual Report 1990–1, 193, at 197.

[116] On these cases and the general question, see Lutz, 355, below.

THE INTER-AMERICAN COURT OF HUMAN RIGHTS

The Inter-American Court of Human Rights came into being in 1979 following the entry into force of the American Convention on Human Rights.[117] The Court is a part-time body that has its seat in San José, Costa Rica.[118] It is composed of seven judges who, by definition, are independent. Judges are nominated by the Convention parties and elected by the same group of states in the OAS General Assembly. As with the Commission, efforts are made to achieve an equitable representation of the legal systems and geographic areas of the region. While all judges have had a legal background, only a limited number have been professional judges at home; most have been academics or, in quite a number of cases, have previously or later had diplomatic or political experience.[119]

The Court differs from the Commission in many ways. Whereas the Commission has various functions, the Court is exclusively a judicial body. It has both advisory and contentious jurisdiction. The Court may render advisory opinions on 'the interpretation of the Convention or of other treaties concerning the protection of human rights in the American states' at the request of the Commission, any OAS member state, whether a Convention party or not, or certain OAS organs.[120] The Court's advisory jurisdiction has proved popular, with the Court averaging nearly one opinion a year in the first seventeen years of its life.[121] Opinions have been requested by states (ten) and the Commission (five). Most have resulted in helpful clarification of the meaning of the Convention, both as to its procedures and the interpretation of its substantive guarantee. In a few cases, states have been tempted to use the Court for their own less than altruistic purposes, as when at odds with the Commission.[122]

Contentious cases may be referred to the Court by the Commission or by a state party to the Convention, generally only against or by a party that has made an optional declaration accepting the Court's jurisdiction. Until recently, cases were slow in coming, partly because few states had made optional declarations,[123] but mostly because the Commission was reluctant to take the initiative. In 1985, in Advisory Opinion No 5, the Court expressed its frustration by criticising the Commission for not referring to it the

---

[117] On the Court, see generally, Trindade, Chap. 5, below.

[118] This was agreed by the parties to the Convention, as Art. 58(1), Convention provides.

[119] See Gomez, 208, below.

[120] Art. 64, Convention. The Court's advisiory jurisdiction is much wider than that of the European Court: see Advisory Opinion No. 3, I/A Court H.R. Series A No. 3, para. 43 (1983), 4 *HRLJ* 339.

[121] Fourteen opinions by the end of 1996, with a fifteenth pending.

[122] Advisory Opinion No. 13 is the classic case of this: see Gomez, 182, below. Another interesting case was Advisory Opinion No. 5, p. 24, n. 124, below.

[123] For the 17 parties that have declarations in force, see Appendix VIII.

individual petition that had triggered the request by Costa Rica for the opinion in that case.[124] The following year, the Commission referred its first cases to the Court.[125] Since then, the Commission has gradually taken a more positive approach and in early 1997 the Court had 16 cases on its docket at various procedural stages.[126] Whether this change will be maintained will depend in part on the Commission's confidence in the Court's jurisprudence.[127]

Whereas the Court has settled a number of important points of interpretation in its advisory opinions, in its jurisprudence in contentious cases the Court has had only a limited opportunity to make a contribution to international human rights law generally and to the interpretation of the Convention in particular. It started impressively in the *Velasquez* case, with a thorough and sound interpretation of the basic obligation of the parties in Article 1 of the Convention and a well-argued treatment of the issues concerning state liability under the Convention for disappeared persons that sets appropriately rigorous standards for state conduct. The Court's judgment on these points has been constantly quoted and followed by the Commission in later cases.[128] Since then, there has been little extended consideration of general questions of interpretation in the Court's judgments, possibly because the cases have mostly followed the gruesome pattern of the *Velasquez* case or have otherwise been so clear cut on their facts as not to call for any grappling with other basic issues;[129] they have not as yet concerned ordinary human rights violations raising points of interpretation of such rights as the right to a fair trial or to freedom of expression.

The Court has been called upon to give most attention to its powers to order reparation. It has tended to deal with the issues that have arisen on a case-by-case basis and has not developed a satisfactory overall approach to

[124] In the *Schmidt* case, the Commission had found that Costa Rica had not infringed Art. 13, Convention when the complainant was refused a licence to practise as a journalist. In its advisory opinion, the Court interpreted Art. 13 differently from the Commission and concluded that the law and practice upon which the refusal was based was in breach of Art. 13.

[125] The Honduran disappeared persons cases (*Velasquez* et al). No case has yet been referred by a state. The Commission has so far only sent cases in which it has found a breach.

[126] The early experience of the European Court of Human Rights was the same, with the European Commission taking a while to get used to the idea of its report on a case not being the decisive document.

[127] The Court has suggested criteria that the Commission should use when deciding to refer a case: see Advisory Opinions Nos. 5 (1985) and 13 (1993), I/A Court H.R. Series A No. 5, para. 25, 7 *HRLJ* 74 and Series A. No. 13. para. 50, 14 *HRLJ* 252. Criteria are also suggested by Trindade, 412, and Vivanco and Bhansali, 425, below.

[128] See, e.g., Report 5/96, Case 10.970 (Peru), IACHR Annual Report 1995, 157, at 189.

[129] All of the cases decided by the Court by the end of 1996 (the *Velasquez, Aloeboetoe, Gangaram Panday, Neira Alegría, Cabellero, El Amparo, Garrido and Baigorria* cases) involved at least one death, and the *Cayara* case, in which the Court declined to take jurisdiction, concerned a massacre. Only in *Gangaram Panday*, by four votes to three, was there no finding that there had been an arbitrary taking of life in breach of Art. 4 by the state.

the subject.[130] As yet, it has declined in most of the cases to award reparation in forms other than monetary compensation. It is to be hoped that the Court may yet take a more expansive approach to its powers in this regard, one that reflects the injuries suffered by the victims of human rights violations or their families, which will not always easily or best be repaired by money. On a more positive note, the defendant state has paid the compensation ordered by the Court in the first contentious cases—the *Honduran Disappeared Persons* cases—to have run the full course.[131] In all of these cases, the facts have been such as to involve acts on the part of the military or other state agents. In none has a law been declared illegal so that the state concerned has been required to amend its legisation.[132] In this connection, it may be noted again that there is no machinery equivalent to that under the European Convention on Human Rights by which an organ of the OAS is responsible for monitoring the execution of Court judgments. The OAS General Assembly could take the initiative in this connection when considering the Court's annual report, but has not done so.[133]

A recent, disturbing tendency in cases that have reached the Court has been for a state to acknowledge liability and thereby avoid a fully reasoned judgment on the merits.[134] Whereas this accelerates the award of compensation, many victims will be at least as much concerned with a public and objective finding of the truth and a statement of responsibility by an independent body after a judicial hearing.

The Court is a young institution and is still in the course of establishing its procedures. One procedural issue that looms large in the minds of those involved in the Court's functioning is the standing of the petitioner to plead his or her case. At present, the Commission has standing before the Court as a party and may, as it were, hide a petitioner's lawyer under its skirts. The lawyer may be a member of the Commission's delegation, subject to any successful objection by the defendant state,[135] and may present the petitioner's arguments in that capacity, though only under the control of the Commission. This is not a satisfactory situation, as the interests of the Commission[136] and the petitioner and their approach as to the legal

---

[130] See Shelton, 153, below. On the questions of costs, see 171, below.

[131] 1996 Annual Court Report, p. 26. Compliance in other cases is pending.

[132] In Advisory Opinion No. 5, I/A Court H.R. Series A No. 5 (1985), 7 *HRLJ* 74 the Court did express the opinion that a compulsory licensing law for journalists, such as that of Costa Rica, which had requested the opinion, was in breach of Art. 13, Convention, and Costa Rica has changed its law accordingly.

[133] See Gomez, 197, below.

[134] See Gomez, 189, below.

[135] For an example, see Vivanco and Bhansali, 436, below.

[136] The Court has stated that the Commission has before the Court a 'quasi-judicial role, like that assigned to the "Ministerio Público" of the inter-American system': *Gallardo* case, No. G 101/81 para. 22 (1981), 2 *HRLJ* 328. In practice, the Commission defends its report in the case.

arguments or the measure of compensation to present or pursue do not always coincide. The experience of the European Court of Human Rights may be of assistance here. That court has, by the amendment of its own rules of procedure and practice, reached the point where the petitioner, who has no standing before the Court in the text of the European Convention, is now an almost equal party to the defendant state in the Court's proceedings[137] and may even seize the Court of the case where the state party has ratified Protocol 9 to the European Convention. There is no reason why such a developement as to standing should not occur in the same incremental way before the American Court;[138] the creation of a power to seize the Court would require political action.

What also needs to be achieved from the standpoint of the petitioner is a means of paying for his or her costs. As yet, the Court has not been sympathetic to using its powers under Article 63(1), Convention to award reparation to this end,[139] and there is no provision in the system as a whole for legal aid for an indigent petitioner's lawyer, in proceedings before either the Commission or the Court. These are gaps that need to be filled.[140]

What the Court has already done in its practice has been to exercise freely its power to issue provisional measures under Article 63(2), Convention, although the measures that have been adopted have by no means always been respected by states.[141]

Another question concerns the interaction between the Commission and the Court. At present, it could not be said that the two institutions work harmoniously together. Understandably, it has taken the Commission some time to adjust to the presence of a new co-actor on the scene. As mentioned, the Commission has been criticised by the Court for its reluctance to refer cases to it, although matters are improving this regard. The Court has also, not surprisingly, rendered an advisory opinion against the Commission for making findings on the merits in cases that it has declared inadmissible[142] and has criticised it for giving a state a further extension of time to submit its observations on a petition.[143] Mention may also be made of the *Cayara* case,

---

[137] See Trindade, 414, below.

[138] On the step taken to give the complainant an independent right of audience at the reparation stage, see Trindade, 415, below.

[139] See Shelton, 171, below. This contrast with the practice of the European Court of Human Rights: see D. Harris, M. O'Boyle and C. Warbrick, *The Law of the European Convention on Human Rights* (London, 1995), 682.

[140] Human rights NGOs, which bring or argue most of the cases, do not have 'deep pockets'.

[141] See Trindade, 145, below. The same is true of the Commission's development and exercise of its power to adopt provisional measures: see Cerna, 107, below.

[142] Advisory Opinion No. 13, I/A Court H.R. Series A No. 13, para. 44 (1993), 14 *HRLJ* 252, 1 IHRR Vol 2 197 (1994).

[143] Advisory Opinion No. 12, I/A Court Series A No. 12, para. 26 (1991), 13 *HRLJ* 149. See also the Court's criticism of the Commission's approach to its friendly settlement role in the *Caballero Delgado and Santana* case: see Cerna, 10, below.

which is the one case that the Commission has referred to the Court which the Court has declined to take.[144] One could be forgiven for thinking that the Court's motivation in this case was to teach the Commission a lesson, for the Commission had undoubtedly handled the case badly. Whether this is a fair assessment or not, the case is one that reflects credit on neither institution, since the end result was an absence of any final judicial[145] resolution of the case for the victims and their families.

Certain other questions concerning the relations between the two institutions go to the boundary between their respective powers. One question is whether the Court may reverse a ruling by the Commission as to admissibility. The Court claims the competence to do so, on the basis that it is the master of its own jurisdiction.[146] As Trindade[147] argues, this leads to an imbalance between the petitioner and the state, unless decisions declaring a petition inadmissible may also be reconsidered by the Court. As Trindade also suggests, it would be preferable in principle for all decisions as to admissibility to be finally disposed of by the Commission.

A final question is whether the Court should accept the findings of fact of the Commission or whether it should, as it does at present, re-examine the facts and make its own assessment of them in the light of the evidence produced before it. As Trindade[148] argues, the former approach is preferable in the interest of husbanding resources. Were the Commission's fact-finding procedures to be made more reliable, the Court might be prepared to review its practice in this regard. Quite apart from any other consideration, it might reduce the period of five years and more that it take for a case to be determined from the point of registration to the final decision by the Court.[149]

---

[144] For an account of the case, see Gomez, 184, below.

[145] The Commission did publish a full report on the case: see Gomez, 185, below.

[146] See the cases referred to by Trindade, 412, n. 29, below.

[147] See Trindade, 411, below. Following an approach that has been widely criticised, the European Court of Human Rights may reconsider a decision declaring an application admissible, although such preliminary objections by states are seldom successful: see D. Harris, M. O'Boyle and C. Warbrick, *The Law of the European Convention on Human Rights* (London, 1995), 675–6.

[148] See Trindade, 412, below. The European Court generally accepts the findings of fact by the European Commission. The question is likely to be important in a higher percentage of cases of gross violations than of ordinary violations. In the latter, the facts may have been found by a national court, or the issue is one not so much of the facts of an incident as of the validity of a state's law.

[149] Note, however, that most of this time is taken before the Commission.

CONCLUSION

The inter-American system for the protection of human rights has already achieved a great deal. Faced in its early years with gross violations of human rights in a number of states, the Commission developed an effective system of *in loco* visits and country reports that threw light upon these tragic events and served as a catalyst for change. The Commission also evolved a system for the consideration of individual petitions that, although far from perfect, has taken root and has the potential for future development. Already it has contributed significantly to international human rights through the Commission's Rule 42, by which 'consistent, specific and credible' allegations by a petitioner will be presumed true in the absence of any government response, and by the increasingly strong stand that the Commission has taken in petition cases in the evaluation of amnesty laws.

A large contribution has also been made by the Court. In the exercise of its broad advisory jurisdiction, the Court has clarified the meaning of certain aspects of the substance and the procedures of the Inter-American human rights system, although others have been left unsatisfactorily obscure. In contentious cases, the Court's judgment in the *Velasquez* case is the leading case in international human rights law on the responsibility of a state in cases of disappeared persons.

But the overriding impression is of arrangements that are in the process of change. The Commission, which remains the workhorse of the system, has a new direction in its work, partly as a result in a change in its membership. It is giving serious consideration to the reform, and greater 'judicialisation', of the procedures by which it considers individual petitions, which are likely to play an increasingly important part in its endeavours. The Commission is already referring more cases to the Court, which will accordingly come to play a more central and significant role in the system. The Court's expanded caseload will lead to an acceleration in the elaboration of the meaning of the substantive guarantee of the Convention and a greater number of legally binding judgments. Increasingly, it can be anticipated, the parallel between the Inter-American and the European Courts of Human Rights will become evident. As with the Commission, the Inter-American Court has the improvement of its procedures under review.

All the achievements of the inter-American system to date have been effected, once the process was initiated, with very little support from the political organs of the OAS. Historically, inadequate funds have been provided for the operation of the system, with, remarkably, additional funding or facilities being provided by the European Community and by gifts from individual states. Similarly, the OAS Assembly has, with few exceptions, not taken the initiative to cause states to comply with Commission reports and Court judgments. Although much can be done by the Commission and the Court to bring the inter-American human rights system to maturity, this absence of political support will need to change for the system to realise its full potential. One immediate fillip that might signal a new mood in this regard would be for the ten missing OAS member states to complete the grand design for the system by ratifying the American Convention on Human Rights.

2

The Rise of the Inter-American Human Rights Regime: No Longer a Unicorn, Not Yet an Ox

TOM FARER

If human rights regimes confirmed the dictum of the Modernist Movement in architecture—'Form follows Function'—then, anatomically speaking, the Inter-American one should resemble the European about as much as the unicorn resembles the ox.

By associating the European regime with an ox, I intend not to insult but rather to celebrate its solid bourgeois virtues: the stolid, efficient application of energy and the consequently consistent production of effective decisions, all within the context of an orderly, stable and prosperous community. The post-war West European setting did not invite, neither did it require, unpredictable improvisation or heroic challenges to the expectations and desires of governing elites.

Latin America, by comparison, has been a feral jungle for most of the Inter-American regime's remarkable life. And although today most of the beasts have withdrawn to their lairs (when they are not off exercising their human right to visit Miami and shop at Gucci), passers-by still see eyes gleaming angrily in the shadows and hear the tense scrape of claws across stony floors.

When, in the second half of the 1970s, the Inter-American Commission began in earnest to test the limits of its authority—descending on countries, probing their viscera and returning with graphic accounts of the stench—it appeared as a fabulous creature to two sets of observers. One was composed by the regimes carrying out murderous political projects. How, they must have wondered, could this organ of an association of governments including their own, an association implicitly consecrated at birth to the defense of the West against the very revolutionary forces they were busily repressing, be calling *them* to account? How could these conservatively dressed, middle-aged gentlemen, nominated and elected by the region's regimes, be harshly indicting various of their electors? It was Dr. Frankenstein and his monster all over again.

Activists and ideologues of the Left, the principal victims of the wave of torture and execution that was engulfing Latin America, formed the other audience where astonishment reigned. I recall a Colombian prison interview in the Spring of 1980. My interlocutor was a thin school teacher with a sweet smile and what looked like a depressed fracture of his cheekbone. He was an admitted member of the M-19 Movement, considered at that point the Government's most dangerous adversary. I began by explaining that I and my Commission colleagues were on a fact-finding trip which would culminate in a report on the condition of human rights in Colombia. And I invoked previously published reports on El Salvador and the Somoza regime in Nicaragua, reports already well known in Latin America, as evidence of our bona fides. After indicating that he was aware of our recent work, he looked at me winningly and asked if I could explain to him the anomaly of the Commission's work, since it was the creature of the OAS and the latter was an institution filled with repressive governments and dominated by my own country, the hegemonic defender of the Latin status quo. He seemed genuinely puzzled.

Some six years after creating the Commission and providing it with a vaguely-worded mandate to assist in the defense of human rights, the OAS had given the Commission explicit authority to investigate individual instances of alleged human rights violations.[1] This competence was to be added to that which the Commission had already teased out of the 1959 resolution that was its precarious authority[2] to investigate and report on the general situation of human rights in OAS member states. Armed with its new mandate, the Commission could have concentrated on individual cases, futilely but respectably pursuing an endless paper trail of victims' complaints and official denials, and occasionally issuing 'reports' on the general condition of human rights in member states that were mere collections of the self-congratulatory no less than imaginative self-assessments sent up to its Washington offices by one or another government. Instead, focusing upon the investigation of the facts and the preparation of country reports on the actual conditions that it found, the Commission converted itself into an accusatory agency, a kind of Hemispheric Grand Jury, storming around Latin America to vacuum up evidence of high crimes and misdemeanors and marshaling it into bills of indictment in the form of country reports for delivery to the political organs of the OAS and the court of public opinion.

---

[1] Resolution XXII of the Second Special Inter-American Conference in 1965 resolves: '. . . to authorize the Commission to examine communications submitted to it and any other available information, so that it may address to the government of any American State a request for information deemed pertinent by the Commission, and so that it may make recommendations, when it deems appropriate, with the objective of bringing about more effective observance of fundamental human rights.' Rio de Janeiro, Nov. 1965, Final Act. OEA/Ser.C/I.13, 32–4.

[2] Resolution VIII of the Fifth Meeting of Consultation of Ministers of Foreign Affairs, Final Act, Santiago, Chile (12–18 Aug., 1959), OAS Off.Rec. OEA/Ser.F/II.5 (Doc 89, English, Rev. 2) Oct. 1959 at 10–11.

Western Europe's human rights institutions, the Commission and the Court, also charged governments with violations of human rights. But the violations almost invariably involved actions undertaken openly on the thinly marked border between the legitimate exercise of public authority on behalf of the community and the irreducible claims of individual liberty. The various European governments employing challenged acts no doubt regarded them as useful but hardly as means essential to the preservation of order or the execution of any other important public function. Moreover, both competitive elections and, in most if not all the countries then subject to the regime, constitutional restraints enforced by independent courts broadly limited their ends and means to those generally consistent in fact with internationally recognized human rights. Thus the European human rights regime largely reinforced national restraints on the exercise of executive and legislative power rather than adding on strong additional ones.

Latin American constitutions also contained long lists of protected rights and corresponding checks on government action.[3] But few, if any, countries had effectively independent judiciaries available and committed to enforcing them. Furthermore, on close inspection constitutional restraints were often riddled with specific exceptions and were for the most part subject to derogation in times of emergency.[4] And the region's constitutional courts had shown little zeal for auditing executive branch claims that the required emergency existed and that the particular suspension of guarantees was reasonably necessary to protect public order.[5] Their determined passivity may

---

[3] See the discussions of constitutional provisions for human rights contained in various IACHR country Reports. For example, IACHR Report on the Situation of Human Rights in Bolivia (1981), Report on the Situation of Human Rights in Colombia (1981), Report on the Situation of Human Rights in Guatemala (1981)

[4] For example, the Chilean government, after the 1973 coup, declared a state of emergency that continued throughout the '70s and into the '80s. Even as the Pinochet regime approached the 1988 plebiscite, two states of emergency were still in effect. Other examples of prolonged or recurrent states of emergency are Paraguay, Guatemala and Uruguay, to name only a few. For further discussion of states of emergency and international human rights law, see J. Fitzpatrick, *Human Rights in Crisis: The International System for Protecting Rights During States of Emergency* (Philadelphia,1994), and Fitzpatrick, Chap. 12 below.

[5] See, for example, the Commission's assessments of judicial passivity or complaisance in Argentina, Chile, and El Salvador, summarized in *Inter-American Commission on Human Rights, Ten Years of Activities: 1971–1981* (Washington: OAS, 1982), 252–6, 274–6, 288–91, 292, and 336–8. The Commission itself eschewed appraisal of the original factual basis for a government's claim of right to suspend constitutional guarantees. Commission restraint had several bases. One was the deference to the judgment of public officials that is virtually instinct in intergovernmental organizations. Another was the desire to avoid wrangles over generally close questions of mixed fact and law when so much that many governments were doing was indisputably illegal. This was, after all, a turbulent period in Latin America. There were subversive movements with varying degrees of external support. And although some Commission members might believe that the government's own policies—its acts and its omissions—sometimes fueled violent opposition, this was a difficult matter to prove. Moreover, some jurists and probably some members, if pressed, would have argued that whatever the cause of domestic violence, even if it were

not have been entirely unconnected to the fact that judges, certainly judges of
the courts with powers of constitutional review, came from the same middle
and upper classes suffused with anxiety about Leftist threats to the established
order of things. Serving in the midst of what luminaries of that order (in the
United States no less than in Latin America) declared to be a global Cold War
and in ideologically polarized societies, judges would be naturally inclined to
concede to governments a very large margin of appreciation about the
requirements of domestic security. In actual fact, however, governments rarely
tested the full measure of that inclination, since they committed the most
flagrant human rights delinquencies secretly or at least behind the often thin
veil of official denial.

So although the norms invoked by the Inter-American human rights
institutions often mirrored those of national constitutions, the conjunction of
multiple exceptions with an auto-restrained judiciary and a secretive state
made constitutional norms ineffective. In actual fact, therefore, the Commission, unlike its European counterpart, was attempting to impose on governments restraints without domestic parallel. It was trying to do this, moreover,
in the face of the conviction held by many regimes and their class supporters
that grave violations of human rights were a regrettable but absolutely
necessary means, if not for survival altogether, then at least for the restoration
of their domestic tranquillity.

Form, then, did not follow function. For in form the European and Inter-
American regimes were quite similar. Both had a body of norms defining in
terms of individual rights the proper limits of Governmental action and the
two sets of norms were almost identical. Both had a Commission with first-
instance jurisdiction over claims of human rights violations and a Court with
jurisdiction to receive cases brought to it by the Commission or by a state
wishing to challenge a Commission decision. The European institutions came
first,[6] preceding the Inter-American Commission by six and the Inter-
American Court by twenty years. They were models for the inter-American
system's architects. Perhaps the very absence of drama in the operation of
these European institutions reassured Latin Governments when in 1959
they joined in nearly unanimous support for the Commission's birth.[7] It is

largely in response to the government's indifference to human misery and its corruption
and the cruelty of its security forces and its failure to maintain democratic order, still
governments had a right to suppress armed challenges to its authority (by means otherwise
consistent with human rights norms). So the Commission, in addition to focusing primarily on the government's clandestine violation of non-derogable rights, would criticize
unreasonable prolongation of emergency measures or *excess* in their application.

[6] *European Convention for the Protection of Human Rights and Fundamental Freedoms*, 213 UNTS 221, ETS 5, UKTS 71 (1953) (signed at Rome, 4 Nov., 1950; entered
into force 3 Sept., 1953).

[7] Paragraph II of Resolution VIII, which created the Commission, was approved with fifteen votes in favor, four against, and two abstentions. See also C. Medina, *The Battle of Human Rights, Gross, Systematic Violations and the Inter-American System* (Dordrecht, 1988)
at 68. *OAS Fifth Meeting of Consultation of Ministers of Foreign Affairs, Final Act*, OEA /
Ser.C/II.

often said of solidly established institutions that if they did not exist, they would have to be invented. Thus they are represented as examples of keen foresight on the part of their founders. By the early 1980s, it was evident that if, on the eve of its birth, the Commission's progenitors had been blessed with foresight, they would have joined in a late-term abortion.

With this bit of foreshadowing, I turn now to a brief history of the Commission's passage from its obscure, anodyne birth to an almost heroic post-adolescence where it is finally joined by the late-emerging Court.

THE RISE OF THE COMMISSION

Although it is the single most cited and celebrated text of the international human rights movement, the Universal Declaration[8] was not the first broadly detailed enumeration of rights to be adopted by an intergovernmental organization. That honor falls to the American Declaration of the Rights and Duties of Man, birthed by unanimous vote of the newly formed Organization of American States some three months before the UN General Assembly acted. But as if exhausted by this essay in norm-making, the Member States did virtually nothing during the next eleven years either to refine and elaborate the rights declared or to establish means for their application to concrete cases. Then in 1959, coincidentally the year in which Fidel Castro began openly to consolidate a socialist-sounding regime ninety miles off the coast of the world's most powerful as well as most unashamedly laissez faire capitalist state, the Organization decided by resolution to establish the Inter-American Commission on Human Rights. It would be composed of seven persons, serving four-year terms, selected by the General Assembly from a pool of supposedly distinguished persons formed by Member State nominees. Assisting these *distinguidos* would be a staff integrated into the OAS bureaucracy headed by the Organization's elected Secretary-General.

The Commission officially began life in 1960 with a vague mandate to promote human rights. Its animating resolution had failed to address, much less clearly to resolve the many basic questions concerning any official human rights enforcement institution.Some of these omissions were made good seven years later by the so-called Protocol of Buenos Aires.[9] It declared the Commission to be a 'principal organ' of the OAS and explicity confirmed

---

[8] *Universal Declaration of Human Rights*, G.A. Res 217 A (III), 10 Dec., 1948, UN Doc A/810, at 71 (1948).

[9] *OAS Charter (as amended by the 1967 Protocol of Buenos Aires)*, Art. 51. For further discussion of the Protocol and its effect on the status and function of the Commission, see T. Buergenthal, 'The Revised OAS Charter and the Protection of Human Rights,' *AJIL*, Oct. 1975, Vol. 69, No. 4, 828–36. Also see Medina, above n. 1, at 87–9.

its jurisdiction over petitions from individuals [10] alleging violations by their governments of rights enumerated in the American Declaration. While making themselves unconditionally vulnerable to individual complaints, with a Gallic delight in paradox OAS members made prior consent a condition of Commission jurisdiction over complaints they might make against each other. Surely this was to swallow a camel and shrink from a fly. For while the former were certain to occur, the latter were improbable at any time, much less among members of a political and military[11] alliance waging a Cold War. Even states without close ties are unlikely to take steps which are certain to aggravate their mutual relations unless those steps concern matters high on the foreign policy agenda. Human rights certainly did not enjoy a place of prominence in 1960s Hemispheric statecraft. Except in relations with Communist-Bloc states, they were hardly on the radar screen of US foreign policy discourse until the 1970s.[12] Also inhibiting interstate complaints is the fact of universal vulnerability: at least isolated instances of abusive action by persons exercising public authority will occur even in democratic states with strong rule-of-law traditions. If, for instance, we were to accept Dostoyevski's dictum that the quality of a country's prisons reveals the quality of its civilization, very few countries would appear very civilized.[13]

The relative probability (and hence risk) of individual and state claims certainly was understood by the European states when, in constructing their own regional regime, they made acceptance of Commission jurisdiction over

---

[10] The Commission does not require the complainant to demonstrate a familial or other close connection to the alleged victim and it characterizes complaints brought by non-governmental organizations such as Amnesty International or Human Rights Watch as 'individual'; indeed a considerable proportion of the Commission's cases, certainly some of its leading ones, have an organizational provenance. Whether brought by an individual in the literal sense or an organization, a single case may concern a number of victims, even entire communities as in complaints alleging grave mistreatment of a named indigenous people.

[11] Coincident with the establishment of the OAS, the member states entered into a mutual security agreement, the Rio Treaty, which committed them to concert their responses to any threat to the peace and security of the Hemisphere. Decision-making procedures in the Treaty were entwined with those of the OAS. The Treaty defined the military just as the Charter defined the political dimensions of the regional anti-communist association of the United States with the states of Latin America. The Treaty-Charter relationship ceased to be integral when the Anglophonic states of the Caribbean joined the OAS but did not become parties to the Treaty.

[12] See L. Schoultz, *Human Rights and United States Policy Toward Latin America* (Princeton, NJ: Princeton University Press, 1981), 3. Also see D. Forsythe, *The Politics of International Law: US Foreign Policy Reconsidered* (Boulder,1990).

[13] Consider Reports such as *Human Rights Violations in the United States: A Report on US Compliance with the International Covenant on Civil and Political Rights* (NY: Human Rights Watch and ACLU, 1993), and *Prison Conditions in Japan* (NY: Human Rights Watch/Asia, 1995). Increasingly elaborate conceptions of what constitutes a 'human right', particularly the growing demands for the recognition of group rights coincident with the growth in the West of a culture receptive to claims of victimization, have made all states progressively more vulnerable to charges that they are human rights delinquents.

individual (but not state) complaints optional for themselves. Not all states rushed to accept it. France, for instance, waited until 1981, nearly thirty years after the system began to function.[14]

While explicitly confirming the jurisdiction of the Commission over individual claims, the Protocol left a deposit of uncertainty on a number of other matters. The most consequential one concerned the intended audience for Commission reports on conditions in particular countries. Was it only the annual General Assembly of the Organization? Or could the Commission publish a report as soon as it was completed and the concerned government had had a chance to respond? If the former interpretation prevailed, then a country report completed around the time of one Annual Meeting, but too late to get on its agenda, would languish in the Commission's offices for another twelve months. In the meantime, the target state could have completed a campaign of extermination waged against persons deemed subversive. In any event, it could plausibly claim that the information on which the report rested—information that would generally be collected some months before the report's preparation—was stale and that any human rights problems had been corrected.

Treating the General Assembly and/or other political organs of the OAS as the only legitimate recipients of its reports could have had a second and still more damaging effect. Although documents presented to the General Assembly customarily become public at the time they are considered, no constitutional provision prevented the Assembly from treating them as confidential and barring public access both to the document and to its discussion of the document's contents, assuming it decided to hold such a discussion rather than simply 'taking note' of the Commission's previous year's work.

From its inception, the international human rights movement has operated on the assumption that the most important means for improving the behavior of delinquent regimes is international public opinion. Although human rights activists often refer merely to the 'shaming effect' of exposure, as if a government shown to be torturing and murdering its opponents may experience a kind of moral epiphany or at least be embarrassed into less malignant behavior, their lobbying efforts imply and their private conversations often confirm belief in a more complex chain of causation. While hoping to trigger pressure from morally sensitive and influential sectors within the target state, in most instances the real targets of shaming campaigns are citizens of liberal democratic states. Today the resources and numbers of private organisations with transnational sympathies have grown to the point where they can themselves sometimes exert influence directly,

[14] [1981] *Yearbook of the European Convention on Human Rights* 32–3.

for instance through economic boycotts.[15] But in the 1960s and '70s, when the human rights movement was in its early adolescence and international civil society as a whole was puny compared to its current physique, governments remained the preeminent, indeed virtually exclusive instruments for influencing the behavior of governments. To be effective, then, private groups had to achieve a multiplier effect by activating the foreign policy establishment in the most influential Western states. The anticipated chain of causation proceeded from exposure to public outrage, to pressure on politicians in democratic states, to pressure on the delinquent regime.

Activists did not always admit this premise of their efforts. In its early years, Amnesty International, for instance, ostensibly relied on grass-roots appeals contained in letters sent to senior government officials respectfully requesting the release of 'prisoners of conscience.' On the surface, then, an appeal to the latent benignity of the letters' recipients. But the letter writing was coordinated from Amnesty's central research office and stemmed from that office's formal conclusion on the basis of an impartial inquiry that the subject of these letters was, indeed, a person imprisoned for his or her political views or associations and hence held in violation of rights guaranteed by the various human rights texts. In fact, then, the letter campaigns were part of a strategy of exposure, of pressure, dressed however in the bland clothing of an appeal to conscience which had, as it were, been momentarily mislaid.[16]

Differences of view concerning the Commission's publications policy finally came to a head in 1978 when after much debate and delay, the members approved a report on the situation of human rights in El Salvador,[17] a report which ripped off the state's electoral facade to reveal brutish military government ruling on behalf of the military caste and a tiny upper-class. Not only did the Report find the government responsible for grave and systematic violation of virtually all political and civil rights, in addition it recounted the discovery of the clandestine cells in which allegedly 'disappeared' persons deemed dangerous to state security had been incarcerated pending, in a number of cases, their execution.

Having at last overcome the resistance of some members to the Report's detailed candor, the Commission wrestled with the question of publication. Resolution came finally on the basis of a compromise. The Report could be published immediately, but with an annex containing the Salvadoran government's denials, objections and explanations. I and some other members objected on the grounds that to the extent the Commission had found any of

[15] See P. Wapner, 'Politics Beyond the State: Environmental Activism and World Civic Politics,' in *47 World Politics*, 3 (1955), 311.

[16] For further discussion of Amnesty International, see E. Larsen, *A Flame in Barbed Wire: The Story of Amnesty International* (NY,1979).

[17] IACHR, Report on the Situation of Human Rights in El Salvador (1978).

the Government's comments on its draft persuasive, it had correspondingly modified its Report and hence in relationship to the final report they were blows against empty space, literally irrelevant. As for the remainder of the Government's many and choleric comments, since the Commission had determined them to be meretricious where not simply mendacious, why dignify them with inclusion even as an Annex? Publication might be taken to imply that the Commission felt that readers of the Report should decide for themselves what was the actual state of affairs in Salvador, an implication at odds with the categorical conclusions of the Report. Moreover, how could readers make a decision on their own when much of the evidence stemmed from direct observation and interrogations conducted by Commission members? Whether because of the force of these objections or a more self-confident Commission or the changed moral and diplomatic environment in the Hemisphere occasioned by the human rights program of US President Jimmy Carter, no such annex was included in subsequent reports.

FROM PROTOCOL TO CONVENTION

After the Protocol of Buenos Aires, the next major landmark in a chronological account of institutional development was the American Convention on Human Rights, completed and signed at a 1969 diplomatic conference in San Jose, Costa Rica.[18] In the very resolution establishing the Commission, OAS members had declared it to be a transitional arrangement pending the adoption of a human rights treaty.[19] When would the transition end? After every state adhered to the treaty or simply after the adherence of the number required to bring it into force? And if the latter, then would non-adhering states slip through the jurisdictional net and escape assessment altogether, a result hardly calculated to encourage universal adherence. Concerning these issues the resolution had nothing explicit to say.

The intervening ratification of the Protocol of Buenos Aires added a new dimension to the legal issues. After being endowed with conditional existence through a resolution subject to amendment by a simple majority of any subsequent General Assembly, under the terms of the Protocol the Commission became a 'Principal Organ' of the OAS with the jurisdictional power described above. By being thus constitutionalized, it had as much legal claim to permanence as the OAS itself which was presumably subject to dissolution by the same two-thirds vote that would be required to dissolve

[18] OAS *Treaty Series*, No. 36. or above n. 4, at 22–41.
[19] Art. 150 of the OAS Charter, as amended by the Protocol of Buenos Aires states that 'Until the Inter-American Convention on Human Rights, referred to in Chapter XVI, enters into force, the present Inter-American Commission on Human Rights shall keep vigilance over the observance of human rights.'

the Commission. But, some legal scholars asked, what exactly had been incorporated into the Charter?[20] Certainly the procedures for electing the Commission and its jurisdiction to examine both individual cases and the general condition of human rights in all members of the OAS. But what about the substantive norms it had been applying, namely those embodied in the American Declaration. Had they too been incorporated?

The affirmative on this issue had a powerful case. National legal systems do recognize a distinction between *in personam* and subject-matter jurisdiction. But that distinction is coherent only where the institution in question has *some* subject-matter jurisdiction. A court is by definition an institution that applies 'the law', that is, determines whether certain behavior is consistent with authoritative norms or, in civil cases, whether such norms authorize public intervention either to maintain or to reverse the status quo. A 'court' without any law to apply is a definitional absurdity. With respect to the Commission, the only law available was the Declaration. The generalities of the OAS Charter itself were insufficiently precise to qualify. Moreover, it was the Declaration that the Commission had been applying since its inception and neither before nor after the adoption of the Protocol did any state suggest that it ought to be finding its law elsewhere.[21] Under the circumstances, silence was eloquent.

From 1969 to 1977, exactly six states ratified the Convention, five less than the number required to activate it. So the question of its effect on the Commission remained moot. Then Jimmy Carter came to Washington with a personal, no less than electoral commitment to the promotion of human rights, and an equally personal aversion to a confrontational or imperious statecraft or one employing sanctions on trade and investment. One way of reconciling these often contradictory impulses was to emphasize multilateral actions and institutions such as the languishing Convention. The most committed delinquents managed to resist President Carter's entreaties. Ironically, so did the United States. Nevertheless, within two years of his assumption of office, Carter had managed to induce ratification by enough of the regimes in the middle of the human rights league table to bring the Treaty into force.

Blindly applauded particularly by legalists in the human rights community, the timing of this happy event was infelicitous. For the issues which had for years been moot now threatened to become real. None of the period's great malefactors—Argentina, Chile, El Salvador, Guatemala, Uruguay, Paraguay

---

[20] See, for example, T. Buergenthal, above n. 9.

[21] In an Advisory Opinion, the Inter-American Court subsequently held that '. . . the advisory jurisdiction of the Court can be exercised, in general, with regard to any provision dealing with the protection of human rights set forth in any international treaty applicable to the American States . . . ' (Advisory Opinion OC-1/82 of 24 Sept., 1982). But it clearly saw these as supplementing Hemispheric human rights norms.

—were parties to the new Convention. All were the subjects of multiple cases before or of investigations initiated by the Commission. All therefore had ample incentive to challenge the Commission's jurisdiction over them and in the months preceding the first General Assembly following the Convention's activation I, then a member of the Commission, uneasily anticipated an argument along the following lines:

The Convention itself had two facets. One was substantive: an enumeration of rights almost identical to those found in the Declaration. The other was institutional: the detailed establishment of a Commission and a Court. The institution hitherto recognized as the Commission was at its birth provisional, a makeshift affair, and as such absorbed through the Protocol of Buenos Aires into the constitutive structure of the OAS. There it sat, unfinished, awaiting the time when the Convention would come into force and establish its final form. Now that had happened. There could be only one Commission. Consistent with the founding vision, it had to be the one described in the Convention. But that Commission, by virtue of its being Convention based, had jurisdiction only over ratifying countries. Ergo, it had no jurisdiction over Argentina et al.

It was a strained, convoluted sort of argument, I believed, a gauzy matter of legal-sounding words; but to delinquent governments not notably concerned with legal niceties or vulnerable to critical domestic commentary, it might appear to offer a cover—however poor—for an essentially crude political challenge to the Commission. Pretending insouciance, the Commission proceeded to draft a new statute and regulations consistent with the view that the Convention's activation resulted simply in *adding* a second sort of jurisdiction to the Commission's armory. Previously its sole source of authority, its sole claim to existence was the 1959 resolution as embedded in the 1967 Protocol. Now it could rely as well on the Convention, invoking and employing its procedural standards with respect to ratifying states; with respect to the rest, the Protocol, incorporating the Declaration, continued to suffice.

To my relief and delight, when we presented the new statute incorporating this latter interpretation to the General Assembly, it passed without a murmur of dissent.[22] The result was not simply to confirm the Commission's continuing jurisdiction over all member states of the OAS, it also confirmed the Commission's reading of words and silences in the Convention which might have been construed as reducing, in relation to Convention states, certain capacities it had chosen to exercise before the Convention came into force. Of these by far the most important was the initiation, at its discretion, of general country reports and the conduct, in connection with those reports, of on-site observations (with the permission of the concerned government).

[22] AG/Res. 447 (IX-0-79).

The Convention, according to the Commission's unchallenged interpretation, largely restated existing practices and policies. Hence, although the Commission flew different jurisdictional flags depending on whether it was approaching a Convention or a non-ratifying state, for the most part it was entitled to use and did use identical strategies and tactics. At least in theory, however, the Convention was not entirely without operational consequence for the handling of individual cases. Yet for years practice remained unchanged. To appreciate why, one needs to turn from *explication de texte* to the actual conditions prevailing in Latin America when the Convention came into force.

STATES OF TERROR

There is no better way of evoking those conditions than through the paradigm petition then arriving at the Commission's offices in Washington. It ran something like this:

My name is Monica Fernandez. Three months ago, around noon, I was walking with my son Juan, who is seventeen years old, near our home when we were approached by a group of heavily armed men in civilian clothes. Their leader identified them as members of the joint-intelligence directorate of the armed forces and said they would like Juan to accompany them to police station number four, the one in our neighborhood, so that they could ask him some questions and show him some photos which might help them to identify certain persons. I begged to accompany my son, but they insisted he come alone, saying he would be home for dinner. They took him away in unmarked cars without license plates. Juan did not come home at dinner time, so I went to the police station. There they denied any knowledge of him. Then I went through the city to every one of its many police stations and in each one I received the same answer. The following morning I went from one military barracks to another in the city in search of my son. But everywhere I went the reply was the same: 'He is not here. We know nothing of this fellow.' Since then I have done everything in my power to find my son. I have gone to the Ministry of Defense. Through our local priest, I sought the intercession of the Cardinal. I hired a lawyer and he filed a habeas corpus petition in the District Court; but the government denied any knowledge of my son and the petition was dismissed. I tried to put a notice in the newspapers, but it was rejected as slanderous to the armed forces and afterwards I received very threatening calls late at night and cars would sometimes follow me down the street when I went out. My son has been disappeared. Please help me.'

At the beginning of 1973, the Commission had fewer than fifty active cases on its docket,[23] fewer than fifty in a Hemisphere pocked by states

[23] T. J. Farer, *The United States and the Inter-American System: Are there Functions for the Forms?* Studies in Transnational Legal Policy, No. 17 (The American Society of International Law, 1978), 71.

habituated to torture and summary execution as instruments of governance, a Hemisphere containing Haiti, El Salvador, and Guatemala, to name but a few. But during the first years of the Commission's life, most of the great army of victims (unknown to the Commission because the Commission was unknown to them) had come, as usual, from the *popular classes*, as the poor are called in Latin America. General immunity from official brutality for the upper-middle, much less the upper classes faded only in the late 1960s when political institutions and social structures began to crack under the combined weight of a rapidly growing population, sluggish economic growth in most countries, swollen and apathetic bureaucracies, rent-seeking capitalism, political parties without roots or ruled imperiously from the top and in either case often without programs or purposes other than the acquisition and retention of power, and the globe's most uneven distribution of wealth.[24] For the growing ranks of young educated people filled with disgust over the condition of their countries, Marxist faiths of one sort or another gave intellectual focus and Cuba provided a deceptively brilliant example. Meanwhile, for the oligarchs and officers feeling the very ground shaking beneath their feet, counter-revolutionary doctrine developed initially by the French during the Indo-Chinese and Algerian wars and then refined and disseminated by the United States gave shape to their fears and direction to their means.

Perhaps the center could not have held and managed incremental reform under any circumstances, inherited attitudes and institutions being what they were. But poor Latin America had the bad luck to rendezvous with social crisis in the midst of a Global Cold War which insinuated itself into the politics and culture of every state in the Hemisphere. Global polarization reproduced itself nationally wherever the center was weak.

By 1973, when the Chilean Armed Forces, under the leadership of General Augusto Pinochet, overthrew the elected government of Salvador Allende and set about terrorizing, exterminating, imprisoning or expelling its opponents,[25] even democracy in the weak sense—periodic elections not grossly corrupt to choose occupants of the legislative branch and the highest executive position in the country—had begun to look like an endangered species. For with the ascension of Pinochet, generals (or, as in Haiti, thugs with civilian clothes and a kept army) now reigned not only in such traditional purlieus of authoritarian rule as Guatemala and El Salvador, but also

[24] For details on global poverty, see E. Oyen, S. M. Miller and S. Abdus Sammad, (eds.), *Poverty: A Global Review: A Handbook on International Poverty Research* (Oslo, 1996). See also G. Myrdal, *Asian Drama: An Inquiry into the Poverty of Nations* (New York, 1972).
[25] For details of the Chilean coup and its aftermath, see P. Sigmund, *The Fall of Allende* (Pittsburgh, 1977) and J. White, *Chile's Days of Terror: Eyewitness Accounts of the Military Coup* (New York, 1974). See also IACHR Report on the Status of Human Rights in Chile (1974) and IACHR Second Report on the Situation of Human Rights in Chile (1976).

in two states, Chile and Uruguay, which had for decades been Latin paragons
of elective governance and in Brazil which, after a long history of oscillation
between civil and military rule, had by the late 1950s seemed committed to
the former. And though elected government survived in Argentina, its
condition was so patently morbid that many observers correctly anticipated
its imminent demise.

It was not simply the rapid spread of military governments (with strong
backing from industrial and land-holding social sectors, and in many cases—
before Jimmy Carter became President—the Executive power of the United
States) that flattened the hopes of democrats throughout the hemisphere.
Beyond the looming ubiquity of such governments was the appearance of
permanence. Previously during the twentieth century, military interventions,
at least in the hemisphere's larger and more economically developed states,
had been heralded as brief interruptions in electoral governance occasioned
by emergencies beyond the coping power of civilians. The intervenors of the
1960s and 1970s adopted a very different stance. They had come, they
seemed to say, not to rescue but to suspend indefinitely both elected regimes
and the frequent associates of such regimes, namely freedom of speech and
association and protection from summary procedures for detention and
punishment. Uninhibited by the dysfunctional constraints of electoral and
constitutional government, they would proceed methodically to heal a feverish national society by cauterizing its leftist infections and enclosing it in a
new political economy. This was, the officers implied, a project of indefinite
duration.[26]

Organized, disciplined, and determined, they set out to eliminate opposition to their political project which was to grow the economy while maintaining the basic social structure and traditional culture of these peripheral
semi-capitalist states and, of course, the military establishment's position as
a state within the national state, a self-governing and policing body, the final
word on the meaning of the constitution and ultimate arbiter of the nation's
destiny. Moderates in the military defined the enemy as the members and
ideological and material supporters of clandestine groups of the Left willing
to employ violence. Radicals added to those categories all persons who
through their teaching and writing and other activities fertilized the roots of
subversion by questioning the traditional institutions of national life, those
who, in the words of one Argentine general, are not with us. Either definition
encompassed large numbers of mostly young people from the middle classes.
And so, in the more developed countries where they had once been more-or-
less safe, they began to visit the torture centres established and methodically
maintained by the new Torquemadas and to experience that world of pain

---

[26] See, for instance, G. O'Donnell, *Modernization and Bureaucratic Authoritarianism:
Studies in South American Politics* (Berkeley, 1973).

disproportionate access to which had hitherto been the unique privilege of the poor.

Brazil was first. With strong if slightly cloaked support from the United States[27] the military had displaced a populist civilian regime in 1964 and imposed its version of order. Initially this seemed to require very little exertion. Political parties were weak[28] and the rest of civil society—other than organisations of industrialists and landowners—only somewhat stronger; recent civilian governments had not been successful either as economic managers or as agents of greater social equity. The country lacked a charismatic civilian leader. In historical context openly authoritarian rule was nothing new. But as (and quite possibly because) economic conditions failed to improve dramatically and the military appeared determined to institutionalize itself as arbiter of the national destiny and to ignore the country's gross inequities, mostly young people, inspired by the still very fresh Cuban example[29] and probably influenced by anti-capitalist explanations of underdevelopment, formed grouplets of armed resistance. The military government's intelligence services responded with the means the French had pioneered in the battle of Algiers, namely pitiless torture of anyone suspected of participating in or having information about the conspirators.[30] Like the French, they won the battle; unlike the French, they did not lose the war.

Brazil's descent into the abyss of systematic torture barely registered on the Commission's radar screen. Perhaps this reflected the relatively limited scope of the torture campaign, although like its predecessors and those still to come, it extended well beyond the virtual handful of people who had chosen violence as a means of resistance. It also suggests that nearly ten years after its creation, the Commission still had a pretty low profile. And perhaps it said something about the underdevelopment of Brazilian civil society at that point, since, as subsequent events would confirm, there is a discernible correlation between the strength of indigenous institutions committed to the defense of civil liberties and the scope of appeals to the Commission for help.

Confirmation came first from Uruguay where in the late 1960s the military launched a 'creeping coup,' that is the progressive evisceration of civil authority accompanied by a spreading net of arbitrary arrest and

---

[27] For a discussion of the US role in the 1964 Brazilian coup, see P. Parker, *Brazil and the Quiet Intervention* (Austin, 1979), see also L. Schoultz, above n. 12, at 168–77.

[28] See L. Diamond, 'Democracy in Latin America: Degrees, Illusions, and Directions for Consolidation,' in *Beyond Sovereignty: Collectively Defending Democracy in the Americas*, T. Farer, (ed.), (Baltimore, 1996) 80.

[29] Which, of course, Fidel Castro was actively promoting, Cuba being an insufferably small stage for the exercise of his swollen ego.

[30] See generally A. Horne, *A Savage War of Peace: Algeria 1954–1962* (New York, 1978).

excruciating torture which in the course of the 1970s would achieve Hemispheric preeminence in terms of the percentage of the population trapped in its folds.[31] No Latin country had a more educated population, a more developed civil society, a broader tradition of culture and civility. Yet nowhere else was so large a proportion of the middle classes and the organized working class scooped up by the state and tossed to the torturers. Unlike chronic objects of state terror isolated in the Andean altiplano or Haitian ghettoes or the interior of Guatemala, this new class of victims and their families and friends were connected to the wider world through a network of personal and institutional ties. They also differed from the traditional class of victims in seeing themselves as the possessors of both constitutionally and internationally guaranteed rights. As the coup crept inexorably forward, the Commission's hitherto exiguous agenda began to swell. Then in September of 1973 came a very different sort of coup— a public, swift, and furiously violent decapitation of Chile's elected government, a government testing (improvidently, to be sure) the possibilities of democratic revolutionary change in a peripheral capitalist country. The Commission's case load quickly metastasized, growing within seven years from about fifty to well over seven thousand with no end in sight.[32]

THE LIMITS OF CASE WORK

In the European system, the vast majority of petitions were regularly dismissed at the door of its Commission on the grounds either that the petitioner had failed to exhaust internal remedies or that the facts as stated did not constitute a violation of the European Convention.[33] Although the Inter-American Commission employed the same conditions of admissibility, they rarely barred the door. With respect to internal remedies, Europe differed qualitatively from Latin America. In most of the European states subject to the Human Rights Convention, its provisions were both embedded and mirrored in domestic law[34] and hence in theory enforceable by local

---

[31] See IACHR Report on the Situation of Human Rights in Uruguay (1978). See also L. Weschler, *A Miracle, A Universe: Settling Accounts with Torturers* (New York, 1990).

[32] *IACHR, Ten Years of Activities: 1971–1981*, above n. 5, at 82.

[33] Almost 90% of all registered petitions are found inadmissible by the Commission. See T. Zwart, *The Admissibility of Human Rights Petitions: The Case Law of the European Commission of Human Rights and the Human Rights Committee* (Dordrecht, 1994), 5.

[34] 'Embedded' because the constitutions of most continental states explicitly declared international agreements to be a part of domestic law. For example, Austria holds international treaties and agreements as equal to the Constitution. Other countries of Europe, such as France, hold international treaties as superior to statutory law, while many others hold them equal to statutory law but give preference to international law when it conflicts with domestic law. (See R. Bernhardt, 'The Convention and Domestic Law' in *The European System for the Protection of Human Rights*, R. St. J. Macdonald, F. Matscher and H. Petzold

courts. Since those courts enjoyed independence and prestige and functioned within a rule-of-law culture, one could assume that in the great majority of instances, theory and fact would coincide. In Latin America, the assumption that the courts would generally apply authoritative norms could not be lightly made even in the case of countries with elected governments; in the case of states whose officials were working overtime to generate petitions to the Commission, it could not be made at all.

As products of a legal culture instinct with respect for the formalities of right procedure and a political one hostile to external audits of internal behavior, the Latin members of the Commission might have been expected to dodge behind notional internal remedies, at the very least by imposing on petitioners a heavy burden of proof that they had exhausted them. To their very great credit, the Commissioners chose to confront reality. Quietly, informally, they simply *presumed* the exhaustion of remedies, leaving governments the option of raising the issue.[35] Few in fact did.

Having driven easily through the Commission's deliberately porous juris-dictional screen, most cases immediately stalled. And this happened even when there were still only a few. After all, while European cases almost always presented issues of law, in Inter-American ones it was almost invari–ably the facts which were disputed. No government claimed that torture and summary execution were permissible even in states of emergency; they simply denied torturing and killing. And precisely because as a matter of high policy Latin governments were using indefensible means, they could hardly be expected to facilitate the Commission's investigations. Hearings conducted with a constitutionally recalcitrant accused and without benefit of compulsory process are generally not a plausible means for determining the truth, except, perhaps, where they follow an intensive investigation which makes a *prima facie* case of guilt. The Buenos Aires Protocol had not explicitly imposed on states any obligation to admit Commission fact-finding missions. Given the manifest attitudes of the ratifying states about their sovereign prerogatives, the Commission could not credibly have implied such an obligation from the vague commitment to facilitate its work, much less could they have expected states to accept so imaginative an interpretation of their original intent.

Once the case load metastasized, practical obstacles to effective investiga-tions made the formal ones largely irrelevant. In 1976, the Commission's professional staff hardly existed, and during the succeeding decade, when it reached the acme of its prominence and efficacy, the effective staff was less

---

(eds.), Dordrecht: 1993, 25–40.) 'Mirrored' in that the Conventions' provisions were much the same as the guarantees of individual liberty enumerated in the various national constitutions.

[35] To be sure, the issue did not frequently arise, because, as I indicated earlier, the sorts of persons likely to file a complaint with the Commission were equally likely to have sought judicial relief in national courts, however slim the prospect of success.

than a dozen. But without the active cooperation of governments, even three or four dozen could have investigated only a tiny fraction of the thousands of cases appearing on the Commission's agenda.

The stunning leap in numbers did not alter the Commission's practice, which was as follows. Each case's allegations were incorporated into a letter addressed to the Foreign Minister of the target state who was asked to solicit comments from his government. Time would pass. Eventually, sometimes after further prodding, the Government would respond. Responses often assumed the form of an opening paragraph in which the Foreign Minister suavely invoked his country's ancient and celebrated commitment to the defense of human rights, a second paragraph congratulating the Commission on its labors, and a third either flatly denying the allegations or indicating that the most scrupulous inquiries were being conducted into the charges. If the latter, then more prodding would often intervene before the arrival of a second letter essentially identical in its first two paragraphs and using the third to convey the government's joy in being able to inform the Commission that the inquiry had demonstrated that the accusation was baseless.

In the case of disappearances, the government might say simply that according to the records of the Ministry of the Interior or the police or the armed forces, the named individual had never been arrested and of course was not presently detained. Or it might garnish this declaration with suggestions that the supposed victim had disappeared himself or herself in order to join a subversive group or had chosen to leave the country in order to escape arrest for subversion or the revenge of subversive groups intolerant of deserters. Normally after receiving a flat denial of responsibility, the Commission would simply transmit it to the petitioner for comment. If the latter had no comment, having already conveyed to the Commission all the available information, the case, while it might remain formally on the agenda, would become inactive.

Occasionally petitioners did respond with new information, for instance, with an account of the place and condition of the disappeared person provided to the petitioner by a person who had been held in the same clandestine torture center and then released. Whereupon the Commission would go through the same process of transmitting the alleged facts to the government which would again deny the allegations. Occasionally, certain governments absolutely failed to respond no matter how often prodded and were finally subjected to the time limit and the presumption of truth set by the Commission's Regulations.[36] Pursuant to the latter, the Commission would accept the allegations as true and include the case in its annual report to the General Assembly. And very occasionally, the government's response was so incredible and/or contradictory or evasive or otherwise

---

[36] Arts. 34.6, 42, *Regulations of the Commission*, see Appendix V.

inculpating that the Commission felt justified in finding a violation of human rights.[37]

With much of the Hemisphere convulsing under a reign of terror, the Commission majority concluded without any formal decision to invest almost all of its resources in reports on the general conditions of human rights in various countries, rather than focus on individual petitions. Accumulated cases from a country would serve as one basis for choosing the target of a general inquiry and as an aid to the structuring of on-site observations where governments allowed them. However, the Commissioners accurately anticipated that in the course of a general inquiry, they might develop sufficient facts to permit a definitive conclusion to a number of individual petition cases.

THE PRIMACY OF COUNTRY REPORTS

The Commission treated country reports as a matter entirely within its discretion. It adopted no criteria for the decision to undertake a general inquiry at least in part because it found no objective correlatives to the gravity of a situation. Numbers of unresolved petition cases before the Commission might be persuasive evidence of difference in conditions between countries at the same level of economic development, but revealed very little about the depth of the human rights abyss in a country like Guatemala with its small middle class and weak and ethnically-polarized civil society. Adoption of formal criteria for triggering investigations would have led to endless and inconclusive disputes over their application and thus fomented excuses for non-cooperation. Their adoption would also have grated against the Commission's claim that it was functioning not as an accusatory but rather as a fact-finding body, as ready to compliment as to condemn, seeking information on behalf of the political organs of the OAS, eager to advise and assist. This stance had a number of virtues. Along with deflecting the charge that it was not investigating countries in the order of their respective degrees of delinquency, it justified a considerable informality of procedure, an informality absolutely required by the determined efforts of governments to hinder the Commission and conceal their crimes and the Commission's lack of coercive investigatory authority. In addition, it allowed the Commission quietly to incorporate into its decisions on the timing of inquiries judgments about how best to influence the behavior of

---

[37] In one Uruguayan case where death by torture was alleged, the government conceded that a young woman had died in detention, but insisted that it was a simple case of suicide by hanging. The Commission noted that under Uruguayan law, when a person died in detention, the state had to perform an autopsy. And so it requested a copy of the autopsy report to which the government responded that the report was classified and hence could not be made available. See *IACHR, Ten Years of Activities*, Case 1870, above n. 5, at 161–3.

governments. It might, for instance, try to use the threat of inquiry to inhibit atrocity.[38]

Once made, the decision to investigate was communicated confidentially to the concerned government which was simultaneously urged to invite the Commission to visit its country. The quid for this quo would be the Commission's feigning acceptance of an 'unsolicited' invitation. Should the government deny itself the opportunity to appear an eager host with nothing to hide, the Commission would then publicly announce its decision to prepare a report on the condition of human rights in the country and would formally request permission to enter and conduct an on-site observation.

Actually, during this period (roughly 1976 to 1984) a few invitations were unsolicited. In 1977, when the treaty relinquishing control of the Panama Canal was before the United States Senate, General Omar Torrijos, the real albeit not formal head of the Panamanian State, urged the Commission to visit his country as quickly as possible. Opponents of the Treaty in the United States claimed that its adoption would strengthen Torrijos' grip on Panama and they labeled him one of the Hemisphere's most egregious human rights delinquents. The Commission, Torrijos declared in a communication to its then chair, was as obligated to vindicate the reputation of governments falsely accused of human rights violations as to condemn the true malefactors. A member of the US National Security Council subsequently informed the author that Torrijos had acted at the suggestion of United States government officials. A second unsolicited invitation came three years later, this time from the President of Colombia responding to a demand from guerrillas then holding a clutch of Ambassadors hostage in Bogota's Dominican Republic Embassy. And a third came from the revolutionary Sandinista-dominated government in 1981 immediately after it replaced the Somoza regime in Nicaragua.

Of the countries approached by the Commission during this period (roughly 1976 to 1983) three—Chile, following the Commission's first report on conditions there, Paraguay and Uruguay—said no. Under varying degrees of direct and indirect pressure from the Carter administration, Argentina, El Salvador, and Haiti consented. The precedents resulting from this combination of unsolicited invitations and acquiescences combined to transform the on-site observation from an extraordinary initiative to a standard Commission practice and this may in part explain why even after Ronald Reagan replaced Jimmy Carter in the White House, the government of Guatemala, then the Hemisphere's most ferocious and assiduous practitioner of terror, consented to a Commission request for entry.

Until 1977 the Commission functioned without any settled rules for the

---

[38] Under the atrocious conditions of the time, the threat did not in fact prove very effective.

conduct of on-site inquiries. This lacuna left every regime room to negotiate the terms of entry with the Commission whose members, although nominally elected in their personal capacity as experts in the field of human rights and persons of moral distinction, enjoyed varying degrees of independence from the influence of their respective governments and held varying ideas about the prerogatives of sovereign states to deal with threats to internal security. Hence when Omar Torrijos solicited a Commission report on Panama, declaring in his zeal that all of the government's doors and windows would be open to facilitate observation of what lay inside, a group of Commission members saw the chance to effect an anticipatory stiffening of its spine so that it could better resist pressure for blinkered inquiries in instances where governments contemplated a Commission inquiry with an enthusiasm less unbuttoned than Torrijos'. So they drafted and secured general consent to a specific set of regulations on observations '*in loco*', acceptance of which would be implied whenever a government invited the Commission or granted permission for entry in response to a Commission request.[39] Essentially, the regulations gave the Commission a virtually absolute discretion to go any-where in the country, including all centres of detention, whenever and however it chose and to collect and preserve evidence by any means it deemed appropriate. In addition, Governments committed themselves to provide any necessary logistical support, to publicize the Commission's visit, and to issue a general assurance that persons testifying before the Com-mission or filing complaints would be protected from reprisal.[40]

Torrijos quickly gave the regulation the force of precedent by accepting its application to his country. Armed with this precedent in an organization formally premised on the sovereign equality of its members, commissioners were better equipped to resist the threats and blandishments of more powerful and less friendly states. Thus when the government of Argentina attempted to neuter a commission visit by proposing that it be limited to study of the country's judicial system, opponents of the gambit quickly marshaled a consensus by invoking the regulation and the principle of equal treatment for all member states.

The Panama report marked the opening of a period of intense activity and ascending prominence for the Commission. It also revealed some potential weaknesses of the general reports as means for influencing elite and public opinion. One was the Commission's studied refusal to compare countries. Arguably this is a natural position for a judicial body to assume. Guilt and innocence are absolute: Did the party charged violate authoritative norms?

[39] *Inter-American Commission on Human Rights, Regulations*, Title 2, Chap. iv, Arts. 54 and 55.
[40] Although the assurances were dutifully if sometimes grudgingly issued, the Commis-sion always warned persons offering information or filing complaints that it could not guarantee their safety.

An affirmative answer leads ineluctably to a finding of guilt. But even conceding that in the generality of cases guilt should be determined without reference to the number and severity of the defendant's crimes relative to the norm for the delinquencies at issue or the norm for all criminals in the jurisdiction, the court will normally make some sort of comparative judgment when it moves to the sentencing stage.

In form, Commission reports approximate the stages of the trial. After marshaling and analyzing the facts in relation to the norms of the American Declaration or later the Convention, the Commission reaches 'Conclusions.' They are in large part an enumeration of the specific rights the concerned government has violated through its acts and omissions. Then follow 'Recommendations', an enumeration of measures for terminating violations and repairing injuries. If the Commission were in fact a Grand Jury reporting to a court empowered to enjoin condemned behavior and order reparations, comparative judgments would be logically and practically irrelevant. For at least in theory, the court's enforcement resources are infinite: injunctions and punishments imposed in one case do not reduce the number available for imposition in others.

The human rights enforcement process is, of course, rather different at least to the extent it relies on agents external to the concerned state. By addressing its recommendations to the subject of a report, and particularly in calling, as it often does, for the punishment of the persons who have perpetrated murder, torture and arbitrary detention, the Commission implies a separation between the state itself or at least its highest officials, on the one hand, and the perpetrators on the other. Or it could be seen as resting its hopes for mitigation and reparation on the shaming effect of exposure. But in the cases where the Commission concluded, during this grim era, that terror was a matter of high state policy, it entertained no such hopes. Nor where civil society was weak and the governing clique strong and ferocious could the Commission hope to catalyse an internal process of correction. No, in such cases the only possible efficacy of a report was in persuading other states, either directly or indirectly through the medium of enlightened opinion, to exert influence on the delinquent.

As a practical matter, public indignation is an exhaustible good. Fatigue can set in rather sharply, particularly where essays in the vindication of moral values threaten to prove costly. Enforcement resources being in fact limited, a rational enforcement strategy—that is one which pursues the largest possible reduction in violations both near and longer term achievable with a given investment of resources—ought to take account of the relative gravity of crimes it seeks to terminate or avert and also the relative susceptibility of delinquents to external pressure. At a given moment, two regimes may be equally vicious. But one may include, or be little more than the public face of, private economic interests dependent for their wealth on access to foreign markets, while the other may be composed simply of thugs with no vocational alternative to public theft or of ascetic fanatics. If the principal enforcement resource available for deployment against both regimes is economic boycott, in a world of limited resources one might rationally choose to concentrate on the first of these not-so-hypothetical regimes.

Relative susceptibility to pressure is a strategic judgment arguably beyond the base competence of human rights experts. But relative viciousness is not. Yet most human rights organs, private no less than official, eschew such judgments. They do so partially on the ground that the judgments are 'political' in character rather than quasi-judicial and partially on the allegedly pragmatic ground that such judgments would tend to minimize the gravity of every violation and the absolute nature of human rights. For the reasons I have suggested, neither ground is unassailable.

The Panama report underscored the risks incident to failure to note at least gross differences among countries or to propose in general terms where a given country stands in the international human rights league table. Panama was not a human rights paragon. The regime led by General Omar Torrijos had come to power by coup d'etat and such electoral activity as it allowed at the time of the Commission's visit posed no threat to its survival. So it plainly violated Article XX of the American Declaration concerning the right to participate in government. In addition, the regime dealt with perceived conspiracies to effect its overthrow by suddenly seizing opponents and putting them free of charge on flights out of the country.[41] And although it had used them only once and that some years ago against an admitted bomber of public facilities, it had issued decrees *permitting* it to convict persons suspected of crimes against state security through an administrative process entirely circumventing the judiciary, decrees that might fairly be assumed to have chilled political activity.[42]

On the other hand, the regime did not torture opponents or disappear them or detain and convict them wholesale without due process. Limits on rhetorical opposition to the government were loose. The regime plainly had a substantial political base and, in part for that reason, in part because of the personality of Torrijos, a relaxed self-confidence. The net result was an atmosphere largely free of that acute fear which then permeated life in much of Latin America. Overall, one had to conclude that Panama was very far

[41] 'Probably it is a violation of human rights,' Torrijos conceded to the Commission. 'But which would you prefer,' he inquired with a smile, 'an extended stay in Miami or in the prison you visited yesterday?' He was referring to the *Carcelo Modelo*, a relic of some forgotten era of liberal penal reform with eight to a cell and beds for four, so people alternated in a kind of time-share arrangement.

[42] Following discussions with the Commission, the Panamanian Government rescinded the decrees in question. See *IACHR, Ten Years of Activities, 1971–1981*, above n. 4, at 272.

from the bloody dictatorship evoked in the United States by opponents of the Canal Treaties. At worst it stood in the middle class of performers. But although the Commission's Report stated that it had found no evidence of systematic torture or summary execution, since it concentrated on the human rights violations which did exist, against its will it lent itself to exploitation by persons wishing to paint a distorted image of Torrijos' government.

Perhaps because Latin America in the 1970s and early '80s offered such vivid contrasts between regimes of limitless terror and the rest, the lack of any explicitly comparative element in Commission reports did not thereafter seem consequential. And given the politics, premises and traditions of the OAS, the Commission could have openly made comparative judgments, however general, only at considerable risk to its authority within the organization. But the danger of communicating a distorted image or an image readily susceptible to distortion remains for all human rights reporting agencies and requires further consideration.

The Panama Report also illustrated the incongruity between the traditionally measured pace of Commission work and the needs of the world it served. By the time of its publication a year had passed and political discourse in the United States about the Treaties and the regime they would no doubt strengthen had frozen. For better or worse, the Commission had failed to communicate with an attentive audience. Its possible contribution to public understanding dissipated. This was not a necessary consequence of a part-time Commission composed by members prominently employed in government or academic position. For they would shortly demonstrate that with the necessary will and resources, they could act with dispatch.

In June of 1978, as a full-scale uprising against the dictatorship of Anastasio Somoza in Nicaragua bubbled toward the surface, the Commission informed the Nicaraguan Ambassador to the OAS in its decorous prose that it had decided to prepare a report on human rights in that country and 'hoped to receive an invitation from his government to make an on-site observation so that the report would reflect as accurately as possible the realities of human rights in Nicaragua.'[43] After securing an affirmative response, the Commission set a November date for its visit. But when, at the end of the summer, resistance to Somoza, led by Sandinista cadres, exploded in virtually all of the country's cities, the supreme organ of the OAS in times of crisis, the 'Meeting of Consultation of Ministers of Foreign Relations,'[44] recommended that the Commission accelerate its visit. Preceded by several staff lawyers, the Commission arrived on the third of October—within days of Somoza's recapture of the rebellious areas and the flight of opposition

---

[43] *IACHR, 10 Years of Activity*, above n. 4, at 277.
[44] See Arts. 61–69 of the OAS Charter.

forces into the hills to prepare for the next round—and plunged into scenes from Goya. After a week collecting evidence all over the country from diplomats, journalists, priests, non-governmental organizations, Red Cross Workers and, above all, occupants of the National Guard's cells, and survivors of the mopping-up operations in the cities completed only days before, the Commission directed its Executive Secretary to prepare a draft report along lines it outlined to him. Completed in a feverish burst of effort, it was ready for Commissioners when they arrived in Washington two weeks later for a special session at which they revised and approved the draft by consensus and immediately forwarded it to the Foreign Ministers, at the same time making certain it was available to the media.

For all the novelty of its expeditious completion, what really distinguished that report on Nicaragua was the harsh, detailed clarity of its descriptions and the categorical smack of its conclusions: 'In the light of the foregoing, the Inter-American Commission on Human Rights, in plenary, has arrived at the conclusion that the Government of Nicaragua has incurred responsibility for the following serious, persistent, and generalized violations:

a) The Government of Nicaragua is responsible for serious attempts against the right to life, in violation of the international humanitarian norms, in repressing in an excessive and disproportionate manner, the insurrections that occurred last September in the main cities of the country. In fact, the bombing of towns by the National Guard was done in an indiscriminate fashion and without prior evacuation of the civilian population, which caused innumerable deaths of persons who were not involved in the conflict, and, in general, a dramatic situation;
b) Likewise, the Government of Nicaragua is responsible for a large number of deaths which occurred after the combats [sic], because of abuses perpetrated by the National Guard during the so-called 'Operation Mop-up' and other actions several days after the cessation of hostilities in which many persons were executed in a summary and collective fashion for the mere reason of living in neighborhoods or districts where there had been activity by the Frente Sandinista de Liberacion Nacional (FSLN) and young people and defenseless children were killed;
. . .
d) The Government of Nicaragua is also responsible for the death and serious abuse, arbitrary detention, and other violations of the human rights of peasant groups;
e) In the events of last September *and even earlier* [emphasis added], there were serious violations to the right to personal security, by means of torture and other physical abuses which were inflicted on numerous detainees; . . . .'[45]

In the final paragraphs of its conclusions, the Commission made it clear that human rights violations were not conjunctural but endemic. With respect to the right to assembly, for instance, it flatly stated that '[e]ven before the emergency regime [declared by Somoza when the insurrection

---

[45] *IACHR, 10 Years of Activity*, above n. 4, at 277.

began] came into effect, the right to associations [sic], in general, and those of political and trade union associations, in particular, had been seriously limited.'

But the truly extraordinary features of the Report came at its very end. Although the Carter Administration in the United States wished to move Nicaragua toward political pluralism, it deeply distrusted the Sandinistas and saw if not Somoza himself then the National Guard as the necessary bulwark against the emergence of a left-wing regime.[46] It wanted government by 'moderate, 'centrist forces' and, to be entirely fair, it wanted to mitigate the gore bound to gush from a continuation of the conflict. But the Guard was not really a national army; it was a personal instrument of the dictator. So when the United States pursued an arrangement under which Somoza would abdicate formal power and possibly even leave the country for a time while the Guard remained in place, it was necessarily working to preserve at least important elements of the existing political order. This was not unintended. On the contrary, precisely what Washington desired was some benign modification of the prevailing political system not its sudden, total overthrow.[47]

To that goal the Report did not contribute when in its final lines the Commission declared that '[t]he damage and suffering caused by these violations have awakened, in a very forceful way, an intense and general feeling among the Nicaraguan people for the establishment of a system which will guarantee the observance of human rights.' Throughout Latin America those words, written by a body six of whose seven members were conservative representatives of Latin American establishments, were read and were intended to be read as a statement of moral conviction that the entire political order, the whole system of public authority in Nicaragua, was root-and-branch rotten. And, as if those words were not enough to make the point, the Commission for the first and only time in its history addressed no recommendations to the government. Within its own traditions and those of the OAS, there was no way it could have more clearly denied that the public authority system built over the years by the Somoza family had either redeeming features or redemptive potential.

AFTER NICARAGUA: TRIUMPH AND DECLINE

Before his death, Anastasio Somoza would cite the Commission report as one of the decisive forces driving him to resign and flee Nicaragua even

---

[46] On the attitude of the Carter Administration, see L. Schoultz, above n. 12, at 104. See also, R. A. Pastor, *Whirlpool: US Foreign Policy toward Latin America and the Caribbean* (Princeton, 1992), 53–4.

[47] See L. Schoultz, above n. 12, at 344–5.

though the Guard was still holding the line in most of the country. Whatever its effect on Somoza, its effect on the Commission's profile and prestige appeared to those of us then inside it as profound. One suggestive sign came in the form of a telephone call from Turbay Ayala, the President of Colombia, in the spring of 1980. He informed the Commission that after weeks of impasse in negotiations with M-19 Guerrillas who were occupying the Dominican Embassy in Bogota and holding hostage a clutch of Ambassadors and lower-ranking diplomats, his government had suddenly been confronted with a demand that the Commission be invited to visit. Until then, the principal issue on the negotiating agenda had been release of over a hundred M-19 activists, including most of the organization's leaders, who were scheduled for trial by a military tribunal. The President, citing constitutional restraints, had been immovable. In this new demand he shrewdly saw a means of breaking the impasse, and to that end he extended an invitation to the Commission which it accepted on the understanding that it would conduct a normal observation *in loco* leading to a report on human rights conditions in the country.

In the course of its subsequent visit, the Commission operated on two tracks: it followed its usual pattern of interviewing prisoners (including in this case the M-19 leaders), receiving petitions, talking with representatives of all sectors of the population and with relevant public officials and investigating individual cases; it also went almost every day to the Embassy for conversations with the occupiers and their hostages. With an eye to breaking the impasse, President Turbay Ayala proposed to enter into an agreement with the Commission whereby it would retain a presence in the country primarily in order to monitor the proceeding against the M-19 militants, but also to observe over time the human rights conditions of the country. As the Commission explained to the embassy occupiers, it was an offer without precedent and one the Commission was prepared to accept if the occupation ended peacefully. Largely on the basis of this novel agreement, the occupiers—its implicit third-party beneficiaries—seemed persuaded that they could depart without dishonor. Very early on a fine Saturday morning, occupiers, hostages and Commission members cavalcaded to the airport through streets lined with cheering crowds (although the exit was supposed to be a closely-held secret). The long, tense siege was over.

Success in facilitating exit from the impasse in Bogota came on the eve of the 1980 OAS General Assembly at which the Commission's President would present its report on the condition of human rights in Argentina where, during the previous Fall, it had conducted a seventeen-day investigation. Having seen and commented (furiously) on a draft of the report, the Argentine military government knew that the President would announce to the assembled foreign ministers and a small army of journalists the Commission's unanimous conclusion that the thousands of Argentines acknowledged to have 'disappeared' during the preceding three years had, in fact, been arrested by the country's armed forces, tortured pitilessly and then murdered.

During the Commission's visit, representatives of respectable society in Argentina had often said privately that 'abuses' committed by overzealous functionaries had no doubt been committed in the course of what amounted virtually to a civil war, a war fought by the government against well-entrenched and sophisticated subversive organizations bent on the evisceration of the established order. But those abuses had to be seen in the light of the violent and anarchic conditions into which the military had moved and the character of its opponents. The Commission was now going to correct that comforting misapprehension. This was no matter of episodic abuses which no government involved in a civil or any other armed conflict can entirely avoid. What had happened, quite simply, was that the high command of the armed forces, acting in the name of Argentina (arguably a synonym for respectable society) had carried out a campaign of extermination against a portion of its own citizens.

As the General Assembly approached, the Argentine government launched a furious initiative to block what had in the prior three years become the standard response to a Commission Report: a resolution thanking the Commission for its work and calling by name upon the subject country to implement the Commission's 'Recommendations.' Since the recommendations flowed from the conclusions, these resolutions implicitly acknowledged their accuracy. Should it be named, Argentina announced, it would walk out of the OAS and it would regard any vote for such a resolution as a hostile act.

Argentina might also have been expected to launch an all-out assault on the Commission itself, particularly on its reporting powers. But coming so soon after the triumph in Bogota— where the Commission had, after all, demonstrated that while it could be a difficult critic it could also be useful to a government—conditions for such an assault were not propitious. Moreover, the Carter Administration had not yet departed Washington. In its wonted way, it wanted to find a formula to assuage the Argentines. Still, having made the strengthening of inter-governmental human rights institutions a principal element of its operationally cautious but rhetorically ebullient essays in the defense of human rights, it could not now withdraw its patronage. Further inhibiting an assault on the Commission was the occupation of El Salvador's normally reactionary seat at the Assembly by a regime sprung from a 1979 coup which according to one of its beneficiaries,[48] a politician of the hitherto repressed centre-left, had been partially catalysed by

---

[48] Communicated in a private conversation with an official of the coalition that briefly governed after the coup.

imminent publication of the Commission's raking indictment of the regime's predecessor.

On the appointed day of the Assembly, the Commission's President laid out before an eerily silent conclave of foreign ministers the evidence which had led the Commission to the moral conviction that the Government of Argentina had waged a war of extermination in violation of its most solemn obligations under international human rights law. The presentation and intent silence continued for over an hour. Nothing quite like it had ever happened before at such an Assembly. Nor would it happen again. Although it did not seem so at the time, the brief heroic age of the Commission was drawing to a close.

THE 1980S AND BEYOND: SLIDING GENTLY FROM THE APOGEE

Argentina's military government won the battle and lost the war. Two wars, to be precise. In the end, the General Assembly did not adopt a separate resolution on the Argentine report. Instead it bundled Argentina into an omnibus resolution calling on all countries mentioned that year by the Commission to cooperate with it. But despite the Government's efforts, the Commission's report circulated through Argentina, wreaking moral damage no doubt aggravated by the disappearing sensation of a subversive threat. For the terror campaign had long since succeeded in smashing the clandestine opposition's spine. Perhaps driven by a sensed loss of prestige, the armed forces high command then launched their doomed assault on the Malvinas/Falklands. Splintered by defeat in this real war, they withdrew at last to their barracks, withdrew in such disarray that they failed to extract a commitment to amnesty from their elected successors.

Gradually, in the course of the decade, other military governments in South America began their own withdrawal. Undefeated, they moved with deliberate speed, yielding power slowly to political leaders chastened by the experience of terror, committed at most to such moderate social and institutional reforms as were tolerable to the armed forces and their class supporters. As the southern cone of the Hemisphere ceased to convulse, the Central America isthmus resumed its natural place at the focal point of human rights concern. Throughout the decade the Commission dutifully reported on the carnage but with little apparent effect particularly on the killing grounds of Guatemala and El Salvador where, in waging wars of extermination against revolutionary forces, the armed forces and their paramilitary associates coincidentally advanced the declared purpose of the Administration of Ronald Reagan to defeat leftist subversion in the Hemisphere. And although initially far more responsive to Commission complaints and qualitatively less abusive than the regimes in Guatemala and

Salvador, the Sandinista Government of Nicaragua became increasingly indifferent to legal restraint as the war with the US-backed 'Contras' escalated.[49]

Sisyphean efforts by the entire human rights community, non- as well as inter-governmental, highlighted the limits of the strategy of exposure. It worked most effectively either when the human rights violators relied on internal support from groups not wholly insensitive to moral claims or international public opinion or when it positively affected the tone and substance of great power diplomacy. In Central America during the 1980s, exposure just . . . well, it just exposed, for it had lost its connection to the levers of real power.

Indifference to the Commission, if not hostility, stemmed from more than the predominance in Ronald Reagan's Washington of Cold War concerns and a fierce determination finally to win. Where the Carter Administration had seen inter-governmental institutions, whether regional or global, as contributors to global order, its successor was inclined to view them as impediments to the exercise of power in the national interest. UN condemnation of the Grenadan intervention[50] could only have strengthened this policy assumption most forcefully voiced by the Administration's principal voice at the United Nations, Ambassador Jeane Kirkpatrick.[51]

Washington's diminished interest in the inter-American human rights system could be felt inside the OAS. A new Secretary-General appropriated a slice of the Commission's space, let its staff diminish and watched its budget shrink. The Commission lost its leading figures from the prior decade, above all the brilliant Venezuelan lawyer-diplomat, Andres Aguilar, who went on to become a World Court Judge. Its reports ceased to be centerpieces of the Annual General Assembly.

Also greasing its descent from the heights of influence was the emergence of new actors on the Inter-American human rights stage, above all a burgeoning non-governmental human rights community. The most influential among them, Americas Watch,[52] had been organized just after Reagan's election by a group of American human rights activists who presciently anticipated the coming inferno in Central America. It quickly acquired a budget larger than the Commission's. Fired by zeal, unencumbered by the inter-state politics and often ponderous procedures and self-limiting ordinances of the Commission (particularly with respect to recommending meas-

---

[49] Compare the 1981 Commission Report, IACHR Report on the Situation of Human Rights in Nicaragua (1981) with the Americas Watch Report, *Human Rights in Nicaragua: 1986* (New York: Americas Watch Committee, 1987).

[50] General Assembly Resolution 38/7 (2 Nov., 1983), declared the 'armed intervention' in Grenada a 'flagrant violation of international law'.

[51] See J. Kirkpatrick, *New York Times*, Oct. 28 and 29 1983. Also, see generally, J. Kirkpatrick, *The Reagan Doctrine and US Foreign Policy* (Washington, DC, 1985).

[52] Now Human Rights Watch/Americas.

ures for pressuring delinquents),[53] Americas Watch began producing reports distinguished as much by their forceful, clear prose as by their unrelenting accuracy. Persuasive reports dispatched by the increasingly professional human rights organizations developing inside Latin states also began to arrive in the public domain. From a riveting star giving solo performances, the Commission now found itself just a bit adrift on a stage crowded with more deft and arresting actors.

WHITHER THE COMMISSION IN A DEMOCRATIC ERA?

At the end of the 1980s even Central America began to step back from remorseless civil war. Throughout Latin America, then, the grosser human rights violations subsided from the old torrent to a trickle, and elected—if not always liberal—democratic regimes[54] began to seem normal. The end of the Hemispheric state of emergency and the proliferation of credible investigating agencies, some with greater competence and drive than the Commission, provided two reasons for it to consider shifting a *modest* proportion of its human and financial resources to individual cases, which continued to arrive. For as an official institution, it had a role denied to the NGOs, namely building a body of doctrine interpreting the American Declaration and Convention.

As long as governments were simply torturing and maiming, interpretation was hardly necessary. But with governments striving with varying degrees of effort to establish the rule of law, the Commission naturally began to receive more cases from the gray borderland where the state's authority to promote the general interest collides with individual rights. From such governments, moreover, one might expect at least a measure of cooperation with the Commission, substituting for brazen denial open legal defense of their position on questions of fact and law.

Unlike the Buenos Aires Protocol with its broad grant of authority to the Commission, the Convention deals in some detail with individual petition cases and, being modeled on the European Convention, arguably envisions a modestly formal presentation of evidence by petitioner and the accused state. Before the Convention came into force, the Commission had occasionally granted audiences to individual petitioners and to governments where

---

[53] Although Commission Reports during the heroic period were almost invariably adopted in the end by unanimity, they were often the product of difficult negotiations among members some of whom were subject to influence by their own or other governments, and who had quite varied views about the quantity and quality of evidence required to overcome what some implicitly saw as a strong presumption in favor of the government's version of events.

[54] See Diamond, above n. 28, at 53.

they could argue their cases *ex parte*. These audiences were as informal as they sounded. There were rules neither of evidence nor procedure. Commission Members might or might not ask questions. There was no record. In effect, audiences were just another means for acquiring information, information to be independently assessed by Commission members.

Once the Convention came into force, then, with respect to ratifying countries, a more formal procedure might have appeared appropriate to Commission members. But with an exiguous staff, numerous cases and a continuing commitment to general reports, the Commission continued to handle cases casually. In doing so, it came under increasing criticism not only from some governments, but from human rights lawyers as well. Like any good lawyers, they wanted to feel that technical competence in the accumulation and presentation of evidence mattered. And they wanted deadlines, so that decisions came predictably and with reasonable dispatch. In addition, they wanted formal precedents that could then be deployed in arguments with governments. And finally, they wanted more than a Commission conclusion in favor of their clients. They wanted injunctions and reparations which they could secure only from the Inter-American Court. And they could not get to that Court until the Commission had finished processing the case and, even then, only if the Commission or the target state decided to invoke the Court's jurisdiction.

From its inception, the Court privately encouraged such invocation, action being necessary for more than a notional existence. And when, in the course of the 1980s, few cases or even requests for interpretive advisory opinions came, even as a growing number of states both ratified the Convention and took the further step of recognizing the Court's jurisdiction 'on all matters relating to the interpretation or application of this Convention,' eyebrows were raised and Judges of the Court complained.

The Commission's seeming indifference to the Court, even reluctance to send it business, had two sources. Before the Court came into existence, the Commission stood alone as interpreter of the Hemisphere's human rights norms *including those governing its own powers and procedures.* Once the Court appeared on the scene, more than one Commission member saw a danger that states might attempt to delay Commission action and undermine its prestige through constant challenges to its authority coupled with demands that it seek an interpretative ruling from the Court before taking another step.[55] While this risk might seem to explain only the Commission's reluctance to ask for interpretive opinions, it probably also acted generally to moderate the Commission's interest in enhancing the Court's profile. However, as suggested earlier, until the mid-1980s the main inhibitor was continuing emphasis on reports; and thereafter it was in part limited time

[55] See Art. 64 of the Convention.

and resources. Preparation for and the conduct of formal hearings for many cases made huge demands on a staff very poorly equipped to respond, not to mention the demands on Commissioners who functioned as it were in their spare time. Nevertheless, pressured by commentators, lawyers and governments, the Commission has gradually begun to move toward a more case-oriented existence and correspondingly to generate much more business for the Court.

Yet there remains a great need for country reports. Despite the spread of elected governments and great improvement in the condition of human rights, indisputable and grave violations continued to occur in many countries, albeit with less international hue and cry, since once again almost all of the victims are drawn from the only episodically visible and relatively mute lower classes. And given an enduring culture of impunity for public security agencies, weak judicial systems, a tradition of broad executive discretion in the exercise of power and a continuing tendency of elites to dismiss non-governmental human rights activists as 'Leftists,' grave violations of basic rights are likely to continue as a feature of life in many countries. Reports, in part because they bring together many cases of abuse and reveal a pattern of delinquency by public officials, attract far more attention than conclusions in individual cases. In addition, they provide members of the target country and the international community with a far more accurate appreciation of the extent and endemic character of human rights violations. *Therefore they must continue to be the central preoccupation of the Commission and its most important contribution to the mitigation of officially inflicted pain and humiliation in the Western Hemisphere.*

Reports must continue. However, the altered and enhanced but not transformed conditions of life in the Western Hemisphere call for additional dimensions to the Commission's reporting efforts. Beyond its traditional single-country focus, peculiarly appropriate where gross violations are epidemic or a country has undergone what appear to be dramatic changes, the Commission should attempt occasional thematic reports. For instance, it might look cross-nationally at the access of the poor to the civil courts or at the output of justice systems in a number of countries. Equally challenging and important would be reports on economic and social rights. The Commission has construed the single reference to them in the Declaration and Convention[56] as creating two obligations for states.[57] One is to develop a serious plan for mitigating extreme poverty. The other is to begin implementing such a plan giving priority to health and nutrition. Compliance with those minimal obligations is measurable.

Human rights lawyers were not the Commission's only critics. As a kind of

---

[56] Arts. XI-XVI and 26 respectively.
[57] *IACHR, 10 Years of Activity*, above n. 4, at 321–3.

peace settled over Latin American societies, democratic governments began lashing out at the one organ of the OAS which had battled with their authoritarian predecessors, battled to create the space in which democracy could grow. This was ironic but not really anomalous. For where in a democratic era is one likely to find greater self righteousness than in the offices of elected leaders? To be elected is to enjoy the Peoples' mandate which, in an age also secular, is as close to heaven's mandate as one can get.

When you accuse an authoritarian government of human rights violations, you arguably accuse only the people who run it. Accuse a democratic one, and you slander the Nation; for what is a nation but the people who comprise it and democratic leaders are their chosen voice. That at least is how some of the newly elected regimes appeared to feel when confronted with adverse Commission rulings.

Two kinds of issues have excited the greatest irritation. One concerns the legality of various sorts of legal immunity coerced from their elected successors by military establishments as they withdrew. In the case of Uruguay, where an electorate threatened with the restoration of military rule had endorsed immunity,[58] the Commission inevitably found that popular majorities could not for any reason deny remedies to the victims of human rights delinquencies, any more than popular majorities could legitimate the denial of due process to or the torture of some despised individual or group.[59] The other issue concerned elections, more particularly the Commission's claim of right to hear and resolve claims that elections had not been conducted fairly. Despite the proliferation of official monitoring missions all over the globe, regimes formed by the winners in contested cases claimed that Commission review constituted an unauthorized interference in their internal affairs, claimed that despite the clear language of the Convention giving to every person a right to 'vote and to be elected in genuine periodic elections, which shall be by universal and equal suffrage and by secret ballot that guarantees the free expression of the will of the voters . . .'[60] In these final years of the Millennium, a time of triumph for liberalism in politics hardly less than economics, elected governments moot projects to discipline the Commission, to clip its jurisdictional wings. Hopefully those projects will come to nothing. For surely it is a little early to conclude either that authoritarian government has forever abandoned the Hemisphere or that elected governments are incapable of terrible acts. What greater irony if, having survived intact the time of night and fog, the Commission were maimed in full daylight by the democracies it struggled to produce.

[58] See L. Weschler, above n. 31. See also, Americas Watch, *Challenging Impunity: The Ley de Caducidad and the Referendum Campaign in Uruguay* (New York: Americas Watch Committee, 1989).

[59] See the IACHR Annual Report 1992–3, at 41.

[60] Art. 23 of the American Convention and 20 of the Declaration.

3

The Inter-American Commission on Human Rights: its Organization and Examination of Petitions and Communications

CHRISTINA CERNA

INTRODUCTION

The Charter of the Organization of American States[1] (OAS) was adopted in 1948 at the Ninth International Conference of American States held in Bogota, Colombia, fifty-eight years after the inter-American system was established.[2] At the same Conference, the States of the American region also adopted the American Declaration of the Rights and Duties of Man (hereinafter 'American Declaration'), a human rights Declaration similar in inspiration and purpose to the United Nations Universal Declaration, but which ante-dated the Universal Declaration by six months.[3] The American States proclaimed the fundamental rights of the individual, but the American Declaration, which defined those rights, was not intended to be legally binding upon the member States of the Organization.

It was not until 1959, the year of the triumph of the Cuban revolution, that a supervisory mechanism to protect the human rights set forth in the American

---

[1] Charter of the Organization of American States, as amended by the Protocol of Buenos Aires in 1967 and by the Protocol of Cartagena de Indias in 1985. OAS publication, Treaty Series No. 1-F (1994), see Appendix I. On 14 April 1990 the inter-American system commemorated its centennial at the OAS headquarters in Washington, DC.

[2] The opinions expressed are those of the author alone and are not to be attributed to the Organization of American States or any of its organs.

[3] All texts of the American Declaration of the Rights and Duties of Man, the American Convention on Human Rights, the Commission's Statute and Regulations and the Court's Statute and Regulations can be found in the OAS publication: *Basic Documents Pertaining to Human Rights in the Inter-American System* (Updated to May 1996) OEA/Ser.L/V/II.92, Doc. 31 rev. 3, 3 May 1996, and appendices to this book. Since 1985 the Organization of American States with the Dutch publishing house, Martinus-Nijhoff, has been issuing a bilingual Yearbook entitled: *Inter-American Yearbook on Human Rights/Anuario Interamericano de Derechos Humanos*, an annual compilation of all Commission and Court documents, edited by the Commission as a companion series to the *Yearbook of the European Convention on Human Rights*.

Declaration was created.[4] The Inter-American Commission on Human Rights (hereinafter 'Commission' or 'IACHR') was established in that year not by a treaty but by a resolution of a political body,[5] a fact that reflects the unwillingness at that time of the member states of the OAS to undertake legally binding obligations as regards human rights. The first seven members of the Commission were elected on 29 June 1960, and the first regular session of the Commission was held from 3–28 October 1960. In February 1997, the Commission held its 95th regular session.

The Commission commenced functioning in 1960 pursuant to the terms of its Statute, which was an improvised set of rules adopted in that year by the member States of the Organization through the Council of the OAS.[6] The Statute permitted the Commission to exercise jurisdiction over all the member States of the Organization. Article 9 gave it the following functions and powers:

a) To develop an awareness of human rights among the peoples of America;

b) To make recommendations to the Governments of the Member States in general, if it considers such action advisable, for the adoption of progressive measures in favor of human rights within the framework of their domestic legislation and, in accordance with their constitutional precepts, appropriate measures to further the faithful observance of those rights;

c) To prepare such studies or reports as it considers advisable in the performance of its duties;

d) To urge the Governments of the Member States to supply it with information on the measures adopted by them in matters of human rights;

e) To serve the Organization of American States as an advisory body in respect of human rights.[7]

---

[4] For the importance of the Cuban revolution in motivating the OAS to create a mechanism to monitor human rights, see G. Connell-Smith, *The Inter-American System* (Oxford, 1966) at 290–6 and J. Dreier, *The OAS and the Hemisphere Crisis* (New York, 1962). For an excellent history of the creation of the Commission and primarily its first twenty years, see, C. Medina Quiroga, *The Battle of Human Rights, Gross Systematic Violations and the Inter-American System* (Dordrecht, 1988). See also L. Leblanc, *The OAS and the Promotion and Protection of Human Rights* (Dordrecht, 1977); A. Schreiber, *The Inter-American Commission on Human Rights* (Leyden, 1970); K. Vasak, *La Commission Interamericaine des droits de L'Homme* (Paris, 1968).

[5] See Resolution VIII of the Fifth Meeting of Consultation of Ministers of Foreign Affairs. Paragraph II of Resolution VIII resolved: 'To create an Inter-American Commission on Human Rights composed of seven members elected as individuals by the Council of the Organization of American States from panels of three names presented by the governments. The Commission, which shall be organized by the Council of the Organization and have the specific functions that the Council assigns to it, shall be charged with furthering respect for such rights.' Res. VIII, Fifth Meeting of Consultation of Ministers of Foreign Affairs, Final Act, Santiago, Chile (12–18 Aug. 1959). OAS Off. Rec. OEA/Ser.F/II.5, (Doc. 89, English, Rev.2) Oct. 1959 at 10–11.

[6] See T. Buergenthal, 'The Inter-American System for the Protection of Human Rights', Anuario Juridico Inter Americano, 1981; R. Norris, 'The New Statute of the Inter-American Commission on Human Rights', *HRLJ*, I (1980), 379.

[7] Art. 9 has since been replaced by Art. 41, American Convention and Arts. 18–20 of the Revised Commission Statute: see below, 74.

Article 2 of the Statute stated that 'for the purpose of this Statute human rights are understood to be those set forth in the American Declaration of the Rights and Duties of Man'. Although the Commission at once began receiving individual petitions alleging human rights violations committed by the Member States of the OAS, it was not granted the authority to examine such complaints until 1965.[8] This reflects the fact that, despite their adoption of the American Declaration and establishment of the Commission, for all practical purposes the member States at this time continued to consider human rights to be exclusively a matter of domestic jurisdiction.

In its early years, the Commission focused not upon the examination of individual complaints but upon investigating the general human rights situation in particular OAS member states. In its quest to identify appropriate measures for promoting and defending human rights, it used its statutory authority to hold meetings in any member State of the OAS[9] as the basis for a power which it claimed to conduct on-site investigations in OAS States. These fact-finding investigations and the ensuing country (or special) reports,[10] which the Commission presented to the OAS General Assembly, became the most significant activity of the Commission during the first years of its history. The position changed with the entry into force of the American Convention and the establishment of the Inter-American Court of Human Rights, whereupon the individual complaint procedure began to acquire greater prominence.

As noted, the Commission did not at the outset derive its powers from a treaty and could easily have been abolished by the member States. Given the political sensitivities connected with the conduct of on-site investigations, it is somewhat surprising that this did not happen. As Professor Buergenthal has observed:

The Commission was designated an 'autonomous entity' of the OAS, no doubt because this was as good a name as any for a body which was not provided for in the OAS Charter or any other treaty, was established by a simple conference resolution and qualified neither as an organ of the OAS Council nor as a so-called 'specialized organization' of the OAS. Moreover, the human rights, the protection and observance of which the Commission was to ensure, were proclaimed in the American Declaration of the Rights and Duties of Man, an instrument not deemed to create binding legal obligations for OAS member States. Consequently, an aura of make-believe attached to the inter-American human

---

[8] See below, 76.

[9] Art. 11(c), Commission Statute provided that the Commission 'may move to the territory of any American State when it so decides by an absolute majority and with the consent of the government concerned.'

[10] The power to adopt reports specific to particular countries followed from the Commission's decision at its first session that the wording 'in general' in Art. 9(b), Commission Statute authorised it to make general recommendations to particular member states, not just recommendations to members states generally: IACHR Report of the Work Accomplished During its First Session, 3–28 Oct. 1960, OEA/Ser.L/V/II.1, doc. 32, 10 (1961).

rights system, denying it the political authority that flows from constitutional legitimacy.[11]

In 1970 the Protocol of Buenos Aires, which amended the OAS Charter, entered into force. The new Charter gave the Commission the lacking 'constitutional legitimacy'. It transformed the Commission into one of the 'principal organs' of the OAS through which the Organization achieves its purposes.[12] As of 1970, the Commission can only be abolished if the OAS Charter is amended to provide for its dissolution.

The new Charter also provided, in Article 111, that an 'inter-american convention on human rights shall determine the structure, competence, and procedure of (the Inter-American) Commission, as well as those of other organs resonsible for these matters.' The 'convention' referred to in Article 111 proved to be the American Convention on Human Rights (hereinafter 'American Convention'), which was eventually adopted within the inter-American system in 1969. Twenty-five of the thirty-five OAS member states are now parties to it. The Convention incorporated into its text the Commission's pre-existing powers under its Statute.[13] It also created the Inter-American Court of Human Rights.

Following the entry into force of this Convention on 18 July 1978, the Commission's Statute was revised by the OAS General Assembly to enable it to continue exercising jurisdiction over all OAS member states, whether they were parties to the Convention or not.[14] Article 1(1) of the Commission's revised Statute states that the IACHR was 'created to promote the observance and defense of human rights and to serve as a consultative organ of the Organization in this matter.'[15] Human rights are identified in Article 1(2) as the rights set forth in the American Convention on Human Rights for States parties thereto, and in the American Declaration of the Rights and Duties of Man for other member States. In respect of all OAS states, the revised Statute confirmed the powers of the Commission to make country reports and to examine individual petitions. The Commission's extra-Convention exercise of jurisdiction over non-Convention parties has not been challenged by OAS member States, since it ante-dates the drafting of the American Convention. Most significantly, the Commission has continued to examine without objection petitions alleging violations of

[11] T. Buergenthal, 'The Revised OAS Charter and the Protection of Human Rights', 69 *AJIL* 828 at 833 (1975).
[12] Art. 52(e), OAS Charter.
[13] See Art. 41, Convention, below, 74.
[14] The revised Commission Statute was approved by Resolution 447 at the OAs General Assembly in La Paz, Bolivia in October 1979. See R. Norris, 'The New Statute of the Inter-American Commission on Human Rights', 1 *HRLJ* 379 (1980).
[15] Cf,. Art. 112, OAS Charter and Art. 41, Convention, below, 74.

the American Declaration by non-Convention parties, such as the United States,[16] since the Convention entered into force.

The Commission drafts its own Regulations, which are internal rules of procedure which may be modified by the members of the Commission without consultation with the political bodies of the Organization.[17] The Regulations provide the details for the dual system of consideration of petitions regarding States parties to the American Convention (Articles 31–50, Regulations) and other OAS member States (Articles 51–54, Regulations).

The inter-American system for the protection of human rights has many elements that lend themselves to comparison with other universal and regional intergovernmental human rights systems. It is a two-tiered system following the model of the European system, comprising both a Commission and Court.[18] For many years, however, the Inter-American Commission functioned alone, as do the African Commission of Human Rights and UN human rights treaty bodies such as the Human Rights Committee. Like some UN and other regional bodies, the Inter-American Commission has the authority to investigate and resolve individual petitions alleging violations of human rights. The most singular characteristic of the Inter-American Commission, however, is its dual function, on the one hand, applying the American Convention to States parties to the Convention and, on the other hand, applying the American Declaration to States that are not parties thereto, in that way continuing to exercise its jurisdiction over all the member States of the Organization, as it has since its creation on 25 May 1960.

ORGANIZATION OF THE COMMISSION

The Commission's Statute provides that the Commission shall be composed of seven members 'of high moral character and recognized competence in the field of human rights.'[19] This is a much smaller body than the eighteen-member UN Human Rights Committee or the thirty-plus member European Commission of Human Rights.[20] There is no specific requirement that the

[16] The United States has objected to the Commission's view that the American Declaration is the source of *legally binding* obligations for it, but not to the power of the Commission to hear cases against it.

[17] In contrast with its Regulations, the Commission's Statute, which is an intermediate set of rules between the American Convention and the Commission's Regulations, can only be modified with the approval of the member States of the Organization.

[18] The European Commission and Court will be replaced by a single institution, a permanent European Court of Human Rights, when the 11th Protocol to the European Convention on Human Rights (ECHR) enters into force.

[19] Art. 2, Commission Statute. Cf. Art. 34, Convention.

[20] Art. 28, International Covenant on Civil and Political Rights establishes an 18 member

members be lawyers or have had legal training, although, due to the political-legal nature of the work, most of the members have had a legal background. Today, approximately half of the members of the Commission hold academic positions. Since membership on the Commission is neither a full-time nor a salaried position, the majority of the members continue to engage in other full-time occupations, such as careers in law, the diplomatic service, academia or politics. Some have held political office or practised journalism and one member was a former president of his country. In the past, the majority of the members of the Inter-American Commission were involved in diplomatic service.[21]

The seven members serve in their 'personal capacity'.[22] They are independent of their countries of nationality, which they do not represent; instead, they 'represent all the member countries of the Organization'.[23] The Commission's Statute provides that membership of the Commission is incompatible with any other function which 'might affect the independence or impartiality of the member or the dignity or prestige of his post' on the Commission.[24] If five of the seven members vote that a case of incompatibility exists, the matter must be submitted to the General Assembly for decision.[25] Incompatibility is a very sensitive matter, and no case has ever been taken to the General Assembly by the members of the Commission regarding one of their own. On several occasions, members of the Commission have been targeted for attack by member States of the Organization, but in each case the attack was purely rhetorical and the member State did not proceed to attempt to have the member removed from the Commission.[26] Such attacks by member States underline the importance of political and diplomatic skills on the part of the members and underscore the political-legal nature of the Commission's functions. Political tact and diplomatic skills are indispensable qualities for an effective member. For example, during an on-site visit to examine the human rights situation in a member State, the members of the Commission meet with the Head of Government and senior cabinet officials regarding matters which are

Committee regardless of the number of States parties to the Covenant. Art. 20, ECHR provides that there shall be one member for every High Contracting Party.

[21] For a list of the names of all the members of the Commission and the periods during which they served since 1960, see T. Buergenthal and R. Norris, 'Procedure for the Election of the Members of the Inter-American Commission on Human Rights', in *Human Rights: The Inter-American System* (Looseleaf, Oceana Publications, 1993) Binder II, Booklet 9. On the background of Commission members, see further, below, Gomez, Chapter 7.

[22] Art. 36(1) Convention; Art. 3(1), Commission Statute.

[23] Art. 35, Convention; Art. 2(2) ('member states'), Commission Statute.

[24] Art. 8(1), Commission Statute.

[25] See Art. 73, Convention and Art. 8(2), Commission Statute.

[26] See T. Buergenthal, R. Norris and D. Shelton, 'How is Impartiality Defined?' in *Protecting Human Rights in the Americas, Selected Problems* (3rd edn.) at 375–8 (Strasbourg, 1990).

extremely sensitive and, in many cases, unpleasant for the government concerned.

In spite of the fact that Commission members are elected to represent all the member States of the OAS, Article 19 of the Commission's Regulations, which was adopted by the Commission itself, prohibits members from participating in the 'discussion, investigation, deliberation or decision' of a matter if they are 'nationals or permanent residents of the State which is (the) subject of the Commission's general or specific consideration', or if they are 'accredited to, or carrying out, a special mission, as diplomatic agents, on behalf of said State.'[27] Article 19 remedied what was perceived by members to be a conflict of interest and establishes a bar in respect of a member's state of nationality or permanent residence. For example, Mr. Francisco Bertrand Galindo, a member of the Commission from 1980 to the end of 1983, and a national of El Salvador, served during his term on the Commission as Salvadoran Ambassador to Guatemala. As a result, he did not participate in decisions involving either El Salvador or Guatemala[28], an unfortunate situation given that there are only seven members on the Commission; when one withdraws there is a greater possibility of a decision being stalemated by a tied vote.

As far as the election of Commission members is concerned, politics plays a role insofar as the candidates must be proposed by the governments of the member States and are elected by secret ballot by the OAS General Assembly.[29] A candidate, therefore, needs the support of a government, although not necessarily his own. Each government may propose up to three candidates for election, who may be nationals of the proposing State or of any other member State. If a State proposes three candidates, at least one is required to be a national of a State other than that of the proposing State. The practice has been that States normally propose no more than one candidate each, and that candidate is generally a national of the proposing State. In the election of members, consideration is given to an equitable geographical distribution and to the representation of the principal legal systems in the hemisphere.[30] No two nationals of one State may be members of the Commission at the same time.

[27] Art. 19 (2)(a), as modified by the Commission during its 90th Session, held on 11-22 Sept. 1995.
[28] See Resolutions 30/81 Case 7378; 31/81 Case 7379; 32/81 Case 7383; 33/81 Case 7403; 34/81 Case 7464; 3581 Case 7490; 36/81 Case 7585 and 38/81 Case 4425 all involving Guatemala in the Commission's Annual Report 1980–1.
[29] Art. 36, Convention; Arts. 3–5, Commission Statute. All of the OAS member states may vote; this differs from the procedure for the election of Inter-American Court judges in which only Convention parties may present candidates and vote: Art. 7, Court Statute. On the election process for Commission members, see T. Buergenthal and R. Norris, loc. cit. at n. 21 above.
[30] On 31 Dec, 1996 there were two members from the Southern Cone (Argentina, Chile), two from the Caribbean (Haiti, Trinidad and Tobago), which now comprises one third

The members of the Commission are elected for a term of four years and may be re-elected only once.[31] Their terms of office begin on 1 January of the year following the year in which they are elected. Since the provision of the Statute limiting the service of members to two four-year terms was only adopted following the entry into force of the Convention, prior to 1978 some members served extensive terms on the Commission. For example, Dr. Carlos Alberto Dunshee de Abranches, from Brazil, was a member of the Commission for over nineteen years until 1983.

In the case of a vacancy occurring on the Commission, the Statute provides that each government may propose a candidate within a period of thirty days from the date of receipt of the notice of the vacancy.[32] In practice, the State of the nationality of the former incumbent proposes a candidate to replace the member who has created the vacancy.

The members of the Commission are entitled to the privileges and immunities of diplomatic agents in countries that are parties to the American Convention.[33] In non-Convention parties, such as the United States, in which the Commission has its seat, they are entitled only to the 'privileges and immunities pertaining to their posts that are required for them to perform their duties with independence.'[34]

The members of the Commission are not salaried and receive only a modest honorarium, travel expenses and a *per diem* to cover the costs of their participation at meetings and in the other activities of the Commission.[35] The expenses incurred come from the annual budget of the Commission which is determined by the OAS General Assembly.

On the first day of the first session each year, the members of the Commission elect a Chairman and two Vice-Chairmen; they may be re-elected only once during a four-year period.[36] The Chairman and two Vice-Chairmen are the officers of the Commission and represent the Commission at the OAS General Assembly, before the Permanent Council and other organs of the OAS and at other institutions, such as the United Nations, the Council of Europe and the Organization of African Unity. It is the Chairman's duty to convoke the meetings of the Commission, as well as to preside

---

of OAS membership, two from the Andean Region (Colombia, Venezuela) and one member from North America (United States). The present members are: Dean Claudio Grossman, Chairman; Amb. John S. Donaldson, First Vice Chairman; Prof. Carlos Ayala Corao, Second Vice Chairman; Dr. Oscar Luján Fappiano; Dr. Alvaro Tirado Mejía; Dr. Jean Joseph Exumé; Prof. Robert Kodod Goldman.

[31] See, Art. 6 of the Commission's Statute. Exceptionally, Professor Gilda Maciel Russomano was elected for two four-year terms with effect from January 1984 after she had been earlier elected to fill the vacancy left by Dr Carlos Alberto Dunshee de Abranches for the few months that remained of his term after he died in June 1983.

[32] Art. 11, Commission Statute.   [33] Art. 70, Convention.
[34] Art. 12, Commission Statute.   [35] Art, 72, Convention; Art. 13, Commission Statute.
[36] Art. 14, Commission Statute.

over them, and to present a written report to the members at the beginning of each session regarding the work and activities undertaken on behalf of the Commission since the previous session. The Chairman designates committees to carry out specific functions, such as on-site investigations or the preliminary study of certain cases, and performs any other function which the Commission confers upon him.

The Secretariat performs the day-to-day work of the Commission.[37] It is composed of a full-time staff: an Executive Secretary, currently two Assistant Executive Secretaries and the professional, technical and administrative staff required to carry out its activities.[38] The Executive Secretary and the two Assistant Executive Secretaries serve at the discretion of the Secretary General of the OAS (in positions of trust), and theoretically can be removed at will, whereas the lower-ranking members of the staff are either in the career service or on fixed-term contracts. The members of the Secretariat, like the members of the Commission, are selected to reflect the geographic diversity of the member States of the Organization. Unlike the members of the Commission, the members of the Secretariat, except for the Executive Secretary, are required to have a law degree from their home countries.

The Secretariat prepares the work programme for each session of the Commission in consultation with the Chairman and implements the decisions taken by the members at the conclusion of each session. The Secretariat processes individual petitions until they are ready for decision by the members of the Commission. It prepares draft reports, resolutions, conventions, protocols, studies and other documents entrusted to it by the Commission or by its Chairman.

The Secretariat prepares the agenda of the Commission's on-site visits and accompanies and assists the members during these visits. The Executive Secretary presents a written report to the Commission at the beginning of each session on the activities of the Secretariat since the previous session and on any general matters of interest to the Commission, such as any new ratifications of the Convention or changes in the staff. The Secretariat is obliged to observe 'strict discretion' with regard to all matters which the Commission considers confidential.[39] In light of the fact that the Commission's sessions are closed to the public, there is no possibility of outside review or analysis of Commission decision-making. Hearings before the Commission on individual petitions are normally behind closed doors but may be public if the parties or their representatives agree.[40]

The seat of the Commission is in Washington, DC.[41] The members meet for eight weeks a year, usually in two three-week regular sessions and then

---

[37] Art. 21, Commission Statute. See further on the Secretariat, below, Gomez, Chapter 7.
[38] Art. 12, Commission Regulations.   [39] Art. 13(3), Commission Regulations.
[40] Art. 70, Commission Regulations.   [41] Art. 16, Commission Statute.

one or two shorter extraordinary sessions.[42] During the regular sessions the members of the Commission examine the individual petition cases and country reports which are ready for consideration.

THE ROLE OF THE COMMISSION GENERALLY

The functions and powers of the Commission, which extend to all OAS member states, are set forth in Article 41, American Convention[43] as follows:

The main function of the Commission shall be to promote respect for and defense of human rights. In the exercise of its mandate, it shall have the following functions and powers:

a.　to develop an awareness of human rights among the peoples of America;

b.　to make recommendations to the governments of the member States, when it considers such action advisable, for the adoption of progressive measures in favor of human rights within the framework of their domestic law and constitutional provisions as well as appropriate measures to further the observance of those rights;

c.　to prepare such studies or reports as it considers advisable in the perform-ance of its duties;

d.　to request the governments of the member States to supply it with informa-tion on the measures adopted by them in matters of human rights;

e.　to respond, through the General Secretariat of the Organization of American States, to inquiries made by the member States on matters related to human rights and, within the limits of its possibilities, to provide those States with the advisory services they request;

f.　to take action on petitions and other communications　pursuant to its au-thority under the provisions of Article 44 through 51 of this Convention; and

g.　to submit an annual report to the General Assembly of the Organization of American States.

Article 41 maintains the functions and powers that the Commission had been carrying out prior to the adoption of the Convention. As already noted, following its creation in 1960, the Commission, by seizing the initiative, had

---

[42] Art. 15(1), Commission Regulations provides that the Commission 'shall meet for a period not to exceed a total of eight weeks a year, divided into however many regular meetings the Commission may decide, without prejudice to the fact that it may convoke special sessions at the decision of its Chairman, or at the request of an absolute majority of its members'.

[43] Whereas Art. 41 generally applies to all OAS members, Art. 41(f) applies in its terms only to Convention parties. This omission is made good by Art. 20, Commission Statute which provides for petitions against non-Convention parties. Art. 41, Convention is generally replicated in Arts. 18, 19, and 20, Commission Statute. Art. 18 of the revised Statute replaces Art. 9 of the original Statute quoted above, 66.

been able to expand the functions originally intended for it, so as to include within its powers the making of country reports and the examination of individual petitions, with its initiatives in these regards being subsequently confirmed by the political bodies when they modified its Statute.[44]

Of the powers spelt out in Article 41, the powers to make country reports and to consider individual petitions have been particularly important in the Commission's work. The processing of petitions is included as only the sixth item in Article 41's list of the Commission's functions. This anomaly, and surely Article 41 is an anomalous provision in a Convention of this nature,[45] reflects the fact that during its early years, the Commission found that the most efficacious way to assist victims of human rights violations was by its on-site visits investigating human rights abuses in the member States and by the special country reports produced as a result of those visits.[46] The processing of individual petitions played a secondary role in the system at that time and continued to do so until the 1980s when more countries returned to a democratic form of government and the possibility of compensation for a human rights violation by a judgment of the Inter-American Court became a more immediate and attractive remedy.

The Commission's powers in respect of country reports are dealt with separately in another chapter of this book (Chapter 4). Suffice it to mention here the importance of this activity and to note its political dimension. The remainder of the present Chapter is concerned solely with the Commission's consideration of petitions and communications.

But before examining this aspect of the Commission's role, the following general comment about the background that shapes all of the Commission's work is appropriate. The functions of the Commission must be understood within the larger institutional context of the inter-American system. It is

[44] See above, 67.

[45] Art. 41 is considered anomalous because the American Convention is a constituent instrument: it 'creates' the Inter-American Commission and the Inter-American Court, although in point of fact the creation of the Inter-American Commission antedated the entry into force of the Convention. The American Convention at one and the same time 'creates' the Commission and yet preserves the Commission's pre-Convention functions (in Art. 41). The same kind of anomaly can be found in the OAS Charter, a constituent instrument which 'creates' the OAS, in spite of the fact that the inter-American system antedated the 'creation' of the OAS by over five decades.

[46] Cf. above, 67. See the article by the former Executive Secretary of the Commission, Edmundo Vargas Carreno, 'Las Observaciones in loco practicadas por la Comisión Inter-americana de Derechos Humanos' in the OAS publication: *Human Rights in the Americas*, Festschrift to Carlos A. Dunshee de Abranches (Washington, DC, 1984) at 290–305 and a similar treatment of the same subject by Dr. Vargas' successor as Executive Secretary, Edith Marquez Rodríquez, 'Visitas de observación in loco de la Comisión Interamericana de Derechos Humanos y sus informes' in *Estudios Basicos de Derechos Humanos III.* (San José, 1995) at 135–44. Also see an article by a former President of the Commission, Cesar Sepulveda, 'The Inter-American Commission on Human Rights of the Organization of American States, 25 Years of Evolution and Endeavour' in 28 *GYIL* 65 at 79 et seq. (1985).

important to note that the primary purpose of the OAS is the maintenance of peace in the region. This is different from the situation in Europe where the Council of Europe has no peacekeeping role, since that function has been assigned to NATO. In the Americas, the member States of the OAS pledge to resolve disputes among themselves by peaceful means and to exercise collective self-defense in order to repel an act of aggression by a non-member State against a member State. Threats to the peace in the Americas historically have involved attempts by one member State of the OAS to overthrow regimes which it charged with denying human rights and representative democracy to their peoples.[47] It is perhaps for this reason that the main institutional recipient of a Commission country report is not the country under examination, but rather the OAS General Assembly, the Meeting of Consultation of Ministers of Foreign Affairs, or the Permanent Council, as appropriate, notwithstanding the fact that the impact of the report will be greatest in the country under examination.[48] It is the role of the OAS political bodies to determine whether the nature of the human rights situation in the country in question, as set forth in the Commission's report, requires that the OAS collectively should take any specific action.

INDIVIDUAL PETITIONS

The Commission's jurisdiction

In 1965, the Commission was authorised by the Second Special Inter-American Conference to examine individual petitions alleging human rights violations by any OAS member state.[49] The Commission interpreted its 1965 mandate as only permitting it to consider alleged breaches of the rights in Articles I-IV, XVIII, XXV and XXVI of the American Declaration.[50] As a consequence of the entry into force of the American Convention in 1978, the examination of individual petitions has become increasingly important in the Commission's work.[51] Pursuant to Article 41(f) of the American Convention, the Commission is empowered to take decisions on individual petitions

[47] See Connell-Smith, above n. 4 at 289 et seq., and Medina Quiroga, above n. 4.

[48] On the role of the OAS political organs in monitoring the Commission's individual petition decisions, see below, Gomez, Chap. 7.

[49] Res. XXII, Second Special Inter-American Conference, Rio de Janeiro, Nov. 1965, Final Act. OEA/Ser.C/I.13, 32–4 (1965).

[50] Res. XXII of the Second Special Inter-American Conference, loc. cit. at n. 49 above, had instructed the Commission to 'pay particular attention' to the observance of those rights.

[51] In 1995, it opened 140 new cases, bringing the number of individual petitions being processed at the beginning of 1996 to 735 pending cases: Annual Report 1995, 31. By the end of 1996, the Commission had registered over 12,000 cases since 1965 and there were 800 cases pending.

brought against any of the parties to the American Convention alleging breaches of the rights protected in that instrument. In addition, in the exercise of the powers under Article 20 of its Statute, the Commission may consider petitions presented against other OAS member States that have not ratified the Convention[52]—in their case by reference to the norms set forth in the American Declaration. These are now understood to be *all* of the norms in that Declaration, not just those in the above-listed Articles.[53]

Pursuant to Article 41(f), Convention, petitions against Convention parties are subject to the procedures concerning admissibility, hearings on the merits, friendly settlement and reports, provided for in Articles 44 to 51, Convention. The procedures governing communications brought against non-Convention parties are set out in Regulations 51–54, Commission's Regulations. In practice, there is not a great deal of difference between the two procedures other than in one essential respect: that the Commission may opt to submit a case presented against a State party to the Convention to the Inter-American Court, providing that the State party has accepted the jurisdiction of the Court.[54] That option is not available as regards complaints presented under the American Declaration. Other provisions set forth in the Commission's Statute and Regulations which distinguish between the two procedures in other less important respects, such as the requirement that a friendly settlement between the parties be attempted,[55] or the possibility of a State requesting reconsideration of a final decision,[56] are procedures that have in fact been used by the Commission in all cases in which the procedure is warranted on the facts, without distinction as to whether or not the State in question is a Convention party. With regard to Commission reports on individual petitions, the reporting requirements in Articles 50 and 51 apply only in Convention party cases; decisions under the Declaration

[52] Art. 51, Commission Regulations. As of 15 August 1996, the ten States that have not ratified the American Convention, but are subject to the American Declaration as OAS member states are Antigua and Barbuda, the Bahamas (Commonwealth of), Belize, Canada, Cuba, Guyana, St Kitts and Nevis, St Lucia, St Vincent and the Grenadines and the United States.

[53] Although Art. 20, Commission Statute, which gives the power to consider individual petitions concerning non-Convention parties, continues to call upon the Commission to pay 'particular attention to the observance of the human rights referred to in Articles I, II, III, IV, XVIII, XXV and XXVI', the wording 'particular attention' is not understood as exclusive: see Art. 51, Commission Regulations, which provides for petitions concerning any Declaration article. On the question whether petitions may be brought against Convention parties under the Declaration in respect of non-Convention rights, particularly economic, social and cultural rights, see Craven, below, 305.

[54] For the 17 States that have accepted the compulsory jurisdiction of the Court, see Appendix VIII.

[55] This procedure is provided for in Art. 48(1)(f), Convention and Art. 45, Commission Regulations for Convention parties only.

[56] This procedure is provided for in Art. 54. Commission Regulations just for States that are not Convention parties.

in non-Convention party cases follow the pattern set out in Article 53 of the Commission's Regulations.

Standing to bring a petition

The individual's right to bring a petition against a Convention party is automatic from the moment the Convention enters into force for it. Similarly, it exists automatically under the Commission Statute as against all other OAS member states. This is stronger than the arrangements under the European Convention on Human Rights (ECHR), by which the right of individual petition extends only to those ECHR states parties that make a separate declaration recognising it.[57]

Any 'person or group of persons, or any non-governmental entity legally recognized in one or more member States of the Organization' may lodge a petition on his own behalf or on behalf of a third person with the Commission alleging a violation of the American Convention or the American Declaration.[58] Again, this is stronger than the equivalent ECHR provision, by which only a 'victim' may bring a claim. The violation may be of the rights of any 'person'.[59] By 'person' is meant 'every human being'; it does not include juridical persons such as corporations or banks.[60]

In the majority of cases presented to the Commission, the applicant is the victim or a family member or representative of the victim, generally a lawyer from a non-governmental human rights organization. There are, however, cases submitted to the Commission by persons or groups who have no contact with the victim, and although the Commission is authorized to open these cases, the follow-up is understandably difficult. Some cases, which are in the nature of a class action, such as Case 2141 (United States),[61] which presented the question whether the abortion of 'Baby Boy' and all other

---

[57] The right of individual petition will become automatic under when the ECHR 11th Protocol enters into force.

[58] Art. 44 of the American Convention and Art. 26 of the Regulations.

[59] Art. 1, Convention.

[60] Art. 1(2), Convention. The rights of the foetus were considered in Case 2141 (United States) below n. 61. As regards juridical persons, cf. Buergenthal: 'But to the extent that an injury to a corporation or association violates an individual's right under the American Convention, it can be assumed to give rise to a cause of action under it. The outlawing of a labor union, for example, may amount to a denial of the right to freedom of association enjoyed by the union members. The union, as such, as distinguished from the injured individual, does not, however, enjoy the protection of the American Convention.' (T. Buergenthal, 'The Inter-American System for the Protection of Human Rights' in T. Meron (ed.) *Human Rights in International Law, Legal and Policy Issues* (Oxford, 1984, p/b 1989) at 441. See also, Res. No. 10/91, Case 10.169 (Peru) of 22 Feb, 1991, involving the deprivation of property of the shareholders of the Banco de Lima in the Commission's 1990–91 Annual Report, 423.

[61] Res. No. 23/81, Case 2141 (United States), 6 Mar. 1981, in the Commission's Annual Report 1980–81, 25–54, 2 *HRLJ* 110.

unborn persons in the United States violated the right to life provisions of Article I of the American Declaration, attract a large number of 'co-petitioners' who, because of their interest in the outcome of the case, wish to be placed on record as co-plaintiffs.

The submission of petitions

A petition must be presented in writing and must contain the name and signature of the petitioner and that of any legal representative.[62] It is required to set forth an account of the act that is denounced, specifying both the place and date of the alleged violation and, where possible, the name of the victim or victims as well as that of any government agent considered responsible. The petition must allege that a member State is considered responsible by its action or inaction (commission or omission), or that of its agent, for the violation of one or more human rights set forth either in the American Convention or the American Declaration.

Information should also be provided on whether the petitioner has attempted to exhaust domestic remedies and what the outcome of those attempts has been. If the petitioner has taken the case to a domestic court, the complaint must include information regarding the judgment of that court, whether the case has been appealed and the date of the final judgment. In addition, the petitioner is also requested to state whether the petition has been brought before any other intergovernmental organisation for settlement. Both kinds of information are needed in connection with the requirements as to admissibility discussed below.

The failure initially to include certain information is not fatal to the petition and the petitioner will be requested to supply whatever further information is required.

Whereas the Council of Europe provides legal aid for petitioners bringing cases under the European Convention, the OAS makes no such provision for petititoners bringing claims under the American Convention or the American Declaration.

Decisions as to admissibility

In contrast with the ECHR arrangements, there is no formal admissibility stage in the inter-American system. Instead, upon receipt of the initial communication from the petitioner and other early information, the Commission Secretariat considers whether the petition is *prima facie* admissible[63] and, if it is, registers it and opens the case. As further facts (for example, as

---

[62] See Art. 46(1), American Convention and Chapter II of the Commission Regulations.
[63] Art. 34(1)c) uses the term admissible 'in principle'.

to the exhaustion of domestic remedies) emerge, a final decision may be taken
by the Commission, or the Secretariat acting for it, to close the case, or the
Commission may adopt a formal report declaring inadmissible a petition that
has earlier been deemed to be *prima facie* admissible. Otherwise, the processing continues and the case is dealt with on the merits, usually without any
separate, final decision declaring that the petition is admissible.

If it is *prima facie* admissible, a petition will be registered and given a case
number; if not, it will be considered as inadmissible and the petitioner will
be informed that the petition does not meet the specific requirements for
admissibility. If the complaint is accompanied by important or extensive
documentation, it is returned.

Petitions deemed prima facie *admissible*

Once a communication (that is, a letter, telegram or fax) has been received
by the Secretariat, the Secretariat lawyer in charge of the country against
which the complaint is directed considers whether the case is *prima facie*
admissible, and hence is to be registered and examined in detail in accordance with the procedure in Article 48, Convention.[64] The Secretariat of the
Commission is administratively authorised by the Commission to decide not
to open a case when the petition is not *prima facie* admissible. This decision
is taken mostly on the basis of the information provided by the petitioner at
the pre-registration phase.[65] Complaints in which it is clear that domestic
remedies have not been exhausted prompt the Secretariat to request further
information from the petitioner regarding the failure or the inability to
exhaust domestic remedies, before it decides whether to open the case or to
declare it inadmissible. This only occurs in cases where the life of the victim
is not in danger. Where there is a risk to life, the Secretariat tends to open a
case, leaving it to the State and the petitioner to provide further information
on the local remedies issue as the petition is processed.

The criteria for the *prima facie* admissibility of a petition are listed in
Article 46(1), Convention and are considered in a separate section on
admissibility requirements below.[66] In practice, petitions are sometimes
disposed of by the Secretariat at the pre-registration stage on grounds other
those in Article 46.[67] Thus the Secretariat may decide not to register a
petition because it is brought against a state which is not a member of the
Organization, or because the violation complained of is not of a right (or

---

[64] In Declaration cases, the same procedure applies: see Arts. 32–43 and 52; Commission
Regulations.
[65] The Government may come to know of the complaint prior to the decision as to *prima
facie* admissibility and present evidence and argument to the Secretariat, which it also takes
into account.
[66] See 83.
[67] As the examples in the following sentence show, these may be ones listed as grounds of
inadmissibility in Art. 47, Convention, as to which see below, 84.

cannot be interpreted as being of a right) set forth in the American Convention or the American Declaration (inadmissible *ratione materiae*)[68] or, most commonly, because the violation is not imputable to the State but is the responsibility of a private individual. Cases which have been rejected on this last ground include cases which impute responsibility for an alleged violation to guerrilla organisations instead of a member state (where the petitioner has not alleged State responsibility on some other ground, such as complicity or failure to investigate alleged violations).

Since most inadmissible cases are rejected by the Secretariat, acting for the Commission, at the *prima facie* admissibility stage, the Commission itself has few opportunities to declare a case inadmissible. However, the Commission may declare inadmissible a case which has been considered to be *prima facie* admissible, where the resulting investigation causes the Commission to reverse this decision.[69] In 1983, for example, the Commission declared the case of Viviana Gallardo (Costa Rica) inadmissible in a final decision as to admissibility under Article 48(1)(c), Convention, on the ground of non-exhaustion of local remedies.[70] It also declared the case of Salvador Jorge Blanco, the ex-President of the Dominican Republic, inadmissible, in spite of the Secretariat's having considered the case *prima facie* admissible, again on the ground of non-exhaustion of local remedies.[71]

Final decisions that a petition is admissible

In only a few cases which the Commission have registered and processed as being *prima facie* admissible and in which the Commission has not, exceptionally, later declared the petition to be inadmissible, has the Commission issued a separate, final decision declaring the petition to be admissible. Normally the Commission just includes a statement confirming the case's admissibility in the final decision on the merits.[72] In the large number of petitions dealing with 'disappeared' persons in Argentina, for example, the Commission never issued separate admissibility decisions, but declared the admissibility of a case when it adopted its decision on the merits. Few governments challenge the failure of the Commission to issue a separate, formal admissibility decision in these circumstances. Exceptionally, the Commission will adopt a separate decision on admissibility where the State disputes the admissibility of

[68] Cases which have been deemed inadmissible by the Secretariat on this ground have included an employee's grievance against his employer for failure to receive a promotion.

[69] Art. 48(1)(c), Convention.

[70] See Res. No. 13/83, in the Matter of Viviana Gallardo and others (Costa Rica), 30 June 1983, Commission's Annual Report 1982–3, at 49–53.

[71] Res. No. 15/89, Case 10.208 (Dominican Republic) 14 Apr. 1989, Commission's Annual Report 1988–9, at 67–103. The notoriety of the victim and the importance of the matter in the Dominican Republic may also have played a part.

[72] This is also the practice of the Human Rights Committee under the International Covenant on Civil and Political Rights.

a petition or the Commission's jurisdiction, and the case cannot proceed to a decision on the merits without a prior admissibility determination, or where the circumstances of the case otherwise appear to warrant it. The United States Government, for example, in response to requests for information regarding alleged violations in cases that have been found to be *prima facie* admissible, will generally present information going to the admissibility of the case rather than the merits, which requires the Commission to issue a separate admissibility decision.[73] An admissibility decision was also issued in 1996 in a non-United States case in which the Commission rejected the defendant State's arguments as to the exhaustion of domestic remedies. It found that the family of murdered Guatemalan anthropologist Myrna Mack had not had 'effective and real access' to domestic remedies since the Guatemalan government refused to provide access to evidence in the case and six years had elapsed since the murder and a final judicial decision was still pending.[74] In another case, in 1987, the Commission adopted and published a decision declaring the case of Osvaldo Antonio Lopez (Argentina) admissible, in order to facilitate a friendly settlement of the case, but in 1988, the Commission closed the case due to the fact that Lopez had been granted an unconditional release.[75]

The Court's confirmation of the Commission's admissibility practice

The Inter-American Court had occasion to consider the Commission's practice in respect of the taking of decisions as to admissibility when the Commission submitted the three disappeared persons cases against Honduras. The Government of Honduras objected to the admissiblity of these cases, *inter alia*, on the ground that the Commission had not issued a formal admissibility decision, which it contended was a procedural requirement under the Convention. The Court rejected this contention, ruling that whereas an 'express and formal act' is only necessary where a petition is declared inadmissible, there being no such requirement in cases that are treated as admissible. The Court's judgment read as follows:

39. There is nothing in the procedure that requires an express declaration of admissibility, either at the Secretariat stage or later, when the Commission itself

[73] See Decisions of the Commission as to the Admissibility of Application No. 9213 (United States), 17 Apr. 1987, Commission's Annual Report 1986–7, at 184–92; Report No. 19/92, Decision of the Commission as to the Admissibility of Case 10.865 (United States), 1 Oct. 1992, Commission's Annual Report 1992–3, at 142–65; Report No. 28/93, Decision of the Commission as to the Admissibility of Case 10.675 (United States), 13 Oct. 1993, at 334–75.

[74] Report No. 10/96, Admissibility, Case 10.636 (Guatemala), 5 Mar. 1996 in Annual Report 1995 (sic), at 125–35. See also Report No. 24/92, Cases 9328, 9329, 9742, 9884, 10.131, 10.193, 10.230, 10.429 and 10. 469 (Costa Rica); The Right to Appeal the Verdict in a Criminal Proceeding, 2 Oct. 1992 in Annual Report 1992–3, at 74–82.

[75] See Res. No. 15/87, Case 6935 (Argentina), 30 June 1987, Commission's Annual Report, 1986–7, at 32–63; Res. No. 25/88, Case 9635 (Argentina), 13 Sept. 1988, Commission's Annual Report, 1987–8, at 82–101.

is involved. In requesting information from a government and processing a petition, the admissibility thereof is accepted in principle, provided that the Commission, upon being apprised of the action taken by the Secretariat and deciding to pursue the case (Arts 34(3), 35 and 36 of the Regulations of the Commission), does not expressly declare it to be inadmissible (Art.48(l)(c) of the Convention).

40.Although the admission of a petition does not require an express and formal act, such an act is necessary if it is found to be inadmissible.[76]

The Court thereby ratified what had been the Commission's practice for many years, even to the extent that the Court interpreted the language of the Convention in ways that are not obvious. This was the first time that the Court had expressed itself on the Commission's procedure. Whether or not the Court's pronouncements as regards the Commission's procedure are binding on the Commission is an issue that has not yet been tested. Since the Commission is created as a co-equal body with the Court, one may speculate whether a contrary decision, challenging the Commission's practice, would require the Commission to change its practice or not.

Power of the Court to overturn a Commission decision as to admissibility

Finally, it may be noted that the Inter-American Court claims the power to reconsider a decision as to admissibility by the Commission in any case that comes before the Court. However, in a dissenting opinion in a recent Court case, Judge Cançado Trindade suggested that the Court should not re-open the questions of 'pure' admissibility, which 'should be resolved definitively by the Inter-American Commission on Human Rights.'[77] Thus, if the Court were to follow Judge Trindade's approach, it would not consider a claim by a defendant state of non-exhaustion of local remedies that has already been rejected by the Commission.

Admissibility requirements and grounds of inadmissibility

There are four admissibility requirements set forth in Article 46(1):[78] the exhaustion of domestic remedies (Article 46(1)(a)); compliance with the six

---

[76] I/A Court H.R., *Velasquez Rodriguez* case, Preliminary Objections, Series C No. 4, at paras. 35, 39 and 40 (1988); I/A Court H.R., *Fairen Garbi and Solis Corrales* case, Preliminary Objections, Series C No. 2 (1987); I/A Court H/R., *Godinez Cruz* case, Preliminary Objections, Series C No. 3 (1987). The decisions on the procedural issues in all three cases are virtually identical.

[77] Order of 18 May 1995 (Art. 54(3), ACHR) in the *Genie Lacayo* case, in the Court's Annual Report for 1995, 83–7 at 85, 3 IHRR 397 (1996). In that case, the Court had joined a preliminary objection that the claim was inadmissible because domestic remedies had not been exhausted, an argument already rejected by the Commission.

[78] These apply also to Declaration cases: see Arts. 32–43, 52 Commission Regulations.

month rule (Article 46(1)(b)); no case pending before another international forum on the same subject (Article 46(1)(c)); and the provision of details of the petitioner or his/her representative (Article 46 (1)(d)). The last of these requires that 'the petition contains the name, nationality, profession, domicile, and signature of the person or persons or of the legal representative of the entity lodging the petition.' (Article 46(1)(d)). The other three requirements are considered below. Of these, the exhaustion of local remedies is by far the most important. Generally a state will argue that domestic remedies have not been exhausted and therefore the Commission should declare the complaint inadmissible. In cases where the state has not alleged that the applicant has failed to exhaust domestic remedies, it has been the Commission's practice to assume that there is no problem in this regard and to continue processing the case and to adopt a decision.

Somewhat curiously, the requirements as to *admissibility* in Article 46, Convention are supplemented by grounds of *inadmissibility* in Article 47, Convention. The latter are that:

(a) any of the requirements (as to admissibility) indicated in Article 46 has not been met;

(b) the petition or communication does not state facts that tend to establish a violation of the rights guaranteed by this Convention;

(c) the statements of the petitioner or the state indicate that the petition or communication is manifestly groundless or obviously out of order; or

(d) the petition is substantially the same as one previously studied by the Commission or another international organization.

The grounds in (b) and (c) above are predictable and necessary to avoid the Commission wasting its time on cases that clearly have no merit in law or on the facts.[79] They are not considered separately in this Chapter. The ground in (d) takes the ground of admissibility in Article 46 (1)(c) (no case pending elsewhere) a stage further.

The relationship between Articles 46 and 47 was explained by the Inter-American Court as being that Article 46 applies to the question of *prima facie* admissibility and that Article 47 applies thereafter. As a result, a decision that a petition is inadmissible on the basis of Article 47 is taken by the Commission, or the Secretariat for it,[80] under Article 48(1)(c) after the petition has been communicated to the defendant government as being *prima facie* admissible by reference to the requirements in Article 46.[81] In

---

[79] Cf. the 'manifestly ill-founded' and 'incompatible with the provisions of the Convention' admissibility requirements in Art. 27, ECHR.

[80] The Secretariat is administratively authorised to close a case after it has been registered when further information reveals that it is inadmissible.

[81] Advisory Opinion No. 13, I/A Court H.R. Series A. 13, 14 *HRLJ* 252, 1–2 IHRR 197 (1994).

practice, the position is less clear cut than this, with the Secretariat taking into account when assessing *prima facie* admissibility under Article 46 considerations that properly arise under Article 47.[82]

Exhaustion of domestic remedies

The most complete preliminary objection which can be invoked by a government in order to block consideration of a complaint by the Commission is to allege that domestic remedies have not been exhausted. In practice, this is what most governments do allege.

The general rule of international law that domestic remedies be exhausted before recourse is had to an international forum has been incorporated into the American Convention (Article 46) and the Commission's Statute (Articles 19 (a) and 20 (c)), and reiterated in the Commission's Regulations (Article 37). It has application to both Convention and Declaration cases. The Commission has stated that the reason for the rule 'lies in the principle that the defendant State must be allowed, before anything else, to provide redress on its own and within the framework of its internal legal system, which must be exhausted before the international instance is brought into play.'[83]

Under Article 46 (1)(a), Convention, a petition is not admissible unless domestic remedies have been exhausted 'in accordance with the generally recognised principles of international law.'[84] These 'principles' only require the exhaustion of such domestic remedies as are 'adequate' and 'effective'.[85] This limitation is to some extent expressly provided for by Article 46 (2) which states that domestic remedies do not have to be exhausted in the following denial of justice situations:

a.   the domestic legislation of the State concerned does not afford due process of law for the protection of the right or rights that have allegedly been violated;

b.   the party alleging violation of his rights has been denied access to the remedies under domestic law or has been prevented from exhausting them; or

c.   there has been unwarranted delay in rendering a final judgment under the aforementioned remedies.

The Commission has developed an extensive jurisprudence in which it has interpreted and applied the Convention's exhaustion of domestic remedies requirement. In a number of cases, it has held that the applicant need not pursue domestic remedies further for reason of 'unwarranted delay'

---

[82]   e.g., that the petition does not relate to a protected right or has no merit whatsoever on the facts: see above, 84.

[83]   See Case No. 10.208 (Dominican Republic) (above) n. 71, at 100. Cf. the Inter-American Court's statement in the *Velasquez* case, I/A Court H.R. Series C No. 4 para. 61 (1988), 9 *HRLJ* 212.

[84]   Art. 46(1)(a), Convention.

[85]   Cf. the Court's judgment in the *Velasquez* case, below, 91.

(Article 46(2)(c)). For example, in a case presented against the Government of Ecuador involving torture, the Commission found that domestic remedies had been exhausted in spite of the Government's allegation that the matter was still before the courts. The Commission, invoking the above denial of justice exception, stated:

That there has been an unwarranted delay in the administration of justice, since three years and six months have elapsed without a court issuing a decision on these violations of human rights—torture and ill-treatment—as established in Article 46.2.c. of the American Convention.[86]

Another 'unwarranted delay' case involved the arrest and deliberate, brutal treatment of two young protesters in Chile. The facts of the case revealed that army personnel seized the two young people, doused them with fuel, set them on fire, loaded them onto a vehicle, drove them to the outskirts of the city of Santiago, and dumped them on an abandoned road. One of the individuals died of his injuries and the other suffered massive burn injuries that required extensive treatment.[87] In response to the Commission's request for information on this case, the Chilean Government replied that the case was still under investigation and for that reason it refused the Commission's request to carry out an on-site investigation. In this case, the Commission was particularly concerned about the savagery of the act committed and the apparent cynicism of the government. The military courts had charged one officer, Fernadez Dittus, with 'manslaughter' and this same official, a short time later, was promoted to captain. The Commission found that domestic remedies had been exhausted, despite the Government's allegation that they were still pending, for the following reasons:

More than twenty months have elapsed since the events that are the object of this case transpired, but as of March 23, 1988, date of the provisional approval of this Resolution, there has been no indication of accountability, and it could, therefore, be considered that there has been an unwarranted delay in the judicial decision under the provisions of Article 37.c. of the Regulations of the Commission which would make it possible to waive the requirement of the exhaustion of domestic remedies.[88]

The Commission did not disguise its irritation as concerns the government's action, for example, the promotion of this official to the rank of captain, in this additional comment:

The very small proportion of military or police personnel who have been convicted in Chile for numerous denunciations of human rights violations, which gives reason to believe that the delay in the judicial proceedings in this case could

---

[86] See Res. No. 14/89 Case 9641 (Ecuador), 12 Apr, 1989, Annual Report, 1988–9, at 104–15.
[87] See Res. No. 1/88, Case 9755 (Chile), 12 Sept. 1988, Annual Report 1987–8, at 132–9. [88] Id. at 137.

become yet another device for assuring the impunity of the perpetrators of a crime that is so reprehensible, especially when one takes into account Lieutenant Fernandez Dittus' promotion to the rank of Captain, and the freedom he enjoys while such extremely serious accusations are under investigation. Added to this are the statements made by high-level Chilean authorities, including the President himself, exonerating the military officers involved, an indication of the negative attitude that exists as regards inflicting the punishment that those responsible for so condemnable an offense deserve.[89]

In a number of cases, domestic remedies that a government claims to be available have been considered to be ineffective, so as not to require exhaustion, for other reasons. For example, in cases where there is good evidence that there is no independent judiciary that is competent to provide an effective remedy for the alleged human rights violation at the domestic level, the practice of the Commission has been to dispense with the exhaustion requirement. In this connection, the Commission will have available to it the comprehensive examination documenting the lack of independence in the judicial system set forth in its country report on the state concerned.[90] The suspension of constitutional guarantees which result in the courts declaring themselves incompetent to hear writs of *amparo* is another situation in which the Commission may regard local remedies as being ineffective. Other such situations include the maintainence by a military regime of a declaration of a state of emergency, even after the 'emergency' has terminated. It will continue, that is throughout the existence of the military regime, during which time civilian courts are closed down, or 'special' or 'secret' tribunals are created which do not provide minimal guarantees of due process. Also, in the thousands of cases dealing with the 'disappeared' in Argentina, the Commission did not analyze the problem of the failure to exhaust domestic remedies because there was an evident denial of justice given the failure of the Argentine judicial system to resolve any of these cases.

A case in which the remedies available were ineffective in the different sense that they did not cover all of the petitioners' complaints involved Haitian nationals, who fled, by boat, in massive numbers to the United States in the early 1980s, seeking political asylum. The petitioners, in their original complaint, alleged a violation of due process, and of discriminatory treatment by the US immigration officials in the processing of these claims.[91] As the influx of the Haitian 'boat people', as they came to be known, continued, the US Immigration and Naturalization Service placed them in detention camps pending hearings on their asylum claims. As a consequence,

---

[89] Id. at 138.

[90] See, e.g., the sections dealing with the judiciary in the country reports on Argentina (1980), Chile (1985), Guatemala (1983), Nicaragua (1981) and Paraguay (1987). For updates on these reports, see the Commission's Annual Reports.

[91] Case 3228 (United States).

the original complaint was supplemented with charges that the Haitians were being discriminated against as compared with nationals of other countries seeking asylum who were not being detained, that their detention was illegal, and that the conditions of detention were both deplorable and inhumane. The petitioners urged the Commission to conduct an investigation of the conditions in which the Haitians were being held in these detention camps in Miami, Puerto Rico and Brooklyn, New York. With the consent of the US Government, Commission visits were conducted on 28–29 June 1982, and on 5–6 August 1982. This was the first time that the Commission had conducted an on-site investigation in the US.

As regards the issue of domestic remedies, a number of lawsuits were simultaneously pending in US courts, and the Commission, during its inspection visit to the Florida camp, attended the proceedings in the federal District Court in Miami, at which Judge Spellman ordered that the Haitians interned in camps and federal prisons in the United States be released.[92] In spite of these on-going actions, the petitioners argued that since the domestic lawsuits did not cover all the allegations raised in their communication, the Commission should not consider itself barred from dealing with the case. In addition, those Haitians who had lost their appeal for political asylum in the US were being deported back to Haiti and were subject to imprisonment and, in some cases, death. Consequently, the pending lawsuits in US courts did not provide an effective remedy for these individuals and their last and only recourse, according to the petitioners, was the Commission. Although the case was not declared inadmissible, it was closed without a decision because of the inability of the members of the Commission to reach a consensus on the merits of the case.

In another case, the question that arose, but was left undecided, was whether the applicant should be expected to pursue judicial remedies, possibly as far as the US Supreme Court, as well as administrative remedies. In the case of Jean Pierre Williams, the applicant alleged a violation of his right to US nationality. Williams was the natural son of a Belgian mother and US father. Under Belgian law, since his father had 'recognized' him, he was considered a US, not a Belgian national. Under US law, however, since he had not complied with the provisions of the US Nationality Act, he was not considered a US citizen. The US maintained that in order to exhaust domestic remedies Williams had to apply for a passport through the US Consulate in Belgium, in spite of the fact that he did not come within the terms of the US law. The processing of the case was suspended while Williams applied for and was duly denied the passport.

---

[92] See the Commission's Annual Report 1981–2, at 17–18. For a later Haitian boat-people case, see Report No. 28/93, Case 10.675 (United States) Decision of the Commission as to the Admissibility, 13 Oct. 1993 in Annual Report 1992–3, at 334–75.

The US then maintained that Williams was required to exhaust not only administrative but also judicial remedies, even if that meant taking the case to the US Supreme Court in order to challenge the constitutionality of the US Nationality Act. The Commission sought the assistance of a non-governmental human rights organization, the International Human Rights Law Group in Washington, DC, which assisted it in providing Williams with a lawyer who was willing to take the case to court on a *pro bono* basis. While the case was pending in the federal District Court for the District of Columbia, the US agreed to give Williams a passport and the case was closed.[93] The Commission could have considered these attempts to exhaust domestic remedies as unduly onerous on the applicant, but since his life and liberty were not at risk and it was possible to assist the petitioner in taking these actions, the Commission did not apply the exception to the exhaustion rule.

Where an application is rejected for non-exhaustion of domestic remedies, it will be open for the applicant to submit a further communication after domestic remedies have been exhausted. In a case involving the former President of the Dominican Republic, Jorge Salvador Blanco, the petition alleged that there had been violations of due process in the proceedings against the former president since the trial had been carried out *in absentia*.[94] The Commission held the complaint to be inadmissible because the former President had returned to the Dominican Republic and appeared before the Dominican court in order to exercise his right to file an appeal against the *in absentia* judgment. The appeal process invalidated all the previous proceedings related to the *in absentia* trial under challenge. Consequently, the Commission held that the case was inadmissible, but without prejudice to its being presented again in the future, depending upon the results of the appeal process.[95]

When applying the exhaustion of local remedies rule, it is important to know who has the burden of proof. Consequently, the Commission, recognizing the difficulty of some applicants of demonstrating that remedies that are apparently available are of no avail in practice, especially those in States with non-functioning judiciaries, has placed the burden of proof as regards exhaustion on the State. The Commission's Regulations (Article 37(3)) state:

When the petitioner contends that he is unable to prove exhaustion as indicated in this Article, it shall be up to the government against which this petition has been lodged to demonstrate to the Commission that the remedies under domestic law have not previously been exhausted, unless it is clearly evident from the background information contained in the petition.

The above paragraphs in this section concern the practice of the Commission in applying the exhaustion of domestic remedies rule. The meaning of the requirement has also been considered by the Inter-American Court. It did

---

[93] Since this case was closed without a decision, it does not appear in any of the Commission's reports.

[94] See above, 81.

[95] Loc. cit. at p. 81, n. 71, 103.

so first in its judgment on the merits in the three disappeared persons cases against Honduras.[96] In these cases, the Honduran Government alleged that domestic remedies, such as habeas corpus, *amparo*, the right of appeal, cassation, etc., were available and had not been exhausted; although claims had been brought, they had not been properly or finally pursued.[97] The Commission argued that the petitioners had exhausted domestic remedies by having presented three writs of habeas corpus and two criminal complaints, which had produced no result.[98] Further, the Commission argued that 'the prior exhaustion of domestic remedies was not required because of the total ineffectiveness of the [Honduran] judiciary.'[99] The proof of this, as presented by the Commission, was documentation showing that not a single writ of habeas corpus had resulted in the release of anyone who had been illegally detained by the governmental authorities and had subsequently 'disappeared'. In addition, the Commission asserted, at least two of the exceptions to the rule set out in Article 46(2) were applicable, because during the period in question there was no due process of law and the petitioner did not have access to any remedy. The Court rejected the defendant state's preliminary objection, holding that the Commission had shown that the remedies that remained to be exhausted were 'ineffective or were mere formalities'.[100] The Court stated:[101]

The testimony and other evidence received and not refuted leads to the conclusion that...although there may have been legal remedies in Honduras that theoretically allowed a person detained by the authorities to be found, those remedies were ineffective in cases of disappearance because the imprisonment was clandestine; formal requirements made them inapplicable in practice; the authorities against which they were brought simply ignored them, or because attorneys and judges were threatened and intimidated by those authorities.

In its judgment on the merits in the Honduran cases, the Court also made certain important statements of principle. As regards the burden of proof on the issue of exhaustion, the Court first recalled that it had stated in its preliminary objections judgment in the cases that a 'state claiming non-exhaustion of local remedies has an obligation to prove that domestic remedies remain to be exhausted and that they are effective.'[102] It continued:

The Court now affirms that if a State which alleges non-exhaustion proves the existence of specific domestic remedies that should have been utilized, the opposing party has the burden of showing that those remedies were exhausted or that the

---

[96] I/A Court H.R., *Velasquez Rodriguez* case, Series C No. 4 (1988), 9 *HRLJ* 212; I/A Court H.R., *Godinez Cruz* case, Series C No. 5 (1989); I/A Court H.R., *Fairen Garbi and Solis Corrales* case, Series C No. 6 (1989).

[97] See *Velasquez Rodriguez* case, Judgment, Id., para. 53.   [98] Id., para. 55.

[99] See *Fairen Garbi and Solis Corrales* case, Preliminary Objections, above n. 76, para. 81.

[100] Judgment on the merits, para. 81.   [101] Id., para. 80.

[102] *Velasquez Rodriguez* case, Preliminary Objections para. 88.

case comes within the exceptions of Article 46(2). It must not be rashly presumed that a State party to the Convention has failed to comply with its obligation to provide effective domestic remedies.[103]

The Court then established a test for the exhaustion of domestic remedies: not only must the remedies exist in the statute books but they must also be both adequate and effective.[104] An adequate remedy is one 'suitable to address an infringement of a legal right'.[105] In reply to the Honduran Government's position, the Court stated that:

For example, a civil proceeding specifically cited by the Government, such as a presumptive finding of death based on disappearance, the purpose of which is to allow heirs to dispose of the estate of the person presumed deceased or to allow the spouse to remarry, is not an adequate remedy for finding a person or for obtaining his liberty.[106]

Habeas corpus would be the appropriate remedy for finding a person in detention. Yet the Honduran Government stated that in order to file a writ of *habeas corpus* under Honduran laws the petitioner must identify the place of detention and the authority ordering the detention. Since this information is unknown in a case involving a 'disappearance', the Court held this remedy to be inadequate.[107]

An effective remedy, said the Court, is one 'capable of producing the result for which it is designed'.[108] The Court found that the record of the case demonstrated that from 1981–4 more than one hundred persons had been illegally detained in Honduras and that most of them had 'disappeared'.[109] Those who reappeared did so not as the result of any of the legal remedies allegedly available to them, but because of other circumstances, such as the intervention of diplomatic missions or actions of human rights organizations. The Government of Honduras, said the Court, 'had the opportunity to call its own witnesses to refute the evidence presented by the Commission, but failed to do so'.[110] It concluded that:

. . . although there may have been legal remedies in Honduras that theoretically allowed a person detained by the authorities to be found, those remedies were ineffective in cases of disappearances because the imprisonment was clandestine; formal requirements made them inapplicable in practice; the authorities against

---

[103] See *Velasquez Rodriguez* case, Judgment, above n. 96, para. 60.
[104] Id., para. 63.
[105] Id., para. 64.
[106] Id.
[107] Id., para. 65.
[108] Id., para. 66.
[109] See Honduras, *The Facts Speak for Themselves*, The Preliminary Report of the National Commissioner for the Protection of Human Rights in Honduras, translation by Human Rights Watch/Americas (formerly Americas Watch), Centre for Justice and International Law (July 1994).
[110] *Velasquez Rodriguez* case, Judgment, above n. 96, para. 79.

whom they were brought simply ignored them, or because attorneys and judges were threatened and intimidated by those authorities.[111]

The Court's pronouncements on the exhaustion of local remedies in the three Honduran cases are in line with the Commission's extensive practice on the subject.

At the request of the Commission, in Advisory Opinion No 11[112] the Inter-American Court pronounced on two other particular aspects of the domestic remedies rule, viz whether Article 46, Convention exempts an individual from exhausting domestic remedies where he/she is unable to do so (i) by reason of indigence or (ii) because an atmosphere of fear prevails within the legal community so that a lawyer cannot be found. On the first point, the Court was of the opinion that under Article 46(2) a person is exempt from exhausting domestic remedies if it can be shown that he/she 'needs legal counsel to effectively protect a right which the Convention guarantees and his indigency prevents him from obtaining such counsel'.[113] On the second point, to the same effect, the Court was of the opinion that 'where an individual requires legal representation and a generalised fear in the legal community prevents him from obtaining such representation, the exception set out in Article 46(2)(b) is fully applicable and the individual is exempted from the requirement to exhaust domestic remedies'.[114]

The Six-months rule

When the Secretariat has satisfied itself that domestic remedies have been exhausted, it looks to the next requirement of admissibility, set forth in Article 46(l)(b), which states that the petition must have been filed within six months from the date on which the party alleging the violation of his rights was notified of the final judgment. This requirement appears straight-forward, especially for those cases in which the applicant was able to go to court and has a final judgment in hand. It is rendered somewhat more complicated, however, when the applicant is unable to exhaust domestic remedies because of one of the denial of justice provisions in Article 46(2), Convention. In such cases, the Commission applies a 'reasonable time' test. Article 38(2) of its Regulations provides that in the denial of justice cases falling within Article 46(2), Convention:

. . . the deadline for presentation of a petition to the Commission shall be within a reasonable period of time, in the Commission's judgment, as from the date on which the alleged violation of rights has occurred, considering the circumstances of each specific case.

---

[111] *Velasquez Rodriguez* case, Judgment, para. 80.
[112] I/A Court of H.R. Series A. No. 11 (1990), 12 *HRLJ* 20.
[113] Id., para. 32.   [114] Id., para. 35.

The six months rule does not prevent the bringing of a claim that concerns an alleged violation that may have commenced more than six months before the claim is brought but that involves a continuing breach. For example, the cases relating to disappeared persons in Argentina were presented to the Commission some time after they had disappeared but while the persons were still 'disappeared' and the families had no information as to their whereabouts.[115] Similarly, cases presented on behalf of individuals held in arbitrary detention in Argentina at the disposal of the National Executive Power (the 'PEN detainees') were admitted while these individuals were still in indefinite detention, since they had no judicial remedy.[116] The Commission also admitted many cases of Chilean exiles who were not allowed to return to their home country and who had no judicial recourse. In determining whether such cases had been presented within a reasonable time, the Commission took into consideration whether the violation was still continuing. If it was, the Commission opened the case, even though the alleged violation may well have commenced many more than six months before.[117]

Certain cases involving the death penalty in Jamaica come within this 'continuing violation' category of exceptions to the six-months rule. The Commission has received a large number of petitions from individuals condemned to death, filed, in some cases, many years after they were tried and sentenced, claiming that they are innocent, and that they were only sentenced to death as a result of a denial of due process in the trial of their case. In view of the continuing risk to the petitioners' right to life, which may be infringed because of the alleged allegations of an unfair trial, the Commission must determine, according to the circumstances of the particular petition, whether it was brought within a reasonable period of time. Many of these cases have been opened by the Commission's Secretariat, since they disclose a *prima facie* violation, and then subsequently closed by the Commission following a consideration of the merits because no lack of a fair trial in breach of the Convention has been proven.[118]

Case pending before another international forum

For a petition to be admissible, Article 46 (1)(c), American Convention requires that 'the subject of the petition or communication is not pending in

---

[115] See, e.g., Res. Nos. 21/78, 22/78 and 27/78, Cases 2209, 2266 and 2484 (Argentina), 18 Nov. 1978 in Annual Report 1979–80, at 49–57.

[116] See, e.g., Res. Nos. 15/81, Cases Nos. 2488 and 3482 (Argentina), 6 Mar. 1981 in Annual Report 1980–81, at 19–25.

[117] See, e.g., Res. Nos. 55/81, 56/81 and 57/81, Cases Nos. 4288 and 5713 and 4662 (Chile) of 16 Oct. 1981 and Res. No. 24/82, *Exiles* (Chile) which involves 50 separate cases, as of 8 Mar. 1982, all in the Annual Report 1981–2, at 57–65.

[118] See, e.g., Res. No. 25/81, Case 3102 (Jamaica), 25 June 1981 in Annual Report 1981–2, at 89–91, Res. Nos. 27/96 and 28/86, Cases 7505 and 9190 (Jamaica), 16 Apr. 1986 in Annual Report 1985–6, at 51–7.

another international proceeding for settlement.' In light of the fact that international standard setting is leading to the creation of many new intergovernmental human rights bodies that are competent to hear petitions from OAS member states, this provision will no doubt become more important in the future. At present the issue of possible conflict of jurisdiction mainly exists for the Inter-American Commission in relation to the Human Rights Committee, certain member States of the OAS having also ratified the International Covenant on Civil and Political Rights and the First Optional Protocol thereto.[119]

The practice of the Inter-American Commission has been to conduct a process of consultation between its Secretariat and the Secretariat of the Human Rights Committee, on a periodic basis, in order to exchange information regarding pending cases. In one case, the alleged victim withdrew his case from the Inter-American Commission in order to present it before the Human Rights Committee.[120] In a second case, the petitioner sought to take his case to the United Nations but, since the case was well advanced in the Commission's procedure, the Commission's Secretariat advised the victim's legal representative not to withdraw it. The government ignored the Commission's recommendation on the merits of the case and the same legal representative subsequently presented the same case to the Human Rights Committee.[121]

In a number of cases dealing with 'disappeared' persons in Peru, the Peruvian Government objected to the Commission's jurisdiction, stating that the cases in question had been examined by the UN Working Group on Enforced or Involuntary Disappearances and therefore should not be examined by the Inter-American Commission. The Commission rejected this argument, hold-

---

[119] The OAS member States concerned, as of 15 Aug. 1996 are: Argentina, Barbados, Bolivia, Chile, Colombia, Costa Rica, the Dominican Republic, Ecuador, El Salvador, Jamaica, Nicaragua, Panama, Peru, Suriname, Uruguay and Venezuela. The Committee against Torture and the Committee against Racial Discrimination are other examples of bodies within the UN system that may hear petitions against OAS member states.

[120] Members of the UN Human Rights Committee and its Secretariat have written that: 'In the majority of such cases (which have concerned examination of the same matter by the Inter-American Commission on Human Rights) the authors have then withdrawn their communications from the IACHR in order to enable the Committee to proceed with its examination.' A. de Zayas, J. Moeller and T. Opsahl, *Application of the International Covenant on Civil and Political Rights under the Optional Protocol by the Human Rights Committee*, in 28 GYIL 9, 21. This was true in the past but not in recent years. A number of cases in the early years were withdrawn from the IACHR because the State (Uruguay) against which the petitions had been presented, had ratified the UN Covenant and the Optional Proocol but had not ratified the American Convention. The petitioners were (mistakenly) advised that the protection afforded by the Covenant would be greater than that under the American Declaration.

[121] See Res. No. 13/84, Case No. 9054 (Jamaica), 3 Oct. 1984, Annual Report 1984–5, at 111–13 and Communications Nos. 210/1986 and 225/1987 *Pratt and Morgan* v. *Jamaica*, final views adopted by the UN Human Rights Committee on Apr. 6, 1989. See also M.Schmidt, 'The Optional Protocol to the International Covenant on Civil and Political Rights: Procedure and Practice', 4 *Interights Bulletin* 27 (1989).

ing that it was not prohibited by Article 46(1)(c) from considering a case 'if the proceeding in progress in another organization is confined to a consideration of the general human rights situation in the country, and no decision has been reached on the specific facts concerning which the petition has been submitted to the Commission, or the decision does not lead to a real settlement of the violation charged.'[122] The Commission stated that it was not within the competence of the UN Working Group 'to decide on the specific facts alleged in the present case' and therefore the Commission was not barred by the American Convention or its Regulations from considering the case.[123]

Similarly, during its 54th Session, held during the period 8–17 October 1981, the Commission held that it was not barred from considering Case 7579 of Jorge Salazar (Nicaragua), just because the same case had been under consideration by the International Labor Organization in Geneva. Although the ILO had published an extensive report on the Salazar case, the ILO procedure was not an 'international procedure of settlement' within the meaning of Article 46 (1)(c) of the American Convention. Today, this issue would not arise in light of the fact that both the Commission and the UN Human Rights Centre consider the prohibition to be solely on the 'simultaneous' examination of a pending case.

Another limit to the rule preventing the consideration of cases pending elsewhere has now been added by the Human Rights Committee, which has opened some cases in spite of the fact that the same case was pending the Inter-American Commission, on the ground that the petitioner before the Inter-American Commission was not the victim or his representative. Since the standing requirement before the Inter-American Commission allows unrelated third parties to present complaints, the Human Rights Committee has, in a sense, 'pierced the veil' of the proceedings before the Commission and concluded that if the applicant before the Commission is not the victim or his representative, then the victim cannot be precluded from having access to the UN Human Rights Committee.[124]

Since the prohibition in Article 46(1) is on 'simultaneous' examination of the same matter by more than one international body, the fact that the same case is subsequently presented to another forum, as a result of the offending State's failure to comply with the first decision, presents no problem of admissiblity under Article 46.[125] However, it is a ground of inadmissibility in Article 47 that the petition is 'substantially the same as one previously

---

[122] See Cases 9501–9512 (Peru), 24 Mar. 1988, Annual Report 1987–8, at 235–9, 263–74.

[123] Id.

[124] See de Zayas, et al. above n. 120, at 13.

[125] A problem of a different kind, of course, would arise if the second international body came down with a decision which contradicted the decision of the first body if the same substantive issue were in question.

studied by the Commission or another international organization'. Whereas this prevents a case being considered by the Commission after it has been before the Human Rights Committee, the reverse is not true.[126]

Examination of petitions declared *prima facie* admissible

If a petition is considered by the Secretariat to be *prima facie* admissible, the procedure in Article 48, Convention and Article 34, Commission Regulations applies. The 'pertinent parts' of the complaint are transmitted by the Commission to the State concerned, without revealing the identity of the petitioner (unless the petitioner indicates otherwise). The State is requested to provide information on the case within 90 days from the date on which the request is sent (Article 34(5), Commission Regulations). This request for information does not prejudice the Commission's final determination regarding the admissibility of the complaint.

When the Secretariat transmits the pertinent parts of the complaint to the government, it specifically requests the government to provide information as to whether the applicant has exhausted domestic remedies. At the same time, the Secretariat informs the applicant that his case has been forwarded to the government for comment, and requests the applicant to submit any supplementary documentation regarding the exhaustion of domestic remedies which may not have been included with the original filing of the complaint (such as copies of court judgments, medical records, etc.).

In practice, many States do not reply within the 90-day period. The Regulations provide that a State may request, 'with justifiable cause', a 30-day extension, but in no case shall extensions be granted beyond six months from the date of the Commission's first request.[127] In part due to the workload of the Secretariat (over 12,000 individual petitions have been registered by a Secretariat which consists of thirteen staff lawyers, and for many years comprised less than half that number), these time limits have been liberally construed. Consequently, when a governmental representative 'promises' the Secretariat a reply on a case provided another extension beyond the 180 days limit is granted, the Secretariat administratively grants the request.

Some examples of abuse of this procedure have involved certain States parties to the Convention never responding to any requests for information by the Commission.[128] However, there are States, not parties to the Convention, which routinely present complete and detailed replies to the Com-

[126] See Art. 5(2)(a), First Optional Protocol, International Covenant on Civil and Political Rights, which contains no such limit.
[127] Art. 34(6), Commission Regulations.
[128] On the presumption of truth that has been developed to deal with this situation, see below, 98.

mission's requests for information on cases involving violations under the American Declaration.

The Secretariat transmits the Government's reply to the petitioner for observations, which must be submitted within 30 days. These are, in turn, transmitted to the Government for its final observations, which are also due within a 30–day period.[129] In practice, the interchange of correspondence goes on for as long as new information is requested and submitted by the parties. In the juvenile offenders death penalty case presented against the United States, after the formal procedure (of the submission of the Government's response and the petitioners' observations thereto) had been completed, the parties submitted written briefs to the Commission summarizing and recapitulating their respective positions. These additional briefs were not required by the Commission but facilitated its review of the issues involved.[130]

As regards the question of the kind of evidence that may be used to prove a case before the Commission, the Convention and the Regulations are silent. In practice, the Commission relies on the written information provided by the parties as supported by documentary evidence, witnesses, admissions (by governments), expert testimony, on-site visits and uncontestable facts (judicial notice) in proving a case.

In the majority of cases, fact-finding has been limited to an evaluation of the written information presented to the Commission by the parties. In some cases this information is enhanced by a hearing, at the Commission's headquarters, at which the representatives of the two parties present their points of view and respond to queries put to them by members of the Commission.[131] In some cases where the facts are particularly complicated, the Commission may hold more than one hearing on a case.[132]

The investigation of a case may also entail an on-site visit by a representative or a special delegation of the Commission or may even result in a special country report on the human rights situation in the State concerned.[133] Whether

---

[129] Art. 34(7), Commission Regulations.

[130] Res. No. 3/87, Case 9647 (United States) in the Commission's Annual Report 1986–7, at 147–84.

[131] Art. 48(1)(e), Convention and Art. 43, Commission Regulations.

[132] See, e.g., Res. No. 24/88, Case 9706 (Mexico), 23 Mar. 1988 in the Commission's Annual Report 1987–8, at 163–73.

[133] Art. 44, Commission Regulations. See, e.g., Res. No. 25/87, Case 9726 (Panama), 23 Sept. 1987 in the Commission's Annual Report 1987–8, at 174–234, involved an investigation by a representative of the Commission; Res. Nos. 18–21/89 and 22/89, Cases 10.116–119 and 124 (Suriname), Annual Report 1988–9, involved an investigation by a delegation of the Commission, and the Commission's Report on the Situation of Human Rights of a Segment of the Nicaraguan Population of Miskito Origin (1983) originally came before the Commission as a petition presented by an Indian rights organization, 'Misurasata', see 10–13 of the Report; see also the Commission's Report on the Situation of Human Rights in Suriname (1983), which had its origin in a petition from Amnesty International requesting the Commission to investigate the killing of 15 prominent Surinamers.

the investigation includes an on-site visit or not depends upon the government's willingness to invite the Commission to visit its territory to investigate the case.

The fact-finding process is rendered nugatory if the government provides no response at all to the Commission's request for information. This occurred in the past in a large number of cases, especially those involving States generating a significant number of petitions, where there was reason to believe that massive violations were taking place. In order to deal with these cases the Commission evolved a practice, codified in Article 42 of its Regulations,[134] which it began employing prior to the entry into force of the American Convention, by which it presumes the facts to be true as presented by the petitioner if the government chooses not to respond. This article was designed to persuade States to cooperate in the procedure or risk the equivalent of a default judgment. The Commission has continued to use this procedure, even after the entry into force of the Convention, as regards both States parties to the Convention and other OAS member states, if they fail to respond to the Commission's requests for information.[135]

However, for the presumption of truth to apply, the petitioner's version of the facts must comply with the criteria of 'consistency, specificity and credibility'.[136] Referring to the judgment of the Inter-American Court in the *Velasquez* case, the Commission stated in a 1996 case:[137]

18 . . . the Commission considers of special importance the case law of the Inter-American Court of Human Rights, that states that 'silence of the accused or elusive or ambiguous answers on its part may be interpreted as an acknowledgment of the truth of the allegations, so long as the contrary is not indicated by the record or is not compelled as a matter of law',[138] which is reaffirmed by Article 42 of the Commission's Regulations.

19. The Commission considers that the petitioner should furnish sufficient infor-

[134] Art. 42 reads: 'The facts reported in the petition whose pertinent parts have been transmitted to the government of the State in reference shall be presumed to be true if, during the maximum period set by the Commission under the provisions of Article 34, paragraph 5, the government has not provided the pertinent information, as long as other evidence does not lead to a different conclusion.'

[135] See, e.g., Res. No. 4/87, Case 7864 and Res. No. 5/87, 9619 (Honduras) Annual Report 1986–7, at 65–88; Res. Nos. 7/88–14/88 and 16/88–19/88, Cases 9501–9512 (Peru) 24 Mar. 1988, Annual Report 1987–8, at 235–59, 263–74; Res. No. 12/86 Case 9289, Res. 13/86, Case 9295, Res. No. 15/86 Case 9341, Res. No. 17/86 Case 9344 (Nicaragua), 16 Apr. 1986, Annual Report 1985–6, at 112–16 and 119–23. Report No. 26/92, Case 10.287 (El Salvador) 24 Sept. 1992 in Annual Report 1992–3, at 83–92; Report No. 5/94, Case 10.574 (El Salvador) 1 Feb. 1994 in Annual Report 1993 (*sic*), at 174–80; Report No. 9/94, Cases 11.105, 11.107, 11.110, 11.111–4, 11.118, 11.120, 11.122 and 11.102 (Haiti) 1 Feb. 1994 in Annual Report 1993 (*sic*), at 224–31. See also Reports Nos. 10/94, Case 10.770 (Nicaragua) 1 Feb. 1994 in Annual Report 1993 (*sic*), at 293–302.

[136] Case 10.948 (El Salvador) 1 Mar., 1996 in Annual Report 1995 (*sic*), at 101–12, 106–7.

[137] Ibid.

[138] *Velasquez Rodriguez*, para. 138.

mation for it to make the analysis called for in Article 46 and 47 of the American Convention and in Article 32 of the Regulations, that is, to determine whether the petitioner has satisfied the requirements for admission and admissibility. Similarly, the Commission must evaluate the petitioner's version of the facts in accordance with the provisions of the American Convention and the Regulations of the Commission.

20. The Inter-American Court has implicitly established the criteria that should be employed to evaluate the petitioner's version in order to determine whether there is other evidence that might lead to a different conclusion. Especially important for that action by the Commission are the criteria of *consistency*[139] and *credibility*.[140] A third requirement that is absolutely necessary before analyzing consistency and credibility is *specificity*, which is deduced as a corollary of those two factors.

21 . . . The petitioners must therefore establish the requirements of admissibility and the minimum elements of consistency, specificity and credibility in their version of the facts for them to be presumed to be true.

Closure of cases by an administrative decision

Pursuant to Article 48(1)(b), Convention, a case shall be closed provided that the grounds for the petition no longer exist. In practice, this procedure, which is distinct from that by which a petition is declared inadmissible, has mostly involved cases of arbitrary detention in which the Commission has been informed that the detainee has been released and the petitioner no longer chooses to continue with the case. Other cases have concerned petitions which were inactive for a long period of time and the petitioners have failed to follow up on their original complaint or can no longer be located by the Secretariat. In recent years, the Commission has taken the position that such 'archiving' of cases is done 'without prejudice' should the petitioners re-appear or produce new information.

The Commission has also closed large numbers of cases pending against a State in which there has been a significant and radical change of government. Cases concerning 'disappearances' in Argentina were individually opened and used to document the systematic practice of the government, specifically, the *modus operandi* of the security forces in carrying out the practice of 'disappearances', in the Commission's country study on Argentina. Following

---

[139] *Velasquez Rodriguez*, para. 143. The determination of consistency is a matter of the logical/rational comparison of the information furnished by the petitioner, to establish that there is no contradiction between the facts and/or the evidence submitted.

[140] *Velasquez Rodriguez*, para. 146. The credibility of the facts is determined by assessing the version submitted, including its consistency and specificity, in evaluating the evidence furnished, taking into account public and well-known facts and any other information the Commission considers pertinent.

the change of government in 1983, when the military turned over power to the elected civilian government, these cases were closed by an omnibus resolution in spite of the fact that separate decisions had not been taken in each case.[141] The cases pending against the Government of Anastasio Somoza in Nicaragua were also closed when the Sandinista Government assumed power. Similarly, cases were closed as a result of the transition from military rule to democracy in Uruguay. While this practice may raise questions under international law in terms of continued state responsibility for human rights violations, in practice the mechanics of processing such a large volume of cases has made this kind of 'housekeeping' a necessity. Because of its small staff and the large number of cases which it receives, the Commission has been forced to rationalize the processing of cases to serve the fundamental purpose of the system, which is to assist the victims of human rights violations in the most efficacious way possible.

The procedure has been for the Secretariat to present the cases which it recommends be administratively closed to the Commission during its regular session and for the Commission to decide which cases are to be closed without the adoption of a formal written decision.

Friendly settlement of cases

Pursuant to Articles 48(l)(f) and 49, Convention, a case is closed if a friendly settlement is reached between the parties. The friendly settlement must be achieved on the basis of respect for the human rights recognized in the American Convention. The Commission draws up a report which is then transmitted to the parties and communicated to the Secretary General for publication. The report must contain a brief statement of the facts and of the solution reached. Some recent cases involving the Argentine Government have resulted in a friendly settlement.[142]

Prior to these cases, the Commission had been disinclined to undertake officially its friendly settlement role. The reason for this was that the Convention procedure revolves around the central notion that human rights violations can be solved by means of a friendly settlement, whereas the Commission historically had been used to documenting violations of a kind which it considered did not lend themselves to a friendly solution. Its

---

[141] See OAS publication, Report on the Situation of Human Rights in Argentina, OEA/Ser.L/V/II.49, doc. 19, 11 Apr. 1980 (Washington, DC, 1980). See also Res. No. 1/83, *Cases of Disappeared Persons in Argentina*, 8 Apr. 1983 in the Commission's Annual Report 1982–3, at 46–7.

[142] Report No. 1/93, Report on the Friendly Settlement procedure in Cases 10.288, 10.310, 10.436, 10.496, 10.631 and 10.771 (Argentina), 3 Mar. 1993 in Annual Report 1992–3, at 35–40; Report No.22/94, Case 11.012 (Argentina), 20 Sept. 1994 in Annual Report 1994, at 40–5. See also Res. No. 5/85, Case No. 7956 (Honduras), 5 Mar. 1985 in Annual Report 1984–5, at 104–11.

disinclination in this regard is part of a more general phenomenon. Having been established 20 years before the entry into force of the Convention, the Commission has generally been slow in adapting its procedures to the requirements of the Convention and has taken time to adjust its philosophy to that inherent in it. The disinclination to use the friendly settlement procedure illustrates this point in that no such procedure was formally operated by the Commission before the Convention came into force and it is still the case that none is provided for in the Commission's Statute for non-Convention parties.[143]

But the language of Article 48(1)(f) of the Convention is mandatory:

The Commission shall place itself at the disposal of the parties concerned with a view to reaching a friendly settlement of the matter on the basis of respect for the human rights recognized in the Convention.

The Inter-American Court had the opportunity to address the issue of the extent of the Commision's obligation under this provision in the three Honduran cases. There the Honduran Government argued that the Commission had violated Article 48(1)(f) of the American Convention by not promoting a friendly settlement between the parties.[144] The Commission, in contrast, argued that the special circumstances of the case made it impossible to pursue such a settlement, for the facts had not been clearly established (due to the Government's lack of cooperation), and the Government had not accepted any responsibility in the matter. Moreover, the Commission contended that the rights to life (Article 4), to humane treatment (Article 5) and to personal liberty (Article 7) violated in these cases, could not be 'effectively restored' by conciliation.[145]

The Court acknowledged that the language of Article 48(1)(f) 'would seem to establish a compulsory procedure'. Inexplicably, however, it interpreted this mandatory language to allow for a discretionary practice, as the Commission had argued:

. . . if the phrase is interpreted within the context of the Convention, it is clear that the Commission should attempt such friendly settlement only when the circumstances of the controversy make that option suitable or necessary, at the Commission's sole discretion.[146]

The Court then suggested that the failure of a government to reply to the Commission's request for information in a case is sufficient, under certain circumstances, to be considered a waiver of the friendly settlement procedure:

Irrespective of whether the positions and aspirations of the parties and the degree of the Government's cooperation with the Commission have been

---

[143] In fact, the friendly settlement procedure is now used in cases concerning any OAS member state, whether a party to the Convention or not.

[144] See *Velasquez Rodriguez*, Preliminary Objections, above n. 76, para. 42.

[145] Id., para. 43.   [146] Id., para. 44.

determined, when the forced disappearance of a person at the hands of a State's authorities is reported and that State denies that such acts have taken place, it is very difficult to reach a friendly settlement that will reflect respect for the rights to life, to humane treatment and to personal liberty. Considering the circumstances of this case, the Court finds that the Commission's handling of the friendly settlement matter cannot be challenged.[147]

This would seem to contradict the language of the Convention, which expressly mandates an attempted friendly settlement in all cases. There is no stated or implicit authority in the Convention to suggest that the Commission may determine which cases are susceptible to settlement and which are not. Since the core notion of the Convention is the conviction that human rights disputes can be settled, the Commission should not place itself in a position, *a priori*, to exclude certain cases because of the nature of the violations involved, since the Convention itself establishes no such hierarchy.

Following the judgment of the Inter-American Court in the three Honduran cases, in a number of cases the Commission included language in its resolutions to the effect that the nature of some complaints was such that they were not susceptible to being resolved by means of the friendly settlement procedure.[148] In 1994, in the *Caballero Delgado and Santana* case, the Court revisited the issue and admonished the Commission for this approach. It stated that whereas the Commission enjoys some discretion as regards a friendly settlement, it does not have 'arbitrary powers' in this regard.[149] The Court continued:

Only in exceptional circumstances and, of course, for substantive reasons may the Commission omit the friendly settlement procedure because the protection of the rights of the victims or of their next of kin is at stake. To state, as the Commission does, that this procedure was not attempted simply because of the 'nature' of the case does not appear to be sufficiently well-founded.[150]

Following this further pronouncement by the Court, the Commission now inquires of each of the parties whether it is interested in a friendly settlement and if one, or both, rejects the offer, then the friendly settlement procedure ends there. It is for the parties, however, and not for the Commission to make that determination. The rationale for this position is evident if one takes into consideration the ultimate sanction available under the system. Were the case to reach the Inter-American Court, and were the Court to find the government responsible for a violation, then the Court would order the

---

[147] *Velasquez Rodriguez*, para. 46.
[148] Case 9641 (Ecuador) above, n. 86 and Res. Nos. 9/89 and 10/89, Cases 9799 and 9802 (Peru), 14 Apr. 1989, in Annual Report 1988–9, at 116–22.
[149] I/A Court of H.R., *Caballero Delgado and Santana* case, Preliminary Objections, Series C No. 17, para. 27 (1994), 15 *HRLJ* 176.
[150] Id., at para. 27.

government to indemnify the victim or his/her relatives. Although the financial award does not 'effectively restore' the victim's right to life or liberty, nonetheless, this financial award and a judgment finding the government responsible is the aim and purpose of taking the case to the Court. If the financial arrangement is understood 'to repair' (in the sense of 'to make reparations') the damage or injury caused by the violation, then the Commission and the victim's representatives save themselves the trouble of having to go before the Court and proving the case all over again.[151]

Final decisions on the merits

Cases are decided on the merits when sufficient evidence has been presented to enable the Commission to take a decision, or where the government in question has not responded and the Commission takes a 'default judgment' based on Article 42 of its Regulations.[152]

Pursuant to Article 50, Convention, if a friendly settlement is not reached the Commission is required in all individual petition cases to 'draw up a report setting forth the facts and stating its conclusions'.[153] This preliminary report is transmitted to the state concerned which is not be at liberty to publish it.[154] When transmitting the report, the Commission 'may make such proposals and recommendations as it sees fit'.[155]

Pursuant to Article 51, Convention, if the case has not been settled or submitted to the Court by the Commission or the State concerned within a

[151] This was particularly relevant in the case of *Fairen Garbi and Solis Corrales*, in which the Court found that there was insufficient evidence to hold the Government of Honduras responsible for their 'disappearance'. Had the Commission sought a friendly settlement in the three Honduran cases, as a package, or as a reparations program to apply to all Honduran 'disappearance' cases, it is possible, although unlikely, that the Honduran Government might have been willing to settle all three cases to avoid having to go before the Court. See, above n. 96.

[152] On Regulation 42, see above, 98.

[153] Art. 50(1), Convention. Art. 53, Commission Regulations provides for a simpler but comparable procedure for American Declaration cases. Instead of the two Art. 50 and 51 reports (the case cannot be referred to the Court), there is a 'final decision' of the Commission which is sent to 'the state in question or the petitioner' (Art. 53(2)) and 'shall include any recommendations the Commission deems advisable and a deadline for their implementation' (Art. 53(1)). If the deadline is not met, 'the Commission may publish its decision' (Art. 53(2)). It may do this in its annual report or elsewhere as it sees fit (Art. 53(4)).

[154] Art. 50(2), Convention. The report may only be transmitted to the state concerned. In Adv. Opin. No. 13, Series A No. 13, Certain Attributes of the Inter-American Commission on Human Rights, para. 49 (1993), 14 *HRLJ* 252, 1 IHRR Vol 2 197 (1994) the Court expressed the opinion that Art. 47(6), Commission Regulations ('the parties concerned') was inconsistent with the Convention insofar as it required the report to be transmitted to the petitioner and the victim as well as the defendant State.

[155] Art. 50(2), Convention.

three-month period[156] from the date of the transmittal of the Article 50 report to the state, the Commission must adopt a final report[157] in which it 'may . . . set forth its opinion and conclusions concerning the question submitted for its consideration' and, where 'appropriate', 'shall make pertinent recommendations and shall prescribe a period within which the State is to take the measures that are incumbent upon it to remedy the situation'.[158] When the prescribed period has expired, the Commission is required to decide whether the State has taken 'adequate measures' and whether to publish the report.[159]

Article 51 reports are not published if the State has complied with the Commission's recommendations, because the act of publishing is considered notice of the government's failure to comply.[160] The Commission, however, has sought ways of remedying the fact that no public notice is given of cases in which governments do comply with the Commission's recommendations. It has taken the view that this should be done in order to encourage greater compliance and also to provide a public record of the effectiveness of the Commission's work. Accordingly, in the Commission's Annual Report, 1988–1989, brief mention was made of a case in which the government in question did comply with the Commission's recommendations, although the fact that the Commission had taken a decision on the merits in this case and the government had complied, are not mentioned.[161]

In the *Caballero Delgado and Santana* case, the Inter-American Court offered an interpretation regarding the normative status of recommendations made by the Commission in its Articles 50 and 51 reports.[162] The Court stated, in dictum:

---

[156] For a controversial case in which the Court refused to take jurisdiction because the Commission had failed to refer the case to the Court within this time limit, see the *Cayara* case, I/A Court H.R., Preliminary Objections, Series C No. 14 (1993), 14 *HRLJ* 159, 1–2 IHRR 175 (1994).

[157] In Adv. Opin. No. 13, Certain Attributes of the Inter-American Commission on Human Rights, Series A No. 13, 16 July 1993, para. 54 (see n. 154), the Court expressed the opinion that the two reports under Arts. 50 and 51 are separate documents that cannot be combined as one report, although they may coincide in their conclusions and recommendations. In fact the two reports are very similar in wording.

[158] Art. 51(2), Convention.

[159] Art. 51(3), Convention. Publication would be in the Commission's Annual Report.

[160] In Adv. Opin. No. 13, para. 54, see n. 154 the Court took the view that the power to publish the report under Art. 51(3) arises only where the Commission's recommendations 'have not been accepted'.

[161] Case 9579 (Grenada), Annual Report 1988–9, at 29.

[162] I/A Court H.R., *Caballero Delgado and Santana* case, published in the Court's Annual Report 1995, at 135, 17 *HRLJ* 24, 3 IHRR 548 (1996). The Court was responding to a claim by the Commission that Colombia should be held to have violated the Convention 'by deliberately failing to comply with the recommendations' made by the Commission, id., para. 67. During the Preliminary Objections stage of this case, the Government of Colombia had argued that 'it was impossible for it to pay compensation because the Commission's Article 50 Report "was not a binding decision, as would be the case of a judgment of the Inter-American Court, but was simply a recommendation", pointing to its domestic legal provisions'. See *Caballero Delgado and Santana* case, above, n. 149, at para. 50.

In the Court's judgment, the term 'recommendations' used by the American Convention should be interpreted to conform to its ordinary meaning, in accordance with Article 31(1) of the Vienna Convention on the Law of Treaties. *For that reason, a recommendation does not have the character of an obligatory judicial decision for which the failure to comply would generate State responsibility.* As there is no evidence in the present Convention that the parties intended to give it a special meaning, Article 31(4) of the Vienna Convention is not applicable. *Consequently, the State does not incur international responsibility by not complying with a recommendation which is not obligatory.* As to Article 44 of the American Convention, the Court finds that it refers to the right to present petitions to the Commission, and that it has no relation to the obligations of the State. (Emphasis added).[163]

It is, of course, not for the Court to define the competence of the Inter-American Commission on Human Rights; that is reserved to the Commission.[164] This dictum on the part of the Court attempts to subordinate the role of the Commission to the Court in spite of the fact that the two were designed to be co-equal bodies.

With regard to the Court's interpretation of the normative status of Commission recommendations made under Articles 50 and 51 of the Convention, it should first be recalled that there is no requirement in the Convention that every case presented to the Commission be transmitted to the Court.[165] The system as currently structured cannot, and was not designed to, bear the wholesale transmission of all petitions from the Commission to the Court. Moreover, Article 51(1) explicitly leaves open the option of the case being finally decided by the Commission's adoption of a final report, to be published in its Annual Report to the General Assembly, as an alternative to reaching a friendly settlement or submitting a case to the Court. What purpose would be served for the Commission to reach 'conclusions' and make 'recommendations' in an Article 51 report in such cases as regards whether the State incurred in a violation of any of the rights set forth in the Convention if the State were not obligated to act appropriately in response to these conclusions? Since the Commission is currently processing approximately 800 petitions and there are less than a dozen cases currently pending before the Court, is the Court suggesting that the efficacy of the system is limited to the few cases before the Court?

A distinction may be drawn here between a preliminary Article 50 report and, for cases that are not referred to the Court, a final Article 51 report. Article 50 of the American Convention refers to the Commission's 'conclusions' on an individual petition. The Commission's 'conclusion' that a State

---

[163] Id., at para. 67.

[164] It is a fundamental principle of administrative law that an administrative body defines the scope of its own competence.

[165] The question of the criteria for the selection of cases to submit to the Court has been an issue of much debate and little resolution, both in the European and the inter-American systems. See Trindade, Chap. 13, below.

has violated a right set forth in the Convention is buttressed by the 'recommendations' which the Commission may issue under Article 50(3), but which are not obligatory, as the State may or may not comply with these recommendations as it chooses. The 'conclusions' and 'recommendations' in an Article 51 report, however, do carry legal consequences. If the State does not respond to them, it has ignored its international obligations under the Convention to remedy the violation which the Commission has found it to have incurred and that is set forth in its Article 51 report.

In this connection, it is interesting to note that the Government of Colombia has recently shown itself to be in the vanguard in recognizing the obligatory character of decisions of the Inter-American Commission on Human Rights. Colombia, recognizing that it has been the object of eleven adverse decisions of the Inter-American Commission during the past nine years and of three adverse decisions of the United Nations Human Rights Committee, all of which make reference to the issue of the payment of an indemnity, has adopted a law by which the State is obliged to implement decisions of the Committee and the Commission.[166] Law No. 000288 of 5 July 1996 posits the establishment of a Committee comprised of the Ministers of Interior, Foreign Relations, Justice and Defense, who would review the decisions emitted by these international bodies. This governmental Committee would have 45 days from the date of official notification of an international decision to issue its opinion.[167] If this governmental Committee is of the view that either of these international bodies has decided a case erroneously, then the law requires the government to take the matter to the Inter-American Court of Human Rights.[168]

This Colombian Law is unique in the hemisphere in proclaiming the obligatory nature of Commission decisions and in instituting an implementation

---

[166] See Palabras del Señor Presidente de la Republica, Doctor Ernesto Samper Pizano, en el Acto de Sancion de la Ley que Establece Instrumentos Para la Indemnizacion de Perjuicios a las Victimas de Violaciones de los Derechos Humanos, en Virtud de lo Dispuesto por Determinados Organismos Internacionales de Derechos Humanos, Santafé de Bogotá, 5 de julio de 1996. Unpublished document received courtesy of the Embassy of Colombia.

[167] Law No. 000288 of 5 July 1966, 'Por Medio de la Cual se Establecen Instrumentos para la Indemnizacion de Perjuicios a las Victimas de Violaciones de Derechos Humanos en Virtud de lo Dispuesto por Determinados Organos Internacionales de Derechos Humanos.'

[168] See Palabras del Señor Presidente, above, n. 166: 'Puede ocurrir que a juicio del Gobierno, como representante del Estado colombiano, las decisiones de la Comisión Interamericana de Derechos Humanos y del Comité del Pacto de Derechos Civiles y Políticos, no reúnan los presupuestos de hecho y de derecho establecidos en la Constitución Política y en los tratados internacionales aplicables. En ese evento, la actitud responsable, que es la que nos traza la ley que he sancionado y que es la que asumiremos, *consistirá en demandar esa decisión ante el organismo jurisdiccional competente: La Corte Interamericana de Derechos Humanos para el caso de las resoluciones de la Comisión Interamericana.*' (Emphasis added.)

mechanism for the payment of indemnity when recommended by the Human Rights Committee or the Commission. It also posits an attractive new role for the Inter-American Court as a forum for serious disputes between the Commission and States and not as a second instance in an international appeals process, which is the role that the Court has intimated for itself in the *Caballero* decision. It will be interesting to see how many other States in the hemisphere follow Colombia's lead.

The increasing legitimacy of the Inter-American System for the promotion and protection of human rights in the American hemisphere is demonstrated by the example of the Colombian Government's change of position from its assertion before the Court in 1992 that the Commission's recommendations were not legally binding, to its adoption of a law in 1996 which creates a mechanism to enforce Commission decisions at the domestic level.[169] It is this progressive and increasing acceptance of the OAS norms and organs which will eventually lead to complete hemispheric acceptance of the American Convention and the functioning of the system as its drafters had originally contemplated.

Provisional measures

Article 63(2), Convention provides that in 'cases of extreme gravity and urgency, and when necessary to avoid irreparable damage to persons, the Court shall adopt such provisional measures as it deems pertinent in matters that it has under consideration'. In addition, '(w)ith respect to a case not yet submitted to the Court, it may act at the request of the Commission.'

In practice, the Commission has assumed for itself a comparable power to request provisional measures on behalf of victims under threat of imminent danger in cases pending before it. It may act ex officio or at the request of the petitioner. It assumed such a power before the entry into force of the Convention and the establishment of the Court. Given the broad language of the Commission's functions and powers under Article 41 of the Convention, the Commission has since determined that it is not only authorized to request the Court to adopt provisional measures, but may itself 'in urgent cases, when it becomes necessary to avoid irreparable damage to persons . . . request that provisional measures be taken . . . in cases where the denounced facts are true'.[170] The Commission, broadly interpreting its own scope of action in this regard, maintains that it is authorized to 'take any action it considers necessary for the discharge of its functions.'[171]

When the Commission requests provisional measures, it does so for

---

[169] See above *Caballero Delgado and Santana* case, n. 162 and Law No. 000288, at n. 167.
[170] Art. 29(2), Commission Regulations.
[171] Art. 29(1), Commission Regulations.

humanitarian reasons, and its action in no way prejudices either the admissibility or the merits of the case. The granting of provisional measures also has an injunctive character where, for example, the Commission requests a stay of execution in a death penalty case that it has under review.

The procedure for carrying out provisional measures is that when the Commission itself is in session, the Commission takes a decision on the measures to be requested. If the Commission is not in session, the Regulations provide that the Chairman, or one of the Vice Chairmen if the Chairman is unavailable, if possible in consultation with the other Commission members, will decide on the measures to be adopted, which are then implemented by the Secretariat.[172]

A typical example is Case 9647 (United States) in which two juvenile offenders were scheduled to be executed.[173] The Commission requested the US Secretary of State and the Governors of the respective states to stay the executions 'in the spirit of [the] major human rights instruments and the universal trend favorable to the abolition of the death penalty.'[174] The Government effectively ignored the request and replied that the individuals had been accorded fair trials and executed them as scheduled.

In another group of cases, the Commission invoked provisional measures and requested the Government of Guatemala to suspend and commute the death sentences pending against three groups of Guatemalans who had been tried by secret tribunals ('Courts of Special Jurisdiction'). The Chairman of the Commission at the time, Professor Cesar Sepulveda, as an eleventh-hour follow-up to the requests sent to the Foreign Ministry, made telephone calls at dawn on the day in question to attempt to convince the Guatemalan authorities to suspend the first group of executions.[175] The Government of Guatemala also ignored the request and carried out the scheduled executions.

In another urgent case involving an alleged Honduran army attack on a group of Salvadoran refugees in Colomoncagua, Honduras, a number of refugees were reported to have been killed, wounded, arrested, raped and tortured. The petitioners in this case requested that the Commission act to secure the safety of the refugees and the persons who had been taken into detention.[176] The Commission requested the Government of Honduras 'to adopt the pertinent precautionary measures to ensure that the acts covered by the denunciation would be actively and rapidly investigated, as well as to safeguard the victims and preserve the existence of other evidence for the corresponding investigation.' It further requested that the Government

[172] Art. 29(3) Commission Regulations.
[173] Case 9647 (United States), above n. 130.
[174] Id., at 149.
[175] Res. No. 5/87, Cases 8094, 9038 and 9080 (Guatemala) 3 Oct. 1984 in Annual Report 1984–5, at 81–4. See also C. Sepulveda, 'The Inter-American Commission on Human Rights', above n. 46.
[176] Res. No. 5/87, Case 9619 (Honduras), above n. 135.

'adopt timely measures to prevent a repetition of such occurrences and to ensure due respect for the principle of "no return" (non-refoulement) stipulated in Article 22(8) of the American Convention on Human Rights.'[177] The information provided by the Government was considered unsatisfactory by the petitioners. The Commission resolved to consider the facts alleged by them to be true and requested the Government to present the results of a complete investigation and to indicate the measures proposed to indemnify the victims or their heirs. The Government ignored this request.

The Commission has also requested that the Court take provisional measures pursuant to Article 63 (2) of the American Convention in cases pending before the Court. During the Court's consideration of the three Honduran cases, the Commission, 'in view of the threats' against two of the witnesses, requested that the Court take provisional measures to guarantee their safety.[178] The Court did so and the Honduran Government informed the Court that it would guarantee these two witnesses 'the respect of their physical and moral integrity (. . .) and the faithful compliance with the Convention. . . .'[179]

Two months later, in January 1988, while the cases were still pending, the Court was informed of the death, by assassination, of two other witnesses in the proceedings. In response, the Court adopted the following provisional measures pursuant to Article 63(2) of the Convention, ordering:

1. That the Government of Honduras adopt, without delay, such measures as are necessary to prevent further infringements on the basic rights of those who have appeared or have been summoned to do so before this Court in the 'Velasquez Rodriguez,' 'Fairen Garbi and Solis Corrales' and 'Godinez Cruz' cases, in strict compliance with the obligation of respect for and observance of human rights, under the terms of Article 1(1) of the Convention.

2. That the Government of Honduras also employ all means within its power to investigate these reprehensible crimes, to identify the perpetrators and to impose the punishment provided for by the domestic law of Honduras.[180]

The Commission, upon receiving notice of these killings, also requested the Court to take provisional measures and, after consideration of the Commission's request, the Court adopted the following additional measures:

1. That the Government of Honduras, within a period of two weeks, inform this Court on the following points:

a. the measures that have been adopted or will be adopted to protect the physical integrity of, and to avoid irreparable harm to, those witnesses who have testified or have been summoned to do so in these cases.

---

[177] Id., at 75.
[178] See, *Velasquez Rodriguez* case, Judgment, above n. 96, para. 39.
[179] Id., para. 41.   [180] Id.

  b. the judicial investigations that have been or will be undertaken with respect
     to threats against the aforementioned individuals.

  c. the investigations of the assassinations, including forensic reports, and the
     actions that are proposed to be taken within the judicial system of Hondu-
     ras to punish those responsible.

2. That the Government of Honduras adopt concrete measures to make clear
that the appearance of an individual before the Inter-American Commission or
Court of Human Rights, under conditions authorized by the American Convention and by the rules of procedure of both bodies, is a right enjoyed by every
individual and is recognized as such by Honduras as a party to the Convention.[181]

The Honduran Government submitted documents to the Court to prove
that it, in fact, had initiated judicial inquiries into the assassinations of these
two individuals, and it produced the autopsy reports and statements by
forensic specialists.

In 1994, the Commission adopted its report in a later case arising out of
this situation.[182] The report included information regarding the identity of
the two perpetrators of the two assassinations provided by a former member
of the batallion 'who declared that he had seen Professor Pavon's name on
the black list of the batallion, as a result of his having testified before the
Inter-American Court of Human Rights in the case of the disappeared of
Manfredo Velasquez Rodriguez and Saul Godinez Cruz'.[183] Despite the fact
that this witness claimed to have been told by the perpetrators that they had
committed the act, the Government did not proceed to investigate the case
against them. The Commission, for its part, adopted an unexpectedly tepid
report, concluding that 'the Government of Honduras failed to comply' with
its obligations under Articles 4, 8, 25, and 1.1 of the American Convention.[184]
It did not recommend that the Government carry out a thorough investigation
of the case and bring the perpetrators to justice or that the heirs of the victims
be compensated by the State.

A further request for provisional measures—this time in a case not
pending before the Court—was made by the Commission to the Court in the
Chipoco case. There the Commission's request to the Court for measures on
behalf of a human rights activist who was receiving threats from the government was unsuccessful.[185] However, in such a case the request itself may
provide the threatened victim with some protection by means of the publicity
afforded the case, even if the measures are not granted.

---

[181] *Velasquez Rodriguez*, para. 45.
[182] Report No. 13/94, Case No. 10.437 (Honduras), 2 Feb. 1994 in Annual Report
1993 (*sic*), at 249–58.
[183] *Id.*   [184] Id.
[185] *Chipoco* case, resolution of the President of the Inter-American Court of Human
Rights, 14 Dec. 1992. Provisional measures requested by the Inter-American Commission
on Human Rights regarding Peru, Annual Report of the Court 1992, at 17–19.

In sum, precautionary or provisional measures, whether taken by the Commission or the Court at the request of the Commission, have produced meager results. They have served, above all, to communicate to the Government the seriousness with which the Commission or the Court considers the violation, and to put the Government on notice. They have been most effective in cases involving arbitrary detention in countries where it is feared that the victim will be 'disappeared' by the authorities. In those cases a written communication to the governmental authorities or a phone call to the Foreign Ministry has, on occasion, resulted in the release of the person detained and the case has been closed.[186]

Requests for Reconsideration

In the inter-American system, a decision taken by the Commission on a case is not necessarily final. The practice has evolved that if the government requests a reconsideration of the decision, the Commission must decide, at its next regular session, whether or not to grant the request. Requesting reconsideration has become an effective tool for governments to delay the publication of the Commission's decision, even if the request is denied, given the fact that the Commission only holds two regular sessions per year.

The practice of reconsideration of Commission decisions is provided for in Article 54, Commission Regulations, which allow either the State or the petitioner the possibility of requesting reconsideration.[187] In order to request reconsideration, pursuant Article 54, the party must invoke 'new facts or legal arguments which have not been previously considered'. Reconsideration is a procedure set forth in the Commission's Regulations to apply to States that are not parties to the American Convention. In practice, the Commission has made this recourse available to any member State (and any petitioner) which requests reconsideration of the decision adopted, whether the petition concerns a Convention party or not.[188] Consequently, States parties to

---

[186] A case of this nature will be presented by the petitioner on behalf of the individual detained. It will generally be presented by means of a phone call from a relative of the victim or by an NGO. The Secretariat will send a fax and, in some cases, will follow up with a phone call to the affected State's Ambassador to the OAS, expressing concern for the victim's safety as set forth in the petition. If the individual is released the file is closed, pursuant to Art. 48(1)(b) of the Convention, and is not included in the Commission's Annual Report. If the victim is not released the case follows the normal procedure.

[187] The Regulations were modified during the Commission's 70th Session (June–July 1987). Prior to the modification of this provision only the State had the right to request reconsideration.

[188] The Convention does not contemplate the right to request a reconsideration of a decision. Art. 50 of the Convention appears to contemplate the issuance of a 'provisional' decision which may then be 'finalized' under the procedure set forth in Art. 51 if a case is not settled or referred to the Court within three months. In practice, this three-month period has also been used by States parties to request reconsideration.

the American Convention, such as Argentina, Chile, Colombia, Nicaragua, Grenada and Peru, have requested reconsideration.[189]

In some cases, governments have requested reconsideration after the 90-day period specified in the Commission's resolution has expired. These requests for reconsideration have generally been denied, but, in some cases, the Commission has accepted the information presented by the government and the original resolution has been modified.

The rationale for the provision for reconsideration is to allow governments the opportunity to correct any errors in the Commission's decisions. Although the reconsideration procedure has, at times, been abused, it has been of use in correcting some inaccuracies. If the case involves a 'disappeared' person, for example, and the government receives new information that the individual is living in another country or has 'reappeared', the reconsideration procedure enables the government to bring this information to the attention of the Commission and to prevent the publication of an erroneous decision. The Commission, when faced with new information of this sort during the reconsideration procedure, will attempt to verify the new information with the victim's representative. In some cases, in spite of the fact that the government has presented new information, for example, that an individual in detention has been released, that information has been impossible to verify in light of the fact that the victim's relatives have had no contact with the victim, or it may turn out to be untrue and is contradicted by the victim's representative. In other cases, the Commission has reconsidered its decision in light of new information obtained but has maintained its decision (for example that the government has violated a specific right), although not in the terms formulated in the original resolution.

INTER-STATE COMMUNICATIONS

As in the European system and under the International Covenant on Civil and Political Rights, the American Convention provides for inter-state as well as individual complaints.[190] This procedure is not automatic following ratification or accession to the Convention. Pursuant to Article 45 of the American Convention, any State party may, when it deposits its instrument of ratification or adherence, or at any later time, declare that it recognizes the competence of the Commission to receive and examine communications in which a State party alleges that another State party has committed a violation of a human right set forth in the Convention.[191] Only a State party that has recognized the

---

[189] See, e.g., Res. No. 24/87, Case 9620 (Colombia), 16 Sept. 1988, Annual Report 1987–8, at 112–31.

[190] There is no provision for inter-state communications under the Declaration against non Convention parties.

[191] For the states that have declarations under Art. 45, see Appendix VIII.

Commission's competence under Article 45 may present an inter-state complaint against another State, and the Commission shall only consider an inter-state complaint against a State party that has recognized its competence under Article 45. A declaration under Article 45 may be made for an indefinite time, a specified period, or for a specific case, and shall be deposited with the General Secretariat of the OAS, which shall transmit copies to the member States of the Organization.

In practice, no State in the inter-American system has yet presented an inter-state complaint, unlike in the European system where this procedure has produced a rich jurisprudence. Given the political sensitivity of filing such a complaint, it is unlikely that States will choose to resort to it unless their own interests are directly involved, which, in proceedings of this kind is infrequent at best. Another possible explanation for the failure of this procedure to be used is that the inter-State complaints presented in the European system, such as the *Greek Case*,[192] are dealt with in the context of the country studies of the Inter-American Commission. The *Greek Case* involved the overthrow of a democratic government in Greece in April 1967 resulting in the military taking power. The Greek Colonels, in Latin American fashion, declared a state of emergency and suspended ten articles of the Constitution in view of the 'internal danger threatening public order and the security of the State'. The Governments of Denmark, the Netherlands, Norway and Sweden, by written application, alleged before the European Commission that the Greek Government had violated numerous Articles of the European Convention.

The European Commission, after investigating the human rights situation in Greece, having carried out fact-finding missions, and having received copious amounts of testimony and evidence, concluded that the Greek military government had not satisfied the Commission in showing that there had been in April 1967 a public emergency threatening the life of the Greek nation to warrant the declaration of a state of emergency and the suspension of part of the Greek Constitution. The Council of Europe's Committee of Ministers had before it a proposal for the suspension of Greece from membership when the Greek Government announced its denunciation of the European Convention and its withdrawal from the Council of Europe.

A similar series of events in the Americas would be treated by the Commission as grounds for requesting consent from the Government concerned to conduct an on-site visit with a view to the adoption of a country report. Alternatively, one of the political bodies (the Permanent Council, a Meeting of Consultation or the General Assembly) would convoke a meeting to consider the deteriorating political situation and would request the Commission to carry out an on-site visit and to report back to it. Given this

---

[192] 'The Greek Case', *European Yearbook* 12 (1969) (Martinus-Nijhoff, 1972).

efficient alternative mechanism it is unlikely that the inter-state complaints procedure envisaged in Article 45 of the American Convention will be invoked in the Americas as it has been in Europe.[193]

[193] In addition, to strengthen the consolidation of democracy in the hemisphere, in 1991, the OAS General Assembly adopted Resolution 1080, which instructs the Secretary General immediately to convene a meeting of the Permanent Council in the event of any occurrence giving rise to sudden or irregular interruption of the democratic process or of the legitimate exercise of power by a democratically-elected government in any of the Organization's member states. The Council is to examine the situation and then decide whether or not to convene an *ad hoc* Meeting of the Ministers of Foreign Affairs or a special session of the General Assembly within ten days. In either forum, the Foreign Ministers are to look into the events collectively, and adopt any decisions they deem appropriate in accordance with the Charter and international law.

4

The Role of Country Reports in the Inter-American System of Human Rights

CECILIA MEDINA

INTRODUCTION

The power to prepare country reports is vested in the Inter-American Commission on Human Rights (hereinafter the Commission), an organ that operates under both the American Convention on Human Rights (hereinafter the American Convention)[1] and the Charter of the Organization of American States (OAS).[2] The Commission has, unlike other international supervisory organs in the field of human rights, an extensive and varied range of powers. These are exercisable in respect of all OAS member states, whether parties to the American Convention or not.

The Commission developed its powers through practice. From its inception and until the American Convention entered into force in 1978, the Commission reigned alone over human rights in the continent and enjoyed an exceptional freedom to establish and develop procedures and mechanisms to fit the specific situation of the countries it had to supervise.[3] The Commission's Statute granted the Commission three powers which allowed it to develop the practice of preparing country reports with all the peculiarities they possess. These were the powers (i) to prepare such studies or reports as it considered advisable in the performance of its duties; (ii) to make recommendations to states in the field of human rights; and (iii), strangely enough, 'to move to the territory of any American State when it so decides by an absolute majority of votes and with the consent of the government concerned'.[4] This last power was used by the Commission to develop its practice of carrying out observations *in loco*, that is to say, visiting a country to collect and verify facts and, in general, to use the various other mechanisms at its disposal in a different location from that of

---

[1] See Appendix III.
[2] See Appendix I.
[3] For an elaboration on this point, see C. Medina, *The Battle of Human Rights: Gross, Systematic Violations and the Inter-American System* (Dordrecht, 1988) particularly Chap. IV.
[4] See original Statute of the Commission, Art. 11.(c), reproduced in IACHR *Basic Documents*, (OEA/Ser.L/V/I.4, 1 Dec. 1960).

the headquarters of the Organization in Washington DC where the Commission's regular meetings are held. With these three powers, which are now contained in Article 41, American Convention and in Article 18(a), Commission Statute, the Commission succeeded in developing the practice of examining the general situation of human rights in a country and preparing and publishing a country report based upon this examination.

THE DEVELOPMENT OF THE PRACTICE OF PREPARING COUNTRY REPORTS

If one were to describe the main features of the Commission when it began to carry out its work, the words 'clarity of purpose', 'determination' and 'creativeness' would come to mind immediately. As an organ, the original Commission seems to have had a keen perception of its ultimate purpose, which was to make life better for the human beings inhabiting the continent. It also seemed determined to fulfill this function and appeared ready and willing to use its apparently meagre powers in novel ways with the aim of achieving what it thought was its duty to achieve.

In the early 1960s, a major objective of the human rights movement was to give individuals a possibility of resorting to the international community when the state under whose jurisdiction they found themselves did not respect their human rights. The European Convention on Human Rights had devised a mechanism that, although requiring an optional declaration of acceptance from the states parties to the Convention, permitted an individual to lodge a complaint before the European Commission on Human Rights, and this was an ideal for which others in other regions also strived.

The American continent was not only lacking in that sort of mechanism; it also had no human rights convention and the Commission was but an 'autonomous entity' of the Organization of American States, created in a legally insecure manner by a resolution of the Fifth Meeting of Consultation of Ministers of Foreign Affairs.[5] It was to be expected then that the Commission would follow the trend and, in appearance this is what the Commission did when, contrary to the attitude of the UN Human Rights Commission concerning petitions,[6] it decided that, although 'it was not

---

[5] Resolution VIII, Fifth Meeting of Consultation of Ministers of Foreign Affairs, *Final Act*, (OEA/Ser.C/II.5, English).

[6] In 1947, the Economic and Social Council of the United Nations (ECOSOC) passed Resolution 75 (V) recognizing that it had no power to take any action in regard to any complaints concerning human rights. A later resolution, Resolution 728 F (XXVIII) of 30 July 1959, created a complicated and useless mechanism to distribute communications to the members of the UN Human Rights Commission. Individuals had to wait until 1970 to have a possibility of seeing their communications examined, and then confidentially and only for the purpose of deciding whether there exists in a given country 'a consistent pattern of gross and reliably attested violations of human rights' (ECOSOC Resolution 1503 (XLVIII) of 27 May 1970).

empowered to make any individual decision with regard to written communications or claims it might receive', it would 'take cognizance of them
for the purpose of using them in fulfillment of paragraphs b) and c)' of
Article 9 of its Statute.[7]

The Commission's move pointed to an attempt to start considering
petitions, and this was further reaffirmed when in 1965 the Commission
was formally granted the power to examine them.[8] The main objective
seemed to have been, however, a different one. The Commission had
discovered very soon that the mere examination of petitions, European-
style, would not lead to an improvement of human rights in the continent,
since the problems to be faced were frequently gross, systematic human
rights violations perpetrated by dictatorial regimes.[9] To deal with these, a
formal judicial or quasi-judicial decision or opinion to the effect that the
conduct of a state amounted to a violation of human rights seemed
pointless; states which perpetrate gross, systematic violations are clearly
aware that what they are doing constitutes a serious infringement of their
international obligations in the field of human rights, and their attitude
vis-à-vis international supervisory organs is one of denial of the facts and
not, as usually happens in the individual petition procedure, one of
disputing the interpretation of the extent and scope of a right and/or its
application to the facts of a particular case.

The difference in the circumstances which the Commission faced, as
compared with those in Europe, made it use individual petitions mainly as
an aid to composing a picture of the general situation of human rights in a
country.[10] The primary objectives pursued by the Commission at the outset

[7] IACHR Report on the Work Accomplished During its First Session, 3 to 28 Oct. 1960
(OEA/Ser.L/V/II.1, doc. 32, 4 Mar. 1961), 13. Paragraphs b) and c) of original article 9
vested the Commission with the following functions and powers: 'b) To make recommendations to the Governments of the Member States in general, if it considers such action
advisable, for the adoption of progressive measures in favor of human rights within the
framework of their domestic legislation and, in accordance with their constitutional precepts,
appropriate measures to further the faithful observance of those rights;   c) To prepare such
studies or reports as it considers advisable in the performance of its duties'.

[8] See Resolution XXII of Second Special Inter-American Conference. English text in
Buergenthal and Norris (Eds.) *Human Rights: The Inter-American System*, (New York, 1984)
Booklet 6 (Apr. 1982), Chap. V, at 163.

[9] Gross, systematic violations of human rights may be defined as 'those violations, instrumental to the achievement of governmental policies, perpetrated in such a quantity and in
such a manner as to create a situation in which the rights to life, to personal integrity or to
personal liberty of the population as a whole or of one or more sectors of the population of a
country are continuously infringed or threatened'. For an explanation of the concept, see C.
Medina, op. cit., n. 3, Chap. II, 7–19.

[10] Evidence of this was the fact that when in 1965 the Commission saw its powers to
examine individual petitions formally established by resolution XXII of the Second Special
Inter-American Conference, it developed a broad and progressive interpretation thereof
with the aim of not forfeiting its power to deal with the general situation of human rights in
the country (See ibid, 77–81).

were, firstly, to create a mechanism that would make it possible to document a situation of gross, systematic violations in a state and, secondly, to encourage the OAS political organs to undertake political action in its respect. To these ends, *in loco* observations and country reports were clearly very well suited. The first objective was achieved very soon: already in 1962 a first report on Cuba was prepared and published[11] which contained the rudiments of what is today a country report. Its best form was reached in 1985 in the fourth report on Chile, which can be considered a model report compared with what had been done before then.[12] The attempts of the Commission to interest the OAS in the serious problems of human rights in the region have been less fortunate; although there has been progress, it has not been steady.[13]

THE DECISION TO PREPARE A COUNTRY REPORT

The decision to prepare a country report lies with the Commission, which may decide on its own motion. Usually the Commission will decide to do so (i) when it has received various individual petitions or reports from states alleging widespread violations of human rights in the territory of a country, almost always including the right to life, to humane treatment and to personal freedom,[14] or (ii) when it has already prepared a country report and wishes to monitor further the situation.[15]

[11] See IACHR Report on the Situation Regarding Human Rights in Cuba (1962).

[12] See IACHR Report on the Situation of Human Rights in Chile (1985).

[13] As early as 1963 the Commission made an indirect call for action to the OAS Council acting as a Provisional Organ of Consultation when it informed the Council 'of its deep concern about the situation regarding human rights in [Haiti] (. . .) and of the refusal of the Government of Haiti to permit the Commission to examine in its own territory the reports it had received of serious and repeated violations of human rights' (IACHR Report on the Work Accomplished During its Sixth Session, 16 Apr. to 8 May 1963 (OEA/Ser. L/V/II.7, Doc. 28 (English), Aug. 21, 1963, 14). However, the Commission had to wait untill 1976 to see a discussion of a country report in a public forum. The Second Chile Report was discussed at the Sixth Regular Session of the General Assembly (Santiago de Chile, 1976)) (IACHR Second Report on the Situation of Human Rights in Chile (1976)). The situation changed for the worse in 1980, when a 'silent diplomacy' approach began to be used, but this gradually started to reverse again in 1984 (See C. Medina, op. cit, n. 3, 293–6 and 303–7).

[14] This was the reason that first prompted the Commission to prepare country reports and the only one invoked for a considerable period of time. See, as example, IACHR Report on the Situation of Human Rights in Guatemala (1981).

[15] In the last reports on Haiti, for example, the Commission acknowledges that it has continued to assign priority to the country in view of the 'critical situation of human rights persisting in Haiti', see IACHR Report on the Situation of Human Rights in Haiti (1994) 1, and that it has continued to give priority to its work in Haiti 'in view of the worsening human rights situation' in that country, IACHR Report on the Situation of Human Rights in Haiti (1995), 3.

In the last report on El Salvador, although it does not say so in so many words, the situation was the same, as the Commission introduced the report with a thorough account of the developments in El Salvador from 1979 to 1992 and the activities the Commission carried out during that period, IACHR Report on the Situation of Human Rights in El Salvador (1994), 7.

The Commission is sometimes prompted to decide on the preparation of a country report at the request of a political organ of the OAS, which will usually make the request after learning that a situation of gross, systematic violations is taking place in a country,[16] or at the request of the state concerned, made probably because that state's government wishes to obtain support for a certain policy it has decided to follow or wishes to have a clean human rights image within the region.[17] The second report on Nicaragua had a slightly different reason; it was prepared some time after Anastasio Somoza had been overthrown and after the new government had ratified the American Convention on Human Rights and had invited the Commission to visit the country. This suggests that the government may have been aware of the need to make an assessment of the major task it had to face to amend laws and practices contrary to human rights which had existed in Nicaragua for many years, and that it wished to put them into effect with the support of the Commission.[18]

The fact that the Commission is the body to select the countries to be examined has been the object of opposition within the OAS membership from the very beginning of the Commission's work. However, in spite of the efforts of some countries, the Commission has not been deprived of its right to make the selection. The resolution passed by the OAS General Assembly on the Commission's 1993 Annual Report and on the country reports of that year has a paragraph that addresses this point. Dispositive paragraph 15 states that: 'in its annual report the Commission should strike a general balance of how human rights have fared in all of the member states of the OAS, taking into account, among other sources, information supplied by member states'.[19] Although this seems to be a mild request, it might be interpreted in the sense that the General Assembly wished the Commission not to examine specific countries but examine all countries each year, a task that the General Assembly and anybody who has some knowledge of the system know the Commission cannot carry out.[20] If this were the Assembly's intention, a difficult thing to assess from only reading the text of the resolution, it would mean a major setback

[16] The Ad Hoc Meeting of Ministers of Foreign Affairs (Haiti) 'reiterated to the Inter-American Commission on Human Rights that it continue its ongoing and close monitoring of the situation in Haiti and keep this Ad Hoc Meeting informed, through the Permanent Council' (See OEA/Ser.F/V.1, MRE/RES. 5/93, 6 June 1993)

[17] See, for example, OAS, IACHR Report on the Situation of Human Rights in Panama (1978).

[18] OAS, IACHR Report on the Situation of Human Rights in Nicaragua (1981).

[19] AG/Res.1213, n. 25.

[20] In the debate at the 24th Ordinary Session of the General Assembly, the Chairman of the Commission stated that the Commission had '10 lawyers to cover 600 million people, and 10 lawyers to cover all the important tasks that the Assembly from time to time assigns to us'. See 51 below, 81.

for the effectiveness of the Commission's supervisory powers, were the Commission to comply.

FACT-FINDING IN THE PREPARATION OF COUNTRY REPORTS

Ideally country reports are the result of observations *in loco*, which are now frequently undertaken. The power to conduct observations *in loco* originated and developed purely as a matter of Commission practice. But now the Commission's powers are set forth in detail in its Regulations.[21] The special commission, composed of Commission members, appointed to carry out an observation *in loco* will organize its work in the manner it sees fit. It has powers to interview people freely and privately, to move around the territory of the country, to visit jails or other detention centres, and to gather information in any form, including written information from the government or oral information obtained from witnesses.

The visit cannot take place without the government's consent, but, once that is given, the government must grant the commission all necessary facilities to fulfil its mission and must undertake to facilitate contact with persons and entities and not to retaliate against those that co-operate with the commission during the visit.

If there is no observation *in loco*, the Commission still may call a hearing to receive testimony, request information from the State, use official or unofficial documents, have resort to reports by experts and make use of individual petitions submitted to it for examination that complain of breaches of human rights.[22]

There seems to have been no objection so far to the modalities used by the Commission for fact-finding, except to its use of the facts of individual petitions. This has been contested by states on the basis that confidentiality is being breached and that the publication in a country report of the facts of individual cases implies the outcome of the Commission's opinion on the petition in the sense that it suggests that the facts constitute a violation of the international obligations of the state. Also contested has been reference to individual situations which have not yet been the subject of a petition registered by the Commission. Again the debate on the Commission's 1993 Annual Report is instructive. The representative of Peru complained about the Commission's reference to individual cases, stating that the American Convention provided that the Commission's report under Article 50 was confidential, and that the Commission had made use

---

[21] Chap. IV of Title II of the Commission's Regulations. See Appendix V.
[22] This is what the Commission did in the seven reports it has issued on the situation of human rights in Cuba. The last full report on Cuba was prepared in 1983 (See IACHR The Situation of Human Rights in Cuba, Seventh Report (1983).

in its country report on Peru of some pending cases on which the Commission had yet to write a report. He also complained about the use of specific examples of alleged violations which had never been submitted to Peru for comment and had not been registered by the Commission as individual cases.[23] The representative of Nicaragua registered similar complaints and the representatives of both countries took the opportunity during the debate to address the individual cases which had been mentioned in the 1992 Annual Report and set forth their position concerning them.[24]

THE CONTENTS OF COUNTRY REPORTS

As to its contents, what one could call typical country reports follow a more or less standard pattern. They begin with a chapter on background information, in which the reasons for issuing the report are stated and the steps taken by the Commission prior to the report, if any, are described. This background information is followed by a description and analysis of the political and legal system in force in the country. Next, specific rights are studied separately, usually those about which the Commission has received petitions. The study of each right begins with a general review of the domestic legal norms regulating the right concerned. The inter-American legal standards on the right, and sometimes other international standards, such as those in the International Covenant on Civil and Political Rights or the Geneva Red Cross Conventions, are also spelt out, and the domestic legal order is reviewed for its conformity therewith.

An examination of the actual situation follows. The report mainly contains a general description and analysis of the practice in the state concerned with regard to the rights under consideration. The Commission uses all the evidence it has gathered, including that which comes from individual petitions. If petitions are still being processed, the Commission usually states at the beginning of the report that 'the inclusion of those cases does not make any pre-judgment with respect to the findings which the Commission will eventually issue on [them]'.[25] The cases quoted are used as examples of the general situation. Obviously, no reference to specific evidence in pending cases is possible and confidentiality in the steps being taken by the Commission is necessary, particularly to protect

---

[23] See OAS, *Transcripción de las actas*, n. 51, 34.
[24] See ibid. 46–52, for the remarks of the representative of Peru, and 63–77 and 91–4 for the statements of the representative of Nicaragua.
[25] IACHR Report on the Situation of Human Right in Colombia (1981), 22.

the witnesses.[26] When examples are used of individual cases in which the Commission has already written a report on the merits, it has to be taken into account that in most, if not all, of them the Commission's opinion has been adopted on the basis of the presumption of truth provided for in Article 42 of the Commission's Regulations.[27] This means that the state has either remained silent in the face of the allegations of the complainant, or has provided counter arguments which are clearly inadequate, or has made only a general denial, and the Commission has found the complainant's allegation *prima facie* well-founded. If this is the case, the Commission will not have examined any evidence. A different situation obtains when the Commission writes a report on a country which has been cooperative and has itself shown a willingness to investigate human rights violations and to follow the Commission's advice. In that case the Commission sets down in more detail the specific evidence supporting its opinion.[28]

Since 1980, some country reports (there has been no consistency in this practice) also contain a chapter on the situation of economic, social and cultural rights regardless of whether there has been a complaint about them.[29]

The reports end with conclusions and recommendations. The contents of recommendations vary. They may request the state to take measures to prevent the occurrence in the future of serious violations of the right to life and of the right to be free from torture and cruel, inhuman or degrading treatment. They may call upon the state to take measures to investigate past violations, to punish those found responsible and to give reparation to the victims or their families. In some cases, the recommendation may be very specific and political.[30] States sometimes object to this type of recommendation on the ground that they violate the principle of non-intervention. Such objections are evidence that there is not yet in the region a firm commitment to international supervision in the field of human rights.

One of the most salient features of country reports is their flexibility.

---

[26] The risk that a person testifying on a human rights case takes should not be underestimated. In the first case before the Inter-American Court of Human Rights, *Velásquez Rodríguez* v *Honduras*, one witness was killed after testifying for the case and another before doing so.   [27] On Art. 42, see above, Cerna, Chap. 3.

[28] One example of this type of report is the Report on Colombia (1981), n. 37.

[29] See IACHR, Report on Guatemala (1981); IACHR Seventh Report on Cuba (1983); and IACHR Report on Nicaragua (1981).

[30] For example, it was recommended to El Salvador in 1980 that it reopen the dialogue among all sectors of society, including the dissident forces of the left and of the right, with a view to establishing the necessary conditions to enable El Salvador to hold elections. See IACHR Annual Report 1979–80 (1980), 147. Similar recommendations were made to Guatemala. See IACHR Report on Guatemala (1981), 133. Haiti was requested to repeal a provision of its Criminal Code and to repeal a Press Law. See IACHR Report on the Situation of Human Rights in Haiti (1979), 81. Colombia was requested to implement Article 62 of its Constitution which required that no less than 10% of the general expense budget be invested in the judicial branch and the public ministry. See IACHR Report on Colombia (1981) 222.

Although what has been described so far is a typical country report, one finds variations. The recent report on El Salvador,[31] which is worth examining in some depth to prove the point, follows a different pattern. The report starts with an overview of the present situation, in which an account is given of the position of the Commission during the armed conflict in that country. Then it goes to identify the key issues of the peace negotiations and to review them in the light of the American Convention on Human Rights.

Thereafter important novelties follow. The first is that the reports adopted by the Commission in a series of individual petition cases between 1983 and 1993 are reproduced,[32] preceded by some words that reflect the frustration of the Commission with the attitude of the authorities of El Salvador in the handling of these cases. The Commission states:[33] 'Unfortunately, in not one of these cases did the authorities respond to the Commission's recommendations, follow up on its requests or recognize the compulsory jurisdiction of the Inter-American Court of Human Rights, despite the Commission's recommendations to that effect'. It is clear that with this statement the Commission is giving notice to the authorities of El Salvador that it continues to expect and demand a response to past violations.

Secondly, the Commission includes some remarks about the Truth Commission. This Commission was created after the Mexico Agreements (27 April 1991) in order to 'investigate serious acts of violence that occurred since 1980, whose impact on society urgently requires that the truth about them be made known to the public'. The parties to these agreements undertook to comply with the Truth Commission's recommendations.[34] The report reveals that the parties had failed to comply with the obligations they had undertaken.[35] It also stated that, inasmuch as the recommendations of the Truth Commission were directly related to the international commitments undertaken by El Salvador under the American

---

[31] IACHR Report on El Salvador (1994).

[32] There are 29 resolutions on cases which sometimes refer to several dozens of victims. In all of them the Commission finds violations of the rights to life and to humane treatment (Arts. 4 and 5, American Convention).

[33] IACHR Report on the Situation of Human Rights in El Salvador (1994), 21

[34] See Report on El Salvador (1994), 42.

[35] The report reproduces the reactions of the Salvadoran Armed Forces, who called the Truth Commission's report 'unfair, incomplete, illegal, unethical, partial and disrespectful'; of the judiciary, whose Supreme Court '[e]mphatically rejected the conclusions and recommendations made against the justice system in El Salvador'; and of the executive branch of the government, which also objected to the Truth Commission's Report, stating that it 'examines only a part of everything that happened in all those years of violence' and that it would be 'unjust to take legal or administrative measures against some but not others, simply because the latter did not figure in the cases examined in the Truth Commission's Report' (See ibid., 69–70).

Convention on Human Rights, the Inter-American Commission was empowered to urge that they be complied with and implemented.

Thirdly, the report contains a number of individual petition cases which were still pending because of lack of information from the government, and which were on the verge of being completed by the application of the presumption of truth in Article 42 of the Commission's Regulations. Before reproducing the cases, the Commission states[36] that it is 'deeply disturbed' that

in a surprising number of cases the Government of El Salvador has disregarded the petitions that the Commission [. . .] has repeatedly filed in exercise of authorities that the Convention gives it for the handling of individual cases.

It further adds that

Salvadoran officials have not paid any attention to many of these cases, and although the Commission has repeatedly requested action and has allowed the deadlines called for in its Regulations to lapse, in order to give the Salvadoran officials more time to prepare their defense and to answer the complaints,[37] those who have the duty under the law to give specific and proper responses to them still have not done so.

Fourthly, the Commission takes the opportunity to publish in this country report a resolution on one individual case (No. 11.238).

Fifthly, the Commission makes observations on the enactment of an amnesty law. It starts by reporting on some steps it had taken when the Amnesty Law was about to be enacted, among which an important one was the letter sent by the Commission to the Salvadoran government before the President's deadline for vetoing the law which had already been approved in Congress.[38] In it the Commission had stated: (i) that the political agreements concluded among the parties to the Salvadoran conflict in no way relieve the state of its obligations under the American Convention on Human Rights; (ii) that, according to the Inter-American Court's interpretation of the Convention, the state had a legal duty to investigate violations committed within its jurisdiction, identify those responsible, impose the appropriate punishment and ensure the victims adequate compensation; (iii) that this legal duty applied to case 10.287;[39] and (iv) that the Commission was confident that the President of El Salvador would not allow domestic laws to violate international commitments undertaken by that state.[40]

---

[36] IACHR Report on El Salvador (1994), 44.
[37] One wonders about the propriety of this decision of the Commission.
[38] IACHR Report on El Salvador (1994), 73.
[39] See Report 26/92 on case 10.287, 'Las Hojas Massacre' in the Commission's Annual Report for 1992–3.
[40] It is interesting to note that the Salvadoran Government replied to the Commission

The Commission further comments on the enactment of the amnesty law in El Salvador in the light of the country's international human rights obligations and concludes that this law violated them 'because it makes possible a 'reciprocal amnesty' without first acknowledging responsibility (despite the recommendations of the Truth Commission); because it applies to crimes against humanity, and because it eliminates any possibility of obtaining adequate pecuniary compensation, primarily for victims'.[41]

Finally, the Commission sets forth its general conclusions of the examination of the situation of human rights in El Salvador. It states that it views with satisfaction the progress made in the economic and social situation, but reiterates its competence to monitor compliance with the obligations under the American Convention, in spite of the fact that there exist special agencies to monitor compliance with the Peace Accords.

As noted above, the report on El Salvador differs from the typical country reports of the first years of the Commission and shows the versatility of this instrument, which allows the Commission to make use of several powers with which it has been vested in order to better fulfil its functions. The report also shows that the Commission does not always use country reports mainly for the purpose of documenting a case of gross, systematic violations of human rights; sometimes it wishes to expose a government and give it notice that the Commission will not cease to demand compliance with international human rights obligations in spite of political negotiations carried out within a country. Although this may be seen as going beyond what should be allowed to an international organ, the message is a very important one for the future of human rights in the American continent, where the precariousness of democracy and respect for human rights seems to be endemic.

THE ROLE OF THE POLITICAL ORGANS OF THE OAS WITH REGARD TO COUNTRY REPORTS

In section II above, it was said that one of the aims of the Commission when it started to develop the practice of preparing country reports was to involve the political organs of the OAS in the supervision of situations of gross, systematic human rights violations, since these cannot be addressed solely through a legal approach. As noted there, the Commission succeeded

stating that it was willing to comply with the recommendations of the Truth Commission 'insofar as they are consistent with the Constitution and laws of El Salvador and serve the interests of national reconciliation', thereby conditioning compliance to political considerations, See IACHR Report on El Salvador (1994) 73–4.

[41] Ibid., 77.

in this when the second report on Chile was discussed at the General Assembly.

The involvement of the political organs of the OAS may serve two different purposes. One is to bring documented gross, systematic human rights violations to the attention of states and non-governmental organizations, both international and national ones. The other is to bring about a discussion on the substance of the matter in a governmental forum with a view to the passing of a resolution, possibly with recommendations to the state concerned and/or to all other OAS member states to take bilateral or joint action, and with measures providing for the monitoring of compliance with these recommendations.

The first purpose has been achieved by the mere fact that country reports have been discussed in public; the second has so far not been realised. Debate on country reports often takes the form of a dialogue between the member of the Commission presenting the report and the representative of the state concerned. The latter usually defends the government by attacking the Commission and accusing it of misusing its supervisory powers. The rest of the states' representatives express their support for the general work of the Commission, or for the state which has attacked it, but refuse to deal with the issues in the country report which are supposedly being under consideration. States neither refer to the facts in the report or the Commission's assessment thereof, nor debate the possible solution to the violations allegedly committed by the state subject to the report. This attitude on the part of states has been constant from the time the Commission's country reports first started to be discussed at the OAS political fora, be it the General Assembly or the Permanent Council, until today.[42]

For example, in the debate at the 24th General Assembly in 1994 on the situation in El Salvador, the Salvadoran representative objected to the Commission's issuance of the report, finding it not opportune due to the substantive progress of the human rights situation in the country, and expressing the view that the Commission was not empowered to make value judgments on the Peace Accords, since they were of a political nature.[43] The debate between the representative of Peru and the Chairman of the Commission with regard to procedural matters will be dealt with below.[44] With regard to the substance of the examination of the human rights situation in Peru by the Commission, the Peruvian representative said, *inter alia*, that Peru could not accept the criticism that the Commission

---

[42] For a thorough examination of the role of the OAS political organs in country reports, see C. Medina, op. cit., n. 3, Chaps. VIII, IX and X, concerning the country reports of Cuba, Nicaragua under the time of Somoza, and Chile.

[43] See *Transcripción de las Actas*, n. 51, 6.

[44] See below, pp. 128–9.

had made of the lack of independence of the judiciary. In his view, the Commission's recommendations were illegitimate, not pertinent and did not respond to the reality of the human rights situation in Peru.[45] In similar vein, the representative of Nicaragua stated, when commenting on the report on his country, that the Commission was not objective and that the report interfered with the internal affairs of Nicaragua. Because of this, the Nicaraguan representative rejected the Commission's report in its entirety. He further accused the Commission of letting itself be influenced by some sectors of Nicaraguan society.[46] No other state spoke with regard to the substance of any of these reports. A refreshing change was the attitude of the representative of Guatemala, who surprisingly was grateful that Guatemala had not been subject of a country report and had only been commented upon in a section in the Annual Report of the Commission, but did not refer to those comments. It should be noted, however, that the situation examined and criticised by the Commission in that Annual Report were attributable to a prior Guatemalan government.

It is regrettable that there has been no change in the OAS in this respect. States seem to forget that the American Convention on Human Rights sets forth a code of conduct for the states parties as well as an international *ordre public*, and that it is, on the one hand, in the interest of each and every state, and, on the other hand, the duty of each and every state, to see to it that this *ordre public* is kept.

THE PRACTICE OF REVIEWING THE STATE OF HUMAN RIGHTS IN SPECIFIC COUNTRIES IN THE ANNUAL REPORTS OF THE COMMISSION

Aside from its practice of preparing country reports, the Commission has for many years included a chapter in its Annual Report examining the general state of human rights in specific countries. This chapter contains usually a shorter version of what could be a proper country report. States have once in a while objected to this practice. When this happened for the first time, the Commission did not include in its next annual report (for 1980–1) a chapter on the situation on human rights in particular countries; instead it included a general report on the general situation of human rights organized on the basis of topics such as 'summary executions', 'disappearances after detention' and 'political rights' rather than by country.[47] The rebellious Commission returned to its usual practice by which it examined the position generally in a few particular countries in its next

---

[45] *Transcripción de les actes*, n. 51, 35–6.
[46] Ibid., 57–8.   [47] IACHR Annual Report 1980–1.

annual report, that of 1981–2,[48] but this provoked strong criticism from the governments of Uruguay and Argentina, countries that were at the time under military rule.[49] The insistence of the Commission, after one further year of apparent obedience in 1982–3, and the change in the political system in Brazil, Uruguay and Argentina, made possible a return to the former practice starting with the Annual Report of 1983–4.[50]

Countries are, however, persistent. In 1993 there was a major attack on the Commission's practice. The representative of Peru gave a reasoned speech before the Legal and Political Affairs Committee of the OAS to sustain the argument that the Commission did not have any power that was separate from and additional to its power to prepare country reports that authorised it to include a section concerning the situation of human rights in specific countries in its annual reports. He started by saying that the Commission could only prepare 'general and special reports' in conformity with Articles 60 to 64 of its Regulations. He went on to say that nothing prevented the Commission from including a section in the annual report concerning the situation of human rights in a country, but that it could only do so after following the procedure of Article 62 of the Regulations, which involves giving the state concerned an opportunity to comment on a report at the draft stage. This was something that the Commission had never done when drafting the sections on the human rights situation in specific countries in its annual report and certainly had not done when including a section about Peru in its Annual Reports of 1992 and 1993.[51] Furthermore, the representative of Peru complained that the Permanent Mission of Peru had learned from a press release that a report on Peru had been prepared, and that although it requested the Commission for a copy thereof it had never received it. Consequently he requested that the General Assembly instruct the Commission to transmit to the State, prior to publication, any report prepared on the country's human rights situation so as to give the State an opportunity to read it and correct any mistakes or furnish an explanation about the events mentioned in that report as constituting violations of the international human rights obligations of that State.[52] A similar complaint was made by the representative of Nicaragua.[53]

[48] IACHR Annual Report 1981–2.
[49] See OEA/AG, Duodécimo Período Ordinario de Sesiones (Washington, DC, 15–21 noviembre 1982), *Actas y Documentos* (OEA/Ser.P/XII.0.2, 29 julio 1983), Vol. II, Part 2, 74, 79–81.
[50] IACHR, Annual Report 1983–4.
[51] See the proceedings of the meeting of the Legal and Political Affairs Committee of the OAS in: Vigésimo Cuarto Período de Ordinario de Sesiones, 6 de junio de 1994, Belem, Brasil, *Transcripción de las actas de las sesiones de la Comisión de Asuntos Jurídicos y Políticos celebradas los días 9, 12 y 26 de abril de 1994* (Versión no editada) (Punto 19 (b) del temario), OEA/Ser.P, AG/doc. 3078/94 add. 1, 17 mayo 1994, Textual, 28–32.
[52] Ibid., 31.
[53] See ibid., 91.

The Chairman of the Commission, who was present at the meeting, took up the issue. He first stated that both the special reports—that is to say, the country reports—and the reports that appear in what is now Chapter IV of the Annual Report 'by which the Commission studies large patterns of behavior within countries are permissible under our rules and under the Convention'. He added that the 'flexibility of these different reports permits the Commission to react rapidly to some cases and more slowly and in a more deliberate fashion in others'. He conceded that the point raised with regard to giving the state an opportunity to comment on the reports or, 'more important, to make adjustments in its own behavior' was a good one and gave an assurance that the Commission would study whether this particular interest of the states could be accommodated with the need for the flexibility that both modes of reports demanded.[54]

Both the position of the representative of Peru and of the Commission are reasonable in their own fashion. It seems only fair that criticisms of a state should first reach that state in order to allow it to react to them before they become public. But it also seems fair that the Commission attempt to remain as flexible as possible, since the experience in the continent gives ample evidence of the need for ingenuity and creativeness on the part of the human rights supervisory organs. From the legal point of view, however, the position of Peru and other states is sound, not only because it is supported by the rules of the system, but also because in international law states must have always an opportunity either to amend their conduct or to give their reasons for a different interpretation of the norms they are supposedly violating and that are being applied to them. The problem is that this legally sound position is premised on the fact that the situation of human rights in the continent is one where the rule of law prevails, at least in general terms, and that states accept the Commission's and the Court's interpretation of the states' international obligations, as so often is the case in Europe. Were this the situation, probably nobody would support or have some sympathy for the Commission's position; also most probably, the Commission's position would not be its current one and therefore there would be no difference of approach to resolve.

Unfortunately this is not the case. Some countries are trying to make a transition to democracy and to fully respect human rights, but they have not actually arrived at their final destination. However, instead of admitting this and allowing the supervisory organs to help them put their house in order, they try to limit the powers of the Commission. This was the purpose, for example, of the request made of the Court unsuccessfully a few years ago for an advisory opinion to the effect that a state's national laws

[54] Ibid., 78.

cannot be controlled by the Commission or the Court.[55] It also underlies the suggestion that the Commission refrain from monitoring democratic states.

This notwithstanding, the Commission should carefully review its current practice in the light of the aims it wishes to achieve. A constant friction between states and the Commission concerning the matter of the 'mini' country reports incorporated into the annual reports, particularly when international law and the very Regulations of the Commission do not seem to support the Commission's position—since states are entitled to have an opportunity to know beforehand the violations of international law they may have committed—may lead to a deterioration of its standing within the OAS, which would be a most undesirable result.

So far, the reaction of the General Assembly does not lend itself to detect a clear view of what will happen in the future. In the resolution passed on the Commission's 1993 Annual Report, the Assembly did not instruct the Commission to follow a different procedure for the special section in its annual reports, as Peru had requested.[56] The Annual Report of 1994 did contain an examination of the situation of human rights in specific countries without any change in the procedure, that is to say the 'mini' reports were not transmitted to the states for comment. The 1995 Annual Report omitted reports on specific states, apparently in order to give the Commission an opportunity to review its practice. The 1996 Annual Report is now (February 1997) being discussed at the 95th Session of the Commission. In his inaugural speech, the President of the Commission stated that the practice of incorporating 'mini' reports in the annual reports was to be continued, but henceforth on the basis of set criteria for selection.[57] The question of allowing the states to comment upon the 'mini' reports was not addressed, so that it is impossible to know whether the Commission will give states this opportunity.

Until the time comes when a very significant majority of OAS member states accept supervision 'European-style', the problem presented by the inclusion of reports on particular states in the Commission's Annual Report will probably continue, to the detriment of the development of

[55] See Advisory Opinion No. 13, I/A Court H.R. Series A No.13 (1993), 14 *HRLJ* 252, 1–2 IHRR 197 (1994) paras. 26–8, where the Court advised that if the legislative organ violated the Convention by enacting a law contrary to it, the Commission and the Court were fully empowered, when dealing with a petition, to examine the situation and decide that a violation had occurred.

[56] See AG/Res.1213 (XXIII-0/93), adopted at the ninth plenary meeting of the General Assembly, on 11 June 1993.

[57] Although the writer does not have a written version of the speech, the criteria to be applied seem to be the following: (i) states where a state of emergency has been declared; (ii) states about which numerous complaints have been lodged regarding the violation of non-derogable rights under the Convention; (iii) states where political rights are suspended; and (iv) states where the situation of human rights has radically and notoriously improved.

the inter-American supervisory system and consequently also to the detriment of the individuals protected by this supervision.

CONCLUSION

Country reports as they are now prepared remain mainly unchanged in their essentials, although it should be noted that their primary characteristic is the opportunity that they offer to carry out different activities and pursue different objectives, so in truth what remains unchanged is the very flexible nature that they possess. They constitute an important instrument for the Commission in carrying out its functions, since they allow it to use all its powers in combination and further various objectives. First, the preparation of a country report is a very effective way in which to monitor situations which amount to more than a mere addition of individual, isolated violations. The latter may be, and increasingly are, addressed through the examination of individual petitions which finishes ideally with an opinion of the Commission recommending steps to be taken to repair the violation. It is difficult in such a context to react to multiple violations, of various human rights, which usually have as their background the clear and large-scale infringement of the rule of law.

Secondly, although it is not the purpose of country reports to deal with isolated violations, it does happen during the course of the preparation of a report that an observation *in loco* of a general nature will be carried out, during which the Commission will informally address the situation of specific individuals, which might result at least in an alleviation of the severity of the violations to which they are subject.

Thirdly, country reports are also a good vehicle for finding out the underlying factors which prevent the people in a country from fully enjoying their human rights. The interdependence of these rights can be best seen when they are examined together, as happens in the course of the preparation of a country report, and any correction of the conduct of the state with respect to certain rights that results from this type of exercise may also improve the guarantee of other rights of others.

Finally, country reports are also necessary in order to carry out some form of control over economic, social and cultural rights which do not form part of the catalog of the American Convention but can be found in the American Declaration of the Rights and Duties of Man.[58]

---

[58] The American Declaration on the Rights and Duties of Man was adopted in 1948 at the Ninth International Conference of American States. See Appendix II in this book. The Declaration is the standard against which OAS member states are measured. Member states which are parties to the American Convention are measured against the catalog of human rights set forth in the Convention so far as the two instruments overlap.

Country reports would better achieve their objectives if states were to carry out their obligations fully. A thorough debate in the political organs of the OAS of the substance of the violations documented in a report, of the causes thereof and of the possible solutions thereto, followed by political recommendations and firm political actions to monitor compliance would most probably do much to improve the situation of human rights in the continent. Unfortunately, this does not seem to be possible in the near future. However, even without the commitment of the OAS political organs and the states that compose them, the goals that may currently be achieved by the preparation of country reports make it particularly important that the Commission does not abandon this activity, which is a major one among its functions.

5

The Operation of the Inter-American Court of Human Rights

ANTÔNIO AUGUSTO CANÇADO TRINDADE

CREATION, INDEPENDENCE AND COMPOSITION.

The Inter-American Court of Human Rights is an autonomous judicial organ, established by the 1969 American Convention on Human Rights for its interpretation and application, whose main purpose is to judge cases of alleged violations of the human rights protected thereunder.[1] Following the entry into force of the American Convention (on 18 July 1978), the States Parties elected, at the Seventh Special Session of the OAS General Assembly (on 22 May 1979), the first Judges to compose the Court, which held its first meetings on 29 and 30 June 1979 at the OAS headquarters in Washington DC. The ceremony of installation of the Court in its seat, San José, Costa Rica, took place on 3 September 1979.

The Statute of the Court was approved during the Ninth Regular Session of the OAS General Assembly (La Paz, Bolivia, 1979), and its first Rules of Procedure were adopted in August 1980. On 10 September 1981, the Court and the Government of the host State, Costa Rica, concluded a Headquarters Agreement, which sets up the regime of privileges and immunities enjoyed by the Court, its Judges, staff and all persons appearing before the Court. Even though the Court, unlike the Inter-American Commission on Human Rights, is technically not an organ of the Organization of American States (OAS), it is nonetheless the judicial organ of the inter-American system of protection of human rights.[2]

Since its first meeting on 29 and 30 June 1979, the Court has so far held 34 regular sessions and 20 special sessions (until the end of 1996). From

[1] On the Court's structure and functioning, see C. A. Dunshee de Abranches, 'La Corte Interamericana de Derechos Humanos', in *La Convención Americana sobre Derechos Humanos* (Washington, 1980) 91–147; A. A. Cançado Trindade, 'Formación, Consolidación y Perfeccionamiento del Sistema Interamericano de Protección de los Derechos Humanos', *XVII Curso de Derecho Internacional Organizado por el Comité Jurídico Interamericano* (Washington, 1991), 9–47; C. M. Cerna, 'The Structure and Functioning of the Inter-American Court of Human Rights (1979–1992)', (1992) 62 *BYIL* 135.
[2] Cf. Inter-American Court of Human Rights (hereinafter I/A Court H.R.), Adv. Opin. No 1. I/A Court H. R Series A No. 1 (1982), 3 *HRLJ* 140.

the start, the Court has on average met three times a year. During its sessions, the Court delivers its judgments and advisory opinions in public hearings, adopts and lifts provisional measures of protection and adopts interlocutory resolutions. Furthermore, it hears the arguments of the parties and the testimonies of witnesses and experts in public hearings, and studies all written material presented to it. The Court also monitors the progress of pending cases, the state of compliance with the provisional measures of protection it has adopted and with its Judgments. It further considers the reports of its President and the Secretariat, prepares and issues its *Annual Report*, approves its budget and tackles other administrative matters.

As the Court and the Commission have their seats in two different places (in San José, Costa Rica and in Washington DC respectively), there have been rather few joint meetings of their members. In fact, the two supervisory organs of the American Convention have had joint meetings on only six occasions so far, namely, in San José, Costa Rica in 1990, in Nassau in 1992, in Belém do Pará (Brazil) in 1994, in Miami in 1994, in Washington DC in 1995, and, finally, again in Washington DC in December 1996. They should certainly meet more often, as the dynamics of a regional *system* of human rights protection requires greater co-ordination between its two international supervisory organs.

The Court is composed of seven Judges, nationals of OAS member States and recognized jurists in the field of human rights serving in an individual capacity,[3] elected in the OAS General Assembly by an absolute majority vote of the States Parties to the Convention.[4] The Judges serve for a term of six years, and may be re-elected only once.[5] There may be Judges *ad hoc*,[6] but no two Judges may be nationals of the same State.[7] The membership of the Court is partially renewed every three years.[8] For its deliberations, the quorum is constituted by five Judges.[9] The Court, which appoints its own Secretary, has established its Secretariat[10] at its seat in San José, Costa Rica. The Court draws up its own budget[11] and administers it.[12]

---

[3] American Convention on Human Rights (hereinafter ACHR), Art. 52(1), see Appendix III in this book.

[4] ACHR, Art. 53(1).   [5] ACHR, Art. 54(1).
[6] Cf. ACHR, Art. 55.   [7] ACHR, Art. 52(2).
[8] Cf. ACHR, Art. 54(1).   [9] ACHR, Art. 56.
[10] Cf. ACHR, Arts. 58(2) and 59.
[11] It submits its budget for approval to the OAS General Assembly; ACHR, Art. 72.
[12] Court's Statute, Art. 26.

Contentious Jurisdiction

The American Convention on Human Rights confers upon the Inter-American Court of Human Rights adjudicatory as well as advisory functions.[13] The former involves the Court's power to adjudicate on contentious cases relating to claims that a State Party has violated the Convention. The contentious jurisdiction of the Court comprises all cases, submitted to it either by the Inter-American Commission on Human Rights or by a State Party,[14] provided that the State or States concerned have recognized its jurisdiction, by means of a special declaration pursuant to Article 62(1) and (2) of the American Convention, or else by a special agreement.[15] The declaration of acceptance of the Court's jurisdiction, presented to the OAS Secretary General, may be made unconditionally, or on condition of reciprocity, for a specified period, or else for specific cases.[16]

Among these modes of acceptance of the Court's jurisdiction, set forth in Article 62(2) of the Convention, it is rather surprising to find the condition of reciprocity, which, in practical terms, could be resorted to only in inter-State cases (none brought before the Court to date), but not in cases referred to it by the Commission. Moreover, considerations of reciprocity have proven utterly inadequate in the present domain of the protection of human rights, where they have been gradually overtaken by the notion of a collective guarantee of human rights and considerations of common or general 'public interest' or *ordre public*.[17]

Although the Court's contentious jurisdiction covers cases concerning the interpretation and application of the provisions of the American Convention,[18] as some of the provisions of the Convention refer to other

---

[13] On these functions, see H. Gros Espiell, 'Contentious Proceedings before the Inter-American Court of Human Rights', 1 *Emory Journal of International Dispute Resolution* (1987) 175–218; A. A. Cançado Trindade, 'El Sistema Interamericano de Protección de los Derechos Humanos (1948–1995): Evolución, Estado Actual y Perspectivas', *Derecho Internacional y Derechos Humanos / Droit international et droits de l'homme*, D. Bardonnet and A. A. Cançado Trindade (eds.) (Costa Rica/La Haye, 1996) 47–95; T. Buergenthal, 'The Advisory Practice of the Inter-American Human Rights Court', (1985) 79 *AJIL* 1; M. Cisneros, 'Algunos Aspectos de la Jurisdicción Consultiva de la Corte Interamericana de Derechos Humanos', *La Corte Interamericana de Derechos Humanos—Estudios y Documentos* (San José, 1985) 53–66; M. E. Ventura and D. Zovatto, *La Función Consultiva de la Corte Interamericana de Derechos Humanos—Naturaleza y Principios (1982–1987)* (Madrid, 1989), 21–463.   [14] ACHR, Art.61(1).
[15] ACHR, Art. 62(3).   [16] ACHR, Art. 62(2).
[17] On the erosion of reciprocity and the prominence of considerations of *ordre public* in the domain of the international protection of human rights, cf. A. A. Cançado Trindade, *A Protecao Internacional dos Direitos Humanos—Fundamentos Jurídicos e Instrumentos Básicos*, (Sao Paulo, 1991), 10–12.   [18] By virtue of ACHR, Art. 62(3).

treaties,[19] these other treaties may be taken into account, despite the fact that the Court's competence *ratione materiae* is, for contentious cases, in principle limited to the American Convention.

For a case to be heard by the Court, it is necessary for it first to be submitted to the Commission for examination and for the procedures set forth in Articles 48 and 50 of the Convention to have been duly completed.[20] It may be recalled in this connection that, in the matter of *Viviana Gallardo et al* (1981),[21] the Court declared inadmissible the request of the Costa Rican government that it adjudicate on a case that had not first been taken to the Commission. The Court stated that the proceedings before the Commission were not established in the exclusive interest of the State. Instead they not only assured the institutional integrity of the system of protection provided for in the Convention, but also acted as a safeguard of the individual rights of the victims.

Of the 25 States Parties to the American Convention at present (end of 1996),[22] 17 have to date accepted the jurisdiction of the Court in contentious cases.[23] The basis of the Court's compulsory jurisdiction provides yet another illustration of the unfortunate lack of automatic application of international jurisdiction. The inter-American system of human rights protection will considerably advance the day that all OAS member States become Parties to the American Convention (and its two Protocols) without reservations and all States Parties to the Convention accept unconditionally the Court's jurisdiction.

The Court's decisions, in the exercise of its adjudicatory function, are binding on all those States which have recognized as obligatory its contentious jurisdiction.[24] The Convention provides that reasons are to be given for the judgments of the Court, which are final and not subject to appeal, and are to be notified to the parties to the case.[25] If the judgment does not represent in whole or in part the unanimous opinion of the Judges, any Judge is entitled to attach to it his dissenting or separate opinion.[26] The Court has the power to rule that the injured party be ensured the enjoyment of the right that has been violated and to award such reparation as may be due, as appropriate.[27] In case of disagreement as to the meaning and scope of the judgment, the Court is to interpret it at the request of a party.[28] Judgments on reparations may be executed in the State

---

[19] ACHR, Arts. 29, 75 and 46(1)(c).   [20] ACHR, Art. 61(2).

[21] I/A Court H. R. Series A&B No. 1 (1981), 2 *HRLJ* 108.

[22] See Appendix VIII.   [23] See Appendix VIII.

[24] ACHR, Art. 68(1).

[25] ACHR, Arts. 66(1), 67 and 69, respectively.

[26] ACHR, Art. 66(2).   [27] ACHR, Art. 63.

[28] Providing that the request is made within 90 days from the date of notification of the judgment; ACHR, Art. 67.

Party concerned in accordance with the domestic procedure governing the execution of judgments against the State.[29]

In the exercise of its adjudicatory function as the judicial organ of the inter-American system of protection, the Court has so far heard or taken cognizance of 22 contentious cases, some of which are still pending. In these cases, the Court has delivered to date (end of 1996) 28 Judgments, relating to preliminary objections, merits, reparations, and interpretation of judgments.[30] By and large, the proceedings in cases before the Court have evolved, in general terms, pursuant to the relevant provisions of the American Convention as well as the Court's Statute and Rules of Procedure (cf. below), into the distinct phases of preliminary objections, merits, reparations, supervision of compliance with judgments and interpretation of judgments.

Preliminary objections have been raised in most contentious cases before the Court, but not in all. Proceedings in this phase have been regarded as *not* suspending the proceedings on the merits, even though delaying a decision on the merits. From the opening of the case with the lodging of the application with the Court until the decision on the merits (following written proceedings and oral hearings), it has taken the Court an average of 28 months to deliver a judgment on the merits.[31] In the practice of the Court, deliberations have occurred in the course of one of its sessions, normally following the one in which the last hearing on the merits was held, and the respective judgment has been delivered shortly afterwards.

Even though reparations can be ordered in the judgment on the merits,[32] in practice, in the great majority of cases, the Court has reserved that decision for a subsequent phase, given the need for further information or argument before a decision can properly be taken. In a recent judgment,[33] the Court systematized the considerations it takes into account in order to rule on the matter of reparations. It has taken an average of 16 months for such judgments to be delivered. [34] In these judgments, the Court has, in general, reserved for itself the faculty of supervising compliance with the judgment. [35] In this connection, it may be noted that recently, the Court,

[29] ACHR, Art. 68(2).

[30] OAS, *The Inter-American Court and the Inter-American System of Human Rights: Projections and Goals* (by Court's Secretariat), OAS Doc. OEA/Ser. G-CP/CAJP-1130, of 26. 11. 1996, 7.

[31] Ibid. , 10.

[32] This occurred in the the case of *Gangaram Panday* v *Suriname* I/A Court H.R. Series C No. 16, (1994), 15 *HRLJ* 168, 2 IHRR 360 (1994).

[33] *Neira Alegría* case (Peru—Reparations, 1996). Annual Report of the Inter-American Court of Human Rights, OAS/Ser.L/V/III.35, doc 5, 3 Feb. 1997, 179.

[34] OAS doc. loc. cit. above n. 30, 11.

[35] See, e.g., *Aloeboetoe* v *Suriname*, I/A Court H. R Series C No. 15 (1993), 14 *HRLJ* 413; 1–1 IHRR 2081 (1994). On the Court's retaining jurisdiction, see, e.g., *Maqueda* v *Argentina*, 16 *HRLJ* 151, 3 IHRR 355 (1996).

with its present composition, adopted an order[36] in the *Velásquez Rodríguez* and *Godínez Cruz* cases (the so-called Honduran cases), in which it found that the State of Honduras had at last complied with the reparations judgment, thus putting an end to the proceedings in the case.

As to the interpretation of judgments, which is a possibility foreseen in the American Convention itself[37], the Court had by the end of 1996 been called upon to interpret judgments on only two occasions.[38]

The following survey of the Court's practice in contentious cases gives an indication of the Convention rights that the Court has been called upon to interpret and the kinds of factual situations that have been presented to the Court. In its judgments in contentious cases so far, the Court has dwelt upon such basic human rights set forth in the American Convention as the right to life, the right to personal integrity, the right to personal liberty, the right to a fair trial (judicial guarantees), the right to judicial protection, and the right to equal protection before the law.[39]

In the cases of *Velásquez Rodríguez*[40] and *Godínez Cruz*,[41] the victims had 'disappeared' at the instance or with the acquiescence of Honduran officials and were presumed to be dead. The Court declared that Honduras had violated, to the detriment of Velásquez Rodríguez and Godínez Cruz, respectively, Articles 7 (right to personal freedom), 5 (right to personal integrity) and 4 (right to life) of the Convention, in combination with its Article 1(1), and decided furthermore that Honduras was under the obligation to pay 'just compensatory damages' to the relatives of the victims. These were the first cases in which the Court decided that a State Party had violated the American Convention. In the case *Fairén Garbi and Solís Corrales*,[42] however, the Court declared that it had not been proved that F. Fairén Garbi and Y. Solís Corrales (both of Costa Rican nationality) had 'disappeared' by a cause imputable to Honduras, whose responsibility accordingly was not established.

In the *Aloeboetoe* case,[43] seven young members of the Saramaca tribe had been killed by Suriname soldiers. Suriname having recognized responsibility, the Court proceeded to the determination of the amount of reparations to be paid to the relatives of the victims or their heirs;

---

[36] Annual Report of the Inter-American Court of Human Rights, OAS/Ser.L/V/III.35, Doc. 5, 3 Feb. 1997, 209, 213.

[37] ACHR, Art. 67.

[38] This happened in the *Velásquez Rodríguez* and *Godínez Cruz* (Honduras–Reparations) cases, in 1990, at the request of the Inter-American Commission on Human Rights, I/A Court H. R. Series C Nos. 9 and 10 (1990), 12 *HRLJ* 14.

[39] ACHR, Arts. 4, 5, 7, 8, 25 and 24, respectively.

[40] I/A Court H. R. Series C No. 4 (1988), 9 *HRLJ* 212.

[41] I/A Court H. R. Series C No. 5.

[42] I/A Court H. R. Series C No. 6 (1989)

[43] I/A Court H. R. Series C No. 15 (1993), 14 *HRLJ* 413; 1–1 IHRR 208 (1994).

furthermore, it ordered the establishment of two trust funds and the creation of a foundation, as well as the reopening of a school located in Gujaba and the functioning of the medical dispensary already in place.

In the *Cayara* case (preliminary objections),[44] it was alleged that the Peruvian army had been responsible for extrajudicial killings, torture, arbitrary detention and forced disappearances of villagers following an ambush of soldiers by the 'Sendero Luminoso'. The Court, in a much-debated decision, dismissed the case without deciding it on the merits, as it found that the Commission had lodged the complaint without complying with the time-limit set forth in Article 51(1) of the Convention.

In the *Gangaram Panday* case,[45] concerning Suriname, the victim had died in state custody after being detained for immigration reasons following his arrival by air from abroad. The Court held that Suriname had violated Article 7(2) of the Convention (illegal detention) in combination with Article 1(1). Although the victim had died in detention, the Court held, by a majority of four to three, that there was no breach of Article 4(1) (the right to life). The dissenting minority considered that Suriname had violated Article 4(1) of the Convention (right to life), in combination with Article 1(1), since the State had not acted on the facts with the degree of care expected of it to protect the life of a person in its (illegal) custody.

In the *Neira Alegría* case,[46] three prisoners had been killed as a result of the blowing up by the army of a prison building held by rioters. The Court held that Peru had violated Articles 4(1) (right to life) and 7(6) (right of habeas corpus, in connection with the prohibition of Article 27(2)), in combination with Article 1(1) of the Convention, for which it was under a duty to pay fair compensation to the relatives of the victims.

In the *Caballero Delgado and Santana* case,[47] the two victims had been captured by an army patrol and were presumed dead. The Court held that Colombia had violated Articles 7 (right to personal liberty) and 4 (right to life), in combination with Article 1(1) of the Convention, and was under a duty to pay fair compensation to the victim's relatives.

In the *Maqueda* case,[48] against Argentina, after taking part in a political demonstration, the victim had been sentenced to ten years imprisonment following his conviction under a special criminal procedure for cases involving acts of violence that threaten constitutional order and democracy. The petition alleged violations, *inter alia*, of Articles 8 (right to a fair trial) and 25 (right to a judicial remedy). The Court, after analyzing the friendly settlement, involving a commutation of sentence, reached by the Commission

---

[44] I/A Court H. R. Series C No. 14 (1993), 14 *HRLJ* 159, 1–1 IHRR 175 (1994).
[45] I/A Court H. R. Series C No. 16 (1994), 15 *HRLJ* 168, 2 IHRR 360 (1995).
[46] I/A Court H. R. Series C No. 20 (1995), 16 *HRLJ* 403, 3 IHRR 362 (1996).
[47] I/A Court H. R. Series C No. 21 (1995), 17 *HRLJ* 24, 3 IHRR 548 (1996).
[48] Resolution of 17 Jan. 1995, 16 *HRLJ* 151, 3 IHRR 355 (1996).

and the parties, and verifying compliance with it, admitted the *désistement* of the complaint, nevertheless reserving the power to re-open and further examine the case should a change in the circumstances which led to the settlement occur.

In the *El Amparo*,[49] fourteen fishermen were shot and killed by members of the military and the police. The Court, given the recognition of international responsibility on the part of Venezuela, decided that Venezuela was under an obligation to provide reparation for damages and to pay 'a fair indemnification' to the surviving victims and to the relatives of those who had died. As the six-month period granted by the Court to the parties to reach an agreement (on reparations and indemnities) expired, the Court ruled on the reparations due.[50]

In the *Garrido and Baigorria* case (1996), the Court took cognizance of the recognition of international responsibility by Argentina for the arrest by the provincial police of Mendoza, and subsequent disappearance, of Adolfo Garrido and Raúl Baigorria. The Court granted the parties a six-month period to reach an agreement on reparations and compensation, which agreement would be reviewed by the Court.

Besides the case of *El Amparo*, the Court has now ruled on reparations also in the cases of *Neira Alegría* and *Aloeboetoe* and, earlier, in the *Velásquez Rodríguez* and *Godínez Cruz* cases (1989–1990). Proceedings on reparations are pending in the *Caballero Delgado and Santana* case.

There are a number of other cases in which judgments have already been rendered on preliminary objections and which are currently pending before the Court on the merits. These are the cases of *Genie Lacayo*[51] against Nicaragua, *Paniagua Morales* and *Blake* against Guatemala,[52] and *Castillo Páez* and *Loayza Tamayo* against Peru. Also pending in the merits phase is the case of *Suárez Rosero* against Ecuador.

Finally, there are other cases of which the Court has only very recently been seized and that are still in the initial phase of proceedings. These are the cases of *Benavides Cevallos* against Ecuador, *Cantoral Benavides* and *Durand and Ugarte* against Peru, and *Bámaca Velásquez* against Guatemala.

In its Judgments on the merits, the Court has related the protected rights in the Convention (Articles 3 to 26) to the general duty of States parties under Article 1 of the American Convention to ensure respect for those

---

[49] Judgment of 18 Jan. 1995, 16 *HRLJ* 149, 3 IHRR 349 (1996).

[50] I/A Court H.R., *El Amparo* case, Judgment of 14 Sept. 1996 Annual Report of the I/A. Court H.R., OAS/Ser./V./III.35, Doc. 5, 3 Feb. 1997, 159; in his Dissenting Opinion, Judge A. A. Cançado Trindade maintained that, besides the reparations ordered, the Court should, in addition, have proceeded to the determination (requested by the Commission) of the incompatibility or otherwise of the Venezuelan Code of Military Justice (Art. 54(2) and (3)) with the American Convention on Human Rights, and of its juridical consequences.

[51] 16 *HRLJ* 414, 3 IHRR 384 (1996).

[52] 3 IHRR 539 (1996).

rights. [53] To that general duty, one may add the other general duty under Article 2 of the Convention to adopt such legislative or other measures as may be necessary to give effect to the rights protected in the Convention. The combination of the first of these two general duties under Article 1 of the Convention with the specific duties vis-à-vis each protected right under the Convention has proven to be one of the most important contributions of the Court's case-law in contentious cases so far. The Court, however, has yet to develop further its case-law on the relationship between the general duty under Article 2 of the Convention to adopt domestic law measures and the duties of protection in respect of the particular rights guaranteed under the Convention.

It should also be noted that, as the exercise of the Court's contentious jurisdiction is still relatively new (the first cases in which the Court found a State Party in breach of Convention provisions dating from 1988, less than a decade ago), the Court has not yet had the occasion to pronounce in its contentious jurisdiction on a number of rights under the American Convention. Such is the case of the right to juridical personality, the right to be free from slavery or involuntary servitude or forced or compulsory labour, the freedom from ex post facto laws, the right to compensation, the right to privacy, the freedom of conscience and religion, the freedom of thought and expression, the right of reply or correction, the right of assembly, the freedom of association, the rights of the family, the right to a name, the rights of the child, the right to nationality, the right to property, the freedom of movement and residence, and the right to participate in the conduct of public affairs (political rights).[54]

But now, after virtually 17 years of continuous functioning and more than a decade of exercise mainly of its advisory jurisdiction (below), the Court's contentious proceedings appear at last to be evolving on a constant and regular basis. With a steady increase in the number of such cases referred to it by the Inter-American Commission, there is reason for hope that the Court will soon have the opportunity to pronounce also upon at least some of these other rights, so that it will in the future have had occasion to interpret all the rights guaranteed in the Convention.

Advisory Jurisdiction

In addition to the adjudicatory function, the Inter-American Court is also endowed with an advisory function.[55] By virtue of Article 64(1) of the

---

[53] The leading case is *Velasquez Rodriguez* (1988).

[54] ACHR, Arts. 3, 6, 9, 10, 11, 12, 13, 14, 15, 16, 17, 18, 19, 20, 21, 22 and 23, respectively.

[55] On the Court's advisory jurisdiction, see the literature cited above, n. 13. See also the Court's exploration of its advisory function in Advisory Opinion No. 3, I/A Court H. R. Series A No. 3 (1983) 70–4 paras. 39–44, 4 *HRLJ* 339.

American Convention, OAS member States—whether or not they have ratified the American Convention—may consult the Court regarding the interpretation of the Convention itself or of other treaties concerning the protection of human rights in OAS member States. Likewise, the organs listed in chapter X of the OAS Charter may also consult the Court, within their respective spheres of competence. In practice, the only organ which has done so to date has been the Inter-American Commission on Human Rights, which has requested advisory opinions from the Court on five occasions. Furthermore, Article 64(2) of the Convention allows the Court to deliver, at the request of a member State of the OAS—again, irrespective of whether it has ratified the Convention or not—advisory opinions on the compatibility or otherwise of any of its domestic laws with the American Convention or other treaties concerning the protection of human rights in OAS member States.

The Inter-American Court is thus vested with a particularly wide advisory jurisdiction, 'more extensive', in the Court's own words, 'than that enjoyed by any international tribunal in existence today'.[56] The Court has delivered fourteen Advisory Opinions to date (end of 1996), there being now a fifteenth request for an advisory opinion pending. Besides the Commission (above), a number of OAS member States have also made use of the power to request an advisory opinion from the Court.[57] In practice, in the exercise of its advisory jurisdiction, the Court has invited all OAS member States as well as the organs concerned to submit their written observations on the subject of the requested opinion; 21 States and six OAS organs have so far presented their viewpoints on the matter at issue.[58]

Moreover, by means of *amici curiae* the Court has secured a considerable amount of participation by academic institutions, non-governmental organizations and individuals in advisory proceedings (a total of 41 *amici* to date).[59] Once written observations are presented, the Court sets a date for a public hearing on further observations that OAS member States and OAS organs may wish to make. The Court carefully considers, first, the effects that the requested opinions may have on protected rights and on the inter-American regional system as a whole, and, secondly, whether the request falls under its advisory function. Only then does the Court deliver its opinion. This process has had an average duration of 10 months.[60]

In its fourteen Advisory Opinions delivered so far, the court has tackled

---

[56] Advisory Opinion No. 1, I/A Court H. R. Series A No. 1 (1982), 29 para. 14, 3 *HRLJ* 140.

[57] These are Costa Rica (four times), Uruguay (three times, including one request together with Argentina), Colombia, Peru and Argentina (once, each); a fifteenth request, now pending before the Court, has been made this time by Chile.

[58] Cf. OAS doc. cit. above n. 30, 13–14.

[59] Cf. ibid., 14–15.

[60] Cf. ibid., 16.

a wide range of issues, as the following survey indicates. The Court has stressed the specificity of the various instruments of international protection of human rights and the interaction between the different systems of protection that exist at regional and global level and has taken the view that the Convention enters into force immediately upon ratification for a state that ratifies it subject to a reservation (first and second Opinions). In underlining the unique character of its wide advisory function, the Court has explained the limitations imposed by the Convention on the death penalty, with a view to its 'final suppression' (third Opinion, of 1983). It has added that its wide advisory faculty enables it to deliver an advisory opinion not only on laws in force, but also on draft legislation (fourth Opinion, of 1984).[61]

With regard to freedom of thought and expression, the Court has warned that the compulsory membership in an association of journalists, to the extent that it hinders the access of any person to the 'full use' of the means of social communication, is incompatible with Article 13 of the American Convention (fifth Opinion, of 1985). [62] The Court has, furthermore, clarified that the word 'laws' in Article 30 of the Convention means a legal norm of a general character, intended for the 'general welfare', that emanates from the legislative organ that is competent under the national constitution and democratically elected and is elaborated according to the procedure for law-making established by the constitution (sixth Opinion, of 1986).[63] The Court has also taken the view that the fact that an Article of the Convention refers to action to be taken by law does not by itself mean that the Article is not directly applicable, and observed that Article 14(1) of the Convention is directly applicable per se (seventh Opinion, of 1986).[64]

In an important opinion, the Court has indicated that the remedies of *amparo* and habeas corpus cannot be suspended in accordance with Article 27(2) of the Convention, as they constitute 'indispensable judicial guarantees' of the protection of the recognized rights; constitutional and legal provisions of the States Parties which authorize, explicitly or implicitly, the suspension of the remedies of *amparo* or habeas corpus in situations of emergency are thus to be regarded as 'incompatible' with the international obligations which the Convention imposes upon those States. Domestic remedies before competent and independent tribunals should not only be formally accessible but also effective and adequate. Due process (Articles 8 and 25) is applicable to 'all judicial guarantees' referred to in the Convention, even under the regime of suspension regulated by its Article 27, also

---

[61] I/A Court H. R. Series A No. 4 (1984), 5 *HRLJ* 161.
[62] I/A Court H. R. Series A No. 5 (1985), 7 *HRLJ* 74.
[63] I/A Court H. R. Series A No. 6 (1986), 7 *HRLJ* 231.
[64] I/A Court H. R. Series A No. 7 (1986), 7 *HRLJ* 238.

subject to a control of legality (closely related to democracy itself), so as to preserve the rule of law (eighth and ninth Opinions, of 1987).[65]

The Court has stated that its advisory function encompasses the rendering of advisory opinions on the interpretation of the 1948 American Declaration on the Rights and Duties of Man in relation to the OAS Charter (its human rights provisions) and the American Convention on Human Rights and other treaties concerning the protection of human rights in the American States (tenth Opinion, of 1989).[66] The Court has, moreover, elaborated upon the extent of the exceptions to the requirement of the exhaustion of local remedies (under Article 46 of the Convention). In a human rights context, these are to be understood and applied in a more flexible way than in other contexts and in favour of the alleged victims. Thus, the requirement does not apply if, by reason of the victim's indigence or a generalized fear on the part of lawyers in the community to represent certain persons, the victim is unable to use or exhaust such local remedies as exist (eleventh Opinion, of 1990).[67]

The Court has also advised that the Inter-American Commission is competent (under Articles 41–42 of the Convention) to determine whether a domestic law of a State Party violates the obligations incumbent upon it under the American Convention, but is not competent to determine whether that law contradicts the domestic law of that State (thirteenth Opinion, of 1993).[68] The Court has further maintained that the adoption, as well as the application, of a domestic law in breach of a state's obligations under the Convention is a violation of the Convention, resulting in that state's international responsibility. If an act pursuant to the application of such a law is an international crime, it generates the international responsibility not only of the State but also of the individual officials or agents who have committed that act (fourteenth Opinion, of 1994).[69] The Court left unanswered the question whether individual responsibility arises on the part of state officials or agents for violations of non-derogable Convention rights (for example, right to life, right not to be subjected to torture or slavery, right not to be incriminated by means of retroactive application of penalties) that do not amount to international crimes.

At present, the Court has pending before it a fifteenth request for an opinion on the interpretation of Articles 50 and 51 of the American Convention (on the Commission's report, opinion, conclusions and recommendations on cases submitted for its consideration).

As will be apparent from the above summary of the Court's practice, its

[65] I/A Court H. R. Series A No. 8 and 9 (1987), 9 *HRLJ* 94, 204.
[66] I/A Court H. R. Series A No. 10 (1989), 11 *HRLJ* 118.
[67] I/A Court H. R. Series A No. 11 (1990), 12 *HRLJ* 20.
[68] I/A Court H. R. Series A No. 13 (1993), 14 *HRLJ* 252, 1–2 IHRR 197 (1994).
[69] I/A Court H. R. Series A No. 14 (1994) 16 *HRLJ* 9, 2 IHRR 380 (1995).

fourteen Advisory Opinions to date have helped to shed light on some central issues of the utmost importance to the operation of the inter-American system of human rights protection.

On only one occasion so far, has the Court declined a request for an opinion; it did so on the ground that for the Court to give the requested opinion would have been to undermine its contentious jurisdiction and impair the human rights of the complainants in cases that were pending before the Commission (twelfth Opinion, of 1991).[70]

Provisional Measures of Protection

Besides the exercise of its contentious and advisory jurisdictions (above), the Court has ordered, on the basis of Article 63(2) of the American Convention, provisional measures of protection in cases of 'extreme gravity and urgency, and when necessary to avoid irreparable damages to persons'.[71] The Court has done so, as foreseen in the American Convention, in relation both to cases pending before it and, upon the request of the Commission, with respect to cases before the Commission which have not yet been submitted to it.[72]

In the first alternative (cases pending before the Court itself), provisional measures have been ordered by the Court to protect the rights to life and to a humane treatment of witnesses in the cases of *Velásquez Rodríguez*, *Godínez Cruz*, and *Fairén Garbi and Solis Corrales* (Honduras, 1988),[73] *Caballero Delgado and Santana* (Colombia, 1994), *Blake* (Guatemala, 1995),[74] *Suárez Rosero* (Ecuador, 1996), and *Loayza Tamayo* (Peru, 1996). In the second alternative (cases pending before the Commission, not the Court, in which the Commission requests provisional measures), provisional measures of protection have been ordered by the Court in the cases of *Bustíos-Rojas* (Peru, 1990–1991),[75] *Chunimá* (Guatemala, 1991–1992), *Reggiardo Tolosa*[76] (Argentina, 1993–1994), *Colotenango*[77]

---

[70] I/A Court H. R. Series A No. 12 (1991), 13 *HRLJ* 149.

[71] On provisonal measures, see, T. Buergenthal, 'Medidas Provisórias na Corte Inter-americana de Direitos Humanos', 84/86 *Boletim da Sociedade Brasileira de Direito Internacional* (1992–3) 11–36; D. Cassel, 'A United States View of the Inter-American Court of Human Rights', in A. A. Cançado Trindade (ed.), *The Modern World of Human Rights—Essays in Honour of Thomas Buergenthal* (Costa Rica, 1996), 209–29, esp. 220–2; J. M. Pasqualucci, 'Medidas Provisionales en la Corte Interamericana de Derechos Humanos: Una Comparación con la Corte Internacional de Justicia y la Corte Europea de Derechos Humanos', 19 *Revista del Instituto Interamericano de Derechos Humanos* 47 (1994).

[72] The Court has recently published a Compendium reproducing all interim measures adopted in the period ranging from 1987 to 1996: Corte Interamericana de Derechos Humanos, *Serie E: Medidas Provisionales—N. 1: Compendio 1987–1996* (Costa Rica, 1996), 1–184.

[73] 9 *HRLJ* 104, 105.   [74] 3 IHRR 539 (1996).

[75] 11 *HRLJ* 257.   [76] 2 IHRR 411 (1995).

[77] 2 IHRR 414, 421 (1995).

(Guatemala, 1994–1996), *Carpio Nicolle*[78] (Guatemala, 1995–1996), *Alemán Lacayo* (Nicaragua, 1996), *Vogt* (Guatemala, 1996), and *Serech and Saquic* (Guatemala, 1996). In such instances of requests by the Commission in cases not pending before the Court, the Court applied a presumption that such measures of protection are necessary.

Provisional measures of protection have been ordered in situations implying an imminent threat to life or of serious physical or mental harm. In practice the Court has not required from the Commission a substantial demonstration that the facts are true, but has proceeded rather on the basis of a reasonable presumption that this is so. In any case, before ordering provisional measures of protection, the Court verifies that the State concerned has recognized its contentious jurisdiction under Article 62(2) of the Convention.

In only two cases so far—*Neira Alegría* (1992), and *Chipoco*, also concerning Perú, (1992)—were measures requested by the Commission not ordered by the Court, either because what was in fact the intention of the request was rather the undertaking of a visit *in loco*, or else because the individual concerned was not in danger (being already out of the country). In another case (*Suárez Rosero*, 1996), given the change of circumstances, the Court decided to lift the urgent measures that had been ordered by its President.

The growing use of provisional measures of protection is a reassuring development. The granting of those measures has become an increasingly important aspect of the contemporary case-law of the Court, given the emergency relief it has secured and indeed the lives it has saved, thus demonstrating clearly the preventive function of the international protec-tion of human rights.

THE EVOLVING RULES OF PROCEDURE

The Inter-American Court has had so far three sets of Rules of Procedure. Its original Rules were adopted in 1980. At that time, the Inter-American Court had had virtually no experience in the handling of contentious cases. It thus took as a model the Rules then in force of the European Court of Human Rights, which, in turn, had found inspiration in the procedure set forth in the Rules of the International Court of Justice (ICJ). These latter, however, had been designed for the *contentieux* between States before the ICJ. They were not always appropriate for the settlement of human rights cases, the vast majority of which involve claims by individual complainants against respondent States (not seldom their own). It was thus not surprising

---

[78] 3 IHRR 529 (1996).

to find, for example, the procedure before the Inter-American Court being divided in its original Rules into a written and an oral phase, the former comprising, as in other international tribunals, of such documents as memorial and counter-memorial, and reply and rejoinder,[79] and the latter consisting of oral hearings before the Court.[80] The Court was thus soon faced with the need to adapt gradually its Rules to the nature of the cases it was later to be called upon to adjudicate.

Bearing this in mind, the Court's second Rules of Procedure were adopted in 1991, and were amended on three subsequent occasions.[81] Further changes in the Court's procedure, to improve and render it more flexible (as required by human rights cases) were introduced by means of resolutions adopted by the Court on specific aspects, subsequently incorporated into the amended Rules of Procedure.

This was the case of two recent resolutions, on the composition of the Court at the reparations phase of proceedings and for supervision of compliance with its Judgments,[82] and on the presentation of evidence[83] respectively. The former determined that all issues relating to reparations and the supervision of compliance with the Court's judgments are to be decided by the Judges serving in the Court when those matters were decided, unless a public hearing had already taken place, in which case the Judges present at the hearing will decide the issues. The latter established that evidence is as a rule to be presented with the complaint (*demanda*), and only exceptionally in other phases. [84] This second ruling will help to avoid an indefinite prolongation of proceedings. Both resolutions were clearly intended to rationalize and simplify the Court's procedure, thus improving it, bearing in mind the peculiar nature of human rights cases and the need to render proceedings less cumbersome and more expeditious.

These changes have been incorporated into the Court's third Rules of Procedure, which were adopted in 1996 and entered into force on 1 January 1997. By and large, in the new Rules, the successive procedural acts in the Court's procedure are at last regulated in a logical order.[85]

To arrive at its current Rules, the Court took into account the experience it had accumulated in the exercise of its contentious jurisdiction to date. A couple of examples may be singled out in this connection. The present rule as to the presentation of the complaint (*demanda*) before the Court is

---

[79] Pursuant to the Rules of Court of 1980, Arts. 26–31 (on written proceedings).

[80] Pursuant to the Rules of Court of 1980, Arts. 32–3 (on oral proceedings).

[81] On 25 Jan. 1993, 16 July 1993 and 2 Dec. 1995, respectively.

[82] Court's resolution of 19 Sept. 1995, 3 IHRR 576 (1996).

[83] Court's resolution of 2 Feb. 1996.

[84] Rules of Court of 1996, Art. 43, see Appendix VII.

[85] Thus, under Title II, general rules of procedure are dealt with in Chap. I, written and oral proceedings in Chaps. II and III and the handling of evidence in Chap. IV.

clearer and simpler, so as to avoid difficulties that have arisen in practice.[86] Also, the rules regulating the situation where the respondent State accepts responsibility (*allanamiento*)[87] have been revised in the light of the Court's experience in recent cases.[88]

In the handling of contentious cases by the Court, one issue is particularly deserving of attention, namely, the degree of overlapping which has taken place between the work of the Inter-American Commission and the Court with regard to fact-finding. Early examples are provided by the Court's handling of the *Honduran* and *Surinamese* cases. Nowadays, as the number of contentious cases referred by the Commission to the Court increases considerably, that duplication of work gives cause for concern.[89] In November 1996, it was predicted by the Court's Secretariat that by the end of the year the Court would have heard no less than 157 witnesses and experts on the merits of nine contentious cases.[90] This aspect of its work is bound to take much of the Court's time in future, raising a problem that is aggravated by the fact that the Court is not in session permanently, meeting on average only three times a year, and by its practice of not working in chambers.

In order to avoid considerable and undesirable delays in the procedure in receiving testimonial evidence (quite apart from the documentary evidence that the Court receives), less time-consuming methods of fact-finding need to be devised,[91] in addition to its practice of using presumptions and of shifting of the burden of proof. The Court, above all, should be enabled to rely more on the fact-finding undertaken previously by the Commission. There are indications in the text of the American Convention that support the view that the task of fact-finding should be entrusted to the Commission,[92] so as to enable the Court to devote most of its time to the final determination of the findings of law. Such a division of labour, leaving the Court to concentrate on the legal issues, is implicit in the relevant provisions of the Convention. The Court is not an appellate tribunal for the Commission's decisions, and the functions of the two

---

[86] e.g., in the case of *Paniagua Morales*, against Guatemala (Preliminary objections, 1996). Cf. Rules of Court of 1996, Art. 26.

[87] Rules of Court of 1996, Art. 52(2).

[88] Namely: cases *Aloeboetoe* (Suriname, 1991), *El Amparo* (Venezuela, 1995), *Garrido and Baigorria* (Argentina, 1996).

[89] OAS/Permanent Council, *Toward a New Vision of the Inter-American Human Rights System*, OAS doc. OEA/Ser. G-CP/doc. 2828/96, of 26. 11. 1996, 9–10.

[90] OAS, doc. cit. above n. 30, 9.

[91] Cf. e.g., M. Reisman and J. K. Levit, 'Fact-Finding Initiatives for the Inter-American Court of Human Rights', in R. Navia (ed.) *La Corte y el Sistema Interamericanos de Derechos Humanos* (Costa Rica, 1994), 443–57; and cf. T. Buergenthal, 'Judicial Fact-Finding: Inter-American Human Rights Court' in R. Lillich (ed.) *Fact-Finding before International Tribunals* (N.Y.,1990), 261–74.

[92] ACHR, Arts. 48, 50 and 61.

international supervisory organs under the American Convention are best viewed as complementary rather than overlapping. Improvement in the present arrangements is not only much needed, but is also quite feasible, since the rules that are currently applied in this area are ones that have evolved anyway through the Court's practice.

Last but not least, a key and recurrent issue has been that of the *locus standi* of the individuals (the alleged victims) before the Inter-American Court in cases referred to it by the Commission. Although, under the American Convention, only the Commission and the States Parties have the right to submit a case to the Court,[93] the Convention also refers to the 'injured party',[94] by that meaning of course the alleged victims. Since the early *Honduran* cases,[95] the representatives of the victims have had some degree of presence in proceedings before the Court. In fact, the Rules of Procedure of 1991 (the second Rules of Court, above) provided that the alleged victims, their representatives or next-of-kin may assist the Delegates of the Commission (Article 22(2)). The Court obtains their viewpoints in certain circumstances,[96] and may invite them to submit briefs regarding the application of Article 63(1) of the Convention (Article 44(2)).

The Rules of Procedure of 1996 (the third Rules of Court, above) have taken a step forward, by providing (Article 23) that in the proceedings before the Court at the stage of reparations 'the representatives of the victims or of their relatives may present their own arguments and evidence in an autonomous way'. It is submitted that there are compelling reasons for granting the alleged victims *locus standi in judicio* before the Court in all phases of the proceedings; such reasons are fully developed in Chapter 13 of this book. After all, the recognition of the international personality and full procedural legal capacity of the human being is proper before a Court whose function is to protect human rights.

[93] ACHR, Art. 61(1).
[94] Cf. ACHR, Art. 63.
[95] *Velasquez Rodriguez, Godinez Cruz, Fairen Gabri and Solis Corrales*.
[96] Namely, when the applicant notifies the Court of its intention not to proceed with the case (Art. 43(1)) or when the parties have reached a friendly settlement (Art. 43(2)).

6

Reparations in the Inter-American System

DINAH SHELTON

International human rights treaties generally require that the States Parties afford an effective remedy to the victim of a human rights violation.[1] Failure to provide a remedy constitutes a separate breach of the treaty, additional to the original violation.[2] Where domestic remedies do not exist or prove ineffectual, international supervisory organs may have jurisdiction to accept petitions meeting stated admissibility criteria in order to decide if a violation has been committed. Two human rights treaties, the European and the Inter-American Conventions, go further and authorize their respective courts to issue judgments on reparations. The Inter-American Convention contains the broader mandate:

If the Court finds that there has been a violation of a right or freedom protected by this Convention, the Court shall rule that the injured party be ensured the enjoyment of his right or freedom that was violated. It shall also rule, if appropriate, that the consequences of the measure or situation that constituted the breach of such right or freedom be remedied and that fair compensation be paid to the injured party.[3]

DRAFTING HISTORY OF ARTICLE 63(1)

The drafting history of Article 63(1) reveals no debate about conferring broad competence on the Court to order reparations. The Inter-American Commission on Human Rights, whose first draft of the Convention was

---

[1] For example, the International Covenant on Civil and Political Rights, Art. 2(3)(a) requires that each State Party undertake 'to ensure that any person whose rights or freedoms as herein recognized as violated shall have an effective remedy, notwithstanding that the violation has been committed by persons acting in an official capacity.'

[2] *Velasquez Rodriguez*, Preliminary Objections, I/A Court H.R. Series C No.1 (1987), para. 91.

[3] Art. 63(1), American Convention on Human Rights, see Appendix III. Contrast the comparable provision in the European Convention on Human Rights: 'If the Court finds that a decision or a measure taken by a legal authority or any other authority of a High Contracting Party is completely or partially in conflict with the obligations arising from the present Convention, and if the internal law of the said Party allows only partial reparation to be made for the consequences of this decision or measure, the decision of the Court shall, *if necessary*, afford just satisfaction to the injured party.' Art. 50, Convention for the Protection of Human Rights and Fundamental Freedoms, 4 Nov. 1950, 312 UNTS 222 (emphasis added).

the basic working document at the Conference of San José, gave the Court the power to award compensation in its draft Article 52(1).[4] The Commission itself had worked from three drafts prepared by the Inter-American Council of Jurists (ICJ), the Government of Chile and the Government of Uruguay. All of these earlier drafts generally replicated the language of Article 50 of the European Convention on Human Rights and were thus more restrictive than the draft finally produced by the Commission.[5] The Commission did not indicate the reasons for or origin of the changes it made.

Guatemala's written comments on the Commission's draft for the San José Conference proposed to strengthen the Article further, to add that the Court might also order remedies for the consequences produced by the act or measure that impaired the injured's rights and that the injured party be guaranteed the enjoyment of his violated right or freedom.[6] Committee II, which dealt with the provisions on the organs of protection, largely accepted these proposals. The Rapporteur stated that Committee II had 'approved a text which is broader and more categorically in defense of the injured party than the Draft.'[7] The Plenary adopted the Committee version of Article 63(1) without discussion, giving the Court the three duties or powers it currently enjoys to order measures that: (1) ensure future respect for the right or freedom that was violated, (2) remedy the consequences of the violation, and (3) compensate for the harm.

JURISPRUDENCE OF THE COURT

The Court began functioning in 1979, after the Convention had entered into force the previous year. It has since issued eight judgments on damages;[8] the matter is pending in two cases.[9] One proceeding was dis-

---

[4] Draft Art. 52(1) contained the language of the last part. of present Art. 63(1), allowing the Court to order that fair compensation be paid. See T. Buergenthal and R. Norris, *Human Rights: The Inter-American System*, Vol. 2 Bk. 13, 20.

[5] OAS, Inter-American Council of Jurists, Fourth Meeting, Santiago, Chile, Aug.-Sept. 1959, OAS doc. 128, rev. (1959), reprinted in T. Buergenthal and R. Norris, *Human Rights: The Inter-American System*, Vol. 3 Bk. 16(1) at 26, 57, 86.

[6] Id. at 132.   [7] Id. at 232.

[8] *Velasquez Rodriguez* case, Compensatory Damages, I/A Court H.R. Series C No.7 (1989), 11 *HRLJ* 127; *Godinez Cruz* case, Compensatory Damages, I/A Court H.R. Series C No.8 (1989); *Velasquez Rodriguez* case, Interpretation of the judgment of compensatory damages, I/A Court H.R. Series C No.9 (1990), 12 *HRLJ* 14; *Godinez Cruz* case, Interpretation of the judgment of compensatory damages, I/A Court H.R. Series C No.10 (1990); *Aloeboetoe et al.* case, Reparations, I/A Court H.R. Series C No.15 (1993), 14 *HRLJ* 413 1–1 IHRR 208 (1994); *Gangaram Panday* case, I/A Court H.R. Series C No.16 (1994), 15 *HRLJ* 168, 2 IHRR (1995); *El Amparo* case, Reparations, judgment of 14 Sept. 1996 (Annual Report of the Inter-American Court of Human Rights, OAS/Ser.L/V/III.35, Doc. 5, 3 Feb. 1997, 159); and *Neira Alegría et al* case, Reparations judgment of 19 Sept, 1996.

[9] *Caballero Delgado and Santana* case, I/A Court H.R. Series C No.22 (1995), 17 *HRLJ* 24, 3 IHRR 548 (1996) and *Garrido and Baigorria* case, Judgment of 2 February 1996 (Annual Report of the Inter-American Court of Human Rights, OAS/Ser.L/V/III.35, doc. 5, 3 Feb. 1997, 179).

missed after the parties reached a settlement approved by the Court.[10] In all but one case, the Court issued its judgment on reparations after the issue was briefed by the parties following the Court's decision on the merits. In *Gangaram Panday*, the Court did not follow this procedure, but awarded a 'nominal' sum in its judgment on the merits.

The Court's jurisprudence on damages reveals less generosity towards victims than might be expected on the basis of the text of Article 63(1) and its drafting history. The opinions are not consistent and indicate a fundamental misunderstanding of the sometimes different interests and roles of the victims and the Commission. Nonetheless, the Court's judgments represent the most wide-reaching remedies afforded in international human rights law. The following discussion reviews each of the Court's decisions on reparations in chronological order. There follows a general comparative analysis and critique of the Court's treatment of the topic.

THE HONDURAN CASES

Velasquez Rodriguez and *Godinez Cruz* were the first contentious cases decided by the Court.[11] The Inter-American Commission on Human Rights submitted these cases against Honduras to the Court, alleging state responsibility for the disappearance of the two named individuals. The Court found the government responsible and asked the parties, viz the Commission and the Honduran Government, to negotiate an agreement on the amount of damages.[12] The Court kept the case open, reserving the right to approve the agreement or, if no agreement were reached, to set the amount and order the manner of payment.[13] The Court noted that in the circumstances of a disappearance it could not order that the victim be guaranteed the enjoyment of the rights and freedoms violated.[14] The Court refused to award costs because they had not been pleaded.[15]

Subsequently, the Court seemed to recognize the importance of the precedent that these cases would set on the subject of reparations, whether

---

[10] *Maqueda*, I/A Court H.R. Series C No.18 (1995), 16 *HRLJ* 151, 3 IHRR 355 (1996).

[11] *Velasquez Rodriguez*, I/A Court H.R. Series C No.4 (1988), 9 *HRLJ* 212; *Godinez Cruz*, I/A Court H.R. Series C No.5 (1989).

[12] *Velasquez*, id. at 191–192. In Godinez Cruz, the Court held it would fix the amount of the compensation in execution of the judgment, after hearing the interested parties, unless they reached an agreement in the interim. As in the *Velasquez* case, the Court reserved the right to approve any such agreement.

[13] Id. [14] Id. at 189.

[15] *Velasquez*, id. at para. 193; *Godinez Cruz*, id. at para. 202, citing Art. 45(1) of the Court's Rules of Procedure. This decision was repeated during the damages phase of the case. See *Velasquez Rodriguez*, Compensatory Damages, paras. 41–2 where the family seeks reimbursement of costs of the investigation to locate the disappeared. The Court notes that the costs were not pleaded nor proven opportunely.

or not the parties reached agreement. By resolution, it authorized the President to initiate whatever studies and name whatever experts might be convenient so that the Court would have the elements necessary to set the form and amount of compensation.[16]

No agreement was reached between the parties: Honduras argued that the compensation given should be 'the most favorable benefits' that Honduran legislation provided for Hondurans in the case of accidental death. The Commission countered that the amount and form of payment constituting just compensation should be determined by the requirements of international law. The two sides did agree on a designation of beneficiaries which was limited to the wife and children of the disappeared, 'once they had fulfilled the requirements of Honduran law to be recognized as heirs of the victims.' The Court rejected even this limited agreement, holding that 'the family members . . . need only show their family relationship. They are not required to follow the procedure of Honduran inheritance law.' In fact, the secretariat of the Court, under instructions from the President, requested information from Honduran officials, including 'the names and status of their wives; and those of any concubines recognized in any official document . . . names and civil status of their children, those of the marriage and any outside the marriage.'[17] The parties returned to Court.

In pleadings, the victims asked for more than monetary compensation: they asked the Court to order Honduras to take various remedial measures. These included an end to disappearances in Honduras; an investigation and public disclosure of what had happened to the disappeared in some 150 cases; trial and punishment of those responsible;[18] 'a public act to honor and dignify the memory of the disappeared. A street, park, elementary school, high school, or hospital could be named for the victims of disappearances'; actions against death squads and in favor of humanitarian organizations; and an end to all forms of pressure against the families of the disappeared 'a public recognition of their honor.'

The monetary compensation sought included establishment of a fund for the primary, secondary, and university education of the children of

[16] *Velasquez Rodriguez*, Compensatory Damages, above n. 9, para. 4.

[17] Id. para. 13(4), (5).

[18] There is a vast literature on the duty to investigate and prosecute, much of it stemming from the impunity and amnesty laws passed in Latin American states after periods of human rights abuses. See: L. Wechsler, *A Miracle, A Universe: Settling Accounts With Torturers* (New York, 1990); C. Nino, 'The Duty to Punish Past Abuses of Human Rights Put into Context: The Case of Argentina,' 100 *Yale LJ* 2619 (1991); D. Orentlichter, 'Settling Accounts: The Duty to Prosecute Human Rights Violations of a Prior Regime,' 100 *Yale LJ* 2537 (1991); J. M. Pasqualucci, 'The Whole Truth and Nothing but the Truth: Truth Commissions, Impunity and the Inter-American Human Rights System,' 12 *Boston U. Int'l. LJ* 321 (1994); N. Roht-Arriaza, Comment, 'State Responsibility to Investigate and Prosecute Grave Human Rights Violations in International Law,' 78 *Cal.L Rev*. 449 (1990).

the disappeared; guaranteed employment of working-age children; and establishment of a retirement fund for the parents of the disappeared.

The attorneys for the victims, designated as 'counselors or advisers to the Commission' in order to permit them a role before the Court,[19] asked for a public hearing to receive a psychiatric report on the moral damages suffered by the victims' families.

The Commission's claims were also extensive. It sought to have Honduras investigate, prosecute and punish those responsible for the disappearances. The request for compensatory damages included payment to the spouse of 'the highest pension recognized by Honduran law' and payments to the children through completion of their university education; title to an adequate house; general damages for the wife and children (200,000 lempiras[20]), damages for lost earnings (2,422,420 lempiras) and emotional harm (4,845,000 lempiras), based upon an expert opinion offered by the victim's family. In addition, the Commission specifically requested punitive damages in the amount of 2,422,000 lempiras. The Commission supported some of the other measures requested by the family under the heading of moral damages: for example, public homage through naming a street, thoroughfare, school or other public place and a public condemnation of disappearances. On its side, the government offered 150,000 lempiras.

The Court considered at length the basis for an award of damages, noting that international law requires restitution of the *status quo ante* where possible and compensation where it is not possible:

It is a principle of international law, which jurisprudence has considered 'even a general concept of law,' that every violation of an international obligation which results in harm creates a duty to make adequate reparation. Compensation, on the other hand, is the most usual way of doing so (Factory at Chorzow, Jurisdiction, Judgment No. 8, 1937 (PCIJ, Series A, No. 17, 29; Reparation for Injuries Suffered in the Service of the United Nations, Advisory Opinion, ICJ Reports 1949, 184).

Reparation of harm brought about by the violation of an international obligation consists in full restitution (*restitutio in integrum*), which includes the restoration of the prior situation, the reparation of the consequences of the violation, and indemnification for patrimonial and non-patrimonial damages, including emotional harm.[21]

---

[19] Only the States Parties and the Commission have the right to submit a case to the Court. Art. 61, American Convention on Human Rights. The Commission is represented by Delegates, who may be assisted by any person of their choice, including attorneys for the victims. Art. 22, Rules of Procedure of the Court. This is the only means by which the victims may directly participate in arguing their case before the Court. See further, Trindade, 149 above.

[20] Two lempiras equal approximately one US dollar.

[21] *Velasquez Rodriguez* above n. 8, paras. 6, 25–6.

The Court seems to suggest that awards for emotional harm are particularly appropriate in cases of human rights violations.[22] Indemnification under this heading is to be based upon the principles of equity. Reparations generally are to be effective and independent of the limitations of national law.

In regard to some of the claims, the Court referred back to the decision on the merits. It noted that some of the measures claimed would constitute a part of the reparation of the consequences of the violation of rights rather than being part of the indemnity. In this regard, it reiterated the continuing Honduran duty stated in the judgment on the merits to investigate the cases, prevent future violations and punish those responsible. The Court also found, like the European Court, that its judgment on the merits is a type of reparation and constitutes moral satisfaction of significance and importance. No requests for non-monetary reparations were granted.

The Court rejected the claim for punitive damages, finding that the expression 'fair compensation' used in Article 63 (1) is compensatory in nature and not punitive. It also found that an award of amounts meant to deter or to serve as an example 'is not applicable in international law at this time.'

In regard to the measure of damages awarded, the Court rejected the notion that criteria for accidental death, such as those in the rules concerning life insurance, should be the measure of a death that was 'the result of serious acts imputable to Honduras'. Instead, the damages must be calculated as a loss of earnings based upon the income the victim would have received up to the time of his possible natural death, adjusted by the fact that the children 'who should be guaranteed the possibility of an education which might extend to the age of twenty-five' could begin work at that time. The starting point was the salary the individuals received at the time of disappearance, adjusted as necessary 'to arrive at a prudent estimate of the damages, given the circumstances in each case.' In *Velasquez Rodriguez*, the amount was set by the Court at 500,000 lempiras.[23]

Moral damages the Court defines as 'the result of the psychological impact suffered by the family . . . because of the violation of rights and freedoms guaranteed by the American Convention, *especially* by the dramatic characteristics of the involuntary disappearance of persons.'[24] The Court seems to be rightly suggesting that one factor in assessing moral damages is the egregiousness of the conduct of governmental authorities. The family demonstrated the existence of moral damages through expert psychiatric testimony which 'the government could not disprove.' Moral damages were set at 250,000 lempiras.

---

[22] Id. para. 27.
[23] The family of Godinez Cruz was awarded 650,000 lempiras.
[24] *Velasquez Rodriguez*, above n. 8 para. 50 (emphasis added).

The final issue dealt with by the Court in the Honduran cases concerned the mode of payment. The Court ordered a lump sum payment within 90 days, free of taxes, or payment in six equal monthly installments, beginning within 90 days. In the latter case, the amount remaining due would be subject to interest at current rates in Honduras. Without any indication of the basis of its judgment, the Court divided all amounts awarded between the wife, who received one-quarter, and the children, who shared three-quarters. The Court ordered establishment of a trust fund for the children, created in the Central Bank of Honduras 'under the most favorable conditions permitted by Honduran banking practice.' The children receive monthly payments from the fund until age twenty-five, when it is to be distributed.

The *Velasquez Rodriguez* and *Godinez Cruz* judgments on compensatory damages were the subject of further proceedings when the Commission asked for a clarification. The problem arose due to high levels of inflation in Honduras and the need to protect the value of the award. The Commission asked that the amount of the award be indexed, calculated in United States dollars of 20 October 1989, and that it maintain that same value throughout the life of the trust.[25] In agreeing with the Commission, the Court repeated that compensation due victims or their families must attempt to provide *restitutio in integrum* for the damages caused by the measure or situation that constituted a violation of human rights.

The desired aim is full restitution for the injury suffered. This is something that is unfortunately often impossible to achieve, given the irreversible nature of the damages suffered, which is demonstrated in the instant case. Under such circumstances, it is appropriate to fix the payment of 'fair compensation' in sufficiently broad terms in order to compensate, to the extent possible for the loss suffered.[26]

The Court interpreted its award concerning the establishment of a trust fund 'under the most favorable conditions permitted by Honduran banking practice' to mean that any act or measure by the trustee must ensure that the amount assigned maintains its purchasing power and generates sufficient earnings or dividends to increase it. The trustee has to perform the task 'as would a good head of family' with the power and the duty to select various investments that will achieve the mandate. The decision of the Court to place the award in a trust fund was precisely because it is an institution that 'is designed to maintain and increase the real value of the assets.' The Court therefore rejected the Commission's request that the government be ordered to disburse additional sums periodically to maintain constant the value of the original award for so long as the trust

---

[25] *Velasquez Rodriguez*, Interpretation of the Compensatory Damages Judgment, above n. 8 para. 20; *Godinez Cruz*, Interpretation of the Compensatory Damages Judgment, above n. 8 para. 20.   [26] Id. para. 27.

remains in effect. However, the Court did order the government to pay lost opportunity costs resulting from its failure to comply with the judgment in the time ordered: interest and the decline in value of the lempira since the date of judgment. This constituted a real loss which must be compensated by the government.

Some eight years later, the Honduran government paid the award.

Aloeboetoe

In the *Aloeboetoe* case[27] the Court dealt only with the issue of reparations, after Suriname accepted responsibility for the kidnapping and deaths of seven young men of the Saramaca tribe. Six of the men were forced to dig their own graves before being killed. One was shot and seriously wounded while trying to escape. He later died of his wounds after testifying about the massacre. On behalf of the victims' families, the Commission sought indemnification for material and moral damages, other non-monetary reparation, and reimbursement of expenses and costs incurred by the victims' next of kin. The Commission also argued that the Saramaca tribe suffered direct moral damage and was entitled to compensation.

The Court faced a difficult issue of identifying the persons in the families of the decedents who would be entitled to compensation. The Saramacas are descendants of African slaves who maintain a traditional culture, including a matriarchal social structure and polygamy. Marriages are not registered with the government, partly due to lack of knowledge and partly because the government has failed to provide accessible facilities to register births, deaths and marriages.

The Court, applying a generally recognized choice of law principle, determined that local law should apply to determine next of kin and beneficiaries of the victims. Surinamese law holds that a victim's next of kin includes the legally recognized spouse, the children, and perhaps dependent parents of the victim. The law does not recognize polygamy. In contrast, Saramaca tribal customary law accepts multiple marriages and the duty of adult children to care for their parents. The Court found that Surinamese family law was not effective in the region and was therefore not the local law for purposes of the case. As a result, the multiple wives and children of the victims were recognized by the Court.[28]

The Commission and the lawyer for the victims argued that the tribe itself had suffered an injury because under tribal customs 'a person is a member not only of his or her own family group, but also of his or her

---

[27] *Aloeboetoe*, above n. 8.
[28] The Court found no issue under the Convention with regard to the recognition of polygamy. In contrast, the all male Court refused to place the monetary compensation under the control of the female head of the family because this would involve gender discrimination.

own village community and tribal group'.[29] It was argued that in the Saramaca culture a communal matrilineal group takes responsibility for the welfare of its members and for such matters as determining which family members are to share in compensation rendered. The attorneys relied on the decisions of earlier international tribunals which found that the right to recover rests on the direct personal loss, if any suffered by each of the claimants.[30] '[T]he direct personal loss referred to is pecuniary in nature and is measured principally by the degree of financial dependence which existed between the claimant and the deceased.' The Court rejected this part of the claim.

Regarding the quantum of compensation, the Commission argued that material damages for each dependent should be based on the total loss to the family members.[31] According to the Commission, the proper formula requires estimating net present value of the amounts (a) which the decedent, had he not been killed, would probably have contributed to the claimant, plus (b) the pecuniary value to such claimant of the deceased's personal services in claimant's care, education, or supervision, and (c) reasonable compensation for mental suffering or shock. Adjusted by a number of additional factors,[32] net present value requires calculating: (i) the age at death of each victim and annual earnings at that time, (ii) the life expectancy of each victim determined by actuarial tables, (iii) annual earnings taking into account inflation rates.

Although it listed the factors applied in the *Lusitania* arbitration, the Commission calculated and demanded only lost revenues: the personal services and value to the family of the decedent were not considered.[33] This factor may have been considered too subjective or difficult to apply. Whatever the reason, the absence of an award for personal services, plus

---

[29] Id. at para. 19.

[30] Arbitral Decision No. II, in Reports of International Arbitral Awards, Vol. VII, 27.

[31] The Commission relied on the *Lusitania* Cases (1923) for its method of calculating damages. See *Opinion in the Lusitania Cases*, Judgment of 1 Nov. 1923, 363.

[32] The additional factors listed in the Commission brief, and taken from the *Lusitania* Cases, are: (a) the age, sex, health, condition and station in life, occupation, habits of industry and sobriety, mental and physical capacity, frugality, earning capacity and customary earnings of the deceased and the uses made of such earnings by him; (b) the probable duration of the life of deceased but for the fatal injury, in arriving at which standard life-expectancy tables and all other pertinent evidence offered will be considered; (c) the reasonable probability that the earning capacity of deceased, had he lived, would either have increased or decreased; (d) the age, sex, health, condition and station in life, and probable life expectancy of each of the claimants; (e) the extent to which the deceased, had he lived, would have applied his income from his earnings or otherwise to his personal expenditures from which claimants would have derived no benefits.... Decedent's pain and suffering, life insurance proceeds, and punitive damages are not included. Commission Brief of 31 Mar. 1992, 7–8.

[33] The Commission has similarly failed to include a valuation for personal services in all of the subsequent cases. Mental suffering and shock are considered the basis for moral damages.

the concededly 'extremely conservative'[34] calculation of lost revenues, resulted in substantially less being claimed in material damages than was actually suffered.

The Commission sought moral damages for the psychological harm resulting from the deaths of loved ones, for being denied information as to the victims' whereabouts and for being unable to bury the bodies. They also sought to repair damage to the family members' position in their culture due to the loss of each husband/father because the traditional standing of each family is based in part on the contributions of working men to their parents and grandparents and their dignity reflects on the family as a whole.

In total, the victims and the Commission sought a lump sum of 5,114,484 Suriname florins, representing the material and moral damages, plus an annual sum representing actual damages of Sf 84,080 to the adult dependents, to be divided among them.[35] The lump sum award consisted of Sf 1,114,484 in material damages to the children; Sf 660,000 in moral damages to the children; Sf 1,340,000 in moral damages to the adult dependents; and Sf 2,000,000 in moral damages to the tribe of the victims.

The victims in *Aloeboetoe* sought measures other than compensation: 1) an apology from the President of Suriname and the Congress, 2) publication of the Court's decision, 3) return of the bodies of six victims to the families, 4) the naming of a park or square or prominent street after the Saramaca tribe, 5) investigation and punishment of the responsible persons. Attorneys for the victims also sought both costs and fees, pleading these to avoid the defect the Court had found in the Honduran cases. They sought amounts for attempting to ascertain the whereabouts of the victims; and for pursuing the claim at the local level, before the Commission and before the Court, including attorney's fees.[36] The requests for legal costs were Sf 715,618 and US$18,533, while the amount of expenses was US$32,375. The government argued that the Commission was working with outside attorneys, listed as attorneys for the victims, who performed work that the Commission should be doing. Further, the Court found that

---

[34] The Commission and the lawyers for the victims underestimated the actual damages, choosing to base their calculations on 'extremely conservative assumptions' about the inflation rate in Suriname. They noted that the actual state of the economy would 'indicate much higher figures' and 'substantially higher' damages. Commission Brief, 9. It is not clear why this approach was taken.

[35] The names and relationships of the family members and other dependents, as well as information relevant to material and moral damages, were obtained in large part through detailed questionnaires prepared by the Commission and administered to the Saramaca.

[36] These costs included a visit to Suriname by the attorney representing the victim, a visit to the interior of the country by part of the non-governmental organization involved, the appointment of research assistants to prepare the three hearings for the case before the Commission and the initial memorandum to the Court, and the hiring of an associate professor to take over the law course of the victims' attorney.

the US$250 per hour fee for services 'bears no relationship to prevailing conditions in the inter-American system.'[37]

The Court accepted some of the claims made by the Commission and the victims, such as the full amount of moral damages, while rejecting others, including the material damages claimed by parents of the decedents. Rather than rely on the Commission, the Court decided to appoint its own experts to assist in acquiring information to fix the amount of the compensation and costs. In addition, the Court sent its own Deputy Secretary to Suriname to gather addition information regarding the economic, financial and banking situation of the country.

In its judgment the Court emphasizes that the law on damages, including its scope and characteristics and the determination of beneficiaries, is governed by international law. Compliance with a judgment on reparations is not subject to modification or suspension by the respondent State through invocation of provisions of its own domestic law.[38] In this regard, the Court distinguishes between future action by the State, which must conform to the Convention and ensure the enjoyment of the right or freedom that was violated, and reparations for past actions of the state. Where, as here, the violation involves a loss of life or other right that cannot be restored, compensation must be in an amount sufficient to remedy all the consequences of the violations that took place.

The Court discusses for the first time the issue of proximate harm, noting that all human actions cause remote and distant effects. It is not clear what the purpose of this discussion is, although it may relate to the denial of the tribe's claim for moral damages or the claims of the parents of the victims. Whatever the underlying reason, the Court is singularly unhelpful in providing guidance to determine what harm will be deemed too remote from the act for the actor to bear responsibility. According to the Court, the responsible party must 'make reparation for the immediate effects of such unlawful acts, but only to the degree that has been *legally* recognized.'[39] This suggests a double limitation: the injury must be 'immediate' (undefined) *and* one that has already been recognized by law. This is an exceedingly difficult test to apply in a new court where there is no precedent. The Court also states that *restitutio in integrum* is 'one way in which the effect of an international unlawful act *may* be redressed, but it is not the only way in which it *must* be redressed, for in certain cases such reparation may not be possible, sufficient or appropriate.[40]

Calculation of compensatory damages followed the approach taken in the Honduran cases and is similar to the Commission's proposals.

---

[37] Aloeboetoe, above n. 8, para. 30. [38] Id. para. 44.
[39] Id. para. 49 (emphasis added). [40] Id. para. 49 (emphasis in original).

Compensation for actual damages is seen to comprise both indirect damages (daño emergente) and loss of earnings (lucro cesante). A 'prudent estimate of damages' is the income that the victims would have earned throughout their working life had they not been killed, based on the income that they would have earned for their economic activities during the month of June 1993.[41] To avoid the problems that arose in the Honduran cases with high inflation in the country, the Court calculated the annual income of each victim in local currency then converted it into dollars at the free market exchange rate. Wages back to 1988 were computed, along with interest, and the resulting amount was increased by the current net value of the expected income during the rest of the working life of each of the victims. The amounts ranged between US$19,986 and US$55,991.

The victims were also found to have suffered moral damages due to abuse by an armed band that deprived them of their liberty and later killed them:

The beatings received, the pain of knowing they were condemned to die for no reason whatsoever, the torture of having to dig their own graves are all part of the moral damages suffered by the victims. In addition, the person who did not die outright had to bear the pain of his wounds being infested by maggots and of seeing the bodies of his companions be devoured by vultures.[42]

As the Court noted, anyone subjected to the aggression and abuse described will experience moral suffering. The Court explicitly decided that such claims are survivable: the Court found that the deceased had 'an inherent' right to compensation that national law generally transmits to their heirs by succession. Successors are also presumed to have suffered their own actual and moral damages due to the loss of life. The burden of proof is on the other party to show that such damages do not exist. Claimants who are not successors, however, must provide specific proof justifying their right to damages. The Court applies this principle as well as 'rules, generally accepted by the community of nations' that designate spouse and children as successors. Only if there is no spouse or children, are the ascendant deemed successors. Nevertheless, the Court presumed that the parents suffered moral injury as a result of the cruel death of their offspring, 'for it is essentially human for all persons to feel pain at the torment of their child.'[43] The Court accepted the total amount of moral damages claimed by the Commission, an equal amount for each victim,

[41] The judgment is dated 10 Sept. 1993; the massacre took place 31 Dec. 1987. June 1993 was selected because in that month a free exchange market was established in Suriname. This made it possible to avoid the distortions produced by a system of fixed rates of exchange in a highly inflationary economy.
[42] Id. para. 51.
[43] Id. para. 76.

except the one who was wounded, who received one-third more than the others in light of his greater suffering.[44] One-half the amount went to the children and one-quarter each to the wives and parents.

The total amount of the reparations ordered in *Aloeboetoe* came to US$453,102. As in the Honduran cases, the Court ordered the establishment of a trust fund, only this time the Court ordered it to be established in dollars and administered by a Foundation. The Court appointed the members of the Foundation, whose duty was to obtain the best returns for the sums received in reparation and to act as trustee of the funds. The government was ordered to make a one-time contribution of US$4000 or its equivalent in local currency to the operating expenses of the Foundation. Suriname was ordered not to restrict or tax the activities of the Foundation or the operation of the trust funds. Each adult beneficiary may withdraw up to 25% of the sum due to them at the time the Government makes the deposit. The duration of the trust fund is between three and seventeen years, with semi-annual withdrawals permitted. The Foundation is permitted to set up a different system in undescribed special circumstances.

In *Aloeboetoe*, unlike the Honduran cases, the Court ordered specific non-monetary remedies, requiring that the government reopen and staff the school and health dispensary in the area where the victims' families lived. The Court did not discuss the other requests made by the Commission, except to note briefly the continuing obligation of Suriname to inform the families of the location of the bodies of the victims.

The Court again rejected the request for fees and costs, except the costs of the next of kin in searching for the victims. The Court stated that the victims did not appoint anyone to represent them, which was a mistake of fact. In fact, the attorney in the case represented two NGOs and was designated 'legal advisor' to the Commission to facilitate his participation in the case.[45] According to the Court, if the Commission fulfilled its function by 'contracting outside professionals instead of using its own staff' it could not demand attorney's fees.[46]

Gangaram Panday

The Court began to change directions dramatically with its decision in *Gangaram Panday*.[47] Gangaram Panday was illegally detained and died

---

[44] Moral damages for the six was calculated at US$ 29,070; the seventh victim was awarded US$ 38,755. Id. at 85.

[45] David Padilla, attorney with the Commission, says 'the Court made a serious mistake of fact,' in the *Aloeboetoe* case. See D. Padilla, 'Reparations in *Aloeboetoe* v. *Suriname*', 17 *Hum. Rts.Q.* 541, 548–9 (1995).

[46] Id., para. 114.   [47] *Gangaram Panday* case, above n. 8.

while in government custody. The complaint alleged that Suriname violated the victim's rights to life, humane treatment, personal liberty and judicial protection, as well as the general obligation to respect and ensure the Convention rights. The Court unanimously found a violation of the right to personal liberty, but, in its first divided opinion, held 4–3 in respect of the Article 4 claim that government responsibility for the victim's death had not been proved. It also noted that the finding of responsibility for deprivation of personal liberty was reached 'by inference.' Seemingly *because* of this, it awarded nominal damages, not including lost earnings or other indirect damages, and did not award costs.[48] The victim's wife and any children were to be paid US$10,000 or its equivalent in Dutch florins within six months of the date of the judgment. The judgment is inexplicable and clearly wrong; the type and quantum of evidence leading to a finding of responsibility has no bearing on whether costs are awarded, nor on the amount of damages. The amount and type of evidence goes to a determination of whether or not the state is responsible and the degree of wrongfulness of a state's conduct may be a variable in awarding moral damages; in no case does the amount and type of evidence affect the amount of loss suffered by the victims.

Apart from theoretical objections to the Court's decision, the Court's approach undermines respect for the Convention. It signals states accused of violations that they can avoid being held responsible[49] or having to compensate victims if they succeed in withholding or concealing evidence that would prove the allegations.

El Amparo

In the *El Amparo* case,[50] the Court held Venezuela liable to make reparations ('obligada a reparar los daños') and to pay fair compensation to the surviving victims and next of kin, after the government of Venezuela accepted responsibility for the deaths of fourteen fishermen and violations of the rights of two survivors. Venezuela decided not to contest the facts referred to in the complaint. The Court ordered that the state and the Commission decide the reparations and the form and amount of compensation by mutual agreement.

---

[48] 'Since Suriname's responsibility has been inferred, the Court decides to set a nominal amount as compensation. . . . Also based on the fact that Suriname's responsibility has been inferred, the Court considers that it must dismiss the request for an award of costs.' Id. para. 70, 71.

[49] In contrast to its treatment of the evidence in the Honduran cases, where the Court held that the state cannot rely on failure of proof as a defense if the evidence cannot be obtained without the state's cooperation, the Court failed to shift the burden to the government to explain how Gangaram Panday died. By not requiring the government to come forward with evidence on the treatment and fate of the victim during the period he was in government custody, the Court imposed a heavy and undue burden on future litigants.

[50] *El Amparo* (Venezuela), 16 *HRLJ* 9, 2 IHRR 349 (1995).

In submitting the case to the Court, the Commission invoked Convention Article 1(1) (obligation to respect rights) together with Articles 2 (domestic legal effects), 4 (right to life), 5 (right to humane treatment), 8(1) (right to a fair trial), 24 (right to equal protection), 25 (right to judicial protection). In addition to a declaration of Venezuelan responsibility, the Commission asked for investigation and punishment of the actual and 'intellectual' authors of the wrong; a declaration regarding the incompatibility of Article 54(2) and (3) of the Military Code of Justice and an order for its revision; and reparations for the victims together with costs and attorneys' fees.

The Court's judgment reserved the right to review and approve any agreement reached on reparations and to determine the scope of reparations and amount of indemnities, court costs and attorneys' fees should no agreement be reached. Although the Court makes no specific mention of the non-pecuniary reparations asked by the Commission, Judge Cançado Trindade, concurring in the judgment, added that the Court was reserving the right to decide on the compatibility of the sections of the Code of Military Justice with the Convention, and should have so stated.

The parties failed to reach agreement and the Court resumed proceedings. The Commission submitted a brief prepared by the attorneys for the victims in which it reiterated its claim for both pecuniary and non-pecuniary relief. The Commission emphasized the objectives of reparations, which are to re-establish respect for international norms by restoring the *status quo ante*, or paying damages when this is not possible. In this regard, the Commission and the victims viewed it as essential to go beyond the payment of compensation to conform to the requirements of Article 63(1) and the earlier judgment. In fact, only in respect of the right to life and personal integrity was compensation required, because of the irreversible nature of the injury. In regard to the other violations, the Commission argued that *restitutio in integrum* could be accomplished and should be ordered by the Court. Specifically, the Commission repeated its call for government action to reform the Code of Military Justice and investigation and punishment of the authors of the harm, as well as monetary compensation. In addition, satisfaction required unequivocal establishment of the truth, and restoration of the honor of the victims and their families. This required a public admission, published in the principal newspapers of the country and abroad, and a memorial or plaque in memory of the victims.

The claim for monetary compensation contained some new elements. Relying on the distinction made by the Court in the *Aloeboetoe* case between indirect damages and loss of earnings, the Commission sought to include in the damages claim the costs incurred by the victims and their families as consequence of the violations.[51] Without proof of the exact amount incurred by each family, due to the conditions in which they live, the attorneys asked for a lump sum of US$240,000 to be divided equally among the 14 families and two survivors.[52] Lost earnings were calculated for the fishermen on the basis of the rural minimum wage in October 1988, incorporating increases during the subsequent period, and adjusted by the index of inflation. Based on a life expectancy of 69 years, this calculation was said to represent a 'prudent estimate of the damages.' The amount claimed for each of the deceased was between US$5508.59 and US$5558.85; on behalf of each of the two survivors US$2773.87 was claimed.[53] The amount of moral damages was set in reference to the Honduran cases. The brief argued that the psychological damage in *El Amparo* was equal to that in the earlier cases because the families knew that their relatives were murdered and additional violations were committed; the amount requested was US$125,000 per family of those who died and half that amount for the two survivors.[54]

The Court issued its judgment on reparations on 14 September 1996. In regard to the indirect damages (daño emergente), the Court was persuaded by the Venezuelan argument that adequate proof of the costs was lacking and that the sum was disproportionate. Instead of the US$240,000 requested, the Court awarded US$2000 to each of the families and each of the survivors for the costs incurred regarding actions taken within the country.

Compensatory damages were assessed, as the Commission proposed, on the basis of the minimum wage for the country at the time of the incident in 1988 and the normal life expectancy of those who died. A twenty-five percent reduction represented the personal expenses of the deceased. In the case of the survivors the amount represented the period during which they could not work. On the basis of this calculation, the Court awarded

---

[51] The brief listed professional fees for legal and administrative actions, medical costs, photocopying costs, telephone charges, the cost of translation of testimony, notary costs and other costs of legal assistance, plus the cost of publication of press communications.

[52] During oral hearings on reparations, Venezuela labelled the sum demanded 'astronomical' and 'disproportionate.' *El Amparo* case, above n. 8, para. 18.

[53] During the hearings, the victims claimed that the Commission had made an error in calculating the damages based on the minimum wage. After further consultations, the Commission re-calculated the sums and arrived at figures between US$67,000 and US$197,000 for the victims and US$5000 for the survivors. The government objected to the revision, calling it a radical modification that was procedurally incorrect.

[54] According to the brief, all compensatory damages would be paid one-third to the surviving spouse and two-thirds to the children. One-half the moral damages would be given to the children, one-quarter to the spouse and one-quarter to the fathers. In response to the Commission's claim, the government cited the practice of the European Court of Human Rights which has repeatedly stated that recognition of a violation by the Court is normally an equitable reparation for all the damages caused.

between US$23,139.44 and US$28,641.52 to each of the families and US$4,566.41 to each of the survivors.

The Court addressed the Commission's argument equating the moral damages in this case with those in the Honduran cases. The Court rejected using prior cases as precedent, stating that each case must be looked at on its own facts. It noted that, like Suriname in the *Aloeboetoe* case, the Venezuelan government recognized its responsibility in this case. It also cited with approval the Venezuelan reference to the practice of the European Court of Human Rights, where declaratory judgment of responsibility is often viewed as sufficient reparation. In doing so, the Court ignored the clear differences between the damages provision in the European Convention and Article 63(1) of the American Convention. In any event, the Court found that such a judgment would not be adequate reparation for moral damages in this case given the gravity of the violations. It awarded each of the families and each of the survivors US$20,000. All damages were ordered distributed according to the Commission's recommendation.

The treatment of non-pecuniary reparations followed the European Court practice. The Court rejected making an 'abstract' pronouncement on the compatibility of the Military Code of Justice with the Convention and thus refused the Commission's request. Investigation and punishment were again referred to as continuing obligations. For the remaining non-pecuniary measures, the Court found that a determination of Venezuelan responsibility and the judgment on damages constituted adequate reparations.[55]

Finally, the Court once more denied costs and attorneys fees for proceedings before the Commission and the Court, continuing to confuse the representation of the victims with the work of the Commission.

Neira Alegría

The *Neira Alegría*[56] case against Peru was submitted by the Commission in 1990. It alleged violations of Articles 1, 2, 4, 7, 8, and 25 of the Convention in regard to two men detained at a Peruvian correctional facility and accused of terrorism. During or after the military suppression of a riot at the prison the two men disappeared. The Commission sought to have Peru declared responsible for the disappearances and consequently for violations of the Convention. The Commission asked that the Court order Peru to investigate, identify and punish those the perpetrators; identify the next of

---

[55] Judge Antonio Cançado Trindade dissented on the issue of non-pecuniary damages, pointing out that reparations go beyond *restitutio in integrum* and indemnification to include rehabilitation, satisfaction and, importantly, guarantees of non-repetition. In his view this adequately supports the requested non-pecuniary measures as laws may *per se* violate the Convention and need to be considered in contentious cases.

[56] *Neira Alegría et al.,* I/A Court H.R. Series C No.20 (1995); Reparations, above n. 8.

kin of the whereabouts of the disappeared; pay monetary damages; and pay the court costs and attorneys' fees.

The Court unanimously found Peru responsible for violations of the rights cited. Consistent with its prior practice, the Court left it to the parties to agree on compensation and retained jurisdiction over the case, whether or not the agreement was reached. The Court held that Peru must pay the expenditures that the victim's next of kin may have incurred during the national proceedings as well as fair compensation. As usual it insisted that

the Commission cannot demand that expenses incurred as a result of its own internal work structure be reimbursed through assessment of costs. The operation of the human rights organs of the American System is funded by the Member States by means of their annual contributions.[57]

The parties failed to reach agreement and on 19 September 1996 the Court issued its judgment on reparations. As in the *Amparo* case, the Court awarded each family US$2000 as compensation for its costs incurred in legal procedures in Peru. No costs were awarded for proceedings before the Commission or the Court. Lost earnings are calculated based on life span and monthly salary, discounted to present value. If the actual salary is not known, the compensation is based on the minimum monthly salary applicable in the country. The amounts awarded for lost earnings were US$31,065.88, US$30,102.38 and US$26,872.48. The Commission sought US$125,000 moral damages per victim, a sum which the government called 'exorbitant'; the Court awarded US$20,000.

Other Cases

In the *Caballero Delgado and Santana* case,[58] the Court found Colombia responsible for the detention and disappearances of the two named persons. It found that 'reparations should consist of the continuation of judicial proceedings inquiring into the disappearance of Isidro Caballero-Delgado and Maria del Carmen Santana and punishment of those responsible in conformance with Colombia domestic law.'[59] It also decided that Colombia was obligated to pay fair compensation to the relatives of the victims and to reimburse the expenses they had incurred in their actions before the Colombian authorities in relation to this proceedings. Once

[57] *Neira Alegría*, id. para. 87, quoting *Aloeboetoe*, above n. 8, para 114.
[58] Judgment of 8 Dec. 1995, Annual Report of the Inter-American Court of Human Rights, OAS/Ser.L/V/III.33, doc 4, 22 Jan. 1996, 125, 17 *HRLJ* 24, 3 IHRR 548 (1996).
[59] Id. para. 69.

more, the Court reminded the Commission that it cannot demand reimbursement of expenses incurred as a result of its own internal work.

The compensation and costs phase of the case remains open.[60] The Commission has asked the Court for reform of the penal law of Columbia as it regulates *habeas corpus* and disappearances; investigation and punishment of those responsible; and actions to repair the damage caused to the honor and good name of the victims and their families. In damages, the Commission has asked for moral damages in the amount of US$125,000 each for the two disappeared, based on the precedents in the Court's jurisprudence to date. In addition, the Commission seeks moral and material damages for the families of the victims.

The Court discontinued the *Maqueda* case due to a friendly settlement achieved after submission of the case to the Court.[61] The victim alleged he was being wrongfully imprisoned by the government of Argentina. The government agreed to release him. In turn, the applicant waived all claims to monetary damages and agreed to petition the Court to discontinue the case. The Court found the agreement to be consistent with the Convention in that the principal matter was the right to freedom which had been restored and granted the petition, although reserving the power to reopen and proceed with the case should any change occur that would so warrant.

SUMMARY AND CONCLUSIONS

The Court has been consistent in several aspects of its treatment of reparations. First, all awards begin with a declaratory judgment regarding the human rights that have been violated. Second, apart from the anomalous *Gangaram Panday* case, the Court has consistently invited the two sides to reach agreement on reparations and the amount of damages. Third, the Court generally awards costs for actual expenditures in internal legal and administrative procedures at the national level, while denying all costs and legal fees for proceedings before the Inter-American Commission and Court.

Other aspects of the Court's decisions are less consistent. Some are hard to justify. First, the Court is reluctant to utilize its power to order non-pecuniary reparations, although these can be extremely important in remedying human rights violations. In some cases, applicants may be more concerned to know the truth, such as the whereabouts of the disappeared

---

[60] The Court also delivered an opinion on 2 Feb. 1996 in the case of Garrido and Baigorria against Argentina. The state accepted responsibility for the disappearances of the two individuals. The Court ordered the parties to negotiate an agreement on reparations. See above, n. 9, judgment in *Garrido Baigorria* case.

[61] *Maqueda* case, Resolution of 17 Jan. 1995, Annual Report, id. at 32, 16 *HRLJ* 151, 3 IHRR 355 (1996).

victim, than they will be about receiving monetary compensation. In addition, an award of financial compensation without requiring remedial action may signal to a government that it is permitted to violate human rights provided it has sufficient tax revenues to pay for the resulting damages. Non-pecuniary measures serve to reinforce the validity of the obligation breached, forcing the responsible state to acknowledge responsibility. They also provide a measure of satisfaction to persons injured by the state and serve to send a message to society that the violations will not be tolerated or repeated.

The Court also has been criticized for not advancing the international law of reparations by creating a general fund to pay victims of gross and systematic human rights abuses.[62] It is argued that the result creates an inequity between similarly situated victims because not all cases can reach the Court and thus only some victims will receive compensation. Honduran Human Rights Commissioner Leo Valladares, in his official report on disappearances in Honduras, called it patently unfair 'that only those whose cases were before the Inter-American Court received reparations, and that all of the proven cases of disappearances should receive economic reparations.'[63] It is questionable, however, whether the Court could award damages to parties not before it. The procedure is designed for individual victims to bring cases, but if the Court decides in one case that compensation must be paid the victims, it serves notice on the government in regard to similar cases that reparations are due. In addition, class actions may be filed on behalf of all victims. The Convention allows petitions to be filed with the Commission not only by the victim or relative of the victim, but by 'any non-governmental entity legally recognized in one or more member states of the OAS'.[64] The Commission must still decide whether to refer the case to the Court, but, should it do so, this type of 'mass tort action' would allow the Court to establish a fund as it did in the *Aloeboetoe* case. United Nations Special Rapporteur Theodoor Van Boven calls for such a procedure, stating it is 'necessary that, in addition to individual means of reparation, adequate provision be made to entitle groups of victims or victimized communities to present collective claims for damages and to receive collective reparation accordingly.'[65]

---

[62] J. Pasqualucci, 'The Inter-American Human Rights System: Establishing Precedents and Procedure in Human Rights Law', 26 *Inter Am. L Rev*. 297, 331–2 (1994–95).

[63] The National Commissioner For The Protection of Human Rights in Honduras: *The Facts Speak For Themselves* (New York, 1994), 234.

[64] American Convention, Art. 44.1

[65] *Study Concerning the Right to Restitution, Compensation and Rehabilitation for Victims of Gross Violations of Human Rights and Fundamental Freedoms, final report submitted by Mr. Theo Van Boven, Special rapporteur to the Sub-Commission on Prevention of Discrimination and Protection of Minorities*, UN Hum. Rts. Comm., 45th Sess., UN Doc. E/CN.4/Sub.2/1993, sec. VII.

The Court's approach to compensatory damages is largely based on the arguments presented by the Commission. From the beginning, the Commission has articulated a standard which it has failed to apply in omitting claims for damages resulting from the loss of personal services of the victim. It also has underestimated the impact of inflation. The Commission in general has relied too heavily on the presentations of victims and their attorneys, failing to develop a coherent and consistent theory and practice of damages.

The standard and approach of the *Lusitania* cases offers a framework for developing a theoretical and practical approach to damages. Compensatory damages should repair all the proximate direct and indirect consequences of the harm. Moreover, with a dual focus on suffering of the victim and wrongfulness of government conduct, it seems that moral damages may partially substitute for punitive damages.

The greatest disappointment in the Court's approach thus far is in regard to costs and attorneys' fees. The recent approach of the Court, awarding US$2000 to each claimant for costs incurred at the national level, is partly due to the lack of proof presented by the Commission and the victims. It also seems that the claims made in the *El Amparo* case were excessive; it is hard to avoid the suspicion that they constituted an effort to receive attorneys fees for work done at the Commission and the Court, as well in national proceedings. If this is the case, the Court itself is largely responsible, due to its persistent denial of attorneys fees for the victims' lawyers in Court proceedings.

The Court apparently fails to see the difference between the interests of the Commission and those of the victims, although this was recognized in the initial proceeding before the Court. In the *Viviana Gallardo* case,[66] the Court spoke of the need to reconcile the interest of the victims that the full enjoyment of their rights be protected and assured; the need to safeguard the institutional integrity of the system; and the interest of the government in a speedy judicial process.[67] In that proceeding, the Court noted that no person is entitled to submit cases to the Court because individuals do not have standing. The system requires 'that the Convention be interpreted in favor of the individual, who is the object of international protection.'[68] The Commission's role is likened to that of the 'Ministerio Publico' which carries out an initial investigation, attempts a friendly settlement and proposes appropriate recommendations to remedy the violation it has found to exist.

Victims need their own attorneys before the Commission and before the

---

[66] *In the Matter of Viviana Gallardo et al.*, I/A Court H.R. Series A and B No.1 (1984), 2 *HRLJ* 108, 238.
[67] Id. para. 13.
[68] Id. para. 16.

Court; indeed, this may be required for due process.[69] Procedures before the Commission 'have not been created for the sole benefit of the States, but also in order to allow for the exercise of important individual rights, especially those of the victims.' The victims and their families also must be able to recover costs and fees, otherwise the goal of *restitutio in integrum* is defeated.

In issuing its judgments on reparations, the Court should recall that Article 63(1) was deliberately expanded to ensure protection for the victims of human rights violations. These persons will only be able to vindicate their rights if they have access to legal assistance and that assistance will only come if it is compensated. To ensure *restitutio in integrum*, the Court must liberalize its views on attorneys fees and costs. The Commission represents the institutional interests in the system; the victims deserve and are entitled to their own representation. Where the state has caused the wrong, it should pay for the procedures necessary to achieve a remedy.

[69] See Article 8, American Convention on Human Rights.

7

The Interaction between the Political Actors of the OAS, the Commission and the Court

VERÓNICA GÓMEZ

INTRODUCTION

International or regional organs for the protection of human rights tend to be prisoners of the unending paradox of having been created and being nourished directly by the subjects they are meant to control. Although they may confer a number of powers on these organs, states both retain control over their functioning, by electing their members and allocating their budgets, and may play an important role in enforcing their decisions. This paradox may create institutional and political tension and thus interfere with the work of these organs and their effectiveness. The inter-American system of human rights protection is an interesting scenario for the analysis of this kind of tension.

This Chapter is an attempt to explore the interaction between the Inter-American Commission on Human Rights (the Commission), the Inter-American Court of Human Rights (the Court) and the Permanent Council and the General Assembly of the Organization of American States (OAS) and individual member States and explain its impact on the functioning and effectiveness of the inter-American system of protection. Three different kinds of tension will be evaluated: those that arise as human rights standards are interpreted and applied during the individual petition procedure before the Commission and in the advisory and contentious jurisdiction of the Court; those that derive from the need to make the work of the Commission and the Court effective; and, lastly, those that result from the exercise by member States of their control over the functioning of the organs, in respect of their composition, budget and, to some extent, mandate. Finally, consideration will be given to current OAS proposals to reform the human rights System. The rules and the players of the system will be briefly described as a prelude to the analysis of their interaction.

The Rules

In 1945, the American States had decided to call for the drafting of a declaration and a convention on the rights and duties of man.[1] The American Declaration[2] was adopted by resolution at the 1948 Bogota Conference where the Charter of the OAS was signed. The American Convention[3] was finally adopted in 1969 and entered into force in 1978. These instruments, together with the Statutes of the Commission[4] and the Court[5] and the resolutions issued by the General Assembly, constitute the legal corpus of the system of protection.

It is pertinent to note that the OAS Charter has been amended several times. The 1967 Protocol of Buenos Aires[6] changed the structure of the Organization and elevated the status of the Inter-American Commission on Human Rights to that of one of the principal organs of the OAS. In 1985, the Protocol of Cartagena de Indias[7] incorporated the promotion and consolidation of representative democracy—based on respect for the principle of non-intervention—as an essential purpose of the OAS and also strengthened the powers of the Permanent Council and the Secretary General. The 1992 Protocol of Washington[8] allows for the suspension of the right of a Member State whose democratically constituted government has been overthrown by force, to participate in the Councils of the Organization. The 1993 Protocol of Managua[9] established the Inter-American Council for Integral Development, which has as its main purpose the promotion of cooperation among the American states with a view of attaining development and eradicating poverty.

As regards the purposes of the OAS, these are presently focused on peace and security, democracy, the settlement of disputes and the promo-

[1] Final Act of the Inter-American Conference on Problems of War and Peace, Mexico City, Feb.-Mar. 1945.
[2] See Appendix II.   [3] See Appendix III.
[4] See Appendix IV.   [5] See Appendix VI.
[6] Protocol of Amendment to the Charter of the Organization of American States 'Protocol of Buenos Aires' adopted at Buenos Aires, Argentina, 27 Feb. 1967 at the Third Special Inter-American Conference. The Protocol entered into force 27 Feb. 1970. OASTS No. 1–A.
[7] Protocol of Amendment to the Charter of the Organization of American States 'Protocol of Cartagena de Indias', adopted at Cartagena de Indias, Colombia on 5 Dec. 1985 at the Fourteenth Special Session of the General Assembly. The Protocol entered into force on 16 Nov. 1988. OASTS No. 66.
[8] Protocol of Amendment to the Charter of the Organization of American States 'Protocol of Washington' adopted at Washington DC, 14 Dec. 1992 at the Sixteenth Special Session of the General Assembly of the OAS. The Protocol entered into force in Sept. 1997.
[9] Protocol of Amendment to the Charter of the Organization of American States 'Protocol of Managua' adopted at Managua, Nicaragua 10 June 1993 at the Nineteenth Special Session of the General Assembly of the OAS. The Protocol entered into force on 29 Jan. 1996.

tion of economic, social and cultural development. The Summit of the Americas, held in Miami in December 1994, entrusted the OAS with a new agenda, including the strengthening of democracy and the system of protection of human rights.[10]

The Players

The inter-American system of human rights protection is in force throughout the 35 Member States of the OAS. Membership extends from North America and the Caribbean—with their prevailing Anglo-Saxon institutional frameworks—to Suriname—the ex-Dutch colony—and Central and South America. The incorporation of the Caribbean States within the OAS has been encouraged by their growing representation within the organs of the Organization, including those of the human rights system. However, the OAS is still largely a Latin American organisation, shaped by the problems and idiosyncrasies of that particular group of States.

The Member States mainly gather in the context of three political organs: the General Assembly, the Permanent Council and the Meetings of Consultation of Ministers of Foreign Affairs. The General Assembly is the supreme organ of the OAS.[11] It meets once a year when the representatives of the Member States meet for its regular session in order to decide on issues of functioning, general action and policy. The Assembly is empowered to determine the structure and functions of the organs of the OAS and, consequently, its decisions have been crucial throughout the history of the Commission. The Assembly created the Commission by resolution in 1959, approved its original statute in 1960 and its amendment in 1979. It elects the members of the Commission and the judges of the Court and approves the budget and annual reports of both institutions.

The Permanent Council is composed of one representative of each Member State of the OAS with the rank of Ambassador.[12] Apart from seeing to the maintenance of friendly relations among the Member States, it takes up any matter entrusted to it by the General Assembly or the Meeting of Consultation of Ministers of Foreign Affairs. Most important, it acts as the preparatory committee of the General Assembly, reviewing, *inter alia*, legal and budgetary matters.[13] By virtue of the amendments to the Charter introduced by the Protocol of Cartagena de Indias,[14] the Permanent Council has assumed the role of reviewing the annual report of

---

[10] See IACHR Annual Report 1994, 215.

[11] Art. 54 of the OAS Charter.   [12] Art. 80 of the OAS Charter.

[13] The Committee on Juridical and Political Affairs of the Permanent Council reviews the annual report of the Commission and the Court and its Committee on Administrative and Budgetary Affairs decides on their budget.

[14] Arts. 54.f and 90.f of the OAS Charter.

the Commission and the Court before its submission to the General Assembly.

Member States also gather in the Meetings of Consultation of Ministers of Foreign Affairs. These *ad hoc* meetings, first established in 1938, are held at the request of any Government whenever problems of an urgent nature and of common interest to the Member States arise.[15]

For the purposes of this analysis, only three of the institutional organs of the OAS will be described: the General Secretariat and, of course, the Inter-American Commission and Court of Human Rights.

The General Secretariat, which is based in Washington DC, is the central and permanent organ of the OAS. It has a number of administrative, secretarial and budgetary functions,[16] besides carrying out the duties entrusted to it by the General Assembly, the Meeting of Consultation of Ministers of Foreign Affairs, or the Councils of the Organization, namely, the Permanent Council and the Inter-American Council for Integral Development.[17] It is directed by a Secretary General[18] elected by the General Assembly for a five-year term.[19] He/she may participate, with a right to speak but without a vote, in all meetings of the Organization and may bring to the attention of the General Assembly or the Permanent Council any matter which, in his/her opinion, might threaten the peace and security of the Hemisphere or the development of the Member States.[20] The Secretary General also has the task of determining the number of officers and employees of the General Secretariat, including those of the Secretariat of the Inter-American Commission on Human Rights, and is responsible for appointing them, regulating their powers and duties and fixing their remuneration.[21]

The Inter-American Commission on Human Rights is an organ with powers of a unique nature. Since its creation in 1959, it has gradually cumulated multiple functions of an advisory, drafting, monitoring and quasi-judicial character by virtue of the OAS Charter,[22] its Statute[23] and the American Convention on Human Rights.[24] Its mandate is very broad and involves tasks which, as time goes by, are more and more difficult to harmonize. These functions are performed by seven independent individuals who meet for eight weeks a year in Washington DC or in the venue of an *in loco* visit.[25] In terms of its workload, in the area of individual

---

[15] Art. 61 of the OAS Charter.
[17] Art. 107 of the OAS Charter.
[19] Art. 108 of the OAS Charter.
[21] Art. 113 of the OAS Charter.
[16] Art. 112 of the OAS Charter.
[18] Art. 109 of the OAS Charter.
[20] Art. 110 of the OAS Charter.
[22] Art. 106 of the OAS Charter.
[23] Arts. 18, 19 and 20 of the Statute of the Commission.
[24] Art. 41 of the American Convention.
[25] Art. 15, Commission Regulations provides that the Commission 'shall meet for a period not to exceed a total of eight weeks' per year.

petitions, the Commission has opened more than twelve thousand cases and published almost five hundred reports. As for its other main area of activity, the Commission conducts several *in loco* visits a year and prepares 'country reports' on the human rights situations in the states concerned in the light of them.

In 1979 the Inter-American Court of Human Rights joined the Commission in the task of interpreting and enforcing the American Convention. The Court has a broad judicial mandate in contentious cases which includes the power to declare a State party in breach of the Convention and to ensure the enjoyment of the right violated and to order reparation.[26] It also has an advisory jurisdiction by which it may render interpretations of the American Convention and of any other human rights treaty to which OAS Member States are parties.[27] This jurisdiction can be invoked by any Member State of the OAS—not only States party to the Convention—and by any of the main organs of the OAS—including, of course, the Commission. These tasks are performed by seven judges who meet on a part-time basis at the seat of the Court in San José, Costa Rica.

PROBLEMS OF LAW AND POLICY IN THE FUNCTIONING OF THE COMMISSION AND THE COURT

From a legal perspective, the most interesting examples of the tension in the interaction between the human rights organs of the inter-American system and the Member States of the OAS are to be found in the course of the study of individual petitions filed with the Commission and the exercise by the Court of its advisory and contentious jurisdiction. Many of the Member States have experienced periods of political instability, terrorism and military dictatorship accompanied by gross violations of fundamental rights. Most of these States have also experienced transitional periods of return to democracy and have faced problems relating to accountability and the restoration of law and order. The role of the Commission is to establish a dialogue with these States as they experience these historic and political developments and to do so on the basis of the human rights standards in the American Declaration and the American Convention. The attempts of the participant States, the Commission and the Court to articulate their position in this dialogue in the interpretation and application of the rules of the inter-American human rights system merit analysis.

The Study of Individual Petitions by the Commission

The interaction between the Commission and a Member State against which a case has been opened can be observed in two consecutive stages of the

---

[26] Art. 63 of the American Convention.   [27] Art. 64 of the American Convention.

consideration of the complaint: those of cooperation in the response to requests for information and of legal debate on the question whether the Declaration or the Convention has been infringed.

Cooperation with the Commission seems to depend mainly on the institutional and political situation of the State involved in a particular case. During many years, particularly during the seventies and early eighties, non-cooperation—meaning not only the silence of the government[28] but also its failure to provide relevant information on the case in its response to the complaint[29]—seemed to be the rule. This was the distinctive reaction of non-democratic or unstable regimes which had never been scrutinized by an international quasi-judicial organ.

As a response, the Commission supplemented the obligation to provide information requested on individual cases[30] with a rule of the presumption of truth. Article 42 of the Regulations of the Commission provides that, as long as other evidence does not lead to a different conclusion, the facts reported in a petition can be presumed to be true whenever the government fails to provide information within the permitted time period.[31] This rule was a crucial procedural tool during the period in which the Commission dealt mostly with gross and systematic violations. It provided the basis for Commission findings in place of a fact-finding stage in an important number of reports published during the seventies—under the Declaration and during the eighties—under the Declaration and the Convention. The rationale for the presumption of truth rule is the assumption that States have complete control over the verification of facts which occur within their territory. Consequently, without their cooperation, the Commission is limited to analysing only the available evidence in order to find whether the Declaration or the Convention have been violated. The

---

[28] See, for instance, Res. 29/82, Case 7473 (Bolivia); Res. 20/82 Cases 2931 (Chile), IACHR Annual Report 1981–2, 34 and 47, respectively.

[29] The Commission has considered as non-cooperation replies which are a mere acknowledgement of receipt (see, for instance, Res. 37/82, Case 2401(Haiti) and Res. 52/82, Case 5154 (Nicaragua) IACHR Annual Report 1982–3, 67 and 102, respectively); protocol answers not providing relevant information (see Res. 12/80, Case 3358 (Argentina), IACHR Annual Report 1979–80, 74); confirmation of facts without further explanation (see Res. 41/83, Case 3405 (Haiti) IACHR Annual Report 1983–4, 48) global denial of the facts alleged in several petitions (see Resns. 20/78, 21/78, 22/78, 27/78, Cases 2155, 2209, 2206, 2884 (Argentina) IACHR Annual Report 1979–80, 46–57). See M. Pinto, *La denuncia ante la Comisión Interamericana de Derechos Humanos* (Buenos Aires, 1993), 101.

[30] See Arts. 48 and 43 of the Convention. See also Report 26/92, Case 10287 (El Salvador), IACHR Annual Report 1992–3, 89.

[31] The Commission is very lenient relating to compliance with procedural requirements and, therefore, this presumption does not operate automatically on the expiry of the permitted 90 day period. Usually, a state receives a warning providing for a further period. See, for instance, Report 9/94, Cases 11102 et al (Haiti), IACHR Annual Report 1993, 313.

Commission has applied this principle confidently, mainly based on its direct knowledge of the general situation of particular countries assessed during *in loco* visits. Recently, it has introduced a three-part criterion to evaluate the facts presented by a petitioner whenever the rule on the presumption of truth applies: the petitioner's statement of the facts will be accepted if it satisfies the criterion of specificity, consistency and credibility.[32]

With the changed political context of the nineties, non-cooperation has become less frequent. During the last two years the Commission has published only three reports where the facts of the case were assessed on the basis of Article 42 of its Regulations, out of a total of 15 reports on individual cases. These cases involved the violation of the right to personal liberty, humane treatment and due process by Guatemala,[33] Peru[34] and El Salvador.[35] After ten years of non-cooperation, the Government of El Salvador expressed its intention to cooperate with the Commission in 1992. However, in spite of receiving an update on the facts of the cases being processed, the Government did not answer the charges against it or comply with the recommendations of the Commission.[36]

Once a dialogue between the petitioner, the Commission and the State involved in a case has been established, the legal debate begins. States have responded to the allegations made before the Commission with a full range of denials, justifications and partial acknowledgments.[37] The arguments used by the governments have varied with the changing political context and with the intended audience. States used also to employ a double discourse. For a domestic audience, they used to justify the righteousness and necessity of their actions. The justification for State-sponsored violence was to send a message to the population to prevent it from collaborating with political opponents. In contrast, in the international arena, they used to deny facts and/or responsibility, particularly before organs such as the Commission and the Court that were applying international human rights standards to the facts. Before the organs of the inter-American human rights system, the literal denial of the allegations made by a petitioner was the standard response during the seventies and early eighties. In recent years the repertoire of State responses has gained in variety. Denial of facts and responsibility appear together with arguments relating to jurisdiction, continuity of the State, State

---

[32] See for instance, Report 13/96, Case 10948 (El Salvador) IACHR Annual Report 1995, 106. See further, Cerna, 98 above.

[33] Report 25/94, Case 10508 (Guatemala) IACHR Annual Report 1994, 46.

[34] Report 5/96, Case 10970 (Peru) IACHR Annual Report 1995, 157.

[35] Report 13/96, Case 10948 (El Salvador) IACHR Annual Report 1995, 101.

[36] IACHR Report on the Situation on Human Rights in El Salvador (1994), 44.

[37] See Cohen, 'Government Responses to Human Rights Reports: Claims, Denials and Counterclaims' 18 *HRQ* 517 (1996).

sovereignty[38] and the separation of powers, all of these arguments including some kind of partial acknowledgment of the facts.

The Dialogue before the Court

Advisory Jurisdiction

The advisory jurisdiction of the Court has provided the Member States with the opportunity of using the System without running the risks involved in an adjudication process. The Commission and the Member States have repeatedly invoked the advisory jurisdiction of the Court, and even non-governmental organisations have been allowed to participate in the legal debate. The Court has been consulted about issues regarding jurisdiction,[39] compatibility of domestic legislation with the Convention,[40] the interpretation of the substantive guarantees[41] and even the procedural rules regarding the study of petitions before the Commission.[42]

The positions of the participants in the dialogue are usually clear: the Commission and non-governmental organisations advocate the widest interpretation of the Convention in favour of human rights; the Member States have heterogeneous positions ranging from the advocacy of restrictive interpretations[43] to support for wide interpretations which do not interfere with their policy or interests.[44] Curiously—yet perhaps predictably—advisory proceedings seem to have developed into a forum where the Member States and the Commission defend antagonistic positions.[45]

---

[38] See, for example, Res. 1/90, where Mexico argued that the authenticity of local elections could not be reviewed by an international jurisdiction. In its view, by opening and analysing the cases at issue, the Commission was infringing the right of self determination and political autonomy of Mexico, therefore violating the principle of non-intervention enshrined in the OAS Charter. IACHR Annual Report 1989–90, 103–5.

[39] See, for instance, *Interpretation of the Meaning of 'Other Treaties' in Art. 63 of the American Convention, Advisory Opinion OC-1/82*, I/A Court H.R. Series A & B No.1 (1982) 3 *HRLJ* 140 (1982).

[40] See, for instance, *Proposed Amendments to the Naturalization Provisions of the Political Constitution of Costa Rica, Advisory Opinion OC-4/84*, I/A Court H.R. Series A & B No.4 (1984), 5 *HRLJ* 161 (1984).

[41] *Character and Scope of the Right to Reply or Correction Recognized in the American Convention, Advisory Opinion OC-7/85*, I/A Court H.R. Series A No.7 (1986), 7 *HRLJ* 238 (1986).

[42] *Certain Attributes of the Inter-American Commission on Human Rights (Arts. 41, 42, 46, 47, 50 and 51 of the American Convention) Advisory Opinion OC-13/93*, I/A Court H.R. Series A No.13 (1993), 14 *HRLJ* 252 (1993). (Hereinafter *OC-13/93.*)

[43] See, for instance, the position of the United States in *Interpretation of the American Declaration on the Rights and Duties of Man within the Framework of Art. 64 of the American Convention on Human Rights, Advisory Opinion OC-10/89*, I/A Court H.R. Series A No.10 (1989), 11 *HRLJ* 118 (1990).

[44] See, for instance, the position of Uruguay, ibid.

[45] On the quasi-contentious nature of the advisory proceedings see M. Reisman, and J. Koven Levit, 'Fact-Finding Initiatives for the Inter-American Court of Human Rights' in R. Nieto Navia (ed.) *La Corte y el Sistema Interamericano de Derechos Humanos* (San José, 1994), 453.

The issues raised in Advisory Opinion No. 13 are a good example. Uruguay and Argentina invoked the advisory jurisdiction of the Court to ask for an opinion on issues 'concern[ing] concrete cases that have been dealt with by the Commission . . .'[46] Certain questions relating to the procedure applicable to complaints filed with the Commission were asked. The two questions that are discussed below dealt with the competence of the Commission. The first question asked whether the Commission is 'competent to assess and offer an opinion on the legality of domestic legislation adopted pursuant to the provisions of the Constitution, insofar as the "reasonableness", "advisability", or "authenticity" of such legislation is concerned.'[47] In the opinion of the Court, the adoption of laws which do not conform to the Convention constitutes a violation of the Treaty and, therefore, where they are adopted the Commission has the same powers that it would have if confronted with other types of violations.[48] The Court noted that a statute adopted according to constitutional requirements is not necessarily compatible with human rights standards[49] and in such cases the Commission could consider the norm which does not conform to the Convention as unreasonable or unadvisable. What the Commission cannot do is rule as to how a norm is adopted in the municipal sphere.[50]

The second question requested an opinion on whether it was appropriate for the Commission to address the merits of an individual petition which has been declared inadmissible. This question was a clear reaction to Report 90/90[51] where the Commission, after declaring the case inadmissible due to lack of exhaustion of domestic remedies, recommended that Uruguay adopt a number of measures.[52] In the Commission's view, its recommendations were justified by 'reasons of moral order and social justice'.[53] Predictably, the Court considered that a declaration of inadmissibility precludes any decision on the merits of a case.[54] The Court explained that Commission should not exercise its general attributes, which empower it to

---

[46] *OC-13/93*, para.3.   [47] Ibid.
[48] Ibid., paras. 26 and 27.
[49] Ibid., para. 28.   [50] Ibid. para., 29.
[51] Report 90/90, Case 9893 (Uruguay), IACHR Annual Report 1990–1, 77. See also Report 27/93, on inadmissibility on the grounds of lack of exhaustion of local remedies, where the Commission 'invited' the government of Canada to consider granting permission to stay to the petitioner—a widow with five children, from Trinidad, trying to avoid deportation—until the conclusion of the succession of her husband. IACHR Annual Report 1993, 62.
[52] The recommendations included the repeal of certain legislation and the revocation of its effects. In order to follow up compliance with its recommendations, the Commission further requested Uruguay to incorporate a chapter on the subject in its annual report to the then Inter-American Economic and Social Council. Report 90/90, Case 9893 (Uruguay), IACHR Annual Report 1990–1, 91.
[53] Ibid.
[54] OC-13/93, para. 42. 'It is a matter of a case which has been closed and to rule on the merits afterwards would be the equivalent of the Commission ruling on a communication without having received it' ibid., para. 43.

make recommendations to the Member States,[55] in the context of the procedure governing the admissibility of an individual petition.[56]

The questions relating to the competence of the Commission discussed above reveal some disagreement regarding the scope if its powers and imply strong criticism of its legal competence. The former Executive Secretary of the Commission, Edith Márquez, has criticized Argentina and Uruguay for trying to subvert decisions taken by the Commission by requesting these opinions from the Court.[57] In her opinion, the attempts to review the work of the Commission by invoking the advisory jurisdiction of the Court constitute 'inconvenient precedents' which could generate 'unsolved disagreements.'[58]

However, this was not the first occasion on which the Court has virtually 'reviewed'—in a broad sense—certain aspects of the decisions of the Commission through its advisory jurisdiction. For instance, in Advisory Opinion No 5, the Court stated that the Commission should have submitted a particular case—the *Schmidt* Case[59] against Costa Rica—to its contentious jurisdiction.[60] It also stated that the Commission had unreasonably delayed its final report on a number of cases by giving repeated extensions to the Government of Costa Rica to comply with the recommendations of its preliminary report.[61] In such instances, the tension on the operation of the inter-American system of human rights is not between the Member States and the Commission and the Court, but between these two supervisory organs themselves.

Contentious Jurisdiction

Predictably, State Parties have been reluctant to submit cases for adjudication. Consequently, the activation of the contentious jurisdiction of the Court has depended on the discretion of the Commission. It has been argued that during this phase the role of the Commission is that of a

---

[55] Art. 41 (b), Convention contains a general power, distinct from the Commission's competence to consider individual petitions, to 'make recommendation to the governments of member states'.

[56] *OC-13/93*, para. 44.

[57] E. Márquez Rodríguez, 'Las relaciones entre la Comisión y la Corte Interamericana de Derechos Humanos' in R. Nieto Navia, (ed.) *La Corte y el Sistema Interamericano de Derechos Humanos* (San José, 1994), 305. [58] Ibid., 306.

[59] Res. 17/84, Case 9178 (Costa Rica), IACHR Annual Report 1984–5, 51.

[60] *Compulsory Membership in an Association Prescribed by Law for the Practice of Journalism, Advisory Opinion OC-5/85,* I/A Court H.R. Series A No.5, paras. 25 and 26 (1985), 5 *HRLJ* 161 (1985).

[61] *Compatibility of Draft Legislation with Art. 8(2) of the American Convention on Human Rights, Advisory Opinion OC-12/91,* I/A Court H.R. Series A. No.12, paras. 26 and 27 (1991) 13 *HRLJ* 149 (1992).

'representative of the social interest',[62] *ministerio público*[63] or 'an initiator or facilitator'.[64] In any event, the Commission is the only vehicle of the interests of the petitioners, who do not have *locus standi* to appear before the Court. Naturally, these interests are antagonistic to those of the respondent State. In this context, the perception of the Commission as a quasi-judicial organ is affected by its role before the Court, which involves it in virtually re-arguing the original case and—sometimes—defending its findings. The best example of the effects of this perception is the tone of the remarks of the Peruvian Government in the context of the *Cayara* Case: 'Once it has filed its suit, the Commission's legal status is transformed, *de facto* and *de jure*, from that of a general investigative agency, impartial both to governments and to petitioners, into that of opponent of the respondent Government. In other words, upon the mere filing of a complaint it becomes the procedural adversary of the government.'[65] In brief, the dialogue which takes place during the contentious procedure is much influenced by the perception of the Commission as a litigator before the Court.

When confronted with the prospect of international adjudication, the first reaction of States usually consists of challenging the jurisdiction of the Court. Apart from the requirements regarding jurisdiction *ratione materiae*, *personae* and *temporis*, the respondent States have challenged compliance with Article 61(2) of the American Convention. This provides that in order for the Court to hear a case, the procedures set forth in Articles 48 to 50, including those concerning admissibility, friendly settlement and the issuance of a preliminary report, must have been completed while the case is before the Commission. Not surprisingly, compliance with this requirement has been challenged before the Court by States since the very first contentious cases.

The Commission and the Court have disagreed on the nature of the Court's role in respect of Article 61(2). In the preliminary objections phase of the Honduran Cases, the Commission argued that the Court did not have jurisdiction to review whether the rules governing the procedure before the Commission had been respected, particularly those related to the admissibility of a case.[66] In contrast, the Court considered that it was empowered to rule upon all matters relating to the Convention, including the proper completion of the procedures before the Commission in Articles

---

[62] H. Fix-Zamudio, 'The Inter-American Court of Human Rights' 20 *Canadian Council of International Law. Proceedings of the Annual Conference* 195 (1991), 211.

[63] See the Separate Opinion of Judge Rodolfo Piza Escalante in *In the Matter of Viviana Gallardo et al*, I/A Court H.R., No G 101/81 Series B (1981), 2 *HRLJ* 328.

[64] M. Reisman, & J. Koven Levit, op. cit., n. 45, 447.

[65] IACHR *Complaints and Report on the Cayara Case* (1993), 53.

[66] *Velásquez Rodríguez*, Preliminary Objections, I/A Court of H.R. Series C No.1, para. 28 (1987).

48 to 50 of the Convention, upon which the Court's jurisdiction in a case depends.[67] Since that time, the Court has reviewed the Commission's decisions on the exhaustion of remedies and its exercise of discretion in the friendly settlement procedure[68] when a challenge is presented by the State Parties during the preliminary objections phase of a case.

So far, the Court has upheld its jurisdiction in all of the cases in which States have challenged the procedures conducted by the Commission, with one exception: the dismissal of the *Cayara* Case.[69] The case is a remarkable one that merits detailed consideration. The records of the case show that in February 1991[70] the Commission issued a preliminary report under Article 50 on four joint cases relating the massacre at Cayara.[71] In its report, the Commission declared Peru to be in violation of the rights to life, humane treatment, personal liberty, judicial protection and property and it expressed its intention to submit the case to the Court.[72] In its reply, Peru highlighted a number of procedural irregularities which, in its view, invalidated the investigation of the case. It argued that the Commission had failed to transmit all of the pertinent parts and attachments of its report to the government, thereby depriving it of its right to defence. On this basis, it requested the Commission to make the appropriate 'procedural corrections' and not to submit the case to the Court.[73] This reply reached the Commission on 3 June 1991, the same day on which the case was referred by the Commission to the Court by fax. A few days later, the Commission requested permission from the Court to withdraw the case in order to 'reconsider it and possibly present it again.'[74] Once the Commis-

---

[67] Ibid., para. 29.

[68] *Caballero Delgado and Santana*, Preliminary Objections, I/A Court H.R., para. 27 (1994), 15 *HRLJ* 176 (1994) 2 IHRR 393 (1995).

[69] *Cayara*, Preliminary Objections, I/A Court H.R. Series C No 14 (1993), 14 *HRLJ* 159 (1993), 1–1 IHRR 175 (1994).

[70] Report 29/91, Cases 10264, 10206, 10276, 10446 (Peru) approved by the Commission at its 1102nd Meeting on 20 Feb. 1991, reproduced in IACHR *Complaints and Reports on the Cayara Case* (1993), 58.

[71] On the night of 13 May 1988, a Peruvian Army convoy was ambushed by Shining Path near Erusco in the district of Cayara. Four soldiers were killed. In a reprisal which lasted for several months, military troops arbitrarily executed 33 people, made seven others disappear and tortured six more persons. In addition to the above, an indeterminate number of peasants from the area were subjected to arbitrary execution, forced disappearance and torture in an attempt to obtain information. The property belonging to the victims was destroyed or damaged, as well as some public buildings. A number of key witnesses were also murdered. The Commission received a complaint about these events on 17 Nov. 1988, IACHR, *Complaints and Reports on the Cayara Case* (1993), 3.

[72] *Cayara*, loc. cit. at n. 69, para.23.					[73] Ibid., para 25.

[74] The Chairman of the Commission, Mr Patrick L. Robinson, sent a note to the President of the Court on 20 June 1991 as follows: 'I take the liberty of informing Your Excellency that the Commission, acting at the request of the Government of Peru and in order to ensure that no questions arise as to the correct application of the proceedings, as well as to protect the interests of both parties (the Government and the petitioners), has decided for the time being to withdraw the case from the Court, in order to reconsider it and possibly present it again at

sion 'regained' jurisdiction, it sent the Article 50 report to the state again, this time with all of the missing parts and attachments, and fixed a period for the submission of final observations by the government.[75] In reply, far from addressing the merits of the case, Peru argued that it had at no time submitted a motion for reconsideration, and that the decision to withdraw the case from the jurisdiction of the Court had been taken unilaterally by the Commission in violation of the procedural rules.[76] In response, the Commission adopted a second preliminary report,[77] to the same effect as the earlier one, which it transmitted to the government, setting a new 90 day period for it to make observations. The Government's response was not to make observations on the report but to maintain its position, stating that the Commission could not insist on going ahead with an irregular proceeding.[78] The Commission filed a new application with the Court on 14 February 1992 which was followed by 12 preliminary objections by the Peruvian government. In a very controversial decision,[79] the Court dismissed the complaint on the ground that it had been referred to the Court after the expiry of the time limit for submission set forth in Articles 50 and 51 of the Convention.[80] In declining jurisdiction in the case, the Court resorted to ambiguous reasoning relating to procedural and factual issues and finally based its decision to reject the case on the need to protect the reliability of the system.[81] When confronted with the hardly excusable procedural gaffes committed by the Commission and the ingenious manipulation of the system by the defendant government, the Court unanimously and expressly chose to give priority to the preservation of its own institutional authority and credibility over the protection of the procedural equity owed to the victims.

It must be said that States have not always appeared before the Court to litigate in good faith. The proceedings in the case *Neira Alegría et al*,[82] are a

---

some future date, after the observations submitted by the Government of Peru with regard to the instant case have been properly assessed', Ibid., para 27.

[75] Ibid., para. 28.   [76] Ibid., para. 29.

[77] It did this in order to recommence the three month period within which it could submit the case the Court following the transmission of the Art. 50 report on a case to the state: see Art. 51(1), Convention.

[78] Ibid., para. 30   [79] See Pinto, op. cit., n. 29, 152.

[80] *Cayara*, loc. cit. at n. 69, paras. 60 and 61. Although this second reference to the Court was out of time as far as the first preliminary report was concerned, it was made within the required three month period in relation to the second preliminary report. The Court took the view that a second report could only be taken into account in a case in which the state had requested the reconsideration of the first report, which was not the case on the facts. The Court indicated that the Commission retained its power to adopt and publish an Article 51 report. In response, the Commission published a document cited in n. 70 above.

[81] Ibid., para. 63.

[82] The case is related to the disappearance of Neira Alegría and Edgar and William Zenteno-Escobar during the crushing of a riot in San Juan Bautista prison, known as *'El Frontón'*. After a long confrontation the inmates gave up resistance but the Joint Command of the Peruvian

striking example of this attitude. In a six year saga,[83] the respondent State, Peru, has used all the means at its disposal to undermine and delay the proceedings before the Commission and the Court. The initial complaint was filed with the Commission by the families of three of the victims following an adverse decision of the Peruvian Court of Constitutional Guarantees. After four warnings by the Commission on the consequences of non-cooperation, and a hearing, the State alleged that a Special Military Tribunal was examining the case and therefore domestic remedies had not yet been exhausted. Although, the preliminary Article 50 report declaring the case admissible and condemning Peru on the merits was issued in 1990,[84] the State insisted on its inadmissibility claim, this time maintaining that the petitioners had failed to present their complaint within six months following the exhaustion of remedies.[85] When this argument was put forward as a preliminary objection,[86] the Court noted that the inconsistency of its assertions regarding its own domestic law estopped Peru from challenging the observance of the Conventional requirements on the exhaustion of remedies. As a second objection, the Government argued that the Commission had failed to submit *Neira Alegría et al* to the Court within the three month time limit provided for in Article 51(1) of the American Convention, that is a three month period following the transmittal of the preliminary report to the respondent State. The case had indeed been submitted to the Court past the original deadline. But the delay was the natural consequence of a request, put forward by Peru itself, for a 30 day extension to present a response to the preliminary report. The State challenged an irregularity to which it had contributed and even disputed the power of the Commission to grant the request for an extension. The Court, resorting to 'elementary principles of good faith', found that the respondent Government could not 'invoke the expiration of a time limit that was extended at its own behest'[87] and 'request something of another and then challenge the grantor's powers once the request has been complied with.'[88]

The judgment on preliminary objections was followed by a special motion by Peru for its revision,[89] which is something not contemplated in the American Convention; a request of interpretation of the same judg-

---

Armed Forces blew up the foundations of the main pavilion killing more than 90 of them. The Court found breaches of the rights to life (Art. 4) and to habeas corpus (Art. 7(b)).

[83] The case was referred to the Court on 10 Oct. 1990, and the Court rendered judgment on reparations on 19 Sept. 1996, I/A Court H.R. Annual Report 1996, 162.

[84] Report 43/90, Case 10.078 (Peru), 14 May 1990 (unreported).

[85] Art. 46.1 (b) of the American Convention.

[86] *Neira Alegría et al.*, Preliminary Objections, I/A Court H.R. (1991), 13 *HRLJ* 146 (1992).

[87] Ibid., para. 34.

[88] Ibid., para. 35.

[89] Filed on 13 Dec. 1991.

ment;[90] and, finally, the withdrawal of the motion for revision just before the hearing on its admissibility and merits. Since the judgment on preliminary objections was extremely clear, predictably the interpretation requested by the respondent State related only to inconsequential wording or concerned Convention provisions which could only be interpreted by the Court in the exercise of its advisory jurisdiction. None of the requests were related to the operative part of the judgment and the Court found them to be manifestly inadmissible.[91] One of the judges described the requests for revision and interpretation put forward by Peru as 'an abuse of the judicial process'[92] and the Court expressed the view that 'the presentation of a request for revision and its withdrawal a few minutes before the public hearing—after a considerable amount of time and valuable resources had been devoted to these proceedings by the Commission and the Court—should be taken into account in determining the court costs to be borne by the parties to this case.'[93] However, in its judgment on the merits, the Court, with a different composition,[94] rejected the claims on costs presented by the Commission.[95]

Peru also resorted to objecting to the witnesses, expert witnesses and to a request that the hearings on the merits should not occur in public, all of which contentions were rejected.[96] After a lengthy trial stage the Court examined the case and drafted its decision on July 1994.[97] However the Court gave an additional six months period to the State to settle the case

---

[90] Filed on 6 Mar. 1992.

[91] *Neira Alegría et al.*, Request for Revision and Interpretation of the judgment of 11 Dec. 1991 on Preliminary Objections, I/A Court H.R., paras. 16 to 21(1992), 14 *HRLJ* 19 (1993).

[92] '. . . I consider the requests by Peru for revision and interpretation of the judgment of December 11, 1991 an abuse of the judicial process. A government that adheres to a human rights treaty and accepts the jurisdiction of a Court established to ensure its interpretation and application, as Peru did in ratifying the Convention and accepting the jurisdiction of this Court, has the right to resort to every legitimate judicial remedy and procedure to defend itself against charges that it has violated the treaty. What it may not do is interpose manifestly ill founded and trivial motions whose sole purpose can only be to disrupt and delay the orderly and timely completion of the proceedings. Such tactics violate the object and purpose of the human rights machinery established by the Convention.' Ibid., Declaration by Judge Thomas Buergenthal.

[93] Ibid., para. 15.

[94] The Court's membership had changed while the case was pending. The new Court (Judges Fix Zamudio, Picado Sotela, Nieto Navia, Montiel Argüello, Salgado Pesantes, Aguiar Aranguren), prompted by a memorandum presented by the *ad hoc* judge appointed by Peru, decided to hear the merits of the case itself, rather than refer it back to the Court as it had been composed when it rendered judgment on the preliminary objections and on the motions relating to it (Judges Fix Zamudio, Picado Sotela, Nieto Navia, Buergenthal and Barberis). *Neira Alegría et al.*, Order of 29 June 1992, I/A Court H.R. 13 *HRLJ* 407 (1992).

[95] *Neira Alegría et al.*, I/A Court H.R., para. 87 (1995), 16 *HRLJ* 403 (1995), 3 IHRR 362 (1996).

[96] See *Neira Alegría et al.*, Orders of 29 June and 30 June I/A Court H.R. (1992), 13 *HRLJ* 407.

[97] I/A Court H.R. Annual Report 1994, 11.

and it only rendered judgment on the merits, in favour of the petitioners, in January 1995.

Needless to say, once a case has been declared admissible, States generally try to avoid an adverse decision on the merits. They do so, *inter alia*, by challenging the Commission's findings of fact. The exercise of jurisdiction *in toto* over the cases submitted to it has led the Court to conduct a *de novo* trial in every single case, including a new fact-finding stage to re-ascertain the facts. In the *Gangaram Panday* case,[98] submitted against Suriname, the Commission requested that the facts of the case as presented by the Commission be considered as verified.[99] Predictably, the Court reaffirmed its full jurisdiction over the case and decided to review most of the factual issues challenged by the Government.[100] The Court has shown reluctance to rely on the factual findings of the Commission with consequences that go beyond a conflicting institutional relationship: a *de novo* trial may result in confirmation of the findings as to compliance with the standards of the Convention[101] but it also means employing scarce resources. It obliges the Commission to produce evidence and witnesses and it requires the Court to conduct its own fact-finding in order to evaluate the evidence presented by the parties. The conduct of *de novo* trials by the Court brings further procedural guarantees to the States Parties, but diminishes the chances of the petitioners having their cases submitted for adjudication, due to the lack of necessary resources for litigation on the part of the Commission. The Court expressed its view in the Honduran Cases that the purpose of exercising full jurisdiction, including fact-finding, over contentious cases was not only to afford greater protection to the rights guaranteed, but also to assure State parties that all of the rules established in the Convention would be strictly observed.[102] Unfortunately, there is a chance that this may have an adverse effect upon procedural equality. States Parties are allowed to re-argue their cases before the Court, now trying to avoid being declared in breach by a judicial decision and being liable to pay large compensation. But the victims, who lack *locus standi* to appear before the Court, cannot defend their position with 'equal arms'. They depend on the precarious intermediation of the Commission.

---

[98] *Gangaram Panday,* I/A Court H.R. Series C No.16 (1994), 15 *HRLJ* 168 (1994), 2 IHRR 360 (1995).

[99] Ibid., para. 30.   [100] Ibid., paras. 41 and 42.

[101] It must be said that the standards of evidence applied by the Commission have been traditionally uncertain. Even in those cases where the State cooperates during the proceedings, the Commission does not conduct a formal fact-finding stage. The holding of a hearing mainly depends on the chances of the petitioner or the victim to appear before the Commission during the bi-annual regular sessions held in Washington DC.

[102] *Velásquez Rodríguez,* Preliminary Objections, I/A Court of H.R., Series C No.1, para. 29 (1987).

From the perspective of the respondent State, there is an alternative which may lead to a result which could appear attractive. Some States have resorted to acknowledgments of responsibility which avoid a fully reasoned judgment on the merits. This involves the full recognition of facts and responsibility and therefore places the State in a difficult position during the reparations phase. However, this gesture may avoid an express condemnation. The first acknowledgment of responsibility took place in the case *Aloeboetoe et al* [103] where Suriname admitted responsibility on the facts alleged by the Commission at the public hearing regarding preliminary objections.[104] In the next case of this kind, the *'El Amparo'*[105] Case, Venezuela decided not to 'contest the facts referred to in the complaint' and accepted international responsibility, in rather vague terms. As a result of this statement, the Court declared that the controversy as to the facts had ceased and closed the merits phase, giving a six month period to the parties to agree on reparations.[106] However, the result was that the judgment of the Court failed to contain a statement condemning Venezuela for the violation of the Convention, thereby omitting the most important satisfaction that a court of law—particularly a human rights court—can bring to the victims and their families. The Court also failed to establish clearly which were the terms of the reparations owed by the State. The absence of a proper judgment on the merits deprived the Commission and the victims of a decision on the claims made in the petitions which, far from stressing monetary compensation, were focused on the obligation of the State to investigate the violations and modify its legislation.[107] In the most recent case of acceptance of responsibility, Argentina acknowledged responsibility for the arrest of Adolfo Garrido and Raúl Baigorria by the police and their subsequent disappearance.[108]

PROBLEMS OF EFFECTIVENESS

The political organs of international organizations such as the UN, the Council of Europe and the OAS are often perceived as carrying ultimate responsibility for the effectiveness of the systems they govern. They are regarded as enforcers, that is organs with the power to take action—such as moral and political condemnation, suspension or expulsion

---

[103] *Aloeboetoe et al*, I/A Court of H.R., Series C No.11, (1991), 13 *HRLJ* 140 (1992).

[104] Ibid., para 22.

[105] *'El Amparo'*, I/A Court H.R. (1995). 16 *HRLJ* 149 (1995), 3 IHRR 349 (1996).

[106] Ibid., para. 20. See *'El Amparo'*, Reparations, I/A Court HR, (1996) I/A Court H.R. Annual Report 1996, 143.

[107] Ibid., para. 14. See also the concurring opinion of Judge A. A. Cançado Trindade.

[108] *Garrido and Baigorria*, I/A Court H.R. (1996), I/A Court H.R. Annual Report 1996, 70.

from membership or the imposition of other sanctions—against States found in breach of a particular set of international commitments.

Since 1960, the OAS has claimed to be a forum for the promotion and protection of human rights. But how effective has the system been in securing compliance with the obligations assumed by the Member States? The previous section of this article explored the dialogue among the petitioners, the respondent Member States, the Commission and the Court. This section explores how Member States acting within and through the political organs of the OAS, particularly the Permanent Council and the General Assembly, have responded to the challenge of making the work of the Commission and the Court effective.

The Political Organs as Enforcers of the System

The last step in the treatment of petitions filed against Member States under the American Declaration, after completion of the procedure set forth in the Statute and Regulations of the Commission, is the inclusion of the Commission's final decision in its annual report. The same is true for reports on petitions filed against State Parties to the American Convention, once the procedure established in the Convention and the Regulations of the Commission has been exhausted. Unless a case is referred to the Court or closed after a successful friendly settlement, the enforcement and effectiveness of the recommendations of the Commission in its reports on individual petitions brought under the Convention depend on the action taken by the General Assembly on the basis of these reports. This is all the more so since the submission of contentious cases to the Court and the making of friendly settlements[109] have not been as frequent as might be hoped. The same position exists in respect of the judgments of the Court, which is also obliged to submit an annual report to the Assembly.[110] The dynamics of enforcement depend to a large extent on the widespread publicity that is afforded by the presentation of the Commission's annual and country reports and the Court's annual report to the General Assembly, the debate on their contents in that body, the Assembly's call to comply with the resolutions of the Commission and the Court's judgments and the measures adopted by it in case of non-compliance.

---

[109] The Commission has only published four friendly settlement reports: Res. 5/85, Case 7956 (Honduras), IACHR Annual Report 1984–5, 104; Report 1/93, Cases 10228 et al. (Argentina) IACHR Annual Report 1992–3, 35; Report 22/94, Case 11012 (Argentina), IACHR Annual Report 1994, 40 and Report 19/97, Case 11212 (Guatemala), IACHR Annual Report 1996, 447.

[110] Art. 65 of the American Convention.

The Legal Framework

There is no provision in the OAS Charter vesting in the General Assembly the task of controlling compliance with the decisions and reports of the Commission under the Declaration or the Convention or the judgments of the Court under the Convenion. It has been argued that, in view of this omission, it was natural for the political organs to refrain, as they have done, from exercising a role which is not expressly provided for in the Charter, particularly in the area of individual freedoms.[111] In fact, the absence of an enforcement role for the political organs is a predictable omission for an instrument which has non-intervention as one of its cornerstone principles.[112] Some of the Member States still consider the protection of such freedoms as an issue relating to the conduct of their internal affairs.

The adoption of Resolution 1080[113] and the Washington Protocol (see Introduction, above) have been crucial steps in the evolution of a movement away from this non-interventionalist approach, at least in the area of promotion and protection of democracy. Resolution 1080 provides a procedure of consultation[114] to be followed by the organs of the Organization in order to take a decision regarding the 'interruption' of the legitimate exercise of power by a democratic government in any of the Member States. In turn, the Washington Protocol has amended Article 9 of the Charter so as to empower the General Assembly to suspend the rights of membership of a State where democracy has been interrupted. The procedure of Resolution 1080—which has already been invoked during the institutional crisis suffered by Haiti, Peru, Guatemala and Paraguay—and the sanction to be applied by virtue of the Washington Protocol are the first steps in establishing a clear mandate regarding the protection of democracy by the OAS.

As regards human rights, the American Convention does not include any specific undertaking relating to the enforcement of the decisions and reports of the Commission and the judgments of the Court by the OAS political organs. State Parties simply undertake to respect and ensure the

---

[111] See S. Chodos, *Informe Final sobre 'Las decisiones de los órganos de justicia supranacionales en el ámbito americano y su relación con los actos de los Estados miembros'* (Universidad de Buenos Aires, 1994) (unpublished research report), 16.

[112] See Art. 1 of the OAS Charter.

[113] AG/Res. 1080 (XXI-0/91) adopted at the Fifth Plenary Session of the General Assembly, held on 5 June 1991 in Santiago, Chile.

[114] The Res. instructs the Secretary General to convoke the Permanent Council in the event of the 'interruption' of the legitimate exercise of power by a democratic government of any of the Member States. In a ten day period either the General Assembly or the *ad hoc* Meeting of Ministers of Foreign Affairs convoked for that purpose should evaluate the event and 'adopt any decisions deemed appropriate in accordance with the Charter and International Law.'

rights set forth in the Conventional text.[115] Neither the Statute nor the Regulations of the Commission make any reference to enforcement either. These instruments only focus on the Commission's duty to submit an annual report to the General Assembly.[116]

As noted, the Court is also obliged to submit an annual report to the General Assembly. Unfortunately, the Convention does not go beyond that to establish a reliable mechanism for the enforcement of court judgments. Although State Parties expressly undertake to comply with them[117] and the Court must specify in its annual report the cases in which States have not done so,[118] no express powers are given by the Convention to the OAS political organs to monitor compliance with Court judgments or impose sanctions for non-compliance with them.

Political Organs as Enforcers in Practice

The tone of the resolution issued by the General Assembly regarding the annual reports—and occasionally country reports—of the Commission, has varied through the years. The resolutions adopted in the early seventies were limited to acknowledging receipt of the annual reports and thanking the Commission for its work. But then three consecutive resolutions issued by the Assembly in 1975, 1976, and 1977 on the basis of the findings of the Commission in its country reports on the situation in Chile, represented a major breakthrough and a much more positive and supportive approach.[119] In its resolution on the First Report on Chile,[120] the General Assembly called upon 'all the governments, including the government of Chile, to continue to give the most careful attention to the suggestion and recommendations of the Commission' and requested a follow-up report on the situation in Chile.[121] The Assembly made sure that Chile had the chance to present its observations on the report. Interestingly, the Assembly evaluated Chile's observations in the light of the follow up report[122] and emphasised that the defence presented by the Government 'fail[ed] to clarify information received by the Commission on affronts to human rights'.[123] This time the Assembly made 'a special appeal' to the Government of Chile to adopt and implement the necessary measures for ensuring full

---

[115] Arts. 1.1 and 2 of the American Convention.
[116] Art. 41(g), American Convention; Art. 18(f), Commission Statute.
[117] Art. 68.1 of the American Convention.
[118] Art. 65 of the American Convention.
[119] For a thorough account of these sessions of the General Assembly see C. Medina Quiroga, *The Battle of Human Rights* (Kluwer, 1988) 275–291.
[120] IACHR Report on the Status of Human Rights in Chile (1974).
[121] AG/Res. 190 (V-0/75).
[122] IACHR Second Report on the Situation of Human Rights in Chile (1976).
[123] AG/Res. 243(VI-O/76).

respect of human rights and to continue cooperating with the Commission, which was requested to continue monitoring the situation. This special appeal was repeated in the next Assembly where the government was also 'urged' to grant the necessary guarantees of security to persons providing evidence to the Commission.[124] The Assembly also ensured that the matter remained on the agenda by requesting the Government to continue to provide information on the situation to be included in the next annual report.

In 1978–9, the General Assembly also addressed the situation in Uruguay,[125] Paraguay[126] and El Salvador.[127] Based on the findings presented in the Commission's country reports on these States, the Assembly appealed in its resolutions for the adoption of the measures recommended by the Commission. The wording found in the Assembly's resolution regarding the 'concern of the Member States over the effective exercise and protection of human rights in the Hemisphere' shown in the 'opinions expressed during the discussions' were an indication that there was a genuine interest on the part of Member States within the Assembly in the effectiveness of the system of protection and that this was gaining momentum.

In 1979, the General Assembly summarized in its resolution the catalogue of serious violations exposed in the Commission's annual report, ranging from forced disappearances—including the situation of children born in captivity—to torture and detention without trial. With very clear and direct language, the Assembly referred to the situation in Chile, Peru and Uruguay and urged each one of them to adopt a particular set of measures, including the lifting of the state of siege.[128] A separate resolution on 'Religious Freedom'[129] was also issued. On the basis of the findings of the Commission, the Assembly requested the Member States to refrain from restraining the exercise of freedom of religion and specifically appealed for the respect of the rights of Jehovah's Witnesses.

At the end of the 1970s, the General Assembly also sought to stimulate cooperation by Member States with the Commission by issuing a number of resolutions relating to the protection of human rights in general. These resolutions called upon Member States to consent to on site investigations[130] and urged Member States to cooperate with the Commission by supplying information on the situation of human rights in their territory and protecting witnesses from retaliation.[131] They also sought to clarify the position of the Organization by stating that 'there are no circumstances that justify torture, summary execution or prolonged detention without due process of law.'[132]

---

[124] AG/Res. 313(VII-0/77).
[125] AG/Res. 369 (VIII-0/78).
[126] AG/Res. 370 (VIII-0/78).
[127] AG/Res. 446 (IX-0/79).
[128] AG/Res. 443 (IX-0/79).
[129] AG/Res. 444 (IX-0/79).
[130] AG/Res. 371 (VIII-0/78).
[131] AG/Res. 315 (VII-0/77).
[132] Ibid.

During this period, the General Assembly was willing to oversee compliance with general human rights standards on the basis of the judgement of the Commission and to enhance the effectiveness of the latter's recommendations. The call to Member States to protect individuals who were cooperating in the Commission's enquiries shows the Assembly's endeavours to prevent further violations and to contribute to the functioning of the system. Statements such as those requesting the lifting of the state of siege in Chile and Paraguay[133] and urging the Member States 'to refrain from adopting or implementing laws that would have the effect of impeding investigations'[134] were unusual for an organisation which has non-intervention in internal affairs as one of its pillars and showed a promising commitment to the protection of human rights. But most significantly, at the end of the 1970s, the political organs not only supported the work of the Commission in the ways indicated but also relied on the authority of its findings to justify one of the crucial statements in the history of the OAS. The Commission's 1979 Special Report on the Situation of Human Rights in Nicaragua[135] was presented as the factual and legal foundation of the decision of the 17th Meeting of Consultation of Ministers of Foreign Affairs declaring that the regional and domestic problems created by the situation in Nicaragua could only be solved by replacing the Government then in power, that is, Anastasio Somoza's regime.[136]

Ironically, shortly after the entry into force of the American Convention and the creation of the Court, the General Assembly's efforts in support of the recommendations of the Commission came to an end. The situation of human rights in Argentina was the subject of a country report issued in 1980.[137] The Argentine Government rejected the Report, questioned the methods of the Commission and—under the threat of leaving the Organization—managed to gain enough support among the Member States to prevent condemnation by the General Assembly.[138] Sadly, the Argentine Government's efforts towards the adoption of a low profile resolution were successful. The Assembly 'took note' of the Annual Report and the country reports on Argentina and Haiti in the same resolution.[139] This time it also took note of the 'observations, objections and comments' made by the Member States that were the subject of these country reports and 'on the

---

[133] AG/Res. 443 (IX-0/79).   [134] AG/Res. 445 (IX-0/79).
[135] IACHR Report on the Situation of Human Rights in Nicaragua (1979).
[136] Res. II adopted by the 17th Meeting of Consultation of Ministers of Foreign Affairs held on 23 June 1979. For a thorough account of the debates held during the Meeting see Medina Quiroga, op. cit., n. 119, 247–56.
[137] IACHR Report on the Situation of Human Rights in Argentina (1980).
[138] Tenth Regular Session of the General Assembly, November 1980. For a reproduction of the debates held see T. Buergenthal, *Protecting Human Rights in the Americas*, 3rd. edn. (1990) 339.
[139] AG/Res. 510 (X-0/80).

measures that, on their own initiative, they have freely taken [. . .] to guarantee human rights in their countries.' Although the Governments of the Member States were requested to take measures to protect a specific range of fundamental rights, they were not urged to comply with the recommendations of the Commission. The language of this Resolution makes the adoption of measures dependent on 'their own free initiative'. Only one specific measure recommended by the Commission was echoed by the Assembly: the creation of central records to register detentions with a view to gathering information relating to the status of persons who were reported as disappeared. Moreover, the recommendations and statements of the Assembly were directed to all Member States, not just those who were the object of the Commission's attention.

By 1981, the Assembly's resolutions lost all of the elements that once made them a vehicle of political condemnation. Member States were merely requested to 'preserve and ensure the full effectiveness of human rights'.[140] The recommendations of the Commission regarding individual cases or the situation of human rights in particular countries addressed in the Annual Report were not even mentioned. In 1983, with the first signs of gradual democratization in some of the Member States, the General Assembly started to call again in general terms for the implementation of the Commission's recommendations.[141] However, these initiatives were far from being a serious attempt at enforcement. The Assembly called upon 'the Member States mentioned in the annual [and] [. . .] special report[s]' without actually mentioning them by name. Furthermore, the appeals made by the Assembly to States to implement its recommendations subject to municipal and not to international law was deceptively ambiguous. It could be said that during the late eighties the General Assembly showed a genuine interest in the work of the Commission[142] and the Court. However, it was not prepared to offer any support for those institutions beyond the level of formal gestures, such as an acknowledgment of receipt of the reports and an instruction to the Commission to undertake some kind of future promotional task.

The amendments to the OAS Charter by the Protocol of Cartagena de Indias[143] introduced some changes in the procedure for dealing with the annual reports by the political organs. Under the new arrangements, which have been in operation since 1991, the Commission presents its annual and country reports to the Permanent Council from where, after a debate, they are sent to the Assembly with a number of comments and recommendations attached. The debates are usually dominated by the responses of the

---

[140] AG/Res. 453 (XI-0/81). See also AG/Res. 618(XII-0/82).
[141] AG/Res.666 (XIII-0/83). See also AG/Res. 742 (XIV-0/84) and AG/Res. 778 (XV-0/85).
[142] See, for instance, AG/Res. 1022 (XIX-0/89).
[143] Arts. 54.f and 90.f of the OAS Charter.

Governments criticised in the annual and/or country reports. Sadly, the strategy that they adopt in their defence is a consistent attack on the Commission, mainly focused on its mandate and its credibility. Some of the young Latin American democracies object to the scrutiny of the Commission for both policy and legal reasons. The policy arguments are mainly based on the change in the political context and on the role of the Commission: democracies should not be judged by the same standards previously applied to authoritarian regimes; the Commission should only have a constructive role towards young democracies instead of condemning their weaknesses and contributing to their lack of stability; and, in any event, member States should only be judged in the light of their domestic context. From the legal point of view, some of the Member States believe that the mandate of the Commission should be limited to the promotion of human rights and the offering of advice. Their arguments mainly involve reprimanding the Commission for its alleged lack of efficiency, accuracy and clear criteria by which to decide which of the member States should have their human rights situation reviewed in the annual reports.[144]

This atmosphere of criticism of the Commission is reflected in the resolutions of the General Assembly which recently only 'take note' of the annual reports in the light of the recommendations of the Permanent Council.[145] The resolutions issued in the last five years have not been aimed at securing compliance with the recommendations of the Commission. Member States are not urged any more to implement the recommendations, quite the contrary. Now the Commission is urged to give special importance to 'the dialogue with the Member States concerning progress made and difficulties encountered in the observance of human rights'.[146] Some of the Assembly's recommendations are strongly critical of the work and the judgment of the Commission. For instance, Member States have recommended that the Commission reconsider whether States assessed in the section of the annual reports updating general situations 'should continue to be mentioned' the next year.[147] Sadly, such a recommendation is intended to silence the Commission in an area which has traditionally been within its realm of discretion, that is, the contents of its annual report.

[144] See Brody, Reed & González, Felipe 'Human Rights Development at OAS General Assembly' 48 *The Review of the International Commission of Jurists* 68 (1992); González, Felipe 'The 1993 OAS General Assembly in Nicaragua' 51 *The Review of the International Commission of Jurists* 44 (1993); González, Felipe & Rodríguez, Diego 'Human Rights and their Treatment in the 1994 General Assembly and Permanent Council of the OAS' 53 *The Review of the International Commission of Jurists* 51 (1994).

[145] See AG/Res. 1102 (XXI-)/91; AG/Res. 1169 (XXII-0/92); Resolución aprobada en la novena sessión plenaria, celebrada el 11 de junio de 1993; Res. adopted at the Ninth Plenary Session held on June, 1994 and AG/Res. 1331(XXV-0/95).

[146] AG/Res. 1331(XXV-0/95).

[147] AG/Res.1169 (XXII-0/92).

Some Member States have expressed their view regarding the role of the Assembly in the enforcement of the reports of the Commission. In their opinion, the task of the Assembly is limited to the approval of the Commission's annual and country reports simply by verifying compliance with the formal requirements[148] with which the annual reports must comply and does not include analysing and acting upon its content.[149] This seems to have been the prevailing interpretation over the years and it has had the effect of limiting the contents of the resolutions adopted by the Assembly to a superficial assessment of the drafting and advisory roles of the Commission. The recognition of the Commission's quasi-judicial role is reduced to a perpetual calling upon member states to ratify the American Convention and upon Convention parties to accept the jurisdiction of the Court. No steps are taken to call for compliance with the Commission's reports on individual petitions.

As regards the annual reports of the inter-American Court, it must be said that the General Assembly has failed to support the adjudicatory process convincingly. This was recently demonstrated in the context of two cases concerning Suriname which are two of the very few attempts of judgment enforcement. In its 1994 Annual Report,[150] the Court requested the General Assembly to 'urge the Government of Suriname to report on the status of compliance' with the cases *Aloeboetoe et al*[151] and *Gangaram Panday.*[152] In its 1995 regular session, in its resolution on the Court's Report, the General Assembly repeated the Court's request in the same terms, but did not support the Court to the point of stressing the need for compliance or using language that demonstrated its own concern.[153]

The General Assembly's recommendations relating to the assessment of human rights in States affected by terrorism deserve separate analysis. In recent years, the General Assembly has issued a number of resolutions in this area, two of which are worth mentioning. First, Resolution 1043, in which it condemned terrorism and recommended the Commission to assess *generally* the impact of irregular armed groups on the enjoyment of human rights.[154] Second, Resolution 1112 on the strengthening of human rights, in

---

[148] For example, Art. 63, Commission Regulations formally requires the annual report to include certain items, such as any 'general or special report that the Commission considers necessary with regard to the situation of human rights in the members states'.

[149] Opinion of Canada and Chile at the Twenty-Third General Assembly held in Managua, Nicaragua, 7–11 June 1993. See F. González, 'The OAS General Assembly in Nicaragua' 51 *ICJ Rev.*44 (1993).

[150] I/A Court H.R. Annual Report 1994, 18.

[151] *Aloeboetoe et al.*, Reparations (Art. 63.1 of the American Convention on Human Rights), I/A Court H.R. Series C No.15 (1993), 14 HRLJ 413, 1–1 IHRR 208 (1994).

[152] *Gangaram Panday,* I/A Court H.R. Series C No.16 (1994), 15 *HRLJ* 168, 2 IHRR 360 (1995).   [153] AG/Res. 1330 (XXV-0/95).

[154] AG/Res. 1043 (XX-0/90) 'Consequences of Acts of Violence Perpetrated by Irregular Armed Groups on the Enjoyment of Human Rights'.

which the Assembly repeated its call to the Commission to assess the actions of irregular armed groups, this time when reporting on the situation of human rights in *particular* Member States. Curiously, this second resolution urged the Member States to condemn and combat terrorism 'while observing full respect for the standards that characterize a state in which the rule of law prevails' without mentioning the standards of the American Declaration, the Convention or international law. The Commission tried to satisfy the request of the General Assembly by including a section on 'Activities of Irregular Armed Groups' in Chapter V of its 1992–1993 Annual Report.[155] It devoted that section to reviewing the remarks concerning the situation created by terrorism in some of the Member States that it had published in its previous annual and country reports. At the same time, it made an important declaration of principle by stating that 'under no circumstances should a sensitivity towards the actions of armed irregular groups leading to violations of human rights be used as a justification for the violation of human rights by governments themselves.'[156] As regards its own role, it explained that it had encountered 'significant procedural problems in implementing its concern' for the action of terrorist groups[157] and 'hoped that the Assembly would turn its attention to the procedural problems in so far as it wishes the Commission to proceed further.'[158] These 'procedural problems' would seem to include the fact that terrorists are not subject to the controls of the the Declaration or the Convention. As explained by the Court, 'as far as concerns the human rights protected by the Convention, the jurisdiction of the organs established thereunder refer exclusively to international responsibility of States and not that of individuals.'[159] The Commission reiterated that its primary function is to promote and defend the human rights set forth in the Declaration and the Convention. Although it declared itself 'willing and anxious to expand its focus' to consider the problem, it reaffirmed its commitment towards its primary function.[160]

Despite this reaction by the Commission to the Assembly's resolutions, Member States have started to use these resolutions as the legal foundation of their own defences. Resolution 1112—together with Resolution 1990/75[161] of the UN Commission on Human Rights—was quoted by Peru as

---

[155] IACHR Annual Report 1992–3, 215.   [156] Ibid., 220
[157] Ibid., 219.   [158] Ibid., 220.
[159] *International Responsibility for the Promulgation and Enforcement of Laws in Violation of the Convention (Art. 1 and 2, American Convention on Human Rights) Advisory Opinion OC-14/94*, I/A Court H.R., Series A No.14 para 56 (1994), 16 *HRLJ* 9 (1995), 2 IHRR 380 (1995).
[160] Ibid..
[161] 'Consequences of Acts of Violence Committed by Armed Groups and Drug Traffickers for the Enjoyment of Human Rights', UN Commission on Human Rights, *Report on the 46th Session (29 Jan.–9 Mar. 1990) to ECOSOC, E/1990/22, ECN.4/1990/94, Official Records, 1990, Supplement No 2.*

evidence of a trend in international law towards a contextual interpretation of the measures taken by a State in the fight against terrorism. According to that State, the Commission should consider '. . . the entire complex of circumstances that impede government action and lead occasionally to violations of human rights by agents of the governments not as a premeditated, deliberate policy on its part, but as an unfortunate consequence of the climate of violence generated by the action of subversive terrorist groups.'[162] This Government has presented a global justification for its actions in the context of the fight against terrorism. In its view, its actions are taken '. . . in the name of the common good, order, safety and legally protected property.'[163] They are a part of its '. . . moral and legal obligation to react and defend itself against terrorism as an illegal, illegitimate and immoral form of political violence.'[164] Its defence strategy is not limited to the justification of the necessity of its acts. It has also accused the Commission of a '. . . double standard and a kind of selective indignation, for protests multiply in the unusual case of a violation of human rights attributable to the government . . . but when such a violation is directly and deliberately committed by terrorists groups, the response is silence.'[165]

There is clearly disagreement between the Commission and some of the Member States regarding compliance with human rights standards in a climate of violence. Much of the work of the Commission is directed towards highlighting the abuses committed by certain governments in their fight against terrorism.[166] These governments have reacted, alleging selectivity and inaccuracy on the part of the Commission. The institutional reaction of the OAS has been translated into a perpetual call to the Commission to make its assessments 'taking into account the information supplied by the Member States, among other sources',[167] which would include information concerning the State's fight against terrorists. In any event, the Member States have already taken the initiative to bring the legal discussion to their own governmental fora: the suppression of terrorism has been specifically included in the new agenda of the OAS and was the object of a special conference held in Lima in April, 1996. The Member States have declared that terrorism constitutes a systematic and deliberate violation of the rights of the individual and an assault on democracy and have expressed their intention to punish severely this crime in their domestic legislation.

---

[162] Note 7–5 M/150 of the Permanent Representative of Peru to the OAS, dated 18 Sept. 1990 in IACHR Report on the Situation of Human Rights in Peru 1993), 72.

[163] Ibid., 66.

[164] Ibid.   [165] Ibid.

[166] The Commission has referred some of these cases to the Court: *Caballero Delgado and Santana*, *Neira Alegría et al*, *Cayara*, *Loayza Tamayo* and *Castillo Páez*.

[167] AG/Res. 1169 (XXII-0/92); Resolución aprobada en la novena session plenaria, celebrada el 11 de junio de 1993; Res. adopted at the ninth plenary session held on June, 1994.

Unfortunately, if one were to assess the impact that the General Assembly has had as enforcer of the inter-American system of protection of human rights, one would have to conclude that it has not been very significant. The Assembly has tempered its approach to the domestic and regional metamorphosis experienced by the Member States and taken full account of their political and strategic vicissitudes. The system of protection has not been immune from the impact of economic and political leadership either.[168] It is not a secret that the role played in the late seventies by the General Assembly in the area of enforcement was sponsored by the US administration of the day. The Commission also received some material and political support from that quarter, leading, for example, to some of the Member States accepting *in loco* visits. The apathy of the following years could also be explained by reference to US foreign policy: during the early eighties the US chose to give priority to the strengthening of its bonds with its 'allies' in the Cold War—dictatorial regimes engaged in an alleged 'fight against subversion' at the cost of gross and systematic violations— over the respect for human rights in the Hemisphere.[169] Fortunately, by the mid eighties, a wave of democratization started to clear away the authoritarian regimes. However, although Member States have shown respect for the work of the Court, the last decade has brought growing tension between the Commission and the political organs of the OAS. Some of the young democracies, although initially supportive of the Commission, have grown particularly sensitive to exposure in the Commission's annual reports. The political organs do not seem to be willing to become the guardians of the effectiveness of the system. Rather, they seem to be the arena in which the Member States re-argue their cases now in political terms. To make matters worse, their arguments are not focused on the human rights situation but on the Commission, its role, its mandate, its efficiency.

But if the political organs of the OAS have generally done little to promote the effectiveness of the inter-American human rights system, the publication of the Commission's annual and country reports and the Court's judgments and advisory opinions, their release to the media and their availability to the public have nonetheless contributed to the development of public awareness of the human rights situation. Fortunately, despite the criticisms, the Commission is still the axis of the process of publicity, which seems to be the only channel open for the System to have

---

[168]   See, for instance, D. Forsythe, 'Human Rights, the US and the OAS' in 13 *HRQ* 66 (1991) and T. Farer, *The Grand Strategy of the US in Latin America* (1988).

[169]   The US Deputy Secretary of State admitted in the Twenty-First Regular Session of the General Assembly held in Chile in 1991 that in previous decades the US had viewed the hemisphere through the 'sometimes distorting prism of the Cold War'. See C. Medina 'The Inter-American System' 3 *NQHR* 322 (1991), 325.

an impact on the protection of human rights. The Commission has retained the discretion to decide on the contents of its reports, including its findings on both the general situation of human rights in a Member State and its observations and recommendations on individual petitions.[170] Ironically, the best example of the effectiveness of publicity is the reaction caused by the 1980 Report on the Situation on Human Rights in Argentina.[171] As explained, this report was neglected by the political organs which, in the name of solidarity and consensus, agreed not to issue a resolution urging the State to adopt measures in response to the situation that the report disclosed. However, the presence of the Commission during the *in loco* visit conducted in 1979 stimulated the families of thousands of disappeared citizens to use the individual petition procedure available within the inter-American system and the publication of the Report helped the population, the local press and the judiciary to wake from their forced lethargy.[172]

PROBLEMS OF FUNCTIONING

The political organs of the OAS have control over the key features that define the profile, work and credibility of the Commission and the Court, namely their composition, budget and technical support. This section will attempt to explore how the Member States have exercised their power over the functioning of the Commission and the Court, either through the allocation of funds and human resources, or through the election or appointment of individuals with the qualities to serve on them.

Control Over Financial and Human Resources

As far as the Commission is concerned, since the initial allocation of funds to the Commission in 1960—a meagre US$ 34,000[173]—the budget has grown to approximately US$ 3 million, still without matching the needs of an organ with multiple functions that are to be exercised in respect of 35 OAS Member States.[174] This increase in budget has not been the result of systematic planning. It has rather been the result of sporadic attempts to

---

[170] Art. 63 (g) and (h) of the Comission's Regulations.

[171] IACHR Report on the Situation of Human Rights in Argentina (1980).

[172] See T. Farer 'The OAS at the Crossroads' 72 *Iowa L. R.* (1987), 402.

[173] OAS Council, Report of the Committee Program and budget of the financial aspects of the establishment of the Inter-American Commission on Human Rights, OEA/Ser. G/II (c1–481 Rev.) 12 Aug. 1960.

[174] The budget of the early nineties was low enough to be depicted as 'a scandal', see Committee on Human Rights 'The Inter-American Commission on Human Rights: a promise unfulfilled' 48 *The Record of the Association of the Bar of the City of New York* 589 (1993), 611.

arm the Commission with the necessary tools to carry out specific missions. It was significantly increased by the mid sixties due to the role of the Commission in the Dominican crisis and the expansion of its functions[175] and by the early seventies with its recognition as an organ of the Organization. By 1976, the Commission had a budget of US$ 338,000, further reinforced by special contributions made by the US Government.[176] The allocation of special funds on the initiative of a particular Member State, without a previous request by the Organization, gave rise to controversy. A group of Member States, some of which did not wish to be scrutinized by a Commission with enhanced capabilities, condemned this gesture as an attack on OAS autonomy.[177] In 1978, with the entry into force of the American Convention, the budget grew by 160 per cent[178] but it did not increase substantially in the next ten years.[179] Although the figures did not grow considerably in the following years either, the Member States did not let the OAS economic crisis of 1990 affect the budget of the Commission. Notwithstanding the cuts in the general budget of the OAS, the percentage allocated grew from 1.6 per cent in 1988 to 2.2 per cent in 1991.[180] Fortunately, this policy has been reaffirmed by the inclusion of the Commission among the organs of the OAS with priority in the allocation of resources.[181] As a result, the budget of the IACHR rose by 58 per cent from 1995 to 1996 and for the Inter-American Court of Human Rights, 33 per cent. Apparently, there will also be an increase in the Commission's budget for litigation before the Court.[182]

It follows from the level of funding described above, that the Commission has never received the necessary support for the achievement of its broad mandate. The lack of an appropriate budget is one of the explanations for its lack of efficiency both as a quasi-judicial organ and as an advocate before the Court. The equation has been further disturbed by the

---

[175] The Budget of the Commission for the biennium 1967–68 was US$ 139,000. See OAS Council, *Report on the Proposed Program Budget of the Pan American Union for the Fiscal Year 1967–1968, submitted by the Committee on Program and Budget* OEA/Ser.G/IV (c-I-783. Rev.2).

[176] IACHR Annual Report 1976, 7.

[177] Meeting of the OAS Permanent Council, 19 Nov. 1975. See B. Wood, 'Human Rights and the Inter-American System' in T. Farer (ed.) *The Future of the Inter-American System* (Praeger,1979), 144.

[178] The numbers increased to US$ 894,000 and allowed for the hiring of more personnel, the acquisition of facilities and the funding of *in loco* visits, IACHR Annual Report 1978, 12.

[179] In 1988, the budget amounted to US$ 1,083,700.

[180] In 1990, the general budget of the OAS was cut from US$ 66 to 60 million. In spite of the crisis, the budget of the Commission grew to US$ 1,305,500.

[181] Program Action for Strengthening the OAS in the Area of Human Rights, AG/Res. 112 (XXI-0/91). See also section on 'Defence and Protection of Human Rights' in the document *The New Vision of the OAS*.

[182] Remarks by Harriet Babbit, US Permanent Representative to the OAS, delivered at the Twenty-Sixth Regular Session of the General Assembly held in Panama City, Panama, 5 June 1996.

changing context. The membership of the OAS has increased and with it the universe of individuals to be protected; the growing ratification of the American Convention has enlarged and refined the jurisdiction of the Commission and the now prevailing democracy has left behind gross and systematic violations and studies of general situations have given way to increasingly sophisticated individual complaints, which take time to examine. Fortunately, the Organization seems to be starting to make an effort towards supplying the Commission with a realistic budget.

Turning to the Court, this institution has endured Spartan finances since its inception. In 1982, its budget amounted to US$ 30,000[183] and, curiously, it did not grow but was cut by approximately 10 percent in 1986.[184] The Court expressed its disappointment with this measure which impaired its capabilities just before the consideration of its first contentious cases.[185] The budget only grew significantly in 1992 with the specific allocation of a 15 per cent increase in its operating expenses. It received further increases by approximately the same percentage in 1995[186] and 1996.[187] Costa Rica, Canada and the European Union have made special contributions to the Court. According to the Convention, the Court has the power to draw its own budget which cannot be modified by the General Secretariat before submission to the General Assembly for approval.[188] Although this provision suggests some kind of autonomy, the situation has obliged the Court to explain its financial needs. Apparently, the 1992 increase—still unsatisfactory—was obtained after the President of the Court appeared in Washington DC to explain the budgetary needs consequent on the presentation of new cases and the travel expenses of a newly composed Court and of the *ad hoc* judges.[189]

As regard human resources, the original Statute of the Commission entrusted the Secretary General of the OAS with the appointment of personnel from the Pan American Union—now the General Secretariat— to provide secretarial services to the Commission during the period of sessions.[190] In 1965 the Commission was formally provided with its own Secretariat, still attached to the General Secretariat of the OAS.[191] The Convention and the new Statute preserved this institutional structure.[192]

---

[183] I/A Court H.R. Annual Report 1982, 8.
[184] I/A Court H.R. Annual Report 1986, 7.   [185] Ibid.
[186] I/A Court H.R. Annual Report 1994, 16.
[187] I/A Court H.R. Annual Report 1995, 15.
[188] Art. 72 of the American Convention and Art. 26 of the Statute of the Court.
[189] I/A Court H.R. Annual Report 1991, 12
[190] Art. 14 of the Statute approved by the Council of the Organization at the Meeting held on 25 May, 1960.
[191] Art. 14 bis of the Statute amended by Res. XXII of the Second Special Inter-American Conference.
[192] Art. 21.1 of the Statute and Art. 40 of the Convention. See also Art. 12 of the Regulations.

The Secretariat of the Commission is composed of an Executive Secretary, two Assistant Executive Secretaries,[193] and a group of professional, technical and administrative staff.[194] From its initial staff of three, the Secretariat has grown to nearly 20 members, of whom a bare majority are lawyers. The numbers show that each lawyer has a workload which is wholly unrealistic. In the area of the quasi-judicial role of the Commission alone, the quantity and complexity of the complaints filed against certain States require a team of professionals.

The Secretary General controls the recruiting and removal of staff, who are considered part of the personnel of the General Secretariat of the OAS. This situation has led one commentator to define the Commission as 'a creature of the OAS bureaucracy'.[195] This portrayal, discounting its fairness or otherwise, is based partly on the image of the Secretariat as a unit visibly governed by the General Secretariat of the OAS.

It is a fact that the functioning and composition of the Secretariat have a strong influence on the overall performance of the Commission. The Secretariat is in charge of general administration, the handling of complaints, research, the drafting of reports and the organisation of special missions, such as *in loco* visits. The 10-months-a-year absence of the Commissioners has, since the early sixties, led to the execution of the initial steps in the quasi-judicial process of the consideration of individual petitions by the Secretariat, generally unsupervised. The formal adoption of a procedure for the study of individual and inter-State complaints in the 1965 and 1979 amendments to the Statute increased the functions of the Commission and the sophistication of the procedural rules involved. However, the length of the sessions—a maximum of eight weeks a year—remained unchanged. Thus, the Commission was forced to continue delegating—and the Secretariat absorbing—the increasing responsibilities of its quasi-judicial role. Nowadays, the Regulations vest in the Secretariat not only the tasks surrounding the receipt of complaints but also the power to treat them as prima facie admissible. In the latter case, the Secretariat initiates the process of requesting information from the government and promoting a friendly settlement.

The functions and appointment of the Executive Secretary deserve separate analysis. The Executive Secretary has the task of assisting the Commission in the performance of its duties, including the preparation of the work schedule for the sessions[196] and executing its decisions.[197] This is in

---

[193] Art. 13.2 of the Regulations provides that the Assistant Executive Secretaries replace the Executive Secretary in the event of his absence or disability.

[194] Art. 12 of the Regulations.

[195] Anon, 'The Inter-American Commission on Human Rights: A Promise Unfulfilled' 48 *The Record of the Association of the Bar of New York* 589 (1993), 614.

[196] Art. 13.1(b) of the Regulations.   [197] Art. 13.1 (e) of the Regulations.

addition to directing, planning and coordinating the considerable work of the Secretariat[198] and even acting as delegate of the Commission before the Court. The performance of these functions on a full-time basis at the Commission's Washington DC headquarters, before the Court in Costa Rica or at the venue of *in loco* visits makes the Executive Secretary both a crucial player in the functioning of the Commission and the inter-American system generally and somebody who must count on the full confidence and trust of the Commissioners. However, his or her appointment is within the realm of the discretion of the Secretary General of the OAS.[199] The provisions of the new Statute—approved by the General Assembly in 1979—reserving this decision to the Secretary General were disappointing for the Commission.[200]

During its 36 years of existence, the Commission has had only four Executive Secretaries. Dr. Luis A. Reque held the position for 17 years, covering the era preceding the entry into force of the American Convention. He was Chief of the Codification Division of the Pan American Union when the Secretary General of the OAS—José A. Mora—appointed him to provide secretarial services to the Commission in 1960. He participated as Technical Secretary in the Specialized Inter-American Conference which adopted the American Convention in 1969 and conducted the *in loco* visit which was the basis of the first *Report on the Status of Human Rights in Chile*.[201] On his resignation, Dr. Edmundo Vargas Carreño was appointed by Alejandro Orfila in 1977. With a diplomatic as well as academic background, he shaped the Secretariat that emerged after the entry into force of the American Convention. He resigned in 1990 to assume the position of Vice-Minister of Foreign Affairs of Chile. Ambassador Edith Márquez Rodríguez was serving as Alternate Representative of Venezuela to the OAS when she was appointed by Joao Clemente Baena Soares to succeed Vargas Carreño in 1990. She left the Commission in 1996. The present Executive Secretary is Jorge Enrique Taiana, an Argentine sociologist with a background in academia, human rights activism and diplomacy.

The profiles of the successive Executive Secretaries show a perspective of management in transition from bureaucracy to diplomacy. In any event, the crucial role played by the Executive Secretary calls for technical excellence and personal integrity. Paradoxically, the achievement of these

---

[198] Art. 13.1(a) of the Regulations.

[199] Art. 21.2 and 3 of the Statute of the Commission.

[200] See R. Norris, 'The New Statute of the Inter-American Commission on Human Rights' 1 *HRLJ* 379 (1980), 382. The author—then a staff member of the Commission—considers the appointment of the Executive Secretary as an issue '. . . in the battle for greater independence from the General Secretariat . . .'.

[201] IACHR Report on the Status of Human Rights in Chile (1974).

standards depends more on the political organs of the OAS than on the Commission itself. Although César Gaviria has been praised for his choice in the appointment of the new Executive Secretary, the Commission should have full discretion to appoint its own Executive Secretary and professional staff.

The position is different in the case of the Court. Fortunately, the Convention empowers the Court to appoint its own Secretary[202] and its Secretariat is subject to the standards of the General Secretariat except 'in all respects not compatible with the independence of the Court'.[203]

Control over the Composition of the Commission and the Court

The human factor has a bearing on the performance of any institution and the Commission and the Court are no exceptions to this rule. The composition of the Commission has been a crucial factor both in the interpretation of its mandate and its functioning. At the very outset, the first members of the Commission seized the initiative to re-define the Commission's original mandate, taking the first step towards the establishment of a quasi-judicial organ in the inter-American system.[204] As regards functioning, the background and personality of the individuals called to serve as Commissioners have contributed greatly to the work accomplished during its 37 years of existence.

The election process starts with the nomination of candidates, six months prior to the completion of the terms of office of the incumbent Commissioners.[205] The list of candidates is presented to the General Assembly where it is subject to secret ballot voting. The candidates elected must comply with the criterion of being 'persons of high moral character and recognized competence in the field of human rights'.[206] The successive patterns of composition reveal that, although the Members of the Commission are elected in their personal capacity,[207] individual merit is not the only factor evaluated by Member States at the moment of casting their votes. One of the factors seems to be the influence of economic and power leadership: US nationals have been consistently elected throughout 36 years.[208] Geographical distribution of membership and representation of the principal legal systems are not provided for as criteria to be followed in

---

[202] Art. 58.2 of the American Convention.
[203] Art. 59 of the American Convention.
[204] IACHR, *Report of the Work Accomplished During its First Session*, 3–28 Oct. 1960, 9.
[205] Art. 4 of the Statute of the Commission.
[206] Art. 34 of the Convention and Art. 2.1 of the Statute.
[207] Art. 36(1) of the Convention and Art. 3(2) of the Statute.
[208] Durward Sandifer (1960–71); Robert Woodward (1972–6); Tom J. Farer (1977–83); Bruce McColm (1984–7); John R. Stevenson (1988–9); W. Michael Reisman (1990–5) and Robert Kogold Goldman (1996–).

the election. However, they seem to be a *de facto* consideration. Half of the 35 Member States of the OAS have had nationals as Commissioners,[209] with Venezuela,[210] Brazil,[211] Mexico[212] and Costa Rica[213]—in that order—leading the numbers. Despite the secrecy of the procedure, the effects of lobbying and block voting are reflected in a geographically balanced result, by which, until recently, both Central and South America are represented. Barbados—which joined the OAS in 1967 and ratified the Convention in 1981—was the first Caribbean Country to have a national on the Commission[214] and has been followed by Jamaica,[215] Trinidad and Tobago,[216] and Haiti.[217] The consolidation of the Caribbean block has somewhat affected the traditional balance and, for the first time, the composition that emerged from the 26th General Assembly[218] in 1995 did not include nationals from Central American Countries. Equilibrium will eventually prevail. In any case, once elected, the Commissioners represent all of the Members States of the OAS, in harmony with the status of the Commission as an organ of the Organization.

As regards the qualifications of the 38 individuals elected so far, almost half of them have had an academic background. The rest had either served as diplomats, ministers or government officials[219] or were political leaders —as was the case of Romulo Gallegos and Adolfo Siles Salinas, former presidents of Venezuela and Bolivia, respectively. Most of these also had an academic profile.

The Judges of the Court are nominated and elected by the States Parties

[209] Besides the US, seventeen other States have had nationals elected to the Commission: Venezuela, Brazil, Mexico, Costa Rica, Colombia, Argentina, Chile, Barbados, Uruguay, El Salvador, Ecuador, Honduras, Jamaica, Guatemala, Peru, Trinidad and Tobago, and Haiti.

[210] Rómulo Gallegos (1960–3); Andrés Aguilar (1972–85); Marco Tulio Bruni-Celli (1986–93); Carlos Manuel Ayala Corao (1996–).

[211] Carlos Alberto Dunshee de Abranches (1965–82); Gilda M. C. M. de Russomano (1983–91).

[212] Gabino Fraga (1960–79); César Sepúlveda (1980–5).

[213] Angela Acuña de Chacón (1960–71); Fernando Volio Giménez (1977–9); Luis Demetrio Tinoco Castro (1980–5).

[214] Oliver Jackman (1986–93).

[215] Patrick Robinson (1988–95). Jamaica joined the OAS in 1969 and ratified the Convention in 1978.

[216] John Donaldson (1994–). Trinidad and Tobago joined the OAS in 1967 and adhered to the Convention in 1991.

[217] Jean Joseph Exhume (1996–). Haiti joined the OAS in 1951 and adhered to the Convention in 1977.

[218] Twenty-sixth Regular General Assembly of the Organization of American States, Haiti, June, 1995.

[219] Just as an example, it is interesting to highlight the case of Luis Demetrio Tinoco Castro (1980–5) who had an extensive official profile as former Ambassador to the UN, the OAS, Canada, Germany, Sweden, and Norway; former Minister of Education, Foreign Affairs and Finance, and founder and Dean of the University of Costa Rica. See *Inter-American Yearbook on Human Rights 1985*, 234.

to the American Convention.[220] They are elected for a term of six years and may be re-elected only once.[221] In practical terms, however, their mandate extends beyond their elected term for as long as it is necessary for the conclusion of the respective procedural phases (preliminary objections, merits and reparations and enforcement) of the cases they have begun to hear.[222]

Each State Party may nominate up to three candidates who can be nationals of any Member State of the OAS.[223] The candidates must have the 'qualifications required for the exercise of the highest judicial functions in conformity with the laws of the state of which they are nationals or of the state that proposes them as candidates'.[224] However, actual experience as a judge is not required. Most of the judges of the Inter-American Court have been prestigious scholars, but only a few of them were career judges when nominated.[225] A judge may not at the same time hold other positions that prejudice their independence or are otherwise incompatible with the office. Thus they may not be 'members or high-ranking officials of the executive branch of government', 'officials of international organisations' or hold other positions that 'might prevent the judges from discharging their duties, or that might affect their independence or impartiality, or the dignity and prestige of the office'.[226] Judges Hernández Alcerro,[227] Gros Espiell,[228] Aguiar Aranguren[229] and Picado Sotela[230] resigned in order to

[220] The composition of the Court, until 31 December 1997, is as follows: Héctor Fix Zamudio (Mexico), President; Hernán Salgado Pesantes (Ecuador), Vice President; Alejandro Montiel Argüello (Nicaragua); Máximo Pacheco Gómez (Chile); Oliver Jackman (Barbados); Alirio Abreu Burelli (Venezuela); Antônio A. Cançado Trindade (Brazil).

[221] Judges Buergenthal (1979–91), Nieto Navia (1982–94) and Fix Zamudio (1987–99) were re-elected and held office for two full terms. Judges Piza Escalante and Nikken (1979–88) were re-elected for a full term after their first half term as two of the original members of the Court.

[222] Art. 54 of the American Convention and Art. 5.3 of the Statute provide that the Judges must sit in the Court after the expiry of their term of mandate to hear the cases they have begun to hear and that are still pending. See *Order of 19 September 1995,* I/A Court H.R.

[223] Art. 53 of the American Convention and Art. 7 of the Statute of the Court.

[224] Art. 52(1) of the American Convention. See also Art. 4 of the Statute of the Court.

[225] The present Court (see n. 220) includes only one member who is a full time judge in his country: Judge Alirio Abreu Burelli, a member of the Venezuelan Supreme Court. Judge Alejandro Montiel Argüello was earlier a member of the Supreme Court of Justice of Nicaragua from 1962–72.

[226] Art. 18, Statute of the Court

[227] Judge Jorge Ramón Hernández Alcerro was elected in 1986 but he resigned on July 1988. The General Assembly elected Policarpo Callejas Bonilla to complete his term of mandate, finishing in December 1991.

[228] Judge Héctor Gros Espiell resigned in March 1990 in order to become Minister of Foreign Affairs of Uruguay. The General Assembly elected Professor Julio Barberis to complete his term of mandate, finishing in December 1991.

[229] Judge Asdrubal Aguiar Aranguren, who had been elected in 1992 to complete the term of deceased Orlando Tovar Tamayo, resigned in February 1994.

[230] Judge Sonia Picado Sotela resigned in June 1994.

accept appointments incompatible with their position at the Court. There is no bar on holding political or diplomatic posts when not a judge. In fact, many of the 22 judges elected so far have held positions as ministers or diplomats before or after their election or even pursued a political career.[231] For instance, Carlos Roberto Reina (1979–1985), the first president of the Court, became president of Honduras in 1993. Apart from the requirements regarding legal qualifications, the candidates must have shown 'competence in the field of human rights' and, most important, they must possess 'the highest moral authority'. The human rights community is the true guardian of compliance with these standards and, not long ago, the nomination of a candidate for the Court who could not gather support from the NGOs as a jurist with either moral authority or competence in the field of human rights had to be withdrawn.[232] However, the lobbying of the human rights organizations has not always been effective and, at least on one occasion, block voting has resulted in the election of a very questionable nominee.[233]

The election of new members is, naturally, a crucial step in the evolution and functioning of both the Commission and the Court. Mindful of the importance of the human factor, NGOs have started to monitor the election process as from the nomination of candidates by the Member States. These organisations have learned that lobbying for the nomination of individuals with the required expertise and independence—and also the necessary motivation—although a long and frustrating process, is the only way to secure the election of suitable candidates regardless of the result of the secret ballot voting in the context of the General Assembly.

THE POLITICAL ORGANS AND THE FUTURE OF THE INTER-AMERICAN COMMISSION

The Commission was originally conceived as a quasi-diplomatic body with promotional, advisory and drafting functions. The gradual expansion of its functions to include the examination of individual petitions allowed for the development of its quasi-judicial role which was further enhanced by the entry into force of the American Convention. Its 'quasi-diplomatic' profile,

---

[231] For example, on the present Court, Judge Alejandro Montiel Argüello had earlier been the Nicaraguan Minister of Foreign Affairs (1957–61 and 1972–8) and had served his country as an ambassador and UN delegate (1979). He is at present an Advisor to the Ministry of Foreign Affairs.

[232] The Argentine Government withdrew the nomination of a candidate who was a member of the Executive Power and had a controversial political background.

[233] See, Douglas Cassel Jr., 'Somoza's Revenge: A New Judge for the Inter-American Court of Human Rights' 13 *HRLJ* 137 (1992).

far from being discontinued, was consolidated.[234] However, the benefits of a broad and tailored mandate also brought some negative consequences. The diplomatic and judicial duality of the Commission was a useful tool when approaching the Member States, almost strategically, during the seventies and the early eighties but its impact can hardly be disguised in the new context. Today, the Commission operates in a context of prevailing democracy, with governments jealous of their fragile image, and where the task of overseeing compliance with human right standards is no longer reduced to findings on gross violations. More than ever, the performance of the quasi-judicial mandate requires transparency, impartiality and efficiency. Thus, the ambivalent profile of the Commission has started to have an impact on its efficiency and its credibility.

The OAS has declared the strengthening of the system for the protection of human rights as one of its priorities. The Secretary General has expressed the intention of the OAS to 'review [. . .] strengthen and if necessary reform' the system of protection.[235] The Permanent Council is presently in charge of evaluating the System with a view to introducing reforms. Apparently, such reforms will be aimed at making the operation of the System more transparent and predictable.[236] However, the modification of the system is surrounded by technical as well as political obstacles.

There are legal problems to be confronted in the making of any alteration to the rules governing the structure and functioning of the Commission. Any amendment to the American Convention regarding the structure of the Commission would only enter into force after 2/3 of the State Parties express their consent through ratification.[237] Amendments are only valid

---

[234] As Patrick Robinson, former Member of the Commission, has explained '. . . New members of the Commission, particularly those from common-law countries, are always surprised at the level and intensity of the quasi-diplomatic role of the Commission. In fact, the prestige and reputation of the Commission in the Inter-American System is due more to its quasi-diplomatic role than to the quasi-judicial function of receiving petitions [. . .] The term quasi-diplomatic should not be understood to imply that the Commission is a political body carrying out political functions; rather it is indeed to indicate that the Commission's work is concerned with much more than the Article 44 function of considering petitions.' P. Robinson, 'The Inter-American Human Rights System' 17 *West Indian Law Journal* 8 (1993), 21.

[235] César Gaviria has expressed that the OAS '. . . hope[s] to undertake a review . . . [to] strengthen and if necessary reform the inter-american system of human rights. In the new democratic context of the Hemisphere, the demands for the services of the system are growing [. . .] there is a greater need for the legal proceedings to be stricter so that the recommendations of the Commission and the decisions of the Court are heeded, the national systems are strengthened, and finally so that the multilateral system be truly complementary, compatible and coordinated to the national systems. . . .' Speech of the Secretary General of the OAS, delivered at the Twenty-Sixth Regular Session of the General Assembly held in Panama City, Panama, June, 1996.

[236] Remarks by Harriet Babbit, US Permanent Representative to the OAS, delivered at the Twenty-Sixth Regular Session of the General Assembly held in Panama City, Panama, 5 June 1996.

[237] Art. 76.2 of the American Convention.

among States Parties consenting to them. *Ergo*, the modifications introduced would be valid, at least for a time, for some but not necessarily for all of the States Party to the Convention. The adoption and entry into force of amendments relating to the Commission by 2/3 of the 25 States Parties would exclude from the new institutional and procedural regime at least eight States Parties, until they ratify the amendment, plus the ten OAS Member States that have not yet ratified the Convention and are subject to the jurisdiction of the Commission through of the OAS Charter and the Commission Statute only. Any attempt to modify the structure or functioning of the Commission should therefore be made against a background of consensus on the part of all of the Member States of the OAS.

The only concrete proposal presented to the General Assembly so far is not very encouraging. The Commission has kept its basic format untouched since 1959, when the Fifth Meeting of Consultation of Ministers of Foreign Affairs decided to create 'an Inter-American Commission on Human Rights composed of seven members elected, as individuals, by the Council of the Organization of American States'.[238] The seven-member feature remained uncontroversial until 1993 when, during the meeting of the General Assembly,[239] Nicaragua proposed increasing the number of Commissioners to eleven. The initiative was presented as an attempt to strengthen the Commission's independence and effectiveness. However, it is evident that—far from enhancing independence—such modification would only affect the competition among States for geographical distribution of seats and would aggravate the difficulties in coordinating the presence of the part-time Commissioners during the four week biannual sessions.[240] The proposal is still under study but the grounds for its rejection are convincing.

The political obstacles and dangers are clear: some of the Member States wish for the mandate of the Commission to be curbed. They prefer the Commission to play a purely promotional and advisory role.[241] The Commission and the Court are aware of the dangers.[242] There is an urgent need for a genuine attempt to improve the effectiveness of the system—particularly the functioning of the Commission and the conditions surrounding litigation before the Court—but it is vital that such attempt is made in good faith.

[238] Final Act of the Fifth Meeting of Consultation of Ministers of Foreign Affairs, Santiago, Chile, 12–18 Aug. 1959, OEA/Ser. C/II.5, 11.

[239] Twenty Third Ordinary Meeting of the General Assembly of the OAS, Managua, Nicaragua, 7–11 June, 1993.

[240] F. González, 'The 1993 OAS General Assembly in Nicaragua' 51 *The Review of the International Commission on Jurists* 44 (1993), 46.

[241] See V. Vaky and H. Muñoz, *The Future of the Organization of American States*, (New York, 1993), 19–20.

[242] When consulted by the Permanent Council about this project to amend the Convention, the Presidents of the Commission and the Court expressed the view that '. . . this was not the proper time to introduce reforms': I/A Court H.R. Annual Report 1995, 20.

8

The Civil and Political Rights Protected in the Inter-American Human Rights System

SCOTT DAVIDSON

INTRODUCTION

The civil and political rights[1] protected by the inter-American human rights system are derived from two sources: the American Declaration of the Rights and Duties of Man and the American Convention on Human Rights. Although the American Declaration was originally adopted as a non-binding resolution of the Ninth International Conference of American States at Bogota in 1948,[2] it has subsequently been confirmed by the Inter-American Court of Human Rights as an authoritative interpretation of the references to human rights in the OAS Charter.[3] All member States of the OAS are thus bound by the Charter references to human rights as interpreted by the American Declaration. In contradistinction to the broad hemispheric application of the Declaration, only States which are party to the American Convention are bound by its provisions. This does not, however, dispose of the relationship between the two instruments. Article 29(d) of the Convention, which falls under the rubric 'Restrictions on Interpretation', states: 'No provision of this Convention shall be interpreted as . . . excluding or limiting the effect that the American Declaration of the Rights and Duties of Man . . . may have.' It thus appears that where a right is stated more broadly in the Declaration than in the Convention, the broader formulation of the former is to be preferred when interpreting the Convention.[4] As to the application of the Declaration to non-Convention parties, since the Declaration is drafted with less precision

---

[1] Economic and social rights within the inter-American system are considered in Chap. 9 of this book.

[2] OAS Resolution XXX, Final Act of the Ninth International Conference of American States, Bogota, Colombia, 30 Mar.–2 May 1948, 48.

[3] Advisory Opinion No. 10, I/A Court H.R Series A No. 10 (1989), 11 *HRLJ* 118, *Interpretation of the American Declaration of the Rights and Duties of Man within the Framework of Article 64 of the American Convention on Human Rights*.

[4] T. Buergenthal, 'The Inter-American System for the Protection of Human Rights' in T. Meron, (ed.), *Human Rights in International Law: Legal and Policy Issues*, (Oxford, 1984), 439–93 at 442. See also *Interpretation of the American Declaration*, loc. cit. above, n. 3 at para. 41.

than the Convention, its more general wording may well permit the opportunity for more creative interpretation of the scope and meaning of the rights in the Declaration by the system's institutions. Where, however, the Declaration's meaning can be determined by reference to the more detailed exposition of the rights in the Convention, the Commission has indicated that it will proceed in this way in its interpretation of the Declaration on the basis that the 'most accepted doctrine' in American international law is to be found in the Convention.[5] It would seem, therefore, that the relationship between the Declaration and the Convention is one of interdependency.

THE RIGHT TO LIFE: ARTICLE I DECLARATION; ARTICLE 4 CONVENTION

Article I Declaration

Every human being has the right to life, liberty and the security of his person.

Article 4 Convention

1. Every person has the right to have his life respected. This right shall be protected by law and, in general, from the moment of conception. No one shall be arbitrarily deprived of his life.

2. In countries that have not abolished the death penalty, it may be imposed only for the most serious crimes and pursuant to a final judgment rendered by a competent court and in accordance with a law establishing such punishment, enacted prior to the commission of the crime. The application of such punishment shall not be extended to crimes to which it does not presently apply.

3. The death penalty shall not be reestablished in states that have abolished it.

4. In no case shall capital punishment be inflicted for political offences or related common crimes.

5. Capital punishment shall not be imposed upon persons who, at the time the crime was committed, were under 18 years of age or over 70 years of age; nor shall it be applied to pregnant women.

6. Every person condemned to death shall have the right to apply for amnesty, pardon, or commutation of sentence, which may be granted in all cases. Capital punishment shall not be imposed while such a petition is pending decision by the competent authority.

---

[5] Inter-American Commission on Human Rights (hereafter IACHR) Report on the Status of Human Rights in Chile (1974), 3. See also IACHR Report on the Status of Human Rights in Chile (1985) 150. And see the *Baby Boy* case, at n. 11, in which the Commission found that the Convention did not intend to deviate from the Declaration. .

The right to life is guaranteed by Article I of the Declaration and Article 4 of the Convention. While Article I of the Declaration simply provides that '(e)very human being has the right to life', Article 4 is considerably more detailed. It first states that '(e)very person has the right to have his life respected'. It then provides that the right 'shall be protected by law' and that such protection is to commence, 'in general, from the moment of conception'. Finally, Article 4 (1) prohibits the 'arbitrary' taking of life by the state. The remaining provisions of Article 4 deal in detail with the question of the death penalty.

Protection of life generally

The requirement in Article 4(1) of the Covention that the right to life be 'protected by law', coupled with the general obligation in Article 1 of the Convention to act positively to 'ensure' the rights guaranteed in the Convention, means that States Parties must take adequate steps in their law and practice to safeguard human life. Applying accepted standards, they must make the taking of life by the State and others illegal, provide for the proper policing of the community to enforce the law and act rigorously after the event to investigate, punish and compensate for any taking of life. These positive obligations were fully considered by the Inter-American Court of Human Rights in the *Velasquez Rodriguez* and *Godinez Cruz* cases (the Honduran Disappearance Cases).[6]

The question of the extent of the positive obligation of a State to protect the life of a person in its custody was in issue in the *Gangaram Panday* case.[7] In that case, the victim had been found dead in his cell, probably, the Court considered, as a result of suicide, after having been detained for some two to three days by the Suriname Military Police following his arrival from abroad at Zanderij Airport. Although holding that the victim's detention was contrary to Article 7 of the Convention,[8] the Court, by four votes to three, held that the victim's right to life under Article 4 of the Convention had not been infringed. The majority took the view that the 'circumstances surrounding this case make it impossible to establish the responsibility of the State'.[9] The minority considered that the State has a duty to act with 'due diligence' to protect life and that this duty becomes stricter in respect of persons who are illegally detained. On the facts, there had been indications that the victim's detention had intensified

---

[6] *Velasquez Rodriguez* v *Honduras* I/A Court H.R. Series C No. 4 (1988), 9 *HRLJ* 212; *Godinez Cruz* v *Honduras*, I/A Court H.R Series C No. 5. On the positive obligations under Art. 1 of the Convention, see above, 15. On the rulings on the facts in the *Velasquez Rodriguez* case, see below, 219.

[7] I/A Court H.R. Series C No. 16 (1994), 15 *HRLJ* 168, 2 IHRR 360 (1995).

[8] See below, 235.

[9] Loc. cit. at n. 7, para. 62.

his 'depression and contempt for life', a factor which led the minority to conclude that more should have been done to safeguard the victim's life. The collective dissenting opinion reads:[10]

The international protection of human rights, as it relates to Article 4(1) of the American Convention on Human Rights, has a preventive dimension, in which the obligation to act with due diligence assumes graver implications when dealing with illegal detentions. Due diligence imposes on the states the obligation to prevent, within reason, those situations which—as in the case now before us—could lead, sometimes even by omission, to the denial of the inviolability of the right to life.

The protection of unborn children

The obligation to protect the right to life applies to all 'human beings' or 'persons'. Article I of the Declaration applies *ratione personae* to 'human beings' while the Convention applies to 'persons'. This difference in drafting is immaterial as Article 1(2) of the Convention provides that for its purposes 'person' means 'human being'. Neither the Declaration nor the Convention defines what is meant by the term 'human being', thus the questions of whether a foetus is a human being and when a human being ceases to exist are not answered by the instruments themselves. While the Commission has considered the former question, neither it nor the Court has been required to rule on the latter.

In the *Baby Boy* case[11] the Commission was required to answer the question whether the overturning of the conviction of a doctor for conducting an abortion on a male foetus under Massachusetts' law and the United States Supreme Court's interpretation of the United States Constitution[12] permitting abortion was in breach of Article I of the Declaration. After reviewing the *travaux préparatoires* of Article I, the Commission held that there had been no breach of this provision. The Commission noted that, during the drafting of Article I, language which would have protected life from the moment of conception had been removed, along with specific language protecting the rights of 'incurables, imbeciles and the insane' and a further provision limiting the application of the death penalty. The reason given by the Commission for the removal of these provisions was that their inclusion would have necessitated derogation from laws already in force in a large number of American States.[13] It thus concluded that the

---

[10] Dissenting opinion, para. 4, of Judges Picado-Sotela, Aguiar-Aranguren and Cançado Trindade.
[11] Case 2141 (USA), IACHR Annual Report 1980–1 25; 2 *HRLJ* 110.
[12] See *Roe* v *Wade* 410 US 113 (1973).
[13] The Commission noted that in the penal codes of a large number of states it was not a criminal offence to effect an abortion in one or more of the following cases; to save the life of

United States was correct in arguing that Article I did not protect life from the moment of conception since 'the conference faced this question but chose not to adopt language which would clearly have stated that principle.'[14] A reading of the *travaux* does not lead ineluctably to this conclusion, and the better view is perhaps that expressed in the concurring opinion case of Dr Aguilar who stated that Article I 'sidesteps' this important issue.[15] He stated that Article I represents a compromise formula which leaves to each State the power to determine whether life begins and warrants protection from the moment of conception or at some other time prior to birth.

The petitioners also sought to rely on Article 4(1) of the Convention as a means of interpreting Article I of the Declaration. While noting that the US was not a party to the Convention and was not therefore technically bound by Article 4(1), the Commission was nonetheless prepared to engage in a theoretical analysis of this provision. Resort to the *travaux* of Article 4(1) revealed that it was a compromise between those States which permitted abortion and those which did not. The phrase 'in general, from the moment of conception' was not intended to deviate from the meaning of the Article I of the American Declaration.[16]

Shelton criticises the way in which the Commission was prepared to resort immediately to the *travaux* of each of the instruments under consideration without first applying the traditional canons of treaty interpretation contained in Article 31 of the Vienna Convention on the Law of Treaties.[17] In her view the two dissenting Commissioners came closer to this technique than did the majority. They applied the ordinary meaning of the words in their context and supported their view of when life begins by reference to medical science and theology. By employing this approach, they concluded that a foetus is a human being from the moment of conception.[18]

Euthanasia

Neither Article I of the Declaration nor Article 4 of the Convention gives any indication of whether euthanasia, or mercy killing, is permitted. Passive euthanasia, by which treatment is withdrawn with the consent of the

the mother, to protect a rape victim or the honour of an honest woman, to prevent the transmission of disease, or for economic reasons.

[14] Loc. cit. at n. 11, para. 19(h).
[15] Concurring Decision of Dr Andres Aguilar M., id. at 44, para. 5.
[16] Loc. cit. at n. 11, at 41–4.
[17] D. Shelton, 'Abortion and the Right to Life in the Inter-American System', (1980) 1 *HRLJ* 316.
[18] Case 2141 (USA), IACHR Annual Report 1980–1, 25, dissenting opinions of Dr. Luis Demetrio Tinoco Castro and Dr. Marco Gerardo Monroy Cabra at 45 and 49.

patient, thereby foreshortening life, would presumably not violate the relevant provisions.[19] Active euthanasia, by which death is brought forward by a positive act, might not satisfy the requirements of Article I of the Declaration or Article 4(1) of the Convention, even with the patient's consent. The Commission has held elsewhere[20] that the right to life is fundamental, and it might well be that neither the Commission nor the Court would be prepared to see a weakening of the fundamental character of this right by a mercy killing exception, even where this is done with the consent of the patient.

No arbitrary taking of life

A reading of the Declaration and Convention provisions reveals some differences in drafting. While Article I is direct and unequivocal, Article 4 appears to import an element of conditionality into the right. The fact that by its terms no-one is to be deprived of his or her life 'arbitrarily' seems to permit the non-arbitrary deprivation of life. However, the Commission's report in Case 10.559 (Peru),[21] contains the following passage:

This prohibition against arbitrary deprivation of human life is at the core of the right to life. The use of the term 'arbitrarily' might appear to indicate that the Convention allows exceptions to the right to life, on the mistaken assumption that life may be taken in certain circumstances provided that this is not done arbitrarily. However, quite the opposite is the case, since the intent of this clause is rather to seek to ensure strengthening of the conditions governing application of the death penalty by states which have not yet abolished it, and at the same time, to serve as a guarantee to prevent summary executions.

The Commission would appear to have been seeking to stress in this passage that Article 4 provided a guarantee 'to prevent summary executions', as on the facts of the case, and that the term 'arbitrary' should not be relied upon to lessen the strict limits on the taking of life set by Article 4. It is submitted that the Commission's statement does not mean that the use of deadly force by state agents may not be excused under Article 4 in some circumstances, for example, where it is absolutely necesssary in self-defence.

Guidance on the approach to be taken in determining whether the use of deadly force by the police, the armed forces and other state agents

---

[19] Passive euthanasia has been found not to be in breach of the European Convention on Human Rights: see D. Harris, M. O'Boyle and C. Warbrick, *The Law of the European Convention on Human Rights*, (London, 1995) 38. There has been no ruling on active euthanasia.

[20] See IACHR Annual Report 1986–7, 271.

[21] See however the Commission's statement in Case 10.559 (Peru), IACHR Annual Report 1995, 136, 147–8.

assertedly for good reason is 'arbitrary' and hence contrary to Article 4 can first be found in the general statements by the Court in the *Honduran Disappearance* cases *(Velasquez Rodriguez et al)*.[22] There, in connection with the right to life and other human rights violations involved in forced disappearances, the Court first acknowledged that the State has both a right and a duty to guarantee its national security, which may involve the use of deadly force, but then noted that there are limits to its freedom of action:

. . . regardless of the seriousness of certain actions and the culpability of the perpetrators of certain crimes, the power of the state is not unlimited, nor may the state resort to any means to attains its ends. The state is subject to law and morality. Disrespect for human dignity cannot serve as the basis for any state action.

It follows from this that the mere fact that the taking of life is by a person acting for the State does not by itself mean that it is not 'arbitrary'. Instead, the use of deadly force by the police or other state actors is 'arbitrary' unless it can be justified as being absolutely necessary for a recognised public interest reason.

This was relevant on the facts of the *Neira Alegria* case.[23] While the Court did not pass on the precise meaning of 'arbitrary' in this case, it did declare that the deaths of three inmates following the disproportionate use of force by Peruvian authorities in quelling a prison riot led to the conclusion that they had been arbitrarily deprived of their lives in violation of Article 4(1).[24] Although the rioters were highly dangerous and armed, the use of dynamite to blow up the building being held by them, leading to the deaths of over 100 prisoners, was a 'disproportionate use of force'.[25] In that case, the public interest justification could be seen in terms of preventing escape or maintaining public order. It is probable that, like other international human rights guarantees,[26] which apply a test of strict proportionality in this context, that self defence and the need to effect an arrest are also good public interest reasons for the purpose of Article 4 of the Convention.

Together with the obligation to act positively to protect human life,[27] the prohibition of the arbitrary taking of life was one of the grounds for the

---

[22] Loc. cit n. 6, above, para. 154.
[23] I/A Court H.R. Series C No. 20 (1995), 16 *HRLJ* 403, 3 IHRR 362 (1996).
[24] Loc. cit. at n. 23, para. 76.
[25] Id., para. 76.
[26] Art. 6, ICCPR prohibits the taking of life 'arbitrarily'.This has been held to permit the taking of life by state action where this is necessary in self defence, to effect an arrest or to prevent an escape: *Guerrero v Colombia*, 1 HRC Sel. Decns. 112 (1979). Cf. Art. 2(2), ECHR, which refers expressly to these reasons and to the 'purpose of quelling a riot or insurrection'.
[27] See above, 215.

finding of a breach of Article 4 of the Convention in the *Honduran Disappearance* cases. In the Velasquez case, the Court found that a practice of forced disappearances existed in Honduras between 1981 and 1984 that was 'carried out or tolerated by Honduran officials' and that Manfredo Velasquez had 'disappeared at the hands of or with the acquiescence of those officials within the framework of that practice'.[28] As far as the right to life was concerned, the Court noted that the 'practice of disappearances often involves secret execution without trial, followed by concealment of the body to eliminate any material evidence of the crime and to ensure the impunity of those responsible'.[29] Where this happens, the Court said, there is 'a flagrant violation' of Article 4 Convention.[30] With regard to the facts of the case, the Court also stated that the 'context in which the disappearance of Manfredo Velasquez occurred and the lack of knowledge seven years later about his fate create a reasonable presumption that he was killed'.[31] The Court continued:[32]

> Even if there is a minimal margin of doubt in this respect, it must be presumed that his fate was decided by the authorities who systematically executed detainees without trial and concealed their bodies in order to avoid punishment. This, together with the failure to investigate, is a violation by Honduras of a legal duty under Article 1(1) of the Convention to ensure the rights recognised by Article 4(1). That duty is to ensure to every person subject to its jurisdiction the inviolability of the right to life and the right not to have one's life taken arbitrarily. These rights imply an obligation on the part of the States Parties to take reasonable steps to prevent situations that could result in the violation of that right.

In the above passage, Honduras's liability under Article 4 is predicated partly upon its failure to fulfil its positive obligation to act preventatively and by way of subsequent investigation to 'ensure' the individual's right to life. Given the finding that Honduran officals were directly or indirectly implicated,[33] the case may also clearly be seen, in terms of the language of Article 1(1) of the Convention, to have involved a breach of Article 4 on the basis of a lack of 'respect' for the right to life by virtue of 'arbitrary' taking of life by the State, as well a lack of protection of the right to life on its part.

More generally, it may be noted at this point that the practice of forced disappearances that was involved in the Honduras cases has presented great problems in Latin America and involves breaches of other basic human rights as well as the right to life. Neither the Declaration nor the

---

[28] *Velasquez Rodriguez* v *Honduras,* para. 148.   [29] Id., para. 157.
[30] Id.   [31] Id., para. 188.
[32] Id., The Commission has also stated that disappearances 'constitute a serious violation of the right to life': Case 10.563 (Peru), IACHR Annual Report 1993, 303, 308.
[33] See para. 148, judgment, quoted above at n. 28. Elsewhere in its judgment, para. 182, the Court stated that it was 'convinced, and has so found, that the disappearance of Manfredo Velasquez was carried out by agents who acted under cover of public authority'.

Convention contain any explicit prohibition of the practice, which has been utterly condemned by the institutions of the OAS.[34] But as the Court has observed, disappearances constitute 'a multiple and continuous violation of many rights under the Convention that the States Parties are obligated to respect and guarantee'.[35] In the *Honduran Disappearance* cases the Court found that disappearances violated Articles 5 and 7 of the Convention, concerning the rights to humane treatment and to personal liberty and security respectively, as well as Article 4.

With regard to the right to life, the Court followed the approach it had spelt out in the Honduran disappearances cases in the *Caballero Delgado and Santana* case.[36] In this case, the Court found that the detention and disappearance of the two victims in an area in which there was intense army and guerrilla activity had been effected by the Colombian army. Since there has been no news of the two victims for more than six years, the Court considered it reasonable to conclude that the two victims were dead, although their bodies had not been found. The Court held, by four to one, that Colombia was in breach of the guarantee of the right to life in Article 4(1) of the Convention.

The Court and, more especially, the Commission have found numerous violations of Article I of the Declaration and Article 4(1) of the Convention which have raised few issues of interpretation. The vast majority of cases which appear in the Commission's reports have involved unambiguous and frequently uncontested violations of the right to life by the State in the form of the 'arbitrary' taking of life by State agents. They typically involve assassinations, extrajudicial executions, massacres and enforced disappearances.[37] The Commission and the Court have been able to classify these as violations of the Declaration and Convention without the need for any analysis of their content.

---

[34] See 'Inter-American Convention on Forced Disappearance of Persons', IACHR Annual Report 1986–7, 277–84. See also the following resolutions of the OAS General Assembly: Res AG/Res.443 (IX–0/79); AG/Res.510 (X–0/80); AG/Res.543 (XI–0/81); AG/Res.618 (XII–0/82); AG/Res. 666 (XIII–0/83); AG/Res.742 (XIV–0/84) and AG/Res.890 (XVII–087). The Inter-American Convention on Forced Disappearance of Persons (1994) 33 ILM 1529; 3 IHRR 226 (1996) was adopted at Belem, Brazil on 9 June 1994. For the purposes of the Convention it defines forced disappearances as 'the act of depriving a person or persons of his or their freedom, in whatever way, perpetrated by agents of the state or by persons or groups of persons acting with the authorization, support, or acquiescence of the state, followed by an absence of information or a refusal to acknowledge that deprivation of freedom or to give information on the whereabouts of that person, thereby impeding his or her recourse to the applicable legal remedies and procedural guarantees'.

[35] *Velasquez Rodriguez v Honduras*, I/A Court H.R. Series C No. 4, para. 155; *Godinez Cruz v Honduras,* I/A Court H.R., Series C No. 5, para. 163. See also *Caballero-Delgado and Santana v Colombia*, 17 *HRLJ* 24; 3 IHHR 548 (1996).

[36] Judgment of 8 Dec. 1995; 17 *HRLJ* 24, 3 IHRR 548 (1995).

[37] See the individual cases cited in connection with Colombia, El Salvador, Guatemala, Haiti, Honduras and Peru in the Commission's 1993 Annual Report, where a number of these practices are denounced as violations of the right to life.

The death penalty

Although Article 4 of the Convention contains numerous provisions concerning the death penalty,[38] Article I of the Declaration is silent on this matter. The original draft of Article I did contain a reference to the death penalty which provided that 'the right to life may be denied by the State only on the ground of a conviction of the gravest crimes, to which the death penalty has been attached.' This provision was, however, excised from the final draft for the same reasons that the reference to the commencement of life at conception was eliminated.[39] Under Article 4 the death penalty may only be imposed for the 'most serious crimes' pursuant to a 'final judgment rendered by a competent court'.[40] Furthermore, the death penalty may not be imposed for 'political offences or related common crimes'[41] and may not be applied retroactively.[42] The death penalty is also limited so as to exclude its application to certain kinds of person. It may not be imposed upon persons under 18 years of age nor upon persons over 70 when the capital offence was committed.[43] Women who are pregnant at the time of the planned execution are also excluded from its application.[44]

The Convention's express recognition of the continuing legality of capital punishment in certain circumstances read in conjunction with the statement by the Commission in Case 10.559 (Peru), quoted above, reveals that the exercise of the death penalty in conformity with the strict requirement of the Convention will not violate Article 4(1). This view was confirmed by the Inter-American Court in *Neira Alegria* v *Peru* in which it stated that the inclusion of the word 'arbitrarily' in Article 4(1) of the Convention excludes legal proceedings leading to the death penalty from its ambit.[45] Nonetheless, it is noteworthy that the American Convention demonstrates an abolitionist trend in relation to the death penalty, since it may not be extended to crimes to which it does not currently apply,[46] and it may not be re-established in states which have abolished it.[47] Despite the express wording of Article 4(2) in this regard, the Commission has been confronted with situations in which States Parties to the Convention have introduced the death penalty for crimes to which it did not hitherto apply. In 1993, Peru amended its constitution to add terrorism to the list of crimes which attracted the death penalty. The Commission considered that

---

[38] On the death penalty in the inter-American system generally see W. A. Schabas, *The Abolition of the Death Penalty in International Law* (Cambridge,1993), 281–2.

[39] See above, 216.　　　　　　　　　　　　　[40] Art. 4(2) American Convention.

[41] Art. 4(4) American Convention.　　　　　[42] Art. 4(2) American Convention.

[43] Art. 4(5) American Convention.　　　　　[44] Id.

[45] Judgment of 19 Jan. 1995, (1995) 16 *HRLJ* 403, (1996) 3 IHRR 362.

[46] Art. 4(2) American Convention.

[47] Art. 4(3) American Convention.

this was a manifest violation of Peru's obligations under the Convention.[48] The abolitionist trend in Article 4 is also supported by the 1990 Protocol to the American Convention Abolishing the Death Penalty[49] which, although not requiring States to abolish the death penalty immediately, requires them not to apply it.[50] The Commission's abolitionist approach is also evident in a number of Jamaican death penalty cases in which allegations of a lack of due process contrary to Articles 8 and 25 of the Convention were made. Although the Commission found no breach of the Convention on the facts of these cases, it nonetheless recommended that the death penalty be commuted for humanitarian reasons and that the government take definite steps to abolish the death penalty 'as has been done in various countries'.[51]

The Commission has also ruled that the application of the death penalty may constitute cruel, inhuman and degrading treatment. In its 1993 'Report on Peru'[52] it stated: 'For the Inter-American Commission on Human Rights, there is no premium that can be placed upon human life. The death penalty is a grievous affront to human dignity and its application constitutes cruel, inhuman and degrading treatment of the individual sentenced to death.' Furthermore, the Commission has held that in no circumstances may the death penalty be used to restore public order.[53]

Although the Convention expressly forbids the execution of persons under the age of eighteen when the offence was committed, the Declaration does not. Since the United States is not party to the American Convention, and since in certain states in the United States persons under the age of eighteen at the time of the commission of the offence are still liable to be executed, the question of whether Article I of the Declaration prevents such executions has been raised before the Commission. Case 9647 (United States of America)[54] concerned the execution of two

---

[48] 'Report on Peru' in IACHR Annual Report 1993, 478. Cf. IACHR Annual Report 1971, 33; Annual Report 1981–2, 106; Report on the Situation of Human Rights in Argentina (1980) 29, Report on the Situation of Human Rights in Chile (1985), 48–50.

[49] PAUTS 73; 29 ILM 1447 (1990). In force 1993. See Appendix VIII for parties.

[50] Id., Art. 1.

[51] Case 9054 (Jamaica), IACHR Annual Report 1984–5, 111. See also Case 3115 (Jamaica), IACHR Annual Report 1981–2, 89; Case 3552 (Jamaica), IACHR Annual Report 1982–3, 99; Case 7604 (Jamaica), IACHR Annual Report 1983–4, 54.

[52] IACHR Annual Report 1993, 478.

[53] IACHR 'Areas in which Steps Need to be Taken Towards Full Observance of the Human Rights Set Forth in the American Declaration of Human Rights and Duties and the American Convention on Human Rights', 1986–7 Annual Report, 271.

[54] IACHR Annual Report 1986–7, 147 at 170. See on this case, Schabas, op. cit. above, n. 38, 254–63; Cerna, 'US Death Penalty tested before the Inter-American Commission on Human Rights', (1992) 10 *NQHR* 155; D. Fox, 'Inter-American Commission on Human Rights Finds United States in Violation', (1988) 82 *AJIL* 601; Shelton, 'The Decision of the IACHR of 27 March 1987 in the case of Roach and Pinkerton: A Note',

seventeen-year olds in South Carolina and Texas for rape and murder and attempted rape and murder respectively. The petitioners argued that the application of the death penalty to persons below the age of eighteen was contrary to customary international law, and that such customary international law was incorporated into Article I of the Declaration. Following a review of the development of customary international law in the field of capital punishment, the Commission found that 'in the member States of the OAS there is a recognized norm of *ius cogens* which prohibits the State execution of children' and that this norm was 'accepted by all of the states of the Inter-American system, including the United States'.[55] The problem which confronted the Commission, however, was the age of majority. The Commission was convinced by the US argument that there was no extant rule of customary international law declaring eighteen to be the age of majority for the purposes of determining whether a person should be tried as a juvenile or an adult. This leads to the curious result that there is a norm of *ius cogens* prohibiting the execution of juveniles which does not stipulate the age of majority at which it ceases to apply. Furthermore, the Commission held that even if there were an emergent norm specifying eighteen as the age of majority, the United States would not be bound by it under the Declaration, since it had signified its intention to enter a reservation on this point to Article 4(5) of the Convention should it ratify the Convention.[56]

Despite this conclusion, the Commission considered that the question of age did not dispose of the case before it. Following a review of practice in this field in the different states within the United States, the Commission determined that whether or not the death penalty applied to persons under 18 depended not upon the nature of the crime itself, but upon the sentencing law in the state concerned, and this varied from one state to another. The Commission therefore concluded that 'the failure of the [US] federal government to preempt the states as regards this most fundamental right—the right to life—results in a pattern of legislative arbitrariness throughout the United States which results in the arbitrary deprivation of life and inequality before the law, contrary to Articles I and II of the American Declaration . . .'[57] It might be remarked that the Commission's reasoning in this case, which is restricted to the question of the juvenile

---

(1987) 8 *HRLJ* 355; and D. Weissbrodt, 'Execution of Juvenile Offenders by the United States Violates International Human Rights Law', (1988) 3 *Am. U J Int'l. L. and Pol.* 339.

[55] Id., para. 56. The Commission quoted the US response in the case that 'all states, moreover, have juvenile justice systems; none permits its juvenile courts to impose the death penalty.' As the Commission noted, the *Roach* and *Pinkerton* cases arose because 17-year olds were tried in the states concerned before an adult criminal court, with the full range of penalties available in such courts, and not before a juvenile court.

[56] Id., at 170.   [57] Id., at 173.

death penalty, might be applied equally to the death penalty *per se* in the United States, since the application of the death penalty will depend upon the *locus* of the crime rather than its nature.

Although the Commission has not otherwise been obliged to analyse the death penalty in detail, certain statements in its annual reports suggest that Article I of the Declaration is further qualified by the requirements that it may only be imposed in accordance with pre-existing laws and the requirements of due process. In a report on Cuba, the Commission condemned the State for executing a number of military officers following conviction for drug trafficking and hostile acts against third countries, since these were not capital crimes under Cuban law and there were doubts about compliance with the requirements of due process.[58] A decision to impose the death penalty that was racially motivated would also be a breach of Article I of the Declaration, as read with Article II.[59]

With regard to the Convention, the Court has had occasion to consider the compatibility of a reservation attached to a state's ratification of the Convention with the requirement in Article 4(4) that the death penalty may not be imposed for a 'common crime' related to a political offence. In *Restrictions to the Death Penalty*,[60] a reservation made by Guatemala at the time of ratification stated that its ratification of the American Convention was subject to Article 54 of the Guatemalan Constitution which excluded political crimes from the death penalty, but not common crimes related to political crimes.[61] Although Article 4 is a provision from which a State Party may not derogate in time of emergency, the Court advised that the reservation was valid as not being one that deprived the guarantee of the right to life of its purpose as a whole. However, having been made as a reservation to Article 4(4), the reservation in question could not, as Guatemala had claimed in a case before the Commission, justify the introduction of capital punishment for a related common crime that did not exist at the time of ratification. In the Court's view, such an act was a violation of the prohibition of new capital offences in Article 4(2), a provision to which Guatemala had not sought to enter a reservation. As the Court noted, the Article 4(4) reservation could only serve to protect capital offences for common crimes that existed at the time of ratification.[62]

---

[58] IACHR 1988–9 Annual Report at 158. Cf. Case No 10.031 (United States) (Celestine case), IACHR Annual Report 1989–90, 575 (requirement of impartial tribunal: no proof of a biased jury on the facts).

[59] Case No 10.031 (United States) (Celestine case), IACHR Annual Report 1989–90, 62. (no breach on the facts: statistics that showed that a black person was much more likely to be sentenced to death not sufficient proof of discrimination).

[60] Advisory Opinion No. 3, I/A Court H.R. Series A No. 3 (1983), 4 *HRLJ* 339.

[61] Id., para. 10.

[62] Id., para. 71.

THE RIGHT TO HUMANE TREATMENT: ARTICLES I, XXV, XXVI DECLARATION;
ARTICLE 5 CONVENTION

Article I Declaration

Every human being has the right to life, liberty and the security of his person.

Article XXV Declaration

. . . Every individual who has been deprived of his liberty has . . . the right to humane treatment during the time he is in custody.

Article XXVI Declaration

Every person accused of an offense has the right . . . not to receive cruel, infamous or unusual punishment.

Article 5 Convention

1. Every person has the right to have his physical, mental, and moral integrity respected.
2. No one shall be subject to torture or to cruel, inhuman, or degrading punishment or treatment. All persons deprived of their liberty shall be treated with respect for the inherent dignity of the human person.
3. Punishment shall not be extended to any person other than the criminal.
4. Accused persons shall, save in exceptional circumstances, be segregated from convicted persons, and shall be subject to separate treatment appropriate to their status as unconvicted persons.
5. Minors while subject to criminal proceedings shall be separated from adults and brought before specialised tribunals, as speedily as possible, so that they may be treated in accordance with their status as minors.
6. Punishments consisting of deprivation of liberty shall have as an essential aim the reform and social readaptation of the prisoners.

The right to humane treatment is protected by Articles I, XXV and XXVI of the Declaration and Article 5 of the Convention. Article I of the Declaration provides that everyone has the right, *inter alia*, to 'security of his person'. While the Declaration nowhere refers to the prohibition of torture and related practices (but see Article XXVI above concerning punishments), the Commission has always assumed that they are subsumed under Article I. There is also the guarantee of 'humane treatment' of persons in custody in Article XXV of the Declaration. The non-derogable Article 5 of the Convention is much more extensive. It provides that every person has the right to 'have his physical, mental and moral integrity respected'[63] and that 'no one shall be subjected to torture or to cruel, inhuman or degrading treatment or punishment'.[64] Moreover, all detainees must 'be treated with respect for the inherent dignity of the human person'.[65] The remaining provisions of Article 5 deal with other aspects of the treatment and punishment of those deprived of their liberty.

The sphere of operation of Article 5 of the Convention is different to that of Article 4 of the Convention. In the *Neira Alegría* case the Commission argued that the deaths of three prison inmates who had been killed by the Peruvian authorities were a violation of Article 5 as well as Article 4(1). The Court rejected this view on the grounds that while the deprivation of a person's life might also be understood as an injury to his or her personal integrity, this was not the meaning of Article 5. In the Court's view, Article 5 was concerned solely with circumstances in which it could be proved that individuals had been subjected to ill-treatment or indignity contrary to the terms of Article 5.[66] Although inhuman treatment might occur in the circumstances surrounding a violation of the right to life, this had to be proved and did not follow simply from the fact that a person has been killed.

As noted above in the discussion of Article 4, the violation of Article 5 is also a constituent element in the phenomenon of enforced disappearances. The Commission has taken the approach that disappearances, even if of a temporary nature, are cruel and inhuman.[67] In the very many cases of disappearances considered by the Commission, there has usually been no actual proof of inhuman treatment, but it has relied substantially on its powers under Article 42 of its Statute[68] to presume the facts alleged by the petitioner, including claims of treatment contrary to Article 5, to be true in the absence of any reply by the respondent State. In the *Honduran Disappearance* cases, however, the Court did have some more positive evidence. It found that the evidence of disappeared persons who had regained their liberty tended to show that they had often been 'subjected to merciless treatment including torture and other cruel, inhuman and degrading treatment in violation of the right to physical integrity recognised in Article 5 . . .'[69] The Court found, in particular, that prolonged isolation and detention incommunicado, which were in themselves cruel and inhuman treatment, were harmful to the psychological and moral

---

[63] Art. 5(1). [64] Art. 5(2).
[65] Id. [66] Loc. cit., above, n. 23, para. 86.
[67] Case 10.508 (Guatemala) IACHR Annual Report 1994, 51 at 54.
[68] On the presumption in Art. 42 of the truth of facts credibly alleged by the petitioner that are not contradicted by the state, see above, 98.
[69] *Velasquez Rodriguez,* loc. cit. above, n. 6 at para. 155; *Godinez Cruz,* loc. cit. above, n. 6 at para. 162.

integrity of the persons detained.[70] Furthermore, the Court found that respect for the physical, mental and moral integrity of the person and freedom from torture, inhuman and degrading treatment had been violated by Honduras in the very act of causing the disappearance of the victim.[71]

In considering whether there has been a violation of Article I of the Declaration or Article 5 of the Convention, the Commission and the Court have so far tended to deal with these provisions as composites and have not attempted to differentiate between their various components. Even so, there are a number of cases in which such differentiation is evident. In Case 10.772 (El Salvador)[72] the Commission held that the rape of a seven year old girl by a soldier violated the 'respect for personal integrity' guarantee in Article 5(1).[73] Similarly a number of cases involving prisoners have been held to have violated the 'respect for the inherent dignity of the human person' guarantee in Article 5(2). Thus overcrowding and the lack of minimum services in El Salvadoran prisons were held to affect the right of prisoners to be treated with the required respect for their dignity.[74] Similar concerns were also expressed about the disciplinary regime in Cuba's prisons, although Article 5(2) was not specifically mentioned.[75]

Most cases, however, have concerned the prohibition of torture and other lesser forms of ill-treatment proscribed by the first sentence of Article 5(2). In general, neither the Commission nor the Court has attempted to define torture, but have been content to describe certain practices as falling within the concept. The Commission has thus found that the following acts are torture within the meaning of the Declaration and the Convention: sitting a victim half-naked and wet in a metal tub and applying electric shocks; standing on his body beating him on the chest and abdomen; putting a hood over a victim's head so he could not breathe and burning him with cigarettes;[76] rape;[77] mock burials, mock executions, deprivation of food and water,[78] threats of removal of body parts; exposure to the torture of other victims;[79] keeping prisoners naked for lengthy periods of time and denying them appropriate medical treatment;[80] 'sub-

---

[70] *Velasquez Rodriguez,* loc. cit. above, n. 6 at para. 156; *Godinez Cruz,* loc. cit. above, n. 6 at para. 163.

[71] *Velasquez Rodriguez,* loc. cit. above, n. 18 at para. 187; *Godinez Cruz,* loc. cit. above, n. 18 at para. 197.　　　　[72] IACHR Annual Report 1993, 186.

[73] Id.　　　　　　　　　　　　　　　　　　　[74] IACHR Annual Report 1994, 178.

[75] 'Report on Cuba' in IACHR Annual Report 1994, 142 at 161.

[76] Case 10.574 (El Salvador), IACHR Annual Report 1993 at 174.

[77] Case 7481 (Bolivia), IACHR Annual Report 1981–2, 36 and Case 10.970 (Peru), IACHR Annual Report 1995, 157 at 182–8.

[78] Case 7823 (Bolivia), IACHR Annual Report 1981–2, 42.

[79] Case 7824 (Bolivia), id. at 44.

[80] Case 7910 (Cuba), IACHR Res No. 13/82, 8 Mar. 1982, OEA/Ser.L/V/II.55. doc. 28, 8 Mar. 1982, Original: Spanish; Case 5154 (Nicaragua), IACHR Annual Report 1982–3, 101.

marine';[81] keeping detainees hooded and naked in cells and interrogating them under the drug pentothal; imposing a restricted diet leading to malnutrition, and simulation of early release.[82]

Although the Commission and the Court have been reluctant to formulate an abstract definition of torture, it should be noted that within the inter-American system a definition is provided by the Inter-American Convention to Prevent and Punish Torture 1985.[83] This states:

For the purposes of this Convention, torture shall be understood to be any act intentionally performed whereby physical or mental pain or suffering is inflicted on a person for purposes of criminal investigation, as a means of intimidation, as a personal punishment, as a preventive measure, as a penalty or for any other purpose. Torture shall also be understood to be the use of methods upon a person intended to obliterate the personality of the victim or to diminish his physical or mental capacities, even if they do not cause pain or mental anguish.

Exempted from this definition are physical or mental pain or suffering which is inherent or solely the consequence of lawful measures, providing that they do not include the acts or use of methods referred to above.[84] Furthermore, Article 5 of the Inter-American Torture Convention indicates that torture may not be justified on grounds of national emergency, the dangerous character of the detainee or prisoner, or the lack of security of the prison or institution where a prisoner is held. This clearly conforms to the non-derogable quality of the right, as expressed in Article 27(2) of the American Convention. It is interesting to note that whereas the first sentence of the definition in the Inter-American Torture Convention follows the UN Torture Convention definition[85] by requiring the intentional infliction of pain or suffering, the second sentence moves away from the UN Torture Convention definition by including drug based techniques which do not of themselves cause pain, but which are designed to obliterate the victim's personality.

The Commission has recently applied the definition of torture in the Inter-American Convention to Prevent and Punish Torture as an aid to

---

[81] Case 9274 (Uruguay), IACHR Annual Report 1984–5, 121. Submarine is the practice of holding a victim's head in foul water until the point of drowning. 'Dry submarine' uses a similar technique of asphyxiating the victim by covering his or her head with a plastic bag.

[82] Case 2530 (El Salvador), IACHR Report on the Status of Human Rights in El Salvador, OEA/Ser.L/V/II.46, doc. 23, rev. 1, 17 Nov. 1978, Original: Spanish, 89.

[83] PAUTS 85 67; 25 ILM 519 (1986). In force 1987. For parties see Appendix VIII. On the Inter-American Convention to Prevent and Punish Torture see F. Kaplan, 'Combating Political Torture in Latin America: An Analysis of the Organization of American States Inter-American Convention to Prevent and Punish Torture' (1989) XV *Brooklyn J Int. L.* 399; S. Davidson, 'No More Broken Bodies or Minds: The Definition and Control of Torture in the Late Twentieth Century' (1995) 6 *Canterbury L. Rev.* 25–55 at 41–9.

[84] Art. 2 of the Inter-American Convention to Prevent and Punish Torture.

[85] See Art. 1, UN Torture Convention.

defining the meaning of torture in Article 5 of the American Convention on Human Rights in a case involving the repeated rape of a woman by members of the Peruvian armed forces.[86] Here, the Inter-American Commission held that three elements must be combined for torture to exist. First, there must be an intentional act through which physical and mental pain and suffering is inflicted on a person. Second, the act must be committed for a purpose. Third, the act must be committed by a public official or by a private person acting at the instigation of the former.[87] The Commission found that all these constituent elements were present in the act of rape by military personnel.[88]

In general the Commission has not differentiated between torture and inhuman or degrading treatment. In its 'Report on the Situation of Human Rights in Panama', however, the Commission found that the disproportionate use of force and violence by the government in putting down a peaceful demonstration was cruel and inhuman treatment.[89] In the same report, the Commission stated explicitly that ill-treatment of opposition politicians held in jail was not torture but was inhuman and degrading treatment.[90] This finding is difficult to reconcile with the Commission's other decisions on torture noted above, for here the victims had been beaten with rubber hoses and had suffered blows with fists and rifle butts. In the Commission's own words, 'the rule has been indiscriminate brutality combined with the withholding of food and drink'.[91] Perhaps if the Commission had formulated a working definition of torture, it might have come to a different conclusion in this case.

Article 5(3) states that 'punishment shall not be extended to any person other than the criminal.' The Commission has had little opportunity to pronounce upon this right, but in Case 11.006 (Peru)[92] it held that the detention of the wife and children of former Peruvian President Garcia by armed military personnel was a violation of Article 5(3). The Commission observed that 'while the Peruvian Government believes that Dr Garcia Perez should have been arrested for the commission of a criminal offence, the inability to apprehend him did not justify applying punishments intended for him to his wife and children instead'.[93] It is noteworthy that the Commission appeared to assume that mere detention in this case was synonymous with punishment. This is a moot point and one which would undoubtedly have benefited from further analysis.

---

[86] Case 10.970 (Peru), loc. cit. above, n. 77.

[87] Id., 185.

[88] Id., 186–8. The Commission also found that rape was a violation of Art. 11 of the American Convention. See below, 256.

[89] [1989] *Inter-American Yearbook on Human Rights* 528 at 560.

[90] Id., at 616.   [91] Id., at 558.

[92] IACHR Annual Report 1994, 71.

[93] Id., 102.

The remaining provisions of Article 5 deal with imprisonment and associated matters. These find parallels not only in Article I of the Declaration, but in Articles XXV and XXVI of that instrument also. In order to ensure that the requirements of these provisions are complied with, the Commission has declared that States must keep a national record of detainees.[94] Article 5(4) requires that, save in exceptional circumstances, convicted and accused persons are to be segregated and that the latter should be accorded separate treatment appropriate to their status as unconvicted persons. The Commission has noted violations of this provision on two occasions. In 1994 it noted that overcrowded prison conditions in El Salvador were such that this had led to the absence of segregation of convicted and unconvicted prisoners in violation of Article 5(4).[95] A similar observation was made in respect of prison conditions in Panama, although here the Commission noted that conditions for both convicted and unconvicted prisoners alike were 'an affront to the dignity every human being deserves'.[96]

FREEDOM FROM SLAVERY : ARTICLE XXXIV DECLARATION;
ARTICLE 6 CONVENTION

Article XXXIV Declaration

It is the duty of every able-bodied person to render whatever civil and military service his country may require for its defence and preservation, and, in case of public disaster, to render such services as may be in his power. It is likewise his duty to hold any public office to which he may be elected by popular vote in the state of which he is a national.

Article 6 Convention

1. No one shall be subject to slavery or to involuntary servitude, which are prohibited in all their forms, as are the slave trade and traffic in women.
2. No one shall be required to perform forced or compulsory labour. This provision shall not be interpreted to mean that, in those countries in which the penalty established for certain crime is deprivation of liberty or forced labour, the carrying out of such a sentence imposed by a competent court is prohibited. Forced labour shall not adversely affect the dignity or the physical or intellectual capacity of the prisoner.
3. For the purposes of this article, the following do not constitute forced or compulsory labour:

---

[94] IACHR Second Report on the Situation of Human Rights in Colombia (1993), 250.
[95] 'Report on El Salvador' in IACHR Annual Report 1994, 267 at 178.
[96] 'Report on Panama' in IACHR Annual Report 1990–1, 479 at 486.

*a) work or service normally required of a person imprisoned in execution
of a sentence or formal decision passed by the competent judicial authority.
Such work or service shall be carried out under the supervision and control
of public authorities, and any persons performing such work or service
shall not be placed at the disposal of any private party, company, or
juridical person;*

*b) military service and, in countries in which conscientious objectors are
recognised, national service that the law may provide for in lieu of military
service;*

*c) service exacted in time of danger or calamity that threatens the existence
or the well-being of the community; or*

d) work or service that forms part of normal civic obligations.

While Article 6(1) of the Convention prohibits slavery and involuntary
servitude in all their forms, as well as the slave trade and traffic in women,
the Declaration contains no similar prohibition. The Declaration does,
however, contain a duty which is analogous to the exception to the right
contained in Article 6(2) of the Convention. This is found in Article
XXXIV which provides that it is the duty of able bodied persons to render
civil or military assistance to their State in cases of public emergency or
disaster. The concepts of slavery, servitude and related practices are not
defined in the Convention, and the Commission and Court have not yet
had the opportunity to elaborate upon these concepts in any detail. In one
case, however, the Commission was required to investigate the alleged use
of prison labour in Panama for the personal benefit of officers of the
Panamanian National Guard.[97] The Commission could not find sufficient
evidence to support the allegation, but it did find that forced and un-
remunerated labour was required from unsentenced prisoners.[98] Although
the Commission did not explicitly declare it to be so, there is little doubt
that this practice would violate Article 6(3)(a) of the Convention which
states that persons imprisoned in execution of a sentence passed by a
competent judicial authority may not be required to undertake such labour.

If the question of interpretation of Article 6 in other respects were to
come before the inter-American human rights institutions for interpretation, it is suggested that they would draw on a number of sources to aid
their interpretation of these concepts. Perhaps their first recourse would
be to the relevant international instruments. These are the Slavery Convention of 1926[99] as amended by the Protocol of 1953,[100] the Supplementary

---

[97] IACHR Report on the Situation of Human Rights in Panama (1978).
[98] Id., n. 28.
[99] 60 LNTS 253; (1927) 21 *AJIL* Supp. 171.
[100] 182 UNTS 51.

Convention on the Abolition of Slavery, the Slave Trade and Institutions and Practices Similar to Slavery 1956[101] and the Convention for the Suppression of Traffic in Persons 1950.[102] A number of ILO instruments are also relevant to the matter of forced and compulsory labour.[103] In this latter area there can be little doubt that the Commission and the Court would have recourse to the jurisprudence of the European Convention institutions under Article 4 of that instrument as an aid to interpretation.[104]

RIGHT TO PERSONAL LIBERTY AND SECURITY: ARTICLES I, XXV DECLARATION;
ARTICLE 7 CONVENTION

Article I Declaration

Every human being has the right to life, liberty and the security of his person.

Article XXV Declaration

No person may be deprived of his liberty except in the cases and according to the procedures established by pre-existing law.

No person may be deprived of liberty for nonfulfillment of obligations of a purely civil character.

Every individual who has been deprived of his liberty has the right to have the legality of his detention ascertained without delay by a court, and the right to be tried without undue delay or, otherwise, to be released. He also has the right to humane treatment during the time he is in custody.

Article 7 Convention

1. Every person has the right to personal liberty and security.

2. No one shall be deprived of his physical liberty except for the reasons and under the conditions established beforehand by the constitution of the State Party concerned or by a law established pursuant thereto.

3. No one shall be subject to arbitrary arrest or imprisonment.

4. Anyone who is detained shall be informed of the reasons for his detention and shall be promptly notified of the charge or charges against him.

5. Any person detained shall be brought promptly before a judge or other officer authorised by law to exercise judicial power and shall be entitled to trial within a reasonable time or to be released without prejudice to the continuation of the proceedings. His release may be subject to guarantees to assure his appearance for trial.

---

[101] 266 UNTS 3.

[102] 96 UNTS 271.

[103] See, in particular, the Forced Labour Convention 1930 (ILO 29), 39 UNTS 55.

[104] See D. Harris, M. O'Boyle and C. Warbrick, *The Law of the European Convention on Human Rights* (London, 1995), Ch. 4.

6. Anyone who is deprived of his liberty shall be entitled to recourse to a competent court, in order that the court may decide without delay on the lawfulness of his arrest or detention and order his release if the arrest or detention is unlawful. In States Parties whose laws provide that anyone who believes himself to be threatened with deprivation of his liberty is entitled to recourse to a competent court in order that it may decide on the lawfulness of such threat, this remedy may not be restricted or abolished. The interested party or another person in his behalf is entitled to seek these remedies.

7. No one shall be detained for debt. This principle shall not limit the orders of a competent judicial authority issued for nonfulfillment of duties of support.

The right to personal liberty is protected by Articles I and XXV of the Declaration and Article 7 of the Convention. Insofar as these provisions seek to protect the individual from abuses in the criminal process, they are closely related to due process rights which are protected by Article XXVI of the Declaration and Article 8 of the Convention. However, they are not limited to detention in the criminal process; these provisions extend to other cases also, including the detention of the mentally ill, persons with infectious diseases and persons being deported or extradited.

As noted above, Article 7 represents the third in the trilogy of rights violated by the practice of enforced disappearances. In the *Honduran Disappearance* cases the Court held that the kidnapping of an individual and the denial of access to judicial authorities by which the legality of the detention could be reviewed constituted a manifest violation of Article 7.[105] Since the delivery of the judgments in the *Honduran Disappearance* cases the Commission has followed the jurisprudence of the Court on the Convention on this matter.[106] In cases involving non-State Parties to the Convention, the Commission has consistently held that both permanent and temporary disappearances violate Articles I and XXV of the Declaration.[107]

It cannot be said that the jurisprudence of the Court or the Commission adds very much to an understanding of these provisions, since it is not fully reasoned nor fully analytical. This, however, is not surprising given the circumstances in which decisions concerning these rights have been rendered. More often than not the Commission and Court have been confronted by recalcitrant States and a paucity of evidence which is capable of direct confirmation.[108]

---

[105] *Velasquez Rodriguez,* loc. cit. above, n. 6 at para. 84. Cf. the *Cabellero-Delgado and Santana* case, Judgment of 8 Dec. 1995; 3 IHRR 548 (1995) (detention and disappearance at the hands of the Colombian army an illegal detention in breach of Art. 7).

[106] See, for example, Case 10.563 (Peru), IACHR Annual Report 1993, 303 at 308–9.

[107] See, for example, Case 10.508 (Guatemala) IACHR Annual Report 1994, 51.

[108] On the question of the difficulty of finding evidence in disappearance cases see Cerna, 'The Structure and Functioning of the Inter-American Court of Human Rights' 62 British

Right to security of the person

Article 7 (1) guarantees the right to 'personal liberty and security'. Whereas 'personal liberty' concerns arrest and detention, in Case 11.006 (Peru),[109] the Commission ruled that threatening persons with arbitrary and unjustified detention can infringe the right to 'personal security'.[110] In that case, the Peruvian army had illegally entered former President Garcia's home to arrest him. Although the former President escaped, the Commission considered that Article 7 had been infringed in respect of him because he 'was threatened with arbitrary and unlawful arrest and therefore his right to personal security' was violated.

Deprivation of physical liberty

Article 7(2) of the Convention provides that persons may not be deprived of their physical liberty except for the reasons and under the conditions established in advance by a State Party's constitution or a law adopted in accordance with that constitution. Article XXV of the Declaration also provides that persons may not be deprived of their liberty except in the cases and according to the procedures established by pre-existing law. In Case 11.006 (Peru) the Commission noted that the attempted arrest of former President Garcia had been carried out by the Peruvian army which had no constitutional authority to undertake such action and was in any event not based upon a reasoned court order, as the Peruvian constitution required. Insofar as the attempt had led to the arrest of President Garcia's wife and children, these arrests were procedurally illegal and hence a breach of Article 7(2).

Article 7(2) was similarly held by the Inter-American Court to have been violated in the *Gangaram Panday* case[111] for lack of compliance with national law.. There the victim was detained at the airport by the Military Police on his arrival in Suriname so that enquiries could be made into his expulsion from the Netherlands. The Inter-American Court found that the procedure followed by the authorities in connection with the victim's detention did not comply with an order of the President. In consequence, the victim had been detained contrary to Suriname law and hence in breach of Article 7(2) of the Convention.

More generally, the Commission has stated that any arrest must be made

---

Year Book of International Law 135 (1992), at 220–1; J. S. Davidson, *The Inter-American Court of Human Rights* (Aldershot, 1992), 80–6; Shelton, 'Judicial Review of State Action by International Courts' (1988–9) 12 *Fordham Int. LJ* 361.

[109] IACHR Annual Report 1994, 71.
[110] Id., at 100.
[111] I/A Court H.R. Series C No. 16 (1994), 15 *HRLJ* 168, 2 IHRR 360 (1995).

by the agency properly authorised by the national constitution and in accordance with the procedures required by international law. Where these conditions are not met, 'arrests cease to be arrests per se and become kidnappings'.[112]

Arbitrary arrest and imprisonment

Article 7(3) of the Convention prohibits the 'arbitrary arrest or imprisonment' of any person. The side-note to Article XXV of the Declaration states that the provision is concerned with the 'right to protection from arbitrary arrest'. Although the Commission has not elaborated upon the concept of 'arbitrary arrest' in its jurisprudence, it seems clear that any unlawful arrest is immediately classified as arbitrary. Support for this view may be derived from the numerous disappearance cases considered by the Commission and from its more explicit ruling in Case 11.006 (Peru). Here, the detention of former President Garcia's wife in a manner which was clearly inconsistent with the provisions of the Peruvian constitution was held by the Commission to be 'unlawful and arbitrary'.[113]

The dicta of the Inter-American Court in the *Gangaram Panday* case[114] take the matter further and suggest that, although lawful under national law, a deprivation of liberty will nonetheless be 'arbitrary' if the reasons for it or procedures followed are 'unreasonable, unforseeable or lacking in proportionality'. In that case, having found that there was a breach of Article 7(2) because the victim's detention was in breach of national law (see above), the Court found no need to 'express an opinion with regard to the reported arbitrariness' of the detention.[115] It commented upon Article 7(3) generally as follows:[116]

(Article 7(3)) addresses the issue that no one may be subjected to arrest or imprisonment for reasons and by methods which, although classified as legal, could be deemed to be incompatible with the respect for the fundamental rights of the individual because, among other things, they are unreasonable, unforseeable or lacking in proportionality.

Notification of charge

Article 7(4) provides that detained persons must be informed of the reasons for their detention and promptly notified of the charges against them. This provision overlaps with the due process rights contained in Article 8(2)(b), which are considered below.

[112] Report on the Situation of Human Rights in Chile (1985), 138.
[113] Loc. cit. at n. 109 at 101.
[114] Loc. cit. at n. 111, above, para. 47.
[115] Id., para. 51.
[116] Id., para. 47.

Presentation before a judge and pre-trial release

Article 7(5) provides that a detained person must be brought before a judge or other appropriate person 'promptly' and 'shall be entitled to trial within a reasonable time or be released without prejudice to the continuation of the proceedings'.[117] Such release may be made subject to guarantees to assure the detainee's appearance for trial at a future date. Article XXV, paragraph 3 of the Declaration similarly provides that a detained person has the right to be tried without undue delay or otherwise released.

The latter part of Article 7(5) guarantees two alternative rights: the right of the accused to be released on bail pending trial unless there is a good public interest reason to the contrary and the right of a person detained on remand to be tried within a reasonable time. As to the right to bail, in Case 10.037 (Argentina),[118] the Commission was obliged to apply Article 7(5) in a case of the pre-trial detention for three and a half years of a person who had been charged with homicide, kidnapping and extortion. The question of his pre-trial detention or release was regulated by Article 380 of the Argentinian Code of Criminal Procedure which stated that in determining the release of a person detained for trial, the judge enjoyed a discretion and could take into account the characteristics of the case and of the accused in order to decide whether he or she would be likely to abscond. In the Commission's view, Article 380 was consistent with the Convention, providing acceptable legal guidelines within which the judge should exercise his discretion objectively.[119] In this connection, the Commission referred to the jurisprudence of the European Court of Human Rights by which account may be taken, *inter alia*, of the length of any possible sentence of imprisonment when assessing whether the accused would abscond if released.[120] Other elements of the European Court of Human Rights' approach to bail, which it is likely that the inter-American institutions would follow, are that there is a presumption that bail should be granted in the absence of public interest reasons to the contrary, which include the risk of interference with witnesses or evidence and the prevention of crime, as well as the likelihood of the accused absconding. But the central issue in Case 10.037 (Argentina) was whether the accused had been brought to trial within a reasonable time. Relying again on the jurisprudence of the European Court of Human Rights,[121] the Commission

---

[117] On the relationship between Art. 7(5) and Art. 8(1) of the Convention, see below, 244–5.

[118] Case 10.037 (Argentina) [1989] Inter-American Yearbook on Human Rights, 52.

[119] Id., at 90.

[120] The Commission referred to the *Stogmuller* case in this point: Eur. Ct. H.R, Series A, No. 9, 76. In that case, the European Court also took into account the local ties of the accused and the weight of the evidence against him when assessing the likelihood of his absconding.

[121] *Stogmuller* case, loc. cit. at n. 120.

stated that such a period could not be established in abstracto, but must be calculated in each case according to the particular circumstances.[122] In the instant case, the proceedings had been prolonged, *inter alia*, because of the length of extradition proceedings in Brazil, in which the applicant had contested his extradition, and of negligence on the part of the defence in the conduct of proceedings. The Commission concluded that 'although four years is not a reasonable period, in this case because of its unique features and the complexity of the reasons affecting its progress such a period is not an unjustified delay in the administration of justice'.[123]

The question of the reasonableness of pre-trial detention has also been analysed extensively by the Commission in Case 11.245 (Argentina). Here, the alleged victim, Jorge Alberto Gimenez, had been held in custody pending trial for automobile theft and other property offences for a period of 49 months, despite a number of applications to the Argentinian courts to secure his release. Gimenez argued not only that pre-trial detention of this length was a violation of Article 7(5) of the Convention. Following its reasoning in Case 10.037 (Argentina), the Commission held that the 'reasonable length of time' referred to in Article 7(5) could not be determined in the abstract, but 'must be based upon the "sound judgment of the judge", using those criteria established by law'.[124] Furthermore, the Commission's assertion in the same case that the concept of 'reasonable time' in the Convention could not be defined with precision but must be analysed according to the facts of the particular case was also followed here.[125] In addition, the Commission observed that the question of whether pre-trial detention has exceeded reasonable limits must be judged in the context of the presumption of liberty which is embodied in Article 7 of the American Convention.[126]

In order to determine whether Gimenez's pre-trial detention was unreasonable, the Commission adopted a two part analysis. First, the Commission stated that preventive detention must be justified by the national judicial authorities using 'relevant and sufficient criteria',[127] and, second, where the criteria are judged to be 'relevant and sufficient' by the appropriate judicial authorities, the Inter-American Commission and, where appropriate, the Inter-American Court would exercise their judgment to determine whether or not those authorities have used 'special diligence' in the conduct of proceedings 'so that the length of detention would not be unreasonable'.[128] As the Commission further observed:[129]

---

[122] Case 10.037 (Argentina) loc. cit., above, n. 118 at 94.   [123] Id., at 100.
[124] IACHR Annual Report 1995, 43, para. 67.   [125] Id., para. 69.
[126] Id., 45, para. 75.   [127] Id., 47, para. 83.
[128] Id., The Commission cited the ruling of the European Court of Human Rights in *Kemmache* Eur. Ct. H.R. Series A No. 218, 36, para. 45 as authority for this proposition.
[129] Id., Here the Commission cited the ruling of the European Court of Human Rights in *Wemhoff* and *Neumeister* as authority for these propositions.

The Convention organs must determine whether the time that has elapsed, for whatever reason, before judgment is passed on the accused has at some stage exceeded a reasonable limit whereby imprisonment without conviction imposes a greater sacrifice than could, in the circumstances of the case reasonably be expected of a person presumed innocent. Thus, where continued detention ceased to be reasonable, either because the justifications for incarceration are not 'relevant or sufficient' or the length of the judicial proceedings is unreasonable, provision release must be granted.

The Commission further reinforced the context in which States might resort to preventive detention by stating that it was an 'exceptional measure' which applied only in cases in which there exists a reasonable suspicion that the accused will either evade justice or impede the preliminary investigation by intimidating witnesses or destroying evidence.[130]

Turning to the application of these principles in the instant case, the Commission held that while the seriousness of the crimes of which Gimenez had been accused and the likely severity of the punishment consequent upon conviction were matters which could, in principle, be taken into account when assessing the detainee's likelihood of abscondment, in the present case it appeared as if Argentina's arguments were motivated by penal retribution rather than a desire to prevent the victim absconding.[131] Furthermore, the Commission held that the likelihood of severe punishment following lengthy pretrial detention was an insufficient criterion for assessing the likelihood of a detainee's absconding.[132] Indeed, this had the effect of heightening the detainee's perception that he or she was already serving part of the likely sentence, and there were other ways of ensuring that individuals appeared for trial without resorting to incarceration.[133] The Commission did not specify what these measures might be, but common, and no doubt acceptable, conditions for bail include the surrender of a passport, restrictions on movement and reporting obligations. The Commission thus concluded:[134]

Given the fact that pre-trial incarceration is a deprivation of liberty of a person who still benefits from the presumption of innocence, it should be based solely on the probablitlity of the accused's abusing conditional liberty and fleeing, and on whether conditional freedom of an accused is likely to result in some significant risk. Preventive detention would not, however, be based solely on the fact that a suspected crime is deemd particularly socially objectionable.

The risk of a detainee absconding was also an issue which informed the Commission's views on the question of the risk of the detainee's repetition of offences and the threat to society from such repetition. Here, the Commission asserted once again that pre-trial incarceration is a depriva-

---

[130] Id., para. 84. [131] Id., para. 86. [132] Id., para. 87.
[133] Id. [134] Id., 48, para. 89.

tion of liberty of one who is still presumed to be innocent and it should therefore be based solely on the probability of the accused abusing his or her conditional liberty and fleeing and on whether conditional freedom of an accused is likely to result in some significant risk.[135] The Commission did not specify to what or to whom this significant risk might be directed, but presumably it refers to risk either to society or to individuals or both. Furthermore, the Commission held that some weight should be given to the likelihood of the accused being rehabilitated and his or her willingness to make some reparation for the crime of which he or she stood accused.[136] Finally, the Commission gave a clear indication that the decision concerning pre-trial detention should be orientated towards the individual rather than society at large. It held:[137]

Given the length of prison time served, the courts should reach a fair balance of those criteria which address the particular interests of the individual rather than those which serve the public order of society at large, when the time comes to decide whether the accused should be released from prison.

Applying these principles to the instant case the Commission found that there was no proof that the crimes of which Gimenez was charged seriously affected public order, nor were the arguments adduced by the Argentinian courts justifying his detention either 'sufficient or reasonable'.[138] In addition to these criteria, however, the Commission was obliged to determine whether the judicial authorities had exercised 'special diligence' in determining whether the period of detention was unreasonable. Citing the decicisions of the European Court of Human Rights in *Toth* and *B* v *Austria*, the Commission held that an accused in detention is entitled to have his or her case given priority and expedited by the proper authorities where this can be accomplished without hindering the overall trial process,[139] and the burden of proof is upon the respondent government to justify any apparently unwarranted delay.[140] In the present case, the Commission found that there had been no undue complexities and that the authorities had failed to act with 'sufficient due diligence' to avoid the prolongation of the victim's remand in custody.[141]

The issue of the length of trials of persons detained on remand has also been considered in a country report on Panama. Here, the average length of pre-trial detention was two to four years, after which certain detainees were found not guilty of the crimes for which they had been arrested. This was held by the Commission, without reasoning, to be a violation of Article 7(5); the criterion of 'reasonable' in this provision had been exceeded as a consequence of the manifest delay in bringing detained persons to trial.[142]

[135] Id., 49, para. 91.   [136] Id., para. 92.
[137] Id., para. 93.   [138] Id.   [139] Id., 50–1, para. 100.
[140] Id., 51, para. 101.   [141] Id., 53, para. 108.
[142] 'Report on Panama' in IACHR Annual Report 1990–1, 479–85.

Recourse to a competent court

Article 7(6) of the Convention provides that persons deprived of their liberty have the right to 'recourse to a competent court'[143] for the purposes of determining the lawfulness of their arrest or detention. If an arrest or detention is unlawful, the court must be competent to order the detainee's release. Article 7(6) also provides that in States which grant a court remedy to persons who believe themselves to be threatened with the deprivation of their liberty, such remedy must be neither restricted nor abolished. Under Article 7(6) remedies must be available to the interested party or a person acting on behalf of that party. The Court has expressed the opinion in its advisory opinion on *Habeas Corpus in Emergency Situations*[144] that the pre-eminent remedies for challenging the legality of detention in the Americas, habeas corpus and amparo, may not be suspended in times of emergency so as to prevent their use to protect a non-derogable right. Responding to the suspension of the constitutionally guaranteed right of habeas corpus by Panama, the Commission ruled that this violated Articles 7(6) and 25(1) of the Convention and was contrary to the Court's advisory opinion expressed in *Habeas Corpus in Emergency Situations*.[145]

Detention for debt

Article 7(7) of the Convention provides that '(n)o-one shall be detained for debt.' This is more restrictive than Article XXV of the Declaration which states that '(n)o person may be deprived of liberty for non-fulfilment of obligations of a purely civil character.' Although Article 7(7) is narrower in scope than its Declaration analogue, it is suggested that Article 29(d) of the Convention would remedy any restrictive interpretation which might be applied to the former provision.

THE RIGHT TO A FAIR TRIAL : ARTICLE XXVI DECLARATION;
ARTICLE 8 CONVENTION

Article XXVI Declaration
Every accused person is presumed to be innocent until proved guilty.
Every person accused of an offence has the right to be given an impartial and

---

[143] On the meaning of a 'competent court', see the due process requirements in Art. 8, below, 245

[144] Advisory Opinion No. 8, I/A Court H.R. Series A No. 8 (1987), 9 *HRLJ* 94.

[145] 'Report on the Situation of Human Rights in Panama' in [1989] Inter-American Yearbook on Human Rights, 528 at 564.

public hearing, and to be tried by courts previously established in accordance with pre-existing laws, and not to receive cruel, infamous or unusual punishment.

Article 8 Convention

1. Every person has the right to a hearing, with due guarantees and within a reasonable time, by a competent, independent, and impartial tribunal, previously established by law, in the substantiation of any accusation of a criminal nature made against him or for the determination of his rights and obligations of a civil, labour, fiscal, or any other nature.

2. Every person accused of a criminal offence has the right to be presumed innocent so long as his guilt has not been proven according to law. During the proceedings, every person is entitled, with full equality, to the following minimum guarantees:

a) the right of the accused to be assisted without charge by a translator or interpreter, if he does not understand or does not speak the language of the tribunal or court;

b) prior notification in detail to the accused of the charges against him;

c) adequate time and means for the preparation of his defence;

d) the right of the accused to defend himself personally or to be assisted by legal counsel of his own choosing, and to communicate freely and privately with his counsel;

e) the inalienable right to be assisted by counsel provided by the state, paid or not as the domestic law provides, if the accused does not defend himself personally or engage his own counsel within the time period established by law;

f) the right of the defence to examine witnesses present in the court and to obtain the appearance, as witnesses, of experts or other persons who may throw light on the facts;

g) the right not to be compelled to be a witness against himself or to plead guilty; and

h) the right to appeal the judgment to a higher court.

3. A confession of guilt by the accused shall be valid only if it is made without coercion of any kind.

4. An accused person acquitted by a nonappealable judgment shall not be subjected to a new trial for the same cause.

5. Criminal proceedings shall be public, except insofar as may be necessary to protect the interests of justice.

Both Article XXVI of the Declaration and Article 8 of the Convention contain detailed provisions on the right to a fair trial. As the Court has noted, Article 8 recognises the concept of 'due process of law', which 'includes the prerequisites necessary to ensure the adequate protection of those persons whose rights or obligations are pending judicial determination'.[146] The Court has also stated that 'the concept of due process' in Article 8 'should be understood as applicable, in the main, to all the judicial guarantees referred to in the American Convention', even where there have been legitimate derogations from certain rights under Article 27.[147] Article 8 and its sibling provision Article 25 have been recognised as fundamental by the Commission,[148] which has also stated that due process rights must exist in a substantive, as well as a formal, sense.[149]

Article 8(1) of the Convention establishes the basic conditions for the right to a fair trial in criminal and non-criminal cases. Article 8(2) deals solely with the conduct of criminal cases. It not only establishes the presumption of innocence, but also lays down a non-exhaustive list of minimum guarantees. Each of these will be dealt with below. It should be remarked, however, that, as with other substantive rights, the Commission has frequently been content to find violations of Article 8 without distinguishing between its various elements.

In its consideration of Article 8 of the Convention, the Commission has been assiduous in making clear that it is not concerned with the correctness of a national court's decision, but whether that decision has been reached in accordance with the principles of due process of law. Thus, where the Argentine Supreme Court had dismissed the petitioner's claim without hearing evidence, the Commission stated that it was not competent to decide whether the Argentine law of evidence had been properly applied by the Court when it failed to hear evidence. However, the Commission found that the Court's behaviour was 'inconsistent with the letter and the spirit of the Convention as regards judicial guarantees and the principles of due process'.[150]

Right of access to a court

In an important ruling concerning Argentina and Uruguay, the Commission has recognised the right of access to a court in the context of amnesty or impunity laws. The Commission has ruled that a law granting amnesty to persons who were to be tried for human rights violations during the regime of the military junta in Argentina breached the rights of victims and their relatives under Articles 8(1) and 25 of the Convention to bring a claim before the courts in respect of the wrongs done.[151] The rationale

---

[146] Advisory Opinion No. 9, I/A Court H.R. Series A No. 9 (1987) para. 28, 9 *HRLJ* 204.
[147] Id., para. 29.
[148] Case 9850 (Argentina) IACHR Annual Report 1990–1, at 74.
[149] Id.   [150] Id., at 75, para. 20.
[151] Cases Nos 10.147, 10.181, 10.240, 10.262, 10.309, 10.311 (Argentina) IACHR Annual Report 1992–3, 41.

underlying this decision was that in Argentina the victim of a crime participates actively in the criminal process and has a 'fundamental civil right to go to the courts'.[152] The Commission noted the importance of this right 'in propelling the criminal process and moving it forward' and declared that the Argentinian decree had obstructed 'the exercise of the petitioner's right under Article 8(1)'.[153] At the same time, the Commission made a similar ruling concerning Uruguay's amnesty laws; these were found to be in breach of Articles 8(1) and 25 for the same reasons.[154] These are important contributions to the debate on the acceptability of amnesty or impunity laws.[155]

Right to a hearing within a reasonable time

In Case 11.245 (Argentina)[156] the Commission was required to consider this matter in the context of the pre-trial detention of a person accused for automobile theft and other property offences for a period of forty-nine months. The main issue here was the question of the lawfulness of such a lengthy pre-trial detention when measured against Article 7(5)of the Convention.[157] The Commission was, however, also obliged to consider the relationship between Article 7(5) and Article 8(1). The Commission noted that although the two provisions were inspired by the principle that the burden of penal procedures upon the individual should not be 'unremittingly protracted' nor 'produce permanent harm',[158] nonetheless the provisions did not coincide in their meaning of what constitutes a reasonable period.[159] Thus, a delay in trial proceedings which might be justified in the context of Article 8(1) may nonetheless constitute a violation of Article 7(5).[160] The decisive factor in the different treatment of these provisions is, in the Commission's view, that an accused person who is held in custody prior to trial is subject to coercive measures by the State and is therefore entitled to have his or her case 'resolved on a priority basis and conducted with diligence'.[161] Furthermore, the Commission noted that the concept of 'reasonable time' in Article 7 and Article 8 differs in that the former provision 'establishes the possibility for an individual to be released without prejudice to continuation of the proceedings' and that 'the period established for detention is necessarily much shorter than the period allotted for the entire trial'.[162] What criteria then can be applied to

---

[152] IACHR Annual Report 1992–3, 48.   [153] Id.
[154] Cases 10.029, 10.036, 10.145, 10.305, 10.372, 10.373, 10.374 and 10.375 (Uruguay), IACHR Annual Report 1992–3, at 154.
[155] On this matter, see Chap. 11 below.
[156] Loc. cit. above, n. 21.   [157] See above 238.
[158] Loc. cit. above, n. 21, 53, para. 109.
[159] Id., para. 110.   [160] Id.
[161] Id.   [162] Id.

the concept of reasonableness for the conduct of a trial according to Article 8? Here, the Commission was unwilling to be specific, but simply noted that a series of factors might determine the length of a trial. These factors included the complexity of the case, the behaviour of the accused and the diligence of the authorities in the conduct of the proceedings.[163] Even allowing for flexibility in the application of these factors, the Commission found that given the absence of complexity in the present case and the failure of the authorities to pursue the case with due diligence led to the conclusion that the prolongation of procedures for more than five years was a violation of Article 8(1) of the Convention.[164]

Competent, independent and impartial tribunal

In analysing the meaning of 'independent' and 'impartial', which are overlapping requirements, the Commission has emphasised the importance of the constitutional doctrine of the separation of powers. This is cogently expressed in a report on the judiciary in Cuba. Here the Commission said:[165]

The effective observance of [judicial] guarantees is based on the independence of the judiciary, which derives from the classic separation of the three branches of government. This is the logical consequence of the very concept of human rights. In effect, to protect the rights of individuals against possible arbitrary actions of the state, it is essential that one of the branches have the independence that permits it to judge both the actions of the executive branch and the constitutionality of the laws enacted and even the judgments handed down by its own members. Therefore, the Commission considers that the independence of the judiciary is an essential requisite for the practical observance of human rights in general.

These principles have been further elaborated by the Commission in a report on the judiciary entitled 'Measures necessary for rendering the autonomy, independence and integrity of the members of the Judicial Branch more effective'.[166] In this report the Commission listed the criteria which member States should implement to satisfy the requirements of judicial independence and impartiality. The list included the following:

a) guaranteeing the judiciary freedom from interference by the executive and legislative branches;
b) providing the judiciary with the necessary political support for performing its functions;

---

[163] Id., para. 111.
[164] Id., 54, para. 112.
[165] IACHR Seventh Report on the Situation of Human Rights in Cuba (1983) 51. Cited with approval in Case 10.006 (Peru), IACHR Annual Report 1994, at 92–3.
[166] IACHR Annual Report 1992–3, at 207. This report was cited with approval by the Commission in 'Report on Nicaragua', IACHR Annual Report 1993, 422 at 456–7.

c) giving judges security of tenure;

d) preserving the rule of law and declaring states of emergency only when necessary and in strict conformity with the requirements of the American Convention;

e) returning to the judiciary responsibility for the disposition and supervision of detained persons.

The lack of separation of powers and absence of certain requirements in the aforementioned list have been evident in a number of cases reviewed by the Commission. In Case 11.084 (Peru)[167] the Commission held that a special military court was not a competent, independent and impartial tribunal because it was subordinate to the Ministry of Defence, part of the executive branch of government. Similarly, the Commission in a report on Nicaragua in 1994 found that, *inter alia*, the 'politicization' of the judiciary was a factor which 'unquestionably' affected the 'right to justice and due process'.[168]

Lack of the separation of the judiciary from the executive leading to a violation of Articles 8 and 25 was also evident in the Panamanian institution of the *Corregidor*. The *Corregidores* were special police officials who could be appointed and removed at will by township mayors. Although under the constitution *Corregidores* had to be over the age of eighteen, the Commission found that they were generally 'illiterate young men who have neither the preparation nor the independence necessary and are easily influenced'.[169] While the *Corregidores* enjoyed jurisdiction over petty crime, they had exercised their powers over citizens who had allegedly disobeyed or wronged members of the armed forces. In theory sentences imposed by *Corregidores* could be appealed to the mayor, but in practice this did not happen.

A reference to the list of criteria in the Commission's report on the judiciary further indicates that the separation of powers and independence of the judiciary should not only be formally guaranteed, but should also obtain in practice. These points were addressed in a report on Guatemala in which the Commission stated:[170]

Apart from the fact that the rule of law must be in full effect with the principle of separation of powers duly observed, and the fact that administrative measures are needed to provide judges with suitable material means for protecting their security, the autonomy, independence and integrity of the members of the judiciary calls for measures that will ensure unrestricted access to the courts and legal remedies, trials conducted in accordance with the principles of due process of

---

[167] IACHR Annual Report 1994, 113, at 125.

[168] Id., 442 at 451.

[169] IACHR Report on the Situation on Human Rights in Panama [1989] Inter-American Yearbook on Human Rights, 528 at 572.

[170] 'Report on Guatemala' in IACHR Annual Report 1993, 442 at 456.

law, and the conclusion of such trials within a reasonable time and with judgments that address all points.

Some of these points were vividly demonstrated in Case 11.006 (Peru)[171] in which the government of Peru had unconstitutionally removed a number of judges prior to the hearing of a case against the former Peruvian president. Here, the Commission, following the judgment of the European Court of Human Rights in *Campbell and Fell*[172] held that a determination of whether a court is independent of the executive depends on the 'manner of appointment of its members, the duration of their terms [and] the existence of guarantees against outside pressures . . .'[173] Furthermore, the Commission stated that 'the irremovability of judges . . . must . . . be considered a necessary corollary of their independence.'[174]

It is also evident that the lack of physical security of judges in a number of American States threatens their independence and impartiality. This was particularly the case in Colombia where a number of judges and their families were subjected to threats by narco-terrorists. In order to protect the judiciary and their relatives, Colombia took a number of security measures, including the establishment of secret courts. Disapproving of the latter, the Commission noted that the judiciary in Colombia required greater political support and that secret courts were generally not in conformity with the principles of due process of law as set forth in Article 8.[175]

Due guarantees

Article 8 of the Convention provides that every person is entitled to a hearing with 'due guarantees'. This is a residual term that has a meaning that is independent of the other particular guarantees in Article 8(1). It applies to both criminal and non-criminal cases. Most significantly, it allows the 'minimum guarantees' that apply by virtue of Article 8(2) to criminal cases to extend to non-criminal cases also, so far as this is appropriate. It was on this basis that, in Advisory Opinion No 11,[176] the Court expressed the opinion that legal representation might be a 'due guarantee' in the sense of Article 8(1) in a non-criminal case where such representation is necessary on the facts of the case for justice to be done.

---

[171] Case 10.006 (Peru), IACHR Annual Report 1994, 71.
[172] Eur. Ct. H.R., Series A, No. 80 (1984).
[173] IACHR Annual Report 1994, at 92–3.
[174] Id.
[175] IACHR Annual Report 1992–3, at 207.
[176] Advisory Opinion No. 11, para. 28.

Presumption of innocence

Article 8(2) of the Convention states that 'every person accused of a criminal offence has the right to be presumed innocent so long as his guilt has not been proven according to law'. Similarly, Article XXVI of the Declaration provides that 'every accused person is to be presumed innocent until proved guilty'. A clear violation of these requirements was evident in Case 11.084 (Peru)[177] in which a number of army officers were arrested following a meeting at which they had discussed the possibility of restoring democratic rule to Peru. They were tried by a military tribunal which presumed their guilt in violation of the State's constitutional requirements.[178] Another breach was identified in a 1981 report on Nicaragua,[179] in which the Commission found that special tribunals established by the Sandanista government to try suspected *Somocistas* took membership of the National Guard, or bodies associated with it, to amount to evidence which warranted a presumption of guilt. The defendants were thus obliged to prove their innocence. The Commission noted that this was a reversal of the requirement in Article 8(2) and thus violated that provision.[180]

The presumption of innocence is also linked to the question of pre-trial detention. In Case 11.245 (Argentina),[181] an individual had been detained prior to trial for property offences for a period of just over four years. The Commission held that pre-trial detention for such a lengthy period effectively amounted to a punishment before a finding of guilt and thus led to a violation of Article 8(2).[182] The Commission said:[183]

The substantiation of guilt calls for the formulation of a judgment establishing blame in a final sentence. If the use of that procedure fails to assign blame within a reasonable length of time and the State is able to justify further the holding of the accused in pre-trial incarceration, based on the suspicion of guilt, then it is essentially substituting the pre-trial detention for the punishment. Preventive custody thus loses its purpose as an instrument to serve the interests of the sound administration of justice, and the means become the end.

Minimum guarantees in criminal cases

Article 8(2) of the Convention provides that persons accused of criminal offences are entitled to certain 'minimum guarantees'. As the term suggests, these are the minimum requirements with which a State is required

---

[177] IACHR Annual Report 1994, 113.   [178] Id., at 121.
[179] IACHR Report on the Situation of Human Rights in Nicaragua (1981).
[180] Id., at 90–1.
[181] Loc. cit. above, n. 124.
[182] Id., 54, para. 114.   [183] Id.

to comply, although it may implement higher standards through its constitutional law if it so wishes. Lower standards will clearly breach this provision. As indicated above, the list of guarantees is non-exhaustive, and 'other, additional guarantees may be necessary in specific circumstances to ensure a fair hearing.'[184]

Right to a translator

Article 8(2)(a) of the Convention provides that persons who do not understand or who do not speak the language of the tribunal or court before which they must appear are to be assisted by a translator or interpreter. The cost of such services is to be borne by the State. Neither the Commission nor the Court have been required to rule on this provision.

Notification of charges

Under Article 8(2)(b) of the Convention accused persons are entitled to 'prior notification in detail of the charges' against them. This provision is the sibling of Article 7(4) which states that detained persons must be notified of the reasons for their detention and be promptly notified of the charge or charges against them. Both these provisions are primarily concerned with pre-trial procedure. Although the Convention institutions have not considered these provisions, it is arguable that they relate not only to the notification of the precise charges which have been laid against an individual, but also to the communication of the details of the prosecution's case. The reason for this is that Article 8(2)(f) stipulates that accused persons have the right to examine prosecution witnesses or experts in court. It is therefore logical to assume that the identity of such witnesses or experts and their materiality to the case must be disclosed in advance.

Adequate time and means for defence

Article 8(2)(c) of the Convention requires that accused persons be given 'adequate time and means for the preparation' of their defence. The concept of 'adequate time and means' is inherently flexible and will undoubtedly turn on the particularities of any case. Generally speaking, it might be assumed that the more complex a case, the more time will be necessary for preparation. In cases where an individual is represented by legal counsel, it is clear that an accused person will require sufficient time to consult with his lawyer in order that the case be properly prepared.

---

[184] Advisory Opinion No. 11, para. 24.

Whether the time allowed for the preparation of the defence is adequate may be determined by inference. In Case 10.198 (Nicaragua)[185] a former National Guardsman was sentenced to thirty years imprisonment on charges of espionage after being held incommunicado for thirty days, forced to make self-incriminating statements and given only six weeks to prepare his case. The Commission held that it could be inferred from the shortness of the time during which he had been detained, tried and sentenced that he had not been accorded the time and means for the preparation of his defence required by Article 8(2)(c).[186] Similarly, in a report on Peru,[187] the Commission noted complaints from a number of attorneys who claimed that they had been given neither sufficient time to acquaint themselves with their clients' cases nor an opportunity to confer with their clients prior to trial. Furthermore, the attorneys claimed that a number of procedural impediments, such as an absence of notification of the date of the trials, had been placed in their way. While the Commission did not refer to Article 8(2)(c), it nonetheless held that these practices were 'detrimental to the most elementary judicial guarantees and due process'.[188]

Assistance by legal counsel and self-representation

Under Articles 8(2)(d) and (e) of the Convention accused persons have the right to defend themselves personally or to be assisted by legal counsel of their choice. It appears that the right to counsel is engaged from the time that the accused is arrested. Accused persons also have the right to be assisted by counsel provided by the State if they neither engage counsel nor defend themselves personally. However, Article 8(2)(e) does not oblige the State to pay for the provision of defence counsel for indigent or other persons.[189]

Where an accused is unable to secure counsel because lawyers are afraid to represent certain clients in view of the climate of violence in a State, and the 'interests of justice' require legal representation, the State will be in violation of Articles 8(2)(d) and (e).[190] A related issue concerns the situation in which lawyers are harassed and vilified because they take cases bearing 'political' overtones. The Commission has ruled that the 'malicious and unfounded' linking of a defence lawyer to the unlawful activities of

[185] Case 10.198 (Nicaragua) [1989] Inter-American Yearbook on Human Rights, 314.
[186] Id., at 348.
[187] IACHR Annual Report 1993, at 493.　　[188] Id.
[189] Advisory Opinion No. 11, para. 25. Although there is no obligation to provide legal aid, its absence means that domestic remedies do not have to be exhausted before a petition is brought before the Commission: id., para. 31.
[190] Id., para. 38.

which his client had been falsely accused constituted a threat to the free exercise of the legal profession and infringed 'one of the fundamental guarantees of the administration of justice and of due process' contained in the right of defence in Article 8(2)(d)'.[191]

The Commission has also had occasion to examine Articles 8(2)(d) and (e) in a number of other contexts. In a report on Peru, the Commission noted that while in theory persons in Peru who were accused of terrorism had the right to defend themselves, the right was so 'seriously shackled' that it was virtually non-existent, contrary to the requirements of Article 8(2)(e).[192] Furthermore, attorneys in Peru were only allowed to defend one person accused of terrorism at a time. The Commission ruled that this was a 'very serious violation' of the right to be assisted by counsel of one's choice under Article 8(2)(d).[193] The conditions under which a trial is held may also violate these rights. In its report on the judiciary cited above,[194] the Commission noted that the conduct of secret trials to protect the judiciary and their families from narco-terrorism violated the right of self-defence, since the fact that the identity of witnesses was not disclosed made it virtually impossible to rebut their testimony.[195]

Right to present and examine witnesses

Article 8(2)(f) guarantees the right of the defence to secure the appearance of witnesses in court and to examine such witnesses and experts or other persons who may be able to throw light on a case. Although there is no jurisprudence on this point, it would seem reasonable to assume that this right is limited by domestic law considerations relating to the presentation of evidence and the materiality of witnesses and experts. Arbitrary exclusion of defence witnesses or experts would probably constitute a violation of this provision, and the Commission has held that the testimony of unidentified witnesses may be incompatible with the Convention since it is virtually impossible to rebut their testimony.[196]

Freedom from self-incrimination

Article 8(2)(g) provides that accused persons have the right not to be compelled to be witnesses against themselves or to plead guilty in criminal proceedings. Neither the Commission nor the Court have examined this provision in detail. It is closely related to Article 8(3), under which an

---

[191] IACHR Annual Report 1994, 113 at 123.
[192] IACHR Annual Report 1993, at 493. [193] Id.
[194] Loc. cit., above, n. 166. [195] Id., at 210.
[196] IACHR Second Report on the Situation of Human Rights in Colombia (1993) 98. National law, however, commonly makes exceptions for police informers.

involuntary confession of guilt or other incriminating statement by an accused person is not admissible as evidence (see below).

Right of appeal

Under Article 8(2)(h) of the Convention convicted persons must be granted the right to appeal against their convictions to a higher court. In the conduct of an appeal, convicted persons are entitled to all the due process safeguards contained in the Declaration and the Convention. As the Commission has noted, the process of appeal is itself a way in which the defects in due process in inferior courts may be corrected by superior courts.[197] It may also be observed that in an appeal the right to counsel may be even more crucial in establishing that the trial has been conducted fairly. Where an appeal turns on a point of law, it is unlikely in most cases that self-representation will be adequate. It may be argued that Article 8(2)(h) implies that full reasons ought to be given for judgments, since appeal is rendered difficult in their absence. Support for this view may be derived from the Commission's report on the judiciary in which it is stipulated that judgments must cover all points in the case.[198] Whether these criteria should attach to summary proceedings is, however, debatable.

Coerced confessions

Article 8(3) provides that a 'confession of guilt by the accused shall only be valid if it is made without coercion of any kind'. In cases involving coercion, the Commission has simply declared that there has been a violation of Article 8 *in toto*. Thus, confessions extracted by torture or other proscribed ill-treatment have been held to be in violation of Article 8.[199] Furthermore, incriminating statements extracted from an individual without the benefit of legal representation after he had been held incommunicado for a period of thirty days have been held to have violated Articles 8(2)(g) and 8(3).[200]

It would seem that confessions or other incriminating statements made on the basis of a breach of these provisions should be excluded by a court, and that any conviction which depends upon them should be overturned. Indirect support for this view can be derived from Case 11.006 (Peru).[201] In this case, the Peruvian army had entered the home of former President Garcia without warrant and seized papers which they alleged related to

---

[197] Case 9850 (Argentina) IACHR Annual Report 1990–1, 41 at 75.
[198] Loc. cit. above, n. 166.
[199] Case 9850 (Argentina), IACHR Annual Report 1990–1, at 41.
[200] Case 10.198 (Nicaragua), [1989] Inter-American Yearbook on Human Rights, 314.
[201] Loc. cit. above, n. 92, at 71.

criminal offences. The Commission held that this violated the inviolability of the home which was one of the due process rights implicit in Article 8(1). In the Commission's view more than a guarantee of privacy was involved; a guarantee of due process was also in issue because due process standards establish what can be seized, including incriminating evidence against an accused person. The Commission said:[202]

When a search of a domicile is conducted without observing the proper constitutional procedures, that guarantee prevents any evidence thus obtained from being used to arrive at a subsequent court decision. Thus in practice it functions as an exclusionary rule, one that eliminates illegally obtained evidence.

Since this is the Commission's stated view on the exclusion of illegally obtained evidence, it is logical to deduce that *a fortiori* it will adopt the same approach to wrongfully extracted confessions, the truth of which must inevitably be suspect.

Double jeopardy

Article 8(4) of the Convention provides that an accused person acquitted by a 'non-appealable judgment' must not be subjected to a new trial for the same cause. This provision represents the general principle of law which is sometimes referred to as *ne bis in idem*. This matter was considered in detail in Case 11.006 (Peru).[203] Here, former President Garcia had been tried and acquitted on the charge of unlawful enrichment, but the same charge was proffered against him at a subsequent trial. Finding that there had been a violation of Article 8(4), the Commission noted that three elements underpin the concept of *ne bis in idem*. First, the accused person must be acquitted. Second, the acquittal must be a final judgment, and third, the new trial must be based on the same cause which prompted the original trial.[204] As to the meaning of 'accused person acquitted', the Commission ruled that this implies someone 'who, having been charged with a crime has been exonerated from all criminal responsibility, since he has been acquitted because his innocence has been demonstrated, because his guilt has not been proven, or because it has been determined that the acts of which he is accused are not defined as a crime'.[205] The Commission next turned to the meaning of 'non appealable judgment'. It defined 'judgment' as 'any procedural act that is fundamentally jurisdictional in nature', while 'non appealable' was defined as 'expressing the exercise of jurisdiction that acquires the immutability and incontestability of *res judicata*'.[206] In analysing these concepts the Commission drew a distinction between preliminary

[202] Id., at 103.
[204] Id., at 105.
[206] Id.

[203] Loc. cit. above, n. 92, at 71.
[205] Id.

hearings and hearings which had been re-opened. In the case of the former, the Commission took the view that where a court rules that an individual cannot be prosecuted because the acts of which the accused is charged are not a crime, another court citing the same acts cannot then conclude that they are.[207] In the case of re-opened proceedings, the Commission noted that Article 8(4) explicitly prohibits the commencement of a new trial on the same facts. Based on a literal interpretation of the text, the Commission acknowledged that the violation of the principle of *res judicata* by re-opening proceedings which had already been closed would not be covered by Article 8(4). The Commission stated, however, that this provision implicitly includes those cases in which re-opening a case has the effect of reviewing questions of fact or law which have come to have the authority of *res judicata*.[208] In the Commission's view, the second case against former President Garcia bore these particular characteristics.[209]

Public hearings

Article 8(5) provides that criminal proceedings must be held in public, although exceptions are permissible 'insofar as may be necessary to protect the interests of justice'. This provision would appear to accord with the practice of most States in which there is some provision for *in camera* proceedings, especially in matters involving State security. Commenting upon the secret courts established in Colombia to prevent attacks upon the judiciary at a time of emergency but later maintained as a part of the ordinary law at least during preliminary proceedings, the Commission declared that such secret proceedings are incompatible with the right of public trial.[210] In taking this view, the Commission may have been swayed by the fact that the secrecy of these proceedings was exacerbated by the further use of the secret witnesses referred to above.[211]

FREEDOM FROM EX POST FACTO LAWS: ARTICLE 9 CONVENTION

Article 9 Convention

No one shall be convicted of any act or omission that did not constitute a criminal offence, under the applicable law, at the time it was committed. A heavier penalty shall not be imposed than the one that was applicable at the time the criminal offence was committed. If subsequent to the commission of

---

[207] Id., at 106.   [208] Id.
[209] Id., at 107.
[210] IACHR Annual Report 1992–3, 207 at 210. See also IACHR Second Report on the Situation of Human Rights in Colombia (1993) at 249.
[211] See above, 251.

the offence the law provides for the imposition of a lighter punishment, the guilty person shall benefit therefrom.

Article 9 provides that no-one shall be convicted of any act or omission which did not constitute a criminal offence under the applicable law at the time it was committed. While Article 9 of the Convention clearly comprehends the principle *nullum poena sine lege,* it is unusual in that it provides for the retroactive application of lighter penalties where these are introduced subsequent to the commission of a crime. It states that a penalty heavier than the one in force at the time an offence was committed must not be imposed. If, however, subsequent to the offence a lighter penalty is to be applied, the convicted person must enjoy the benefit of this.

RIGHT TO COMPENSATION FOR A MISCARRIAGE OF JUSTICE: ARTICLE 10 CONVENTION

Article 10 Convention
Every person has the right to be compensated in accordance with the law in the event he has been sentenced by a final judgment through a miscarriage of justice.

Under Article 10 of the Convention, every person who has been sentenced by a final judgment through a miscarriage of justice is entitled to compensation. It is required that such compensation be 'in accordance with the law', suggesting that a State must adopt specific laws to deal with both the award and quantum. A practice of ad hoc payment of compensation on an ex gratia basis would not meet the requirements of Article 10.

RIGHT TO PRIVACY : ARTICLES IX, X DECLARATION: ARTICLE 11 CONVENTION

Article IX Declaration
Every person has the right to the inviolability of his home.

Article X Declaration
Every person has the right to the inviolability and transmission of correspondence.

Article 11 Convention
1. Everyone has the right to have his honour respected and his dignity recognised.

2. No one may be the object of arbitrary or abusive interference with his private life, his family, his home, or his correspondence, or of unlawful attacks on his honour or reputation.

3. Everyone has the right to the protection of the law against such interference or attacks.

The right to privacy which is protected by Article 11 of the Convention is broad ranging. The Commission noted in Case 11.006 (Peru) [212] that the rationale for all of its provisions is to prevent the State from interfering arbitrarily in the lives of individuals. [213]

Article 11(1) provides that everyone has the right to 'have his honour respected and his dignity recognized'. The Commission has ruled that the forcible recruitment of a soldier may offend the dignity of the individual in violation of this provision. [214] Protection of the honour and dignity of a person applies not only in its intangible but also in its tangible form. In Case 10.772 (El Salvador), [215] the Commission held that the rape of a seven year old girl by a soldier was a violation of Article 11 as infringing her honor and dignity. Again, in Case 10.970 (Peru), [216] which involved the repeated rape of a woman by a member of the Peruvian armed forces, the Commission held that: '(s)exual abuse, besides being a violation of the victim's physical and mental integrity, implies a deliberate outrage to their dignity. In this respect, it becomes a question that is included in the concept of "private life" '.

In reaching this holding the Commission, cited the decision of the European Court of Human Rights in *X and Y* v *Netherlands*, [217] in which the latter has observed that the concept of a person's private life extends to his or her physical and moral integrity, including that of his or her sex life.

Article 11(2) provides that '(n)o one may be the object of arbitrary or abusive interference with his private life, his family, his home, or his correspondence, or of unlawful attacks on his home or reputation'. As the Commission has noted, [218] this provision has its counterpart in Articles IX and X Declaration. Despite the breadth of protection it provides, the right to privacy is not absolute in this respect: 'exercise of this right is routinely restricted by the domestic laws of states'. [219] Thus, the right to privacy must give way to the normal criminal investigative process. In such circumstances, however, interference with the inviolability of a person's domicile and private life may only be impeached pursuant to a 'well-substantiated

---

[212] Loc. cit. above at n. 92, 71.   [213] Id., at 102.

[214] Case 10.975 (Guatemala) IACHR Annual Report 1993, 216 at 222. The Commission refers to Art. 11 generally.

[215] IACHR Annual Report 1993, 181 at 186. Again, the reference is to Art. 11 generally.

[216] Loc. cit., above, n. 77.   [217] Eur. Ct. H. R., Series A, No. 167.

[218] Case 11.006 (Peru), loc cit. n. 92, 71 at 102.   [219] Id.

search warrant issued by a competent judicial authority, spelling out the reasons for the measure being adopted and specifying the place to be searched and the objects that will be seized'.[220] Clearly, any search must occur in strict accordance with requirements set out in the national law.

While neither the Commission nor the Court have been required to rule on the protection of a person's honour or reputation as protected by Articles 11(2) and (3), it is nonetheless apparent that these provisions are intimately related to issues of freedom of expression which are manifested in Articles 13 and 14 of the Convention.[221] As will be demonstrated below, the Convention generally prohibits prior censorship of expression, which suggests that normally only appropriate post hoc controls are permitted. In the case of defamation, the protection of a person's honour and reputation must be effected by legislation or other appropriate legal provision. Furthermore, Article 14 permits the right of reply to persons who have been injured by inaccurate or offensive statements or ideas which have been disseminated by the mass media. These issues will be considered under Article 14 below.

FREEDOM OF CONSCIENCE AND RELIGION: ARTICLE III DECLARATION;
ARTICLE 12 CONVENTION

Article III Declaration

Every person has the right freely to profess a religious faith, and to manifest and practise it both in public and in private.

Article 12 Convention

1. Everyone has the right to freedom of conscience and of religion. This right includes freedom to maintain or to change one's religion or beliefs, and freedom to profess or disseminate one's religion or beliefs, either individually or together with others, in public or in private.
2. No one shall be subject to restrictions that might impair his freedom to maintain or to change his religion or beliefs.
3. Freedom to manifest one's religion and beliefs may be subject only to the limitations prescribed by law that are necessary to protect public safety, order, health, or morals, or the rights or freedoms of others.
4. Parents or guardians, as the case may be, have the right to provide for the religious and moral education of their children or wards that is in accord with their own convictions.

---

[220] Id.   [221] Cf. the right to have one's dignity 'recognized' in Art. 11(1).

Article 12(1) of the Convention provides that everyone has the 'right to freedom of conscience and of religion'. That right includes the 'freedom to maintain or change one's religion or beliefs', as well as the 'freedom to profess or disseminate one's religion or beliefs either individually or together with others, in public or in private'. This provision is consistent with Article III of the Declaration which recognises everyone's right 'freely to profess a religious faith, and to manifest and practice it both in public and in private'.

These guarantees of freedom of thought and religion are clearly related to other substantive rights namely, the right to freedom of thought and expression, freedom of assembly and freedom of association, all of which are necessary if one is to be permitted to hold religious beliefs and to practice them either individually or with others. Article 12, however, grants the State a margin of discretion to control religious or pseudo-religious practices which may prove harmful to individuals. While Article 12(2) provides that in general no one shall be 'subject to restrictions that might impair his freedom to maintain or change his religion or beliefs', Article 12(3) states that the freedom to manifest these may be subject to limitations 'prescribed by law that are necessary to protect public safety, order, health, or morals, or the rights and freedoms of others'. Any such limitations must be 'prescribed by law' which indicates that they must conform to the principle of legality. While States Parties are entitled to adopt the necessary measures of restriction, these measures are subject to the control of the Commission and Court. Indeed, the Commission has already ruled on this matter in cases involving Jehovah's Witnesses in a number of Latin American States. In Argentina, Jehovah's Witnesses were prosecuted for being unwilling to swear oaths of allegiance, to undertake military service or to recognise the State and its symbols. The Commission held that such prosecutions violated the rights of individuals under Article III and other related rights.[222]

When deciding whether a restriction is 'necessary to protect public safety' or for any of the other purposes listed in Article 12(3), it can be supposed that the Inter-American Court would follow the same approach as it follows when interpreting similar wording in Article 13(2) of the Convention that permits restrictions on freedom of expression.[223] If so, a concept of proportionality applies: the restriction 'must be proportionate and closely tailored to the accomplishment of the legitimate governmental objective necessitating it'.[224]

Under Article 12(4) of the Convention parents or guardians have the

---

[222] IACHR Annual Report 1978–9, 251. The other rights violated were those contained in Arts. I, V, XII, XXI and XXV of the Declaration.

[223] See below, 263–4.

[224] *Compulsory Membership* case, para. 46, see below, 260.

'right to provide for the religious and moral education of their children or wards that is in accordance with their own convictions'. Given the context of this provision, it may be assumed that the word 'convictions' refers to the parents' or guardians' own religious or philosophical convictions. There is no similar provision to this in the Declaration, but in a case involving the expulsion of the children of Jehovah's Witnesses from schools in Argentina for failing to salute the flag, the Commission held that this violated Article XII of the Declaration which provides for the right to education.[225]

FREEDOM OF THOUGHT AND EXPRESSION: ARTICLE IV DECLARATION; ARTICLE 13 CONVENTION

Article IV Declaration

Every person has the right to freedom of investigation, of opinion, and of the expression and dissemination of ideas, by any medium whatsoever.

Article 13 Convention

1. Everyone has the right to freedom of thought and expression. This right includes freedom to seek, receive, and impart information and ideas of all kinds, regardless of frontiers, either orally, in writing, in print, in the form of art, or through any other medium of one's choice.

2. The exercise of the right provided for in the foregoing paragraph shall not be subject to prior censorship but shall be subject to subsequent imposition of liability, which shall be expressly established by law to the extent necessary to ensure:

    a) respect for the rights or reputation of others; or

    b) the protection of national security, public order, or public health or morals.

3. The right of expression may not be restricted by indirect methods or means, such as the abuse of government or private controls over newsprint, radio broadcasting frequencies, or equipment used in the dissemination of information, or by any other means tending to impede the communication and circulation of ideas and opinions.

4. Notwithstanding the provisions of paragraph 2 above, public entertainments may be subject by law to prior censorship for the sole purpose of regulating access to them for the moral protection of childhood and adolescence.

5. Any propaganda for war and any advocacy of national, racial, or religious hatred that constitute incitements to lawless violence or to any other similar illegal action against any person or group of persons on any grounds including

[225] *Id.*

those of race, colour, religion, language, or national origin shall be considered as offences punishable by law.

Freedom of thought and expression are guaranteed by Article IV of the Declaration and Article 13 of the Convention. Article IV provides exiguously that 'every person has the right to freedom of investigation, of opinion, and of the expression and dissemination of ideas, by any medium whatsoever'. Article 13 is more detailed and provides that '(e)very person has the right to freedom of thought and expression'. It then continues to elaborate upon the nature of the right by providing that it includes the 'freedom to seek, receive, and impart information and ideas of all kinds, regardless of frontiers, either orally or in writing, in print, in the form of art, or through any other medium of one's choice'.

Before analysing the meaning of this right, it is perhaps pertinent to comment upon the pivotal position which freedom of expression has assumed in the Commission and Court's understanding of the inter-American human rights system and its relationship to the proper functioning of democratic government. The Court has said:[226]

Freedom of expression is a cornerstone upon which the very existence of a democratic society rests. It is indispensable for the formation of public opinion . . . it represents, in short, the means that enable the community, when exercising its options, to be sufficiently informed. Consequently, it can be said that a society that is not well-informed is not a society that is truly free.

It is also the Court's view that since this right plays such an important role in the functioning of the democratic system, it should be 'scrupulously respected'.[227]

The Court's ideology is also reflected by the Commission which has stated that the right has a 'universal character' since freedom to impart and receive information without distortion is in itself universal.[228] It is significant in this connection that transnational communication is protected by the Convention. This ensures that ideas expressed in media originating in one State may not be interfered with by another, save in accordance with the principles established by Article 13 itself.

In analysing Article 13(1) of the Convention, it is pertinent to note that, since it guarantees the freedom both to transmit and to seek and receive information and ideas of all kinds, it has, in the Court's view, 'a special scope and character' which enhances the free interchange of ideas required for effective public debate within the political arena.[229] As the Court has

---

[226] Advisory Opinion No. 5, *Compulsory Membership in an Association Prescribed by Law for the Practice of Journalism,* I/A Court H.R. Series A No. 5, para. 70 (1985), 7 *HRLJ* 74.

[227] Id., para. 69.   [228] IACHR Annual Report 1980–1, 122.

[229] *Compulsory Membership,* loc. cit. above, n. 226 at para. 30.

also stated, Article 13 both protects an individual right which 'requires . . . that no one be arbitrarily limited or impeded in expressing his own thoughts' and 'implies a collective right to receive any information whatsoever and to have access to the thoughts of others'.[230] The practical application of this proposition was evident in Case 10.325 (Grenada).[231] In this case, a number of books from the left wing Pathfinder Press about the former Prime Minister of Grenada, Maurice Bishop, Fidel Castro of Cuba and Nelson Mandela of South Africa were confiscated by government officials at Point Salines airport pursuant to Grenadian law.[232] Despite attempts to secure release of the books by application to the Grenadian courts, no court order was forthcoming. The Commission held, therefore, that confiscation and retention of the books violated Article 13 since this guaranteed the petitioners' right to transport the books to, and receive the books in, Grenada.[233]

It should be noted that the medium or form in which the expression is made is irrelevant. Article 13(1) provides a non-exhaustive list of potential media which has the capacity to embrace new forms of communication, such as the Internet, and, indeed, other forms of communication yet to be invented. Moreover, freedom of expression supposes non-discrimination in access to the media. It 'requires, in principle, that the communication media are potentially open to all without discrimination or, more precisely, that there be no individuals or groups that are excluded from access' to the media.[234] A fortiori, there must not be a monopoly situation. As the Court stated, 'it is the mass media that make the exercise of freedom of expression a reality' and this entails that there 'must be, *inter alia*, a plurality of means of communication, the barring of all monopolies thereof, in whatever form, and guarantees for the protection of the freedom and independence of journalists'.[235]

Article 13(2) provides that freedom of expression may not be subject to prior censorship. The only exception is indicated in Article 13(4), which permits the prior censorship of public entertainments 'for the sole purpose of regulating access to them for the moral protection of childhood and adolescence'. This prohibition against prior censorship is also reinforced by Article 14 which guarantees the right of reply to anyone injured by the dissemination of inaccurate or offensive statements or ideas. The Commission has said:[236]

The prohibition against prior censorship assures that certain ideas and information will not be automatically excluded from the public arena. Thus people will not only

---

[230] Id. [231] IACHR Annual Report 1995, 113.
[232] Apparently the novel *Our Man in Havana* by Graham Greene was also confiscated. The reason for this is not clear. [233] Loc. cit. above, n. 231 at 123, para. 8.
[234] Compulsory Membership case, loc. cit. at n. 226, para. 34. [235] Id.
[236] 'Report on the Compatibility of "Desacato" Laws with the American Convention on Human Rights' in IACHR Annual Report 1994, at 204.

be free to express their own ideas but will have access to the ideas of others so as to broaden their understanding of the political debate within society. In addition, the right of reply provided for in Article 14 guarantees access to an appropriate medium of communication for those injured by inaccurate or offensive statements.

The Convention prohibits indirect as well as direct forms of censorship. Article 13(3) contains a non-exhaustive list of indirect means of imposing censorship. These include 'the abuse of government or private controls over newsprint, radio, broadcasting frequencies, or equipment used in the dissemination of information, or by any other means tending to impede the communication and circulation of ideas and opinions'. It is significant that this provision deals not only with public, but also with private means of control over the dissemination of information. This would seem to suggest that it is incumbent upon States to adopt appropriate laws for controlling media monopolies tending to impede the free flow of ideas. This view is also supported by the Court's holding in *Compulsory Membership*.[237]

An example of prior public censorhip which was held to be a violation of Article 13(3) was the seizure of a number of books published by a left wing press banned under Grenadian law by Grenadian officials.[238] The Commission held:[239]

The Government's act of seizing and banning the books has the effect of imposing 'prior censorship' on the freedom of expression and therefore has violated the two-fold aspects of the right to receive and impart information to 'everyone' both within and outside of the community, regardless of frontiers as provided by Article 13 of the American Convention.

The Commission also noted that the action taken by the Grenadian government with respect to these books was not saved by the post publication restrictions contained in Article 13(2) of the Convention.[240] It should be noted, however, that the Grenadian government did not argue the merits of this case and that the Commission's decision, while perhaps correct in principle, did not enjoy the benefit of full argument.

Instead of censorship, Article 13(2) of the Convention generally permits the 'subsequent imposition of liability'. Such post-publication restrictions must be 'expressly established by law' and are permissible only 'to the extent necessary to ensure (a) respect for the rights or reputations of others; or (b) the protection of national security, public order, or public health or morals'.

The issues of prior censorship and indirect control of the mass media, as well as that of the approach to post-publication restrictions permitted by Article 13(2), arose in Case 9178 (Costa Rica).[241] In this case, a United

---

[237] *Compulsory Membership,* loc. cit., above, n. 226 at para.56.
[238] Case 10.325 (Grenada) loc. cit., above, n. 231.
[239] Id.   [240] Id.

States journalist, Stephen Schmidt, was convicted of practising the profession of journalism in Costa Rica without belonging to the Colegio de Periodistas (Association of Journalists) as required by law. Under the law, access to the 'Colegio' was limited to persons 'holding a bachelor's degree in journalism of the University of Costa Rica or of universities or equivalent institutions abroad'. Although Schmidt argued that the legal requirement of membership of the Colegio violated Article 13, the Commission held that since Article 13 was not an absolute right, and as long as the Colegio protected the freedom to seek, receive and distribute information without imposing conditions leading to the restriction or curtailment of the right, there would be no violation of this provision.[242]

Although the Commission decided not to remit this case to the Court, Costa Rica sought an advisory opinion on whether compulsory membership of the Colegio was a violation of Article 13.[243] The Court was of the opinion that, since the expression and dissemination of ideas were indivisible concepts, the mass media should, in principle, be open to all.[244] The Court was careful to point out, however, that this did not mean that all restrictions on freedom of expression necessarily violated Article 13, since that provision itself specifically provided for the legitimacy of post hoc controls.[245] Such controls, however, were not unlimited and must meet the requirements of procedure and form which, in turn, 'depend upon the legitimacy of the ends that such restrictions are designed to accomplish'.[246] The Court specified four requirements which any post-publication restriction would have to meet in order to be valid:[247]

1. The existence of previously established grounds for liability;
2. The express and precise definition of these grounds by law;
3. The legitimacy of the ends sought to be achieved;
4. A demonstration that these grounds of liability are 'necessary to ensure' the aforementioned ends.

The Court continued:[248]

Article 13(2) is very precise in specifying that the restrictions on freedom of information must be established by law and only in order to achieve the ends that the Convention itself enumerates. Because the provision deals with restrictions . . ., the legal definition must be express and precise.

The Court also stressed that in assessing any restriction upon freedom of expression, it must take into account the 'object and purpose' of the Convention, which was stated in its preamble to be 'the consolidation of

[241] IACHR Annual Report 1984–5, 51.
[242] Id., at para. 59. [243] Compulsory Membership, Loc. cit., above, n. 226.
[244] Id., para. 34. [245] Id., para. 35.
[246] Id., para. 37. [247] Id., para. 39.
[248] Id., para. 40.

democratic social justice based on respect for the essential rights of man.'
The Court therefore concluded that any restrictions on freedom of expression must be judged by reference to the legitimate needs of democratic
societies and institutions.[249]

Furthermore, following an examination of the comparable provisions of
the European Convention on Human rights and the Civil and Political
Covenant, the Court ruled that the 'necessity' of any restrictions, and hence
their legality under Article 13(2), depends upon a demonstration that the
restrictions are 'required by a compelling governmental interest'.[250] They
must also be 'proportionate and closely tailored to the accomplishment of
the legitimate governmental objective necessitating it'.[251] Interestingly,
there is no mention of any allowance to states of a 'margin of appreciation'
when they decide on the need for a restriction in the public interest. In
contrast, such a 'margin of appreciation' doctrine plays a large part in the
interpretation of the freedom of expression guarantee in Article 10,
European Convention on Human Rights.[252]

Of particular importance in *Compulsory Membership* on the facts of the
case was the Court's analysis of the prohibition in Article 13(3) of indirect
controls imposed by private means. Here the Court declared that the State
has an obligation to ensure that a violation of Article 13(1) 'does not result
from the "private controls" referred to in Article 13(3)'.[253] It would seem that
such private controls may be economic in the form of monopoly ownership
of the media with the attendant restrictions which that may bring (such as
control of ideas by the owner) or they may include professional bodies such
as the Colegio. While it was acknowledged that the requirement of
compulsory membership restricted the dissemination of information and
ideas by certain classes of person, it was nevertheless argued that this was
justifiable under Article 13(2)(a) for the maintenance of professional and
ethical standards and to prevent employer interference with the
independence of journalists. The Court was not convinced by this argument
and stated that any justification must be rooted in Article 13(2)(b) on
grounds of 'public order' or as a 'just demand of the general welfare in a
democratic society' as permitted by Article 13(2) of the Convention.[254]

In order to determine whether compulsory licensing of journalists fell
within either of these categories, the Court found it necessary to explicate
their meaning. It defined 'public order' as 'a reference to the conditions
that assure the normal and harmonious functioning of institutions based
on a coherent system of values and principles',[255] while 'social welfare'

---

[249] Id., para. 42.   [250] Id., para. 46. Cf. the Court's third requirement quoted above.
[251] Id., Cf. the Court's fourth requirement quoted above.
[252] See above, 10.
[253] Compulsory Membership, loc. cit. n. 226, para. 48.
[254] Id., para. 63.   [255] Id., para. 64.

meant the 'conditions of social life that allow members of society to reach the highest level of personal development and the optimum achievement of democratic values'.[256] Although the Court acknowledged that the compulsory membership of journalists might achieve these ends, given the fundamental importance of freedom of expression to democratic life, the same criteria demanded the guarantees of 'the widest possible circulation of new ideas and opinions as well as the widest access to information by society as a whole'.[257] Since journalism was the 'primary and principal' manifestation of freedom of thought and expression, and since its restriction was not justifiable on public order grounds, the requirement of compulsory licensing of journalists could not be justified since this deprived non-members of the *Colegio* of their rights under Article 13(1).[258] Furthermore, the Court ruled that the regulation of ethical and professional standards in the practice of journalism could be achieved by other less restrictive means, presumably including post hoc controls.[259]

Much of the Court's reasoning in *Compulsory Membership* has been approved by the Commission in a report on desacato laws.[260] These laws, which exist in a number of Latin American States, criminalise expression which offends, insults or threatens a public functionary in the performance of his or her duties. Their rationale is to protect public functionaries in the exercise of their duties. The Commission found that these laws violated the American Convention for a number of reasons. First, they invert a fundamental principle of democratic systems which requires the government to be subject to controls, such as public scrutiny, in order to preclude or control abuse of power.[261] The fear of criminal sanctions discourages people from voicing their opinions on matters of public concern, particularly where they involve value judgments.[262] Second, where desacato laws allow truth as a defence, the burden of proof is generally placed on the utterer of the statement, thus further inhibiting the free flow of ideas and opinions.[263] The Commission was particularly concerned that proving the veracity of these statements might be impossible given that political debate involves value judgments that are not susceptible to proof.[264] Finally, the Commission noted that the rationale behind desacato laws reverses the principle that a properly functioning democracy is itself the best guarantee

---

[256] Id., para. 66.   [257] Id., para. 69.

[258] Id., para. 70. The Court drew a distinction here between the licensing of journalists, who played a part in the realisation of the Convention right to freedom of expression, and the licensing of other professions, where there was no such link.

[259] Id., para. 79.

[260] 'Report on the Compatibility of "Desacato" Laws with the American Convention on Human Rights', loc. cit. above, n. 236.

[261] Id., at 207.   [262] Id.

[263] Id., at 208.   [264] Id., at 209.

of public order, since they seek to preserve public order by 'restricting a fundamental human right which is recognised internationally as a cornerstone upon which democratic society rests'.[265] Commenting upon Articles 13(2) and (3), the Commission stated that these provisions recognise that the zone of legitimate State intervention begins at the point where the expression of an opinion or idea interferes directly with the rights of others or constitutes a direct and obvious threat to life in society.[266] The Commission observed that in a democratic society the threshold should be high, given the pivotal role which freedom of thought and expression plays.[267]

In another case involving limitations upon the use of freedom of expression to criticise governments, the Commission held that there had been a violation of Article 13 where a critic of the government was wrongfully denied the right to reacquire his citizenship and was deported to silence his criticism.[268]

As noted above, Article 13 prohibits indirect means of control on freedom of expression through restrictions on the allocation of radio broadcasting frequencies or of equipment used in the dissemination of information or 'by any other means tending to impede the communication and circulation of ideas and opinions'. Such 'other means' were present in a case in which the closure of a radio station was effected by State agents threatening the station manager and his family, interfering with transmissions, and causing power cuts.[269]

Specific limitations on the right to freedom of expression are contained in Article 13(5) of the Convention. This provides that 'any propaganda for war and any advocacy of national, racial or religious hatred that constitute incitements to lawless violence or to any other similar illegal action against any person or group of persons on any grounds including those of race, colour, religion, language or national origin' must be made criminal offences punishable by law. This provision clearly requires States to outlaw hate speech and other forms of expression which are aimed at the destruction of the rights of others. To date, there is no Commission or Court jurisprudence on any of these matters.

---

[265] Loc. cit., above, n. 236.
[266] Id., at 211.
[267] Id.
[268] Case 9855 (Haiti) IACHR [1988] Inter-American Yearbook on Human Rights, 244.
[269] Case 9726 (Paraguay) IACHR Annual Report 1987–8, 110.

RIGHT OF REPLY : ARTICLE 14 CONVENTION

1. Anyone injured by inaccurate or offensive statements or ideas disseminated to the public in general by a legally regulated medium of communication has the right to reply or to make a correction using the same communications outlet, under such conditions as the law may establish.
2. The correction or reply shall not in any case remit other legal liabilities that may have been incurred.
3. For the effective protection of honour and reputation, every publisher, and every newspaper, motion picture, radio, and television company, shall have a person responsible who is not protected by immunities or special privileges.

Part of the system of post hoc control in the area of freedom of expression is the granting of the right of reply to persons who have been injured by the dissemination of inaccurate or offensive statements or ideas. The Court has noted the 'inescapable relationship' between Articles 13 and 14.[270] As to the balance between the two, it has stated that in regulating the right to reply, states parties 'must respect the right to freedom of expression guaranteed by Article 13', but, at the same time, must not 'interpret the right to freedom of expression so broadly as to negate the right to reply'.[271]

Under Article 14, persons who have been injured are entitled to the right of reply or correction using the same medium as that in which the injurious statement was uttered. Furthermore, the right is to be enjoyed 'under such conditions as the law may establish'. This latter does not mean that the establishment of the right of reply is optional. As the Court has noted, Articles 1(1) and 2 of the Convention require States to take all the necessary measures to give effect to the right under their domestic law.[272] In giving effect to the right, however, it is apparent that there is some measure of discretion. Although Article 14 requires that the injured person should be given access to the same medium as that in which the injurious statement was uttered, it does not specify whether beneficiaries of the right are entitled to the same amount of space, the time within which the right is to be exercised, what language is admissible and so on. While the Court has not spelled out the precise limits of the right, it has stated that it must be established by law, but other than this it must fall 'within certain reasonable limits and within the framework of the concepts stated by the Court'.[273] The vagueness of this pronouncement is unlikely to be of assistance to States seeking to implement this right in their domestic law.

[270] Advisory Opinion No. 7 *Character and Scope of the Right to Reply or Correction Recognized in the American Convention*, I/A Court H.R. Series C No. 7, para. 25 (1986), 7 *HRLJ* 238.
[271] Id.   [272] Loc. cit. at n. 270, para. 24.
[273] Id., para. 27.

Article XXI Declaration

Every person has the right to assemble peaceably with others in a formal public meeting or an informal gathering, in connection with matters of common interest of any nature.

Article 15 Convention

The right of peaceful assembly, without arms, is recognised. No restrictions may be placed on the exercise of this right other than those imposed in conformity with the law and necessary in a democratic society in the interest of national security, public safety or public order, or to protect public health or morals or the rights or freedoms of others.

The right of peaceful assembly is recognised by Article XXI of the Declaration and Article 15 of the Convention. Article XXI is slightly fuller than Article 15 in providing that everyone is to enjoy the right in concert with others either 'in a public formal meeting or in an informal gathering, in connection with matters of common interest of any nature'. In addition to simply protecting the right of peaceful assembly, Article 15 stipulates that, in order to qualify, those assembling must do so 'without arms'. This supposes that an armed assembly is unlikely to remain peaceful for very long or that the carrying of arms implies the potential use of violence. It should also be noted that Article 15 may be restricted by limitations which are imposed 'in conformity with the law' and which are 'necessary in a democratic society in the interest of national security, public safety or public order, or to protect public health or morals or the rights or freedoms of others'. It can be taken that, as with restrictions under the comparable wording of Article 13, 'the restriction must be proportionate and closely tailored to the accomplishment of the legitimate governmental objective necessitating it'.[274] Despite the importance of this right to the proper functioning of democracy, the Commission and the Court have had little opportunity to analyse it in detail. Their comments have been restricted to findings of violations in cases involving religious groups.[275]

Article XXII Declaration

Every person has the right to associate with others to promote, exercise and protect his legitimate interests of a political, economic, religious, social, cultural, professional, labour union or other nature.

[274] See above, 264.   [275] See above, 258.

Article 16 Convention

1. Everyone has the right to associate freely for ideological, religious, political, economic, labour, social, cultural, sports, or other purposes.
2. The exercise of this right shall be subject only to such restrictions established by law as may be necessary in a democratic society, in the interest of national security, public safety or public order, or to protect public health or morals or the rights and freedoms of others.
3. The provisions of this article do not bar the imposition of legal restrictions, including even deprivation of the exercise of the right of association, on members of the armed forces and the police.

Although there are some notable differences in the categories of association mentioned in Article XXII of the Declaration and Article 16 of the Convention (the Convention does not mention professional associations for example), the wording 'or other purposes' in Article 16, when taken with Article 29(d) of the Convention, would seem to remedy any obvious omissions in this area. Although Article 16 includes the right to form and join a 'labour union', the Commission has held that Article 16 should not be interpreted as including the negative right not to join a trade union.[276] Generally, Article 16 should be read in conjunction with the San Salvador Protocol to the American Convention concerning trade union rights.[277]

Article 16(2) permits restrictions on certain listed public interest grounds. It can be taken that, as with the comparably worded restrictions in Article 13, 'the restriction must be proportionate and closely tailored to the accomplishment of the legitimate governmental objective necessitating it'.[278]

Article 16(3) allows States to impose 'legal restrictions, including even deprivation of the exercise of the right of association, on members of the armed forces and the police'. This allows a state to bar unionisation by the armed forces and the police entirely, although no such limitation applies in respect of the civil service. With regard to the impact of Article 16 on the regulation of professional associations, the Court acknowledged in the *Compulsory Membership* case[279] that the organisation of professions into professional associations is not per se contrary to the Convention, since such associations can ensure compliance by members with ethical standards and thus enhance public order. While the Court found in that case that the demands of freedom of expression had a higher value than the need to regulate the profession of journalism by such associations, it nonetheless

---

[276] 'Report on Cuba', loc. cit. above, n. 64 at 148–52.
[277] See below, 309.
[278] See above, 258.
[279] Compulsory Membership, loc. cit., above, n. 226, paras. 69–79.

indicated that in professions such as medicine and the law it was permissible to adopt norms of a public character in order to secure proper regulation of ethical standards. It further observed that law and medicine could be differentiated from journalism in that these were not activities which were guaranteed by the Convention.[280] Although the Court conceded that the practice of law might be associated with certain Convention rights, such as the right to due process, no one right embraced the practice of law as Article 13 did the practice of journalism.[281] In a case involving the regulation of advocates in Argentina, the Commission held that a requirement that an advocate be a member of a bar association was not a breach of Article 16.[282]

RIGHTS OF THE FAMILY: ARTICLE VI DECLARATION; ARTICLE 17 CONVENTION

Article VI Declaration

Every person has the right to establish a family, the basic element of society, and to receive protection therefor.

Article 17 Convention

1. The family is the natural and fundamental group unit of society and is entitled to protection by society and the state.
2. The right of men and women of marriageable age to marry and to raise a family shall be recognised, if they meet the conditions required by domestic laws, insofar as such conditions do not affect the principle of nondiscrimination established in this Convention.
3. No marriage shall be entered into without the free and full consent of the intending spouses.
4. The States Parties shall take appropriate steps to ensure the equality of rights and the adequate balancing of responsibilities of the spouses as to marriage, during marriage, and in the event of its dissolution. In case of dissolution, provision shall be made for the necessary protection of any children solely on the basis of their own best interests.
5. The law shall recognise equal rights for children born out of wedlock and those born in wedlock.

The rights of the family are hybrid rights which span the categories of both first and second generation human rights. Article 17(2) of the Convention provides that 'men and women of marriageable age' have the 'right to

---

[280] Compulsory Membership, loc. cit., above, n. 226, paras. 69–79   [281] Id.
[282] Cases 9777 and 9718 (Argentina), [1988] Inter-American Yearbook on Human Rights 60 at 132.

marry and to raise a family', while Article VI of the Declaration states that every person has the 'right to establish a family'. Article 15 of the San Salvador Protocol to the American Convention[283] further provides that everyone has the right to form a family, 'which shall be exercised in accordance with the provisions of the pertinent domestic legislation'. The language of the Declaration and Protocol appears to be broader than that of the Convention and would seem to contemplate the possibility of single parent families and same sex parent families, but it should be borne in mind that Article 29(d) Convention would give precedence to the broader formulation of the Declaration should such be the case.

Nevertheless, all the instruments appear to support the traditional concept of the family. Article VI states that 'the family is the basic element of society' while the Convention and Protocol state that it is the 'natural and fundamental group unit ['element' in the Protocol] of society'. In each case the State is to protect the family, and in the Convention this obligation is also imposed upon society, although it is not indicated how society is to fulfil its responsibility in this field. Probably the better view is that the State is to create the conditions in which the family finds protection within society, although this may not be derived from a literal interpretation of the provision. Article 15 of the Protocol also provides that the State is to take measures for the improvement of the spiritual as well as the material aspects of the family.

Among the matters to which the State is to pay attention are the provision of special care and assistance to mothers during a reasonable period before and after childbirth; the provision of adequate nutrition for children in their early years; the adoption of special measures for the protection of adolescents in order to ensure the full development of their physical, intellectual and moral capacities; and, finally, the undertaking of special programs of family training in order to help create a climate in which children will receive and develop the values of 'understanding, solidarity, respect and responsibility'. It should be noted that the provision of maternity care in the Protocol is almost identical to the formulation of a similar requirement in Article VII of the Declaration which, through the application of Article 29(d), is incorporated into the Convention.

Some mention should be made of the difference in terminology used in each of the three instruments. While the Declaration states that everyone has the right to 'found' a family, the Convention provides that men and women of marriageable age have the right to 'raise' a family, and the Protocol provides that everyone has the right to 'form' a family. Each of these words has a slightly different nuance, although whether this is of any significance has yet to be addressed by the Court or Commission.

---

[283] On the San Salvador Protocol, see Chap. 9.

Article 17 of the Convention is the only provision which explicitly seeks to regulate the marital relationship. Article 17(3) prohibits forced marriages, while Article 17(4) requires States to take appropriate steps to ensure the equality of rights and a balancing of spousal responsibilities within marriage, during marriage and in the case of dissolution of marriage. In the case of the last of these, this provision also makes clear that the welfare of any children of the marriage must be the dominant concern. Finally, Article 17(4) of the Convention makes it clear that children born out of wedlock are to ensured equal rights by law.[284]

RIGHT TO A NAME: ARTICLE 18 CONVENTION

Article 18 Convention

Every person has the right to a given name and to the surnames of his parents or that of one of them. The law shall regulate the manner in which this right shall be ensured for all, by the use of assumed names if necessary.

Article 18 provides that everyone has the 'right to a given name and to the surnames of his parents or that of one of them'. To this end, persons must to allowed to use an assumed name 'if necessary'. Taking Article 18 as a whole, it would seem that no-one is to be denied the use of a name of his or her own choosing. This would appear to require States to adopt the necessary legal measures to facilitate the change of a person's name should he or she wish to do so. While the Commission and the Court have not yet been asked to rule specifically on this issue, the former has declared that kidnapping and irregular adoption of the children of *desaparecidos* during Argentina's 'dirty war' was a violation of, *inter alia*, Article 18.[285]

RIGHTS OF THE CHILD: ARTICLE VII DECLARATION; ARTICLE 19 CONVENTION

Article VII Declaration

*All women, during pregnancy and the nursing period, and all children have the right to special protection, care and a*Id.

Article 19 Convention

Every minor child has the right to the measures of protection required by his condition as a minor on the part of his family, society, and the state.

---

[284] Art. 17(4), Convention. .
[285] IACHR 'A Study about the Situation of Minor Children who were Separated from their Parents and are Claimed by Members of their Legitimate Families', [1988] Inter-American Yearbook on Human Rights 476 at 480.

Like family rights, the rights of the child are another category of hybrid right. They are protected by Article VII of the Declaration, Article 19 of the Convention and Article 16 of the San Salvador Protocol to the Convention.[286] As noted above under family rights, Article VII provides not only for the pre and post-natal care of women, but also deals with the right of children to special protection. Article 19 of the Convention is short and simply provides that '(e)very minor child has the right to the measures of protection required by his condition as a minor on the part of his family, society and the State'. Article 16 of the Protocol, however, while largely reiterating the Convention provision, spells out in detail what this entails. It provides that every child has the right to grow under the protection and responsibility of its parents and that, save in exceptional judicially recognised circumstances, children of young age ought not to be separated from their mothers. This creates a presumption in favour of maternal custody in the case of marital separation or divorce. Article 16 further provides that every child has the right to free and compulsory education, at least during elementary schooling, and to continue his or her training at higher levels of the educational system.

There has been little formal legal analysis of these provisions by the Commission or Court, but the Commission has found violations of Article 19 Convention in a number of cases. In Case 11.006 (Peru)[287] the Commission ruled that the detention by force of the children of former President Garcia by the Peruvian army was a violation of Article 19 which it viewed as particularly repugnant.[288] The Commission has also held that the rape of a seven year old girl by a soldier in El Salvador was a violation of Article 19 of the Convention.[289] Furthermore, in a number of disappearance cases, although the Commission has not specifically referred to Article 19, it has held that the violations of other provisions have been aggravated by the fact that the victim was a minor.[290]

In a wide ranging report on the treatment of the children of the disappeared in Argentina, the Commission analysed which provisions of the Convention and Declaration had been violated.[291] The cases investigated fell into two categories: first, where the children were given to parents who were unaware of their origins and, second, where the adoptive parents were cognisant of the provenance of the children. Of the latter the Commission commented that 'the cases in which the new parents are

---

[286] On the San Salvador Protocol, see Chap. 9.

[287] Loc. cit., above, n. 92, 71.

[288] Id., at 101.

[289] Case 10.772 (El Salvador) IACHR Annual Report 1993, 181 at 186.

[290] Cases 9936, 9948 and 9960 (Guatemala) IACHR Annual Report 1990–1, 136.

[291] IACHR 'A Study about the Situation of Minor Children who were Separated from their Parents and are Claimed by Members of their Legitimate Families', [1988] Inter-American Yearbook on Human Rights, 476.

themselves the captors, torturers and executioners of the natural parents . . . constitute . . . one of the most unusual manifestations of a repressive pathology'.[292] In both cases, however, the Commission found that the norms which had been violated by the kidnappings and irregular adoptions were: first, Article 18 of the Convention giving the child the right to an identity and a name; second, Article XVII of the Declaration and Article 1 of the Convention recognising the right to be legally recognised as a person; third, Article VII of the Declaration and Article 19 of the Convention concerning the right of pregnant women and children to special measures of protection; and, finally, Articles V and VI of the Declaration and Articles 11 and 17 of the Convention concerning protection of the rights of the family.[293] The Commission also noted that none of these rights were derogable and that, even assuming a state of civil war existed in Argentina at the time, these acts would still violate the norms of humanitarian law contained in the Geneva Conventions of 1949 and their Additional Protocols of 1977.[294]

RIGHT TO A NATIONALITY : ARTICLE XIX DECLARATION; ARTICLE 20 CONVENTION

Article XIX Declaration
Every person has the right to the nationality to which he is entitled by law and to change it, if he so wishes, for the nationality of any other country that is willing to grant it to him.

Article 20 Convention
1. Every person has the right to a nationality.
2. Every person has the right to the nationality of the state in whose territory he was born if he does not have the right to any other nationality.
3. No one shall be arbitrarily deprived of his nationality or of the right to change it.

Article XIX provides that every person has the right to the nationality to which he is entitled by law and to change it, if he so wishes, for the nationality of another State that agrees thereto. Article 20(2) similarly provides that all persons are entitled to the nationality of the State in whose territory they are born in the absence of any other. This last provision clearly gives preference to the *ius soli* in the absence of nationality based on the *ius sanguinis*. Article 20(3) provides that no one may be

---

[292] Inter-American Yearbook Human on Rights, at 480.
[293] Id., at 490.　　　　　　　　　　　　　[294] Id.

'arbitrarily deprived of his nationality or of the right to change it'. Article 20 was found by the Commission to have been violated when an individual who had lost his Haitian nationality when he became an American citizen was denied the right to recover his Haitian citizenship, as he was entitled to do by Haitian law.[295]

Article 20 has also been considered in the context of certain proposed legislation amending the criteria for naturalisation in Costa Rica.[296] Costa Rica had sought to make its law governing naturalisation more restrictive than it had been previously. While the Court confirmed that the conferral of nationality was primarily a matter for a State's discretion, its law nonetheless had to conform to the genuine link requirement established by the International Court of Justice in the *Nottebohm* case.[297] In the case of Costa Rica, it was clear that the reason for the proposed amendments was to make Costa Rican nationality more difficult to acquire, and this was within that State's reserved domain as long as the requirements complied with international law. Although the Court did not comment on this issue, it seems apparent that the proposed Costa Rican legislation was designed to strengthen the genuine link between Costa Rica and those who sought its nationality. The Court did, however, observe that it could identify no potential infringement of Article 20, since no Costa Rican citizen would be deprived of his or her citizenship by an application of the proposed amendments.[298] Furthermore, there was nothing in the amendments which would prevent them from acquiring a new nationality if they wished to do so.[299]

RIGHT TO PROPERTY: ARTICLE XXIII DECLARATION; ARTICLE 21 CONVENTION

Article XXIII Declaration

Every person has a right to own such private property as meets the essential needs of decent living and helps to maintain the dignity of the individual and of the home.

Article 21 Convention

1. Everyone has the right to the use and enjoyment of his property. The law may subordinate such use and enjoyment to the interest of society.

2. No one shall be deprived of his property except upon payment of just compensation for reasons of public utility or social interest, and in the cases and according to the forms established by law.

---

[295] Case 9855 (Haiti), [1988] Inter-American Yearbook on Human Rights, 244.
[296] Advisory Opinion No. 4 *Proposed Amendments to the Naturalization Provisions of the Political Constitution of Costa Rica*, I/A Court H.R. Series A No. 4 (1984), 5 *HRLJ* 161.
[297] Id., para. 32.
[298] Id., para. 42.   [299] Id.

3. Usury and any other forms of exploitation of man by man shall be prohibited by law.

Both the Declaration and the Convention protect the right to property. Article XXIII of the Declaration simply provides that every person has the 'right to own such private property as meets the essential needs of decent living and helps to maintain the dignity of the individual and the home', while Article 21 of the Convention provides that everyone has the 'right to the use and enjoyment of his property'. This 'use and enjoyment' may, however, be subordinated to the interests of society. The apparently broad reach of this proviso is limited by Article 21(2) which states that no one 'shall be deprived of their property except upon payment of just compensation, for reasons of public utility or social interest an in the cases and according to the forms established by law'. Article 21(3) also requires that usury and 'any other form of exploitation of man by man' be prohibited by law. What this last formula means in the context of the right to property is unclear, but it would seem that it is aimed at any exploitative practice such as debt bondage, although it is arguable that this is covered by Article 6 of the Convention.

The Commission has held that the right to property is fundamental and inalienable and that no State, group or person may undertake or conduct activities to suppress the rights upheld in Articles XXIII and 21.[300] The Commission has also stated that the international instruments establishing the right to property 'have become rules of customary international law, and as such are considered obligatory in the doctrine and practice of international law'.[301] Moreover, the Commission has given its approval to the view of the United Nations Special Rapporteur[302] that the ownership and possession of property protects the individual from becoming 'a mere pawn of an excessively powerful State authority'.[303] Indeed, the Commission has further affirmed that the right to property is of special importance in fostering the general enjoyment of all other human rights.[304]

Although the American Convention is said by the Commission to follow 'a more progressive approach'[305] to the right to property than other international instruments, its social interest proviso also provides better protection than those instruments against arbitrary expropriation without compensation or illegal confiscation.[306]

---

[300] Case 10.770 (Nicaragua), IACHR Annual Report 1993, 293 at 299, para. 13. See also 'Report on Nicaragua', id. 442 at 465.

[301] Id.

[302] ECOSOC E/CN. 4/1993/15 at 35 and 85. Luis Valencia Rodriguez, Special Rapporteur.

[303] Case 10.770 (Nicaragua) IACHR Annual Report 1993, 293 at 300, para. 13.

[304] 'Report on Nicaragua', id. 442 at 465–6.

[305] Id., at 466.   [306] Id.

The Court and Commission have had little opportunity to apply these theoretical observations to actual cases. The confiscation of an individual's mine without compensation in Nicaragua was held to be a breach of Article 21.[307] Destruction of property has been held to violate Article XXIII of the Declaration, so that a breach was held to have occurred in Case 10.116 (Suriname) [308] in which the dwelling of a terrorist suspect was incinerated with the loss of his family's possessions. Creeping expropriation may also infringe Article 6. Thus there was a breach by Paraguay when a private radio station had been closed down through intimidation of the station manager and his family and by interference with broadcasts and power cuts caused by agents of the State.[309]

FREEDOM OF MOVEMENT AND RESIDENCE: ARTICLE VIII DECLARATION; ARTICLE 22 CONVENTION

Article VIII Declaration

Every person has the right to fix his residence within the territory of the state of which he is a national, to move about freely within such territory, and not to leave it except by his own will.

Article 22 Convention

1. Every person lawfully in the territory of a State Party has the right to move about in it, and to reside in it subject to the provisions of the law.

2. Every person has the right to leave any country freely, including his own.

3. The exercise of the foregoing rights may be restricted only pursuant to a law to the extent necessary in a democratic society to prevent crime or to protect national security, public safety, public order, public morals, public health, or the rights or freedoms of others.

4. The exercise of the rights recognised in paragraph 1 may also be restricted by law in designated zones for reasons of public interest.

5. No one can be expelled from the territory of the state of which he is a national or be deprived of the right to enter it.

6. An alien lawfully in the territory of a State Party to this Convention may be expelled from it only pursuant to a decision reached in accordance with law.

7. Every person has the right to seek and be granted asylum in a foreign territory, in accordance with the legislation of the state and international conventions, in the event he is being pursued for political offences or related common crimes.

---

[307] IACHR Annual Report 1986–7, 89 at 10.
[308] [1989] Inter-American Yearbook on Human Rights 190 at 204.
[309] IACHR Annual Report 1986–7, 110 at 113.

8. In no case may an alien be deported or returned to a country, regardless of whether or not it is his country of origin, if in that country his right to life or personal freedom is in danger of being violated because of his race, nationality, religion, social status, or political opinions.
9. The collective expulsion of aliens is prohibited.

Although a number of petitions has been brought in relation to freedom of movement and residence, the jurisprudence of the Commission on this subject has not been particularly analytical.

Under Article VIII of the Declaration individuals have the right to fix their residence within the territory of the State of which they are nationals, to move freely within that territory and not to leave it except by their own will. Although Article VIII does not specify that everyone has the right to return to their own country, the Commission has implied such a right. Thus, the Commission has found violations of Article VIII in numerous cases in which Cuba has both prevented citizens from leaving and returning to the State. The Commission has also declared a number of cases concerning other countries involving involuntary exile and refusal to allow persons to return home to violate Article VIII of the Declaration.[310] In this context the Commission has remarked that 'the right of every person to live in his homeland, to leave it and to return to it when he so desires . . . is a basic right that it is recognised by all international instruments for the protection of human rights'.[311] A refusal to grant a passport, thereby depriving citizens of the right to leave their State has been held to violate Article VIII of the Declaration.[312]

Article 22 of the Convention is more detailed than its Declaration counterpart. Article 22(1) provides that every person—including aliens—'lawfully in the territory of a State Party has the right to move about in it and to reside in it subject to the provisions of the law'. The final phrase seems to leave the way open for States to apply certain restrictions. Thus it is not unusual for the movement of aliens to be restricted in certain states, nor for legitimate restrictions to be placed on those on bail awaiting trial. While Article 22(3), which provides for limitations to the right on public interest grounds, appears to support this view, Article 22(4) also permits States to restrict the right of residence in designated zones 'for reasons of public interest'. This would seem to conform to the practice of restricting

---

[310] See, for example, Cases 2509 (Panama), IACHR Annual Report 1979–80, 63; 2777 (Panama) IACHR Annual Report 1979–80, 67; Case 2719 (Bolivia), IACHR Annual Report 1978, 83; Case 2794 (Peru), OEA/Ser.L/V/II.49, doc. 36, 3 Apr., 1980, Original: Spanish; Case 3411 (Chile), IACHR Annual Report 1978, 83; Case 7378 (Guatemala), IACHR Annual Report 1980–1, 57; Case 4288 (Chile), IACHR Annual Report 1981–2, 57.

[311] 'Report on Cuba' in IACHR Annual Report 1994, 142 at 155–6.

[312] Case 2711 (Uruguay), Resolution 22/81, 6 Mar. 1981, OEA/Ser.L/V/II.52, doc. 32, 6 Mar. 1981, Original: Spanish.

residence next to sensitive military installations or penal institutions for both aliens and citizens alike. It is likely that the 'proportionality' requirement spelt out by the Court under Article 13[313] will apply when assessing restrictions sought to be justified under Articles 22(3) and (4) also. Acts of unlawful detention and kidnapping have been held by the Commission to interfere with persons' freedom of movement and residence. In Case 10.574 (El Salvador)[314] the Commission found a violation of Article 22 when a petitioner was kidnapped, tortured and told he would be permanently 'disappeared' if he returned to his native town. Any unlawful detention or deprivation of an individual's liberty will constitute a violation of the right to freedom of movement and residence.[315]

Unlike Article VIII of the Declaration, Article 22(2) of the Convention expressly recognises the right of every person 'to leave any country freely, including his own'. Article 22(5) explicitly gives nationals a right to remain in and return to their own country. This provision is unconditional and thus appears to prevent the use of exile as a punishment. Noting in its 1980–1 Annual Report that a number of states (Bolivia, Chile, Guatemala, Haiti and Paraguay) had administratively expelled nationals as a means of eliminating political dissidents,[316] the Commission expressed itself in very forceful terms on this clear breach of the Declaration and the Convention, although seemingly accepting that nationals may be expelled as an alternative to imprisonment provided that due process requirements are observed:

The Commission considers that all of these expulsions, that were not subject to control by the judiciary, constitute a serious violation of human rights and, when carried out without the consent of the state to which these persons were transferred, a serious violation of international law. Therefore, the Commission urges all states to put an end to this practice and to limit expulsion of nationals only to those cases that have been reviewed by the judiciary, as an alternative to the penalty of privation of freedom and always for a definite period of time.

The remaining provisions of Article 22 deal exclusively with the rights of aliens in a host State. Article 22(6) provides that 'an alien lawfully within the territory of a State Party to the Convention may only be expelled from it pursuant to a decision reached in accordance with law'. It appears that this decision may be either an executive or a judicial decision in accordance with the law of the State in question. Article 22(6) says nothing of the right to appeal such a decision, but the practice of the Commission (see below) indicates that due process must be followed and it is submitted that the

---

[313] See the *Compulsory Membership* case, above, 258.
[314] IACHR Annual Report 1993, 174.
[315] Id., at 179.
[316] At 120. Cf. Case 2794 (Peru), IACHR OEA/Ser.L/V/II. 46, doc. 37, 8 Mar. 1979, reprinted in T. Buergenthal, R. Norris and D. Shelton, 3rd edn, 139 (exile of political dissidents without any domestic remedy a breach of Article VIII Declaration).

procedural guarantees in Article 8 of the Convention must apply in such proceedings. This may therefore require access to counsel and, in certain circumstances, the right to an interpreter.

Article 22(8) includes a guarantee of *non refoulement* by providing that an 'alien may not be deported or returned to a country, regardless of whether or not it is his country of origin, if in that country his right to life or personal freedom is in danger of being violated because of his race, nationality, religion, social status or political opinion'. Under Article 22(7) such a person 'has the right to seek and be granted asylum in a foreign territory, in accordance with the legislation of the State in question and international conventions, in the event he is being pursued for political offences or related common crimes'. Article 22(9) further prohibits the mass expulsion of aliens for any reason whatsoever. The mass expulsion from Honduras of nationals of El Salvador resident there, many of them illegal immigrant agricultural workers, after violence that followed a World Cup football match between the two countries in 1969, was condemned by the Commission as a 'violation of human right'.[317]

RIGHT TO PARTICIPATE IN GOVERNMENT: ARTICLE XX DECLARATION; ARTICLE 23 CONVENTION

Article XX Declaration

Every person having legal capacity is entitled to participate in the government of his country, directly or through his representatives, and to take part in popular elections, which shall be by secret ballot, and shall be honest, periodic and free.

Article 23 Convention

1. Every citizen shall enjoy the following rights and opportunities:
   a) to take part in the conduct of public affairs, directly or through freely chosen representatives;
   b) to vote and to be elected in genuine periodic elections, which shall be by universal and equal suffrage and by secret ballot that guarantees the free expression of the will of the voters; and
   c) to have access, under general conditions of equality, to the public service of his country.
2. The law may regulate the exercise of the rights and opportunities referred to

[317] IACHR Preliminary Report of the Subcommittee on Violations of Human rights in Honduras and El Salvador, OAS Doc. OEA/ Ser.L/V/II.22, doc. 2 of 15 Jul. 1969, reprinted in T. Buergenthal, R. Norris and D. Shelton, op. cit. at n. 316, above, 133. This case occurred before the Convention entered into force; the Declaration does not specifically protect aliens from expulsion, although the right to 'security of the person' in Art. I may apply.

in the preceding paragraph only on the basis of age, nationality, residence,
language, education, civil and mental capacity, or sentencing by a competent
court in criminal proceedings.

Article XX of the Declaration provides that all persons having 'legal
capacity' are entitled to participate in their national government, directly
or through their representatives, and to take part in popular elections by
secret ballot, which shall be 'honest, periodic and free'. Article 23 of the
Convention provides that every citizen is to enjoy certain 'rights and
opportunities', including participation in the conduct of public affairs of
his country, directly or through freely chosen representatives; the right to
vote in genuine periodic elections which are to be conducted by universal
and equal suffrage and by a form of secret ballot which guarantees the free
expression of the voters; and access, under general conditions of equality,
to the public service of his or her country.

There are clearly differences in the drafting of these extensive provisions
which require some analysis. The Declaration states that it is persons
having 'legal capacity' (undefined) who are entitled to participate in
government and elections, while the Convention provides that it is 'citizens' for whom the political rights in Article 23 are guaranteed. The rights
in Article 23 are not unlimited. An examination of Article 23(2) reveals
that the law may regulate them by reference to 'age, nationality, residence,
language, education, civil and mental capacity, or sentencing by a competent court in criminal proceedings'. The list of potential restrictions in
Article 23(2) is exclusive, that is, there are no other grounds upon which
the rights in Article 23(1) may be limited. It should also be observed that
Article 23 guarantees a right which may not be suspended or derogated
from even in time of war or public danger. As the Commission has stated
in the context of electoral rights, 'the exercise of these rights is so essential
if societies are to function normally that Article 27 of the Convention
prohibits their suspension regardless of the circumstance'.[318]

Personal application of electoral rights

Both Article XX of the Declaration and Article 23 of the Convention
provide that individuals have a right to elect and to be elected. As noted
above, however, limitations are permitted by Article 23(2) by reference to
age, nationality, etc. A case that did not fall easily within any of the
permitted grounds of limitation was Case 10.804 (Guatemala)[319] In this
case, the former President Rios Montt was prohibited from standing for

---

[318] Case 10.596 (Mexico), IACHR Annual Report 1993, 259 at 269.
[319] Id., 206 at 210, para. 19.

election because of his participation in a regime which had been established contrary to the Guatemalan constitution. The Commission, having regard to the OAS commitment to democratic organisation, found that the principle of ineligibility appears in other constitutions of the hemisphere and that it was included in the General Treaty of Peace and Friendship concluded by Guatemala, El Salvador, Honduras, Nicaragua and Costa Rica. The Treaty also provided that these States would not recognise any government established by unconstitutional means. The Commission ruled that 'these principles rejecting the breach of the constitutional order, the disqualification of these leaders for high office and non re-election were adopted because they were considered as juridical principles of international relations and common defense of the democratic consolidation of the region'.[320] From this it concluded that the provisions of the Guatemalan constitution represented a 'customary constitutional rule' in Central America.[321] The Commission also considered whether ineligibility established a discriminatory principle contrary to Article 23. It held, however, that since ineligibility arose in a number of circumstances for democratically elected heads of State who have held office for a certain period of time, it was acceptable under a State's constitutional law to apply ineligibility to those who led a breach of the constitution. In the light of these factors, the ruling of ineligibility to stand for office in the case of Rios Montt was not a violation of Article 23.[322]

As well as the declaration of ineligibility of Rios Montt, there was a similar declaration in respect of the vice-presidential candidate who stood with him.[323] In addition to being declared ineligible for election, this candidate was also denied the right to challenge this declaration by an application for *amparo*. The Commission held that a denial of the rights of this candidate based on the ineligibility of the presidential candidate could only be interpreted as a violation of his electoral rights.[324]

The Commission has also held that Article 23(2) does not prohibit the imposition of conditions upon candidates for elections. A requirement that membership of a political party is a necessary precondition to candidature has been accepted by the Commission.[325] Indeed, the Commission has shown itself to be strongly in favour of party organisation, saying that parties are necessary in a democracy 'if chaos and anarchy are not to reign'.[326]

---

[320] IACHR Annual Report 1993, 212, para. 28. [321] Id., para. 29.
[322] Id., 213, para. 35.
[323] Case 10.804(b) (Guatemala), IACHR Annual Report 1994, 46. [324] Id.
[325] Case 10.109 (Argentina), [1988] Inter-American Yearbook on Human Rights, 172.
[326] Id., at 184.

Election criteria

The Commission has stated on a number of occasions that 'any mention of the right to vote and to be elected would be mere rhetoric if unaccompanied by a precisely described set of characteristics that the elections are required to meet'.[327] In its report entitled 'Human Rights, Political Rights and Representative Democracy in the Inter-American System',[328] the Commission reviewed these characteristics in some detail. It stated that a review of all major human rights instruments revealed that truly democratic elections should possess the following criteria: they should be 'authentic or genuine', periodic, by universal suffrage, and conducted in such a way that they preserve the free expression of the will of the electorate.[329]

Authenticity of elections

In order for elections to be authentic or genuine, the Commission has said that there must be no interference which tampers with the will of the citizenry as expressed through the election process.[330] The Commission has stated that in order to achieve this the 'fundamental currents of political thought' must be reflected in the drafting of a State's electoral laws.[331] Such laws must also reflect a consensus and must not be imposed by a legislative majority. In addition, the Commission has also stated that there must be a maintenance of 'general conditions' under which the election unfolds. This is defined as conditions in which there are a plurality of political parties which are entitled to conduct the election under the same basic conditions.[332] Thus fairness in elections appears to imply that no party should be given an advantage over another, such as limiting access to the media in the case of opposing parties.[333]

Universal suffrage

Universal suffrage implies that all those of voting age who are not rendered ineligible from voting in accordance with one of the permitted exceptions in Article 23(2) must be entitled to take part in periodic elections. The Commission has, however, noted that in certain cases impediments are

---

[327] Case 10.596 (Mexico), IACHR Annual Report 1993, 259 at 270. See also Cases 9768, 9780 and 9829 (Mexico) IACHR Annual Report 1989–90, Chap. V, Section III.

[328] 1993 Annual Report, at 514.

[329] Id.   [330] Id., at 524.

[331] IACHR 'Report on the Situation of Human Rights in Panama' [1988] Inter-American Yearbook on Human Rights, 528 at 598.

[332] 'Human Rights, Political Rights and Representative Democracy in the Inter-American System', IACHR Annual Report 1990–1, 514 at 525.

[333] Id.

caused to voters by political interference or repression by way of unwarranted police action and prosecution. Such action has been condemned by the Commission which has noted that it exemplifies the relationship of political rights to other rights such as the right to a fair trial and to personal liberty, and their relationship to a system in which the rule of law and an independent judiciary exist to protect these rights.[334] Such a situation occurred in Case 9855 (Haiti)[335] in which the petitioner, a political opponent of General Namphy, the President of Haiti, was denied the opportunity to recover his nationality as permitted by law and was thus denied candidature in a forthcoming election. The Commission held that the denial of the right of the petitioner to initiate judicial proceedings to recover his nationality was a breach of Article 25, which in turn led to a denial of his political rights under Article 23.[336]

Periodicity and secrecy of elections

In order to allow the electorate to express its will freely, it is necessary that ballots be held with reasonable frequency and in circumstances which will allow voters to cast their votes in secret. Although the Commission has indicated that this requirement is intimately related to a range of other human rights, it has not specifically commented on the appropriate period within which an election must be held. It has, however, ruled that the postponement of an election for ten years violated Article XX of the Declaration.[337]

RIGHT TO EQUAL PROTECTION: ARTICLE II DECLARATION;
ARTICLE 24 CONVENTION

Article II Declaration

All persons are equal before the law and have the rights and duties established in this Declaration, without distinction as to race, sex, language, creed or any other factor.

Article 24 Convention

All persons are equal before the law. Consequently, they are entitled, without discrimination, to equal protection of the law.

Article 24 of the Convention is clearly designed to prohibit discrimination in the application of the law and in legal proceedings, but nowhere does it include a list of the prohibited grounds of discrimination. This, however,

---

[334] IACHR Annual Report 1990–1, at 532.
[335] [1988] Inter-American Yearbook on Human Rights, 244.
[336] Id.   [337] IACHR Annual Report 1977, 93.

may be remedied by reference to both Article II of the Declaration and Article 1(1) of the Convention which provide extensive catalogues of prohibited discrimination. Indeed, the Court has declared that the meaning of discrimination in Article 24 must be interpreted by reference to the list of prohibited grounds contained in Article 1(1).[338] Article II provides that there must be no discrimination on grounds of race, sex, language, creed 'or any other factor', while Article 1(1) states that, in addition to these grounds, discrimination is prohibited on the grounds of colour, political or other opinion, national or social origin, economic status, birth or any other social condition. The Court has noted that although Articles 1(1) and 24 overlap, their conceptual origins are different. While Article 1(1) is a parasitic provision which is designed to ensure that the rights proclaimed in the Convention are implemented without discrimination by States Parties, Article 24 provides a free-standing and general prohibition against discrimination arising from the application of any domestic legal norm in any subject area.[339] The underlying rationale for the prohibition of discrimination has been expressed by the Court in the following way:[340] 'Equality springs directly from the oneness of the human family and is linked to the essential dignity of the individual'. Because of this, the Court has held that no group has a right to superior treatment over another, nor must other groups be treated as inferior. At first sight, this might seem to preclude any form of discrimination, but the Court, citing a dictum of the European Court of Human Rights in the *Belgian Linguistics* case,[341] has acknowledged that on occasions different treatment for different groups might not offend this principle since 'not all differences in treatment are in themselves offensive to human dignity'.[342] Indeed, the Court has acknowledged that certain factual inequalities might legitimately give rise to inequalities in legal treatment which do not violate principles of justice, and which may, in fact, be necessary to secure redress for those who are disadvantaged in some way.[343] As examples of circumstances in which difference in treatment would be justified, the Court cited the cases in which limits were placed on the legal capacity of minors or mentally incompetent persons.[344] The Court went on to hold:[345]

Accordingly, no discrimination exists if the difference in treatment has a legitimate purpose and if it does not lead to situations which are contrary to justice, to reason or to the nature of things. It follows that there would be no discrimination in differences in treatment of individuals by a state when the classifications

---

[338] Advisory Opinion No. 4 *Proposed Amendments to the Naturalization Provisions of the Political Constitution of Costa Rica,* I/A Court H.R. Series A No. 4, para. 54 (1984), 5 *HRLJ* 161.

[339] Id.   [340] Id., para. 55.

[341] Eur. Ct. H.R., Series A, No. 2 (1968).

[342] *Proposed Amendments,* loc. cit., above, n. 338, para. 56.   [343] Id., para. 56.

selected are based on substantial factual differences and there exists a reasonable relationship of proportionality between these differences and the aims of the legal rule under review. These aims may not be unjust or unreasonable, that is, they may not be arbitrary capricious, despotic or in conflict with the essential oneness and dignity of human kind.

In *Advisory Opinion No.4, Proposed Amendments,* the Court was required to apply these abstract principles in the context of proposed legislation by the Costa Rican government to regulate the acquisition of Costa Rican citizenship. The proposed legislation envisaged a much shorter period of residency for persons of Central American, Ibero-Spanish or Spanish citizenship than those of other national origin, but not all those who possessed such citizenship were treated identically. Those who had acquired citizenship through naturalisation rather than the *ius soli* were required to serve a longer qualification period. The Court found that the different treatment in each of these cases was justified. Commenting on the first category of persons, the Court noted that those of Central American, Ibero-Spanish or Spanish citizenship shared close historical, cultural and spiritual bonds with the people of Costa Rica and would therefore be more likely to assimilate easily and quickly with the national community.[346] The difference in treatment of those having acquired such nationality through naturalisation or birth, although much more difficult to maintain, was also held to be permissible since the Court took the view that Costa Rica might entertain legitimate doubts about the ease with which individuals might acquire the nationality of other American States.[347] Finally, the Court was obliged to consider the difference in treatment between a foreign woman who married a Costa Rican man who was treated more favourably than a foreign man who married a Costa Rican woman. The Court held that this putative provision was based on outdated notions of paternal authority and conjugal inequality and could now no longer be regarded as a legitimate reason for different treatment. This potential discrimination of the grounds of sex would therefore violate Article 23.[348]

A case of discrimination on the grounds of sex has also arisen before the Commission. In a report on El Salvador, the Commission held that a violation of Article II had occurred where adultery alone was a sufficient ground for a man to divorce his wife, but public scandal and abandonment had to be proved in addition to adultery where a woman was seeking to divorce her husband.[349]

---

[346] Loc. cit., above, n. 338, para. 60.
[347] Id., para. 61.
[348] Id., para. 64.
[349] IACHR Report on the Situation of Human Rights in El Salvador (1978), 160.

RIGHT TO JUDICIAL PROTECTION: ARTICLE 25 CONVENTION

Article 25 Convention

1. Everyone has the right to simple and prompt recourse, or any other effective recourse, to a competent court or tribunal for protection against acts that violate his fundamental rights recognised by the constitution or laws of the state concerned or by this Convention, even though such violation may have been committed by persons acting in the course of their official duties.

2. The States Parties undertake:

a) to ensure that any person claiming such remedy shall have his rights determined by the competent authority provided for by the legal system of the state;

b) to develop the possibilities of judicial remedy, and

c) to ensure that the competent authorities shall enforce such remedies when granted.

Article 25 guarantees the right of all persons to 'simple and prompt recourse, or any other effective recourse, to a competent court or tribunal for protection against acts that violate their fundamental rights'. These rights may be those recognised by the constitution of the State concerned or by the Convention. It is immaterial for the purposes of Article 25 that the acts called into question were performed by an agent of the State acting in the course of his or her official duties. As the Court has noted, Article 25 incorporates the principle of international human rights law that the procedural instruments for the protection of human rights must be effective.[350] It has also stated that it creates an obligation for States to provide effective judicial means to permit the vindication of rights violated.[351] Failure to provide such recourse will lead to the responsibility of the State which is in breach of its obligation.[352] The practical result of the application of these principles has been a finding by the Court that the remedies of habeas corpus and *amparo* may not be suspended, even in times of public emergency.[353]

Article 25(2) requires that States must ensure that any person claiming a remedy to vindicate his or her rights must have these rights determined by 'the competent authority provided for by the legal system of the state'. This provision must also be read together with Article 8 of the Convention which requires the principles of due process to be satisfied. Thus, proceedings to vindicate rights must be heard by an independent and impartial

---

[350] *Judicial Guarantees in States of Emergency,* loc. cit., above, n. 146, para. 24.
[351] Case 11.006 (Peru), IACHR Annual Report 1994, 71.
[352] Id.
[353] *Judicial Guarantees in States of Emergency,* loc. cit., above, n. 146 at para. 30.

tribunal which is free from executive interference. As noted above, the
Commission has had occasion to comment on the lack of political support
for the judiciary in the execution of its functions in this area. This has been
particularly apparent in the field of 'disappearances' where the judiciary in
certain States has been unable or unwilling because of political intimidation to carry out its functions in the proper manner. Since Article 25(2)
also requires States to develop judicial remedies to protect human rights
and to enforce these remedies when granted, it should be noted that there
has also been a failure in this area where the conditions referred to above
have obtained in various States.

Despite these observations on the ineffectiveness of access to, and
enforcement of, judicial remedies, not all violations in this area have been
so stark. The Commission detected a violation of Article 25 in Peru where
the military exercised judicial jurisdiction in half the country and a state of
emergency existed for the civil courts in the other half. The Commission
ruled that this state of events deprived individuals of simple and swift
recourse to the courts for protection of their rights.[354] Article 25 has also
been held to have been violated where an individual is denied recourse to
judicial procedures to challenge an expulsion order[355] and where a court
refuses to review a case where there appears to be sound reasons for so
doing.[356] Of particular importance, however, has been a finding by the
Commission that Article 25(2) will be breached by the application of
impunity or so-called caducity laws to members of the military who have
violated human rights, since these deny individuals the opportunity to
secure a judicial remedy.[357] These cases also illustrate the point that in the
practice of the Commission and the Court, Article 25 is closely linked with
the right to a fair trial in Article 8: where the two provisions overlap in
their field of application, a breach of both will commonly be found where
domestic procedures are deficient, as on the facts of the amnesty cases.

[354] IACHR Annual Report 1992–3, 207 at 211.
[355] Case 9855 (Haiti), [1988] Inter-American Yearbook on Human Rights, 244.
[356] Case 9260 (Jamaica), [1988] Inter-American Yearbook on Human Rights, 256 at 270.
[357] Cases 10.147, 10.181, 10.240, 10.262, 10.309, 10.311 (Argentina) IACHR Annual
Report 1992–3, 41 at 48, para. 39. See also the Uruguayan amnesty cases, considered with
the Argentinian cases, above, 243, under Art. 8. .

9

The Protection of Economic, Social and Cultural Rights under the inter-American System of Human Rights

MATTHEW CRAVEN

INTRODUCTION

In a region beset by political strife and instability and marked by widespread violence, it is perhaps not surprising that the predominant focus of human rights concerns has been the traditional 'liberal' rights and freedoms. The almost endemic problems of torture, arbitrary detention, forcible disappearances, and denial of political participation have all tended to encourage a myopic vision of human rights that has excluded from view problems of a broader nature, and particularly those relating to economic, social and cultural rights.

Although the inter-American system was the first to give express recognition to economic, social and cultural rights, for much of the early period of its work the inter-American Commission on Human Rights treated those rights as a marginal and diversionary concern. In general they were regarded 'more as byproducts of economic development than as values in themselves'.[1] This view continued to prevail during the drafting of the American Convention of Human Rights and in the work of the inter-American Commission until the late 1970s. Since that time, there has been a growing recognition within the Organization of American States (OAS) that it is no longer feasible to set aside considerations of poverty or social justice in its approach to human rights. Not only has it become apparent that questions of inequality underlie many of the broader problems of political violence, but it has also been accepted that minimum benchmarks should be established for the implementation of all human rights.

Specific recognition of economic, social and cultural rights is to be found in all of the major human rights instruments of the inter-American system, namely, the Charter of the OAS, the American Declaration, the American

---

[1] L. LeBlanc, 'The Economic, Social and Cultural Rights Protocol to the American Convention and its Background', 2 *NQHR* (1992) 130.

Convention on Human Rights and its Additional Protocol on Economic, Social and Cultural Rights. The relationship between these instruments and the associated role of the inter-American Commission on Human Rights and the inter-American Court on Human Rights is intricate, but significant nonetheless for the protection of economic, social and cultural rights.

THE CHARTER OF THE OAS

The Charter of the OAS,[2] adopted in 1948, contained only a few human rights provisions of a general nature,[3] and lacked the necessary machinery for supervision. The Protocol of Buenos Aires, however, which amended the Charter and came into force in 1970, added to it a number of provisions relating to the economic, social, scientific and cultural development of Member States, and outlined certain obligations of international co-operation. Within these provisions, several individual economic, social and cultural rights found recognition. Article 45, in particular, speaks of the right of all human beings to 'material well being' and to 'spiritual development', the right to work and the right of employers and workers to associate for the defense and promotion of their interests. Article 49 similarly mentions the right to education. In no sense, however, do these and other articles of the Charter that relate to the economic, social and cultural well-being of the populations amount to a coherent body of rights. Use of the term 'right' is for the most part incidental and more often than not can only be inferred from the existence of State obligations.[4] The obligations themselves are both vague and imprecise. In the case of Article 45, for example, States are not required to 'ensure' or 'guarantee' the relevant rights, rather they agree to 'dedicate every effort to the application of the . . . principles and mechanisms' that are enunciated. The right to work (incidentally expressed not only as a right but as a 'social duty') and the right to freedom of association, are therefore treated as mere 'principles' which States will endeavour to apply, suggesting that they have less the characteristics of individual rights than of objectives of social and economic development.

That the economic and social rights in the Charter were primarily conceived as objectives of national development rather than individual human rights, is borne out by two further points. First, Chapter VII of the

---

[2] Charter of OAS, see Appendix I to this book

[3] Art. 5(j) (now 3(l)) provides: 'the American States proclaim the fundamental rights of the individual without discrimination as to race, nationality, creed, or sex.'

[4] For example Art. 45(i) mentions 'adequate provision for all persons to have due legal aid in order to secure their rights'.

Charter in which these rights are to be found is itself entitled 'Integral Development', suggesting that the particular concern of member States was to promote development co-operation,[5] and ensure that States in the region did not seek to procure economic advantage over others by reducing labour costs.[6] Secondly, in Chapter XIII, the Charter specifically provides for the creation of an inter-American Economic and Social Council charged with promoting 'cooperation among the American countries in order to attain accelerated economic and social development'. It would appear to have been the intention that ECOSOC should have primary responsibility for implementing the objectives in Chapter VII rather than the inter-American Commission of Human Rights (the 'Commission').[7] This confirms the impression that the rights in Chapter VII are merely incidental concerns. As the Commission itself has noted:

the rights incorporated in to the Charter are considered in the context of the standards of international law applicable to relations among the American states, for which reason they do not constitute a base of standards that makes possible their international protection. In other words, that instrument does not recognize human rights, compliance with which may be claimed against a state, but rather it establishes objectives of economic and social development to be reached by the states through internal effort and international cooperation.[8]

Ultimately it was in the form of the American Declaration of the Rights and Duties of Man, and the later American Convention on Human Rights, rather than the Charter, that the Organization sought to pursue its human rights objectives. That being said, the Charter does remain of considerable importance, particularly insofar as it provides the normative foundations for the American Declaration and for the activities of the inter-American Commission as a Charter organ.

THE AMERICAN DECLARATION OF THE RIGHTS AND DUTIES OF MAN

The American Declaration of the Rights and Duties of Man was adopted as a Resolution of the Ninth International Conference of American States in 1948[9] together with a Charter of Social Guarantees.[10] It had been

---

[5] e.g., Art. 48 which provides for cooperation between States to meet educational needs.

[6] See e.g., Art. 46 which relates to harmonization of labour and social security legislation.

[7] This view is more than substantiated by the later system developed for the American Convention. Art. 43 of the Convention, which concerns the implementation of economic and social rights, merely provides for the Commission to receive copies of the Reports submitted to the I/A ECOSOC.

[8] IACHR Annual Report 1983–4, 138.

[9] Res. XXX, Ninth International Conference of American States, Bogotá, Colombia, 30 Mar.–2 May 1948, Final Act. 38.

[10] Res. XXIX, Final Act, 29.

conceived in 1945[11] and the initial draft had been prepared by the inter-American Juridical Committee.[12] That draft, which invoked a conception of the State as a 'cooperative commonwealth', gave recognition not only to civil and political rights but also to a range of economic, social and cultural rights including the rights to work, to just conditions of employment and to social security. Although the Conference substantially amended the draft articles,[13] the Declaration as adopted does contain a number of economic, social and cultural rights. Specific recognition is given, *inter alia*, to the right to health (Article XI), the right to education (Article XII), the right to the benefits of culture (Article XIII), the right to work (Article XIV), the right to rest and leisure (Article XV), and the right to social security (Article XVI). In addition, the Declaration contains a number of rights that might be closely associated with an individual's economic and social interests, such as the right to associate for the protection of labour-union interests (Article XXII), the right of women and children to special protection (Article VII), the right to the inviolability of the home (Article IX), and the right to property (Article XXIII).

When it was adopted, the American Declaration was considered, like the Universal Declaration of Human Rights, to have no binding force in law.[14] It was adopted as a resolution of the Conference and was intended merely as a statement of moral, or political, principle. Since that time, however, the Declaration has, by virtue of institutional recognition[15] and subsequent State practice, acquired some 'normative force'. Although its significance has certainly declined since the entry into force of the American Convention, it remains of particular importance, in terms of the rights it contains. Indeed, pending the entry into force of the Additional Protocol to the American Convention (the San Salvador Protocol),[16] the Declaration remains the only instrument in the inter-American system that gives detailed recognition to economic, social and cultural rights.

The formal legal status of the Declaration was considered in some depth

---

[11] Res. XI, I/A Conference on the Problems of War and Peace, Mexico City, 1945.

[12] Pan American Union, IAJC, 'Draft Declaration of the International Rights and Duties of Man and Accompanying Report' (1946).

[13] See generally, LeBlanc, above, n. 1, 131–4.

[14] As Buergenthal has commented, some of the language of the Declaration has 'the ring of political manifesto and, in large measure, the Declaration certainly is political manifesto'. T. Buergenthal, 'The American Human Rights Declaration: Random Reflections' in K. Hailbonner, G. Ress, T. Stein (eds.) *Staat und Völkerrechtsordunung* (1989), 133, 134. See also, L. LeBlanc, *The OAS and the Promotion and Protection of Human Rights* (1977), 16.

[15] In 1960 the Council of the OAS approved the statute of the Inter-American Commission which provided in Art. 1(2) that the 'human rights' for which the Commission would be responsible were those set forth in the American Declaration. Statute of the Inter-American Commission on Human Rights, Approved by GA/Res. 447, OAS 9th Sess., La Paz, Bolivia 1979, amended by Res. 508, 10th Sess., (1980).

[16] See, below, text acc. nn. 84–103.

by the inter-American Court in its advisory opinion OC-10/89.[17] In that case, the Government of Colombia sought an interpretation of Article 64 of the American Convention[18] enquiring specifically as to the status of the American Declaration of the Rights and Duties of Man and the Court's jurisdiction in relation to the Declaration. In their written observations on the question, Costa Rica, the USA, and Venezuela all pointed out that the Declaration was not a treaty under international law but a non-binding declaration of moral principles, and that therefore the Court was not empowered to interpret the Declaration under the terms of Article 64.[19] The Court agreed that the Declaration was not intended to be a treaty as defined by the Vienna Convention on the Law of Treaties 1969[20] and that it could not be considered a treaty within the meaning of Article 64(1). It went on to note, however, that the Declaration could be relevant in the interpretation of the American Convention and the Charter of the OAS, both of which were treaties, and that accordingly the Court could 'render an advisory opinion relating to [the Declaration] whenever it is necessary to do so in interpreting those instruments'.[21]

The Court's reasoning in relation to the OAS Charter is particularly significant. As the Court noted, the OAS Charter does not list or define the fundamental rights of man to which it refers,[22] but does instruct the inter-American Commission to 'keep vigilance over the observance of human rights'.[23] The Statute of the Commission, which was approved by Resolution 447 of the OAS General Assembly in 1979, provides a definition of those 'human rights' over which it was to exercise its competence.[24] Article 1(2) of the Commission's Statute specifies that

---

[17] Interpretation of the American Declaration of the Rights and Duties of Man within the Framework of Art. 64 of the American Convention on Human Rights, Advisory Opinion No 10. I/A Court H.R. Series A No.10 Appendix IV. 109, 11 *HRLJ* 118. Cf. T. Buergenthal, 'The Inter-American Court of Human Rights', 76 AJIL (1982) 231, 242–4.

[18] Art. 64(1) empowers OAS member states to request an opinion 'regarding the interpretation of this Convention or of other treaties concerning the protection of human rights in the American states'.

[19] Paras. 11–12, 15, 17–18. It was suggested, however, that the Court may have resort to the Declaration as a relevant instrument in the interpretation of other treaties and insofar as its provisions have become customary international law. Costa Rica and Uruguay, paras. 11 and 14.

[20] 1155 UNTS 331.   [21] Above, n. 17, para. 44.

[22] See e.g., Preamble, Art. 3(k), Art. 17, OAS Charter.

[23] Art. 145, OAS Charter. See also, Arts. 53, 106, OAS Charter.

[24] One has to pursue a circuitous argument to establish the significance of the Statute. Art. 106 of the OAS Charter provides that '[a]n inter-American convention on human rights shall determine the structure, competence, and procedure of th[e] Commission [on Human Rights]'. The Convention itself provides, in Art. 39, that the Commission 'shall prepare its Statute, which it shall submit to the General Assembly for approval'. Since the Convention establishes the 'structure, competence, and procedure' of the Commission for all member States (whether or not they are party to the Convention) in virtue of the Charter, the Statute may also be treated as a definitional instrument.

[f]or the purpose of the Statute, human rights are understood to be:

(a) The rights set forth in the inter-American Convention in relation to the States parties thereto;

(b) The rights set forth in the American Declaration of the Rights and Duties of Man, in relation to the other Member States.

By this act of approval, and by a number of subsequent similar acts,[25] the Court concluded that the member states of the OAS had 'signaled their agreement that the Declaration contains and defines the fundamental human rights referred to in the Charter'.[26] The approach taken by the Court largely reflected the established practice of the Commission on Human Rights. The Commission had been using the Declaration as the focal point of its activities for many years (an approach which had been endorsed by the OAS General Assembly[27]) and had itself found the Declaration to be legally binding on member states of the OAS back in 1981.[28]

From a fairly early stage in its operation the Commission had been in the receipt of communications relating to putative violations of the rights in the American Declaration.[29] These it had initially used informally as a source of information of which it could 'take cognizance' in the preparation of recommendations, studies and reports as provided in Article 9(b) and (c) of its Statute.[30] Then, in Resolution XXII of 1965, it was formally given the power to handle communications, request information and make appropriate recommendations to states.[31] The same Resolution, however, asked the Commission to focus upon a number of specific civil and political rights in the Declaration.[32] The Commission interpreted the Resolution as granting it the power to 'examine' communications concerning violations of those rights which had been cited in the Resolution. With respect to the other rights in the Declaration, such as all the economic, social and cultural

---

[25] See, Res. 314 (VII-O/77), 22 June, 1977; Res. 371 (VIII-O/78), 1 Jul. 1978; Res. 370 (VIII-O/78), 1 Jul. 1978.

[26] Para. 43. Cf. Buergenthal (1989), above, n. 14, 136.

[27] See e.g. Res. XXII, OEA/Ser.E/XIII.I doc. 150, rev (1965) in which the Commission was authorised to consider communications and to focus specifically upon certain rights in the Declaration.

[28] See Res. 23/81, Case 2141 (US) 6 Mar. 1981, in IACHR Annual Report 1980–1, 25, paras. 16–17 2 *HRLJ* 110. See also D. Shelton, 'Abortion and the Right to Life in the Inter-American System: The Case of "Baby Boy" ', 2 *HRLJ* (1981) 309; N. 8 *HRLJ* (1987) 355; D. Weissbrodt, 'Execution of Juvenile Offenders by the United States Violates International Human Rights Law', 3 *Am. Uni. J Int L Pol.* (1988) 339; D. Fox, 'Inter-American Commission on Human Rights Finds United States in Violation' 82 *AJIL* (1988) 601; C. Cerna, 'US Death Penalty tested before the Inter-American Commission on Human Rights', 10 *NQHR* (1992) 155.

[29] The Commission was first established in 1959 and was charged with 'furthering respect' for human rights, Res. VIII, Final Act of 5th mtg., OAS doc. OEA Ser. C/II. 5 (1960) 10–11.

[30] OEA/Ser.L/V/II.1, doc.32, 14 Mar. 1961.

[31] OAS doc. OEA/Ser. C/I.13/Final Act (1965) 32–4.

[32] It was authorised to pay 'particular attention' to the observance of the rights in Arts. I, II, III, IV, XVIII, XXV, and XXVI of the American Declaration.

rights, it considered itself as retaining its right to 'take cognizance' of communications for the purpose of identifying gross and systematic violations of human rights.[33] The procedure of taking cognizance, however, eventually evolved and became part of general case procedure and was later used in the examination of the general human rights situation in a country. The Commission was therefore in a position to receive, and act upon, complaints relating to economic, social and cultural rights.[34]

Between the years of 1978 and 1982 the Commission received and considered a number of communications concerning putative violations of economic, social and cultural rights in the Declaration. Since that time, however, the Convention has largely replaced the Declaration in the Commission's work *vis a vis* Convention parties (following the terms of Article 2(1) of the Commission's Statute), and the number of communications on these rights has declined dramatically. This in itself does not mean that the level of protection within the inter-American system for economic, social and cultural rights has necessarily declined. Even though the American Convention pays little attention to them as such, economic, social and cultural rights may receive protection through provisions that essentially concern civil and political rights. For example, during the Declaration's active period, a good number of complaints related to the ill-treatment of prisoners in detention involving the deprivation of food and health care.[35] Although this was treated as a violation of the right to health and well being under the Declaration (Article XI), it now falls under the terms of the Convention which guarantees the humane treatment of prisoners. That being said, it is undoubtedly the case that the protection of economic, social and cultural rights has in general suffered as a result of the apparent replacement of the Declaration by the Convention.

Perhaps the most significant claims relating to economic, social and cultural rights that have been considered under the Declaration by way of individual petitions have been those involving the persecution and mistreatment of minorities and indigenous populations. In Case 1802 the Commission considered complaints regarding the persecution of the Aché Tribe in Paraguay, which included complaints of murder, torture, the withholding of medical attention, inhuman conditions of work, the sale of

---

[33] Arts. 37, 53, 1970 Regulations, OEA/Ser.L/V/II.23, doc. 21 (1970)

[34] Art. 51 of the Commission's current regulations provide that '[t]he Commission shall receive and examine any petition that contains a denunciation of alleged violations of the human rights set forth in the American Declaration of the Rights and Duties of Man, concerning member states of the Organization that are not parties to the American Convention on Human Rights'.

[35] e.g. Case 2029 (Paraguay) OEA/Ser.L/V/II.41, doc.9 12 May 1977; Case 4402 (Cuba) IACHR Annual Report 1980–1, 94–5; Case 2300 (Cuba) IACHR Annual Report 1981–2, 65–8; Case 6091 (Cuba) ibid., 71–6; Case 6093 (Cuba) ibid., 77–9; Case 7899 (Cuba) ibid., 70–1. See also, Res. 13/82, OEA/Ser.L/V/II.65 doc. 28, 18 Mar. 1982.

children, and acts aimed at the destruction of culture.[36] Since Paraguay did not respond to the request for information, the Commission presumed the facts to be established and consequently found violations not only of the right to life, liberty and security (Article I), but also of the right to the protection of the family (Article VI), the right to the preservation of health and well-being (Article XI), the right to work and fair remuneration (Article XIV) and the right to leisure time (Article XV).[37] A similar case of persecution arose in Case 2137 which concerned a number of steps that had been taken by the Argentinian government against Jehovah's Witnesses, including the closure of their meeting halls and the exclusion of their children from schools.[38] The Commission found a violation, *inter alia*, of the right to education (Article XII). Both of these cases involved claims to freedom from interference and non-discrimination and as such did not differ in any great respect from other civil and political claims.

In a contrasting case, concerning the Yanomami Indians in Brazil, the Commission addressed the violation not only of obligations of abstention, but also of positive obligations in respect of a minority group. It found that in sanctioning the exploitation of the Amazonas, the Brazilian government had allowed the displacement of the Yanomami Indians from their ancestral land, had failed to establish a park for the protection of their heritage, and had failed to protect them from disease and ill-health. As such, the Commission found violations both of their right to residence (Article VIII) and their right to health (Article XI).[39] What might have been significant in this case is the fact that the problems had arisen as a result of an act of (government sanctioned) intervention. In other words any positive obligations recognized by the Commission may have been seen to arise as a consequence of that initial act of intervention rather than having existed *a priori*.

What is particularly significant about these cases is that they represent a small sample of the endemic problems that face indigenous populations in the region. It is particularly apparent that the concerns of indigenous populations relate most closely to social and cultural rights, and that pending the entry into force of an instrument directly related to the rights of indigenous populations it is the Declaration that will remain of greatest utility as a normative instrument for the protection of their interests.[40]

---

[36] Case 1802 (Paraguay), IACHR Annual Report 1977, 30–44, 55–7.
[37] Ibid.
[38] Case 2137 (Argentina), IACHR Annual Report 1978, 43–7.
[39] Case 7615 (Brazil), IACHR Annual Report 1984–5, 24–34.
[40] For further discussion of the position of indigenous peoples see Hannum, Chap. 10.

THE AMERICAN CONVENTION ON HUMAN RIGHTS
(THE PACT OF SAN JOSÉ)[41]

It was clear from a very early stage that States were interested in drafting and ratifying a binding international human rights instrument for the American region.[42] That vision did not become a reality until the adoption of the American Convention on Human Rights in 1969.[43] During the drafting of the Convention there was some debate as to whether, and to what extent, economic, social and cultural rights should be given specific recognition within the Convention.[44] Although each of the draft Conventions presented by the American Committee of Jurists,[45] by Panama,[46] and by Chile,[47] gave extensive recognition to economic, social and cultural rights (all of which were more or less adaptations of the International Covenant on Economic, Social and Cultural Rights (ICESCR)), the final 'working draft' presented by the inter-American Commission virtually excluded all reference to them.[48] The Commission's reasoning was predictable if somewhat self-justificatory. It argued that the Convention should only cover those rights to which American States were actually willing to extend protection[49] and noted, in that respect, that both the Council of Europe and the United Nations had decided to address economic, social and cultural rights in separate instruments with specially tailored implementation procedures.[50]

[41] American Convention on Human Rights (Pact of San José), See Appendix III.

[42] In 1954, for example, the 10th I/A Conference passed Res. XCV in which the Conference resolved to 'unite the efforts of all the American States to apply, develop, and perfect the human rights principles in the OAS Charter, the Declaration and the Universal Declaration of Human Rights'.

[43] The drafting of a human rights convention had first been entrusted to the Inter-American Council of Jurists in 1959, Res. VIII, 5th Meeting of Consultation of Ministers of Foreign Affairs, Final Act, OEA/Ser.C/II.5, (1959) 10–11. See generally, C. Bauer, 'The Observance of Human Rights and the Structure of the System for their Protection in the Western Hemisphere', 30 *Am.ULR* (1980) 5; M. Cabra, 'Rights and Duties Established by the American Convention on Human Rights', 30 *Am.ULR* (1980) 21.

[44] See, Cabra, ibid., 58–61; J. Peddicord, 'The American Convention on Human Rights: Potential Defects and Remedies', 19 *Texas ILJ* (1984) 139.

[45] OEA/Ser.I/II.4, doc. 119, (1959) 62. This draft devoted a full Chap. (Arts. 20–33) to economic, social and cultural rights.

[46] Panama, OEA/Ser.K/XVI/I.1, doc. 6 (1969)

[47] Chile, OEA/Ser.K/XVI/I.1, doc. 7 (1969)

[48] doc. OEA/Ser.L/II.19/doc.48 Rev. 1 (1968).

[49] Ironically enough, one criticism of the Convention as adopted is that it 'overreaches the actual consensus of the American states', Peddicord, above, n. 44, 147.

[50] It appears that the Commission was swayed by the fact that the Inter-American ECOSOC statute had just been revised and by the fact that there were proposals to include in the OAS Charter a declaration of ESC rights to be protected by ECOSOC (Preliminary Draft of Economic and Social Standards, approved in Washington DC, 18 June 1966). See, Cabra, above, n. 43, 60.

The Commission's Draft Convention provided in Article 25 that States parties recognize the need to adopt and guarantee those rights in the American Declaration that were not included in the Convention. Although not explicit, this of course referred almost exclusively to economic, social and cultural rights. Paragraph 2 of that draft article then listed a wide range of policy objectives that were to be pursued by member states. These objectives, although covering the general field of economic, social and cultural rights, were not in fact framed in terms of 'rights' at all. Weak though they may have been, these provisions still attracted an almost exclusively negative response from the States concerned. The USA, for example, objected to any reference to the rights at all.[51] Mexico expressed 'serious doubt as to the advisability of including' the draft article on the basis that determining responsibility would always be a difficult task.[52] Only Chile objected that insufficient recognition had been given to economic, social and cultural rights.[53]

Given the differences of opinion on this most crucial (and controversial) question, a working group was convened to discuss and revise the initial Commission draft.[54] The working group texts, which consisted of two articles (later to become Articles 26 and 42) were adopted without comment by the drafting Committee. They were also supplemented by the addition of a further article (ultimately Article 77) providing for the drafting of additional protocols to the Convention.

According to Article 26 as it was to appear in final form (in which it was elliptically entitled 'Progressive development'):

The States parties undertake to adopt measures, both internally and through international co-operation, especially those of an economic and technical nature, with a view to achieving progressively, by legislation or other appropriate means, the full realization of the rights implicit in the economic, social, educational, scientific and cultural standards set forth in the Charter.

Although largely modelled upon the terms of Article 2(1) of the ICESCR,[55] Article 26 is peculiar in a number of respects. First, it refers not to a list of rights enumerated within the American Convention itself, but to rights found in another instrument—the OAS Charter. Even then, it does not allude to rights that have gained specific recognition in the OAS Charter,

---

[51] USA, OEA/Ser.K/XVI/I.1, doc. 10 (1969).

[52] Mexico, OEA/Ser.K/XVI/I.1, doc. 11 (1969).

[53] Chile, OEA/Ser.K/XVI/I.1, doc. 7 (1969).

[54] OEA doc. 53, Corr. 1, 30 Jan. 1970.

[55] Art. 2(1) ICESCR reads: 'Each State Party to the present Covenant undertakes to take steps, individually and through international assistance and cooperation, especially economic and technical, to the maximum of available resources, with a view to achieving progressively the full realization of the rights recognized in the present Covenant by all appropriate means, including particularly the adoption of legislative measures.'

but rather to the 'rights *implicit* in the economic, social, educational, scientific and cultural standards set forth in the Charter' [emphasis added]. What is particularly curious about this formulation, apart from the fact that there appears to have been a conscious effort not to provide a coherent enumeration of the rights concerned,[56] is that reference was made not to the Declaration of Rights and Duties of Man (as had been suggested in several drafts) but to the Charter itself. One reasonable explanation may be that the Declaration was perceived to be an authoritative statement of the human rights provisions in the Charter and that therefore, a reference to the Charter, would necessarily legitimate the invocation of the Declaration.[57]

Secondly, unlike the ICESCR the obligation is not specifically made contingent upon the availability of material resources. It may well be that States perceived it to be implicit in the nature of the rights that their progressive implementation is dependent upon States having the necessary material resources available, but the absence of the phrase 'to the maximum of available resources' does appear to imply two things. First, that so long as States are making progress in the realization of the rights, they need not commit all available resources to that end. Secondly, that even where resources are manifestly available, for example where implementation is non resource-dependent, States are still entitled to implement the rights in a progressive manner. Neither one of these options is available to States party to the ICESCR.[58]

Ultimately, Article 26 of the American Convention is a disappointment. Although it provides some recognition of the existence of economic, social and cultural rights, it does little to give that recognition substance. The fact that reference is made back to the OAS Charter appears to confirm the view that they are to be treated as objectives of social and economic development rather than individual rights in any real sense. Given that the Convention was drafted only shortly after the adoption of the ICSECR, one might have expected a little more, especially since the inadequacies of the substance of the guarantee are in no way remedied by the implementation procedure envisaged for economic, social and cultural rights.

The second draft article put forward by the Commission for inclusion in the Convention would have obliged States parties to report periodically to the Commission on the measures taken to develop their domestic legislation in ways most conducive to achieving equitable distribution of national income and other economic and social objectives of public policy.

---

[56] As the Commission itself noted, Art. 26 tends to view economic, social and cultural rights as 'objectives of development and not as values in themselves', Annual Report 1983–4, 138

[57] See above, n. 26.

[58] See, M. Craven, *The International Covenant on Economic, Social and Cultural Rights: A Perspective on its Development*, (Oxford,1995) 136–44.

Moreover, it would have authorized the Commission to 'make appropriate recommendations' regarding the achievement of these objectives.[59] Criticism of this provision was largely directed towards the assumed role of the Commission. It was argued that for the Commission to make recommendations to States would be something 'above and beyond its competence and capabilities',[60] it being questioned whether such a role was well suited to the Commission as a 'juridical or quasi-judicial organ'.[61] Indeed, it was pointed out that as the inter-American Economic and Social Council already had a role in that area, the Commission would merely be duplicating its work.[62]

As a result of these criticisms the Commission's draft was revised and Article 42 was eventually to read as follows:

The States Parties shall transmit to the Commission a copy of each of the reports and studies that they submit annually to the Executive Committees of the inter-American Economic and Social Council and the inter-American Council for Education, Science, and Culture in their respective fields, so that the Commission may watch over the promotion of the rights implicit in the economic, social, educational, scientific, and cultural standards set forth in the Charter of the Organization of American States as amended by the Protocol of Buenos Aires.

Unlike the draft, Article 42 does not empower the Commission to make recommendations to States parties. Rather, the Commission is merely authorized to 'watch over the promotion' of the rights.[63] The main role in implementation appears to be reserved for the I/A Economic and Social Council (ECOSOC) and the I/A Council for Education, Science, and Culture (CESC). Nevertheless, that the Commission was given any role in implementation appears to have been gratefully received by some commentators at the time.[64]

Despite the clear intentions of the drafters in relation to Article 42, there does remain a technical question as to whether the general provisions of the Convention relating to the submission and consideration of petitions or communications (Articles 44-51) are equally applicable to the economic, social and cultural rights recognized, albeit indirectly, in the Convention. The Commission's power to act upon petitions is governed initially by

---

[59] Draft Convention, above, n. 54, 58.

[60] Mexico, above, n. 52, 59

[61] Chile, above, n. 53, 59–60.

[62] USA, above, n. 51, 62.

[63] The suggestion had been made that the term 'verify' should be used. Some States, however, considered this word to be too strong. See, 'Report of the United States Delegation to the Inter-American Conference on Protection of Human Rights', 9 *ILM* (1970), 710–57.

[64] See e.g., F. Volio, 'The Inter-American Commission on Human Rights', 30 *Am.ULR* (1980) 65, 70, where he comments that 'the Commission will have a great opportunity to broaden its range of activities beyond the limits indicated by the Convention, which is circumscribed by the scope of the norms related only to civil and political rights'.

Article 41(f) of the Convention. Its competence in that regard is spelt out in more detail in Article 44 of the Convention, which specifies initially that persons, groups or Non-Governmental Organizations may lodge petitions with the Commission 'concerning denunciations or complaints of violation of this Convention by a State party'. This would appear to allow for the submission and receipt of complaints in relation to purported violations of Article 26, as, for example, when a State arbitrarily legislates against trade union membership or discriminates against a social group by refusing its members access to public educational facilities.[65]

Volio points out, however, that Article 45 provides that complaints may only be considered if they allege a violation of the rights 'set forth' in the Convention. He concludes that as the economic, social and cultural rights are not specifically 'set forth' in the Convention, they may not be the subject of complaints.[66] Whilst this is true of Article 45, which relates exclusively to the system of inter-State complaints and which is subject to special acceptance, different wording is used in Article 47 which governs admissibility in general. That article refers to the rights 'guaranteed' by the Convention (Article 48, in addition, refers to the rights 'protected' by the Convention). This language, it is considered, does not necessitate the conclusion that petitions are excluded in relation to economic, social and cultural rights. Nevertheless, that position has been the one adopted by the Commission. Article 31 of the Commission's Regulations,[67] provides that the Commission shall take into account alleged violations by a State party of the 'human rights *defined* in the American Convention' [emphasis added]. Only in a remote sense are any economic, social and cultural rights actually 'defined' in the American Convention.[68]

Given the obvious limitations of both Articles 26 and 42, it would appear that economic, social and cultural rights are afforded greater protection under the terms of the American Declaration than under the Convention. This raises an interesting question as regards the precise relationship between these two instruments, particularly as to whether the Declaration obligations subsist even for States parties to the Convention. There are essentially two views on the question, each of which has certain distinct consequences in terms of the protection of economic, social and cultural rights. The first approach is to view the inter-American human rights system as one in the process of organic development in which the later

[65] This would presumably violate the terms of Art. 26 read together with Art. 48 OAS Charter (which provides for the right to education).

[66] Volio, above, n. 64, 72.

[67] Approved by the Commission at its 49th Sess., 169th mtg., 8 Apr. 1980. Modified at the Commission's 70th Sess., 938th mtg., 29 June 1987.

[68] The Commission has found them not to have been incorporated into the Convention: Cases 9718 and 9777 (Argentina), below, n. 73.

instruments are taken to provide the most complete expression of the human rights to which they all refer. The Convention, as such, is taken to supersede the Declaration both chronologically and normatively, with the effect that once a State becomes party to the Convention, the Declaration no longer has legal significance. This view gains some support from the terms of Article 2(1) of the Commission's Statute, which provides that in the exercise of its functions the Commission is to treat 'human rights' as being those contained in the Declaration for member states which are not yet party to the Convention, and those in the Convention for those States which have duly ratified that instrument.

The second approach would be to view the Convention, not as a replacement of the Declaration, but rather as a complementary instrument. Just as much as the Universal Declaration forms part of the International Bill of Rights alongside the UN Covenants, the Declaration would therefore retain its full effect and stand alongside the American Convention. This approach has some support in the terms of Article 29(d) of the Convention, which provides that: 'No provision of this Convention shall be interpreted as: . . . (d) excluding or limiting the effect that the American Declaration of the Rights and Duties of Man and other international acts of the same nature may have.' On this view, any obligations that might have been assumed in relation to the Declaration will therefore subsist for all States, even for those that have become party to the Convention. This would enable the Commission to continue its 'Charter role' in supervising the implementation of the economic, social and cultural rights in the Declaration even in relation to States parties to the Convention on the basis of their Charter obligations concerning human rights.

Neither of the two approaches to the relationship between the Declaration and the Convention—one supposing a complementary relationship, the other one of normative substitution—can be preferred on a strictly textual analysis. As suggested above, the terms of Article 2(1) of the Commission's Statute appear to conflict with those of Article 29(d) of the Convention.[69] Some commentators have taken the intermediate view that, whilst it does not necessarily preserve the full integrity of the Declaration, Article 29(d) does make the Declaration a relevant material source for the interpretation of the Convention. Buergenthal suggests that, given the development of the inter-American system,[70] 'it is difficult to escape the

---

[69] The fact that the provisions are found in different instruments is of little relevance given the fact that the Convention itself specifically forsees the adoption of the Statute of the Commission. In other words, the terms of the Statute are to be read into those of the Convention.

[70] The evolution of the inter-American system was stressed at great length by the Court in Advisory Opinion OC-10/89. See n. 17 paras. 37–43. Cf. Legal Consequences for States of the Continued Presence of South Africa in Namibia (South West Africa) notwithstanding Security Council Res. 276 (1970), Advisory Opinion, ICJ Rep. 1971, 16, where it was stated (p. 31): 'an

conclusion that the American Declaration is designed to serve as a major normative source in the interpretation and application of the Convention and that, as such, it may be resorted to fill the normative *lacunae* of that instrument'.[71] Although Buergenthal was not specific on the point, one would imagine that if there is any normative *lacuna* to be filled by the Declaration it is in relation to economic, social and cultural rights. Whilst this may be stepping over the putative boundary between *lacunae* below *legem* and *lacunae extra legem*, there is a textual case for utilizing the Declaration. Since Article 26 of the Convention specifically refers to the economic, social and cultural rights found in the OAS Charter, and since the Declaration is considered to be an authoritative interpretation of the human rights obligations in the Charter,[72] a body applying the terms of the Convention may presumably apply the economic, social and cultural rights found in the Declaration. Whether or not this is the case, it is apparent nevertheless that resort to the Declaration as a material source for the interpretation of the Convention does not remedy the defects found in the Convention implementation procedures, viz that petitions relating to economic, social and cultural rights can only be addressed through the Charter mechanisms.

The attitude of the Commission towards the application of the Declaration in relation to States parties to the Convention has been largely negative. In general, the Commission has interpreted the terms of Article 2(1) of the Statute in a strict manner, only having reference to the terms of the Declaration in relation to States which have yet to become parties to the Convention. In relation to the States parties themselves, it has either not received any communications relating to Article 26 or it has treated such communications as being beyond its competence to consider. An example of the latter approach is found in a case in which the Commission considered the petitioners' claim that the Convention had incorporated the rights in the Declaration into the Convention by way of Article 2(1) of the Statute.[73] The Commission noted that to take this view was inconsistent with the terms of Article 31(2) of the Vienna Convention[74] and ran counter

international instrument must be interpreted and applied within the overall framework of the juridical system in force at the time of the interpretation.'

[71] Buergenthal, above, n. 14, 138. As a supporting argument, Buergenthal notes that the same principles find recognition in the preambles to the Declaration, the Charter and the Convention, and that in the latter case, reference is made back to the Declaration and the Charter.

[72] See above at n. 26.

[73] Cases 9718 and 9777 (Argentina), IACHR Annual Report 1987–8, 31–81.

[74] The Commission suggested that since States had not agreed to make the Declaration part of the Convention it could not be incorporated in this way. Art. 31(2) reads: 'The context for the purpose of the interpretation of a treaty shall comprise in addition to the text . . . (a) any agreement relating to the treaty which was made between all the parties in connexion with the conclusion of the treaty'.

to the structure of the Statute which distributed the competences of the Commission according to whether or not States were party to the Convention.[75] It concluded that in relation to States party to the Convention, 'the IACHR can only, in accordance with its own Regulations (Article 31), take into consideration the petitions on presumed violations of rights defined in the American Convention on Human Rights'.[76] It added that '[t]he right to work is still not incorporated into the Convention which does not include economic, social and cultural rights'.[77]

Even if these arguments were to be accepted as sound, which it is considered they are not,[78] it appears that the Commission has subsequently modified its position. The Commission has now adopted the view that it can, in certain circumstances, consider petitions referring to rights in the Declaration even in relation to States parties to the Convention. This change of heart on the part of the Commission was undoubtedly brought about by, and certainly followed on from, an earlier opinion of the inter-American Court.[79] The Court considered some of the implications of Article 29(d) of the Convention in Opinion OC-10/89 where it was determining the scope of its own competence in relation to the Declaration. Having found that for States parties to the Convention 'the specific source of their obligations with respect to the protection of human rights is, in principle, the Convention itself', it went on to note that 'given the provisions of Article 29(d), these States cannot escape their obligations they have as members of the OAS under the Declaration'.[80] Although the Court was not altogether unambiguous in its comments, this wording does suggest at least that States retain their substantive obligations in relation to the Declaration, obligations which, in the scheme of the Charter arrangements, would carry with it supervision by the Commission.

The context in which the Commission came to reconsider the matter was one in which it was reviewing an application relating to events occurring prior to Argentina's ratification of the Convention. The question was raised whether, in light of Article 2(1) of its Statute, the Commission was competent to apply the Declaration in relation to Argentina despite the

---

[75] Cases 9718 and 9777, above, n. 73 para. 6.
[76] Ibid.   [77] Ibid.
[78] The suggestion that because the Statute differentiates between States party to the Convention and those not, it excludes the application of Charter procedures in relation to States parties is not a logical necessity. Nor is it quite so simple to say that the right to work is not incorporated into the Convention when Art. 26 implicitly refers to Art. 44 of the OAS Charter which speaks of the right to work.
[79] Note also that Buergenthal argues that the Declaration has maintained its 'normative force' even as regards the States parties to the Convention. Buergenthal, above, n. 14, 139. This, Buergenthal argues is 'implicit' in the language of Art. 1 of the Statute of the Commission because the Convention makes specific reference to the Declaration and the rights that are inherent to the human person. Ibid.
[80] OC-10/89, above, n. 17 paras. 45–6.

fact that it was now a State party to the Convention. In light of its previous practice, one might have assumed the question to have been answered in the negative. However, the Commission, taking note of the opinion of the Court in OC-10/89, took the view that '[r]atification of the Convention by Member states at least complemented, augmented or perfected the international protection of human rights in the inter-American system, but did not create them *ex novo*, nor did it extinguish the previous or subsequent validity of the American Declaration'.[81] It therefore concluded that Argentina remained bound by the terms of the Declaration and found it to have violated Articles I, XVIII, and XXVI of the Declaration.[82] What is particularly surprising is that the Commission need not have gone as far as it did in order to come to this conclusion. It could quite easily have declared the American Declaration to be relevant only insofar as the case concerned events that had occurred prior to ratification of the Convention which was inapplicable *ratione temporis*. To suggest, however, that the Convention did not extinguish the subsequent validity of the Declaration appears to be a distinct departure from the Commission's previous practice, and is potentially propitious for the protection of the economic, social and cultural rights.

The Commission has yet to confirm or deny whether or not it is now willing to entertain petitions relating to rights in the Declaration in relation to States parties to the Convention. It has addressed itself to a case in which both Declaration and Convention rights were at issue, but since domestic remedies had not been fully exhausted, did not comment in detail upon the merits.[83] It is considered that even if the Statute of the

---

[81] Report No. 74/90, Res. 22/88, Case 9850 (Argentina), Annual Report 1990–1, para. 6. Arts. I, XVIII and XXVI protect the rights to life, liberty and personal security; a fair trial and due process of law.

[82] Ibid., para. 7.

[83] Report No. 90/90, Case 9893 (Uruguay), Annual Report 1990–1, 77. The substance of the petition was essentially that decree 193/86 (but also the earlier decree 137/85) of the government of Uruguay, which set increases in retirement pensions for the year 1986, had employed discriminatory scales and therefore was in breach *inter alia* of Arts. II, XVI and XXIII of the American Declaration and Art. 24 of the American Convention. (Also mentioned were Arts. 7, 17, and 22 UDHR; the ICESCR; Art. 26 ICCPR; and ILO Convention No. 128.) The main concern was that for the majority of beneficiaries, retirement payments were to increase at a rate considerably lower than that of the Average Wage Index (IMS) of the preceding year.

Although the Commission came to the conclusion that all available domestic remedies had not been exhausted, and that the petition was therefore inadmissible, it did consider it appropriate to add a number of comments on the case before it. It noted that the matter concerned 'a sizeable social group that is particularly sensitive and economically weak to which the society should extend special protection' (p. 89, para. 23), and that despite its formal lack of competence the Government had impliedly admitted the justice of the complaint. (p. 90, para. 25) It went on to comment that 'it is not possible to establish adjustments of pension payments owed that are lower than a common index, in this case, the Average Wage Index, without creating discriminations that would violate the principle of

Commission does appear to point in a different direction, it would be contrary to the object and purpose of the various human rights instruments and antithetical to the idea of the development of the system as a whole, to suggest that States have in fact dispensed with obligations in relation to the implementation of economic, social and cultural rights in the Charter merely in virtue of ratifying the Convention. Unless the Convention is seen as entirely superseding the Declaration in a legal sense, a point which has never been seriously contemplated, it must be concluded that the Declaration retains its normative force. The only conceivable argument then is that ratification of the Convention, whilst not changing States' existing obligations, does alter the competence of the Commission in relation to supervision. In other words, while States would retain their obligations in relation to the Declaration, the Commission would no longer exercise any supervisory role in that regard. This again would amount to a surrender of advances previously achieved in the inter-American system and for that reason should not be lightly presumed. It would also run counter to the general scheme of the Charter, which supposes that its human rights provisions fall within the remit of the Commission.

equality before the law as embodied in Art. 24 of the Convention. ' (Ibid.) Noting that a satisfactory solution would 'depend on the amount of resources available and in the final analysis, steady economic growth' (p. 90, para. 27) the Commission appended a recommendation to its formal finding of inadmissibility:

> 'for reasons of moral order and social justice. . . to the extent that the economic-financial resources of the state allow, [the government] consider the adoption of legislative or other measures that revoke decree 137/85 and its effects and make it possible to set the adjustments of pension payments owed for 1985 as a function of the Average Wage Index to all retired and pensioned persons and that they be adjusted to the amounts received at present . . .'. (p. 91, para. 3.)

Apart from the highly unusual procedure of discussing the merits of a case which was found to be formally inadmissible, the Commission's determination that the implementation of retirement rates below the Wage index would be discriminatory is a curious one. In coming to this conclusion, the Commission was clearly concerned with establishing some form of equity between pensioners and society as a whole, by stipulating that increases in retirement pensions should not fall below the percentage increase in the average wage of the previous year. Whilst this might seem an appropriate and just stipulation (it indeed being one that the State itself came to accept) one might question whether such a policy is one which logically derives from the terms of Art. 24 of the Convention. Art. 24 is concerned with the 'equal protection of the law' which, as such, would naturally prohibit laws which were in purpose or effect discriminatory. This may prohibit differential rates of retirement payments being imposed (such as were imposed in decree 193/86) but a flat rate would not necessarily discriminate within the group. What the Commission appears to suggest is that Art. 24 prohibits the disadvantagement of the retired vis a vis those who earned the average national wage. If this is the case, the Commission would also logically oppose any difference between the actual rate of the average wage and the retirement pension. It also suggests that the Commission would similarly oppose the idea of compulsory retirement.

THE PROTOCOL ON ECONOMIC, SOCIAL AND CULTURAL RIGHTS

Much of the discussion above assumes that the Convention remains the sole human rights treaty currently in force in the inter-American system. This is not to say that no other treaty has been adopted, or that no other treaty deals with economic, social and cultural rights. Indeed, a Protocol on Economic, Social and Cultural Rights was adopted by the OAS General Assembly in 1988 (the San Salvador Protocol) and has thus far attracted three instruments of ratification or accession. As yet, however, the Protocol is short of the necessary 11 ratifications for it to enter into force.

Although it was agreed during the drafting of the American Convention that only passing reference would be made to economic, social and cultural rights, it was always clear that the matter would have to be considered again at a later date.[84] Thus after the entry into force of the American Convention the Commission began to discuss strategies to deal with the implementation of economic, social and cultural rights.[85] It considered, *inter alia*, three possibilities: amending the existing Convention, drafting an Additional Protocol, or, following the UN example by drafting a separate Convention. In the end, the Commission considered that the Protocol option was the best. This suggestion was ultimately approved by the OAS General Assembly which, in 1982, requested the OAS Secretariat to prepare a draft Protocol.[86] The Secretariat produced a preliminary draft based *inter alia* upon the UDHR, the American Declaration, the ICESCR, the inter-American Convention and various other draft human rights instruments. This draft emphasized the priority of what it called social rights over and above economic and cultural rights and established a system of reporting for which the Commission would be responsible.[87] Various member states, the inter-American Commission and the inter-American Court all presented their comments and suggestions on the draft.

[84] Art. 77 of the Convention is relevant in this connection. It provides that 'the Commission may submit proposed protocols to this Convention for consideration by the States Parties at the General Assembly with a view to gradually including other rights and freedoms within its system of protection'.

[85] M. Cabra, 'Rights and Duties Established by the American Convention on Human Rights', above, n. 43 at 62.

[86] Res. AG/Res. 619 (XXII-0/82).

[87] The rights to which it gave recognition included the right to work (Art. 2) and to fair conditions of employment (Arts. 3–6), the right to social security (Art. 7), the right to join and form trade unions (Art. 9), the right to establish a family (Art. 10), the right to an adequate standard of living (Art. 11), the right to education (Arts. 14–16), academic freedom (Art. 17), the right to take part in cultural life (Art. 18). States parties are also to pledge themselves to ensure dynamic and balanced development and to take steps towards that end (Arts. 12 and 13).

The Commission responded to the Secretariat draft in its Annual Reports for 1983-84 and 1984-85 and pursuant to Resolution 778 (XV-0/85) produced a draft Additional Protocol in 1986. This was transmitted to States parties for their comments and formed the working document upon which a Working Group of the Committee on Juridical and Political Affairs based the final text.[88] As far as the Commission was concerned, it stressed first of all that the rights should be considered 'as the regulating axis of the economic, social and political systems, and not as an aleatory result of the greater or lesser success of the development policies implemented'.[89] Accordingly, it should not include questions such as industrialization, private investment, land tenure systems and other factors instrumental in economic development which had been included in the original draft. It considered that the Protocol should be structured around three basic rights—the right to work, the right to education and the right to health—and should include, as associated with them, other related rights.[90] In addition to these rights, the Commission argued that the Protocol should be supplemented with rights relating to special groups such as the handicapped and the elderly.[91] In terms of implementation, the Commission argued in favour of entrusting supervision to an independent body, such as the Commission itself, rather than to a political body as had occurred in the case of the ICESCR. Although it envisaged that supervision should be undertaken primarily by means of State reports, it did suggest that individuals might also be granted a right of petition in relation to certain specific rights, such as the right to strike.[92] This latter point was also taken up by the Court, which stressed that although not all economic, social and cultural rights could be the subject of complaints mechanisms, some rights could be considered 'jurisdictionally enforceable' and therefore could be subject to the system of protection operated by the Court under the American Convention.[93]

The Working Group, consisting of representatives of fourteen States parties to the American Convention, prepared the final draft that was adopted by the General Assembly in 1988. The final Protocol was largely based upon the Commission text modified in several places to bring it more into conformity with international standards (the terms of the ICESCR being particularly influential). It was mainly in respect of the supervision system that the Working Group diverged substantially from the initial proposals put forward by the Commission.

---

[88] AG/Res. 836 (XVI-0/86)
[89] IACHR Annual Report 1983–4, 144.   [90] Ibid., 171.
[91] Ibid., 140. See also, Peru, OEA/Ser.G CP/CAJP-622/85, add. 3, 9 Jul. 1986.
[92] IACHR Annual Report 1983–4, 142.
[93] I/A Court H.R.Annual Report 1985, Appendix III, 17, 18. See also, Annual Report of 1986, Appendix IV, 41.

The rights recognized in the Protocol by and large follow those in the International Covenant on Economic, Social and Cultural Rights. Articles 6 to 9, for example, bear remarkable similarities in form and terminology to the same articles in the Covenant. They recognize the right to work (Article 6), the right to just, equitable and satisfactory conditions of work (Article 7), trade union rights (Article 8) and the right to social security (Article 9). Such differences in wording as do exist are for the most part superficial.[94] Similar comments could be made about Article 10 (the right to health), Article 13 (the right to education) and Article 14 (the right to the benefits of culture). In several places the Protocol improves upon the wording of the ICESCR. For example, Article 9 spells out the content of the right to social security in considerably greater detail, including, in particular, a right of beneficiaries to social security. It also expands upon the right to food (using the broader notion of adequate 'nutrition') and provides more specific objectives in relation to the right to health (Article 10). The principle difference between the instruments, however, lies in the fact that the Protocol gives recognition to a number of rights in addition to those in the Covenant. In particular, the Protocol gives recognition to the right to a healthy environment (Article 11), the right to the formation and the protection of the family (Article 15), the rights of children (Article 16), the protection of the elderly (Article 17) and the protection of the handi-capped (Article 18).

This is not to say, however, that the Protocol is an improvement on the Covenant in all respects. It is less demanding of States in a number of ways. First, whereas the Covenant provides recognition of the right to housing no such recognition is to be found in the Protocol. This is a particularly significant omission given the extent to which housing has become a major issue in the work of the UN Committee.[95] Secondly, in places the Protocol has reproduced obligations in a somewhat diluted form. In Article 13, for example, the Protocol merely states that 'primary education *should* be compulsory and accessible to all without cost' [emphasis added] whereas the Covenant uses the stricter term 'shall' in the equivalent provision.[96] Similarly, in Article 7 the right to equal remuneration for work of equal

[94] Some notable differences not mentioned elsewhere are: i) Art. 6 of the Protocol specific-ally mentions the development of vocational training programmes for the disabled; ii) Art. 7 of the Protocol includes the additional right of every worker to 'follow his vocation'; iii) Art. 7 of the Protocol speaks of the right to promotion, rather than equal opportunity for promotion; iv) Art. 8 speaks of the right of workers (not everyone) to join and form trade unions; v) Art. 8 of the Protocol specifically provides that 'no one may be compelled to belong to a trade union'; vi) Art. 8 provides that everyone has the right to strike—not merely limiting the right to members of trade unions. For comments on these provisions see, Working Group Report OEA/Ser.G CP/CAJP-694/87, 2 Oct. 1987.

[95] See, Craven, above, n. 58, 329–49.

[96] It is notable that the Commission's draft Convention did use the term 'shall' but that this term was changed by the working group.

value, has been reduced to the considerably weaker 'equal wages for equal work' to emphasize that comparison should only be made within the same place of work.[97]

What is perhaps most surprising about the Protocol is the fact that it does not appear to have been especially tailored to suit the problems of the region. For the most part, the rights in the Protocol would not be entirely out of place in, for example, a comparable European text. As Peru pointed out in the early stages, it was unfortunate that the instrument gave no recognition to the rights of indigenous populations.[98] One might add that some recognition of the rights of migrant workers would also have been appropriate in the circumstances. It would appear that too great an emphasis was placed upon ensuring that the Protocol was compatible with the terms of the ICESCR at the expense of developing a text which truly represented regional values and interests.

As regards the mechanism of supervision, the terms of the Protocol similarly reflect a desire to mimic the Covenant, in spite of the suggestions of the Commission otherwise. States undertake to submit 'periodic reports' to the Secretary General of the OAS 'on the progressive measures they have taken to ensure due respect for the rights set forth' in the Protocol[99] which are then to be transmitted to the inter-American Economic and Social Council (I/A ECOSOC) and the inter-American Council for Education, Science and Culture (I/A CESC) for 'examination'.[100] Parts of the reports may also be sent to the specialized organizations of the OAS for their input.[101] The I/A ECOSOC and I/A CESC will then communicate, in their annual reports to the General Assembly, a summary of the information received and any 'general recommendations they consider to be appropriate'.[102] That the primary responsibility for implementation appears to lie with the I/A ECOSOC and the I/A CESC, both of which are bodies composed of government representatives and concerned with predominantly matters of technical assistance and cooperation, does not augur well. As the experience of supervising the ICESCR has shown,[103] bodies composed of governmental representatives are notably poor in terms of their ability to supervise human rights treaties adequately, especially in cases where the representatives have no real human rights expertise.

The main saving grace, as far as supervision of the Protocol is concerned, is the subsidiary role retained for the Commission in Articles 19(6) and

---

[97] Working Group Report OEA/Ser.G CP/CAJP-694/87, 2 Oct. 1987.
[98] Peru, OEA/Ser.G CP/CAJP-622/85, 9 Jul. 1986.
[99] Art. 19(1), Additional Protocol. See Appendix VIII.
[100] Art. 19(2)
[101] Arts. 19(3) and (4).
[102] Art. 19(5)
[103] See, Craven, above, n. 58, 39–42.

19(7). Article 19(6) provides that the individual petition system of the American Convention (in Articles 44-51 and 61-69) may be operated in cases where a violation of Article 8(a) or Article 13 has occurred and is 'directly attributable to a State Party to this Protocol'. That this additional protection has been created in the case of the right to join and form trade unions (Article 8(a)) and the right to education (Article 13) is probably a reflection of the fact that they are similarly protected under the European Convention on Human Rights and that States therefore had a clearer understanding of what they entailed. Although it suggests an unusually selective approach to the implementation of the rights in the Protocol, this provision is nevertheless to be welcomed. Article 19(7) provides, in addition, that the Commission may formulate 'such observations and recommendations as it deems pertinent' concerning the status of the rights in the Protocol and may include such observations in its annual report to the General Assembly. Depending on the approach of the Commission, this provision may well become the most significant in the Protocol's supervision system.

SUPERVISION OF ECONOMIC, SOCIAL AND CULTURAL RIGHTS THROUGH COUNTRY REPORTS—THE PRACTICE OF THE I/A COMMISSION ON HUMAN RIGHTS

Given the limited recognition of economic, social and cultural rights in the American Convention, it is not surprising that the inter-American Court has only incidentally referred to economic, social and cultural rights in its Judgments or Opinions, the substance of which has been dealt with above.[104] It has therefore been the Commission that has been at the forefront of developments in relation to economic, social and cultural rights. That being said, until the late 1970s the Commission almost entirely ignored the question of economic, social and cultural rights despite the fact that they formed an integral part of the American Declaration. It dealt with the occasional individual petition in relation to such rights, but did not deal with them in any detail in its annual report. The Commission's almost exclusive concern with civil and political rights was the implicit consequence of a particular logic. It was considered that:

---

[104] The Inter-American Court has, however, suggested that it might be competent to deliver an advisory opinion on universal human rights treaties, presumably including the International Covenant on Economic, Social and Cultural Rights. See, Advisory Opinion No.1, I/A Court H.R. Series A No.1, 12 (1982), 3 *HRLJ* 140. See generally, T. Buergenthal, 'The Advisory Practice of the Inter-American Human Rights Court' 79 *AJIL* (1985) 1; M. Parker '"Other Treaties": The Inter-American Court of Human Rights Defines its Advisory Jurisdiction', 33 *Am. UL Rev.* (1983) 211.

a political order or representative democracy, by its very nature, should be translated into substantive improvements in the quality of life of the great majority, if not all, of the population. Work, health, education, suitable housing, and the like would flow necessarily and naturally as a result of the preservation of certain individual guarantees and of the rule of democratic institutions.[105]

Since that time, however, the Commission's attitude has changed considerably.[106] It has become more aware of the importance of the issues involved and has begun to develop its own approach to implementation.

The first occasion upon which the Commission addressed economic, social and cultural rights in any meaningful way was in 1978 following an on-site investigation of human rights violations in El Salvador.[107] Although the majority of the Commission's report was concerned with the widespread violations of civil and political rights, including torture and inhuman treatment, the Commission felt constrained to make comment upon the economic and social conditions that appeared to be one of the major causes of social tension. It noted that the 'tremendous concentration of land ownership and of economic power in general, as well as political power, in the hands of the few' meant that the large majority of the population lived in 'desperation and misery'.[108] These economic and social conditions, as far as the Commission was concerned, served to explain 'to a considerable extent', the serious violations of human rights that had occurred. It therefore recommended that the necessary measures be taken to improve the economic and social situation so that the inequalities would not 'constitute an obstacle to the observance' of human rights and that the violations themselves would be 'lessened and eventually disappear'.[109]

The idea that economic and social conditions underlie many violations of civil and political rights has since remained a consistent theme for the Commission. In its 1979-80 annual report, for example, the Commission noted the existence of an 'organic relationship between the violation of the rights to physical security on the one hand, and neglect of economic and social rights . . . on the other'. It asserted that 'neglect of economic and social rights, especially when political participation has been suppressed, produces the kind of social polarization that then leads to acts of terrorism by and against the government'.[110] This point was reiterated a decade later in the Commission's study on economic, social and cultural rights where it

[105] IACHR Annual Report 1983–4, 137.
[106] LeBlanc, above, n. 1, 140.
[107] Report on the Situation of Human Rights in El Salvador (1978).
[108] Ibid., 165–8.
[109] Ibid., 168.
[110] IACHR Annual Report 1979–80 151. Similarly in its 1981 Report, the Commission noted with respect to Guatemala that the socio-economic disparities within the country contributed to the 'generalized violence' that existed. Report on the Situation Regarding Human Rights in Guatemala.

commented that 'it is evident that in many cases poverty is a wellspring of political and social conflict'.[111]

This may, of course, be an important point for the Commission to make, but it should be noted that there is a difference between giving specific recognition to economic, social and cultural rights *qua* rights, and recognizing them as background conditions, or contextual constraints. The argument that an improvement in economic and social conditions may be necessary to ensure the enjoyment of civil and political rights is to assert the teleological necessity of economic or social development in a general sense but not such as to individuate the correlative interests, or to make them 'rights' in any meaningful way. Indeed, it is a line of thought that tends to reinforce, rather than reduce, the arbitrary and categorical distinctions that are commonly made between economic, social and cultural rights and civil and political rights.

With the exception of a few reports, such as that of Cuba in 1983[112] and 1994[113] or that of Guatemala in 1993,[114] the Commission has only infrequently ventured into the field of economic, social and cultural rights in its country studies.[115] Indeed on those occasions in which socio-economic interests have been mentioned, they have rarely been accompanied by findings of non-compliance and have frequently lacked any mention of rights at all.[116] Thus, when it was considering the case of Haitian sugar cane workers living in 'unhealthy, overcrowded conditions, where potable water and latrines are lacking',[117] the Commission did not speak about the right to health or favourable conditions of employment, but merely noted that the conditions were reportedly 'very akin to slavery, though not slavery in the strict sense'.[118] A similar situation arose during the Commission's consideration of the situation in Panama in 1990-1.[119] During its on-site

[111] Status of Economic, Social and Cultural Rights in the Hemisphere, IACHR Annual Report 1991, 287, 305. In the context of Panama, the Commission noted that the pervasive problem of land ownership—namely that many rural peasants who depended for their livelihood upon land either controlled insufficient amounts of land to work or were deprived of land—was a source of 'actual or potential violence'. Annual Report 1989–90, 173–5 (Panama).

[112] Seventh Report on the Situation of Human Rights in Cuba (1983). In addition to the Commission's traditional concerns, such as freedom of expression or freedom from arbitrary arrest and detention, it also examined the enjoyment of the right to work, the right to remuneration, the right to strike and collective bargaining and even the right to food.

[113] IACHR Annual Report, 148–53 (the right to work and freedom of association); 161–64.   [114] IACHR Annual Report 1993, 409–14, 441.

[115] In the case of Nicaragua, for example, it expressly refrained from commenting on the economic and social conditions prevailing on the basis that the Sandinista government had recently begun the process of 'reconstructing' Nicaragua. Report on the Situation of Human Rights in Nicaragua (1981).

[116] e.g., in the Report of Haiti in 1979, the Commission concentrated on the miserable living conditions in the country. Report on the Situation of Human Rights in Haiti (1979).

[117] IACHR Annual Report 1991, 264.   [118] Ibid., 265.

[119] IACHR Annual Report 1990–1, 490 (Panama).

visit, the Commission discovered that approximately 15,000 people had had their homes destroyed during the US intervention and that they had been sheltered in private housing or in encampments.[120] Reflecting on this situation, the Commission expressed its deep concern 'over the precarious situation of the refugees' and noted that their lives had been 'seriously torn apart by the bombing and armed conflict', and that 'the loss of relatives and neighbours and of their own personal effects and property was compounded by the reclusive lifestyle, unemployment, and the state of indefinite dependence in which they found themselves.'[121] It therefore recommended that Panama 'step up and complete its efforts to provide reparation to families that have suffered human and medical losses as a result of the invasion and the armed fighting of December 1989'.[122] What is remarkable, however, is that during the whole of its examination, the Commission failed to specify which rights gave it cause for concern, or indicate what was expected of the State concerned.[123] Its failure to come to any real conclusions on the matter stand in stark contrast to the observations of the UN Committee on Economic, Social and Cultural Rights when it was considering the same set of events.[124]

Perhaps reflecting upon the haphazard way in which the Commission had dealt with the issues arising, in Resolution AG/Res. 1044 of 1990[125] the General Assembly of the OAS recommended that the I-A Commission prepare a study on the status of economic, social and cultural rights, in the hemisphere. The Commission initially produced a preliminary report in 1991 drawing upon reports presented by member States to international agencies and a study conducted by the Pan American Health Organization. Although it made a number of comments in relation to the implementation of economic, social and cultural rights most of the 1991 report consisted of a summary of reports submitted to the UN Committee on Economic, Social and Cultural Rights by seven States (Chile, Mexico, Argentina, Colombia, Jamaica, Dominican Republic, Costa Rica).[126] Unlike the UN Committee, however, the Commission did not have any mechanism for discussing, or enquiring further into, the information provided by the reports. The reports

---

[120] Ibid., 491.   [121] Ibid.

[122] Ibid. In the following year the Commission continued its examination of the situation in Panama remarking that although 2,860 families had been provided with new dwellings, 54 families still lived in temporary accommodation. Annual Report 1991, 249 (Panama).

[123] The same set of events were the substance of a petition against the US, Report No. 31/93, Case 10.573 (US) 14 Oct. 1993, Annual Report 1993, 312. The complainants alleged, *inter alia*, that US military forces acted in an indiscriminate manner 'with reckless disregard for the safety of Panamanian civilians during the US military operations in Panama' in violation of Arts. I, VII, IX, XIV, XXIII, XXVIII of the American Declaration.

[124] See, UN doc. E/1992/23 UNESCOR Supp. 3, 32 (1992).

[125] 20th Sess., 4–9 June (1990).

[126] Status of Economic, Social and Cultural Rights in the Hemisphere, Annual Report 1991, 290–305.

were therefore summarized for information alone, and were not subject to critical analysis. Indeed, the conclusions drawn by the Commission reflect the cursory consideration given to the reports. The Commission, taking into account 'the adverse economic and financial situation that prevails', urged member states to 'step up their efforts to achieve a minimum level of development'.[127] Much of the Commission's subsequent report in 1992 retained the same format and replicated much of the same information. The main difference was that the State reports, on this occasion, were drawn from information provided by the member States directly to the Commission.[128] The conclusions of the Commission, however, were almost identical. In 1993, the Commission began to take the issue a little more seriously, and devoted several pages of its annual report to analysis of the general obligations and made a number of specific recommendations.[129] Unfortunately, the Commission did not continue the development of this theme in the following year.

The Commission has, on more than one occasion, explained its caution with respect to evaluating State performance in the implementation of economic, social and cultural rights. In considering the matter back in 1980, the Commission perceived there to be two main difficulties. First, the Commission considered there to be a general difficulty with the exercise of its supervisory role in relation to the subject matter of economic, social and cultural rights in that it perceived '[e]conomic policy and national defense policy' to be 'closely related to national sovereignty'.[130] Secondly, although it was possible to identify a process of cause and effect, the Commission 'recognized the difficulty of establishing criteria that would enable it to measure the states' fulfillment of their obligations' in the field of economic, social and cultural rights not least because it had seen the 'very difficult options that the governments face when allocating resources'.[131]

Despite its initial caution, the Commission later expressed its willingness to come to terms with both issues. With respect to the question of sovereignty, in its 1991 report on economic and social rights (see above), the Commission responded both in a general and a more specific manner. As a general point, it noted that the notion of sovereignty in international law is not unlimited and may, for example, be modified by the acceptance of instruments for the protection of human rights.[132] More specifically, the

---

[127] Ibid., 305.
[128] Status of Economic, Social and Cultural Rights in the Hemisphere, Annual Report 1992–3, 220–38.
[129] The Realization of Economic, Social and Cultural Rights in the Region, Annual Report 1993, 519.
[130] Annual Report 1979–80, 151–3.   [131] Ibid.
[132] See e.g., Annual Report 1991, 276.

Commission dismissed the assumption that the implementation of economic, social and cultural rights makes any undue demands upon state sovereignty by reason of requiring a specific form of government or specific economic policy. In its 1980 report, the Commission commented that:

[e]fforts to eliminate extreme poverty have been made under radically different political, economic and cultural systems. . . . To date, there is no political or economic system or individual development model that has demonstrated a clearly superior capability to promote economic and social rights; but whatever the system or model it may be, it must assign priority to attaining those fundamental rights that make it possible to eliminate extreme poverty.[133]

The Commission's claims in this respect now form part of international human rights orthodoxy. It has long been maintained that, in order to avoid invoking the spectres of cold-war ideological confrontation, the implementation of economic, social and cultural rights does not require the creation or maintenance of any particular system of government.[134] This, of course, is an oversimplification and a misleading one. As is implicit in the structure of human rights law, the recognition of economic, social and cultural rights is in part a recognition of the responsibility of the State for the welfare of all its inhabitants. In a strict sense, this is incompatible with 'liberal' conceptions of the minimal State which emphasize individual autonomy, and view redistributionalist activities as being in principle illegitimate. At the same time, as the Commission itself has recognized, 'a democratic framework' may be considered an 'essential element for establishment of a political society where human values can be fully realized'.[135] In other words, popular participation in national decision-making processes can be considered to be an essential prerequisite not only for the protection of civil and political rights, but also for the effective promotion of economic, social, and cultural rights.[136] It seems clear then that human rights, by their nature, do make demands as to the basic framework of government. What is true, however, is that within the framework of a liberal democracy committed to welfare provision, States are free to choose the type of economic or social policies that they perceive to be best for the achievement of human rights. All this suggests is that there is no single panoramic solution for all classes of problem that are likely to arise in the course of implementing human rights.

[133] Annual Report 1979–80, 152.
[134] See e.g., CESCR, General Comment no. 3 (1990), UN doc. E/1991/23, Annex II, para. 8.
[135] Annual Report 1979–80, 151–3.
[136] The Commission has noted, however, that the transition to democracy is not enough alone—as evidenced by the increasing incidence of poverty in some newly democratic regimes. By the same token, the Commission has noted that implementation of economic, social and cultural rights themselves 'creates the condition in which the general population is able . . . to participate actively and productively in the political decision-making process.' Annual Report 1993, 521–2.

As to its second reason for caution, namely the absence of adequate criteria for assessment, the Commission has on several occasions attempted to describe what it took to be the 'essence' of the legal obligation undertaken with respect to economic, social and cultural rights. First, in 1980, the Commission determined that States should 'strive to attain the economic and social aspirations of its people by following an order that assigns priority to . . . the "rights of survival" and "basic needs"'.[137] The Commission did not define what it understood to be 'rights of survival' or 'basic needs', nor their relationship with other human rights. The main difficulty with the invocation of the concept of 'basic needs' is that they tend to translate only imperfectly into human rights—not only are some needs not recognized as rights (and vice versa), but also the priority of needs asserts a particular hierarchy of rights not recognized in existing human rights practice.[138] In light of the difficulties raised, it is not surprising that the Commission has since shifted its emphasis to what has been termed the 'minimum threshold approach' to implementation.[139] As the Commission explained the position in 1993, the obligation to observe and defend the human rights of individuals in the American Declaration and the American Convention: 'obligates them [States], regardless of the level of economic development, to guarantee a minimum threshold of these rights'.[140]

Rather than creating any *a priori* hierarchy of rights or emphasizing categorical differences in implementation, the minimum threshold approach advocates the necessity of action being taken across the board to ensure for all a minimum level of enjoyment of the whole range of human rights. As such, it encapsulates a number of basic principles which are fundamental to the implementation of economic, social and cultural rights and which the Commission itself has come to recognize. First, and foremost, although economic, social and cultural rights are, in principle, subject to progressive implementation, this does not absolve States of the responsibility of taking immediate steps towards that end. The Commission has recognized that implementation of economic, social and cultural rights is 'a progressive process, in step with each member country's development'.[141] But at the same time it has emphasized that this 'does not mean that governments do not have the immediate obligation to make efforts to

---

[137] Annual Report 1979–80, 151–3.

[138] See generally, P. Alston, 'Human Rights and Basic Needs: A Critical Assessment' 12 *HRLJ* (1979) 19.

[139] See B.-A. Andreassen et al., 'Assessing Human Rights Performance in Developing Countries: The Case for a Minimum Threshold Approach to Economic and Social Rights', in B.-A. Andreassen and A. Eide (eds.), *Human Rights in Developing Countries 1987/88* (1988), 333. [140] Annual Report 1993, 524.

[141] Status of Economic, Social and Cultural Rights in the Hemisphere, Annual Report 1991, 287.

attain the full realization of those rights'.[142] It explained that the rationale behind the principle of progressive implementation was merely to allow States to 'advance gradually and consistently toward the fullest achievement of these rights'.[143]

Secondly, the minimum threshold approach assumes that in the creation and implementation of economic and social policies, states should place emphasis as a priority upon assisting the poorest and most vulnerable in society. This, as the Commission noted, was particularly important in a region in which, for most states, the huge disparity in the distribution of wealth was a major social and economic problem.[144] The Commission explained further that:

in view of the unequal distribution of wealth within the states in the region . . . an increase in national revenues does not automatically translate into an improvement in the general welfare of the entire population. The commitment of states to take steps with the aim of achieving progressively the full realization of economic, social and cultural rights requires an effective use of resources available to guarantee a minimum standard of living for all.[145]

In other words, as far as the Commission is concerned, in the implementation of economic, social and cultural rights States have broadly committed themselves to the principle of redistribution on the basis of need. This basic principle has also found recognition in the Commission's comments with respect to Structural Adjustment Programmes. It noted that in a number of States the disadvantaged in society had tended to suffer as a result of Structural Adjustment Projects which had cut public spending and led to an increase in the incidence of poverty.[146] In that respect it commented that '[e]conomic adjustments should not entail a decreased observance of human rights. Instead, they can be used to redress social imbalances and correct the structural violations that are built into the economic and social structures of countries in the region.'[147] In determining whether adequate measures have been taken, the Commission observed therefore that it would 'pay close attention to the equitable and effective use of available resources and the allocation of public expenditures to social programs that address the living conditions of the more vulnerable sectors of society which have been historically excluded from the political and economic process'.[148]

Thirdly, the notion of a minimum threshold assumes either the existence of an international minimum standard of achievement, or the establishment

---

[142] Annual Report 1993, 523.   [143] Ibid., 523.
[144] Ibid., 524–6
[145] Ibid., 524. Cf. also Annual Report 1979–80, 151–3.
[146] Ibid., 524–6
[147] Ibid., 526.   [148] Ibid., 533.

of differential national standards. It has to be assumed that, since the Commission has not seen fit to establish its own minimum standards by which States should be judged, it is willing to let States maintain their own standards. The obvious problem with this approach is that it suggests that what is presented as a minimum standard will in fact merely be what States are willing to concede. Moreover, that it envisages differing standards of achievement among different States runs counter to the assumed universality of human rights. This latter point is actually directly conceded by the Commission which suggested that:

[a] state's level of development may be a factor that is calculated into the analysis of its implementation of these rights, but this is not a factor that precludes the state's obligation to implement, to the best of its abilities, these rights. Rather the principle of progressivity demands that as the level of development in a state improves, so must its level of commitment to guaranteeing economic, social and cultural rights. This follows because the guarantee of economic, social and cultural rights requires in most instances, public expenditure for social programs.[149]

In theory, the more resources a state has, the greater its ability to provide services that guarantee economic, social and cultural rights. This idea is affirmed in Article 32 of the OAS Charter which describes development as the 'primary responsibility of each country and should constitute an integral and *continuous process* for the establishment of a *more just* economic and social order . . .' (emphasis supplied).[150]

Whether or not States will be willing to accept the principle of differential 'targets' in relation to economic, social and cultural rights remains to be seen. The difficulty, of course, is that the acceptability of any such a thesis will only become clear in specific contexts and in relation to particular issues. Unless the Commission puts itself in the position whereby putative violations of economic, social and cultural rights are brought before it, many of its pronouncements in this regard will remain at an abstract level and be devoid of real significance. As the Commission noted in its 1993 Report, there is a 'lack of political commitment regarding economic and social rights'[151] within the region. The question for the Commission therefore is whether or not it has the will or ability to change the prevailing view in a context where the problems of high mortality rates, high unemployment, economic instability, high malnutrition, scarcity of decent housing, and environmental degradation are rife,[152] and where solutions present themselves more in the form of 'trade-offs' than of decisions based upon 'Pareto optimality'.

It appears that the Commission has gone some way towards developing a

---

[149] Ibid., 524. [150] Ibid., 524.
[151] Ibid., 538. [152] Ibid., 289.

general understanding of the concept of the economic, social and cultural rights in the inter-American system. That it has drawn heavily upon the work of the UN Committee on Economic, Social and Cultural Rights is also apparent. However, it has yet to match the UN Committee in its willingness to apply general principles to specific cases or situations and to deal with economic, social and cultural rights in a methodical and consistent manner. In fact only exceptionally will the Commission deal with economic, social or cultural rights in its country studies at all. The failure of the Commission in this regard is not because there is little to say about economic, social and cultural rights in the region. Numerous examples may be found in which the UN Committee has identified significant matters for concern and where the Commission has not. To take but one example, in its report on Colombia in 1994, the Commission failed even to register the existence of problems concerning economic, social and cultural rights. In 1995, the UN Committee, by contrast, adopted a set of concluding observations following its consideration of the Colombia report which included a list of twelve subjects of concern. Included in the list were matters such as: the excessive restrictions imposed upon the right to join and form trade unions and the right to strike; the failure of the government to combat sufficiently the problem of child labour; the insufficient number of labour inspectors to monitor the implementation of health and safety measures in the workplace; the excessive shortfall of adequate housing; and the failure to ensure effective access to education, particularly primary education.[153] None of these matters was of so little importance that it did not deserve to be mentioned in the Commission's report.

CONCLUSIONS

Whilst the human rights we now refer to as economic, social and cultural rights gained their first recognition on the international plane in the American Declaration, they were for some time regarded as marginal concerns. In their approach, the organs of the inter-American system regarded economic, social and cultural rights either as contextual considerations in the implementation of civil and political rights or as interests that would be met once the protection of civil and political rights was ensured. As far as the Commission on Human Rights was concerned this meant that it could safely ignore those rights in the American Declaration that did not form part of the traditional category of liberal rights and freedoms.

Since that time, the prospects for the protection of economic, social and cultural rights have improved. First, the Commission has not only recog-

[153] UN doc. E/C.12/1995/12, paras. 9–20. 3 IHRR (1996) 452, 453–4.

nized the essential interdependence of the full range of human rights, it has started to take a more concerted effort to integrate them into its work. It has endeavoured to concentrate upon such concerns in certain of its country reports, and has also recently conducted a study on the implementation of economic, social and cultural rights. Secondly, the adoption of an Additional Protocol to the Convention on economic, social and cultural rights represents a considerable advance in terms of the potential of the system. Although it is not yet in force, it still remains a salutary reminder to States in the region of the existence and continuing importance of economic, social and cultural rights.

That being said, there remains considerable room for progress. In the short-term, it is clearly open for the Commission to take a more active stance in the implementation of the American Declaration. As much of the discussion in this paper suggests, there is no real legal obstacle to prevent the Commission from receiving, or dealing with petitions relating to the economic, social and cultural rights in the American Declaration. The restrictions that exist in relation to States parties to the Convention are more apparent than real and, in the final analysis, largely self-imposed. Equally, there are clearly opportunities for the Commission to develop a more systematic approach to monitoring the implementation of economic, social and cultural rights whether acting as a Charter organ or as a Convention organ. Its current approach in this respect remains largely haphazard and lacking in direction. All too often, economic, social and cultural rights are overlooked, or treated as merely parenthetic concerns. The simplest of methodological techniques, such as ensuring that in each country report a section is dedicated to the subject of economic, social and cultural rights, would itself substantially improve the current practice.

The Protection of Indigenous Rights in the Inter-American System

HURST HANNUM[1]

Indigenous, native, or tribal peoples exist in every region of the world, but they are perhaps most visible—and have become most politically active—in the Americas.[2] Indeed, the European settlement of the Western Hemisphere and resulting displacement and marginalization of the peoples living on the continent at the time has become a classic example of colonization. Today, approximately 400 indigenous groups of varying sizes remain in the Americas, comprising more than 30 million people—roughly 10 per cent of the population of the entire continent.[3]

Of course, there are countless examples of the conquest or incorporation of geographically contiguous peoples by states throughout Europe, Asia, and Africa, but only Australia and New Zealand offer comparable examples of overseas colonization. If there are few 'problems' with indigenous people in contemporary Europe, it is because most of the conquests or assimilation of the original inhabitants occurred hundreds rather than scores of years ago. With rare exceptions, most ethnically or culturally distinct groups in Europe have based their claims for power on their status as minorities or on a purported right of ethnic self-determination, without classifying themselves as 'indigenous'.

Most indigenous peoples have not only been attacked militarily but have subsequently seen their culture and way of life systematically assaulted. Colonial powers and nineteenth-century states in the Americas attempted to conquer and exterminate hostile tribes, force the assimilation of more acculturated indigenous groups, erode traditional culture and landholdings, and expand private property at the expense of the collective or

---

[1] The author would like to thank Osvaldo Kreimer, of the Commission's staff, for his comments on an earlier draft of the present chapter; of course, sole responsibility for the material contained herein rests with the author.

[2] On the international level, the Maoris in New Zealand and Aboriginals in Australia also have played a major role, but their situation is beyond the scope of the present chapter.

[3] Annual Report of the Inter-American Commission on Human Rights 1988–9, at 247. (The Commission's Annual Reports are hereinafter cited as 'IACHR Annual Report'.)

communal holdings of indigenous peoples.[4] Early European colonists in Latin America, for example, used indigenous labor first as slaves and subsequently as forced wage laborers. Religious missionaries often played a prominent role, frequently intervening to protect indigenous populations from abuse and lobbying for more effective protective measures. At the same time, however, missionaries saw their own role as one of 'civilizing' and 'converting' the 'heathen' natives and showed relatively little concern for preserving indigenous culture.[5]

The fact that many North American Indian nations entered into treaties with various governments, including Canada, France, Great Britain, and the United States, made little difference in terms of the discrimination and land seizures to which they were subjected.[6] While the existence of treaties has had significant domestic legal impact in recent years in some countries, their breach has been of no more concern to the international community than the breach of countless treaties among European states, many of which were created or destroyed by acts of so-called Great Powers irrespective of treaty obligations.

The North American Indian nations that entered into treaties with the European settler states from the seventeenth to nineteenth centuries obviously were subjects of international law, but their status as 'indigenous' nations or states had no international legal relevance.[7] Indigenous rights, unlike the rights of religious and other minorities, were never recognized as a separate issue of international concern. The Organization of American States (OAS), within the jurisdiction of whose members many of the world's indigenous peoples are found, adopted only one formal instrument concerned with indigenous peoples, prior to adoption of the Draft Inter-

---

[4] It is, of course, impossible to generalize about an entire continent or to enter into much detail given the limited focus and length of the present chapter. Much of the impetus for international action on indigenous issues was provided by a massive study prepared in the 1980s, United Nations, *Study of the Problem of Discrimination Against Indigenous Populations* (José R. Martinez Cobo, Special Rapporteur), UN Doc. E/CN.4/Sub.2/1986/7 & Adds. 1–4 (1986) (hereinafter cited as UN Indigenous Study). In addition to this study, reference might be made to Independent Commission on International Humanitarian Issues, *Indigenous Peoples, A Global Quest for Justice* (Zed Books, 1987); J. Brøsted et al., *Native Power* (Universitetsforlaget, 1985); and the various reports published by nongovernmental organizations such as Survival International (London), Cultural Survival (Cambridge, MA), the International Work Group for Indigenous Affairs (Copenhagen), and Minority Rights Group (London) on indigenous groups in the Western Hemisphere.

[5] For a discussion of the philosophical justifications for the conquest of the Americas, see generally R. A. Williams, Jr., *The American Indian in Western Legal Thought: The Discourses of Conquest* (New York: Oxford Univ. Press, 1990).

[6] The Working Group on Indigenous Populations of the UN Sub-Commission on Prevention of Discrimination and Protection of Minorities is engaged in a much-delayed study on 'treaties, agreements and other constructive arrangements between states and indigenous peoples'; the first progress report on the study is contained in UN Doc. E/CN.4/Sub.2/1992/32 (1992).

[7] But compare J. H. Clinebell and J. Thomson, 'Sovereignty and Self-Determination: The Rights of Native Americans Under International Law,' 27 *Buffalo L. Rev.* 669 (1978).

American Declaration on the Rights of Indigenous Peoples by the Inter-American Commission on Human Rights (the 'Commission') in 1995.[8]

The one exception to this lack of formal action by the OAS with respect to indigenous peoples generally was the creation of the Inter-American Indian Institute in 1940.[9] The Institute is now a specialized agency of the OAS; it acts as a standing committee to organize periodic Inter-American Indian Congresses (which are considered organs of the OAS) and also provides advisory services and technical services to OAS member states.[10] However, it was not until 1985 that indigenous people were able to attend the Institute's periodic congresses without invitations from their national governments.[11] The Institute was among the intergovernmental organizations that participated in drafting ILO Convention No. 169,[12] and it hosted an initial meeting to discuss the draft Inter-American declaration on indigenous rights.

In 1949, Bolivia did propose establishing a sub-commission of the UN Social Commission to study 'the social problems of the aboriginal populations of the American continent', but the resolution ultimately adopted only called upon the Economic and Social Council to undertake a study on the situation of indigenous peoples. Even this was too much for some countries (including the United States, Brazil, Peru, and Venezuela), and a subsequent resolution effectively barred any such studies unless requested by affected member states.[13] No requests were forthcoming, and this initiative ended UN concern with the general problems of indigenous peoples for two decades.

The mandate of the Inter-American Commission on Human Rights extends to all OAS member states,[14] but the Commission has had no special authority or obligation to concern itself with the rights of indigenous peoples. It is only through complaints to the Commission and the Commission's country reports that a few specific indigenous situations have been examined.

Faced with a number of individual petitions concerning indigenous people in the late 1960s and early 1970s, the Commission in 1972 did adopt a resolution on 'special protection for indigenous populations'. The

[8] The draft is discussed more fully below, at 334–42.

[9] See International Convention relating to Inter-American Indigenous Meetings and to the Institute, opened for signature 1 Nov. 1940, 56 Stat. 1303, T.S. No. 978.

[10] Cf. 1 UN Indigenous Study at 140–45; Inter-American Commission on Human Rights, *Inter-American Yearbook on Human Rights 1969–1970*, at 73–83 (OAS, 1976).

[11] See R. L. Barsh, 'The IXth Inter-American Indian Congress', 80 *Am. J Int'l L* 682, 683–4 (1986).

[12] International Labour Organisation Convention Concerning Indigenous and Tribal Peoples in Independent Countries (No. 169), adopted 27 June 1989, entered into force 5 Sept. 1991, Preamble.

[13] See 1 UN Indigenous Study at 25–7.

[14] See Cerna, Chap. 3 above.

resolution states that the protection of indigenous populations is a 'sacred commitment' of OAS member states and calls upon states, in particular, to train and monitor public officials so that they will deal with indigenous people appropriately.[15] Unfortunately, until 1995 the resolution remained the only general statement on indigenous rights adopted by the Commission, and it appears to have had little practical impact.

SPECIFIC CASES AND SITUATIONS

Individual cases

Although the Commission has discussed indigenous rights in the context of several reports on human rights situations in particular countries,[16] to date the Commission has reached written conclusions dealing specifically with indigenous rights in only four cases in its nearly 40-year existence. In the cases of the Guahibo in Colombia, the Aché in Paraguay, and the Yanomami in Brazil, the Commission adopted rather cursory statements or resolutions, finding violations in the last two cases. A case concerning the Miskito Indians in Nicaragua resulted in a major report, which is discussed in greater detail below. Many other cases have been filed, but the Commission apparently has not taken formal action to resolve them.[17]

The first case considered by the Commission, that of the Guahibo Indians in eastern Colombia, demonstrates the problems faced by the Commission in ascertaining the facts of allegations made to it, as well as its early tendency to accept the explanations offered by governments.[18] The case involved clashes between colonists and Indians, with the former aided by elements of the Colombian army. The government, responding to several Commission requests for information, claimed that the military was merely restoring public order and denounced as 'false and tendentious' any allegations of human rights violations.[19] After three years of investigation, the Commission implicitly accepted the government's explanations and decided to discontinue its consideration of the case without making formal findings of fact.

[15] See IACHR Annual Report 1972, at 63–5. This and the 1973 recommendations regarding indigenous populations are summarized in Inter-American Commission on Human Rights, *Ten Years of Activities 1971–1981* (OAS, 1982) at 328–9.

[16] See discussion below at 332–4

[17] For example, the Commission did not act on several cases brought in the late 1960s and early 1970s, at approximately the same time as the Guahibo case. See S. H. Davis, *Land Rights and Indigenous Peoples: The Role of the Inter-American Commission on Human Rights* 8–9 (Cambridge, MA: Cultural Survival, 1988).

[18] Case No. 1690 (Colombia), IACHR Annual Report 1973, at 21–2. The case is discussed in Davis, above n. 17, at 16–26.

[19] Davis, above n. 17, at 22.

The next case concerned alleged genocide against the Aché Indians in Paraguay.[20] Filed in 1974, the complaint alleged a number of serious violations of human rights against the Aché, as population pressures and attacks by settlers reduced their original land base. By the early 1970s, a national Indian colony for the Aché was described by one knowledgeable observer as having become 'a disease-infested dumping ground for the remaining members of the Aché tribe',[21] and the dire situation of the Aché had received a great deal of international publicity.

The Paraguayan government never responded officially to the complaint (although it launched political attacks against the Commission's investigation[22]), and, as a result, the Commission eventually decided under its Regulations 'to presume the occurrence of the events denounced to be confirmed',[23] It recommended that the government 'adopt vigorous measures to provide effective protection for the rights of the Aché tribe' and concluded that there had been 'very serious violations' of the rights to life, liberty, security, family, health, fair remuneration for work, and leisure.[24] However, the Commission did not retract its earlier 'provisional' conclusion that 'the policy of the Government of Paraguay is not a policy aimed at eliminating the Aché Indians, but rather a policy aimed at promoting assimilation and providing protection',[25] thus casting some doubt as to the government's ultimate responsibility for the broad range of violations imputed to it.

The third individual complaint that led to adoption of a resolution by the Commission was brought by a number of nongovernmental organizations and concerned the Yanomami Indians in Brazil.[26] The aim of the complaint was to protect the Yanomami, 'the largest unacculturated Indian tribe in South America',[27] from the destruction of their land base by an invasion of Brazilian peasants, miners, and others, which began with construction of a new highway through traditional Yanomami territory in 1973 and accelerated with the discovery of various mineral resources later in the decade. The Brazilian government participated actively in the case and announced several initiatives—including creation and demarcation of a large Yanomami Park advocated by pro-Indian groups—designed to protect the Yanomami's health and territory.

As in previous cases, the Commission seemed inclined to accept the government's assurances that the situation was being appropriately

---

[20] Case 1802 (Paraguay), IACHR Annual Report 1977, at 36–7. See Davis, above, n. 17, at 27–40.   [21] Davis, above, n. 17, at 31.
[22] See id. at 33.   [23] IACHR Annual Report 1977, at 37.
[24] Id.   [25] Id. at 36.
[26] Case No. 7615 (Brazil), IACHR Annual Report 1984–5, at 24–34. This case also is discussed in Davis, above, n. 17, at 41–62.
[27] Davis, above, n. 17, at 41.

addressed. However, unlike previous resolutions it had adopted, the resolution in the Yanomami case was much more substantive and contained conclusions both of law and of fact.

After noting the various legal protections that existed under Brazilian law, the Commission nonetheless concluded that exploitation of natural resources in the Amazon compelled thousands of Yanomami to abandon their homes; that the civilian invasions 'were carried out without prior and adequate protection for the safety and health of the Yanomami' and adversely affected 'the lives, security, health, and cultural integrity of the Yanomamis'; and that the government had violated the rights of the Yanomami to life, liberty, personal security, residence, movement, and health because of its failure 'to take timely and effective measures' on behalf of the Yanomami.[28] The Commission also recognized 'the important measures that the Government of Brazil has taken in the last few years, particularly since 1983, to protect the security, health, and integrity of the Yanomami Indians' and recommended that the government continue to take appropriate measures to protect the Yanomami and to demarcate the boundaries of the Yanomami Park.[29]

The Commission's conclusions rested, as they had to, on the rights found in the American Declaration on the Rights and Duties of Man. However, the Commission also implied that indigenous peoples might be guaranteed additional rights specific to their needs, when it noted that 'international law in its present state, and as it is found clearly expressed in Article 27 of the International Covenant on Civil and Political Rights, recognizes the right of ethnic groups to special protection on [sic] their use of their own language, for the practice of their own religion, and, in general, for all those characteristics necessary for the preservation of their cultural identity.'[30] Destruction of the Yanomami's identity was clearly at the forefront of the Commission's concerns, even if its conclusions were expressed in the narrower language of the American Declaration.

An individual complaint also was at the origin of the Commission's fullest consideration of a case involving indigenous issues, which was ultimately entitled *Report on the Situation of Human Rights of a Segment of the Nicaraguan Population of Miskito Origin*.[31] Although the proximate cause of the complaint was violence in Nicaragua that led to the forced

---

[28] See IACHR Annual Report 1984–5, at 25, 32, 33.

[29] Id. at 33.

[30] Id. at 31. This is a somewhat broader articulation of Art. 27 than is found in the text itself, which reads in its entirety: 'In those States in which ethnic, religious or linguistic minorities exist, persons belonging to such minorities shall not be denied the right, in community with the other members of their group, to enjoy their own culture, to profess and practise their own religion, or to use their own language.'

[31] OAS Docs. OEA/Ser.L/V/II.62, doc. 10 rev. 3 (1983) and OEA/Ser.L/V/II.62, doc. 26 (1984) (hereinafter 'Miskito Report').

relocation of a large number of Miskito Indians, the case became much more complex due to divisions among the original complainants (none of whom was deemed by the Commission to represent adequately the entire Miskito community[32]) and expansion of the complaint to include broader issues of indigenous rights to autonomy and self-determination. The Sandinista government of Nicaragua, which was engaged in a civil war with the U.S.-backed *contras* at the time, participated actively in the Commission's proceedings and invited the Commission to conduct an on-site investigation into the complaints.

After numerous unsuccessful attempts to negotiate a friendly settlement, the Commission reached conclusions with respect to the situation of Miskitos in Nicaragua from December 1981 through September 1983, that is, just prior to adoption of its report. With respect to non-indigenous-specific human rights, the Commission found violations of the right to life and liberty, but it also found that some of the forced relocations were justified as permissible derogations from normal human rights guarantees, in light of the military situation in Nicaragua at the time.

Of greater interest is the Commission's treatment of Miskito claims 1) that they had inherent rights to the lands they had traditionally occupied, and 2) that they enjoyed additional political rights because of their status as indigenous peoples, in particular the right to self-determination.

With respect to land rights, the government categorically rejected the argument that the Miskitos had rights any different from those accorded to all other citizens of Nicaragua and observed that '[t]erritorial unity stands above any other consideration and is not subject to discussion of any kind.'[33] Without addressing the substance of the land rights issue, the Commission noted that 'this kind of problem is neither novel nor exclusive to Nicaragua, since there is a large number of similar situations in America, where vast groups of the Indian population have seen their development potential diminished, due to the absence of a political response that would adequately take into account the peculiarities of their social and economic organization.'[34] Stating that it was 'not in a position to decide on the strict legal validity of the claim of the Indian communities to their ancestral lands',[35] the Commission concluded by recommending that a 'just solution' be found that would meet 'both the aspirations of the Indians and the requisites of territorial unity' of Nicaragua.[36]

The Commission adopted a similar position of encouraging compromise with respect to the broader political claims put forward by the Miskitos, although its legal conclusions were somewhat more precise. After first

---

[32] See the Commission's summary of the various interests and groups involved, id. at 45–6.

[33] Id. at 126.   [34] Id.

[35] Id. at 127.   [36] Id.

noting that the American Convention on Human Rights prohibits discrimination but contains no specific provision related to 'ethnic groups'
(the Commission's term for the Miskitos), the Commission proceeded to
analyze Article 27 of the Covenant on Civil and Political Rights, to which
Nicaragua was also a party.[37] After finding that the Covenant guaranteed
to minorities the rights to use their own language, practice their own
religion, and enjoy their own culture, the Commission then went on to
consider 'whether or not ethnic groups also have additional rights [beyond
those set forth in Article 27], particularly the rights to self-determination
or political autonomy'.[38] Its conclusion remains the only statement to date
by a quasi-judicial or judicial international human rights body to address
directly the question of indigenous self-determination:

The present status of international law does recognize observance of the principle
of self-determination of peoples, which it considers to be the right of a people to
independently choose their form of political organization and to freely establish the
means it deems appropriate to bring about their economic, social and cultural
development. This does not mean, however, that it recognizes the right to self-
determination of any ethnic group as such.[39]

Citing, *inter alia*, UN General Assembly resolutions 1514 of 14 December 1960[40] and 2625 of 13 October 1970,[41] the Commission concluded that
the right to self-determination could never justify disrupting the territorial
integrity of a sovereign state.

Clearly uncomfortable with the conservative reading of international law
it had just given, however, the Commission went on to note that the
absence of any legal right to autonomy or self-determination did not grant
to Nicaragua 'an unrestricted right to impose complete assimilation on
those Indians'.[42]

Although the current status of international law does not allow the view that the
ethnic groups of the Atlantic zone of Nicaragua have a right to political autonomy
and self-determination, special legal protection is recognized for the use of their
language, the observance of their religion, and in general, all those aspects related
to the preservation of their cultural identity. To this should be added the aspects
linked to productive organization, which includes, among other things, the issue of
the ancestral and communal lands. . . . [I]t is fundamental to establish new condi-

---

[37] The examination of the Covenant was justified by referring to Art. 29(b) of the
American Convention, which directs the Commission to interpret the Convention in a way
that does not restrict rights recognized by virtue of any other convention to which a state may
be a party. The text of Art. 27 is set out above, at n. 30.
[38] Miskito Report at 78.
[39] Id. at 78–9.
[40] Declaration on the Granting of Independence to Colonial Countries and Peoples.
[41] Declaration on Principles of International Law concerning Friendly Relations and Cooperation among States in accordance with the Charter of the United Nations.
[42] Miskito Report at 81.

tions for coexistence between the ethnic minorities and the Government of Nicaragua, in order to settle historic antagonisms and the serious difficulties present today. In the opinion of the IACHR the need to preserve and guarantee the observance of these principles in practice entails the need to establish an adequate institutional order as part of the structure of the Nicaraguan state.[43]

This call to establish 'an adequate institutional order' to respond to indigenous demands was at least partially met by Nicaragua, which adopted an autonomy statute for the Atlantic Coast in 1987.[44]

Both the Miskito and Yanomami cases represented significant breaks with earlier cases, in that they did begin to address (albeit superficially with respect to the Yanomami) the larger issues of the political relations between indigenous peoples and the state. The relatively conservative conclusions drawn by the Commission in the Miskito report with respect to self-determination may not be welcome to indigenous rights advocates, but they were amply supported by the state of international law in the mid-1980s and by the limited nature of the texts the Commission was called on to interpret.

It also should be borne in mind that, in at least three of the four situations considered by the Commission, complaints of violations of the rights of indigenous peoples were being investigated in the context of wider human rights violations which affected the entire country (Paraguay), the transition from a repressive military regime to a democratically elected one (Brazil), or a civil war (Nicaragua). Without in any manner diminishing the suffering of indigenous peoples raised before the Commission, the Commission's focus on issues such as personal security and democracy was understandable, given its mandate.[45]

Furthermore, the role of the Commission is not primarily judgmental or condemnatory; it lacks enforcement power, and its success rests largely on its ability to convince governments that a change in policy is necessary. To achieve this end, it is much more likely to accept promises of change made by a government (as it did with Brazil and Nicaragua) than to insist on condemning past violations. It is thus unlikely that the Commission will stretch beyond the facts of a particular case to address broader issues.[46]

[43] Id. at 81–2.

[44] For an account of the process which led to the autonomy statute and references to subsequent criticisms of the law, see H. Hannum, *Autonomy, Sovereignty, and Self-Determination: The Accommodation of Conflicting Rights* (Philadelphia: Univ. of Pennsylvania Press, rev. ed. 1996) at 203–25, 485–7.

[45] In its 1978 report on the general situation in Paraguay, for example, the Commission merely referred in a footnote to the Aché case, without any further discussion of indigenous issues. See IACHR Report on the Situation of Human Rights in Paraguay, (1978), at 9, n. 8. A report several years later did not mention indigenous issues at all. See IACHR Report on the Situation of Human Rights in Paraguay (1987).

[46] The Commission's discussion of self-determination in the Miskito case was in response to specific arguments put forward by the complainants.

Country reports

Given the attacks on indigenous peoples that continue to occur in many
American countries, it is surprising that the Commission has only rarely
addressed indigenous issues in the context of its general reports on the
human rights situation in various states.[47] Of course, indigenous peoples
are often victims of human rights violations that affect society at large,
particularly peasants. However, issues specific to indigenous peoples have
been considered in only a few cases. In addition to the individual cases
discussed above, the most relevant country reports include those concerning Colombia and Peru; it is anticipated that reports on Mexico and Brazil
to be adopted in 1997 also will contain substantial discussions of
indigenous issues.

The Commission adopted two reports concerning the situation of human
rights in Colombia, in 1981 and 1993. The first report discussed the impact
of military operations on indigenous communities and summarized then-
pending proposals to amend Colombian legislation on Indian rights, including the Indian Development Plan to be implemented in 1981–83.[48] The
1993 report summarized the theoretically improved status of indigenous
peoples under the 1991 Colombia constitution, including rights to communal lands and special political participation rights.[49] However, despite
noting that indigenous rights were often violated in practice and describing
as 'typical' a case in which 20 indigenous peasants were massacred by
paramilitary civilians, the Commission recommended only that '[i]t is
essential that the necessary measures be taken to enable . . . [ethnic and
minority] groups to survive and develop, and that their ethnic and cultural
diversity be acknowledged.'[50]

The Commission has considered the decades-old civil war in Guatemala
and its impact on human rights in several reports. Indigenous Maya-Quiche
Indians constitute roughly half of the population of Guatemala, and the
great majority of them live below the poverty line. In its 1985 report, the
Commission observed that 'no other sector has suffered as much from the
violence of the past few years as the farmers and indigenous communities .

---

[47] See generally Medina, chap. 4 above; Anaya, below, n. 56, at 158. The Commission's
inactivity might be compared to the more aggressive approach taken by the Committee on the
Elimination of All Forms of Racial Discrimination, which has raised questions concerning the
treatment of indigenous people in the context of its periodic review of country reports
submitted under the Convention on the Elimination of All Forms of Racial Discrimination. See
Hannum, above, n. 44, at 82, n. 308; M. Banton, 'International Norms and Latin American
States' Policies on Indigenous Peoples', 2 *Nations and Nationalism* 89, 95–9 (1996).

[48] See IACHR Report on the Situation of Human Rights in Colombia (1981), at 208–17.

[49] See IACHR Second Report on the Situation of Human Rights in Colombia (1993), at
229–37.

[50] Id. at 233–44, 251.

. . . In the rural areas, the war has left an unprecedented trail of death and destruction.'[51]

As the Commission noted, this widespread destruction affected both indigenous and non-indigenous peasants, and it is often difficult to identify human rights violations in Guatemala that relate primarily to indigenous peoples *per se*. Again, the Commission did not so much analyze the kind of rights violated by the military and others but simply catalogued the violations of life, security, person, movement, and property of which indigenous and non-indigenous civilians were victims.

The one violation found by the Commission to have been directed specifically against the Maya-Quiche was the 'centuries-old prejudice'[52] against them manifested in nearly every facet of Guatemalan political, economic, and cultural life. Despite recognition of indigenous culture, dress, and language in the Guatemalan constitution, the Commission found inequality and de facto discrimination to be widespread:

> The reality—which the Government openly acknowledges—shows that Guate-mala's indigenous people cannot exercise the same rights and do not have the same opportunities that the *ladino* population or the people of European descent enjoy. . .
>
> Those who retain characteristics that identify them as Mayas—language, community structure, dress, religious practices—are not only excluded from positions of power and prestige in the nation, but in general are scorned by politicians, conservatives, liberals or marxists.
>
> The overall policy of the State has been aimed at keeping them [indigenous people] out of jobs and ignoring their 'backward' traditions, to allow some of the more 'civilized' to become *ladinos*, and to brutally 'mow down any who pose a direct challenge to Creole or *Ladino* dominance.[53]

Seizures of land and forced resettlement also appear to have had a disproportionate effect on indigenous people, but all peasant communities in Guatemala have suffered from similar usurpations. Thus, as in many other countries, most of the widespread human rights violations committed in Guatemala are not directed only at indigenous peoples.

As is true with respect to its investigation of individual cases, the Commission's relative inattention to indigenous rights in the context of country reports may be due to several factors. First, the lack of normative OAS standards specifically concerning indigenous peoples (or even minorities or ethnic groups) has made it difficult for the Commission to focus on these issues. Second, there have been massive human rights violations in most of the countries concerning which reports have been published, and the Commission has been understandably preoccupied with broader issues

---

[51] IACHR Third Report on the Situation of Human Rights in Guatemala (Oct. 1985).
[52] IACHR Fourth Report on the Situation of Human Rights in Guatemala (1993), at 36.
[53] Id. at 33–4 (citation omitted).

of personal security and, more recently, democracy and the rule of law. Third, as noted above, the Commission often is inclined to accept government promises of improvement—and it seems that every government is prepared to promise legislative or even constitutional revisions to improve the lives of indigenous peoples. However, the effective implementation of such promises has often proved problematic.

Inter-American Court of Human Rights

The Court has not yet been seized of a case which relates primarily to indigenous rights, although it has addressed indigenous issues indirectly in at least two cases. The *Chunimá* Case concerned alleged murders of indigenous rights activists in Guatemala but did not raise issues specific to indigenous peoples.[54] In the *Aloeboetoe* Case, the Court considered traditional tribal law in determining the amount of compensation to be paid by the Suriname government to the victims' families.[55]

The American Declaration on the Rights of Indigenous Peoples

The Commission's original mandate gave it no reason to focus on indigenous issues in the Americas. However, international concern with the situation of indigenous peoples has increased tremendously in the past two decades, and the OAS has not been immune from the increasingly effective lobbying carried out by indigenous organizations and other NGOs to force international human rights bodies to devote greater attention to the plight of indigenous peoples around the world.[56]

In 1989, the year in which the ILO adopted Convention No. 169, the Inter-American Commission recommended to the OAS General Assembly that it entrust the Commission with preparing 'a juridical instrument'

---

[54] See *Chunimá* case (Emergency Provisional Measures), 15 July 1991, Order of the Pres. of the I/A Court H.R., reprinted in *1991 Inter-Am. Y.B. Hum. Rts.* 1104. The case was settled without a final judgment having been adopted.

[55] See *Aloeboetoe* case (Reparations), I/A Court H.R., Ser. C No. 15 (1993), 11 *HRLJ* 413. This aspect of the case is briefly summarized in J. M. Pasqualucci, 'The Inter-American Human Rights System: Establishing Precedents and Procedure in Human Rights Law,' 26 *U Miami Inter-Am. L Rev.* 297, 329–31 (1995).

[56] This chapter will not address those activities, but discussions of the development of indigenous rights internationally may be found in, e.g., S. J. Anaya, *Indigenous Peoples in International Law* 39–71 (Oxford Univ. Press, 1996); L. Barsh, 'Indigenous Peoples in the 1990s: From Object to Subject of International Law?' 7 *Harv. Hum. Rts. J* 33 (1994); H. Hannum, above, n. 44, at 74–103, 501; id., 'New Developments in Indigenous Rights', 28 *Virginia J Int'l L* 649 (1988); K. Roy and G. Alfredsson, 'Indigenous Rights: The Literature Explosion'. 13 *Transnat'l. Persp.* 19 (1987); UN Indigenous Study, above, n. 4; and the Annual Reports of the Working Group on Indigenous Populations to the UN Sub-Commission on Prevention of Discrimination and Protection of Minorities.

defining indigenous rights.[57] Noting the common problems faced by many indigenous peoples in the Americas and the inadequacy of international law at the time, the Commission proposed that a declaration or convention be adopted by the General Assembly in 1992, the 500th anniversary of Columbus' arrival on the American continent.

The Commission's recommendation was adopted by the General Assembly,[58] although the proposed timetable proved to be overly optimistic. A meeting of governmental and nongovernmental experts held jointly by the Commission and the Inter-American Indian Institute in 1991 concluded that a declaration would be the most appropriate form for the instrument and that consultations on the declaration should be as wide as possible. In 1992, the Commission sent a questionnaire to all OAS Member States to solicit opinions on the issues and approaches that the future instrument should include; a fairly extensive summary of the responses received (from eleven governments and 20 indigenous organizations) was included in the Commission's 1992–93 Annual Report.[59]

After further internal discussions, the Commission adopted an initial draft declaration in September 1995, which was again sent to OAS governments and indigenous organisations, and others for their comments.[60] The Commission revised the draft in February 1997, based on comments received from governments, indigenous groups, and others;[61] it was hoped that a final declaration would be adopted by the OAS General Assembly in 1997 or 1998.[62]

As the most comprehensive attempt to date to define the scope of indigenous rights in the Americas, the Commission's draft declaration merits detailed attention. Although one might expect the final declaration adopted by the OAS General Assembly to differ from the Commission's draft, a discussion of the latter will highlight many of the areas on which

[57] See IACHR Annual Report 1988–9, at 245–52.

[58] OAS General Assembly Res. AG/Res.1022 (XIX-0/89).

[59] IACHR Annual Report 1992–3, at 263–310.

[60] Draft Inter-American Declaration on the Rights of Indigenous Peoples, OAS Doc. OEA/Ser.L/V/II.90, doc. 9 rev. 1, reprinted in IACHR Annual Report 1995, at 207–18 (hereinafter '1995 Draft Declaration').

[61] Proposed American Declaration on the Rights of Indigenous Peoples, approved by the IACHR on 26 Feb. 1997 (hereinafter '1997 Draft Declaration'). The unofficial English text cited in this chapter is that posted on the Commission's World Wide Web site, http://www.oas.org/EN/PROG/indigene.htm.

[62] Even if this timetable were to slip somewhat, it is likely that the OAS declaration will be adopted before the UN Declaration on the Rights of Indigenous Peoples. Following its adoption by the UN Sub-Commission on Prevention of Discrimination and Protection of Minorities, a body of independent experts, the latter was first considered by a working group of the UN Commission on Human Rights only in late 1995. The second session was held in October 1996, but no substantive progress was made. The text of the UN draft is found in UN Doc. E/CN.4/Sub.2/1993/29, Annex I (1993), and is reprinted in 34 *ILM* 541 (1995).

consensus has been achieved, at least within the relatively narrow confines of the Commission itself.

The draft declaration is divided into six sections, dealing respectively with a definition of indigenous peoples; human rights; cultural development; organizational and political rights; social, economic, and property rights; and general provisions, including the observance of treaties between indigenous peoples and states.

The issue of defining 'indigenous peoples' has long been contentious. ILO Convention No. 169 does define indigenous and tribal peoples, although it notes that use of the term 'peoples' 'shall not be construed as having any implications as regards the rights which may attach to the term under international law'.[63] The UN draft declaration does not presently contain a definition of 'indigenous', although many governments have indicated that this omission is problematic.[64]

The Commission draft adopts the ILO approach, including a caveat with respect to international legal implications that is essentially the same as that set forth in ILO Convention 169, a position opposed by most indigenous organizations. The 1997 draft rejects an earlier proposal for a narrow definition, which would have been limited to the particular circumstances of the Americas: 'indigenous peoples are those who embody historical continuity with societies which existed prior to the conquest and settlement of their territories by Europeans.'[65] Indeed, the latest draft expands the scope of the declaration to include not only indigenous peoples but also 'peoples whose social, cultural and economic conditions distinguish them from other sections of the national community, and whose status is regulated wholly or partially by their own customs or traditions or by special laws or regulations',[66] The one issue on which there is widespread agreement is that self-identification as indigenous should be regarded as a fundamental criterion.[67]

The expanded scope of the 1997 draft may be problematic, as many minority groups also would appear to qualify for the special protections originally designed to respond to the specific needs of indigenous peoples. It would seem to the present author that a narrow definition would more accurately reflect the reality of the Americas, since the protection and recognition of Indian, Inuit, and tribal communities that existed prior to European settlement have been at the heart of international and hemispheric efforts to advance the cause of indigenous rights. Such an approach

---

[63] ILO Convention No. 169, above, n. 12, Art. 1.

[64] See, e.g., the discussions at the first session of the UN Commission on Human Rights Working Group on the UN draft declaration, UN Doc. E/CN.4/1996/84 (1996), at 6–8.

[65] 1995 Draft Declaration, Art. 1(1).

[66] 1997 Draft Declaration, Art. 1(1).

[67] See id., Art. 1(2).

would not necessarily set a precedent for a global declaration, such as that under consideration by the United Nations, but it would more clearly distinguish between indigenous communities and other minority groups within states.

The issue of collective versus individual rights has bedeviled nearly every international discussion of the rights of minorities, indigenous peoples, and other groups.[68] Both the 1966 UN Covenant on Civil and Political Rights and the 1992 UN Declaration on minority rights[69] carefully refer to the rights 'of persons belonging to' minorities. In contrast, neither ILO Convention No. 169 nor the draft UN declaration on indigenous rights hesitates to recognize collective rights.

Two articles of the Commission draft specifically accept the appropriateness of collective rights for indigenous peoples:

Indigenous peoples have the collective rights that are indispensable to the enjoyment of the individual human rights of their members. Accordingly the states recognize *inter alia* the right of the indigenous peoples to collective action, to their cultures, to profess and practice their spiritual beliefs, and to use their lan guages.[70]

Indigenous peoples have the right to have their legal personality fully recognized by the states within their systems.[71]

In addition, the concept of collective rights would seem to be implicit in the declaration's recognition of indigenous rights to autonomy and self-government (Article 15), maintenance of customary law (Article 16), ownership and control over land and intellectual property (Articles 18 and 20), approval of national development plans (Article 21), and the observance of treaties (Article 22).

It is difficult to give priority to any of the next three sections, which deal respectively with culture, political rights, and economic rights, but the emphasis on cultural integrity is most reflective of the Commission's traditional concerns. Although they may not be the strongest legal injunctions, perhaps the most important political and philosophical statements in the declaration are those found in Articles 7 and 8:

Indigenous peoples have the right to their cultural integrity, and their historical and archeological heritage, which are important both for their survival as well as for the identity of their members.[72]

---

[68] See generally J. Crawford, (ed.), *The Rights of Peoples* (Clarendon Press, 1988); N. Lerner, *Group Rights and Discrimination in International Law* (Martinus Nijhoff, 1991); J. B. Muldoon, 'The Development of Group Rights', in J. A. Sigler, (ed.), *Minority Rights, A Comparative Analysis* 32–66 (Greenwood Press, 1983).

[69] Declaration on the Rights of Persons belonging to National or Ethnic, Religious or Linguistic Minorities, GA Res. 47/135, 18 Dec. 1992.

[70] 1997 Draft Declaration, Art. 2(2).

[71] Id., Art. 6 (entitled 'Legal status of communities').   [72] Id., Art. 7(1).

The states shall recognize and respect indigenous ways of life, customs, traditions, forms of social, economic and political organization, institutions, practices,
beliefs and values, use of dress, and languages.[73]

Indigenous peoples have the right to indigenous languages, philosophy and outlook as a component of national and universal culture, and as such, [states] shall
respect them and facilitate their dissemination.[74]

Section Three goes on to address more specifically issues of language,
education, religion, family, health, and the environment. In most cases, the
declaration imposes affirmative obligations on states to promote or facilitate the exercise of the rights by indigenous peoples, as opposed to the
more typical 'negative' formulation of other human rights instruments. For
example, states are to 'take measures' to support the creation of indigenous
media and to ensure that radio and television programs are broadcast in
indigenous languages in regions where there is a strong indigenous presence.[75] States are to 'take effective measures' to enable indigenous peoples
to understand administrative, legal, and political procedures and 'shall
endeavor to establish' indigenous languages as official languages in areas
in which they predominate.[76]

Indigenous peoples are guaranteed the right to establish their own
educational institutions, and states must provide adequate financial and
other assistance to ensure that indigenous educational systems are equal to
non-indigenous education.[77] The precise scope of this article is unclear, in
that it requires that indigenous educational systems 'are equal in quality,
efficiency, accessibility and in all other ways to that provided to the general
population'.[78] Would this require, for instance, state support for indigenous
universities in every indigenous community, or does this simply mean that,
in general, similar financial and other support should be given to indigenous and non-indigenous schools?

States also are to adopt 'necessary' or 'effective' measures to prevent the
imposition of others' religious beliefs on indigenous peoples and to protect
indigenous sacred sites,[79] as well as to enable indigenous peoples to meet
internationally accepted health standards within their communities.[80]

Article 11, which is concerned with family relations, addresses the
sensitive issue of the adoption of indigenous children. Unlike the UN draft
declaration, which currently prohibits the removal of indigenous children
'from their families and communities under any pretext',[81] the Commission
draft only requires that courts and other institutions give consideration to

---

[73] Id., Art. 8(3).   [74] Id., Art. 8(1).
[75] Id., Art. 8(2).   [76] Id., Art. 8(3).
[77] Id., Art. 9.   [78] Id., Art. 9(3).
[79] Id., Arts. 10(2) and (3).   [80] Id., Art. 12(4).
[81] UN Draft Declaration, above, n. 62, Art. 6.

the views of the indigenous individuals, families, and communities concerned.[82]

Finally, Article 13 gives indigenous peoples the right to 'conserve, restore and protect' their environment, with the additional right to 'assistance' from states. In many respects, however, the environmental provisions may be subsumed in the broader land rights set forth in Section Five of the draft.

Section Four, on 'organizational and political rights', is perhaps most notable for what it omits, that is, any reference to the right of self-determination. However, Article 15(1) does reiterate the language of common Article 1 of the two UN covenants on human rights, which addresses the right of 'all peoples' to self-determination, by stating that indigenous peoples have the right 'to freely determine their political status and freely pursue their economic, social, spiritual and cultural development'. The paragraph goes on to specify that 'accordingly they have the right to autonomy or self-government with regard to *inter alia* culture, religion, education, information, media, health, housing, employment, social welfare, economic activities, land and resource management, the environment and entry by nonmembers; and to determine ways and means for financing these autonomous functions.'[83] This latter language parallels that of Article 30 of the UN draft declaration and provides a more useful articulation of indigenous governmental powers than mere incantation of the phrase 'self-determination'.[84] A later article implicitly recognizes the principle of the territorial integrity of states, which usually accompanies international references to self-determination, although the draft's reference to not ignoring interstate boundaries could be clarified.[85]

Complementing the right to self-government is the right of indigenous peoples to participate 'in all decision-making, at all levels, with regard to

---

[82] 1997 Draft Declaration, Art. 11(2).

[83] A useful description of many existing self-governing arrangements may be found in W. J. Assies and A. J. Hoekema, (eds)., *Indigenous Peoples' Experiences with Self-Government* (Int'l. Work Group for Indigenous Affairs and Univ. of Amsterdam, 1994).

[84] There are a great number of recent articles and books addressing the issue of self-determination, including its applicability to indigenous peoples. For contrasting views, compare, e.g., Anaya, above, n. 56, at 75–125; R. L. Barsh, 'The Challenge of Indigenous Self-Determination', 26 *U Mich. J L Ref.* 277 (1993); L. Brilmayer, 'Secession and Self-Determination: A Territorial Interpretation', 16 *Yale J Int'l. L* 177 (1991); A. Cassese, *Self-Determination of Peoples, A Legal Reappraisal* (Cambridge Univ. Press, 1995); H. Hannum, 'Rethinking Self-Determination', 34 *Virginia J Int'l. L* 1 (1993); M. C. Lâm, 'The Legal Value of Self-Determination: Vision or Inconvenience?' in *People or Peoples; Equality, Autonomy and Self-Determination* 79–142 (Montreal: International Centre for Human Rights and Democratic Development, 1996); D. Suagee, 'Self-Determination for Indigenous Peoples at the Dawn of the Solar Age', 25 *U Mich. J L Ref.* 671 (1992); and D. L. Van Cott, 'Prospects for Self-Determination of Indigenous Peoples in Latin America: Questions of Law and Practice', 2 *Global Governance* 43 (1996).

[85] 1997 Draft Declaration, Art. 25.

matters that might affect their rights, lives and destiny'.[86] This right to participate does not grant to indigenous peoples a general right of veto over national policies, but it does ensure that their voices will be heard. Again, some clarification with respect to the scope of this right to participation would be useful, as one can imagine that many national or regional policies could potentially affect indigenous peoples. The assumption may be that special participatory rights would only attach where the exercise of self-government powers is affected. Of course, the right of indigenous individuals to participate in the national political system without discrimination is guaranteed both under general international human rights law and Articles 2, 6, and 15 of the Commission draft.

Articles 16 and 17 concern the status of customary indigenous law and institutions. The former is to be deemed 'part of the states' legal system' and should be applied in all matters arising within indigenous communities.[87] State courts are directed to observe indigenous law and custom in proceedings concerning indigenous peoples or their interests.[88] Article 17 runs counter to the general trend of the declaration to empower separate indigenous institutions, in that it calls on states to facilitate inclusion of indigenous institutions and traditional practices in states' 'organizational structures' and provides that state institutions 'relevant to and serving indigenous peoples' should be designed so as to promote indigenous identity and values.

The draft declaration's Preamble recognizes that 'traditional collective systems for control and use of land, territory, and resources . . . are a necessary condition' for the survival of indigenous peoples, and indigenous organizations constantly emphasize the importance of land rights in statements before international bodies. As demonstrated by the Aché and Yanomami cases discussed above, seizures of land by settlers or by the state are at the center of most attacks on indigenous cultures and ways of life. At the same time, of course, countries faced with widespread poverty and an expanding population are likely to covet land which may be only sparsely populated by indigenous peoples, as well as the potential natural resources contained within such regions.

Section Five of the draft declaration addresses these issues of land rights, as well as intellectual property, development, and special measures to protect indigenous workers. Indigenous rights to land and territories[89] include 1) legal recognition of the various forms of collective ownership and use of territory by indigenous peoples; 2) ownership of lands and

---

[86] 1997 Draft Declaration, Art. 15(2).
[87] Id., Art. 16(1) and (2).
[88] Id., Art. 16(3).
[89] The latter term includes waterways, ice floes, and other aspects of the natural environment that might not be included within a narrow definition of 'land'.

territories 'historically occupied' by indigenous peoples; 3) use of territories to which indigenous peoples 'have historically had access for their traditional activities and livelihood'; and 4) the inalienability of these indigenous ownership and usufruct rights.[90] The draft grants indigenous peoples the right to restitution of 'lands, territories and resources' taken from them, or, where restitution is impossible, to compensation 'on a basis not less favorable than the standard of international law'.[91] States are prohibited from relocating indigenous peoples without their consent, '[u]nless exceptional and justified circumstances so warrant in the public interest', and are obligated to 'take all measures' to prevent outsiders from interfering with indigenous peoples ownership and use of their lands.[92]

Timber, oil, gold, and other mineral resources have proved to be almost irresistible attractions to indebted governments, individual peasants, wealthy landowners, and transnational corporations, and the exploitation of natural resources in areas traditionally inhabited or used by indigenous peoples has often led to explosive clashes between indigenous peoples and either settlers or government forces. Although the resources themselves may not have been important to traditional indigenous cultures, their exploitation inevitably results in substantial disruption of indigenous cultural and economic life. At the same time, many Latin American constitutions or laws reserve ownership over all subsoil resources within the national territory to the state, whether the land itself is in public or private hands.

The draft declaration attempts a compromise between the land rights of indigenous peoples and the exploitation of natural resources by the state. It first declares the basic principle that '[i]ndigenous peoples have the right to an effective legal framework for the protection of their rights with respect to the natural resources on their lands.'[93] However, the succeeding paragraph appears to allow the state to exploit these resources, so long as indigenous peoples are consulted and so long as they participate in the benefits of exploitation, including receiving compensation for any damages caused.[94] These provisions should be read in conjunction with those concerning the environment, which provide that indigenous peoples 'have the right to conserve, restore and protect their environment, and the productive capacity of their lands, territories and resources'.[95]

Provisions on an indigenous right to development seem to tilt the balance back towards indigenous peoples themselves, whose development priorities are to prevail 'even where they are different from those adopted

---

[90] 1997 Draft Declaration, Art. 18(1)-(3).   [91] Id., Art. 18(7).
[92] Id., Art. 18(6) and (8).   [93] Id., Art. 18(4).
[94] Id., Art. 18(5).   [95] Id., Art. 13(3).

by the national government or by other segments of society'.[96] Unless 'exceptional circumstances' exist, no development plan affecting indigenous peoples may be adopted without their 'free and informed consent'.[97]

Finally, Article 22(6) confirms that treaties between indigenous peoples and states should be observed and enforced and calls for disputes to be submitted to 'competent bodies', although it does not identify which bodies those might be.

This brief summary of most of the provisions in the Commission's draft declaration is necessarily incomplete and somewhat cursory. As might be expected in a draft instrument, there are several areas in which greater clarification should be sought and important issues which remain to be resolved.

At the same time, however, some preliminary observations can be made. First, the scope of the draft declaration goes well beyond the concerns for cultural integrity and personal security which have characterized the Commission's statements in the past. Adoption of a final declaration along the lines of the present draft would constitute a significant expansion of indigenous rights presently recognized in the American hemisphere, including much more specific recognition of the rights of indigenous communities and peoples to economic and political self-management.

Second, while the OAS draft declaration is progressive, its language is more moderate and its goals somewhat more modest than those found in the UN draft declaration. Although it might be expected that an OAS declaration on indigenous rights, as a regional instrument, could be more specific and more expansive than a global instrument, the present draft is, in fact, less detailed than the UN draft. Nonetheless, it does address the areas of primary concern to indigenous peoples and organizations, such as control over lands and resources, cultural protection, and the right to be self-governing in a wide range of substantive areas.

CONCLUSION

The inter-American system for protecting human rights has paid only scant attention to indigenous peoples until relatively recently, but that inactivity has been due more to the limited nature of the mandate of the Inter-American Commission on Human Rights than to any conscious desire to avoid problematic issues. Creation of the Inter-American Indian Institute evidenced early OAS interest in Indian affairs, and the OAS' non-confrontational approach to the 'Indian problem' was typical of most non-indigenous thinking during the 1950s and 1960s.

---

[96] 1997 Draft Declaration, Art. 21(1).   [97] Id., Art. 21(2).

The Commission did consider violations of the rights of indigenous peoples when they were properly raised in the context of individual complaints, but the normative standards against which indigenous complaints were measured were those applicable to all individuals within the Americas, not just to indigenous peoples. Even though the Commission attempted to expand the cultural rights of indigenous peoples, by appealing to the norms found in Article 27 of the Covenant on Civil and Political Rights, it remained constrained by the more traditional nature of the rights set forth in the American Declaration on the Rights and Duties of Man and the American Convention on Human Rights.

Since the 1980s, however, the Commission has exhibited a willingness to go beyond the narrow confines of the Declaration and Convention, at least informally, and to attempt to mediate serious disputes between governments and indigenous communities. In both the Yanomami and Miskito cases, the Commission attempted to bring political pressure to bear on governments to lend a sympathetic ear to legitimate indigenous grievances, even if it was on weaker ground in trying to find legal norms which could be applied to specific cases.

Approval by the OAS General Assembly of the Commission's proposal to draft a declaration on indigenous rights represented formal recognition of the need to articulate more meaningful standards to protect indigenous peoples than currently exist. The process of adopting the declaration has benefitted from substantial participation by indigenous organizations, and one hopes that the consultations which led to adoption by the Commission of a revised draft in February 1997 will make it relatively easy for a final text to be approved by the General Assembly.

Of course, adoption of a declaration does not guarantee that rights will be respected. The real test will come when the Commission (or another body) attempts to hold governments accountable for the political obligations they have assumed under the declaration. Many of the rights articulated in the draft, particularly those concerned with political and economic autonomy, must be balanced against competing government interests and, in some instances, arguments based on the competing rights of others.

At the same time, however, few rights are absolute, and balancing individual (or group) rights against the power of government is a task which should be familiar to the Inter-American Commission and Court. In any event, the legitimacy that the concept of indigenous rights will acquire once the declaration is adopted, as well as the necessary articulation of the specific content of those rights, will be important steps towards guaranteeing that the relationship between indigenous peoples and the states which surround them is based on greater equality and mutual respect in the next century than has been the case in the preceding five centuries.

11

Responses to Amnesties by the Inter-American System for the Protection of Human Rights

ELLEN LUTZ

INTRODUCTION

Widespread violations of human rights have a profound effect not only on those directly involved—decision-makers, perpetrators, those targeted for abuse, and unintended casualties—but on everyone living in the impacted society. After the abuses cease, these societies must go through a healing process that includes coming to terms with what happened, grieving for what was lost, condemning those who caused the suffering, and rebuilding.

Since Nuremberg, policy-makers, human rights organizations, and victims have heralded trials for those responsible for human rights abuses as the catalyst for this healing process. They argue that trials reveal the truth about what happened and ensure that the historical record is preserved; defuse social tension and ethnic conflict by individualizing responsibility for widespread abuses; provide a legitimate outlet for those who suffered to condemn those responsible; restore confidence in the judiciary and the rule of law by demonstrating that the judicial process is fair and no one is above the law; and prevent future human rights violations by strengthening democratic institutions.[1] In these ways, trials not only shield nascent democratic governments from allegations of complicity after-the-fact, but contribute to democratic consolidation through affirmation of the rule of law.[2]

Despite the force of these arguments, trials of perpetrators of widespread human rights violations are rare. More often than not, pressure from senior politicians or military or police officials facing trial, financial realities, or distracting new political concerns motivate decision-makers to obstruct trials or limit their reach.[3] Such moves often are justified on the grounds that they promote national reconciliation or encourage the society

---

[1] See, The Justice and Society Program of The Aspen Institute, *State Crimes: Punishment of Pardon*, 1989.

[2] D. Orentlicher, 'Settling Accounts: The Duty to Prosecute Human Rights Violations of a Prior Regime', 100 *Yale LJ* 2537 (1991).

[3] In addition to formal amnesty statutes, de facto amnesties or pardons were routine during

to move forward and leave the past behind.[4] Some states have argued that it is amnesties, not trials, that best lead to the consolidation of democratic government and the prevention of future violations of human rights.[5]

While the complex moral and legal dilemmas surrounding the granting of amnesties or pardons to perpetrators of human rights violations have arisen in all regions of the world, the issue has had a particularly high profile in Latin America. As one dictatorial military regime after another returned to the barracks, the democratically-elected governments that replaced them have been challenged to respond both to the needs of human rights victims and to the demands of unified and still well-armed military officers. In many cases military officers believed themselves to be shielded from prosecution by self-amnesty laws that they passed prior to leaving power.[6] In these states subsequent governments have had to grapple with whether such amnesties should be nullified or repealed, and if so, to what extent. In other states the question of amnesty did not emerge before or during the negotiations leading to civilian rule. Here problems arose when civilian governments attempted to prosecute, or did not block individuals from seeking redress in the courts, and military officers threatened to topple the still-fragile democracies if impunity for past abuses was not assured.[7]

A third scenario emerged in those states in which long-standing armed conflicts, in which both sides engaged in human rights abuses, were ended through negotiations brokered by international actors or intergovernmental bodies. In these cases each party to the negotiations had reason for wanting immunity from prosecution, and all participants in the negotiation process had an interest in achieving rapid results, even if doing so compromised justice.[8] Similarly, where intergovernmental organizations have intervened to achieve a transition from military to elected civilian rule or to shore up a floundering democracy, popular desires for prosecution have been trumped by the intergovernmental organization's interest in expeditious, decisive action.[9]

---

the dictatorial era. Frequently these were provided by courts that themselves were implicated in human rights violations during the prior regime. While no less significant, these informal impunity mechanisms lie outside the scope of this article.

[4] President Menem justified the pardons as a gesture toward reconciliation and insisted that his own past as a prisoner of the military dictatorship conferred on him legitimacy to grant them. Americas Watch, *Truth and Partial Justice in Argentina: An Update* (New York: 1991), 69.

[5] See T. Farer, 'Consolidating Democracy in Latin America: Law, Legal Institutions and Constitutional Structure', 10 *Am. UJ Int'l. L & Policy* 1295, 1308–09 (1995) referring to aguments made by Uruguay before the Inter-American Commission on Human Rights.

[6] Self-amnesties by military officials were passed in Chile (1978), Argentina (1983), and Guatemala (1982, 1983, and 1986).

[7] This occurred in Honduras (1981), Uruguay (1986), Argentina (1986, 1987, and 1989–90), and Suriname (1989).   [8] This was particularly true in Nicaragua and El Salvador.

[9] This occurred in Haiti (1994) and Peru (1995).

As governments backed away from trials for perpetrators of human rights abuses,[10] victims and non-governmental human rights organizations turned to the Organization of American States' (OAS) human rights machinery.[11] Some brought the issue to the attention of the Inter-American Commission on Human Rights (Commission) in conjunction with its mandate to promote human rights in the Americas.[12] Others filed petitions with the Commission alleging that their governments had violated international human rights obligations by retaining or passing amnesty measures.[13]

This article surveys the response of the Commission and other OAS human rights organs to amnesty measures generally and in specific countries, and the jurisprudence that has emerged therefrom. Three overlapping contexts are discernible. The first predates the active engagement of the Inter-American Court of Human Rights on contentious questions when the Commission was the only organ of the OAS seriously concerned with human rights matters. The second begins in 1988 after the Inter-American Court of Human Rights decided the merits of the *Velásquez Rodríguez* case.[14] While the Court has not addressed the issue in a case in which an amnesty provision was challenged, that decision and subsequent ones have leant support to the views expressed by the Commission in the exercise of its quasi-judicial functions under the American Convention on Human Rights. The third follows the OAS' adoption of Resolution 1080 in

---

[10] Trials occurred in very few countries. In Argentina, a handful of the most senior military officers responsible for abuses during that country's 'dirty war' were tried and some convictions were returned. But the trials prompted lower ranking officers to unite in their opposition and demand legal protection from prosecution. See Americas Watch, above, n. 4; Amnesty International, *Argentina: The Military Junta and Human Rights: Report of the Trial of the Former Junta Members*, 1987. In Chile, the post-Pinochet government did not challenge the amnesty law passed during the dictatorship that barred prosecution of members of the armed forces for acts committed during the first five years after Pinochet came to power. The government did, however, prosecute those responsible for the murder of the former Chilean Foreign Minister Orlando Letelier and a US citizen in Washington, DC, a crime that was specifically exempted from the amnesty law. Jose Zalaquett, 'Balancing Ethical Imperatives and Political Constraints: The Dilemma of New Democracies Confronting Past Human Rights Violations', 43 *Hastings LJ* 1425, 1436 (1992).

[11] They similarly turned to the various human rights procedures available to them through the United Nations.

[12] See C. Medina, 'The Inter-American Commission on Human Rights and the Inter-American Court of Human Rights: Reflections on a Joint Venture', 12 *Human Rights Quarterly* 439 (1990).

[13] The IACHR has jurisdiction to consider amnesty laws in the exercise of its jurisdiction to examine petitions alleging violations of the American Declaration of Human Rights (see Org. Am. States, Resolution XXII of the Second Special Inter-American Conference, OEA/Ser.E/XIII.I doc. 150 rev. (1965)). It also has jurisdiction to consider petitions alleging violations of the American Convention on Human Rights (American Convention on Human Rights, Arts. 44–51, see Appendix III.

[14] *Velásquez Rodríguez*, I/A Court H.R. Series C No. 4 (1988), 9 *HRLJ* 212.

Santiago in 1991,[15] in which the Organization committed itself to adopting a more active role in promoting democracy throughout the region. Such action has led the Organization's political organs to be more interventionist in contexts involving human rights violations and more accepting of decisions of other regional or international actors where they are acting to end armed conflict or restore democracy. This, in turn, has had an impact on the Commission's response to amnesty measures.

Before *Velásquez Rodríguez*

In a region in which gross violations of human rights have been commonplace, it is no surprise that the OAS, an international organization composed of sovereign states, traditionally placed low priority on measures to remedy those violations. As an organ of the OAS, the Commission has had to balance its mandate and the political environment in which it operates. It also has had to contend with significant budgetary and personnel constraints. For much of its history, the Commission adapted to these circumstances by emphasizing its political functions to investigate and document gross and systematic violations of human rights, through its country report procedure, over its individual petition functions.[16] In its efforts to bring pressure to bear on responsible states to halt such practices, it relied more on moral persuasion and what political influence it could marshal than on legal authority.

By the mid 1980s, new amnesty laws had been adopted in several countries in the region that had been the subject of intensive Commission scrutiny. The Commission thus considered it propitious to examine the issue generally in the context of its evaluation of steps that need to be taken to achieve full observance of human rights in the region. In its 1985-1986 Annual Report, the Commission recognized the difficulties newly democratic states face when they try to balance national reconciliation and

---

[15] Resolution 1080 created an automatic procedure for convening the hemisphere's foreign ministers in the event of a *coup d'état* or other interruption of the legitimately elected government of a member state 'to look into the events collectively and adopt any decisions deemed appropriate'. OEA/Ser.P/AG/doc. 2739/91 rev. 1 (Resolution 1080), adopted 4 June 1991. Resolution 1080 was followed by subsequent action in Washington in 1992 and Managua in 1993. In the Protocol of Washington, OAS members agreed to further amend the OAS Charter to give the General Assembly the power to suspend from membership by a two-thirds vote a government that overthrows a democratic regime. Protocol of Amendments to the Charter of the Organization of American States, 'Protocol of Washington', 15 May 1949, PAULTS 31, adopted at the Sixteenth Special Session of the General Assembly, Dec. 1992. The Declaration of Managua declares the OAS mission is not simply to defend democracy when it is attacked but 'to prevent and anticipate the very causes of the probems that work against democratic rule'. Protocol of Amendments to the Charter of the Organization of American States 'Protocol of Managua', 15 May 1949, PAULTS 31, adopted at the Nineteenth Special Session of the General Assembly, June 1993.

[16] See Medina, above, n. 12, 442–3.

social pacification with exposing the truth and achieving justice.[17] Because of the sensitivity of this issue, it concluded that this was an area in which international bodies could make only a minimal contribution. It did not pronounce on the legality of amnesty laws promulgated by democratically-elected governments. Instead it adopted the view that it was up to the appropriate democratic institutions of the state concerned—usually the legislature—to determine whether and to what extent amnesty was to be granted.[18] The Commission did conclude, however, that self-amnesties proclaimed by non-democratically accountable regimes that had engaged in rights abuses had no juridical validity.[19]

At the same time, the Commission declared that societies had an unconditional right to know the truth about past events, as well as the motives and circumstances that led to them, in order to prevent repetition of such acts in the future.[20] It also declared that family members of victims had the right to information about what had happened to their relatives. To that end, it recommended that states establish committees to undertake whatever investigations are necessary. It concluded 'that the observance of the principles cited above will bring about justice rather than vengeance, and thus neither the urgent need for national reconciliation nor the consolidation of democratic government will be jeopardized'.[21]

Although amnesty measures previously had been adopted by Brazil, Chile, and Honduras, the first country in which the Commission seriously addressed the amnesty question was Guatemala. Human rights violations, including extrajudicial executions and forced disappearances by security forces and paramilitary groups working in collaboration with government authorities,[22] were a frequent feature of Guatemala's long-standing civil war.[23] During the 1980s successive Guatemalan governments attempted to protect security forces from liability for those violations by passing amnesty laws. The first was a decree promulgated by General Efrain Rios Montt shortly after he seized power in March 1982. It granted amnesty for past political and related offenses to persons who applied for it to appropriate

---

[17] IACHR Annual Report 1985–6, 192–3.
[18] Id.   [19] Id.
[20] Id.
[21] Id., 193.
[22] Inter-American Commission on Human Rights, Report on the Situation of Human Rights in Guatemala (1981), 132.
[23] See e.g., Americas Watch, 'Creating a desolation and calling it peace', May 1983 Supplement to the Report on Human Rights in Guatemala, New York: 1984; Americas Watch, 'Guatemala, a Nation of Prisoners', New York: 1984; Americas Watch, 'Little hope: Human Rights in Guatemala, January 1984 to January 1985', New York: 1985; Amnesty Internatioal, 'Memorandum to the Government of Guatemala following an AI mission to the country in April 1985', New York: 1986; Amnesty International, 'Guatemala: the human rights record', London: 1987; Americas Watch, 'Closing the Space: Human Rights in Guatemala, May1987–October 1988', New York: 1988.

civilian or military authorities within thirty days.[24] A similar amnesty decree was passed the following year to cover acts committed during the interim period.[25] Without ruling on their legality under international law, the Commission determined that they did not provide protection for persons responsible for the most serious violations of human rights. It recommended that Guatemala investigate and punish with the full force of the law those responsible for serious violations of human rights.[26]

The Commission was confronted by the amnesty issue again in 1985 when, days before handing over the reins of power to an elected civilian government, the Guatemalan armed forces decreed an automatic amnesty for both private persons and government agents responsible for or accused of having committed political or related crimes between March 23, 1982 and January 14, 1985.[27] The Commission, at that point optimistic about the prospects for democracy in Guatemala, accepted at face value the justification offered by its authors: the amnesty decree is 'geared to create a climate of social peace and to avoid difficulties to the new administration's actions'.[28] In its comments the Commission expressed concern that the law could hinder judicial action to investigate and sanction subversive and anti-subversive terrorist acts and their legacy of serious human rights abuses.[29] But it did not condemn the amnesty outright. Instead, recalling its prior reports on Guatemala, the Commission expressed hope that judicial processes set in motion by human rights groups with respect to the fate of thousands of disappeared persons would result in the investigation and sanctioning of disappearances and other human rights abuses.[30]

On 24 October 1987, the Guatemalan legislature adopted yet another narrowly drafted amnesty law.[31] This time the Commission, now less generously disposed to the elected civilian regime, admonished Guatemala for doing nothing to fulfill its recommendation to investigate cases of forced disappearances.[32] It again reminded Guatemala of its 1983 recommendation to investigate and sanction those responsible for disappearances and other serious human rights abuses.[33]

---

[24] Inter-American Commission on Human Rights, Report on the Situation of Human Rights in Guatemala (1983), 34. See also R. E. Norris, 'Leyes de Impunidad y los Derechos Humanos en las Americas: Una Respuesta Legal', 15 *Revista Instituto Interamericano de Derechos Humanos* 47, 66.   [25] Id.

[26] IACHR Report on Guatemala, above, n. 24, 133.

[27] Annual Report of the IACHR, above, n. 17, 157.   [28] Id.

[29] Id., 157–8.   [30] Id., 161.

[31] This law was justified by Guatemalan authorities as necessary to fulfil Guatemala's obligations under the amnesty provisions of the Arias Plan to establish peace in Central America. Norris above, n. 24. See also, Americas Watch, 'Closing the Space', above, n. 23, 103.

[32] IACHR Annual Report 1986–7, 248. A similar admonishment was made the following year. IACHR Annual Report 1987–8. See also Norris, above, n. 24.

[33] Id.

The Commission's approach to amnesty during this period was more measured than that pressed upon it by human rights lawyers and non-governmental organizations that placed high priority on solidifying states' legal obligation to punish at least the most senior perpetrators of human rights abuses.[34] As advocates for victims, they had difficulty comprehending the Commission's differentiation between self-amnesties decreed by dictators and amnesties enacted through more democratic processes. They argued that states should only have the power to amnesty those who violate the state's sovereignty since in such cases the state's authority to grant amnesty flows from the state's status as victim. Even democratically elected governments lack the authority to amnesty those who violate individual rights, they asserted, because it is the individual, not the state, who is injured.[35] They further argued that the very purpose of non-derogable provisions in human rights treaties is to protect individuals from the tyranny of the majority.[36]

The influence of these lawyers and non-governmental organizations on the Commission is palpable. Even in this early period they convinced the Commission to include provisions imposing on states the duty to investigate and prosecute grave violations in draft treaties relating to the enforcement of physical integrity rights.[37] And, as will be discussed below, they were an important catalyst for the expansion of the Commission's views about amnesty in the post-*Velásquez Rodríguez* context. In sum, even before its legal authority to interpret the American Convention crystallized, the Commission embraced the view that amnesties should not be used as a shield to prevent victims from obtaining information about human rights abuses. It also endorsed the progressive development of international law towards making amnesties illegal. But it stopped short of declaring that a general norm against amnesties existed, opting instead to defer to genuine popular will. This approach gave the Commission a political advantage with new governments trying to grapple with past abuses, and provided a principled rationale for its opposition to self-amnesties.

---

[34] Most of the scholarly literature addressing amnesties at that time supported the duty to prosecute argument. See above, n. 1, 2. But see J. Zalaquet, 'Confronting Human Rights Violations Committed by Former Governments', in The Justice and Society Program of The Aspen Institute, *State Crimes: Punishment or Pardon* (1988); C. S. Niño, 'The Duty to Punish Past Abuses of Human Rights Put Into Context: The Case of Argentina', 100 *Yale LJ* 2619 (1991).

[35] R. K. Goldman, 'Amnesty Laws, International Law and the American Convention on Human Rights', 6 *International Human Rights Law Group Docket* 1 (1989).

[36] See Farer, above, n. 5, 1309.

[37] Inter-American Convention to Prevent and Punish Torture, Inter-American Convention on Forced Disappearance, reprinted in IACHR, *Basic Documents Pertaining to Human Rights in the Inter-American System*, OEA/Ser.L.V/II.90, doc. 31 rev. 2, 22 Sept. 1995.

The *Velásquez Rodríguez* Decision and the Opening it Created

With the entry into force of the American Convention on Human Rights and the establishment of the inter-American Court of Human Rights in 1979, the Commission, still under-funded and inadequately staffed, was called upon to balance an expanded quasi-judicial role with its ongoing investigation and documentation functions. Moreover, while charged with the lion's share of tasks to ensure the protection of human rights in the region, the Commission was no longer the only or most authoritative human rights organ in the inter-American system. The Commission's adjustment to its new circumstances was uneasy and along the way it encountered difficulties both with the Court and with OAS member states. But as the Commission and the Court wrestled with their respective roles each has made accommodations in ways that have increased the confidence of the Commission to adopt tougher recommendations when confronted with popularly-supported amnesty measures.

The Inter-American Court has binding jurisdiction to resolve cases presented to it by the Commission or states that are party to the American Convention on Human Rights that allege violations of the treaty by a state that has accepted the Court's jurisdiction. It also has advisory jurisdiction to interpret the Convention or other treaties concerning the protection of human rights in the American states if so requested by any member state or competent organ of the OAS.[38] To date, the Court has not considered the legality of amnesty laws in either capacity, but has reflected on the duty of states to ensure the full and free exercise of human rights under Article 1(1) of the American Convention.[39]

In April 1986, the Commission submitted to the Court its first trio of contentious cases. These involved four of some 140 cases submitted to the Commission alleging disappearances in Honduras between 1981 and 1984. The Commission found the Government of Honduras responsible for violations of the American Convention on Human Rights based on Honduras' denial of any knowledge of the victims' whereabouts, its unwillingness to investigate, and its failure to cooperate with the Commission.[40]

Since disappearances are not mentioned specifically in the Convention, the Commission asked the Court to determine that Honduras had violated

---

[38] American Convention on Human Rights, Arts. 61–5.

[39] *Velásquez Rodríguez* case, above, n. 14.

[40] J. E. Mendez and J. M. Vivanco, 'Disappearances and the Inter-American Court: Reflections on a Litigation Experience', 13 *Hamline L Rev.* 507, 535 (1990). The Court found the connection between the disappearances of two Costa Ricans and the Honduran government had not sufficienty been proved. *Fairen Garbi and Solis Corrales* Judgment, I/A Court H.R. Series C No. 6 (1989) at para. 158. It then proceeded to consider the merits of the *Velásquez Rodríguez* case, above, n. 14, and the parallel *Godíñez Cruz* case, I/A Court H.R. Series C No. 5 (1989). For convenience, this chapter will refer only to the *Velásquez Rodríguez* case.

Articles 4, 5 and 7 of the Convention which guarantee the right to life, the right to humane treatment, and the right to personal liberty and security. In its decision on the merits in the *Velásquez Rodríguez* case, the Court concluded that these rights must be interpreted alongside Article 1(1) of the Convention which establishes the duty of governments to respect the human rights of individuals and to guarantee the enjoyment of the rights recognized in the Convention. The Court held that under Article 1(1) states have a duty to organize the governmental apparatus so that it is capable of legally ensuring and actually ensures the free and full enjoyment of human rights.[41] As a consequence of this obligation, 'states must prevent, investigate and *punish* any violation of the rights recognized by the Convention. . . .' (emphasis added)[42] Failure to do so may result in a finding that the state is liable for the alleged human rights violations because it failed to perform its duties under Article 1(1).[43]

Despite the Court's repeated reference in its opinion to the duty of states to punish human rights violators, the Court acknowledged, without elaborating, that there might be legitimate circumstances in which states are unable to do so.[44] This unexplained loophole in states' obligation to punish perpetrators is coupled with the Court's determination that states have an absolute obligation to use the means at their disposal to inform relatives of the fate of the victims.[45]

In the *Velásquez Rodríguez* case, the Court did not need to reach the question whether Honduras' breach of the American Convention included its failure to prosecute those responsible for the disappearances, because Honduras' liability was established on the basis of its failure to investigate the crimes at all. Moreover, because Honduras had not raised the defense that its amnesty provisions blocked investigation or punishment, the Court did not consider the effect of such laws.

In the compensation phase of *Velásquez Rodríguez* the representatives of the families asked the Court, in addition to fair compensation, for 'ethical reparation'. Lawyers for the Commission and family members argued that ethical reparation should include an order that the Honduran government conduct an exhaustive investigation and prosecute those responsible for the disappearances.[46] They further argued that Honduras should publicly repudiate the policy of forced disappearances and publicly apologize to the families.[47] The Court rejected these demands on the ground these fell outside the scope of Article 63(1) of the American Convention.[48] It did,

---

[41] *Velásquez Rodríguez*, above, n. 37, paras. 166–7.
[42] Id., para. 166.
[43] Id., para. 182.
[44] Id., para. 181.
[45] Id., para. 181.
[46] Mendez and Vivanco, above, n. 40, 567.
[47] Id.
[48] 'Measures of this sort would constitute part of the reparation for the consequences of the situation in violation of the rights and freedoms, but not of the compensation cited in Article 63.1 of the Covention.' *Velásquez Rodríguez* Compensation Judgment, I/A Court H.R. Series. C No. 7 (1989), at para. 33, 11 *HRLJ* 127.

however, refer to its decision on the merits to remind Honduras of its obligation to prevent, investigate, and punish the perpetrators of violations, and to disclose all information available to the families. The Court held that this duty remains binding until the Honduran government fully complies.[49]

Since *Velásquez Rodríguez*, the Commission routinely has recommended in its reports on individual petitions that states investigate and punish those responsible for the most serious violations of physical integrity rights.[50] The Court has adopted a more mixed approach. In cases in which the government has admitted responsibility for the abuses, the Court has limited itself to determining or supervising the determination of pecuniary damages.[51] The Court has adopted a similar stance in cases in which the government has taken any action to prosecute the alleged perpetrators, even if the result has been an acquittal by a military court with questionable jurisdiction.[52] In one case, however, involving the disappearance of two persons by members of the Colombian army and civilians acting as soldiers, the Court both acknowledged efforts by the Colombian government to prosecute and ordered that reparations include continuation of the judicial proceedings and punishment of those responsible in conformance with Columbian domestic law.[53]

Action by the Commission after *Velásquez Rodríguez* in Petitions Relating to Amnesty Measures

As more and more states passed amnesty laws, the Commission was inundated with petitions from victims alleging that those laws violated their rights to judicial protection. The Commission's first published recommendation on an amnesty provision came in September 1992 in response to a request by petitioners to address El Salvador's reliance on its amnesty provisions to immunize from prosecution members of its security forces implicated in the Las Hojas massacre. On 22 February 1983, approximately 74 people were assassinated near Las Hojas, Sonsonate. Although evidence implicating Salvadoran security forces was overwhelming, El Salvador's

---

[49] *Velásquez Rodríguez*, above, n. 37, at paras. 34–6. See also Mendez and Vivanco, above, n. 40, 569.

[50] *Gangaram Panday* case, I/A Court H.R. Series C No. 16 (1994), 43, 15 *HRLJ* 168, 2 IHRR 360 (1995), *Neira Alegría et al.* case, I/A Court H.R. Series C. No. 20 (1995), 43, 16 *HRLJ* 403, 3 IHRR 362; *Caballero Delgado and Santana* case, I/A Court H.R. Series C No. 22, 61, 17 *HRLI* 24, 3 IHRR 548.

[51] *Aloeboetoe et al.* case, Reparations, I/A Court H.R. Series C No. 15 (1993), 14 *HRLJ* 413.

[52] *El Amparo* case, I/A Court H.R. Series C No. 19 (1995), 16 *HRLJ* 149, 3 IHRR 349 (1996). The Venezuelan military has since promoted one of the officers who was in charge of the battalion that committed the murders. J.-M. Pasqualucci, 'The Inter-American Human Rights System: Establishing Precedents and Procedure in Human Rights Law', 26 *U Miami Inter-Am. L Rev.* 297, 333–4, n. 196 (1995).

[53] *Caballero Delgado and Santana* case, above, n. 50, 87.

Supreme Court concluded that the amnesty law provided complete protection from prosecution for all those who participated.[54]

The Commission, invoking the Court's analysis in *Velásquez Rodríguez*, concluded that the application of the amnesty law constituted a 'clear violation of the obligation of the Salvadoran Government to investigate and punish the violations of the rights of the Las Hojas victims. . . .'[55] Although it did not recommend repeal of the amnesty law, it recommended that El Salvador investigate the events in order to identify all the victims and those responsible, and submit the latter to justice and appropriate sanctions.[56] It also recommended that El Salvador adopt measures necessary to avoid similar acts in the future and that it remedy the consequences of the situation resulting from the violation and pay fair compensation to the family members of the massacre victims.[57] Because El Salvador had not accepted the compulsory jurisdiction of the Inter-American Court, the Commission could not refer the case to the Court. For its part, El Salvador chose not to seek judicial review of the Commission's recommendation.

A week later the Commission issued recommendations with respect to amnesty laws in two other countries—Argentina and Uruguay. Following the restoration of democracy in 1983, President Raúl Alfonsín moved quickly to establish accountability for the grave violations of human rights, including the forced disappearance of at least 10,000 people, committed under the prior military regime. He established the independent National Commission on Disappeared Persons (CONADEP) to investigate the fate of the disappeared, nullified a self-amnesty law passed by the military before leaving office, passed other laws and ratified treaties aimed at preventing any recurrence of abuses, and set in motion the legal steps that would lead to the trials of nine senior commanders alleged to be responsible.[58]

The trial, which occurred in the summer of 1985, was held in public and was widely regarded as procedurally fair. In a lengthy decision issued on 9 December 1985, the court found that the dictatorship had discharged a deliberate, concerted policy of covert repression, including the use of murder, forced disappearance, torture and prolonged arbitrary detention, as its principle weapon in its campaign to defeat subversion. Five of the generals were convicted and sentenced to prison terms. A year later the Supreme Court upheld the lower court's decision. Subsequently several other senior military officers were tried.[59]

---

[54] *Massacre Las Hojas* v. *El Salvador*, Case 10.287, Report No. 26/92 (24 Sept. 1992), IACHR Annual Report 1992–3, 83.
[55] Id.   [56] Id., Conclusion 5(a).
[57] Id.
[58] Americas Watch, above, n. 4; Amnesty International, above, n. 10.
[59] Id.

As it became clear that trials would not stop with the most senior officers, the military initiated a campaign of intimidation aimed at preventing further trials of those responsible for human rights abuses. Yielding to the pressure, President Alfonsín first pushed through Congress 'full stop' legislation that set a deadline on the filing of cases that could lead to the prosecution of persons accused of human rights violations during the prior regime.[60] Instead of its intended effect of bringing the process to an end, that bill encouraged prosecutors, human rights groups, and relatives of victims to move more rapidly to file cases. This, in turn, increased the apprehension of military officers that they would face trial. Succumbing to threats of a coup over the issue, President Alfonsín sent to Congress a statute permitting military officers the absolute defense of due obedience to superior orders. That statute effectively barred all pending and future prosecutions.[61]

In late 1987, in the wake of these laws, victims of human rights abuses began filing petitions with the Commission alleging violations of their right to judicial protection and to a fair trial under the American Convention. In all, six cases involving multiple petitioners were consolidated for consideration. All alleged that the statutes that curtailed and ultimately extinguished criminal proceedings for egregious violations of human rights during the 'dirty war' violated the Convention.[62] Argentina replied that inasmuch as the cases involved rights violations that had occurred prior to Argentina's ratification of the American Convention, they were time-barred.[63] This argument was rejected by the Commission.

The Commission began its examination of the merits of petitioners' claims by referring to Article 29 of the Convention which precludes a state party from using its laws to restrict or suppress any of the rights guaranteed in the Convention. It then considered the alleged violations of petitioners' right to a fair trial under Article 8(1) of the Convention. The Commission noted that Argentine domestic law provides the victim of a crime with the right to initiate a criminal prosecution. It further cited Article 1(1) of the Convention which obliges state parties 'to respect the rights and freedoms recognized herein and to ensure to all persons subject to their jurisdiction the free and full exercise of those rights and freedoms. . . .' The Commission concluded that Argentina's amnesty laws obstructed petitioners' full

---

[60] 'Full Stop' Law, No. 23,492, 24 Dec. 1986, reprinted in 8 *HRLJ* 476 (1987).

[61] 'Due Obedience' Law, No. 23,521, enacted 8 June 1987, reprinted in 8 *HRLJ* 477 (1987). Alfonsín's successor, President Menem, went further and pardoned everyone still facing prosecution or convicted for political crimes associated with Argentina's 'dirty war'. Presidential Decree of Pardon No. 1002, 7 Oct. 1989.

[62] IACHR Annual Report 1992–3, 41 Report No. 28/92—Cases 10.147, 10.181, 10.240, 10.262, 10.309, and 10.311 (Argentina), 2 Oct. 1992, reprinted in 13 *HRLJ* 336 (1992).

[63] Id., para. 7. Argentina ratified the Convention on 5 Sept. 1984, after democratically-elected government was restored.

exercise of their right to a fair trial under the Convention.[64] It further found that Argentina had violated petitioners' right to seek a judicial remedy under Article 25(2).[65] Finally, referring to the Court's interpretation of Article 1(1) in *Velásquez Rodríguez*, the Commission found that Argentina had failed to fulfill its legal duty to investigate and punish any violation of the rights recognized in the Convention.[66]

The Commission recommended that Argentina pay the petitioners just compensation for its violations of Articles 1, 8 and 25 of the Convention, and that it adopt measures necessary to clarify the facts and identity those responsible for the human rights violations that occurred during the past military dictatorship.[67] It did not, however, call upon Argentina to repeal the amnesty legislation.

That same day, the Commission announced its decision in eight consolidated petitions brought by victims of human rights abuses in Uruguay who similarly alleged that that country's amnesty laws violated Articles 8 and 25 of the American Convention on Human Rights.[68] State terror in the form of widespread suppression of civil and political rights and the routine use of torture, and incommunicado and prolonged arbitrary detention gripped Uruguay several years ahead of Argentina. While the practice of disappearances never emerged on a large scale, at the height of the repression Amnesty International reported that Uruguay had the highest per capita incidence of torture and political prisoners of any country in the world.[69]

The military's grip on state power was eroded in November 1980 when the country's population voted overwhelmingly against a draft constitution that would have provided legal justification for the rights abuses committed by the regime. Four years later, after intensive negotiations between the generals and civilian politicians they hand-picked, the military permitted elections to restore civilian control of the government.

Upon assuming office, democratically-elected President Sanguinetti made no effort to prosecute military leaders responsible for rights abuses.[70] Yet many victims, accustomed from the pre-dictatorship era to seeking remedies for wrongs from an independent judiciary, lodged complaints

---

[64] Id., paras. 32–7.   [65] Id., paras. 38–9.

[66] Id., para. 40.   [67] Id.

[68] Like their Argentine counterparts, the Uruguayan petitioners could not petition under the American Convention on Human Rights for the underlying human rights violations they suffered because Uruguay was not party to the treaty at the time the acts occurred. The treaty entered into force for Uruguay on 19 Apr. 1985.

[69] See L. Weschler, *A Miracle, A Universe* (New York, 1990).

[70] According to some reports, the subject of amnesty was not raised during the negotiations that led up to the elections. Other reports suggest that during the negotiations Sanguinetti adopted the view that while he had no plans to prosecute, he would not interfere with efforts by private citizens to seek redress through normal judicial means. Id., 166–7.

against specific officers alleging torture and other rights abuses. As it became clear that these cases would be prosecuted seriously, the military put pressure on President Sanguinetti to seek a blanket amnesty.[71] Although not technically an amnesty statute, in December 1986 Uruguay's Congress adopted a law that effectively canceled all trials against perpetrators of human rights violations during the dictatorship.[72] Uruguayans opposed to the de facto amnesty succeeded in putting the impunity statute to a referendum. In response, the military waged a campaign of intimidation aimed at defeating it. Although the referendum to overturn the statute was defeated, its margin of failure was modest.

With judicial remedies in Uruguay foreclosed first by the statute and then by the referendum, victims of human rights violations turned to the Commission for a remedy for the denial of their right to seek recourse in Uruguayan courts. Uruguay replied that the Commission should view the amnesty question in the political context of national reconciliation,[73] the need for which was ratified by the majority of the country's population in the referendum.[74] It further pointed out that unlike in Argentina, individuals cannot initiate criminal prosecutions against alleged perpetrators of crimes and that the statute did not impair the right of individuals to seek damages.

In finding the Uruguayan law in violation of Article 8 of the American Convention, the Commission considered not only the possible outcomes of criminal prosecutions but the value of knowing the truth about past events in order to prevent their repetition.[75] It determined that where a state does not establish an alternative investigatory mechanism, it lies with the courts to undertake the investigations necessary 'to establish the crimes denounced and to identify their authors, accomplices, and accessories after the fact'.[76]

In addition, the Commission noted that while individuals cannot initiate indictments in Uruguay, victims do actively participate in criminal proceedings beyond the indictment phase. By reading Article 8 of the American

---

[71] Weschler, above, n. 69.

[72] Ley de Caducidad de la Pretensíon Punitiva del Estado (Law Declaring an Expiration of the State's Punitive Authority). The text of the statute is reproduced in the decision of the IACHR Annual Report 1992–3, 154 Report No. 29/92, Cases 10.029, 10.036, 10.145, 10.305, 10.372, 10.373, 10.374, and 10.375—Uruguay—2 Oct. 1992, reprinted in 13 *HRLJ* 340 (1992).

[73] In arguments before the IACHR, Uruguay argued that it was entitled to a broad margin of appreciation in how best to fulfill its legal commitments, and that in its opinion the best means for preventing future violations of human rights was to consolidate elected government. Uruguay contended that the amnesty legislation was necessary to further this consolidation. Farer, above, n. 5, 1308–9.

[74] Uruguay's electoral system makes voting mandatory. Thus the votes cast genuinely represent the views of its citizenry.

[75] IACHR Report, above, n. 72, citing its earlier Annual Report 1985–6, 205.

[76] IACHR Report, above, n. 72.

Convention with Article 1(1), it found that Uruguay's law denied victims the full and free exercise of this right. It also found a violation of the right to judicial protection guaranteed by Article 25(1).[77]

With respect to the obligation to investigate, the Commission reached a similar conclusion to that reached in the Argentine case. It found no mitigation of the violation in the fact that the statute did not apply to civil actions. To the contrary, it pointed out that although still possible, civil actions had been frustrated because vital testimony from military and police personnel could not be adduced or used.[78]

The Commission did not confront directly Uruguay's argument that the statute was legally sustainable because it had been ratified by the majority of the country's population. By this time, the Commission was convinced by the arguments of human rights lawyers and non-governmental organizations that the process by which amnesty was granted was not significant to determining the legal validity of the amnesty under the American Convention. Had it addressed Uruguay's arguments, the Commission would have had to disclaim its past view that it was up to the appropriate democratic institutions of the state concerned to determine whether and to what extent amnesty was to be awarded.[79] Moreover, states throughout the region, the Inter-American Court, and intergovernmental negotiation processes such as the Arias Peace Plan had embraced the view that it was up to newly established democracies to resolve issues of impunity. As a subordinate organ of the OAS, the Commission must have perceived substantial political and legal constraints against finding Uruguay's democratically-supported amnesty illegal.

Thus, the Commission did not recommend that Uruguay rescind its amnesty law. Further, in both the Uruguayan and Argentine cases, it stopped short of recommending that those responsible for the abuses be punished. Instead it limited itself in each case to recommending that the government 'adopt the measures necessary to clarify the facts and identify those responsible for the human rights violations'.[80]

---

[77] Robert Weiner argues that by making a states' international law obligations concerning amnesties dependent on its domestic laws governing the extent to which individuals can participate in the criminal process, the Commission may have placed itself in the position of having to reach conflicting results on similar amnesty provisions solely on the basis of whether a State's domestic law provides victims an opportunity to so participate. R. Weiner, 'Trying to Make Ends Meet: Reconciling the Law and Practice of Human Rights Amnesties', 26 *St. Mary's LJ* 857, 867, n. 37 (1995). [78] IACHR Report, above, n. 72, para. 53.

[79] See above, n. 17 and accompanying text.

[80] IACHR Report, above, n. 62, Recommendation 3; IACHR Report, above, n. 72, Recommendation 3. One commentator has suggested that the Commission may have stopped short of doing so to make it easier for the new democracies to comply with its recommendations and therefore avoid pressure to send the cases to the Inter-American Court. She further suggests that the Commission's recommendation that the government submit those responsible to justice in the Las Hojas Massacre case may have been made easier by the fact that El Salvador had not accepted the Court's compulsory jurisdiction. Pasqualucci, above, n. 52, 362.

Moreover, although both Argentina and Uruguay had accepted the Court's compulsory jurisdiction, the Commission did not refer either case to the Court. One commentator surmised that the Commission may have been concerned that had it done so it would have placed the Court, with its binding jurisdiction and its supreme responsibility for interpreting inter-American human rights law, in the awkward position of having to choose between barring fledgling civilian governments that were trying to ease out from under abusive military rule from granting amnesty, and wiping away without legal process crimes that deprived thousands of basic human rights.[81] He reasoned that perhaps the Commission decided that allowing international practice to continue under its watchful eye, in the hope that it would 'voluntarily' evolve in the right direction, was preferable to risking losing the issue by submitting it for a final determination by the Court.[82] Political sensitivity about taking two of the region's newest democracies, and, with respect to Argentina, one of the region's more powerful states, to the Court for human rights violations may also have played a part in the decision not to seek a judicial resolution.

The fact that at the time the Argentine and Uruguayan cases were decided the Court had issued rulings only in the Honduran disappearances cases, and was thus largely an unknown quantity where contentious cases were concerned, may have added to the Commission's wariness.

Nonetheless, under the same conditions, the Commission sent the *Aloeboetoe* case to the Court, even though one aspect of that case involved a challenge to an amnesty measure introduced by Suriname. Following a 1980 military coup, Suriname's armed forces were responsible for numerous acts of extrajudicial execution and torture. In one incident, soldiers detained seven unarmed Bushnegroes (Maroons), forcibly dragged them out of a military vehicle at a remote roadside, made them dig their own graves, shot them and left them for dead. One of the seven, who was wounded but escaped, survived long enough to provide eyewitness evidence of the assault.

After the Commission had begun to consider the victims' petition, Suriname adopted an amnesty law that protected members of the armed forces from prosecution for acts committed between 1 January 1985 and 4 June 1989.[83] On 15 May 1990, the Commission adopted a recommendation in *Aloeboetoe* in which it found Suriname in breach of its obligations under the American Convention and recommended that the government investigate the case, try and punish those responsible, take measures to prevent similar violations, and pay just compensation to the families. When Suriname failed to reply to the Commission, it sent the case to the Court.[84] In

---

[81] Weiner, above, n. 77, 868.   [82] Id., 869.
[83] Norris, above, n. 24, 108.   [84] Id.

its memorial, the Commission challenged Suriname's right to invoke its amnesty laws as a defense against fulfilling its international obligations. The Court, however, was never seized of the amnesty issue because at its first preliminary hearing on the case the government of Suriname announced that it accepted full responsibility for the alleged violations. The jurisdiction of the Court was thereby limited to determining damages.[85]

Following publication of the Commission's recommendations with respect to their amnesty laws, Uruguay and Argentina, while evading a judicial determination of the legality of their amnesty measures, tried to undermine the persuasive force of the Commission's recommendations by requesting an advisory opinion from the Inter-American Court. The two countries asked the Court to determine the extent to which the Commission had jurisdiction to interpret the legality of domestic legislation. The Court interpreted this request to refer, in part, to the Commission's authority to interpret whether a domestic law violates the international obligations assumed by the state by virtue of a treaty. In a decision that substantially bolstered the Commission's confidence in its authority to interpret the Convention, the Court concluded that this is something 'the Commission can and should do upon examining the communications and petitions submitted to it concerning violations of human rights and freedoms protected by the Convention.'[86]

While the Commission has yet to issue a blanket determination that all amnesties are illegal, its recommendations in response to individual petitions reveal that it is close to adopting this view. Political and institutional considerations, however, continue to be a barrier to the Commission's comprehensive assertion of this proposition.

AMNESTIES IN THE CONTEXT OF ENDING ARMED CONFLICT OR RESTORING DEMOCRACY

The Commission's greatest challenge in responding to amnesty laws has come in cases in which those laws have been given the imprimatur of legitimacy by regional or intergovernmental actors whose aims are to end armed conflict or restore democracy. In Central America and Haiti, the OAS' political organs have either relinquished or shared decision-making authority with such other actors, and in both places amnesty to perpetrators of serious violations of human rights was accepted as part of the cost for peace and democracy. In the context of such cases, the Commission, in exercising its functions to investigate and document human rights abuses,

---

[85] Id., 109.
[86] *Certain Attributes of the Inter-American Commission on Human Rights* (Arts. 41, 42, 44, 47, 50, and 51 of the American Convention on Human Rights), Advisory Opinion No. 13 I/A Court H.R. Series A No. 13 (1993), 36, 14 *HRLJ* 252, 1–2 IHRR 197 (1994).

has had to maneuver within these political constraints. This has resulted in the appearance of inconsistency where Commission recommendations in this sphere of activity are less forceful than those taken in the exercise of its quasi-judicial duties.

On 7 August 1987, in Esquipulas, Guatemala, the Presidents of Costa Rica, El Salvador, Guatemala, El Salvador and Nicaragua pledged themselves to a common procedure for ending conflict and establishing a lasting peace in war-torn Central America.[87] Under the agreement, the parties promised an 'improvement of representative and pluralist democratic systems', and 'authentic political processes of a democratic nature based on justice, freedom, and democracy'.[88] The agreement also included a loosely-worded amnesty provision, one major purpose of which was to ensure that prisoners held by the irregular forces of the respective countries would be liberated.[89] Shortly thereafter the governments of Nicaragua, Guatemala,[90] El Salvador, and Honduras[91] passed amnesty laws.

In Central America, the amnesty issue was complicated by the fact that in each case, despite differences in extent, intensity, and duration, both parties to the armed conflicts had committed serious violations of human rights or humanitarian law. By including amnesties in the peace agreements, the parties in effect pardoned each other in the interests of peace.[92] In addition, by the end of the 1980s, not only had the wars exacted an enormous toll on the civilian population, but they were an impediment to improved regional cooperation in a post-Cold War era. There was thus great motivation on the part of intergovernmental organizations, other states, and nongovernmental organizations to temper criticism of domestically declared amnesties that included persons responsible for gross violations of human rights and humanitarian law.[93] This was so even though the amnesties effectively deprived civilian victims of avenues for redress.

---

[87] J. L. Moore, Jr., 'Problems with Forgiveness: Granting Amnesty under the Arias Plan in Nicaragua and El Salvador', 43 *Stan. L Rev.* 733, 734 (1991).

[88] Id.   [89] IACHR Annual Report 1988–9, 218.

[90] The IACHR's response to Guatemala's 1987 amnesty law is examined above, n. 22 and accompanying text.

[91] Honduras did not refer explicitly to the Arias Peace Plan in its amnesty law, nor did the IACHR publicly criticize Honduras for this amnesty. According to the National Commissioner for Human Rights, whose office was established in 1992 to study and report on human rights abuses in Honduras, the amnesty laws passed by the Honduran military 'do not expressly prohibit the trial and punishment of military or security personnel implicated in disappearances'. Preliminary Report on Disappearances of the National Commissioner for the Protection of Human Rights in Honduras: *The Facts Speak for Themselves* (1994) at 234–5, discussed in Pasqualucci, above, n. 52, 343.   [92] Farer, above, n. 5, 1306.

[93] Some NGOs, particularly Americas Watch, were unequivocal in their insistence that the Arias Peace Plan amnesty provision had to be interpreted consistent with each government's obligation to promote human rights and punish those quickly of torture, murder, rape or disappearance. But even these tended to bury that criticism in the back pages of their reports. Cf., Americas Watch, *Human Rights in Nicaragua: August 1987 to August 1988* (New York: 1988), 80–2.

Nicaragua

In Nicaragua, the Arias Peace Plan led to an end to the fighting and to talks mediated by the Archbishop of Managua and Joao Baena Soares, Secretary General of the OAS. But here the amnesty issue took the reverse form to that in other countries in the region; the Sandinista government was reluctant to honor the amnesty provisions called for in the Arias Plan and had to be pushed by human rights activists and intergovernmental organizations to do so. With time, Nicaragua declared a general amnesty for the approximately 1600 prisoners held in Nicaragua's prisons and accused of Contra activity. But there was no ambiguity that amnesty for the Contras was traded for an end to their US support; rather the Sandinistas timed prisoner releases to coincide with funding decisions by the US Congress.[94]

The Sandinista government was even more reluctant to amnesty prisoners serving sentences for crimes amounting to human rights and humanitarian law violations committed by Somoza's National Guard before July 1979. These prisoners had been tried and convicted by Special Tribunals that had been repeatedly criticized by the Commission as lacking validity under international law. An agreement finally was reached to enlist the Commission to review these prisoners' cases and distinguish between those in which, notwithstanding the irregularities inherent in the Special Tribunals, there was overwhelming evidence of serious human rights violations, and those in which the evidence was insufficient to justify conviction. The Commission efficiently completed this review and recommended amnesty for the latter, and judicial review by Nicaragua's regular courts for the former. The government, some months after receipt of the Commission's report, freed most of those prisoners whose release the Commission recommended.[95] Then, before leaving office, the Sandinistas freed all remaining political prisoners and made the amnesty complete by granting an amnesty to all officials for crimes committed in public office.[96] This self-amnesty remains intact and has not publicly been criticized by the Commission.

El Salvador

In El Salvador, President Duarte enthusiastically pushed through a broad, 'forgive and forget' amnesty law immediately after signing the Arias Peace

---

[94] Moore, above, n. 87, 746.

[95] In March 1989 the government freed all but 39 of the prisoners recommended by the IACHR for release. It released the remaining 39 in February 1990 after an appeal from Cardinal Obando Bravo to release them in advance of the 1990 presidential elections.

[96] Moore, above, n. 87, 758.

Plan. Yet there, neither the regional negotiations nor the amnesty served to promote peace. To the contrary, afterwards both the war and indiscriminate human rights abuses escalated. Following the murder of six Jesuit priests and a renewed FMLN offensive in November 1989, it became clear to all parties that neither side had the capacity to win militarily and negotiations ensued. Both sides asked the United Nations Secretary General to assist them negotiate a settlement of the conflict and eliminate its root causes. In July 1990, the parties to the conflict signed the San José Agreement on Human Rights which called for an end to attempts on the life, integrity, security or freedom for the individual, an end to disappearances and the punishment of persons found guilty of such acts, and the establishment of a United Nations verification mission, ONUSAL, to oversee the human rights situation.[97] The following year, in an accord signed in Mexico City, the parties agreed to the establishment of an international truth commission composed of independent experts under the auspices of the United Nations and pledged to comply with its recommendations.[98]

The Truth Commission's report, which was released on 15 March 1993, sparked an outcry from senior military officers and government officials, the President of the Supreme Court, and other targets of the report who vehemently rejected the Commission's findings and recommendations. Fear was voiced that the report would provoke violence and destabilize the peace process and ONUSAL forces received anonymous threats.[99] President Alfredo Cristiani sought to defuse the situation by announcing a general amnesty in the following terms:

> . . . one also has to consider that the Report of the Truth Commission examines only a part of everything that happened in all those years of violence. . . . What is most important now is to see what has to be done to erase, eliminate and forget everything in the past. . . . Therefore, we are again calling upon all sectors in the country to support a general and absolute amnesty so that we can turn that painful page in our history and seek a better future for our country.[100]

On 20 March 1993, the Salvadoran Legislative Assembly passed a law that grants a 'full, absolute and unconditional amnesty' to all those who prior to 1 January 1992 participated in the commission of political crimes or common crimes linked to broadly defined political crimes.[101]

---

[97] M. Popkin, 'El Salvador: A Negotiated End to Impunity?' in N. Roht-Arrieza, *Impunity and Human Rights in International Law and Practice* (Oxford, 1995), 201.

[98] IACHR Annual Report 1994, Report of the Situation of Human Rights in El Salvador; The United Nations Blue Book Series, Vol. IV, The United Nations and El Salvador: 1990–1995 (UN Pub., 1995).

[99] Id. (United Nations Report), 37.

[100] Address of President Duarte, 18 March 1993. Cited in IACHR Annual Report 1994, Report on the Situation of Human Rights in El Salvador, 69.

[101] Id., citing General Amnesty Law for the Consolidation of Peace, Decree 486.

In its strongest response to any amnesty measure, the Commission condemned El Salvador's amnesty as incompatible with its obligations under international law. In a message to the Salvadoran Government on 26 March 1993—before the deadline for a presidential veto of the Amnesty Law—the Commission underscored that under Article 27 of the Vienna Convention on the Law of Treaties, a state cannot unilaterally invoke provisions of its domestic law as justification for its failure to perform the legal obligations imposed by an international treaty. The Commission further pointed out that, both as a matter of international law and domestic constitutional law, because El Salvador was a party to the American Convention prior to passing the amnesty law, the former prevailed.[102] It also quoted from the Court's decision in *Velásquez Rodríguez*: 'if the state apparatus acts in such a way that the violation goes unpunished . . . the state has failed to comply with its duties to ensure the free and full exercise of those rights to the persons within its jurisdiction.'

In a report on the Situation of Human Rights in El Salvador issued the following year, the Commission took an even harsher view of the amnesty law. It emphasized, in particular, how the law undermines the recommendations in the Truth Commission's report aimed at preventing the recurrence of such events.[103] It particularly condemned those provisions of the amnesty law that extinguished civil liability because they undermined the ability of victims to discover the truth in particular cases and to obtain reparations.[104] In its 1994 Annual Report, the Commission went a step further and recommended that 'the Salvadoran Government take the necessary steps to repeal the amnesty law in order to investigate and punish those responsible for violating the basic rights of persons and to compensate the victims.'[105]

The Commission undoubtedly felt it had the political flexibility to be so critical because El Salvador's amnesty was so broad it undermined subsequent truth determination, private access to judicial remedies, and reparations. The amnesty also embarrassed the United Nations which had been enlisted to assist El Salvador make the transition from armed conflict to genuine democracy.

Haiti

The intervention of the OAS, the United Nations, and the United States government largely preempted Commission action with respect to the

---

[102] Art. 144, para. 2 of the Salvadoran Constitution states that 'the law shall not modify or derogate that agreed upon in a treaty in effect in El Salvador. In the event of a conflict between the treaty and the law, the treaty will prevail.'

[103] IACHR Annual Report 1994, Report on El Salvador, above, n. 100. See also 1992–3 IACHR Annual Report, 185.

[104] Id., 71.   [105] IACHR Annual Report 1994, 181.

amnesty measures promulgated in Haiti. Following the ouster of President Aristide on 30 September 1991, the OAS Foreign Ministers held an emergency session, in accordance with the Santiago Commitment to Democracy, in which they refused to recognize the new government and instituted a trade embargo. These measures were backed by the United Nations. As time passed, reports documenting human rights atrocities in Haiti and the refugee crisis it precipitated, caused the two organizations to step up their efforts to pressure the government to step down. In late 1992, the UN and the OAS jointly named former Argentine Foreign Minister Dante Caputo to mediate between the de facto military regime and the Haitian government in exile. During negotiations Haiti's military rulers made it clear that they would not budge from power without amnesty. While Aristide was reluctant, an amnesty provision was inserted into the 3 July 1993 Governors Island Agreement.

The Haitian military's failure to comply with the terms of the Governor's Island Agreement did not dampen the willingness of either the intergovernmental organizations or the US government to exchange amnesty for the restoration of democracy in Haiti. Indeed, US officials have acknowledged that during August and September 1993, they presented the de facto government with drafts of amnesty laws that covered not just crimes against the state but also serious human rights abuses against civilians.[106]

Even when international exasperation with the Haitian military reached such a pitch that the Security Council authorized an invasion of Haiti, amnesty remained negotiable. Indeed it was in exchange for a gilded amnesty that included transport to a new home in Panama on a US-supplied jet, the release of restrictions on access to their US bank accounts, and other financial favors that Haiti's military leaders ceded power thereby preventing armed intervention.[107]

The Clinton administration justified the deal cut by its negotiating team led by former President Carter on the grounds that by ridding Haiti of the leaders of the military regime, the new government would avoid the politically destabilizing effects of trials. But President Clinton was clearly more concerned about the political consequences of putting US troops in Haiti without the consent of the military regime, especially given the loss of life and extended occupation that probably would have resulted.[108]

A subsequent amnesty law adopted by the Haitian legislature was ambiguously limited to 'political matters,' and President Aristide announced at the time that he would not grant amnesty to anyone engaged in

---

[106] M. Scharf, 'Swapping Amnesty for Peace: Was There a Duty to Prosecute International Crimes in Haiti?', 31 *Texas J Int'l. Law* 1, 7 (1996).

[107] Id., 9.

[108] Id.

'general or criminal actions'.[109] In practice, while there have been a handful of trials in absentia for persons accused of political assassination, the amnesty has been very broad.[110] But it does not extend to private lawsuits against members of the military regime and it is coupled with other healing measures including a truth commission, purges of military officers, and a program of victim compensation.[111]

Since the signing of the Governor's Island Agreement, the Commission has been circumspect about calling for prosecutions of those responsible for human rights crimes in Haiti. In its 1994 Report on the Situation of Human Rights in Haiti, it urged, as a measure to protect the population from abuses by the military, the substantial reform of Haiti's legal system so that perpetrators of criminal acts could be brought to justice. But it made no mention of the amnesty provision in the Governor's Island Agreement.[112]

After President Aristide was restored to power, the Commission noted that the Haitian military denied victims of human rights violations their right to a fair trial guaranteed by the American Convention. It did not, however, call for trials or repudiation of the amnesty. Instead it underscored the government's inescapable duty to investigate and determine responsibility for human rights violations during the dictatorship and praised the government's decision to establish a Truth Commission.[113]

In the Haitian case, the Commission must certainly have been influenced by the widespread international support for the amnesty bargain. The short-term advantages of offering amnesty were undeniable. Haiti was rid of abusive military rulers and benefitted from the restoration of a democratic government that had broad international support and the necessary technical assistance to institute the reforms needed to consolidate democracy. The United States avoided a controversial extended troop deployment and halted a refugee crisis at a time of high anti-immigrant sentiment. The UN and OAS benefitted from the favorable publicity associated with bringing a lingering crisis to a positive conclusion. The Commission was able, in the exercise of its quasi-judicial functions in the Argentina, Uruguay and Las Hojas, El Salvador cases, to assert that those states have a duty under the American Convention to prosecute and punish persons responsible for human rights abuses. But such a recommendation was beyond its reach in the Haitian case even though Haiti ratified the American Convention in 1977 and legally is bound by the same obligations under the treaty as other states. In Haiti, the Commission had to function

---

[109] Id., 17, citing K. Freed and M. Fineman, 'Haitian Senate Sends Amnesty Bill to Aristide', *Los Angeles Times*, 8 Oct. 1994, at A12.
[110] Id., 18.   [111] Id., 28.
[112] IACHR Report on the Situation of Human Rights in Haiti (1994), 152.
[113] IACHR Report on the Situation of Human Rights in Haiti (1995), 81, 97.

in a political environment in which an immediate solution was valued over the long-term benefits of trials for perpetrators of serious human rights violations. Politics thus militated against any public call for rescission of the amnesty.

CONCLUSION

Although they have come close to doing so, the Inter-American Commission and Court have been reticent to declare illegal all amnesties for perpetrators of human rights abuses. On the record to date, states have an absolute obligation to investigate the truth about past violations of human rights, including identifying those responsible, and to share their findings with victims. They also have an obligation to provide victims with judicial remedies or other means to obtain meaningful reparation. Of course, if a state has ratified a treaty that requires the prosecution of persons who are responsible for specific types of human rights abuses, that treaty obligation must be honored.

While self-amnesties by dictatorial regimes have been declared juridically null by the Commission, amnesties adopted essentially at gunpoint by democratically-elected bodies have stood uncriticized. Even amnesties adopted by popular referendum have not been declared illegal. Instead, where such amnesties have been found to violate rights in the American Convention, the state concerned has only been called upon to pay reparation for the Convention violations, not to repeal the amnesty.

Mutual amnesties between parties to an armed conflict, on the other hand, have been encouraged, even though these tend to have the effect of relieving persons who engaged in serious violations of human rights or humanitarian law from responsibility for their acts. However, mutual amnesties that are so broad as to undermine truth investigations, private access to judicial remedies, or reparations, or that have caused embarrassment to international actors enlisted to assist the state concerned make the transition from armed conflict to genuine democracy, go too far and are likely to be declared illegal.

The human rights organs of the inter-American system are not finished with this question. In a development shortly before this volume went to press, the Commission issued its report in response to a petition challenging Chile's amnesty decree which was adopted by the Junta on 19 April 1978. Decree Law No. 2191 is a blanket amnesty law covering most crimes from the September 1973 coup through 10 March 1978.[114] This law and numerous other laws which transferred vital state-controlled evidence

---

[114] The amnesty decree did not apply to most common crimes nor to those individuals involved in the car-bomb assassination in Washington, DC of former Chilean foreign minister

about human rights abuses out of civilian control were made preconditions for transferring power to elected civilians.[115]

In 1978, the Relatives of Disappeared Detainees, a non-governmental organization, grouped together seventy of the best-documented cases and submitted them together to a civilian court. The cases were transferred to military jurisdiction (Segundo Juzgado Militar de Santiago) where they languished for eleven years. Finally, on 30 November 1989, the military tribunal closed thirty-five of the cases by declaring the Amnesty Law excused the crimes.[116] Plaintiffs then presented a special petition to the Chilean Supreme Court seeking a declaration that the amnesty law was unconstitutional.

President Aylwin took office on 11 March 1990. The following month he announced the creation of a special eight-member commission to investigate the truth about grave violations of human rights committed during the Pinochet dictatorship. Chile ratified the American Convention on 21 August 1990.[117] Three days later, the Supreme Court unanimously upheld the constitutionality of the amnesty law, stating that the law terminated the judicial investigative process.[118] With their domestic remedies exhausted, the Relatives of Disappeared Detainees turned to the Commission, which responded favourably. Whittling away at its previous willingness to tolerate amnesties adopted by democratically-elected bodies, the Commission declared that failure to revoke an amnesty decree issued by a usurping regime violated the American Convention. It therefore called upon Chile to 'amend its domestic legislation so that violations of human rights by the "de facto" military government may be investigated, with a view to identifying the guilty parties, establishing their responsibilities and effectively prosecuting them, thereby guaranteeing to the victims and their families [their] right to justice. . . .'[119]

On 14 June 1995, Peru's legislature adopted a comprehensive amnesty law absolving those in the security forces who committed human rights abuses while combatting terrorism between May 1980 and June 1995.[120] In addition, the law cleared the records of security forces personnel who had already been convicted of human rights abuses. The law was adopted in a summary manner without full notice or Congressional debate, yet it has

---

Orlando Letelier and his associate Ronnie Moffit. R. J. Quinn, 'Note: Will the Rule of Law End? Challenging Grants of Amnesty for the Human Rights Violations of Prior Regime: Chile's New Model', 62 *Fordham L Rev.* 905, 913 (1994).

[115] Id.

[116] Id., 919.

[117] See 30 *ILM* 575 (1991).

[118] Suprema Declaro Constitucional Decreto Ley de Amnistia del 78, *El Mercurio*, 25 Aug. 1990.

[119] Report No. 36/96, Case 10.843, 15 Oct. 1996, in IACHR Annual Report (1996).

[120] US State Department Country Reports, Peru, Mar. 1996.

since been upheld by Peru's Supreme Court, and judicial challenges of the amnesty's scope have been barred by a second law.[121] The Commission condemned these laws but in doing so did not reconsider the political circumstances under which such laws may be passed.

Finally, now that comprehensive peace accords ending Guatemala's thirty-six-year long civil war have been realized, the Commission is likely to be faced, in its investigation and documentation functions, if not through the petition process, with the question of amnesty for past violations of human rights in Guatemala. The amnesty question, which was deliberately omitted from the final peace accord, was resolved ambiguously by the legislature in December 1996. The Law of National Reconciliation extinguishes penal responsibility for crimes committed during the prolonged conflict. While it contains a provision declaring that it does not apply to genocide, torture, forced disappearances or acts not reasonably and objectively related to a bone fide war effort, that provision is not fully tested.[122] Moreover, the previous laws that grant amnesty to the military for political crimes committed between 1982 and 1986 remain in force.[123] Even if the political will to punish criminal acts by Guatemalan military and police officials is present at the moment,[124] dissent from officers who until now have enjoyed impunity remains a threat that hangs over a permanent transition from war to peace.[125]

Ultimately, however, the legality of amnesties in the Americas is likely to be determined not by impartial human rights bodies like the Commission and the Court, but as a result of the political decisions of sovereign states. While the Commission has been forceful in asserting that states have a legal obligation to punish perpetrators of human rights abuses and provide victims with other judicial remedies, it has been rebuffed in practice. The international political actors that are in a position to put pressure on amnesty-granting states to meet their obligations have been silent. While justice may require legal norms prohibiting amnesties for serious violations of human rights, in the Americas it appears that black letter law to underpin that principle of justice will remain, for the foreseeable future, a muted shade of grey.

[121] Id., IACHR Annual Report (1996), p. 740.

[122] UnitedStates Department of State, 'Guatemala, Country Report on Human Rights Practices for 1996', Washington, DC 1997.

[123] R. Rodriguez and P. Gonzales, 'Truth remains peace obstacle in Guatemala', *The Fresno Bee*, 10 Feb. 1997.

[124] Since President Alvaro Arzu took office in January 1996, his administration has cracked down on military impunity by shaking up the army hierarchy and arresting dozens of military officers and some police personnel accused of human rights violations. NotiSur, Latin American Political Affairs, 'Guatemala: New Peace Accord Signals End to War', 17 Sept. 1996.

[125] Id. See also Victor Perera, 'Guatemala: After 36 Years of War, Is Peace Really at Hand?', *Los Angeles Times*, 22 Sept. 1996.

12

States of Emergency in the Inter-American Human Rights System

INTRODUCTION

Among the members of the Organization of American States (OAS), the association between human rights abuse and states of emergency has been strong. Several characteristics of the legal and political culture contribute to this phenomenon—periodic seizures of power by the military from civilian authorities, formalistic legal systems with weak traditions of separation of powers, and economically and racially polarized societies producing insurgent or terrorist groups. Human rights catastrophes occurred so frequently that the very concept of a 'state of siege' took on a Latin-American countenance during the 1970s and 1980s. The peculiar strengths of the inter-American human rights system—the discretionary authority of the Inter-American Commission on Human Rights (IACHR) to undertake on-site visits and to issue critical country reports, along with the analytical capacity and broad jurisdiction of the Inter-American Court of Human Rights—have, in turn, made the OAS a prime innovator in monitoring emergency-related human rights violations.

The dramatic return to democracy in Latin America following its 'near death experiences'[1] may diminish interest in the link between states of emergency and human rights protection. Between 1978 and 1991, fifteen of twenty Latin American states 'returned to or established elected civilian government after experiencing one form or another of authoritarian rule'.[2] *Golpes de estado* (forcible seizure of power by anti-democratic means) strikingly decreased[3] while apparently implacable military regimes

---

[1] T. Farer, 'Consolidating Democracy in Latin America: Law, Legal Institutions and Constitutional Structure', 10 *Am. U J Int'l. L & Pol.* 1295, 1295 (1995).

[2] D. Scott Palmer, 'Peru: Collectively Defending Democracy in the Western Hemisphere', in Farer, (ed.), *Beyond Sovereignty: Collectively Defending Democracy in the Americas* (Baltimore, 1996), 257, 258.

[3] Id. (in the 1980s only seven such incidents occurred, four being 'carried out by militaries to open up the political process to democratic elections [while] only two were mounted to thwart them'.) Between the 1930s and the 1970s, 38% of regime changes in Latin America occurred by means of *golpes*; in the 1980s this declined to 19%, with a very small percentage involving seizure of power from freely elected democratic administrations.

collapsed and were replaced by vigorous if flawed elected governments.[4] American states, drawing on their tragic experiences with military *juntas* and an attachment to the democratic ideal rooted in the romantic revolutionary movements of the nineteenth century, increasingly emphasize the emerging 'right to democracy'[5] as a means to prevent gross violations of fundamental human rights. Adding to the flexible capacities of the IACHR and the Court to confront emergency situations, the OAS requires its political organs to respond expeditiously to disruption of formal democracy in any member state under the Santiago Commitment of 1991[6] and AG Res. 1080.[7] The 1992 Protocol of Washington, in force as of 1997, authorizes the suspension of OAS members whose democratic governments have been overthrown.[8]

Despite these advances, OAS action against human rights violations during states of emergency remains limited. The Western Hemisphere's painful history of external interference by hegemonic states has cultivated a heightened sensitivity to intervention in domestic affairs. Many OAS members are leery of forceful action to restore democracy or to halt rampant human rights violations, and, unlike the United Nations Charter, the OAS Charter makes no provision for the collective use of force. On the contrary, the OAS Charter stresses the principle of non-interference in its Articles 19[9] and 20.[10] Economic sanctions, though occasionally imposed in

---

[4] T. Farer, 'Collectively Defending Democracy in the Western Hemisphere: Introduction and Overview', in Farer, (ed.), *Beyond Sovereignty: Collectively Defending Democracy in the Americas* (Baltimore, 1996), 1, 2.

[5] See generally, T. M. Franck, 'The Emerging Right to Democratic Governance', 86 *Am. J Int'l. L* 46 (1992).

[6] Santiago Commitment to Democracy and the Renewal of the Inter-American System, OAS 3d plenary sess., 4 June 1991. See generally, S. J. Schnably, 'The Santiago Commitment as a Call to Democracy in the United States: Evaluating the OAS Role in Haiti, Peru, and Guatemala', 25 *U Miami Inter-Am. L Rev.* 393 (1994).

[7] Representative Democracy, AG Res. 1080 (XXI–0/91), OEA/Ser.P, OAS Doc. AG/Res.1080 (XXI–0/91) (1991), established a trigger mechanism requiring response by the OAS within ten days of 'any occurrence giving rise to the sudden or irregular interruption of the democratic political institutional process or of the legitimate exercise of power by the democratically elected government in any of the Organization's member states.'

[8] Texts Approved by the General Assembly at its Sixteenth Special Session in Connection with the Amendments to the Charter of the Organization, OEA/Ser.P, OAS Doc. AG/doc. 11 (XVI–E/92).

[9] 'No state or group of States has the right to intervene, directly or indirectly, for any reason whatever, in the internal affairs of any other State. The foregoing principle prohibits not only armed force but also any other form of interference or attempted threat against the personality of the State or against its political, economic, and cultural elements.' Charter of the Organization of American States, signed at Bogotá in 1948, amended by the Protocol of Buenos Aires in 1967 and the Protocol of Cartagena de Indias of 1985.

[10] 'No State may use or encourage the use of coercive measures of an economic or political character in order to force the sovereign will of another State and obtain from it advantages of any kind.'

response to emergencies, have a diluted impact because they depend upon voluntary compliance.[11]

OAS concern with the effects of states of emergency on human rights has evolved significantly over the past four decades. The early efforts of the IACHR focused on reporting and analysis of extensive human rights violations associated with military regimes with a highly formalistic approach to emergency powers. Evincing a keen interest in the conceptual aspects of emergency suspension of rights,[12] the IACHR attempted to counteract the absolutist doctrine of national security propagated by military authorities to justify derogations. The massive scale of violations and the energetic disinformation campaigns by those responsible contributed to the marginalization of the individual complaint mechanism as a vehicle for the IACHR to redress emergency-related abuse.

In the meantime, the entry into force of the American Convention on Human Rights[13] and the establishment of the Court opened new avenues for elucidation of substantive issues relating to states of emergency. These included the definition and scope of non-derogable rights[14] and attribution of responsibility for patterns of serious human rights violations, such as disappearances,[15] a practice often associated with emergency rule. The return to democracy in the region transformed the OAS role—new demands to establish an election-monitoring capacity;[16] new dilemmas concerning transitional justice, amnesty and impunity; and new imperatives to collaborate with the UN in brokering and monitoring peace settlements in situations of internal conflict. Renewed confidence in multilateralism and in democracy at the end of the Cold War produced the Santiago Commitment, calling for prompt, joint response to democratic crises.[17] One result of these trends has been an increased role for OAS political bodies in human rights matters. Threats to democracy in the early 1990s in Haiti, Peru and Guatemala posed a difficult test for these new OAS capacities. Moreover, the 'work of the IACHR [became] both more

---

[11] For a critique of OAS economic sanctions imposed to restore President Aristide to power in Haiti, see D. E. Acevedo, 'The Haitian Crisis and the OAS Response: A Test of Effectiveness in Protecting Democracy', in Damrosch, (ed.), *Enforcing Restraint: Collective Intervention in Internal Conflicts* (New York: 1993), 119, 133–38; V. P. Vaky and H. Muñoz, *The Future of the Organization of American States* 28 (New York, 1993) ('The OAS sanctions on Haiti were too indiscriminate and too leaky to have any impact on the supporters of the military coup').

[12] See discussion of D. H. Martins study, below n. 23.

[13] American Convention on Human Rights, Appendix III.

[14] See below at nn. 151–70.

[15] See below at n. 115.

[16] The OAS Secretariat established a Unit for Democratic Development to provide advisory services and undertook fifteen election monitoring missions between 1989 and 1993. Vaky and Muñoz, above n. 11 at 24.

[17] See above n. 6.

complicated and more sensitive'. as '[d]ealing with abuses by dictatorial governments is one thing, [while] dealing with human rights considerations in democratic regimes is something else.'[18]

Inter-American norms concerning protection of human rights during states of emergency are unusually demanding; the first section of this chapter will describe the content and evolution of those norms. Thereafter, the discussion will turn to the functions and contributions of various OAS bodies to the prevention and redress of human rights violations associated with states of emergency.

SUBSTANTIVE REGIONAL NORMS GOVERNING SUSPENSION OF HUMAN RIGHTS
DURING STATES OF EMERGENCY

The American Declaration of the Rights and Duties of Man[19] was drafted at the same conference that produced the OAS Charter, but it was adopted as 'a simple conference resolution and did not form part of the Charter itself'.[20] Predating the adoption of the Universal Declaration of Human Rights (UDHR) by several months,[21] the Declaration resembles the UDHR in being a general statement of rights with only broadly phrased limitations clauses. Article XXVIII of the Declaration provides that: 'The rights of man are limited by the rights of others, by the security of all, and by the just demands of the general welfare and the advancement of democracy.' The Declaration, unlike the UDHR, also defines the individual's 'duties', but these are not closely related to suspension of fundamental rights during states of emergency.[22]

Despite the paucity of textual guidance on protection of human rights during states of emergency in the Charter and Declaration, the IACHR manifested an early interest in the subject that was to bear fruit in the later drafting of the Convention. The IACHR commissioned a study on the problem of protecting human rights during states of emergency by one of its members, Daniel Hugo Martins, in 1966,[23] with three aims: (1) to examine the history of states of siege within the region in order to categorize related human rights violations; (2) to assess the feasibility of

---

[18] Vaky and Muñoz, above, n. 11 at 20.

[19] OAS Res. XXX, adopted by the Ninth International Conference of American States, Bogotá, 1948.

[20] Buergenthal and Shelton, *Protecting Human Rights in the Americas: Cases and Materials* (4th ed. Kehl, 1995), 39.

[21] Id.

[22] The sole allusion in the American Declaration to emergencies is Art. XXXIV's reference to the obligation of citizens to render services to the community in public disasters.

[23] *La Protección de los Derechos Humanos frente a la Suspensión de las Garantías Constitucionales o 'Estado de Sitio'*, OEA/Ser.L/V/II.15, doc. 12 (1966).

articulating general principles limiting the suspension of rights during emergencies, for uniform incorporation into national law; and (3) to evaluate the possibility of establishing international organs to control the juridical and practical aspects of states of siege.[24] The IACHR recognized the tendency of repressive governments to rely upon the existence of a real or claimed emergency to justify serious violations of fundamental rights and sought to establish a framework for confining the suspension of rights within clear limits. Among other recommendations, the Hugo Martins study favored making only certain, narrowly defined rights suspendable in emergencies.[25]

By the time the Convention was drafted, model derogation clauses could be found in both regional[26] and universal[27] instruments. Article 27 follows the outline of the European Convention for the Protection of Human Rights and Fundamental Freedoms and the International Covenant on Civil and Political Rights (ICCPR) in permitting derogations only under strictly defined circumstances, preserving from invasion a core set of non-derogable rights, and requiring notification of derogations to other states parties.[28] Article 27 is distinguished from the earlier provisions primarily by its broader delineation of non-derogable rights.

In 1966 the OAS Council forwarded to the IACHR three draft human rights conventions,[29] each of which included a specific derogation clause.

---

[24] Above, n. 23 at iv.

[25] These rights would be limited to prohibitions on arbitrary detention, prompt notice of criminal charges, interference with private life and correspondence, and prior restraint on publication. Id., at 30, 37–44.

[26] European Convention for the Protection of Human Rights and Fundamental Freedoms, Art. 15.

[27] International Covenant on Civil and Political Rights, Art. 4.

[28] Art. 27 provides:
'1. In time of war, public danger, or other emergency that threatens the independence or security of a State Party, it may take measures derogating from its obligations under the present Convention to the extent and for the period of time strictly required by the exigencies of the situation, provided that such measures are not inconsistent with its other obligations under international law and do not involve discrimination on the ground of race, color, sex, language, religion or social origin.
'2. The foregoing provision does not authorize any suspension of the following articles: Article 3 (Right to Juridical Personality), Article 4 (Right to Life), Article 5 (Right to Humane Treatment), Article 6 (Freedom from Slavery), Article 9 (Freedom from *Ex Post Facto* Laws), Article 12 (Freedom of Conscience and Religion), Article 17 (Rights of the Family), Article 18 (Right to a Name), Article 19 (Rights of the Child), Article 20 (Right to Nationality), and Article 23 (Right to Participate in Government), or of the judicial guarantees essential for the protection of such rights.
'3. Any State Party availing itself of the right of suspension shall immediately inform the other States Parties, through the Secretary General of the Organization of American States, of the provisions the application of which it has suspended, the reasons that gave rise to the suspension, and the date set for the termination of such suspension.'

[29] The three were submitted by the Inter-American Council of Jurists, Chile and Uruguay. Buergenthal and Norris, (eds.), *Human Rights: The Inter-American System* (Kehl, 1982), 27–31.

The IACHR prepared a draft treaty, drawing upon these instruments, and presented it in 1968 to the Council to serve as the working draft for the Conference of San José.[30]

The bases for permissible derogation under the Convention include 'war, public danger, or other emergency that threatens the independence or security of a State Party'. The IACHR had a strong hand in drafting this language, which differs more in form than in substance from the concept of 'public emergency threatening the life of the nation' in the European Convention and the ICCPR.[31] The reference to 'public danger' was added at the initiative of El Salvador to accommodate exceptional measures during natural disasters.[32] In practice, emergency suspension of rights in the Americas since the drafting of Article 27 derives more often from real or purported threats to internal security, than from international armed conflict, territorial dismemberment or natural disaster.

Article 27 contains an unusually extensive list of non-derogable rights, including fundamental judicial guarantees and the right to participate in a democratic, freely elected government. The list is eclectic, reflecting three distinct though compatible principles—that rights most essential to human life and dignity should never be sacrificed and must always be protected by effective judicial remedies, whatever the price in political stability; that certain rights are highly unlikely to impede the preservation of public order under even the most extreme conditions; and that democracy itself is among the highest values in the Americas. Despite OAS commitment to this generous list, gross and persistent violations of non-derogable rights have been a distinguishing characteristic of states of emergency in the Western Hemisphere, where the practice of 'disappearing' political enemies first achieved international notoriety.[33]

The obligation of notification under Article 27.3 is, on the surface, quite demanding. It requires immediate communication to the other states parties through the intermediary of the Secretary General of the OAS of the fact of derogation, identification of the provisions that have been suspended, the reasons justifying the suspension, and the expected date for full restoration of rights.

However, the practice has been uneven, if not lax. Notices of derogation are not systematically published in any official[34] or even unofficial

[30] Buergenthal and Norris, above, n. 29.

[31] J. Fitzpatrick, *Human Rights in Crisis: The International System for Protecting Rights During States of Emergency* (Philadelphia, 1994), 58.

[32] Norris and Reiton, 'The Suspension of Guarantees: A Comparative Analysis of the American Convention on Human Rights and the Constitutions of the States Parties', 30 *Am. U L Rev.* 189, 198 (1981).

[33] This tragic history is reflected in the Inter-American Convention on the Forced Disappearance of Persons, OEA/Ser.P AG/doc.311/94 rev. 1, 8 June 1994.

[34] Notices of derogation are not included in compilations of documents relating to ratification or accession to the Convention, in the annual reports of the IACHR or in the Inter-American Yearbook on Human Rights, all logical locations for such publication.

sources.[35] Notices are sometimes disclosed in the course of the IACHR's supervisory activities, and may attract critical comment for lateness, deficiency in content or revelation of excessive derogations.[36] The IACHR on occasion has requested information concerning unnotified derogations from states parties to the Convention, having learned of the crisis from other sources.[37] However, in its special reports the IACHR frequently analyzes states of emergency occurring in various states parties to the Convention, without commenting on whether the state complied with its obligation to provide immediate and adequate notification pursuant to Article 27.3.[38] In general, the IACHR seems uninterested in strict compliance with Article 27.3. Oráa states:[39]

[T]here was a special section in the IACHR *Annual Report 1980-1* on states of emergency in ten countries; among these were six States parties to the American Convention. However, there was no reference at all to the obligation of notifying, although only two out of these six States parties had partially complied with the notification procedure. Moreover, there is a set of recommendations at the end of the report on states of emergency, but, surprisingly enough, there is no mention of the need of notifying.

OAS BODIES WITH COMPETENCE TO PROTECT HUMAN RIGHTS
DURING STATES OF EMERGENCY

The Inter-American Commission on Human Rights

The IACHR has actively exposed human rights violations in emergencies both prior to and following the entry into force of the Convention. Although the Declaration is silent on the specifics of emergency suspension of rights, the IACHR has determined that Convention Article 27 expresses a common framework applicable to all OAS members, as it 'embodies the

---

[35] e.g., the six-volume looseleaf treatise edited by Thomas Buergenthal and Robert E. Norris does not include notices of derogation among its collection of vauable OAS documents relating to human rights. *Human Rights: The Inter-American System*, above n. 29. However, two examples of derogation notices, filed by El Salvador and Nicaragua in 1980, are reprinted in Buergenthal and Shelton, above n. 20 at 484–5.

[36] For example, in 1983 the IACHR criticized Guatemala for filing a notice of derogation nine months after the declaration of a state of emergency. However, the critical comment was made in a footnote. Report on the Situation of Human Rights in the Republic of Guatemala, at 33 n. 11 (1983).

[37] The most frequently cited example is the IACHR's communication to Bolivia in1981. See Oráa, *Human Rights in States of Emergency in International Law* (Oxford 1992), 69, 82.

[38] For example, Report on the Situation of Human Rights in Panama (1989); Report on the Situation of Human Rights in Peru (1993); Report on the Situation of Human Rights in Haiti (1995).

[39] Oráa, above n. 37 at 82.

most received doctrine on this subject'.[40] The IACHR confronts the sometimes massive human rights violations associated with states of emergency
primarily through four mechanisms: (1) special reports on the situation of
human rights in particular states; (2) annual reports containing brief
summaries of country situations and general comments; (3) reports on
individual cases; and, (4) following the establishment of the Court, invocation of its advisory and contentious jurisdiction.

Special Country Reports

Shortly after its establishment, the IACHR began issuing country reports
on human rights violations connected with states of emergency, the initial
case being Paraguay.[41] The ill-defined status and authority of the early
IACHR operated in this regard to its benefit. Under its Statute, the
IACHR retained an open-ended mandate 'to prepare such studies or
reports as it considers advisable for the performance of its duties'.[42]
Because the IACHR sets its own agenda, rather than being bound to a
fixed cycle of reviewing state-generated reports on treaty compliance, it
has long been empowered to transform its reporting capacity into a rapid-
response mechanism, scheduling an investigation and report on a fairly
short timetable following the eruption of emergency conditions in any
member state.

   While special reports are not limited to states undergoing a formal
emergency, a *coup d'état* or similar sudden event has often triggered the
IACHR's reporting function. For example, the IACHR took up the situation of human rights in Haiti in June 1988, shortly after the military
takeover of the government by General Henri Namphy, visited the country
and rapidly issued a comprehensive and critical report.[43] The IACHR
sometimes responds to a request from another organ of the OAS[44] in
launching an on-site investigation, though it may also act upon its own

---

[40] Report on the Situation of Human Rights in Chile, para. 93 (1985); Report on the
Status of Human Rights in Chile, para. 5 (1974).

[41] The initial report on Paraguay was issued in 1961, OEA/Ser.L/V/II.10, doc. 2 (1961).
See also, OEA/Ser.L/V/II.13, doc. 5 (1964); and OEA/Ser.L/V/II.43, doc. 13, corr. 1 (1978)
(subsequent reports on Paraguay).

[42] This power was confirmed in the 1965 Statute of the Inter-American Commission on
Human Rights and its 1979 revision. Statute of the Inter-American Commission on Human
Rights, reprinted in *Handbook of Existing Rules Pertaining to Human Rights in the Inter-
American System*, OEA/Ser.L/V/II.26, doc. 10 at Art. 18(c) (1979).

[43] Report on the Situation of Human Rights in Haiti, at 1–2 (1988). The killings of twelve
persons in San Juan Bosco Church in September 1988, shortly after the issuance of the
IACHR's report on Haiti, led the Permanent Council of the OAS in February 1989 to ask the
IACHR to make a further on-site visit, which took place in April 1990. Report on the
Situation of Human Rights in Haiti, at 1–4 (1990).

[44] The OAS Permanent Council requested the IACHR to conduct a study in Bolivia in
1980 following a military coup displacing the elected government. Report on the Situation of
Human Rights in Bolivia (1981).

knowledge gained through complaints from individuals,[45] the suggestion of a non-governmental organization[46] or the invitation of a government. Special country reports remain the pivotal IACHR tool to expose and deter human rights violations during states of emergency.

The on-site visits conducted by the IACHR distinguish it from other human rights treaty bodies and provide unusual depth, concreteness and immediacy to many of its reports. The greatest drawback to the on-site visit is the necessity of securing the government's permission.[47] Governmental invitations to conduct an on-site visit may be negotiated behind the scenes at the initiative of the IACHR.[48] Ironically, the recent proliferation of human rights bodies with a capacity to operate *in situ* may undercut this traditional IACHR strength. The Haitian military regime in 1993 used the field presence of the OAS human rights monitoring mission as an excuse to exclude the IACHR, despite the strong support of the exiled Aristide government for the IACHR's entry.[49]

The IACHR has established a protocol for its on-site visits, requiring the government to provide adequate facilities and to protect witnesses against reprisals.[50] The IACHR typically appoints a special commission consisting of several IACHR members to conduct the visit, accompanied by staff. The itinerary includes interviews with government officials, victims, witnesses, and local experts, as well as travel to significant sites. Large numbers of new denunciations are sometimes added to the IACHR's docket when victims complete IACHR complaint forms during an on-site visit.[51]

IACHR on-site visits have occasionally produced immediate improvement in the human rights situation.[52] But instant reduction in human rights violations and restoration of democratic government have neither been the typical result, nor the expectation, of the IACHR in conducting on-site investigations. Despite its precautionary protocol, the IACHR has sometimes undertaken visits knowing that its presence may trigger a crackdown

---

[45] Report on the Situation of Human Rights in Argentina, at 1 (1980).

[46] A report on Suriname was initiated in response to a cable from Amnesty International concerning fifteen summary executions in December 1982. Report on the Situation of Human Rights in Suriname 1 (1983).

[47] Art. 18(g) of the Statute of the IACHR requires governmental consent for on-site visits. See Appendix IV.

[48] See, e.g., Report on the Situation of Human Rights in the Republic of Nicaragua (1981); Report on the Situation of Human Rights in El Salvador (1978); Report on the Situation of Human Rights in the Republic of Colombia (1981).

[49] Report on the Situation of Human Rights in Haiti, 13–16 (1993). The IACHR later gained entry and issued additional special reports in 1994 and 1995. Report on the Situation of Human Rights in Haiti (1994); (1995).

[50] IACHR Regulations, above, n. 47 at Arts. 55–9.

[51] See, e.g., five hundred seventy-six denunciations were received in 1974 by the IACHR delegation at the Hotel Crillon in Santiago, Chile. Report on Chile (1974), above, n. 40 at 65.

[52] See, e.g., Report on Nicaragua (1981), above, n. 48 at 14 (release of women prisoners).

against those whom it seeks to protect. In Argentina, the offices of several human rights groups were raided and files were seized just as the IACHR was poised to visit.[53]

An on-site visit may have symbolic impact beyond its immediate results and may turn the tide of international and national public opinion against an emergency regime. In the midst of the 'dirty war', when the military government of Argentina was enjoying remarkable success in staving off scrutiny by UN human rights bodies,[54] it consented to a visit by the IACHR.[55] The IACHR's detailed report[56] undercut the regime's efforts to mask its atrocities, while IACHR President Tom Farer added to the public pressure on Argentina by making a formal presentation of the report to the OAS General Assembly in 1980.[57] Such efforts not only respond to the desperation of victims whose voices have been silenced by a government's clever manipulation of emergency powers, but may sow seeds of doubt among complacent sectors of the national community willing to tolerate emergency restrictions as long as their severity is hidden.[58]

On-site visits also infuse drama into an investigatory undertaking that has its humdrum and frustrating aspects:[59]

Although much of its visit is taken up by interviews with government officials and a wide variety of persons familiar with the particular country's human rights situation, the IACHR can also be adventurous, such as when it located secret cells in El Salvador, examined corpses from clandestine graves in Guatemala, sent staff members to interview Guatemalan refugees in Mexico, and provided safe passage for M-19 guerrillas from Colombia who had been holding hostages at an embassy in Bogotá.

The IACHR is typically candid, even condemnatory,[60] in its special reports about a state's human rights practices and suggests specific improvements. For example, a trenchant 1985 report on Chile critiqued legal developments since General Augusto Pinochet's *coup* in September 1973,

---

[53] The connection between the raid and the IACHR visit was apparent in the warrant's listing of the OAS office in Buenos Aires as a location to be searched. Report on Argentina, above n. 45 at 260.

[54] Iain Guest, *Behind the Disappearances: Argentina's Dirty War Against Human Rights and the United Nations* (Philadelphia, 1990).

[55] Buergenthal and Shelton, above n. 20 at 321 (quoting John Simpson and Jana Bennett for the point that pressure from US Vice President Mondale led Argentina to consent to IACHR visit).

[56] Above n. 45.

[57] Buergenthal and Shelton, above n. 20 at 320–1.

[58] Id. at 322 (quoting Emilio Mignone, Cynthia Estlund and Samuel Issacharoff).

[59] Fitzpatrick, above n. 31 at 181 (citations omitted).

[60] The report on the Somoza regime in Nicaragua condemned a variety of 'serious, persistent and generalized violations'. Report on the Situation of Human Rights in Nicaragua, at 77 (1978). The OAS Permanent Council went further and in an extraordinary resolution in June 1979 called for the 'immediate and definitive replacement of the Somoza regime'. Report on Nicaragua (1981), above n. 48 at 20–3.

the values and perspective of the regime, the creeping institutionalization of the emergency, and restrictions imposed on human rights under the transitional 1980 Constitution.[61]

The IACHR has often responded with skepticism to claims by emergency regimes to act on behalf of the nation. Criticizing the suspension of Haiti's 1987 Constitution by General Namphy, the IACHR stated:

A military *coup d'état* and the summary deportation of the head of state cannot be legitimized by the destruction of the nation's fundamental charter or by unsupportable claims, made under the threat of the use of force, that one is acting in the name of democracy and human rights.[62]

When an on-site visit discloses an unusually grave situation, the IACHR makes 'preliminary recommendations' to the government to halt grave violations prior to issuance of its final report.[63]

At other times, however, the IACHR may express sympathy for a government coping with unusual stresses, such as the Sandinista regime in Nicaragua[64] or the beleaguered government of Colombia.[65] Even in these relatively friendly circumstances, the IACHR makes selective findings of violations[66] and recommendations for change.[67] On rare occasions, the IACHR may undertake a series of on-site visits as part of a formal 'friendly settlement'. During the civil war in Nicaragua, the relocation of the Miskito Indians became a matter of great controversy. Despite prolonged efforts, the IACHR was unsuccessful in mediating a solution.[68]

While critical in its conclusions and recommendations, the IACHR rarely attempts a serious or detailed interpretation of Article 27 in a country report. Special reports might include factual observations suggesting a lack

[61] Report on Chile (1985), above n. 40. This report was prepared without an on-site visit and against the strong objections of the Chilean Government, which attempted to block it by seeking a ruling on the IACHR's competence from the Inter-American Juridical Committee. Id. at 3.

[62] Report on Haiti (1988), above n. 43 at 51.

[63] Report on Argentina, above n. 45 at 7–9.

[64] Report on Nicaragua (1981), above n. 48.

[65] Report on Colombia, above n. 48.

[66] The Colombian visit was exceedingly unusual, involving an IACHR negotiating role in a dramatic hostage rescue at the joint request of the government and the M-19 guerrilla organization. Id. at 12–15. Though respectful of the government's claimed good intentions, the IACHR identified violations of the right to life, abusive arrests and detentions, denial by the military justice system of the right to fair trial, military excesses against indigenous people in rural areas, and a systematic failure to punish security force members responsible for human rights violations. Id. at 219–22.

[67] In Nicaragua the IACHR found violations of the right to life, inadequate due process in special courts for 'Somocistas', poor prison conditions, excessive restrictions on expression and political rights, and 'unjustifiable obstacles' in the path of human rights groups. Report on Nicaragua (1981), above n. 42 at 168–71.

[68] Report on the Situation of Human Rights of a Segment of the Nicaraguan Population of Miskito Origin (1984).

of proportionality between the threat faced by the government and the breadth of emergency measures, or findings that non-derogable rights have been violated, but with little discussion of the subtleties of Article 27. The emphasis is descriptive and prescriptive rather than conceptual. Though it may critique particular emergency laws for their negative impact on fundamental rights, the IACHR has never been preoccupied by the forms of emergency rule. For example, the IACHR questioned whether the celebrated lifting of a long-prolonged state of emergency in Paraguay had yielded any real improvement in human rights.[69]

The primary theoretical contribution to understanding the relation between states of emergency and the protection of human rights in the IACHR's country reports is found in exchanges between emergency regimes and the IACHR, especially over the assertion that terrorism justifies suspension of human rights. Argentina provoked the IACHR's initial two-part answer.[70] First, the IACHR refused to consider denunciations against non-governmental actors, limiting its competence to human rights practices of governments. Second, recognizing that governments have an obligation to maintain order, the IACHR insisted that emergency measures be confined to 'extremely serious circumstances' and never involve suspension of non-derogable rights. Only governments lacking broad popular support would resort to state terrorism; democratic governments maintain the rule of law when confronting terrorism.[71]

This approach brought the IACHR into tension with OAS political organs. A resolution of the OAS General Assembly in 1990 requesting the IACHR to report on actions of irregular armed groups[72] was initially met by a dismissive IACHR response that there was 'nothing new' about such acts.[73] The IACHR conceded that a pervasive atmosphere of violence can be considered[74] in order to 'depict the general setting' and 'when analyzing the causes invoked as grounds for suspending the exercise of certain rights, in accordance with the provisions of the American Convention on Human Rights'.[75] However, the IACHR indicated a reluctance to investigate violations of international humanitarian law by guerrilla forces,[76] observing:

[T]he Commission has often heard the argument that human rights violations are inevitable because they are the consequence of the 'war' created by armed groups, who are generally portrayed as terrorists. . . . In the Commission's judgment, this is an invalid argument; consequently, it has repeatedly asserted that unqualified

---

[69] Report on the Situation of Human Rights in Paraguay (1987).
[70] Report on Argentina, above n. 45 at 25–7.
[71] Id.
[72] OAS Resolution AG/Res. 1043 (XX–0/90), *reprinted in* IACHR Annual Report 1990–1 at 504–5.
[73] Id. at 504.   [74] Id. at 505.
[75] Id. at 508.   [76] Id. at 509.

respect for human rights must be a fundamental part of any anti-subversive strategies. . . .[77]

Since 1990, however, the IACHR has paid increasing attention to terrorism. In 1993 the IACHR defensively noted that it had criticized abuses by irregular armed groups in El Salvador (1978), Argentina (1980), Colombia (1981), Guatemala (1981, 1983, 1985), Nicaragua (1983) and Peru (1989, 1993).[78] Observing that it had been 'sensitive' to the problem of terrorism and had 'taken account of it in due fashion',[79] the IACHR nevertheless cautioned:[80] '[U]nder no circumstances should a sensitivity toward the activities of armed irregular groups leading to violations of human rights be used as a justification for the violations of human rights by governments themselves.'

The value of IACHR special reports derives primarily from their effect in marshalling, sometimes with great speed and efficacy, international and national pressure to moderate emergency-related human rights violations. Even after the Santiago Commitment brought OAS political organs into a more direct role in emergency situations, timely and critical on-site visits by the IACHR remain an integral aspect of OAS reaction to emergency-related human rights violations. The *ad hoc* Meeting of Ministers of Foreign Affairs held on 13 April 1992, in response to Peruvian President Fujimori's *autogolpe* of 5 April 1992, specifically requested consent to an IACHR visit.[81] An initial IACHR staff visit occurred on 23–24 April 1992, shortly followed by an IACHR mission on 11–12 May 1992,[82] and the issuance of a detailed and critical special report on 12 March 1993.[83] These contributions by the IACHR reinforced the political pressure exerted by the OAS on President Fujimori to reinstate at least the forms of democratic government.[84]

The IACHR's larger jurisprudential objectives relating to states of emergency are pursued primarily through its increasingly important interaction with the Court. Several advisory opinions and contentious cases, profiled in Section III.3, have markedly advanced understanding of Article 27, state responsibility for violations of non-derogable rights and other issues pertinent to protection of human rights during states of emergency.

[77] Id. at 512.
[78] IACHR Annual Report 1992–3 at 218–19 (1993).
[79] Id. at 219.   [80] Id. at 220.
[81] Report on the Situation of Human Rights in Peru, at para. 44 (1993).
[82] Id. at Appendices VII and VIII.   [83] Above n. 81.
[84] The OAS Secretary-General and the President of the *ad hoc* Meeting of Foreign Ministers visited Peru on 20–23 Apr. 1992, and again on 4–5 May 1992. Report on Peru, above n. 81 at 14. This high-level persuasion no doubt contributed to President Fujimori's decision to appear at the OAS General Assembly on 18 May 1992, and to pledge the early convening of a constitutional congress and holding of municipal elections. Id.at 15.

Annual Reports

The IACHR's annual reports include general observations concerning its conceptual approach. Its 1981 discussion of 'States of Emergency' linked that phenomenon to patterns of violations of certain rights, including detention without due process, expulsion of nationals and limitations on thought and information.[85] This topic was particularly pressing at the time, when formal states of emergency and military governments prevailed in Argentina, Chile, El Salvador, Paraguay, and Uruguay, with *de facto* or *de jure* emergencies operative in other states as well.[86] The IACHR noted that '[f]rom a quantitative point of view, detentions without due process constituted the largest number of violations' linked to emergencies, and that many detentions involved torture.[87] It recommended that OAS states limit 'periods of exception to the time strictly necessary' and permit judicial authorities to act as a check upon executive detention.[88] The IACHR wryly observed that many states of emergency are maintained by governments claiming a climate of social peace, presumably to establish legitimacy and reassure investors, while contradictorily insisting upon the need for extraordinary measures of control.[89]

IACHR annual reports typically include brief descriptions of human rights conditions in several member states, sometimes selected because they apply emergency measures or because they have previously been the subject of a special report.[90] The IACHR's brief comments can be highly critical and may focus on specific emergency laws that it regards as excessive. For example, the IACHR condemned Chile's limitations on judicial remedies to challenge exercises of emergency powers under the 1980 Constitution as 'provisions that institutionalize arbitrary political power'.[91] Addressing the situation in El Salvador, the IACHR 'deplore[d] the enactment of a new emergency procedural law [Decree Law 618], which, like the previous one [Decree Law 50], violates elementary legal principles and guarantees as well as international human rights rules that are binding on the Republic of El Salvador'.[92] Observations in annual reports may occasionally delve, at least superficially, into the question whether a country situation meets the threshold of severity for application of emergency measures. One example is the IACHR's comment in 1987 that 'facts that are a matter of public knowledge show, in the Commission's

---

[85] IACHR Annual Report 1980–1 at 114–22.
[84] Id. at 115–17.   [87] Id. at 117.
[88] Id. at 129.   [89] Id. at 115.
[90] See, e.g., IACHR Annual Report 1986–7, 200–27, 234–67 (Chile, El Salvador, Haiti, Nicaragua, Suriname); IACHR Annual Report 1994 at 129–95 (1995) (Colombia, Cuba, El Salvador, Guatemala).
[91] Annual Report 1986–7, above n. 90 at 203.
[92] Id. at 223.

view, that the Nicaraguan Government is facing a threat to State security',
and that the rights suspended in Nicaragua are 'in keeping with the
provisions of Article 27.2 [of the American Convention], except with regard
to the suspension of the remedy of *amparo* or *habeas corpus*'.[93] The IACHR
cautioned that the unavailability of *amparo* or *habeas corpus* during the
emergency created a 'grave contradiction between the Nicaraguan Constitution and the system of the American Convention',[94] a conclusion reinforced
by the Court's advisory opinions on the non-derogability of those remedies.[95]
The restoration of *habeas corpus* in Nicaragua was favorably noted in the
IACHR's 1989 annual report.[96]

Individual Complaints

In 1965 IACHR authority was extended to receipt of individual petitions,[97]
and in 1979 the Statute of the IACHR conferred upon it new responsibilities under Article 44 of the American Convention on Human Rights.[98]
But until recently, the IACHR's handling of individual petitions arising in
emergency contexts was generally disappointing. It did not take timely
action on many petitions and its annual reports contained a comparatively
small number of case reports.[99] Decisions on admissibility were sometimes
prolonged.[100] During the heyday of formal states of emergency in the OAS,
the IACHR was more likely to use denunciations as illustrative incidents
in its special reports[101] or as the trigger for an on-site visit[102] than to
adjudicate them promptly. As Cecilia Medina explains:[103]

[T]he Commission was the sole guarantor of human rights in a continent
plagued with gross, systematic violations, and the Commission was part of an
international organization for which human rights were definitely not the first
priority. . . . [T]he Commission viewed itself more as an international organ with a

---

[93] Id. at 258.   [94] Id. at 256.
[95] See below nn. 151, 152.   [96] IACHR Annual Report 1988–9 at 194 (1989).
[97] Resolution XXII of the Second Special Inter-American Conference, OEA/Ser.E/XIII.1,
doc. 150 rev. (1965). Art. 9 (bis) of the Commission's Statute permits receipt of individual
communications. *Handbook of Existing Rules Pertaining to Human Rights in the Inter-American
System* OEA/Ser.L/V/II.26, doc. 10 at 24 (1979).
[98] See IACHR Annual Report 1979–80 at 11–13.
[99] In each of its Annual Reports for 1983–4 and 1984–5, for example, only 17 case
resolutions were published. But in 1990–1 a startling eighty-six individual cases were resolved.
Annual Report 1990–1, above n. 72 at 251–422. The IACHR decided to refer to case
dispositions as 'reports' rather than 'resolutions'. Id. at 33.
[100] Prolongation of IACHR disposition of a number of Uruguayan cases eventually
induced the Human Rights Committee to assume jurisdiction over these cases under the
ICCPR. See Fitzpatrick, above n. 31 at 98–105.
[101] Report on Argentina, above n. 45 at 10–12.
[102] Report on the Situation of Human Rights in Guatemala (1981).
[103] C. Medina, 'The Inter-American Commission on Human Rights and the Inter-
American Court of Human Rights: Reflections on a Joint Venture', 12 *Hum. Rts. Q* 439, 442–
3 (1990).

highly political task to perform than as a technical body [of] quasi-judicial supervision. . . .

The IACHR's handling of emergency-related individual cases has improved in recent years. A turning point occurred in 1991, when it published
reports on fifty-one cases from Peru, almost all of which concerned disappearances in the emergency zones.[104] While the legal analysis in the
Peruvian cases lacked depth, the Commission pressed the Peruvian government for greater cooperation in responding to denunciations of emergency-
related violations.[105]

The IACHR's fact-finding approach is especially valuable where governments are unresponsive. A formal presumption under Article 42 of the
IACHR's Regulations specifies that credible allegations to which the
government fails to respond will be presumed to be true.[106] The IACHR
provides governments with ample opportunity to reply, adding delay to the
process. The total control enjoyed by government authorities in emergency
zones makes the presumption particularly apt:[107]

The petitioners have presented a detailed and consistent version in which they state
the date on which and place in which the events occurred. . . . [A]t the time the acts
denounced occurred, Raquel Mejía was living in an area under state of emergency
legislation. In such areas the military customarily assume control of the population
and set themselves up as the supreme authority, even above the duly elected and
constituted civil authorities. As a consequence, they commonly perpetrate numerous human rights violations in these areas.

The IACHR occasionally conducts on-site visits to establish facts in
individual cases[108] and has codified this practice in Article 44 of its Regulations.[109] While this technique is limited by its expense and the need for
government consent, it has illuminated the facts in several contested
cases.[110] Sometimes on-site visits conducted for more general reasons

---

[104] Above n. 99.

[105] Report on Peru, above n. 81 at 3–5. The Government asserted that the irregular
lifestyles of Andean peasants and the tactics of armed insurgents impeded investigation into
disappearances. Id. at 4–5, annex IV.

[106] Art. 42 states: 'The facts reported in the petition whose pertinent parts have been
transmitted to the government of the State in reference shall be presumed to be true if,
during the maximum period set by the commission under the provisions of Article 34
paragraph 5, the government has not provided the pertinent information, as long as other
evidence does not lead to a different conclusion.' Regulations of the IACHR, above n. 47.

[107] IACHR Annual Report 1995 at 157, 174.

[108] R. Norris, 'Observations *In Loco*: Practice and Procedure of the Inter-American
Commission on Human Rights', 15 *Texas Int'l. L J* 46, 54 (1980).

[109] See above n. 47.

[110] One unusual case concerned the massacre of twenty-one peasants in El Aguacate,
Guatemala. Word of the massacre first reached the IACHR from the government of Guatemala, which claimed that anti-government guerillas were responsible. The government brought
two peasants from the region to detail this story in person to the IACHR. An NGO questioning
this account filed a denunciation, alleging Guatemalan military complicity in the massacre. The

corroborate claims in individual denunciations, for example with regard to the case of former Peruvian President Alan García Pérez and his family concerning the 1992 *autogolpe*,[111] and that relating to Georges Izméry's 1992 assassination in Haiti.[112]

In resolving individual claims concerning non-derogable rights, the IACHR increasingly draws upon the jurisprudence of the Court. Regarding President García's denunciation, the IACHR noted:[113]

The obligation to guarantee access to prompt and effective remedy [sic] is not only applicable in times of political stability but during states of emergency as well.

Under the provisions of Article 27.2 of the Convention both remedies—namely, *amparo* and *habeas corpus*—are, in essence, indispensable judicial remedies. They cannot be suspended, not even during a state of emergency.

[T]he Commission is led to conclude that by denying Dr. García Pérez access to a simple and prompt remedy to prevent violation of his rights, the Government of Peru has failed to honor its obligations under the Convention. . . . [N]ot even if the Government were to claim that there was a state of emergency would a suspension of indispensable remedies such as *habeas corpus* be justified.

The non-derogability of the right to life and to humane treatment was similarly stressed in a case concerning the killing of twenty-one villagers by Peruvian armed forces in 1990.[114] The Court's construction of an evidentiary framework for attributing responsibility to the state for disappearances in the *Velásquez Rodríguez* case[115] has guided the IACHR in subsequent individual denunciations.[116]

The restoration of democracy following a period of emergency rule sometimes comes at the price of amnesty for perpetrators of violations of non-derogable rights. The IACHR had occasion to consider impunity in Argentina and Uruguay in a noteworthy pair of 1992 case reports.[117] The IACHR found Argentina's *punto final*[118] and 'due obedience'[119] laws to

---

government then authorized an on-site visit, which was conducted by two IACHR members and two staff. The IACHR concluded that 'grounds for the petition do not exist'. Annual Report 1990–1, above n. 72 at 193–223.

[111] Annual Report 1994, above n. 90 at 71–112.
[112] IACHR Annual Report 1993 at 239, 243. [113] Above n. 90 at 86–7.
[114] Annual Report 1995, above n. 107 at 136–56.
[115] *Velásquez Rodríguez* case, I/A Court H.R. Annual Report 1988 at 35 (1988), 9 *HRLJ* 212.
[116] See, e.g., the *Izméry* case concerning Haiti, Annual Report 1993, above n. 106 at 246–7; Id. at 303, 308–11 (disappearance in Ayacucho Region of Peru).
[117] Annual Report 1992–3, above n. 78 at 41 (Argentina) and 154 (Uruguay). See Lutz, Chap. 11 of this book for further discussion of this.
[118] Law No. 23,492 of 24 Dec. 1986 established a 60 day deadline for termination of all criminal proceedings arising out of the 'dirty war'; Presidential Decree of Pardon No. 1002 of 7 Oct. 1989 terminated criminal proceedings against persons who had not benefitted from the earlier law. Id. at 42.
[119] Law 23,521 of 8 June 1987 established an irrebuttable presumpttion that military

violate the victims' right to fair trial under Article XVIII of the Declaration and the state's obligation to investigate human rights violations under Article 1 of the Convention, the right to fair trial under Article 8 and the right to judicial protection under Article 25.[120] Uruguay's popular referendum granting amnesty for military and police crimes committed prior to 1 March 1985,[121] was similarly found by the IACHR to violate Article XVIII of the Declaration and Articles 1, 8 and 25 of the Convention.[122] These case reports are remarkable because they involved the IACHR in a fairly abstract assessment of the legality of emergency-related laws, a departure from its more typical factual focus on non-derogable rights.

Political Organs as Human Rights Bodies

The IACHR long enjoyed the distinction of being the rare human rights body able to work at the scene of gross violations, through its program of on-site visits. Increased recognition of the link between respect for human rights and international peace, and the inclusion of a human rights monitoring dimension in negotiated conclusions to civil conflict, require the IACHR to adapt to an increasingly crowded field. The IACHR must work collaboratively with UN human rights monitors, such as ONUSAL in El Salvador;[123] with joint UN/OAS monitors, as in Haiti;[124] with Truth Commissions;[125] and with the political organs of the OAS, especially the Permanent Council. The IACHR insists that 'the duties and authorities assigned to it by the American Convention cannot be modified or suspended by the presence of a temporary international agency'[126] protecting human rights in a member state. The IACHR attempts to construct productive avenues of information-sharing between itself and these special agencies.[127]

Three situations, the *coup d'état* in September 1991 in Haiti and the *autogolpes* in April 1992 in Peru and in May 1993 in Guatemala, illuminate the advantages and dangers of direct involvement by OAS and UN political organs in human rights emergencies and the effect of this activity on the

---

personnel who committed crimes during the 'dirty war' were acting in the line of duty and were thus immunized from criminal responsibility. Id.

[120] Id. at 51.

[121] Law No. 15,848 of 22 Dec. 1986. Id. at 154–5.   [122] Id. at 165.

[123] Annual Report 1994, above n. 90 at 170.

[124] Report on Haiti (1993), above n. 49.

[125] Annual Report 1994, above n. 90 at 170 (El Salvador); Annual Report 1992–3, above n. 78 at 50–1 (acknowledging value of CONADEP in Argentina but insisting on IACHR role in assessing legality of *punto final* and 'due obedience' laws).

[126] Annual Report 1994, above n. 90 at 170 (referring to ONUSAL, Truth Commission and Joint Group in El Salvador).

[127] Id. at 171.

IACHR, whose members are non-political experts committed to human rights. The Haitian *coup* occurred within months of the adoption of the Santiago Commitment and AG Res. 1080. The OAS reaction was vigorous, in part because close OAS involvement in monitoring the 1990 elections gave the organization a stake in the success of Aristide's experiment.[128] The OAS refused recognition to the *de facto* authorities[129] and imposed economic sanctions to isolate and pressure the military government.[130]

While the Haitian case reflects well on the seriousness of the Santiago Commitment, it also exposes continued weaknesses. OAS sanctions had little bite until reinforced by the UN Security Council,[131] OAS human rights monitors had little presence until joined by the UN,[132] and the restoration of President Aristide was delayed until the region's hegemon employed military force under UN auspices.[133] The UN/OAS monitoring mission in Haiti experienced severe frustration due to the shifting priorities of key political actors and was required to withdraw on several occasions when the military government perceived high-level support eroding for its efforts.[134] IACHR consideration of the US policy of interdiction and forced repatriation of Haitian asylum-seekers seemed little more than a side-show,[135] even though the refugee situation influenced the United States' eventual decision to intervene forcefully. However, IACHR reports remained an integral aspect of the OAS response to the Haitian crisis.[136]

OAS reaction to the 1992 situation in Peru raises doubt about the depth and meaning of the Santiago Commitment. Fujimori capitalized on public disgust with corrupt and ineffectual legislators and judges by abruptly dismissing the Congress and many jurists.[137] Concentration of power in an authoritarian executive being characteristic of states of emergency, Fujimori's actions were widely criticized. The Permanent Council and *ad hoc* Meeting of Ministers took quick action, prompting Fujimori to appear at the OAS General Assembly and promise a constitutional convention and municipal elections.[138] The adverse reaction of international funders

---

[128] Farer, *Introduction*, above n. 4 at 15.

[129] William G. O'Neill, 'Human Rights Monitoring vs. Political Expediency: the Experience of the OAS/U.N. Mission in Haiti', 8 *Harv. Hum. Rts. J* 101 (1995).

[130] Above n. 11. [131] Id.

[132] O'Neill, above n. 129; I. Martin, 'Haiti: Mangled Multilateralism', 95 *Foreign Policy* 72 (1994).

[133] Perusse, *Haitian Democracy Restored 1991–1995*, (1995), 97–11.

[134] 'Civilian Human Rights Observers Return; UN Mission Faces Obstacles', 31 *UN Chronicle* 20 (1994).

[135] Annual Report 1993, above n. 112 at 334 (decision on admissibility).

[136] Above n. 49.

[137] F. Rospigliosi, 'Democracy's Bleak Prospects' in Tulchin and Bland (eds.), *Peru in Crisis: Dictatorship or Democracy?*, (Boulder, 1994), 35, 50–1; P. Oliart, 'A President Like You: Fujimori's Popular Appeal', XXX *NACLA Rep't. on the Americas* 18–19 (1996).

[138] Above n. 84; see also Rospigliosi, above n. 137 at 46–50.

reinforced pressure from OAS bodies,[139] but Fujimori's serendipitous capture of *Sendero Luminoso* leader Abimael Guzmán reinvigorated direct popular support as a buffer against external human rights criticism.[140] In the end, the revised Constitution extended the death penalty in violation of a non-derogable provision of the American Convention,[141] while the new Peruvian judiciary included 'faceless' judges dispensing punishment without fair process.[142] That Fujimori placated the OAS, despite these draconian measures, raises doubt whether the new focus on democratic governance genuinely reinforces concern for human rights.[143]

The rapid and unseemly collapse of the effort by President Jorge Serrano Elias to mimic Fujimori in Guatemala casts a more optimistic glow on the framework of the Santiago Commitment.[144] Immediate reaction by the Permanent Council and Foreign Ministers to Serrano's attempt to seize power from the legislative and judicial branches induced abandonment by his expected military allies and led to his replacement by the human rights ombudsman Ramiro de León Carpio.[145] Again, loss of foreign financial support added heft to OAS pressure.[146] Similar failed *golpes* in Venezuela reinforce the conclusion that, at least where popular support is lacking,[147] the rapid-response mechanism of the Santiago Commitment significantly reduces the risk that American states will revert to past violent patterns of regime change.

[139] Palmer, above n. 2 at 273–6; C. Graham, 'Introduction: Democracy in Crisis and the International Response', in Tulchin and Bland (eds.), *Peru in Crisis: Dictatorship or Democracy?* (Boulder, 1994), 1, 7–8.

[140] G. Rochabrún, 'Deciphering the Enigmas of Alberto Fujimori', XXX *NACLA Rep't. on the Americas* 16, 20 (1996).

[141] Art. 140 of the new Constitution extended the death penalty from 'treason against the state in time of external war' to 'the crime of treason against the state in time of war, and for the crime of terrorism', adding the ambiguous caveat that this extension be 'in accordance with the laws and treaties to which Peru is a party'. Convention Art. 4.2 prohibits expansion of the death penalty. The Fujimori government has refrained from enacting implementing legislation and acknowledges that the price for expansion of the death penalty may be renunciation of the Convention. Human Rights Watch/Americas: *The Two Faces of Justice* 7, n. 11 (1995).

[142] Id. at 3, 7, 20–5.

[143] R. J. Bloomfield, 'Making the Western Hemisphere Safe for Democracy: The OAS Defense-of-Democracy Regime', 17 *Wash. Q* 157 (1994) (OAS accepted authoritarian system with forms of democracy in Peru because of fears of instability).

[144] As D. E. Acevedo and C. Grossman conclude: 'The OAS's swift response was essential to the failure of the *autogolpe*. The presence of the high-level OAS mission in Guatemala dramatized the message that the *autogolpe* would not be recognized. . . . [T]he somehow accommodating reaction in the case of Fujimori could not be taken for granted: if a swift reaction was considered politically possible, the OAS would employ such action.' 'The Organization of American States and the Protection of Democracy', in Farer (ed.), *Beyond Sovereignty: Collectively Defending Democracy in the Americas* (Baltimore, 1996), 132, 142.

[145] S. Berger, 'Guatemala: Coup and Countercoup', 27 *NACLA Rep't. on the Americas* 4 (1993).

[146] Schnably, above n. 6 at 472–6.

[147] Id. at 395, n. 2.

The Inter-American Court of Human Rights

The Court may preside over contentious interstate cases involving states parties accepting this optional jurisdiction;[148] individual cases referred by the IACHR or a state party;[149] or requests for advisory opinions filed by the IACHR or any OAS member state.[150] To date, the Court has not had opportunity to address the threshold of severity for derogation under Article 27.1 or procedural issues such as notification under Article 27.3. However, non-derogability has featured in several advisory opinions and, more tangentially, in contentious individual cases.

Two path-breaking advisory opinions in 1987 gave a powerful reading to Article 27.2, holding that the remedies of *amparo* and *habeas corpus* are among 'the judicial guarantees essential for the protection of [non-derogable] rights',[151] that these essential judicial guarantees also include judicial proceedings inherent in representative democracy under Article 29.c and that all judicial proceedings must be consistent with due legal process as defined in Article 8.[152] The non-derogability of *amparo* and *habeas corpus,* if respected by OAS states, could substantially reduce violations of fundamental rights during states of emergency.

The IACHR requested Advisory Opinion OC-8/87 because suspension of *habeas corpus* characterizes many states of emergency and because incommunicado detention facilitates violations of non-derogable guarantees against torture and inhuman treatment.[153] The IACHR urged that elimination of a judicial role in assessing the reasonableness of administrative detention violates the principle of separation of powers inherent in the rule of law in democratic societies.[154]

The Court declared that the preservation of democracy was the only legitimate basis for a suspension of rights under the Convention,[155] which could never countenance suspension of the rule of law itself.[156] A derogating government is still legally constrained, even though it may exercise broader flexibility to restrict rights than in normal times.[157] The extent and nature of the judicial guarantees preserved by Article 27.2 depend upon

---

[148] Convention Arts. 45, 62.
[149] Convention Arts. 44, 61.
[150] Convention Art. 64.
[151] *Habeas Corpus in Emergency Situations (Arts. 27(2), 25(1) and 7(6) of the American Convention on Human Rights)*, Advisory Opinion No. 8, I/A Court H.R. Annual Report 1987 at 17, 9 *HRLJ* 94.
[152] *Judicial Guarantees in States of Emergency (Arts. 27(2), 25 and 8 American Convention on Human Rights)*, Advisory Opinion No. 9 I/A Court H.R. Annual Report 1988 at 13, 9 *HRLJ* 204.
[153] Advisory Opinion No. 9, above n. 150 at para. 12.
[154] Id.
[155] Id. at para. 20.
[156] Id. at para. 24.
[157] Id.

which non-derogable rights are jeopardized by emergency measures,[158] but where the right to life and basic human dignity and physical integrity are threatened, *habeas corpus* and *amparo* must remain available.[159] Constitutions and laws of states parties that authorize the suspension of *habeas corpus* and *amparo* during emergencies are thus fundamentally incompatible with the terms of the Convention.[160]

The recently democratized Government of Uruguay requested Advisory Opinion OC-9/87,[161] in which the Court attempted a general definition of the phrase 'essential judicial guarantees'. Noting that the lack of a concrete case was not a barrier to its rendering an opinion, the Court observed that 'the question raised in the request of the Government is related to a specific juridical, historical and political context, in that states of exception or emergency, and of human rights and the essential judicial guarantees in those moments, is a critical problem in the Americas.'[162] The Court's approach stressed both the text and structure of the Convention. Remedies that are 'judicial' require a decisionmaker reasonably independent from the political actors imposing emergency measures.[163] The norm of proportionality in Article 27.1 can realistically be effectuated only if national measures of control exist to insure that strict limits between the public danger and rights-suspensive measures are kept.[164] The Convention does not permit elimination of judicial remedies essential to protect either non-derogable rights or other rights not actually suspended;[165] indeed, the non-existence of effective judicial remedies itself violates the Convention.[166] From Article 8 the Court concludes that due legal process is a requirement of all judicial guarantees under the Convention, including those mentioned in Article 27.2.[167]

The distinct attachment of the inter-American system to 'representative democracy as a form of government' in Article 29.c suggests that meaningful judicial protection, as well as democratic political structures, are mandatory under all circumstances.[168] In addition to *habeas corpus* and *amparo*, Article 27.2 thus requires the preservation of judicial guarantees 'necessary to the preservation of the rule of law, even during the state of exception that results from the suspension of guarantees'.[169] Advisory

---

[158] Advisory Opinion No. 8, above n. 150 at paras. 27–9.

[159] Id. at paras. 42–4. In the *Neira Alegría* case, I/A Court H.R. Series C No. 22, 16 *HRLJ* 403, 3 IHRR 362 (1966) the Court held that Peru had violated the right to *habeas corpus* in Art. 7(6), Convention in relation to the prohibition of derogations for certain rights in Art. 27(2), Convention. This was because the declaration of a state of emergency in parts of Peru and the application of a restricted military zone in certain prisons had impliedly suspended the application of *habeas corpus* to the detriment of three prisoners.

[160] Id.

[161] Above, n. 151.

[162] Id. at para. 17.

[163] Id. at para. 20.

[164] Id. at para. 21.

[165] Id. at para. 25.

[166] Id. at para. 24.

[167] Id. at para. 29.

[168] Id. at para. 37.

[169] Id. at para. 38.

Opinion OC-9/87 does not specify precise judicial remedies, in addition to *habeas corpus* and *amparo*, that can never be suspended; these remedies will vary depending upon the judicial organization of the state concerned and the circumstances of a particular emergency.[170]

The Court's advisory jurisprudence has touched additional issues relevant to non-derogable rights, although none of its other opinions have dealt so deeply with states of emergency. For example, in the aftermath of his 1992 *autogolpe*, President Fujimori of Peru sought to extend the death penalty to acts of domestic terrorism in contradiction to Convention Article 4.2.[171] The IACHR mounted an elliptical attack upon this step, yielding the rather abstract Advisory Opinion OC-14/94.[172]

The Court's delineation of doctrines of state responsibility for violations of non-derogable rights in contentious cases such as *Velásquez Rodríguez*[173] and its practice of ordering provisional measures pursuant to Article 63.2 of the Convention[174] have great potential relevance to the protection of human rights during states of emergency. However, the decided cases do not dwell upon the nuances of Article 27 or the dynamics of emergency rule.

CONCLUSION

As Article 27.1 of the American Convention recognizes, authentic states of emergency may justify restrictions on human rights that are intolerable under ordinary circumstances. But emergency rule consistent with the terms of Article 27 has been the rare exception in OAS experience. States of emergency in the Americas have been tragically linked with large-scale violation of non-derogable rights and authoritarian government directly at odds with the regional norm of democracy. During the 1970s and 1980s when repressive military governments controlled much of Latin America, the human rights organs of the OAS pioneered bold techniques to expose and deter emergency-related violations. Especially noteworthy were the on-site visits and special country reports of the IACHR and the advisory opinions of the Inter-American Court. These mechanisms focused primarily on the protection of non-derogable rights.

---

[170] Id. at para. 40.   [171] See above n. 141.

[172] *International Responsibility for the Promulgation and Enforcement of Laws in Violation of the Convention (Arts. 1 and 2 of the American Convention on Human Rights)*, Advisory Opinion No. 14, I/A Court H.R. Annual Report 1995 at 89–101, 16 *HRLJ* 9, 2 IHRR 380 (1995).

[173] Above n. 115.

[174] See, e.g., *Provisional Measures Requested by the Inter-American Commission on Human Rights in the Matter of Guatemala (Colotenango case)*, I/A Court H.R. Annual Report 1994 (1995), 2 IHRR 414, 421 (1995) (threats against witnesses to violent attack by civil patrol against demonstrators in Guatemalan village).

The dramatic return to democratic government in the Americas has presented new challenges for the OAS, while diminishing the profile of states of emergency as *the* human rights problem of the region. The IACHR and Court must now collaborate with human rights and election monitors, the Permanent Council and Foreign Ministers, as well as various *ad hoc* bodies. Old-style *golpes de estado*, while now rare, have not been entirely banished. OAS response to the overthrow of President Aristide in Haiti in 1991 was prompt and vigorous but ineffectual without UN reinforcement. The Santiago Commitment to Democracy shifts focus from states of emergency *per se* to those that threaten to topple a democratically elected government. In essence, it is a mutual solidarity pact among governments, many of which are beneficiaries of the recent wave of re-democratization. Democracy being ill-defined, authoritarian 'outsider' politicians with strong popular support and a credible terrorist threat, such as Peru's President Fujimori, may deflect human rights scrutiny despite large-scale violations of non-derogable rights. Even with the end of the dark 'state of siege' era, the OAS continues to battle emergency-related human rights challenges.

13

The Inter-American Human Rights System at the Dawn of the New Century: Recommendations for Improvement of its Mechanism of Protection

ANTÔNIO AUGUSTO CANÇADO TRINDADE

EVOLUTION AND PRESENT STATE OF THE SYSTEM

The idea of a general revision of the inter-American system of human rights protection seems to have lately been gathering momentum in the American continent, aiming at the improvement of its mechanism of protection. A Seminar of Experts to that effect was held by the Inter-American Commission on Human Rights on 2–3 December 1996 at the headquarters of the Organization of American States in Washington DC. This Seminar was preceded by another event, the Conference of Experts on the Future of International Human Rights, co-sponsored by the Inter-American Institute of Human Rights and the International Rule of Law Institute of George Washington University,[1] which was held in Washington DC, 20–22 May 1996, and which also dwelt upon the subject of the perspectives of the inter-American system of protection in particular. Other related initiatives are likely to follow, and discussions are bound to develop in the forthcoming months; as this takes place, any projection as to the future of the inter-American system of human rights protection cannot but take into account the experience accumulated in this domain over the last decades.

A reassessment of this regional human rights system requires a clear understanding of its formation and development which, in turn, leads, in our view, to the identification of five stages in its evolution, namely: that of the origins of the system; that of the formation of the system (with the gradual expansion of the powers of the Inter-American Commission on Human Rights); that of the conventional institutionalization of the system

---

[1] This Conference was coordinated, on behalf of the two institutions, by Professors Thomas Buergenthal, Antônio A. Cançado Trindade and Michael Singer. The Conference Report was published in December 1996.

(as from the entry into force of the American Convention on Human Rights); that of the consolidation of the system (with the development of the case-law of the Inter-American Court of Human Rights and the adoption of the two Protocols to the American Convention and of other 'sectorial' inter-American Conventions); and that of the improvement of the system, a stage that has recently commenced. The first part of this Chapter will survey these stages of evolution, and the present state of the system. This will be followed by the presentation of recommendations *de lege ferenda* for the improvement of the system and its perspectives at the dawn of the new century.

Origins

The 1948 American Declaration on the Rights and Duties of Man, accompanied by the 1948 Inter-American Charter of Social Guarantees,[2] represent the starting point of the process of generalization of human rights protection in the American continent. The American Declaration, like the Universal Declaration of Human Rights of the same year, comprised a wide range of human rights (civil, political, economic, social and cultural), aiming at the protection of human beings not only under certain circumstances or in circumscribed sectors as in the past, but in all circumstances and in all areas of human activity. The following may be considered to have been, in historical perspective, the major contributions of the 1948 American Declaration to the development of the inter-American system of protection: a) the conception of human rights as inherent to the human person; b) the integral conception of human rights (encompassing civil, political, economic, social and cultural rights); c) the normative basis of protection vis-à-vis States not Parties to the (subsequent) American Convention on Human Rights; and d) the correlation between rights and duties.[3]

---

[2] Ninth International Conference of American States, *Final Act* , Resolution XXIX, 29.

[3] In recent years, the 1948 American Declaration has been referred to, on distinct occasions, by the Inter-American Court of Human Rights, e.g.: a) in the first Advisory Opinion (of 1982), for the integration between the universal and regional systems of protection; b) in the sixth Advisory Opinion (of 1986), in relation to the concept of the common good (Article 32(2) of the American Convention); c) in the tenth Advisory Opinion (of 1989), as to the interpretative interaction between the Declaration and the American Convention. On the American Declaration, cf., generally: Buergenthal, 'La Relación Conceptual y Normativa entre la Declaración Americana y la Convención Americana sobre Derechos Humanos', *Revista del Instituto Interamericano de Derechos Humanos*—special issue [May 1989] 111–19; A. A. Cançado Trindade, 'El Sistema Interamericano de Protección de los Derechos Humanos (1948–1995): Evolución, Estado Actual y Perspectivas', *Derecho Internacional y Derechos Humanos/Droit international et droits de l'homme* (D. Bardonnet and A.A. Cançado Trindade (eds.), San José de Costa Rica/La Haye, Académie de Droit International de La Haye/Instituto Interamericano de Derechos Humanos, 1996, 47–95; A. A. Cançado Trindade, 'Reflexiones sobre las Declaraciones Universal y Americana de Derechos Humanos de 1948 con Ocasión de

In this first stage, the 1948 Declaration and Charter of Social Guarantees were preceded or accompanied by other instruments of varying content and legal effects, generally oriented to certain situations or categories of rights.[4] Some were binding, others purely recommendatory, instruments (treaties and resolutions respectively). They formed a complex normative corpus, disclosing a diversity of ambits of application (for example, as to its beneficiaries) and paving the way to the devising of distinct means of implementation. This was to mark the operation of the future inter-American system of human rights protection in the years to follow.

Formation

One decade after the adoption of the American Declaration, the Inter-American Commission on Human Rights was created in 1959 by a resolution[5] (and not a treaty), with a mandate originally limited to the promotion of human rights, and enjoying a *sui generis* position within the regional system. Soon it endeavoured to enlarge its own competence, as an organ of *in loco* investigation of situations of human rights and of examination of petitions alleging violations of human rights. Its enlarged attributions and powers were also to comprise the reporting system (reports of distinct kinds, such as session and annual reports, and reports on specific countries). With the 1967 Protocol of Reform of the OAS Charter (which entered into force in 1970) the Commission was at last established as one of the main organs of the OAS and thus endowed with a conventional basis. With the entry into force of the American Convention on Human Rights, the Commission has had a duality of functions, exercising jurisdiction over States Parties to the American Convention as well as States not Parties to the Convention (as to these latter, on the basis of the OAS Charter and the 1948 American Declaration).

The Inter-American Commission on Human Rights has developed its vast practice through the application of the three methods of implementation, namely, the petitioning system (examination of complaints or petitions), the reporting system (elaboration of country reports on the human

Su Cuadragésimo Aniversario', *Revista del Instituto Interamericano de Derechos Humanos—* special issue [May 1989] 121–9; H. Gros Espiell, 'La Declaración Americana: Raíces Conceptuales y Políticas en la Historia—Filosofía y el Derecho Americano', *Revista del Instituto Interamericano de Derechos Humanos—*special issue [May 1989], 41–64; D. Uribe Vargas, *Los Derechos Humanos y el Sistema Interamericano*, (Madrid, 1972).

[4] These were the conventions on the rights of aliens and naturalized citizens (1902, 1906 and 1928), on asylum (1928), on the rights of women (1948); resolutions adopted at inter-American Conferences on various aspects of human rights protection (1938 and 1945); and declarations of inter-American Conferences referring to the subject (1945 and 1948).

[5] Resolution VIII, of the Vth Meeting of Consultation of Ministers of External Relations (Santiago, 1959).

rights situations in particular countries in the region), and the fact-finding system (undertaking of missions of observation *in loco* in various countries).[6] On several occasions the Commission has called upon OAS member States to incorporate certain rights into the texts of their Constitutions and to harmonize their national legislation with the provisions contained in human rights treaties. In its Annual Reports, particularly in recent years, the Commission has related the question of the protection of human rights to its concern about the political organization itself of OAS member-States and the effective exercise of representative democracy as a principle enshrined in the OAS Charter.

The observations *in loco* have been undertaken by the Commission either in the course of the examination of petitions (so as to determine or prove the facts denounced) or else in the investigation of general situations of human rights in given States. Some of those missions became particularly important at different times in the Commission's history, such as those in the case of the Dominican Republic (1965–1966), in the armed conflict between Honduras and El Salvador (1969), in the case of Chile (starting in 1973) and in the enforced or involuntary disappearances in Argentina (report of 1979). By the end of the seventies, the Commission had undertaken eleven such missions, a total which had doubled by the end of the eighties. The Commission is certainly one of the human rights international supervisory organs which has made most use of missions of *in loco* observation.

As for individual petitions, while by the late seventies the Commission

---

[6] On the work of the Commission in general, cf., e.g.: Comisión Interamericana de Derechos Humanos, *Diez Años de Actividades—1971–1981*, (Washington DC, 1982; K. Vasak, *La Commission Interaméricaine des Droits de l'Homme*, (Paris, 1968); A. Schreiber, *The Inter-American Commission on Human Rights*, (Leyden, 1970); Cançado Trindade, 'The Evolution of the OAS System of Human Rights Protection: An Appraisal', 25 *German Yearbook of International Law* (1982), 498–514; C. Grossman, 'Proposals to Strengthen the Inter-American System of Protection of Human Rights', 32 *German Yearbook of International Law* (1989), 264–75. On the methods of operation of the Commission in general, cf., e.g.: A. Aguilar, 'Procedimiento que Debe Aplicar la Comisión Interamericana de Derechos Humanos en el Examen de las Peticiones o Comunicaciones Individuales sobre Presuntas Violaciones de Derechos Humanos', *Derechos Humanos en las Américas—Homenaje a la Memoria de C.A. Dunshee de Abranches,* (Washington DC,1984), 199–216; B. Santoscoy, *La Commission interaméricaine des droits de l'homme et le développement de sa compétence par le système des pétitions individuelles* (Paris, 1995); M. Pinto, *La Denuncia ante la Comisión Interamericana de Derechos Humanos* (Buenos Aires, 1993); Goldman, 'Uruguay: Amnesty Law in Violation of Human Rights Convention', 49 *Review of the International Commission of Jurists* (1992), 37–45; C. Sepúlveda, 'El Procedimiento de Solución Amistosa ante la Comisión Interamericana de Derechos Humanos', *Derechos Humanos en las Américas—Homenaje a la Memoria de C.A. Dunshee de Abranches*, (Washington DC, 1984), 242–52; E. Vargas Carreño, 'Las Observaciones *In Loco* Practicadas por La Comisión Interamericana de Derechos Humanos', *Derechos Humanos en las Américas—Homenaje a la Memoria de C.A. Dunshee de Abranches*, (Washington DC,1984), 290–305; E. Márquez Rodríguez, 'Visitas de Observación *In Loco* de la Comisión Interamericana de Derechos Humanos y Sus Informes', in Cançado Trindade, G. Elizondo and J. Ordóñez (eds.), *Estudios Básicos de Derechos Humanos, Vol. III* (San José, 1995), 135–44.

had examined more than three thousand cases, by the early nineties that total had surpassed ten thousand communications. In its vast practice on the matter, the Commission has adopted resolutions that vary in content according to the facts of the cases. In these resolutions, the Commission has, for example, declared that the alleged acts constitute *prima facie* violations of human rights, or recommended a full investigation of what appeared to constitute violations of human rights, or decided to adjourn consideration of the cases until the results of ongoing investigations are known, or else declared that the alleged violations of human rights have not been proved.

In its decisions on individual cases, or in its *in loco* observations, or else in its country reports on human rights situations, the Commission has dwelt upon such topics as the right to minimal conditions in prisons, the prevalence of judicial guarantees and the due process of law, the characterization of arbitrary detention, the restrictions on death penalty, the requisites of states of emergency and control of suspension of guarantees, the rights to personal freedom and political participation, the presumption of innocence and the absolute condemnation of torture, among others. The Commission has recently indicated that it would be prepared also to survey economic, social and cultural rights. To the concrete results obtained in numerous cases, one may add the preventive function exercised by the Commission. By virtue of its general recommendations addressed to some governments or formulated in its reports, changes have been introduced in national laws or other provisions which violated human rights and domestic remedies and procedures have been set up or perfected so as to ensure the observance of and respect for human rights in the countries of the region.

Conventional Institutionalization

The entry into force in mid-1978 of the 1969 American Convention on Human Rights[7] represented the conventional institutionalization of the regional inter-American system of protection, bringing about the placing of the competence of the Commission (and the newly established Court) on a firm treaty basis as well as legal effects in the domestic law of States Parties. The Convention was largely devoted, like its European counterpart, to the protection of civil and political rights. The Convention contains only one general provision (Article 26) on the 'progressive development' of economic, social and cultural rights. The historical normative gap vis-à-vis economic, social and cultural rights was to be filled and remedied only

[7] On the preparatory work of this latter (not always as illuminating as it might be), see Organización de los Estados Americanos (OAS), *Conferencia Especializada Interamericana sobre Derechos Humanos—Actas y Documentos* (San José de Costa Rica), OEA doc. OEA/Ser.K/XVI/1.2 (1969).

later, with the adoption of the 1988 San Salvador Protocol, which has not yet entered into force. A second Protocol, on the abolition of the death penalty, was adopted in 1990. The two Protocols expand in a significant way the scope of the rights protected in the American Convention system (cf. below).

The Convention provides for a general obligation to 'respect' the protected rights and to 'ensure' their full exercise (Article 1(1)). The scope of this general obligation has been the object of jurisprudential interpretation, notably in the judgments of the Inter-American Court of Human Rights in the *Honduran cases* (merits, 1988–1989).[8]

It cannot pass unnoticed that the draftsmen of the Convention took trouble to include a provision (Article 29) which contains clear norms of interpretation: they expressly rejected an interpretation of the provisions of the Convention which would involve suppressing or limiting the enjoyment and exercise of the protected rights under the Convention by reference to the domestic law of States Parties, or to other international instruments on human rights. The essentially objective character of the obligations entered into by States Parties as to the protection of human rights is beyond question.

The extent of obligations under the American Convention[9] can be measured by its legal effects in the domestic law of States Parties. It is acknowledged today, for example, that Article 2 of the Convention contains an obligation to harmonize national legislation with the provisions of the Convention, a duty which is added to the general obligation under Article 1 of the Convention. Article 2 is certainly not meant to deny the self-executing character of the provisions of the Convention, but, on the contrary, it is intended to single out the general duty of States Parties to harmonize their domestic law with the Convention, or to incorporate the provisions of this latter into their domestic law, in addition to the specific duties that states parties have in relation to each of the protected rights. Moreover, the Convention recognizes the right of everyone to an effective

---

[8] *Velásquez Rodríguez* case, I/A Court H.R. Series C No.4 (1988), 9 *HRLJ* 212; *Godínez Cruz* case, I/A Court H.R. Series C No.5 (1989).

[9] Cf., in general, e.g.: T. Buergenthal, R. Norris and D. Shelton, *Protecting Human Rights in the Americas—Selected Problems*, 3rd. rev. ed.(Kehl/Strasbourg, 1990); A. A. Cançado Trindade, 'Formación, Consolidación y Perfeccionamiento del Sistema Interamericano de Protección de los Derechos Humanos', *XVII Curso de Derecho Internacional Organizado por Comité Jurídico Interamericano (1990)*, (Washington DC, 1991), 9–47; H. Gros Espiell, 'Le Système Interaméricain comme Régime Régional de Protection Internationale des Droits de l'Homme', *Recueil des Cours de l'Académie de Droit International* II (1975), 7–11; E. Vargas Carreño, 'Algunos Problemas que Presentan la Aplicación y la Interpretación de la Convención Americana sobre Derechos Humanos', *La Convención Americana sobre Derechos Humanos,* Washington DC, CIDH/OAS General Secretariat, 1980, 149–69; C. Medina, 'The Inter-American Commission on Human Rights and the Inter-American Court of Human Rights: Reflections on a Joint Venture', 12 *Human Rights Quarterly,* 439–64 (1990).

remedy before national courts to protect the rights guaranteed by the Convention or by the Constitution or domestic laws (Article 25, and Article 8 on the right to a fair trial).

As the American Convention entered into force, the Inter-American Commission, as already indicated, was endowed with a duality of functions, vis-à-vis States Parties (on the basis of the Convention itself) as well as non-Parties which were OAS members (on the basis of the OAS Charter and the 1948 American Declaration). The Commission has undertaken its work by making use of the above-mentioned methods of examination of individual petitions, preparation of reports (of distinct kinds) and conduct of *in loco* observations (fact-finding). The American Convention also provides for 'friendly settlement' on the basis of respect for human rights (Articles 48–50), a possibility which has been resorted to in some cases.

The American Convention confers the right of individual petition in an expansive and unqualified way, to any person (Article 44), without the petitioner having to claim to be himself/herself a victim of a violation of the Convention. This simplified formula has enabled a greater number of persons to lodge complaints with the Inter-American Commission than is the case under some comparable international petition procedures. The Commission has, in turn, applied the conditions of admissibility of petitions with particular sympathy for the need to protect human rights. For example, in the application of the local remedies rule, the Commission has adopted a diversity of solutions (such as requests for further information or the postponement of the examination or the taking of a decision in a case), instead of an early rejection of a complaint and the subsequent re-opening of the case. In the so-called 'general cases' the Commission has dispensed with the exhaustion rule and has applied presumptions (for example, the non-existence or ineffectiveness of local remedies) in favour of the alleged victims.[10] This practice demonstrates that the exhaustion of domestic remedies rule does not have an absolute character, and may be applied with flexibility in the present context of human rights protection.

In its turn, the Inter-American Court has likewise dwelt upon the extent of the exceptions to the local remedies rule, going beyond the generally recognized exceptions of undue delays and denial of justice (for example, by allowing exceptions in cases of indigence and of generalized fear in the legal community to represent victims), as well as upon the issues of the shifting of the burden of proof with regard to exhaustion and the express or tacit waiver of the local remedies rule. The Court has, furthermore, applied the criterion of the reasonable probability of success in the utilization of a remedy, and has insisted on the need for effectiveness of local remedies. It

---

[10] The 'general cases' are ones in which the local situation is such that it can be assumed that adequate and effective remedies are generally not available. See Cerna, 87, above

has rightly pointed out, for example, that in cases of disappearances of persons as a 'state practice' or of negligence or tolerance on the part of public authorities there must be a presumption in favour of the victim, and that there is no point in insisting on the application of the exhaustion rule (as there are in effect no remedies to exhaust). More recently, the Court has rightly ruled[11] that, if the respondent government has failed to invoke the preliminary objection of non-exhaustion in the admissibility proceedings before the Commission, it may not raise it subsequently before the Court (estoppel).

The contribution of the Commission and the Court on this matter point in the right direction, paving the way for developing the application of the local remedies rule so as to pay special attention to the overriding need to protect human rights and the particularities of the context of international implementation of human rights. That contribution shows that the incidence of the local remedies rule in human rights protection is certainly distinct from its application in the practice of diplomatic protection of nationals abroad (in customary international law), and that the rule is far from being an immutable or sacrosanct principle of international law. We are here in a domain of protection which is fundamentally victim-oriented, concerned with the rights of individual human beings rather than of States. Generally recognized rules of international law (to which the formulation of the local remedies rule in human rights treaties refers), besides following an evolution of their own in the distinct contexts in which they apply, necessarily suffer, when inserted in human rights treaties, a certain degree of adjustment or adaptation, dictated by the special character of the object and purpose of those treaties and by the widely recognized specificity of the international protection of human rights.[12]

In recent years, attention has been given to the issue of the relationship of the inter-American human rights system with other systems of protection,[13] be it in order to avoid the conflict of competences, the undue

---

[11] Cases *Castillo Páez* and *Loayza Tamayo* (1996).

[12] See A. A. Cançado Trindade, *The Application of the Rule of Exhaustion of Local Remedies in International Law*, (Cambridge, 1983), 1–443; A. A. Cançado Trindade, *El Agotamiento de los Recursos Internos en el Sistema Interamericano de Protección de los Derechos Humanos* (San José, 1991); A. A. Cançado Trindade, *O Esgotamento de Recursos Internos no Direito Internacional*, (Brasilia, 1984), 19–285. And, on the role of domestic remedies, cf., e.g. : H. Fix-Zamudio, 'La Protección Judicial de los Derechos Humanos en Latinoamérica y en el Sistema Interamericano', 8 *Revista del Instituto Interamericano de Derechos Humanos* (1988), 7–64; H. Fix-Zamudio, 'El Derecho Internacional de los Derechos Humanos en las Constituciones Latinoamericanas y en la Corte Interamericana de Derechos Humanos', in Cançado Trindade (ed.), *The Modern World of Human Rights—Essays in Honour of Thomas Buergenthal* (San José, 1996), 159–207; E. Jiménez de Aréchaga, 'La Convención Interamericana de Derechos Humanos como Derecho Interno', 69/71 *Boletim da Sociedade Brasileira de Direito Internacional (1987/1989)*, 35–55.

[13] On the question of their co-ordination, cf., e.g.: A. A. Cançado Trindade, 'Co-existence and Co-ordination of Mechanisms of International Protection of Human Rights (At

duplication of proceedings and the diverging interpretation of corresponding provisions of co-existing international instruments on the part of the supervisory organs (petitioning system), or to achieve uniform guidelines concerning the form and contents and the standardization of reports (reporting system), or to obtain the regular exchange of information and reciprocal consultations between the supervisory organs (fact-finding system). In so far as the petitioning system is concerned, the early practice of the Inter-American Commission on Human Rights, prior to adoption of the American Convention on Human Rights, disclosed considerable flexibility on the question of the relationship with other procedures, as well as complying with the test of the freedom of choice of procedures on the part of the complainants.

With the entry into force of the American Convention, the relevant provisions of this Convention (Articles 46(1)(c) and 47(d)) are complemented by the guidelines on 'duplicity of procedures' found in the Commission's Regulations (Article 39). The criteria indicated in the Regulations are the following: the Commission will not refrain from taking up and examining a complaint when another international procedure is 'limited to an examination of the general situation on human rights in the State in question and there has been no decision on specific facts that are the subject of the petition submitted to the Commission, or is one that will not lead to an effective settlement of the violation denounced'; and the Commission will not refrain from taking up a complaint when 'the petitioner before the Commission or a family member is the alleged victim of the violation denounced' and the petitioner in the other procedure 'is a third party or a nongovernmental entity having no mandate from the former'.

These are precise guidelines, which, in so far as the petitioning system is concerned, allow the Commission to proceed with the examination of the case, to the benefit of the alleged victims. As for the system of fact-finding or observations *in loco*, there are examples of the concomitant application of two or more mechanisms of protection. Thus, the situation of human rights in El Salvador was the object of examination on the part of a Special Representative of the UN Commission on Human Rights as well as of the

Global and Regional Levels)', 202 *Recueil des Cours de l'Académie de Droit International de La Haye* (1987), 21–435; C. A. Dunshee de Abranches, 'Comparative Study of the United Nations Covenants on Civil and Political Rights and on Economic, Social and Cultural Rights and of the Draft Inter-American Convention on Human Rights', *Inter-American Yearbook on Human Rights* (1968), 169–213; H. Gros Espiell, 'La Convention Américaine et la Convention Européenne des Droits de l'Homme—Analyse Comparative', 218 *Recueil de Cours de l'Académie de Droit International* (1989), 175–411; R. Piza, 'Co-ordination of the Mechanisms for the Protection of Human Rights in the American Convention with Those Established by the United Nations', 30 *American University Law Review* (1980), 167–87; A. H. Robertson, 'The American Convention on Human Rights and the European Convention: A Comparative Study', 29 *Annuaire européen/European Yearbook* (1981), 50–76.

Inter-American Commission on Human Rights (period 1982–1985). Likewise, the situation of human rights in Bolivia was investigated both by a Special Envoy of the UN Commission on Human Rights and by the Inter-American Commission on Human Rights (period 1981–1983). The case of enforced or involuntary disappearances in Argentina was the object of observations *in loco* on the part of the Inter-American Commission as well as the Working Group of the United Nations on the subject (period 1979–1984). The Chilean case was likewise examined at global and regional levels by the Ad Hoc Working Group and the Special Rapporteur on Chile of the United Nations, the ILO Committee on Freedom of Association, and the Inter-American Commission on Human Rights (observations *in loco* in the period 1974–1979).

In sum, the mechanisms of human rights protection at global and regional levels are essentially complementary, and the inter-American system of protection has been no exception to that.

Consolidation

The consolidation of the inter-American system of human rights protection can be taken to have occurred with the development of the case-law of the Inter-American Court, as well as the adoption of the two Protocols to the American Convention and of other 'sectorial' inter-American Conventions. The Inter-American Court, it may be recalled, exercises, under the American Convention, two types of jurisdiction:[14] contentious (Article 62) as well as advisory (Article 64), this latter being particularly wide in scope (cf. below).

---

[14] See, e.g., T. Buergenthal, 'The Advisory Practice of the Inter-American Human Rights Court', 79 *American Journal of International Law* (1985), 1–27; M. Cisneros, 'Algunos Aspectos de la Jurisdicción Consultiva de la Corte Interamericana de Derechos Humanos', *La Corte Interamericana de Derechos Humanos—Estudios y Documentos*, (San José de Costa Rica, 1985), 53–66; H. Gros Espiell, 'Contentious Proceedings before the Inter-American Court of Human Rights', 1 *Emory J. Int. Dispute Res.* (1987), 175–218; A. A. Cançado Trindade, 'El Sistema Interamericano de Protección de los Derechos Humanos (1948–1995): Evolución, Estado Actual y Perspectivas', in Bardonnet and Cançado Trindade (eds.), *Derecho Internacional y Derechos Humanos / Droit international et droits de l'homme* (San José de Costa Rica/La Haye, 1996), 47–95. On other aspects of the Court's faculties, cf., e.g.: C. M. Cerna, 'The Structure and Functioning of the Inter-American Court of Human Rights (1979–1992)', *British Year Book of International Law* (1992), 135–229; A. A. Cançado Trindade, 'Formación, Consolidación y Perfeccionamiento del Sistema Interamericano de Protección de los Derechos Humanos', *XVII Curso de Derecho Internacional Organizado por el Comité Jurídico Interamericano (1990)* (Washington DC, 1991), 9–47; T. Buergenthal, 'Judicial Fact-Finding: Inter-American Human Rights Court', in R. Lillich (ed.), *Fact-Finding before International Tribunals*, (Ardsley-on-Hudson; N.Y.,1990), 261–74; J. E. Méndez and J. M. Vivanco, 'Disappearances and the Inter-American Court: Reflections on a Litigation Experience', 13 *Hamline L Rev.* (1990), 507–77; F. O. Salvioli, 'Algunas Reflexiones sobre la Indemnización en las Sentencias de la Corte Interamericana de Derechos Humanos', in Cançado Trindade, Elizondo and Ordóñez (eds.), *Estudios Básicos de Derechos Humanos Vol. III*, (San José of Costa Rica, 1995), 145–64.

In its fourteen Advisory Opinions delivered to date, the Court has been called upon to pronounce upon a wide range of legal issues that are of the utmost importance to the operation of the inter-American system for the protection of human rights. An account of the Court's opinions is given in Chapter 5 above.

In the exercise of its contentious jurisdiction, the Court has on a number of occasions found violations of certain guaranteed rights under the American Convention, in particular the rights to life, to personal freedom and to personal integrity.[15] On three occasions the respondent States recognized their international responsibility for violation of guaranteed rights under the American Convention.[16] There has been one case of friendly settlement to date.[17] And there have been judgments on reparations in five cases so far.[18] In addition, the Court has very recently been seized of some other new cases.

Thus, in the mid-nineties, after more than a decade of exercising mainly its advisory jurisdiction, contentious proceedings now take place on a regular basis before the Inter-American Court. After more than fifteen years of continuous functioning of the Court, the number of contentious cases sent to it by the Commission is now at last clearly and steadily growing. In relation to the Court's case-law in such cases to date, the contribution of three of its judgments may be singled out as being particularly significant: the two judgments as to the merits in the cases of *Velásquez Rodríguez* and *Godínez Cruz*, and the judgment on reparations in the *Aloeboetoe* case.

In the first two, the contribution of the Court consisted in pointing out the threefold duty of States to prevent, investigate and punish the violations of protected rights, as well as to provide redress, and in linking the substantive provisions on violated rights to the general obligation under Article 1(1) to *respect* and to *ensure* the exercise of the rights provided for in the Convention. Ever since, this link has been invoked systematically in other cases by both the Court and the Commission. The next step forward would appear to be a similar exercise in combining the substantive provisions on violated rights with the general obligation under Article 2 to harmonize domestic law with the American Convention. In the third judgment above-mentioned, in the *Aloeboetoe* case, the contribution of the Court consisted in placing reparations for the violations of the protected rights within the social context to which they apply, taking sensibly

---

[15] See the account of the Court's jurisprudence in contentious cases in Chap. 5, above.
[16] Cases *Aloeboetoe* (1991, concerning Suriname), *Garrido and Baigorria* (1996, concerning Argentina), and *El Amparo* (1995, concerning Venezuela).
[17] Case *Maqueda* (1995, concerning Argentina).
[18] Namely, cases *Velásquez Rodríguez* and *Godínez Cruz* (1989–90), *Aloeboetoe* (1993), *Neira Alegría* (1996), and *El Amparo* (1996).

into account the cultural practices in the community of the saramacas (maroons) in Suriname.

Besides the exercise of its advisory and contentious jurisdictions (above), the Court has ordered (under Article 63(2) of the American Convention) provisional or interim measures of protection in cases of extreme gravity and urgency and in order to avoid irreparable damages to the persons.[19] Those measures have been ordered in situations implying an imminent threat to life or of serious physical or mental harm. The granting of provisional measures of protection is assuming an increasingly great importance in the practice of the Court, given their eminently preventive function.

Two Additional Protocols to the American Convention have been adopted to date, namely, the Protocol on Economic, Social and Cultural Rights (of 1988), and the Protocol on the Abolition of Death Penalty (of 1990). As to the former, the old dichotomy between civil and political rights and economic, social and cultural rights (which found expression in the two UN Covenants on Human Rights) had left its traces also in the inter-American system of protection of human rights. The 1969 American Convention on Human Rights was to cover only civil and political rights, and to contain but one provision (Article 26) on the 'progressive realization' of economic, social and cultural rights. If in the course of the preparatory work of the American Convention the projects submitted by Chile and Uruguay in 1965, and by the Inter-American Council of Jurists six years later, had been adopted, economic, social and cultural rights would have been included in the American Convention. Thus, in spite of the existence of the 1948 Inter-American Charter of Social Guarantees, there remained a historical gap in the inter-American system of protection with regard to economic, social and cultural rights.

The gradual overcoming of the old dichotomy, inaugurated by the reassessment of the matter by the 1968 Teheran Proclamation followed by the landmark UN General Assembly resolution 32/130, of 1977, advocating the interrelatedness or indivisibility of all human rights, led quickly to developments on the American continent. The Inter-American Commission on Human Rights, which had taken account of the situation of some economic, social and cultural rights in some Latin American countries (for example, reports on El Salvador, 1978, and Haiti, 1979), acknowledged, in its Annual Report of 1979–1980, the 'organic relationship' between civil and political rights, and economic, social and cultural rights. The field was open for the next step, that is, the preparation of an international instrument for the protection of the latter. Such work, initiated in 1982, culminated in the adoption in 1988 of the Additional Protocol to the American

---

[19] See the account of the Court's jurisprudence on provisional measures in Chap. 5. above.

Convention on Human Rights in the Area of Economic, Social and Cultural Rights ('Protocol of San Salvador').

The 1988 Protocol opens new courses of action: it contemplates (Article 19(6)), for example, the application of the system of individual petitions or communications (regulated by Articles 44–51 and 61–69 of the American Convention) to the right of association and trade union freedom (Article 8(1)(a)) and the right to education (Article 13). Furthermore, it provides for the formulation, by the Inter-American Commission, of such observations and recommendations as it may deem pertinent concerning the situation of economic, social and cultural rights enshrined in the Protocol (Article 19(7)).[20] Such measures disclose a new perspective for the protection of those rights.

It so happens, however, that the San Salvador Protocol has not yet obtained the number of ratifications sufficient for its entry into force; the probability that this may happen in the near future is uncertain. In spite of that, Article 42 of the American Convention opens a possibility of future action while the San Salvador Protocol does not enter into force: it provides that States Parties to the Convention are to transmit to the Inter-American Commission a copy of each of the reports and studies that they submit annually to the Executive Committees of the Inter-American Economic and Social Council (CIES) and the Inter-American Council for Education, Science and Culture (CIECC), so as to enable the Commission to watch over the promotion of the rights ensuing from the economic, social, educational, scientific and cultural norms or provisions of the amended OAS Charter. In fact, the Commission's Annual Report of 1991, for example, contains indications to the effect that the Commission will from now on be devoting closer attention to the situation of economic, social and cultural rights in the American States.

The second Protocol to the American Convention, pertaining to the abolition of the death penalty, adopted in 1990, constitutes a step forward in relation to the provisions of Article 4(2) to (6) of the American Convention. Article 1 of the Protocol determines that the States Parties will not apply the death penalty in their territory to any person subject to their jurisdiction. The Protocol gives a new impetus to the tendency towards the abolition of the death penalty, expressly acknowledged in its preamble. The Protocol does not admit reservations, and makes exception only for the pertinent provisions of domestic law applicable in wartime—

---

[20] For a study of the San Salvador Protocol of 1988, cf., e.g.: A. A. Cançado Trindade, *La Questión de la Protección Internacional de los Derechos Económicos, Sociales y Culturales: Evolución y Tendencias Actuales* (San José of Costa Rica, 1992); A.A. Cançado Trindade, 'La question de la protection internationale des droits économiques, sociaux et culturels: évolution et tendances actuelles', 94 *Revue générale de Droit international public* (1990), 913–46.

thus paving the way for the largest possible number of ratifications by States of the region.

The contemporary inter-American system of human rights protection does not exhaust itself in the American Convention on Human Rights and its two Protocols adopted to date. To them the three new Inter-American Conventions are to be added, concerned with the protection in particular of human rights of certain persons or in given situations, which could thereby be called 'sectorial'. The Inter-American Convention to Prevent and Punish Torture (adopted one year after the UN Convention, and two years before the European Convention, on this matter),[21] establishes individual responsibility for the crime of torture (Article 3) and establishes obligations on the part of States Parties to prevent and punish torture within their jurisdiction (Articles 6–8 and 11–14). To these latter obligations, it adds the duty to pay suitable compensation for victims of torture (Article 9). Its mechanism of international supervision (Article 17) consists in the submission by States Parties to the Inter-American Commission of Human Rights of information on legislative, judicial, administrative, or other measures they adopt in application of the Convention. The Commission, in its turn, will 'endeavour' to analyse the existing situation in its Annual Reports. It is the weakest mechanism of the three existing Conventions against torture.

The Inter-American Convention on Forced Disappearance of Persons, adopted in 1994, had its preparatory work[22] marked by the prolonged debate as to whether the forced disappearance of persons should be considered a crime against humanity or whether such denomination should correspond only to its systematic practice;[23] the latter was the view that prevailed. The Convention provides for the principle of individual respons-

---

[21] For a comparative study, cf. e.g., H. Gros Espiell, 'Las Convenciones sobre Tortura delas Naciones Unidas y dela Organización de los Estados Americanos', *XIV Curso de Derecho Internacional Organizado por el Comité Jurídico Interamericano (1987)* (Washington DC, 1988), 221–42.

[22] See, e.g., Organización de los Estados Americanos (OAS)/Consejo Permanente, *Informe del Presidente del Grupo de Trabajo Encargado de Analizar el Proyecto de Convención Interamericana sobre Desaparición Forzada de Personas*, doc. OEA/Ser.G/CP/ CAJP/925/93/rev.1, of 25 Jan. 1994, 1–49; OAS, *Informe de la Comisión de Asuntos Jurídicos y Políticos acerca del Proyecto de Convención Interamericana sobre Desaparición Forzada de Personas*, doc. OEA/Ser.G/CP/doc.2458/94, of 22 Feb. 1994, 1-65; OAS, *Report of the Permanent Council on the Draft Inter-American Convention on Forced Disappearance of Persons*, doc. OEA/Ser.P/ AG/doc.3072/94, of 29 Apr. 1994, 1–56, and doc. OEA/Ser.P/AG/doc.2821/92, of 22 Apr. 1992, 1–22.

[23] On gross violations of human rights and the inter-American system of human rights protection, cf., in general, e.g., C. Medina Quiroga, *The Battle of Human Rights—Gross, Systematic Violations and the Inter-American System* (Dordrecht, 1988); and cf. G. Peytrignet, 'Acción Humanitaria Convencional y Extraconvencional del CICR en América Latina: Evaluación y Proyecciones', in Irigoin (ed.), *Nuevas Dimensiones en la Protección del Individuo* (Santiago, 1991), 143–50; H. Hey, *Gross Human Rights Violations: A Search for Causes*, (Dordrecht,1995).

ibility in the crime of forced disappearance (as do the Inter-American Convention against Torture, the 1948 Convention against Genocide, and the 1973 Convention against Apartheid). Besides the individual responsibility of the perpetrators and the international responsibility of the State, the new Convention sets forth the following other legal consequences of its characterisation of the crime of forced disappearance of persons[24] as an international crime (Article II): universal jurisdiction and the obligation to extradite or judge those responsible for the crime; the obligation not to grant political asylum to those responsible for the crime; the imprescriptibility of the action; the obligation of the States to investigate and punish those responsible for the crime; the inadmissibility of the excuse of obedience to superior orders; the inadmissibililiy of benefiting from the condition of being a member of the Executive or Legislative power from which impunity may result from acts constitutive of forced disappearance of persons. As to its international supervision, the Convention refers to the procedures of the Inter-American Commission and Court of Human Rights (Articles XIII-XIV).

The Inter-American Convention on the Prevention, Punishment and Eradication of Violence against Women (Convention of Belém do Pará), also adopted in 1994, covers the subject in both public as well as private ambits (Articles 1 and 3), from an integral outlook encompassing civil, political, economic, social and cultural rights (Articles 4, 5 and 6). To the obligations of States Parties (Articles 7–8), bearing especially in mind the 'situation of vulnerability to violence' which women may suffer (Article 9), it adds a mechanism for international supervision, with provision for a system of reports to the Inter-American Commission on Women (Article 10), and referral to the procedures of the Inter-American Commission and Court of Human Rights (Articles 11–12).

The Inter-American Commission has recently appointed a special rapporteur for the above subject. The mandate of this latter covers an evaluation, in the light of the inter-American norms on the human rights of women, of national legislation and discriminatory practices in the countries of the region. The Inter-American Commission is now concluding the [Inter-American] Declaration of the Rights of Indigenous Peoples (the adoption of which has been postponed in the last four years); its preparatory work has taken into account the endeavours of codification in this area within the United Nations and the International Labour Organization (ILO). Another subject which has recently attracted attention is that of the independence and integrity of members of the Judiciary,[25] resulting in the

---

[24] See, recently, Inter-American Court of Human Rights, *Blake* case (concerning Guatemala), Judgment of 2 July 1996 (Preliminary Objections), and Separate Opinion of Judge A. A. Cançado Trindade.

[25] See Commission Annual Report 1992–3, 207–15.

conclusion that there are deficiencies in the administration of justice in several countries of the American continent.

As to the major question of the preservation and strengthening of representative democracy in the American continent, the OAS Charter itself, it may be recalled, refers to democracy as one of its pillars (preamble and Articles 2(b) and 3(d)). But it was above all by means of Resolution 1080 of the OAS General Assembly of 1991, in combination with the so-called Compromise of Santiago (of the same year), that was intended to instrumentalize the inter-American system so as to promote and enhance representative democracy in the region. The monitoring procedure created has since been applied in the cases of Haiti (1991), Peru (1992) and Guatemala (1993).[26] The subject has been the object of attention also in the Declaration of Nassau (adopted by the 1992 OAS General Assembly) and the 1992 Protocol of Washington of Reform of the OAS Charter.

Under the American Convention on Human Rights, the Inter-American Commission on Human Rights itself has affirmed its competence to examine such matters. For example, in its decision of 1990 in the case of the Mexican elections of 1985–1986, in spite of not having pronounced on the merits, the Commission pointed out that representative democracy presupposes the 'observance of other basic human rights'. In its Annual Reports of 1985–1986 and 1990–1991, the Commission again underlined the direct relationship between representative democracy and the guarantee of the observance of human rights.

RECOMMENDATIONS *DE LEGE FERENDA* FOR THE IMPROVEMENT OF
THE SYSTEM

A new stage in the evolution of the inter-American system of protection is now under way: that of its improvement. To this end, we shall present our thoughts and personal recommendations *de lege ferenda*, in a constructive spirit. There is, in our view, room for improvement in several respects in the contemporary operation of the mechanism of the American Convention on Human Rights.

To begin with, in so far as the composition of the two supervisory organs

[26] For a study of the matter, see, e.g.: A. A. Cançado Trindade, 'Democracia y Derechos Humanos: Desarrollos Recientes, con Atención Especial al Continente Americano', *Federico Mayor Amicorum Liber—Solidarité, Égalité, Liberté; Livre d'hommage, vol. I*, (Bruxelles, 1995), 371–90; D. Shelton, 'Representative Democracy and Human Rights in the Western Hemisphere', 12 *Human Rights L J* (1991), 356–8; W. M. Reisman, 'Humanitarian Intervention and Fledging Democracies', 18 *Fordham Int. L J* (1995), 794–805; J. Crawford, 'Democracy in International Law' (Inaugural Lecture, 5 Mar. 1993), Cambridge, Cambridge University Press, 1994, 1–43; C. M. Cerna, 'Universal Democracy: An International Legal Right or the Pipe Dream of the West?', 27 *N Y U J Int'l. L and Pol.* (1995), 289–329.

is concerned, besides the strict observance of the requisites set forth in the American Convention, there is need to establish clear rules of incompatibility of function (for example, avoiding undue accumulation of jobs or professional activities), expressly defined, for the members of both organs (the Commission and Court), as an additional safeguard of the total independence and impartiality of those organs. As to their conditions of work, which are at present precarious, it is essential that considerably more resources (human and material) are attributed to the Commission and the Court, so that they may fully exercise their functions and satisfy the increasingly varied demands placed upon them to protect human rights.

As to the procedures under the American Convention, they can be improved at virtually all stages. First of all, the opening of cases should be prompt, avoiding all unnecessary delay, and uniform vis-à-vis all States Parties to the Convention (non-selectivity). To the extent that one achieves the 'universal ratification' of human rights treaties by all of the states of the American continent to which the inter-American system is intended to apply, the much-needed and desirable 'jurisdictionalisation'[27] of the mechanisms of human rights protection, and their consequent and equally necessary and desirable depolitization, are bound to accelerate. With the integral ratification by all States[28]—without reservations or interpretative declarations and comprising optional instruments and clauses—of all human rights treaties, the universality of human rights will find expression not only in theory but also in practice, entailing the application of the same norms and criteria to all countries (bearing in mind that the supervisory organs are endowed with clear mandates). The 'jurisdictionalisation' of the procedures of protection constitutes a guarantee for all, against the temptations of selectivity, discretion and casuism. It secures the primacy of the rule of law in the endeavours to realize justice.

With regard to the decisions of the Inter-American Commission as to the admissibility of communications or petitions, these ought to be pronounced *in limite litis*, and not postponed. The decision of admissibility falls, of course, within the exclusive competence of the members of the Commission; the secretariat cannot but assist them. Such decisions ought to be very well founded, as they should not be susceptible of reopening or revision. To allow decisions of admissibility of the Commission to be later reopened and questioned before the Court by the respondent governments generates an unbalance between the parties, in favour of governments (even more so as individuals currently do not even have direct access to the Inter-American Court). If admissibility decisions

[27] By this is meant that the supervisory organs (the Commission and the Court) should emphasise and operate on the basis of the functions and procedures specifically attributed to them by the American Convention.

[28] See Appendix VIII for a list of those states which have ratified the Convention.

continue, as now, to be capable of being reopened by governments before the Court, decisions of inadmissibility of the Commission should also be capable of being reopened by the alleged victims and submitted to the Court. Either all the decisions of the Commission—whether declaring a petition admissible or inadmissible—are reopened before the Court, or they are all kept within the exclusive domain of the Commission.

Once the examination of a case on the merits is concluded by the Commission, if the case is not referred to the Court by the Commission, there is a need for a follow-up procedure for verification and monitoring of the degree of compliance by the State concerned with the decisions of the Commission. If, however, the Commission decides to submit the case to the Court, the dossier must then be very well prepared and founded, so as, for example, to avoid the Court having most of its time consumed with a repetition of the process of fact-finding, and to enable the Court to concentrate on the task of developing its case-law, especially now that new and successive contentious cases begin to be regularly submitted to it by the Commission.

Moreover, clear criteria need to be devised for the referral of cases by the Commission to the Court, so that the present situation of uncertainty on the matter no longer persists. The following elements could be taken into consideration for the formation of such criteria: a) whether fundamental rights (for example, non-derogable rights) are at stake; b) whether there exist questions which could generate a jurisprudential contribution to the interpretation and application of the American Convention; c) whether the questions at issue are susceptible of adequate judicial settlement (for example, 'individualized' cases that are justiciable); d) whether the questions at issue disclose new aspects requiring, or deserving of, judicial determination; e) non-selectivity as between the States Parties to the American Convention which have recognized the compulsory jurisdiction of the Court.

There is also a pressing need to search for a greater balance between the parties at distinct procedural stages. Such balance, for example, should encompass the notification to *both* parties of all and any information on the handling of the case, at all stages, it being incumbent upon the parties to comply with the conventional requisites (including those as to confidentiality). In order to attain that balance, one needs to reconsider more critically the question of re-opening the examination of preliminary objections as to admissibility before the Court which have already been decided by the Commission.[29] Likewise, the joinder of those objections to the merits

---

[29] See I/A Court H.R., *Castillo Páez* case (Preliminary Objections), Judgment of 30 Jan. 1996, Separate Opinion of Judge A. A. Cançado Trindade; I/A Court of H.R., *Loayza Tamayo* case (Preliminary Objections), Judgment of 31 Jan. 1996, Separate Opinion of Judge A. A. Cançado Trindade.

should be avoided, except in very exceptional situations, and on good legal grounds.[30]

The Court should further seek to avoid the situation in which the parties (complainant or respondent), by lack of care or for other reasons, make procedural errors—for example, by the 'withdrawal' of the case—especially when this may render the alleged victims wholly defenceless.[31] Once seized of a case, the Court is master of its own jurisdiction; faced with procedural 'incidents' which may render the alleged victims defenceless, the Court can and ought to retain jurisdiction over the case,[32] even more so because there exist superior interests—of international *ordre public*—at stake.

Last but not least, a point of capital importance ought to be made, one that is closely linked to the doctrinal issue of the procedural capacity of the individual in international law and, more particularly, before international tribunals. In so far as the two existing international courts of human rights—the European and the Inter-American Courts of Human Rights—are concerned, the developments on the matter within the European Court of Human Rights are instructive. As the result of a process beginning in the very first case before the European Court and culminating in the 1980s, the individual is now treated in effect as a party to proceedings before the Court. He may 'request the adoption of interim measures or measures for obtaining evidence, file written pleadings, appear at oral hearings, claim just satisfaction under Article 50 and negotiate friendly settlements'.[33] In addition, by virtue of the Ninth Protocol,[34] which entered into force in 1994, the applicant may, in a case brought against a state party to the Protocol, refer his or her case to the Court after the Commission has reported on the merits; he or she does not have to depend upon the European Commission on Human Rights doing so. In so far as the inter-American system of protection is concerned, the participation of non-

---

[30] See I/A Court H.R., *Genie Lacayo* case, Order of 18 May 1995, 17 *HRLJ* 24, 3 IHRR 397 (1996) Dissenting Opinion of Judge A. A. Cançado Trindade.

[31] See *Cayara* case (Preliminary Objections), I/A Court H.R. Series C No.14, 14 *HRLJ* 159, 1 IHRR Vol 1 175 (1994).

[32] See Art. 43(3) of the 1991 Rules of Procedure of the Court.

[33] D. Harris, M. O'Boyle and C. Warbrick, *The Law of the European Convention on Human Rights* (London, 1995), 661. What the applicant can still not do before the Court is lodge preliminary objections and file a request for revision or interpretation of a judgment.

[34] ETS 140. 18 parties. For comment, see Council of Europe, *Protocol n. 9 to the Convention for the Protection of Human Rights and Fundamental Freedoms—Explanatory Report*, Strasbourg, C.E., 1992, 8–9, and cf. 3–18. For other comments, cf. J.-F. Flauss, 'Le droit de recours individuel devant la Cour européenne des droits de l'homme—Le Protocole n. 9 à la Convention Européenne des Droits de l'Homme', 36 *Annuaire français de droit international* (1990), 507–19; M.-A. Eissen, *El Tribunal Europeo de Derechos Humanos* (Madrid, 1985), 26–43; G. Janssen-Pevtschin, 'Le Protocole Additionnel n. 9 à la Convention Européenne des Droits de l'Homme', 2 *Revue trimestrielle des droits de l'homme* (1991), n. 6, 199–202; M. de Salvia, 'Il Nono Protocollo alla Convenzione Europea dei Diritti dell'Uomo: Punto di Arrivo o Punto di Partenza?', 3 *Rivista Internazionale dei Diritti dell'Uomo* (1990), 474–82.

governmental organizations and other *amici curiae* in the proceedings for Advisory Opinions before the Inter-American Court is well known. The question which can today be raised is in relation to the procedure for contentious cases: can or should the alleged victims (or their legal representatives) have *locus standi in judicio* before the Inter-American Court?

The Court's concern to secure an equitable and fair procedure ought necessarily to lead it to seek to ensure that some form of *locus standi* is granted to the alleged victims (or their legal representatives) before the Court in cases which have already been referred to it by the Commission. This can be achieved pursuant to criteria and rules clearly and previously defined, and with the necessary adaptations to the present procedures and practices (for example, foreseeing ex officio legal assistance on the part of the Commission whenever the victims or other petitioners are unable to provide their own legal representative). This requires the reform of the pertinent provisions of the Statute and Rules of Procedure of the Court. The consequence would be to remedy some distortions brought about by the present system, which inadequately considers, as 'parties' before the Court, the Commission—instead of the victims themselves, as should be the case—and the respondent State (cf. below).

No one better than the victims themselves (or their legal representatives) can defend their rights before the Court, pursuant to previously and clearly defined criteria. No one better than the victims themselves are well motivated to avoid and overcome procedural 'incidents' which may render them defenceless. The *locus standi* of the victims (or their legal representatives) is the logical consequence, at procedural level, of a system of protection providing for individual rights at international level. It is not reasonable to conceive of rights without the procedural capacity to vindicate them. The insufficiencies and deficiencies of the paternalistic mechanism of intermediation by the Commission between the individual and the Court has already been clearly demonstrated in practice. This mechanism was fed by considerations developed in another epoch under the spectrum of State sovereignty, in order to avoid the direct access of the individual to the international legal organs.

It is a mechanism which belongs to the past, as shown by the experience of the European Court of Human Rights and the Ninth Protocol thereto. Once the Eleventh Protocol (of 1994) to the European Convention, on the reform of the mechanism of the European Convention on Human Rights and the establishment of a new European Court as the sole jurisdictional organ of supervision of the European Convention, enters into force, the Ninth Protocol will cease to apply and will become only of historic interest in Europe.[35] However, the Ninth Protocol retains great utility as a model

---

[35] Under the Eleventh Protocol, all states accept an automatic right of individual petition against them upon becoming ECHR parties, with cases being processed by the new single Court

during the current consideration of an eventual revision of the inter-American system of protection, given that the two regional systems are at different stages of development.

Endeavours to improve the inter-American system of protection in this respect would do well to take into consideration the experience of the European Convention, with necessary adaptions to allow for the realities of the operation of our system. Such evolution should take place *pari passu* with the gradual judicialisation of the mechanism of protection: it can hardly be denied that judicial protection is the most advanced form of safeguard of human rights, and the one which best abides by the imperatives of law and justice.

In practice, those who currently act in fact as the lawyers of the victims before the Inter-American Court are euphemistically designated 'assistants' to the Inter-American Commission, and are incorporated as such in the delegation of the Commission appearing before the Court. This pragmatic solution was, so to speak, 'endorsed' by a joint meeting of the Inter-American Commission and the Court (held in Miami) on 24–25 January 1994. Rather than solving the problem, this expedient has created ambiguities, which have lasted ever since. This is not surprising, bearing in mind that the roles of the Commission (as guardian of the Convention assisting the Court) and of the individuals (as the true complainant party) are clearly different.

In the last joint meeting of the Inter-American Court and the Commission (held in Washington DC) on 12 April 1995, support was voiced—although not conclusive—for granting individual complainants *locus standi* before the Court, in cases already referred to it by the Commission. An initial step in this direction has in fact just been taken by the Inter-American Court, in its XXXIV ordinary session, in adopting its new Rules of Procedure on 16 September 1996. The new Rules of Court contain, for the first time, in addition to the provisions on the representation of the respondent States (Article 21) and of the Commission (Article 22) before the Court, a specific provision on the 'representation of the victims or of their relatives' (Article 23), which reads as follows:—'At the stage of reparations the representatives of the victims or of their relatives may present their own arguments and evidence in an autonomous way'.[36]

This is a significant first step, but it is only the first. This provision paves the way for further developments in the same direction. In cases of proven or substantiated violations of human rights, it is the victims themselves—

---

to the point of a final legally binding decision by it in all admitted cases, with there being no need for individual applicants or others (the European Commission will disappear) to refer cases to the Court for a final decision. Individual applicants will continue to have their now established rights as parties to their case before the Court at all stages in the proceedings.

[36] Unofficial translation from the original Spanish.

the true complainant party before the Court—(or their relatives or heirs) who receive, or are entitled to receive, the reparations and indemnities. As the individual victims are present at the *beginning* (before the Commission) as well as at the *end* of the process, there is no sense in denying their presence (before the Court) *during* the process. Coherency is here necessary: the right of access to international justice is to be accompanied by the guarantee of equality of arms in the proceedings before the Court, which is essential to any judicial system of international protection of human rights. The opposition of individual victims of human rights violations to respondent governments—the adversarial element in the arguments of the parties —is of the essence of contentious cases involving the international protection of human rights.

To the acknowledgment of rights, at national as well as international levels, corresponds the capacity to vindicate or exercise them. Without such capacity, any system of protection is ineluctably flawed; in those circumstances, the parties are in flagrant unbalance, and the procedure is partly devoid of an essential element in the search for truth and justice. The 'jurisdictionalisation' of the procedure greatly facilitates the process of remedying this situation and putting an end to those insufficiencies and deficiencies, which can no longer find any justification at the present time.

The full participation of the alleged victims in the procedure before the Court contributes, furthermore, to the more effective presentation of evidence relevant to the case, as no one better than they (or their legal representatives) know how to defend their interests. The exercise of the right of freedom of expression, which the human rights treaties determine to be respected at the level of the domestic law of the States Parties, finds application also at the international level. The precepts of due process of law, which the human rights treaties require to be observed within the legal systems of the States Parties, find application equally at international level. The equity and transparency of the procedure, which are equally applicable to the international supervisory organs, are beneficial to all, including the complainants and the respondent governments.

As if these considerations of principle were not sufficient, there are others, of a more practical nature, that equally militate in favour of the direct access of individuals to the Court, in cases already submitted to it by the Commission. Such advance, on the basis of previously and clearly defined criteria and rules, is convenient not only to the alleged victims but to all concerned: to the governments, to the extent that it contributes to the 'jurisdictionalisation' of the mechanism of protection; to the Court, to enable it to count on more precise and complete information on the facts; and to the Commission, to put an end to the current ambiguity of its role and to enable it to concentrate on its proper function of guardian of the correct and just application of the American Convention (and no longer with the additional function of 'intermediary' between the individual petitioner and the Court).

An advance in this direction is, in the present stage of evolution of the inter-American system of protection, ultimately the *joint* responsibility of both the Court and the Commission. The latter ought always to be prepared to express its point of view before the Court, even if it is not entirely coincident with that of the representatives of the victims; and the Court ought to be prepared to receive, examine and evaluate the arguments of the delegates of the Commission and of the representatives of the victims, even if they are diverging. As the roles of those delegates and representatives are distinct (above), differences in their arguments in the hearings before the Court are normally bound to happen, and are to some extent inevitable.

Finally, only through the *locus standi in judicio* of the alleged victims before the international courts of human rights (in the regional systems of protection) will human beings attain full international procedural capacity to vindicate their rights, when the national organs are incapable of securing the realization of justice. In the improvement of the mechanism of protection under the American Convention, the emphasis ought to fall upon the 'jurisdictionalisation' of that mechanism, particularly in so far as the operation of the method of petitions or complaints is concerned, without prejudice to the continued use by the Inter-American Commission of the methods of reporting and fact-finding. The improvement of the mechanism of the inter-American system of protection ought to be the object of considerations of an essentially juridico-humanitarian character, even as an additional guarantee to the parties in contentious cases of human rights. Every international lawyer, faithful to the historical origins of his/her discipline, will surely contribute to rescue the position of the human being in the law of nations, and sustain the recognition and crystallization of the international personality and full legal capacity of the human being.

The much-needed recognition of the *locus standi* of the alleged victims (or their legal representatives) before the Inter-American Court constitutes an important step forward, but not necessarily the final stage of improvement of the inter-American system of protection. From the *locus standi in judicio* of the individuals before the Inter-American Court one ought to evolve towards the recognition in the foreseeable future of the right of the individuals to lodge a case directly with the [future] Inter-American Court, as the sole organ of protection of the inter-American system of tomorrow. To this end, we wait for the day when, in the parallel regional European system, the Eleventh Protocol to the European Convention on Human Rights enters into force, showing the way to the recognition of the full international legal capacity of the human being to vindicate his/her own rights.

PERSPECTIVES OF THE SYSTEM AT THE DAWN OF THE NEW CENTURY

Despite the undeniable advances of the inter-American system of protection of human rights, from 1948 to 1996, there still remains a long way to go. Until the early eighties, attention was turned mainly to gross and massive violations of human rights (for example, practice of torture, enforced or involuntary disappearances of persons, inhuman or degrading treatment or punishment, illegal or arbitrary detentions) committed by oppressive regimes. Nowadays, there appears to be a diversification in the sources of violations of human rights (for example, those perpetrated by clandestine or assassination groups, or those perpetrated in inter-individual relations, or those resulting from corruption and impunity). To this phenomenon—which stresses in particular the relevance of the preventive dimension of human rights protection—one ought to add the problems of human rights which result not necessarily from political confrontation or repression, but appear rather as endemic or chronic problems of the social milieu of Latin American countries, aggravated by the iniquities of concentration of income and the growing socio-economic disparities. It is necessary to equip the inter-American system of protection, within its possibilities and the parameters of its mandate, so as to be able to face these new or aggravated situations of denial or violation of human rights.

The work of international protection of human rights in the American continent has been transformed in the sense that, after confronting violations of human rights in authoritarian regimes in the recent past, it ought today to focus on violations in the context of the so-called democratic 'transition' or 'consolidation'. This requires a systemic or global outlook of human rights, encompassing the protection of the person in all domains of human activity (civil, political, economic, social and cultural). If one looks towards the future, one ought also to reckon that special emphasis is needed, within States, upon the role of public organs, and in particular of the judiciary, in the protection of human rights. In this respect additional resources are needed so that such national organs may fully exert the functions (for example, the duty of investigation) conferred upon them by human rights treaties such as the American Convention (for example, the guarantee of access to justice and the right to an effective local remedy before national tribunals).

The incorporation of the international norms of human rights protection into the domestic law of the States of the region is of paramount importance today. The contemporary Constitutions of Latin American countries, in growing number, contain in fact express references (in the form of a *renvoi*) to the rights protected under treaties and conventions on human rights protection to which the State concerned is a Party.[37] It is necessary to give practical expression to the present-day coincidence of purpose of international law and internal public law as to the protection of the human being; the consequences of this reassuring coincidence of purpose between international law and municipal law still remain legally unexplored to date.

One ought to keep in mind that each of the three regional systems of human rights protection in operation (that is, the inter-American, the European and the African) is at a distinct stage in its historical development. In Africa, the possible creation of an African Court of Human Rights to complement the work of the African Commission on Human and Peoples' Rights is being discussed. In the ambit of the inter-American system, ways and means of achieving a closer coordination between the Inter-American Commission and Court of Human Rights are being contemplated. And in the European system, the Eleventh Protocol to the European Convention foresees the merging of the European Commission and Court of Human Rights towards the establishment of a sole—judicial—supervisory organ, which would in fact come to function as a true European Constitutional Court.

Each regional system of protection has evolved and operates at its own pace, and lives its own historical moment. But all current efforts point to the gradual strengthening of each system. The existing regional systems have lately been followed by the 1994 Arab Charter on Human Rights. The perspectives of the regional systems of protection ought to be considered necessarily within the framework of the universality of human rights. Universality does not amount to uniformity; on the contrary, it is enriched by regional particularities. Universality prevails at both normative and operational (non-selectivity) levels.

The lessons and results of the Second World Conference on Human Rights (Vienna, 1993) are valid also for the inter-American system as well as for other regional systems of protection of human rights. They are marked, above all, by the integrated and global outlook of all human rights; by the special attention to those in greater need of protection (the weaker and more vulnerable); by the temporal dimension (with measures of prevention and follow-up) of protection; and by the omnipresence of human rights. This last consideration finds expression in the recognition that human rights entail obligations *erga omnes* (binding on States, as well as international organizations, private groups and individuals), everywhere and at all times.

[37] Cf., e.g., in South America: Constitution of Brazil of 1988, Art. 5(2); Constitution of Chile (after the reform of 1989), Art. 5(II); Constitution of Colombia of 1991, Art. 93; Constitution of Argentina (after the reform of 1994), Art. 75(22); Constitution of Peru of 1978, Art. 105, followed by the Constitution of 1993, 4th. final and transitory provision; and, in Central America: Constitution of Guatemala of 1985, Art. 46; Constitution of Nicaragua of 1987, Art. 46.

Human rights violations continue to occur virtually everywhere, but the prompt responses to them are indeed much stronger today than they used to be in the past. We have reached a stage of evolution characterized today by the recognition of the legitimacy of the concern of the whole international community with the promotion and protection of human rights by everyone and everywhere. This corresponds to a new ethos, universally acknowledged, bringing about, as already pointed out, obligations *erga omnes*. We are, ultimately, in the course of a process of construction of a universal culture of observance of human rights. In the pursuance of this goal, a significant role is reserved, in the American continent, to the inter-American system of protection of human rights in general, and to its international supervisory organs in particular.

14

Procedural Shortcomings in the Defense of Human Rights: An Inequality of Arms

JOSÉ MIGUEL VIVANCO AND LISA L. BHANSALI*

INTRODUCTION

Despite the transitions to democracy that have taken place over the past fifteen years, grave human rights violations continue to occur in Latin America and the Caribbean. Further most democratically-elected, civilian governments have failed to establish accountability for past and present violations; in fact, the region's judiciaries are in crisis, and impunity is too often the norm for human rights violations and common crimes alike. Given this reality, a regional system of human rights protection is more needed than ever.

If we could point to one positive change across the hemisphere, it would be the willingness of governments to acknowledge serious human rights problems and that impunity indeed poses the greatest obstacle to their respect. While such an acknowledgment is remarkable, most Latin democracies also employ a double discourse: they recognize the importance of human rights principles, but when confronted with a case before the Inter-American Commission on Human Rights (the 'Commission'), they question the necessity of the system and sometimes even work to undermine its effectiveness. Defendant states frequently act as if their 'honor' were in question in matters before the Commission and the Inter-American Court of Human Rights (the 'Court'). With notable exceptions, states usually deny all facts without conducting in-depth investigations to establish the truth, attempt to discredit the petitioner, and even pressure the Commission with extralegal, political arguments.

These factors undoubtedly affect the current international protection of human rights in the region generally, and the way in which the Commission implements its mandate specifically. In practical terms, it certainly cost the Commission much less to condemn discredited military regimes for human rights violations than it does to condemn the civilian powers which govern the

* The authors express their thanks to Steven Hernández, Associate, Human Rights Watch.

region today. Thus, the Commission must make every effort to limit the debate in human rights cases to good-faith arguments based on solid factual and legal analyses. Indeed, there exists a clear need to create a stronger legal culture within the inter-American system.

One aspect of the development of such a culture is the institutionalization and refinement of the procedures followed by the two supervisory organs of the system, namely the Commission and the Court. With this in mind, and writing from the point of view of those who use, and rely on, the inter-American system of human rights protection, we have chosen to concentrate this Chapter on the following procedural issues: the rationale for rules and regulations; depoliticization; admissibility before the Commission; exhaustion of domestic remedies; friendly settlement; individual participation before the Court; and confidentiality. Though there exist several other procedural areas on which to comment, we believe the aforementioned issues to be the most pressing in terms of the development of the inter-American system at this time.

THE RATIONALE FOR RULES AND REGULATIONS

An international system of human rights protection, like any domestic judicial system, requires clear rules and procedures that inspire confidence in all the actors, petitioners and states alike. A set of rules of procedure and regulations should ensure or facilitate effectiveness and predictability, rather than permit abuse or increase the possibility of arbitrary and capricious decision-making.[1] Any system which aspires to attain credibility and prestige requires the existence of an objective set of procedures that serve to protect due process of law. Essentially, the parties in a case should know their rights in advance and share the conviction that their interests will be fairly heard by an impartial, independent quasi-judicial authority such as the Commission. Obviously, these principles are not foreign to the inter-American system, which has been in existence for more than three decades. Nonetheless, it has only been in the last ten years that the Commission has really begun to actively pursue the examination of large numbers of individual petitions, in addition to exercising its mandate before the Court. As a result, attention has increasingly and appropriately begun to focus on issues of fairness in the procedures of the Commission. If the Commission hopes to establish itself as the human rights organ for the hemisphere that its own mandate outlines, it must develop and implement objective and updated procedural rules which serve to guide petitioners and states in individual cases.

The existing, now somewhat outdated, Regulations of the Commission (the 'Regulations') were adopted some fifteen years ago to interpret and

---

[1] In discussing legal predictability, we seek to refer to the well-known principle in the continental legal system in the Americas known as *seguridad jurídica*.

implement the American Convention on Human Rights (the 'Convention'), with few modifications since.[2] The inter-American system was modeled after its European predecessor, which also granted the individual petitioner the right to have his/her case heard by an international organ as part of its monitoring of state conduct. Even though the procedures for dealing with individual petitions established in the American Convention[3] in the 1960s are somewhat abstract, they reflect a time in which states had begun to recognize not only substantive rights, but also the novelty of procedural rights for petitioners bringing human rights claims (though still short of the right of individual participation when the claim is heard). Today, these procedural rules need a thorough evaluation to assure that petitioners' interests are adequately represented in cases before both the Commission and the Court. The mere fact that the system does not allow for individual participation before the Court demonstrates the need to improve the position of the petitioner to allow for an equality of arms. When a petitioner seeks relief before an international organ, s/he should have the conviction that the system will respect the due process of law and that s/he will have a fair chance to be heard.

The Regulations seek to establish guidelines for the administration of complaints filed before the Commission. The criteria they contain should be periodically reviewed and updated in the interests of efficiency, and to filter out arbitrariness, which regardless of the existence of objective guidelines, seems to make its way into the decision-making process. All too often the Commission has allowed discretion to play a major role in its substantive as well as its procedural decisions, particularly at the important step of registration of a petition or when a complaint is received by staff attorneys of the Executive Secretariat. Overall, the Commission has failed to understand that in a fairly politicized atmosphere of the Organization of American States (OAS), the best way to protect human rights is to develop and consistently apply a pre-established and public set of rules and procedures.

DEPOLITIZATION

Every international system of human rights protection, in one way or another, has been accused of being politicized. In the case of the inter-American system, there appears to be a growing consensus among many actors, including members of intergovernmental bodies, states, and non-governmental organizations (NGOs), that politization is a serious and generalized problem that threatens the system's credibility. Nevertheless, the meaning of politization varies for each of these actors, so much so that the concept

[2] See Appendix V.
[3] See generally Arts. 44 and 48–51 of the American Convention on Human Rights.

requires examination, with a particular focus as to how it manifests itself and affects human rights concerns.

In the inter-American context, the perception of many states is that the Court is less political than the Commission and thus there exists greater respect for the Court's authority. The fact that most governments do not question the binding effect of the Court's judgments might help to explain this phenomenon, particularly when their legally binding quality is contrasted with the apparent lack of enforceability of the Commission's recommendations. Another factor that may support this perception is the existence of multiple and broad functions assigned to the Commission under the Convention, which include not only the examination of individual petitions, but also the potentially more political functions of promoting human rights and reporting on general human rights conditions in the hemisphere.[4]

As a structural concern, the lack of transparency in the election process of members of the Commission and judges of the Court also contributes to the problem of politization. This phenomenon is aggravated by the re-election process in which states, the subjects of monitoring, determine and cast their votes based on the track record of a commissioner or judge, thus threatening the autonomy of the Commission and the Court. Furthermore, the relic of defendant states being permitted to appoint ad hoc judges in cases before the Court should be eliminated in an effort to minimize political influences,[5] and strengthen the Court's impartiality.

Another sign of the system's politization is the visible lack of consistency in the Commission's decisions on individual petitions, in which historically little attention has been paid to developing doctrine and precedent that would establish predictability.

Since the Convention accords certain political, diplomatic and quasi-judicial powers and responsibilities to the Commission, states and petitioners must also work to depoliticize the system by limiting their actions to legal arguments when representing their respective sides in a case. Unfortunately, experience shows that in its deliberations, the Commission has at times taken into account extra-legal arguments, usually introduced by states.[6] The facts, applicable law, and evidence presented by the parties constitute the basic elements that the Commission ought to consider in its decision-making process in cases. Once the Commission succumbs to pressures and considers extralegal factors in the evaluation and decision of a case, it exposes itself to an almost inevitable loss of credibility. As long as the

---

[4] Art. 41 of the Convention.

[5] See Art. 18 of the Rules of Procedure of the Court; see also Art. 10 of the Statute of the Inter-American Court of Human Rights.

[6] States frequently try to introduce the political context of the country to explain a lack of accountability, while petitioners attempt to limit the discussion to the facts and evidence of the case.

Commission can consistently point to objective criteria in its analysis of the merits of a case, and systematically base its findings on a faithful interpretation and application of the Convention, it shields itself from any attempt to discredit its work on the grounds that it has been motivated by political, and not legal, reasons.

The Commission must make an effort to depoliticize its practice with the goal of strengthening not only its credibility, but also its effectiveness in specific individual petitions. This principle of 'depoliticization' should equally apply to the other functions performed by the Commission, including the promotion of human rights. For instance, during on-site missions, as one of the methods of investigation used by the Commission, commissioners collect information about alleged human rights violations, update their knowledge of the facts of individual petitions and meet with high-level governmental officials. At the end of these missions, the Commission is expected to make an assessment of the human rights conditions in the country. If this assessment is not formulated using careful, objective and legal language, without advancing judgment on individual petitions still under consideration, the Commission necessarily exposes itself to the accusation of engaging in purely political debate. In their interactions with government officials, commissioners should also effectively explain the mandate under which they act and refer to established rules that govern their work in response to political discourse.[7]

Not only should the work of the Commission be depoliticized, but it ought to appear as such. In this regard, it is important that the Commission develop and promptly publish the criteria applied and the reasons behind its decision to refer a case to the Court. For more than 10 years, there has been speculation about the reasoning applied in referrals of cases to the Court, thus supporting the view that this decision is overly discretionary and subject to political influences. Reasons for referral might include the following: (i) the potential of a case for the development of jurisprudence; (ii) new legal issues raised by a case for domestic and international human rights law; and (iii) a case involves a pattern of violations or the most pressing human rights issues at a given time. According to the Court, in Advisory Opinion No. 13, the Commission's decision to refer cases is '. . . not discretionary but must be based upon the alternative that would be most favorable for the protection of the rights established in the Convention.'[8] Although the Court's criterion may appear

---

[7] Sometimes the strategy used by certain governments has been to call the Commission's attention to the presumably devastating consequences that condemnation or referral of a case to the Court could have on the state's political stability, thereby exaggerating the scope of the Commission's influence.

[8] I/A Court H.R., *Certain Attributes of the Inter-American Commission on Human Rights (Arts. 41, 42, 44, 46, 47, 50 and 51 of the American Convention on Human Rights)*, Advisory Opinion No. 13, Series A No. 13, para. 50 (1993), 14 *HRLJ* 252, 1–2 IHRR 197 (1994).

explicit in that its language is clear, as a practical matter it fails to establish guidelines and leaves ample room for subjective, rather than objective, interpretation by the Commission. However, in Advisory Opinion No. 5, the Court set out concrete factors for the Commission to consider when deciding to refer cases, such as: (i) 'conflicting domestic judicial decisions' (which could permit the inter-American system to make a significant contribution to the region's continental laws); (ii) 'where the Commission cannot reach unanimous decision on legal issues; and, (iii) where there exists special importance to the hemisphere.'[9]

The Commission should make a serious effort to minimize discretion and increase predictability in the application of rules of procedure in individual cases. Moreover, the Commission should apply the same criteria and rationale in deciding cases regardless of the political conditions of the state concerned, thereby protecting its credibility through the consistency of its practice in the protection of human rights in the hemisphere. The Commission should consistently provide the same protection to victims from country *x* as for victims from country *y*.[10] Furthermore, the Commission does not have the power to select which cases it will move forward. It cannot choose between cases, except when deciding to refer a case to the Court and, as suggested above, this decision should be made in accordance with a well-established and publicized criteria for referral.

ADMISSIBILITY STANDARDS BEFORE THE COMMISSION

The practical problems faced by the Commission when applying its rules on admissibility[11] are very instructive. Many states in the inter-American system are concerned that once the Commission opens a case, having deemed it to be *prima facie* admissible,[12] it is very likely that a petition will be declared admissible in its final decision, and a condemnation of the defendant state will be forthcoming. Given this likelihood, some states have developed two, unfortunate practices: (i) to pressure the Commission not to open cases, and/ or (ii) to prolong the case as long as possible once it has been opened.

---

[9] I/A Court H.R., *Compulsory Membership in an Association Prescribed by Law for the Practice of Journalism (Arts. 13 and 29 of the American Convention on Human Rights)*, Advisory Opinion No. 5, Series A No. 5, para. 25 (1985), 7 *HRLJ* 74.

[10] For example, the Commission enters into dangerous political field when it takes into account the willingness of the state to grant permission for the Commission to conduct an on-site investigation in its own decision to condemn the state or refer a case to the Court. Under such circumstances, the victim, who is entitled to have his/her case heard and decided on the strength of the evidence and by reference to the Convention or Declaration provisions, may find instead that political considerations, extraneous to the case, play a part.

[11] These are set out in Arts. 15–48 of the Convention and Arts. 30–41 of the Commission's Regulations.

[12] On *prima facie* admissibility, see Chap. 3 by Cerna in this book, at 80.

Given the high rates of *prima facie* admissibility,[13] some states may believe that they do not stand a fair chance in the system. But to some degree, the states themselves have played a role in bringing about the current state of affairs. It has recently been the practice of some governments to pressure the Commission into accepting such anomolies as exchanges of information that are not provided for in the Convention, prior to the formal opening of a case (*prima facie* admissibility). At this stage, the state involved seeks the opportunity to provide the Commission with exculpatory information, hoping that it will not open the case against it. While this exchange takes place, the petitioner suffers a violation of due process and an unwarranted delay in his/her case and, of course, a heightened distrust of the Commission as an impartial authority.

To make the system fair for all parties, the Commission should adopt a public, consistent doctrine of admissibility. By setting out the appropriate criteria, the parties know beforehand whether a petition has a future with the Commission. As part of this practice, *every* petition should be registered and, since the Commissioners only meet twice a year for three weeks, the Secretariat should open every case, unless the petition is inadmissible *in limine*.[14] An example of such a petition would be one that alleges violations committed at the hands of a non-inter-American state, a clear case in which the Commission would not have jurisdiction to act. Should a petition be inadmissible *in limine*, it should be rejected with a brief communication to the petitioner, explaining the reasons that support the decision. If the complaint is in principle admissible, but still presents some kind of procedural problem, the Executive Secretary, together with the Commission's President, should request the petitioner to amend the petition, correcting the necessary sections to pass this pre-screening by the staff attorneys, and to file the amended petition again.

After verifying that the complaint describes: (i) a human rights violation under the Convention, (ii) involves a State Party to the Convention, and (iii) makes *some reference* to the exhaustion of domestic remedies, the case should be immediately opened by the Secretariat's staff attorney, and sent to the state concerned for its response. Any further, unwarranted examination of the issues could prematurely affect the interpretation of the merits of the case, particularly if the staff attorney attempts to examine the exhaustion of domestic remedies, which is in itself a line of defense for the state involved to advance.

---

[13] The practice of the Commission for many years has been to maintain a flexible and open policy on the *prima facie* admissibility of cases, which has resulted in the great majority of petitions being held admissible. This is in sharp contrast with the European system, in which some 70% are declared *prima facie* inadmissible and some 15% are formally declared inadmissible later on in the process.

[14] *In limine*, meaning 'on or at the threshold; at the very beginning'. *Black's Law Dictionary* (5th Ed.).

Generally, the Commission has failed to establish detailed procedures and clear practices on the question of admissibility. A problematic practice of the Commission has been that of not establishing a clear phase of admissibility before deciding on the merits of a case.[15] Instead, the Commission should make an admissibility determination using a two-tier procedural approach: (i) *prima facie* and (ii) proper admissibility, leaving open the possibility of dismissing the case later on the merits.[16] This admissibility determination would protect the Commission's integrity from governmental pressures to pre-screen petitions because it would allow them a real chance to have a case held inadmissible, rather than attempt the same through ex-partite communication. Such an approach would also help develop legal predictability as well as further judicial economy in the inter-American system. To avoid further delay in an already slow system, the proper admissibility decision should occur at an early stage, and within a *predictable* time frame, such as at the first session of the Commission after the complaint has been lodged and the state has had an opportunity to respond.

The decision on proper admissibility or inadmissibility should be made by the full Commission and should be published. This decision should also not be subject to appeal by the petitioner or the state. Of course, this would not preclude a petitioner from refiling the petition on the same facts after properly exhausting domestic remedies (if such was the reasoning behind the inadmissibility decision).[17] In fact, the requirement of prior exhaustion of domestic remedies is a benefit established in favor of the state—the state may raise it in its defense. If the state fails to do so, it may be taken as a tacit waiver. As a matter of procedural law, a preliminary objection must be raised at the admissibility stage; a state should be estopped from raising it for the first time before the Court.[18] Indeed, this would trigger issues of fairness if the state were to raise it since the petitioner does not have *jus standi* before the Court.

---

[15] In the *Velásquez, Godinez,* and *Fairén Garbi and Solis Corrales* cases, the Honduran government raised as a preliminary objection before the Court the fact that the Commission had not formally declared the cases admissible. The Court dismissed the objection, ruling that whereas a formal decision that a petition was inadmissible was required, there was no such requirement where a petition was considered admissible. See *Velásquez* Judgment, I/A Court H.R. Series C No.4 (1988), 9 *HRLJ* 212; *Godinez* Judgment, I/A Court H.R. Series C No. 5 (1989); *Fairén Garbi and Solis Corrales* Judgment, I/A Court H.R. Series C No.6 (1989) (emphasis added).

[16] See I/A Court H.R., *Certain Attributes of the Inter-American Commission on Human Rights (Arts. 41, 42, 44, 46, 47, 50 and 51 of the American Convention on Human Rights)*, Advisory Opinion No 13, Series A No. 13 (1993), 14 *HRLJ* 252, 1 IHRR Vol 1 (1994) (hereinafter referred to as 'Advisory Opinion No.13').

[17] In this situation, the Commission returns the case to the petitioner, who must seek relief from domestic tribunals. After domestic courts have made their determinations, and the petitioner still believes that there exists a violation of the Convention, s/he ought to be able to refile before the Commission.

[18] A state may not do so within the European system: see D. Harris, M. O'Boyle and C. Warbrick, *The Law of the European Convention on Human Rights* (London, 1995), 675.

An early decision on admissibility can also help move the parties closer to a friendly settlement. Clearly, a declaration from the Commission that a case is admissible sends a strong message to the state, and could well serve the interests of justice by resolving a case earlier on, with the direct involvement of both sides.

EXHAUSTION OF DOMESTIC REMEDIES

The exhaustion of domestic remedies should not only be perceived as a formal requirement of international human rights protection, but also as obligation of a State Party under the Convention to upgrade and maintain the effectiveness of its judicial system according to international standards. The alternative leads to a situation where the state is flooded with international complaints against it since petitioners can make a fairly easy showing that effective remedies are not available. The premise that domestic judicial systems function and offer adequate remedies is based on the principle that ratification also requires a state to bring its domestic laws into compliance with its international human rights obligations.

Today, the requirement that domestic remedies be exhausted constitutes the most formidable challenge that a petitioner must meet in filing a case before the Commission. Under accepted standards of international law, the petitioner in the inter-American system must show that s/he has made a good faith effort to exhaust domestic remedies when filing a petition with the Commission. This includes presenting specific information as to how, where, and when the petitioner sought a remedy at the domestic level and failed to obtain redress.[19] At this point, if the state so chooses, it may argue that the petitioner has failed to meet his/her burden; that is, that there remain remedies to be exhausted. The state may meet its burden by explaining *which* remedies might have been exhausted, and *how* that ought to have been accomplished. The state must essentially show that domestic remedies were available, adequate and effective.[20] The Commission should then issue an admissibility decision regarding the case.

In the inter-American system, some states contend that today's democratic governments offer effective remedies in individual cases for human rights violations. They argue that the Commission's standard for examining the exhaustion of domestic remedies ought to change from one that supposes that domestic remedies were not effective, as in the case of military dictatorships, to a stricter standard on the basis that domestic remedies are now available, adequate and effective under the region's democratic governments.

---

[19] *Velásquez* Judgment at paras. 59, 60 and 63 et seq.
[20] Id.

Unfortunately, the record in most cases clearly shows that such levels of deference to domestic judiciaries would be a mistake. Even with democratic governments, most of the region's judicial systems today suffer from problems of inefficiency, corruption, and a lack of material and human resources. In fact, some of these issues are being partially addressed by the multilateral lending institutions in projects on judicial reform and public sector management. Ironically, states have invoked these very problems in their own defense as the reasons for not being able to meet their international human rights obligations.[21]

Given these circumstances, it is particularly opportune that the Commission has recently offered petitioners guidance on the subsidiary role of the inter-American system in providing a remedy, compared to the primary role that national courts must play. In determining the inadmissibility of *Marzioni* v. *Argentina*,[22] the Commission made it clear that where petitioners can litigate before domestic tribunals and do have access to justice, they must do so in compliance with the rule of exhaustion of domestic remedies.[23] The function of the Commission is not to act as a court of appeal from the national courts, but only to consider whether the procedure that was followed by the national court or the decision infringes on the right to a fair trial or other guarantees under the Convention. Essentially, the Commission based its decision on the well-known 'fourth instance' doctrine developed in Europe, by which an international supervisory body such as the Commission cannot act as a court of review to overturn domestic decisions applying national law, unless there is a violation of the Convention in the procedures that were followed by the national court.

However, in the case of ineffective judiciaries, the principle of subsidiarity, by which the primary responsibility for human rights protection is entrusted to domestic courts (with international organs as secondary actors) should be closely evaluated. It is precisely in this situation that an international system of human rights protection is meant to offer support to do what domestic remedies cannot. After all, the aim and purpose of regional systems is the effective prevention of and protection from human rights violations. The principle of subsidiarity should not be applied mechanically to every regional system. Europe's judiciaries, for example, enjoy a measurable degree of independence from their executive branches, and impunity is a rare exception. Indeed, the democratic and economic development of states should be considered in deciding the level of deference to be given to domestic judicial systems. In industrialized democracies (where there usually exists a consolid-

---

[21] For example, Colombia has referred to the level of violence in the country and the fears of judges in its arguments in cases before the Commission.

[22] Report No. 39/96, Case 11.673 (*Marzioni* v. *Argentina*), 15 Oct. 1996 at paras. 50–2.

[23] Art. 47 of the Convention.

ated rule of law, independent judiciaries, and effective remedies), regional human rights bodies may well argue for stricter standards on the exhaustion of domestic remedies. Thus, domestic courts serve as the primary triers of fact, presumably because they are in the best position to administer justice to the victim. The European Commission on Human Rights is thus a secondary actor on the scene. To accept such a premise for Latin America is to fail to recognize the reality that there are fundamental differences between the two regions.

Whether advanced or less developed democracies are concerned, if access to an international human rights remedy is to be limited, the Commission should conduct a rigorous examination to ascertain whether derogable or non-derogable rights are involved. In the latter case, the Commission should be less demanding in its application of the exhaustion requirement inasmuch as that requirement should never become an obstacle to the effective exercise of fundamental rights. In the case of derogable rights, where irreparable harm would not occur, the Commission could be stricter in requiring the exhaustion of domestic remedies.[24]

In any event, the general obligation to exhaust domestic remedies is not a bar where remedies are not available, or the petitioner has been intimidated from exhausting them or is unable to do so because of a lack of economic resources, a situation not exceptional in Latin America.[25] In addition, the petitioner may also be relieved from the exhaustion requirement by showing that, although his/her case is still pending before domestic courts, there is an unwarranted delay in the administration of justice such as to amount to a denial of justice.[26] Finally, in some circumstances, a 'consistent pattern of gross human rights violations' may create a presumption against the state that domestic remedies did not exist or were ineffective, and thus unnecessary to exhaust.[27]

As mentioned, Latin American judicial systems suffer under a heavy weight of corruption and a lack of independence, making the petitioner's burden of proof that domestic remedies are inadequate, unavailable or ineffective fairly easy to satisfy. Thus, once the petitioner demonstrates what are largely evident inadequacies of justice in his/her country, the Commission ought to

---

[24] However, some exceptions may still exist. For example, how does one determine which other rights ought to be incorporated into this category—should personal liberty qualify? Though it is suspended from membership of the OAS, the example of Cuba may be instructive: there are still systematic violations of political rights, such as the right to privacy and freedom of expression in Cuba. The United Nations Working Group on Arbitrary Detentions still reports that most political prisoners are arbitrarily detained in Cuba because of the criminalization of legitimate activities for which there is no effective domestic remedy.

[25] I/A Court H.R., *Exceptions to the Exhaustion of Domestic Remedies (Art. 46(1), 46(2) and 46(2)(b) American Convention on Human Rights)*, Advisory Opinion No. 11, Series A No. 11 (1990), 12 *HRLJ* 20.

[26] Art. 46.2(c) of the Convention.

[27] See Art. 46 of the Convention.

act on the case. Should such issues present themselves in preliminary objections by the state, the Court could even take 'judicial notice' of the inadequate state of domestic remedies in the country and reject the objection.[28]

Under international human rights law, the exhaustion of domestic remedies should not pose an insurmountable obstacle for the petitioner. Nor should the state be permitted to hide behind the domestic remedies rule by invoking minor procedural technicalities, while still recognizing the legitimacy of the substantive claim against it.[29]

FRIENDLY SETTLEMENT

The friendly settlement mechanism contained in the Convention permits the parties in a case to directly negotiate an effective solution to their dispute, with the Commission acting as a mediator.[30] The friendly settlement mechanism is an opportunity open to the parties for as long as necessary, and so long as there exists a genuine interest on both sides to negotiate. Although the parties may enter into negotiations at any time during the process, friendly settlements have usually been pursued following some kind of indication that a final decision by the Commission is forthcoming. Nonetheless, the terms of a friendly settlement must be approved by the Commission to assure that they are in accordance with the object and purpose of the Convention. Following this approval, the parties also normally agree that the Commission will monitor the parties' compliance with the terms of the settlement.

Once a settlement has been reached and approved, the Commission issues a report, stating the facts of the case and the terms of the agreement.[31] Although the Convention states that a brief statement should be published,[32] the Commission should make use of this opportunity to analyse publicly the importance of the case and its applicability to similar situations.

---

[28] The taking of judicial notice, a well-known practice in common law systems, is 'the act by which a court, in conducting a trial, or framing its decision, will, of its own motion, and without the production of evidence, recognize the existence and truth of certain facts, having a bearing on the controversy at bar, which, from their nature, are not properly the subject of testimony, or which are universally regarded as established by common notoriety.' *Black's Law Dictionary*, Fifth Ed.

[29] In practice, state reactions vary in this area: some states, such as Peru and Mexico offer a blanket denial of the legitimacy of a claim and raise all types of technicalities to obtain dismissal. However, there have been exceptions like Argentina, which, by working within the procedures of the system, has established the practice of discussing in good faith the merits of a case and the possibility of entering into negotiations toward a friendly settlement.

[30] Art. 49 et. seq of the Convention.

[31] Art. 49 of the Convention. If the Court is involved, it issues a resolution explaining the facts and closing the case. See generally, *Maqueda* case, I/A Court H.R., Series C No.18 (1995), 16 *HRLJ* 151, 3 IHRR 355 (1996).

[32] Ibid.

Should negotiations break down, the case resumes its normal course before the Commission.

The mechanism of friendly settlement has recently gained favor with parties in the inter-American system due to the Commission's generally pro-active role as a mediator. It has only been in recent years that the Commission has understood that pursuing a friendly settlement is a mandatory phase of the process, and has begun inviting the parties to attempt negotiations in every case, thus performing a 'conciliatory' role before a case is referred to the Court or the Commission's decision in the case is published.[33]

Since the Commission only refers a few cases to the Court per year, and the petitioner cannot take his/her own case to the Court, the system's own limitations offer the best incentive for the petitioner to negotiate a friendly settlement. Further, although states have questioned the binding effect of the Commission's recommendations,[34] they have not done so with regard to the friendly settlement mechanism.

The incentives for states to consider entering into negotiations are varied. A state may wish to demonstrate its good faith commitment to human rights by discussing directly with the petitioner the substance of his/her claim and seeking to resolve the matter by arranging for reparations and/or compensation. Some governments may also pursue friendly settlements so as to avoid the embarrassment and stigma which may accompany decisions of the Commission and Court, which are not only made public by the national and international media but published in OAS reports as well. If a state believes that there is a good chance that a case may be referred to the Court, it may attempt to negotiate a friendly settlement.

As previously proposed, an early decision on admissibility by the Commission would also encourage the state to enter into negotiations to settle the case. An admissibility decision would send a clear signal to the state concerned that the Commission is taking the case seriously and that the likelihood of a negative outcome is high. It is interesting to note that the regular practice of the European Commission, once an application has been declared admissible,

---

[33] The Court in its decision on the Preliminary Objections in the *Caballero Delgado and Santana* case recommended that the Commission adopt the mechanism of friendly settlement as a regular practice. According to the Court, before issuing its Art. 50 report, the Commission should invite the parties to enter into negotiaitons under Art. 48(1)(f) of the Convention. *Caballero Delgado and Santana* Case, *Preliminary Objections*, I/A Court H.R. Series C No.17 (1994), 15 *HRLJ* 176, 2 IHRR 393 (1995) at para. 27 et seq. The *Caballero* decision significantly changed the previous practice, in which the Commision considered its role in engaging the parties in a friendly settlement as 'discretionary', and, in some cases, not advisable. See *Velásquez Preliminary Objections,* I/A Court H.R., Series C No.1 (1987) at para. 44 et seq.

[34] The Court in the *Caballero et al.* case declared that 'recommendations of the Commission are not binding'. See I/A Court H.R., Judgment of 8 Dec. 1995 at para. 67, 17 *HRLJ* 24, 3 IHRR 548 (1996). Nonetheless, we believe that the Court was referring to the recommendations made in Art. 50, and *not* recommendations in the report referred to in Art. 51.

is to inform the parties, on a confidential basis, of the Commission's provisional view as to whether a Convention violation has occurred so as to encourage a friendly settlement.[35] To encourage a candid discussion of the issues which would advance meaningful negotiations, the parties, particularly states, should be assured confidentiality. Any statement that is made during the course of the negotiations by a party that is against its interest should not be permitted to be used against it subsequently.

Although the terms of some friendly settlements may be immediately implemented, in the majority of cases the first step is usually a preliminary agreement, followed by a complex process of implementation. In such cases, the parties sould incorporate a timetable for implementation, monitored by the Commission, until full compliance is achieved, at which point a proper settlement has been reached, and the Commission's report may be published.

Petitioners have realized that the quality and binding effect of the outcome of a friendly settlement, in which they directly participate, could be considerably better than a delayed decision by the Commission, or even a final judgment of the Court. In effect, petitioners may be able to negotiate terms in a friendly settlement not ordinarily available to them in the inter-American system.[36] For example, when the parties agree on the points to be discussed at negotiation, petitioners may be able to pursue larger issues which would not only resolve the facts of the case, but extend its effect to other victims who are similarly situated.[37] Under the terms of settlement in the *Verbitsky* v. *Argentina* case,[38] the state not only agreed to drop the charges against the petitioner, but repealed the legislation criminalizing the 'contempt' of public figures. In *Garrido and Baigorria* v. *Argentina*,[39] the parties are still negotiating a friendly settlement regarding the issue of compensation and reparation, while the case is pending before the Court. As a result of the negotiations, the state agreed to include discussions about the *Guardatti* case, which is still before the Commission. In these two cases, Argentina has agreed to investigate the whereabouts of three disappeared individuals, as well as to seek to establish the criminal responsibility of the perpetrators. Also, during negotiations the

[35] See D. Harris, M. O'Boyle and C. Warbrick, *The Law of the European Convention on Human Rights* (London, 1995), 599.

[36] At the international level, the primary purpose is to determine whether the state has complied with its human rights responsibilities under the Convention, and not to establish the individual responsibility of the perpetrators, the latter being something that may be pursued as a part of a friendly settlement.

[37] See e.g. Caso 11.625 regarding the alleged *de jure* violations of the Convention based on those articles of Guatemala's Civil Code which discriminate against women, which is currently in friendly settlement negotiations, the outcome of which may include legislative reform.

[38] IACHR Annual Report 1994, Report No.22/94, Case 11.012 on the Friendly Settlement reached in the *Verbitsky* case (20 Sept. 1994), 40.

[39] In this case, Argentina accepted international responsibility and agreed to enter into friendly settlement negotiations with the petitioners. See *Garrido y Baigorria* Judgment of the Court, 2 Feb. 1996.

petitioners requested, and Argentina agreed, to pursue the enactment of legislation currently before Congress which would grant federal jurisdiction for human rights violations.[40] Such legislation would also include language requiring Argentina to either comply with the Commission's decisions or file a contentious case before the Court.

INDIVIDUAL PARTICIPATION BEFORE THE COURT

In the inter-American system, when the Commission decides to refer a case to the Court, the petitioner loses his/her status and is technically barred from participating in the proceedings. Only the Commission and the defendant state are considered parties to the case before the Court.

Unlike the inter-American system, the European system allows the petitioner to fully participate before the Court, once proceedings have been initiated by the European Commission or a State Party.[41] This is a result of the European Court's own initiatives; at the outset, the applicant had no standing before it. Today, petitioners are directly and independently involved as soon as proceedings are initiated before the Court, designating their advisers, and intervening in all legal procedures. For instance, they are granted rights equal to those of the states and the European Commission in submitting evidence to the European Court. More recently, with the adoption of Protocol 9 by the Council of Europe, those petitioners filing claims against states that have ratified the Protocol may even refer their case to the European Court.

Unfortunately, even with the benefit of European example, the inter-American system has failed to achieve substantial progress in establishing true procedural equity between the petitioner and the defendant state. To date, petitioners in the inter-American system have only been able to participate to a very limited extent in proceedings before the Court. Attorneys for the petitioners are limited to the role of advisors to the Commission and, in that capacity, are under the strict supervision and control of the Commission. The Rules of Procedure of the Court provide that when attorneys for the petitioners are among those individuals selected by the Commission to assist them in litigation before the Court, their participation must be brought to the Court's attention.[42]

The Commission acts as an intermediate for the petitioner and, at the same time, as a 'ministere public', protecting the integrity of the inter-American

---

[40] In Argentina, which has a federal legal system in which the provinces are fairly autonomous, such legislation allowing for federal prosecution would represent a tremendous advancement for the protection of human rights.

[41] See D. Harris, M. O'Boyle and C. Warbrick, *The Law of the European Convention on Human Rights*, (London, 1995), 659ff.

[42] Rule 22(2), Rules of the Court.

system. As a result, petitioners must overcome numerous obstacles in working with the Commission. In this regard, the absence of any right to autonomous participation before the Court is of critical importance, particularly when the interests of the petitioner and the Commission differ or are at odds. For example, the lack of standing before the Court gravely prejudiced the *Cayara* case. In *Cayara*, the Court dismissed the case due to the Commission's procedural irregularities, against the petitioners' interests. This was also the case regarding the question of compensation in *Velásquez et. al.* when the Commission and petitioners differed as to the amount of compensation and the appropriate remedy.[43] Some small progress occurred after the *Velásquez et. al.* cases were decided when the Court amended its regulations and granted formal recognition to the petitioners' attorneys. As a result of this amendment, the rules now permit the Court, at its discretion, to invite the petitioners' attorneys to submit independent briefs at the compensation stage of the proceedings.[44]

Nevertheless, the Court's recent resolution in *Genie Lacayo*[45] is indicative of the Court's apparent lack of interest in achieving equity between the parties and in advancing a system which guarantees the rights of the petitioner. In *Genie Lacayo*, the Court opted to bar the appointment and participation, in a public hearing, of the petitioner's attorney. The attorney was already a recognized member of the Commission's delegation and its adviser, yet the Court upheld the defendant government's objection to his accreditation, which was made on the ground that it allegedly violated the state's 'right to defense'.

Granting independent status for petitioners would provide greater equity between the parties and ensure the due process of law in cases before the Court. An international system which protects fundamental human rights must concern itself with respect for the most basic legal guarantees, such as that of due process. Individual participation before the Court would also give greater balance to the system's proceedings by permitting the direct confrontation of interests (state and petitioner), without third party interference.

Finally, it is worth noting that there is another development in the inter-American system, which permits individuals whose rights are affected to express their view before the Court. The Court has decided on three occasions to permit non-governmental organizations (NGOs) to participate as *amicus curiae*, independent of the Commission, in public hearings relating to advisory opinions.[46]

[43] See *Cayara Preliminary Objections*, I/A Court H.R., Series C No. 14 (1993). See also Méndez and Vivanco, 'Disappearances and the Inter-American Court: Reflections on a Litigation Experience', 13 *Hamline L Rev.*, 565 (1990).

[44] Art. 44(2) of the Rules of the Court.

[45] See *Genie Lacayo* case, Resolution of the Court, 27 Nov. 1995.

[46] See Arts. 34.1 and 54.4 of the Rules of Procedure of the Court. Both non-governmental organizations, the Center for Justice and International Law (CEJIL) and Human Rights

CONFIDENTIALITY

One of the characteristics which for many years distinguished the inter-American system from other international systems of human rights protection was the transparency with which the system operated. The Commission always used to keep the petitioner informed regarding the status of his/her case by automatically transmitting all briefs submitted by the state as well as Commission decisions relating to the case, without any restrictions on publicity.

Under state pressure in the early 1990s, the Commission became so concerned about the question of confidentiality that it began imposing restrictions on publicity concerning pending cases. For instance, for a few years the Commission, with no legal basis in the Convention, its Regulations or any other source (or even as an articulated policy) warned only petitioners that any publicity regarding their case could result in final termination of the matter.[47] Further, as a result of states being publicly embarrassed, on various occasions the Commission scolded petitioners when the contents of hearings were made public.[48]

A serious setback for the petitioner occurred when the Court, in an unfortunate interpretation of the Convention, ruled that an Article 50 report, which contains the preliminary findings of the Commission on the merits, should be transmitted only to the state involved, and not the petitioner. According to the Court, the Regulations of the Commission allowing the petitioner to receive a copy of the preliminary report (and be properly notified), violated the Convention's requirement of confidentiality.[49] In effect, the Court confused giving a copy to the petitioner, which respects the principles of due process, with the need to keep information confidential. The Court's decision was apparently motivated by the complaints of several states that contents of the Commission's preliminary reports were being leaked to the press by petitioners.[50]

Supposedly the purpose of keeping the Commission's preliminary Article 50

Watch/Americas appeared independently before the Court to express their observations in Advisory Opinions No.13 and 14.

[47] Fortunately, this practice was changed as of May 1996.

[48] Regarding the confidentiality of information submitted by the parties, the President of the Court, speaking on behalf of its members and without citing any legal authority, informed the Commission that documents related to what are normally public proceedings before the Court were confidential. See Letter of Héctor Fix-Zamudio, President of the Inter-American Court of Human Rights, Ref. CDH-10 792/150, 20 May 1995.

[49] See Advisory Opinion No.13 of the Court, paras. 48 and 49. Art. 50(2) of the Convention reads: 'The report shall be transmitted to the states concerned, which shall not be at liberty to publish it'. The petitioner is not mentioned.

[50] To our knowledge, there is no evidence to date which shows that petitioners have been responsible for leaks to the press regarding Art. 50 reports.

report confidential is to offer an incentive to the state involved to comply with the Commission's recommendations, before a condemnation ensues. But pursuing this political objective does not justify sacrificing the obligation to respect due process at all stages of the litigation, especially by a human rights body. By not being able to receive a copy of the preliminary report, the petitioner is handicapped at a critical moment in the process. To resolve this matter equitably, the Commission should act to prevent unwanted publicity without violating due process. The preliminary report should be sent to the state and the petitioner with a note reminding both parties that the document is confidential. If the Commission concludes that the preliminary report has been leaked to the press (or otherwise made public) by the petitioner, the Commission can still decide under Article 51(3) of the Convention not to publish its final report.

Without conducting the necessary analysis, the Commission has unfortunately applied the Court's opinion in such a manner as to marginalize petitioners from the very moment the Commission decides to issue its preliminary report until its final Article 51 report is published. Without doubt, the Court's regrettable decision and the Commission's formalistic implementation constitute to date the greatest threat to the inter-American system's development.

Unless the Convention is modified or the Court changes its interpretation of the treaty, the Commission ought to narrow its confidentiality requirement by submitting preliminary reports exclusively to the state for a reasonable period (e.g. sixty days), and sending a note informing the petitioner of the Commission's decision, so that s/he at least knows of the status of the case.[51] Following a reasonable period, the report should then be forwarded to the petitioner. In the case that the state responds within the allotted time, the petitioner's rights are directly triggered, and it is paramount that s/he receive a confidential copy for observations *while* the Commission makes its decision regarding referral to the Court. If the Commission decides to affirm its preliminary report in its Article 51 final report, the latter should be sent simultaneously to both sides.[52] By following this practice, the Commission would still remain faithful to the concerns about leaks and adverse publicity expressed by the Court while still respecting due process.[53]

---

[51] At its October 1996 session, the Commission decided to incorporate this step into its practice so as to address the above-mentioned due process problem.

[52] There is no provision in the Convention that states that Art. 51 reports are confidential.

[53] At this writing, the Commission is in the process of reviewing proposed amendments to correct this unfortunate practice.

CONCLUSION

We have addressed the need to depoliticize the inter-American system by minimizing discretion, and increasing predictability and consistency in the Commission's practice through the application of public rules and guidelines. However, even with substantial reform, those involved in the inter-American system must be attentive to possible abuse. States should not be allowed to misuse the privileges accorded to them by the Convention, such as the exhaustion of domestic remedies requirement. Similarly, states should not distort the advisory authority of the Court. Such was the case when Argentina and Uruguay, both condemned by the Commission for legislation granting blanket amnesties for past human rights abuses, requested an advisory opinion on questions related to the Commission's decisions in these cases, instead of taking their cases as contentious matters before the Court.[54] Fortunately, while these states sought to have the Court overrule the Commission's decision, the Court reaffirmed the Commission's authority to examine and decide whether internal legislation may constitute *de jure* violations of the Convention.[55] However, the Court should also have addressed the *way* in which these states approached the Court. The Court's own jurisprudence indicates that requests for the exercise of advisory opinion jurisdiction should not undermine its contentious jurisdiction, particularly against the petitioner's interests. According to the Court, states should reserve its advisory jurisdiction for legitimate queries about the Convention.[56]

With regard to the issues of admissibility, exhaustion of domestic remedies and confidentiality, the Commission should re-examine its rules and procedures with the aim of reforming the system to ensure full respect for an equality of arms and greater equity between the parties.

Perhaps a central issue still requiring attention concerns the enforceability of the Commission's decisions and verification that they have been respected. The tragic case of *Lalinde* and the behavior of the state concerned exemplify the importance of this issue. In 1988, in its review of a petition alleging the forced disappearance of Luis Fernando Lalinde, the Commission adopted an Article 50 report condemning Colombia.[57] The state then acknowledged the

---

[54] IACHR Annual Report 1992–3, Reports 28/92 (Argentina) and 29/92 (Uruguay), 42 and 162, respectively, 13 *HRLJ* 336. Lamentably, in the *Francisco Martorell* case, after being condemned by the Commission, Chile sought review under the Court's advisory, rather than contentious, jurisdiction,

[55] Advisory Opinion No.13 of the Court at para. 26.

[56] *'Other treaties' subject to the advisory jurisdiction of the Court (Art. 64 American Convention on Human Rights)*, Advisory Opinion No.1 I/A Court H.R., Series A No.1, para. 24 et seq.; see also Advisory Opinion No.13 at para. 15.

[57] *Lalinde* case, Resolution No. 24/87, Case 9620, Colombia, IACHR Annual Report 1987–8, 112.

facts and even declared that an individual, allegedly the victim, was 'cruelly attacked' and killed by an army patrol. By accepting responsibility for an extrajudicial execution as a result of the killing that it acknowledged, and not the crime of disappearance, the state was able to avoid having the case referred to the Court.[58] Following the state's response, and essentially rubber-stamping the state's position, the Commission changed the terms of its report. Whereas it had in its preliminary report declared that Colombia had violated the right to life through the disappearance of the victim, it now categorized the violation as, and condemned Colombia for, an extrajudicial execution under the Convention. Moreover, the Commission never verified that the 'extra-judicially executed' individual was indeed Lalinde, as the state had claimed. Although it followed up with the petitioner on the question of the victim's identity, in fact the body was produced just a few months ago. To date, the petitioner (the victim's mother) maintains that Colombia is responsible for Lalinde's forced disappearance, (not an extrajudicial execution).[59] The *Lalinde* case should act as an incentive to all those concerned with human rights in the inter-American system to press for the verifiable enforceability of the Commission's decisions.

[58] Although Colombia accepted the contentious jurisdiction of the Court in 1985, and Lalinde disappeared in 1984, under the international law theory that disappearance is a continuing violation of human rights, which the Commission supported, the case could still have reached the Court.

[59] IACHR Annual Report 1987–8, 112.

Select Bibliography on the American Human Rights System

1. BOOKS

AMNESTY INTERNATIONAL, *Argentina: The Military Junta and Human Rights: Report of the Trial of the Former Junta Members*, 1987.

BUERGENTHAL, T. & SHELTON, D., *Protecting Human Rights in the Americas: Cases Materials*, 4th edn., Engel, Kehl, 1995 .

CANÇADO TRINDADE, A. A., *A Proteçao Internacional dos Direitos Humanos— Fundamentos Juridicos e Instrumentos Básicos*, Editoria Saraiva, Sao Paulo, 1991.

—— 'Formación de los Derechos Humanos', XVII *Curso de Derecho Internacional Organizado po.r el Comité Juridico Interamericano*, OAS General Secretariat, Washington D.C., 1991.

—— *The Application of the Rule of Exhaustion of Local Remedies in International Law. Its Rationale in the International Protection of Individual Rights*, Cambridge University Press, Cambridge, 1983.

CERDAS CRUZ. & NIETO LOAIZA (Comp.), *Estudios Básicos de Derechos Humanos I*, Instituto Interamericano de Derechos Humanos & Comisión de la Comunidad Europea, San José, 1994.

CONNELL,-SMITH, Gordon, *The Inter-American System,* Oxford University Press, New York, 1966.

DAVIDSON, Scott, *The Inter American Court of Human Rights*, Dartmouth, Aldershot, 1992.

—— *The Inter-American Human Rights System*, Dartmouth, Aldershot, 1996.

DUNSHEE DE ABRANCHES, C. A., 'La Corte Interamericana de Derechos Humanos', *La Convención Americana sobre Derechos Humanos*, OAS General Secretariat, Washington D.C., 1980.

FARER, Tom (ed.), *The Future of the Inter-American System*, Praeger, New York, 1979.

—— *The Grand Strategy of the US in Latin America*, Transaction Books, NJ, 1988.

FAÚNDEZ LEDESMA, Héctor, *El sistema interamericano de protección de los derechos humanos. Aspectos institucionales y procesales*, Instituto Interamericano de Derechos Humanos, San José, 1996.

GUEST, Iain, *Behind the Disappearances: Argentina's Dirty War Against Human Rights and the United Nations*, University of Pennsylvania Press, Philadelphia, 1990.

LE BLANC, L. J., *The OAS and the Promotion and Protection of Human Rights*, Nijhoff, The Hague, 1977.

MEDINA QUIROGA, C., *The Battle of Human Rights*, Kluwer, Dordrecht, 1988.

MOWER, A. G., *Regional Human Rights: A Comparative Study of the West European and Inter-American Systems*, Greenwood, New York, 1991.

O'DONNELL, G., *Modernization and Bureaucratic Authoritarianism: Studies in South American Politics*, Institute of International Studies, University of California, Berkeley, 1973.

PINTO, M., *La denuncia ante la Comisión Interamericana de Derechos Humanos*, Ediciones del Puerto, Buenos Aires, 1993.

SANTOSCOY NORO, B., *La Commission Interaméricaine des Droits de l'Homme et le développement de sa compétence par le système des pétitions individuelles*, Publications de l'Institute Universitaire de Hautes Études Internationales, Geneva, 1995.

SCHREIBER, A., *The Inter-American Commission on Human Rights*, Sitjhoff, Leyden, 1970.

STOETZER, O. C., *The Organization of American States*, 2nd edn., Praeger, New York, 1993.

VAKY, V. & MUÑOZ, H., *The Future of the Organization of American States*, Twentieth Century Fund, New York, 1993.

VASAK, K., *La Commission Interamericaine des Droits de l'Homme*, P.U.F., Paris, 1968.

VENTURA, M. & ZOVATTO, D., *La función consultiva de la Corte Interamericana de Derechos Humanos: naturaleza y principios*, Instituto Interamericano de Derechos Humanos, San José, Civitas, 1989.

WESCHLER, L., *A Miracle, A Universe: Settling Accounts with Torturers*, Pantheon Press, New York, 1990.

WILLIAMS, R. A. Jr., *The American Indian in Western Legal Thought: The Discourses of Conquest*, Oxford University Press, New York, 1990.

2. ARTICLES, CHAPTERS IN BOOKS, ETC.

ANON., 'Damage Awards for Human Rights Violations in the European and Inter-American Courts of Human Rights', 31 *Santa Clara Law Review*, 1127 (1991).

ANON., 'The Inter-American Commission on Human Rights: A Promise Unfulfilled', 48 *Record of the Association of the Bar of the City of New York*, 589 (1993).

ANON., 'Peru's Failure to Make the Military Subservient of Civilian Law: The Absence of Prosecution after the 1988 Cayara Massacre', 12 *Boston College Third World Law Journal*, 433 (1992).

ACEVEDO, D. E., 'The Haitian in Crisis and the OAS Response: A Test of Effectiveness in Protecting Democracy', in Damrosch, L. (ed.), *Enforcing Restraint: Collective Intervention in Internal Conflicts*, Council on Foreign Relations Press, New York, 119 (1993).

AGUIAR, A., 'La responsabilidad internacional del Esta do por violación de derechos humanos' (Apreciaciones subre el Pacto de San José), *Estudios Básicos de Derechos Humanos I*, Cerdas Cruz & Nieto Loaiza, Comp., Instituto Interamericano de Derechos Humanos & Comision de la Comunidad Europea, San José de Costa Rica, 117 (1994).

AGUILAR, A., 'Procedimiento que debe aplicar la Comisión Interamericana de Derechos Humanos en el examen de las peticiones o comunicaciones individuales sobre presuntas violaciones de derechos humanos', *Derechos Humanos en las Americas/Direitos Humanos nas Americas/Human Rights in the Americas. Homenaje a la Memoria de Carlos A. Dunshee de Abranches*, CIDH, Washington, 199 (1984).

AGUILAR URBINA, J., 'An Overview of the Main Differences Between the Systems Established by the Optional Protocol of the ICCPR and the ACHR as Regards Individuals', (1991–92) *Canadian Human Rights Yearbook*, 127.

BAENA SOARES, J. C., 'Some Reflections on the OAS and its Contribution to the Development of International Law', 14 *Canadian Council on International Law, Proceedings of the Annual Conference*, 90 (1986).

—— 'The Organization of American States', 80 *American Society of International Law Proceedings*, 1 (1986).

BANTON, M., 'International Norms and Latin American States' Policy on Indigenous Peoples', 2 *Nations and Nationalism*, 89 (1996).

BARSH, R. L., 'The IX Inter-American Indian Congress', 80 *American Journal of International Law* 682 (1986).

BIDART CAMPOS, G., 'La interpretación del sistema de derechos humanos', 19 *Revista del Instituto Interamericano de Derechos Humanos* (1994), 11.

—— 'El agotamiento de los recursos internos antes de acceder a la jurisdicción supraestatal organizada por el Pacto de San José de Costa Rica', *El Derecho*, 140: 186.

BLOOMFIELD, R. J., 'Making the Western Hemisphere Safe for Democracy: The OAS Defense-of-Democracy Regime', 17 *Washington Quarterly* 157 (1994).

BUERGENTHAL, T., 'The Inter-American System for the Protection of Human Rights' in Meron, T. (ed.), *Human Rights in International Law, Legal and Political Issues*, Oxford, Oxford University Press, 439 (1984).

—— 'The American Human Rights Declaration: Random Reflections' in Hailbonner, K., Ress, G., Stein, T. (eds.), *Staat und Vokerrechtsordunung* 133 (1989).

—— 'Judicial Fact-Finding: The Inter-American Human Rights Court', in Lillich, R. (ed.), *Fact-Finding before International Tribunals, Eleventh Sokol Colloquium* 261 (1991).

—— 'International Human Rights Law and Institutions: Accomplishments and Prospects', 63 *Washington Law Review*, 1 (1988).

—— 'Human Rights in the Americas: View from the Inter-American Court', 2 *Connecticut Journal of International Law*, 303 (1987).

—— 'The Inter-American Court of Human Rights and the OAS', 7 *Human Rights Law Journal*, 157 (1986).

BUERGENTHAL, T., 'The Advisory Practice of the Inter-American Court of Human Rights', 79 *American Journal of International Law*, 1 (1985).

—— 'The Inter-American Court of Human Rights', 76 *American Journal of International Law*, 231 (1982).

—— 'The Inter-American System for the Protection of Human Rights', *Annuario Juridico Interamericano*, 80 (1981).

—— 'The American and European Conventions on Human Rights: Similarities and Diffeand Doand Differences', 30 *American University Law Review*, 155 (1980).

—— 'The Revised OAS Charter and the Protection of Human Rights', 69 *American Journal of International Law*, 828 (1975).

BUERGENTHAL, T. 'The American Convention on Human Rights: Illusions and Hopes', 21 *Buffalo Law Review*, 121 (1971).

—— 'La Relación Conceptual y Normativa entre la Declaración American y la Convención Americanea sobre Derechos Humanos', *Revista del Instituto Interamericano de Derechos Humanis* (1989).

CABRA, M., 'Rights and Duties Established by the American Convention on Human Rights', 30 *American University Law Review*, 21 (1980).

CAMARGO, P., 'The American Convention on Human Rights', 3 *Human Rights Law Journal*, 333 (1970).

CANÇADO TRINDADE, A. A., 'Coexistence and Coordination of Mechanisms of International Protection of Human Rights', 202 *Recueil des Cours, Academie de Droit International, 9* (1987–II).

—— 'A Aplicaçao da regra do esgotamiento dos recursos internos no Sistema Interamericano de Proteçao dos direitos humanos', *Derechos Humanos en las Americas/Direitos Humanos nas Americas/Human Rights in the Americas. Homenaje a la Memoria de Carlos A. Dunshee de Abranches*, CIDH, Washington, 217 (1984).

—— 'The Evolution of the OAS System of Human Rights Protection: An Appraisal', 25 *German Yearbook of International Law*, 498 (1982).

—— 'El Sistema Interamericano de Protección de los Derechos Humanos (1948–1995): Evolución, Estado Actual y Perspectivas', in Bardonnet, D. and Cançado Trindade, A. A. (eds.), *Derecho Internacional y Derechos Humanos/ Droit International et droits de l'homme* (1996).

—— 'Reflexiones sobre las Declaraciones Universal y Americana de Derechos Humanos de 1948 con Ocasión de Su Cuadragésimo Aniversario', *Revista del Instituto Interamericano de Derechos Humanos* (1989).

CARRENO, E. V., 'Las observaciones *in loco* practicadas por la Comisión Interamericana de Derechos Humanos', *Derechos Humanos en las Americas/ Direitos Humanos nas Americas/Human Rights in the Americas. Homenaje a la Memoria de Carlos A. Dunshee de Abranches*, CIDH, Washington, 290 (1984).

—— 'Some Problems Presented by the Application and Interpretation of the American Convention on Human Rights', 30 *American University Law Review*, 127 (1980).

CASSEL, D., 'Somoza's Revenge: A New Judge for the Inter-American Court of Human Rights', 13 *Human Rights Law Journal*, 137 (1992).

—— 'The Inter-American System Put to the Test: The Interpretation Judgments in the Honduran Disappearance Cases', 13 *Revista del Instituto Interamericano de Derechos Humanos*, 315 (1991).

CERDAS CRUZ, R., 'Democracia y Derechos Humanos', *Estudios Básicos de Derechos Humanos I*, Cerdas Cruz & Nieto Loaiza, Comp., Instituto Interamericano de Derechos Humanos & Comisión de la Comunidad Europea, San José de Costa Rica, 295 (1994).

CERNA, C., 'The Structure and Functioning of the Inter-American Court of Human Rights (1972–1992)', 63 *British Yearbook of International Law*, 135 (1992).

—— 'US Death Penalty tested before the Inter-American Commission on Human Rights', 10 *Netherlands Quarterly of Human Rights* 155 (1992).

CLINEBELL, J. H.& THOMSON, J., 'Sovereignty and Self-Determination: The Rights of Native Americans under International Law', 27 *Buffalo Law Review* 669 (1978).

CORBERA, M. J., 'In the Wrong Place at the Wrong Time: Problems with the Inter-American Court of Human Rights', 25 *Vanderbilt Journal of Transnational Law*, 919 (1993).

CORNELL, A. & ROBERTS, K., 'Democracy, Counterinsurgency and Human Rights: the Case of Peru', 12 *Human Rights Quarterly*, 529 (1990).

CORREA, J., 'Dealing with Past Human Rights Violations: The Chilean Case after Dictatorship', 67 *Notre Dame Law Review*, 1455 (1992).

DAVIDSON, S., 'Remedies for Violations of the American Convention on Human Rights', 44 *International and Comparative Law Quarterly*, 405 (1995).

DIAB, J., 'United States Ratification of the American Convention on Human Rights', 2 *Duke Journal of Comparative & International Law*, 323 (1992).

DIAMOND, L., 'Democracy in Latin America: Degrees, Illusions, and Directions for Consolidation', in Farer, T., (ed.), *Beyond Sovereignty: Collectively Defending Democracy in the Americas*, Johns Hopkins University Press, Baltimore, (1996).

DONNELLY, J., 'International Human Rights: a Regime Analysis', 40 *International Organization*, 625 (1986).

DRUCKER, L., 'Government Liability for Disappearances. A Landmark Ruling by the Inter-American Court on Human Rights', 25 *Stanford Journal of International Law*, 289 (1988).

DUNSHEE DE ABRANCHES, C. A., 'Comparative Study of the United Nations Covenants on Civil and Political Rights and on Economic, Social and Cultural Rights and of the Draft Inter-American Convention on Human Rights' (1968), *Inter-American Yearbook on Human Rights*, 169.

—— 'The Inter-American Court of Human Rights', 30 *American University Law Review*, 78 (1980).

DWYER, A., 'The Inter-American Court of Human Rights. Towards Establishing an Effective Regional Contentious Jurisdiction', 13 *Boston College International and Comparative Law Review*, 127 (1990).

ENSALACO, M., 'Truth Commission for Chile and El Salvador: A Report and Assessment', 16 *Human Rights Quarterly*, 656 (1994).

FARER, T., 'Consolidating Democracy in Latin America: Law, Legal Institutions and Constitutional Structure', 10 *American University Journal of International Law and Policy*, 1295 (1995).

—— 'The OAS at the Crossroads', 72 *Iowa Law Review*, 401 (1987).

FARRELL, N., 'The American Convention on Human Rights: Canada's Present Law and the Effect of Ratification', 30 *Canadian Yearbook of International Law*, 233 (1992).

FEINRIDER, M., 'Judicial Review and the Protection of Human Rights under Military Governments in Brazil and Argentina', 5 *Suffolk Transnational Law Journal*, 171 (1981).

FENWICK, C., 'The OAS: The Transition from an Unwritten to a Written Constitution', 59 *American Journal of International Law*, 315 (1965).

—— 'The Charter of the OAS as the Law of the Land', 47 *American Journal of International Law*, 281 (1953).

FIX-ZAMUDIO, H., 'The Inter-American Court of Human Rights', 20 *Canadian Council on International Law, Proceedings of the Annual Conference*, 195 (1991).

—— 'El Derecho Internacional de los Derechos Humanos en las Constituciones Latinoamericanas y en la Corte Interamericana de Derechos Humanos', in Cançado Trindade, A. A. (ed.), *The Modern World of Human Rights—Essays in Honor of Thomas Buergenthal*, IIDH, San José (1996).

FOX, D., 'The IACHR Finds US in Violation', 81 *American Journal of International Law*, 601 (1988).

FROST, L., 'The Evolution of the Inter-American Court of Human Rights: Reflection on Present and Former Judges', 14 *Human Rights Quarterly*, 171 (1992).

FROWEIN, J., 'The European and American Conventions on Human Rights', 1 *Human Rights Law Journal*, 44 (1980).

FURUKAWA, J., 'The Death of Dr. Hugo Spadafora: Human Rights Investigative Responsibility Is Past Due', 4 *American University Journal of International Law and Policy*, 377 (1989).

GANNESSIAN, G., 'Effect of Reservations on Entry into Force of American Convention on Human Rights: Advisory Opinion OC–2/82', 77 *American Journal of International Law*, 840 (1983).

GARCÍA AMADOR, F., 'Attribuciones de la Comision Interamericana de Derechos Humanos en relacion con los Estados miembros de la OEA que no son parte en la Convencion de 1969', *Derechos Humanos en las Americas/Direitos Humanos nas Americas/Human Rights in the Americas. Homenaje a la Memoria de Carlos A. Dunshee de Abranches*, CIDH, Washington, 177 (1984).

GARCÍA BAUER, 'The Observance of Human Rights and the Structure of the System for their Protection in the Western Hemisphere', 30 *American University Law Review*, 5 (1980).

GOLDMAN, R. K., 'Amnesty Laws, International Law and the American Convention on Human Rights', 6 *International Human Rights Law Group Docket* 1 (1989).

—— 'Uruguay: Amnesty Law in Violation of Human Rights Convention', 49 *Review of the International Commission of Jurists* 37 (1992).

GROS ESPIELL, H., 'Le système interaméricain comme régime regional de protection international des droit de l'homme', 145 *Recueil des Cours, Académie de Droit International*, 1 (1975–II).

—— 'Contentious Proceedings before the Inter-American Court of Human Rights', 1 *Emory Journal of International Dispute Resolution*, 175 (1987).

—— 'Las Convenciones sobre Tortura de las Naciones Unidas y de la Organizacion de los Estados Americanos', *XIV Curso de Derecho Internacional Organizado por el Comite Juridicio Interamericano* (1987).

—— 'Derechos humanos: etica, derecho y politica', 9 *Revista del Instituto Interamericano de Derechos Humanos* 45 (1989).

GROSSMAN, C., 'The Inter-American System: Opportunities for Women's Rights', 44 *American University Law Review*, 1305 (1995).

—— 'Régimen hemisférico sobre situaciones de emergencia', *Estudios Básicos de Derechos Humanos I*, Cerdas Cruz & Nieto Loaiza, Comp., Instituto

Interamericano de Derechos Humanos & Comisión de la Comunidad Europea, San José de Costa Rica, 155 (1994).

—— 'A Framework for the Examination of States of Emergency under the American Convention on Human Rights', 1 *American University Journal of International Law and Policy*, 35 (1986).

—— 'Proposals to Strengthen the Inter-American System of Protection of Human Rights', 32 *German Yearbook of International Law* 264 (1989).

GUTIÉRREZ, C. J., 'Conflicts Between Domestic and International Law', 30 *American University Law Review*, 147 (1980).

HARPER, P., 'Fifteen Truth Commissions—1974 to 1994: a Comparative Study', 16 *Human Rights Quarterly*, 597 (1994).

HARRIS, C., 'Advisory Jurisdiction: "Other Treaties" Subject to the Consultative Jurisdiction of the Court', 77 *American Journal of International Law*, 637 (1983).

HILLING, C., 'La protection des droits de peuples autochtones et de leurs membres dans les Amériques', 41 *McGill Law Journal*, 855 (1996).

JIMÉNEZ DE ARÉCHAGA, E., 'La Convencion Interamericana de Derechos Humanos como Derecho Interno', 69/71 *Beletim da Sociedade Brasileira de Direito Internacional* (1987/1989).

KAPLAN, F. H., 'Combating Political Torture in Latin America: An Analysis of the Organization of American States Inter-American Convention to Prevent and Punish Torture', 15 *Brooklyn Journal of International Law*, 339 (1989).

KOKOTT, J., 'No Impunity for Human Rights Violators in the Americas (Inter-American Commission on Human Rights rulings on Argntinian, Uruguayan and El Savadoran Amnesty Laws)', 14 *Human Rights Law Journal*, 252 (1993).

LAUCHLAN WASH, J., SUAGEE, D. SCHLANGER, P., 'Conference Report: The Inter-American Human Rights System: Into the 1990s and Beyond', 3 *American University Journal of International Law and Policy*, 517 (1988).

LE BLANC, L., 'The Economic, Social and Cultural Rights Protocol to the American Convention and its Background', 2 *Netherlands Quarterly of Human Rights*, 130 (1992).

LEIGH, M., 'American Convention on Human Rights: Advisory Jurisdiction; Effect of a Reservation; Death Penalty', 78 *American Journal of International Law*, 881 (1984).

LOCKWOOD, B. Jr., 'Advisory Opinions of the Inter-American Court of Human Rights', 13 *Denver Journal of International Law and Policy*, 245 (1983–4).

MALAMUD-GOTI, J., 'Soldiers, Peasants, Politicians and the War Against Drugs in Bolivia', 6 *American University Journal of International Law and Policy*, 35 (1990).

MARQUEZ RODRIGUEZ, E., 'Visitas de Observacion *In Loco* de la Comision Interamericana de Derechos Humanos y Sus Informes in Cançado Trindade, A. A., Elizondo, G., and Ordonez, J. (eds)., *Estudios Basicos de Derechos Humanos*, Vol. III, IIDH (1995).

McCANN, T., 'The American Convention on Human Rights: Towards Uniform Interpretation of Human Rights Law', 8 *Fordham International Law Journal*, 810 (1982–3).

McCOMIE, V., 'Practical Considerations on Human Rights within the OAS', 4 *American University Journal of International Law and Policy*, 275 (1989).

MEDINA QUIROGA, C., 'The Inter-American Commission on Human Rights and the Inter-American Court of Human Rights: Reflections on a Joint Venture', 12 *Human Rights Law Quarterly*, 454 (1990).

MÉNDEZ, J. E., 'La participación de la Comisión Interamericana de Derechos Humanos en los conflictos entre los Misikitos y el gobierno de Nicaragua', *Derechos Humanos en las Americas/Direitos Humanos nas Americas/Human Rights in the Americas. Homenaje a la Memoria de Carlos A. Dunshee de Abranches*, CIDH, Washington, 306 (1984).

—— & VIVANCO, J. M., 'Medidas de protección para testigos en casos ante la Corte Interamericana de Derechos Humanos', 19 *Revista del Instituto Interamericano de Derechos Humanos* (1994), 157.

—— —— 'Disappearances and the Inter-American Court: Reflections on a Litigation Experience', 13 *Hamline Law Review*, 3, 507 (1990).

MOLTENI, A., 'El derecho de petición y el Sistema Intramericano de protección de los derechos humanos', *Derechos Humanos en las Americas/Direitos Humanos nas Americas/Human Rights in the Americas. Homenaje a la Memoria de Carlos A. Dunshee de Abranches*, CIDH, Washington, 188 (1984).

MOORE, J. L. Jr., 'Problems with Forgiveness: Granting Amnesty under the Arias Plan in Nicaragua and El Salvador', 43 *Stanford Law Review*, 733 (1991).

NETHERLANDS INSTITUTE OF HUMAN RIGHTS, 'Seminar on the Right to Restitution, Compensation and Rehabilitation for Victims of Gross Violations of Human Rights and Fundamental Freedoms', Maastricht 11–15 March, 1992', *SIM Special* 12, Utrecht.

NINO, C., 'The Duty to Punish Past Abuses of Human Rights Put into Context: The Case of Argentina', 100 *Yale Law Journal*, 2619 (1991).

NORRIS, R., 'Observations *in loco*: Practice and Procedure of the Inter-American Commission on Human Rights, 1970–1983', 19 *Texas Internatioal Law Journal*, 285 (1984).

—— 'Bringing Human Rights Petitions before the Inter-American Commission', 20 *Santa Clara Law Review*, 733 (1980).

—— 'The New Statute of the Inter-American Commission on Human Rights', 1 *Human Rights Law Journal*, 379 (1980).

—— 'Leyes de Impunidad y los Derechos Humanos en las Americas: Una Respuesta Legal', 15 *Revista del Instituto Interamericano de Derechos Humanos*, 47 (1992).

—— & DESIO REITON, P., 'The Suspension of Guarantees: a Comparative Analysis of the American Convention on Human Rights and the Constitutions of the States Parties', 30 *American University Law Review*, 189 (1980).

NIETO NAVIA, R., 'La Corte Interamericana de Derechos Humanos', *Estudios Basicos de Derechos Humanos I*, Cerdas Cruz & Nieto Loaiza, Comp., Instituto Interamericano de Derchos Humanos & Comision dela Comunidad Europea, San Josè de Costa Rica, 251 (1994).

O'NEILL, W. G., 'Human Rights Monitoring vs. Political Expediency: the Experience of the OAS/UN Mission in Haiti', 8 *Harvard Human Rights Journal*, 101 (1995).

ORENTLICHTER, D., 'Settling Accounts: The Duty to Prosecute Human Rights Violations of a Prior Regime', 100 *Yale Law Journal*, 2537 (1991).

ORREGO VICUÑA, F., 'A la recherche d'un nouveau rôle pour l'organisation des Etats Américaines: le Protocole d'Amendements de 1985 de la Charte', 33 *Annuaire Française de Droit International*, 784 (1987).

PADDICORD, J., 'The American Convention on Human Rights: Potential Defects and Remedies', 19 *Texas International Law Journal*, 130 (1984).

PADILLA, D., 'The Inter-American System for the Promotion and Protection of Human Rights (the US Constitution and the Adoption of International Human Rights Instruments: Freeing the Political Logjam)', 20 *Georgia Journal of International and Comparative Law*, 305 (1990).

—— 'La Comision Interamericana de Derechos Humanos', *Estudios Basicos de Derechos Humanos I*, Cerdas Cruz & Nieto Loaiza, Comp., Instituto Interamericano de Derechos Humanos & Comision de la Comunidad Europea, San José de Costa Rica, 1994, 227–50.

PAN, J., 'Antecedents y presentación del Informe NO. 29/92 de la Comisión Interamericana de Derechos Humanos', *Impunidad y Derechos Humanos*, Editorial Universidad, Montevideo, 21 (1993).

PARKER, M., 'Other Treaties: The Inter-American Court of Human Rights Defines its Jurisdiction', 33 *American University Law Review*, 211 (1983).

PASQUALUCCI, J. M., 'The Inter-American Human Rights System: Establishing Precedents and Procedure in Human Rights Law', 26 *University of Miami Inter-American Law Review*, 297 (1994/95).

—— 'The Whole Truth and Nothing but the Truth: Truth Commission, Impunity and the Inter-American Human Rights System', 12 *Boston University International Law Journal*, 321 (1994).

—— 'Provisional Measures in the Inter-American Human Rights System: An Innovative Development in International Law', 26 *Vanderbilt Journal of Transnational Law*, 803 (1993).

PIN-BERLIN, D., 'To Prosecute or to Pardon? Human Rights Decisions in the Latin American Southern Cone', 16 *Human Rights Quarterly*, 105 (1994).

PIZA ESCALANTE, R., 'Coordination of the Mechanisms for the Protection of Human Rights in the American Convention with Those Established by the United Nations', 30 *American University Law Review*, 187 (1980).

POPKIN, M., 'El Salvador: A Negotiated End to Impunity?', in Roht-Arrieza, N. (ed.), *Impunity and Human Rights in International Law and Practice*, Oxford University Press, 201 (1995).

REQUE, L., 'The Organization of American States and the Protection of Human Rights', *Inter-American Yearbook on Human Rights* 1968, OAS, 220 (1973).

ROBERTSON, A., 'Revision of the Charter of the Organization of American States', 17 *International & Comparative Law Quarterly*, 346 (1968).

—— 'The American Convention on Human Rights and the European Convention: A Comparative Study', 29 *Annuaire Europeen/European Yearbook* 50 (1981).

ROBINSON, P., 'The Inter-American Human Rights System', 17 *West Indian Law Journal*, 8 (1992).

ROHT-ARRIAZA, N., 'State Responsibility to Investigate and Prosecute Grave

Human Rights Violations in International Law', 48 *California Law Review*, 449 (1990).

ROSPIGLIOSI, F., 'Democracy's Bleak Prospects', in Tulchin, J. S. and Bland, G. (eds.), *Peru in Crisis: Dictatorship or Democracy?* 35, 50–1 (1994).

ROWLES, J., 'The US, the OAS and the Dilemma of the Undesirable Regime', 13 *Georgia Journal of International and Comparative Law*, 385 (1983).

SANDIFER, D., 'Human Rights in the Inter-American System', 11 *Howard Law Journal*, 508 (1965).

SCHABAS, W., 'Substantive and Procedural Hurdles to Canada's Ratification of the American Convention on Human Rights', 12 *Human Rights Law Journal*, 405 (1991).

SCHNABLY, S., 'The Santiago Commitment as a Call to Democracy in the US: Evaluation of the OAS role in Haiti, Peru and Guatemala', 25 *University of Miami Inter-American Law Review*, 393 (1994).

SCHARF, M., 'Swapping Amnesty for Peace: Was there a Duty to prosecute International Crimes in Haiti?' 31 *Texas International Law Journal* 1 (1996).

SCHEMAN, L. R., 'The Inter-American Commission on Human Rights', 59 *American Journal of International Law*, 335 (1965).

—— 'The OAS and the Quest for International Cooperation: American Vision or Mirage', 13 *Case Western Reserve Journal of International Law*, 83 (1981).

SCHREIBER, A., 'Human Rights in Revolutionary Cuba: The Work of the Inter-American Commission on Human Rights', 2 *Journal of International and Comparative Law*, 139 (1969).

SEPÚLVEDA, C., 'El procedimiento de solución amistosa ante la Comisión Interamericana de Derechos Humanos', *Derechos Humanos en las Americas/ Direitos Humanos nas Americas/Human Rights in the Americas. Homenaje a la Memoria de Carlos A. Dunshee de Abranches*, CIDH, Washington, 242 (1984).

—— 'The Inter-American Commission on Human Rights of the Organization of American States: 25 Years of Evolution and Endeavour', in 28 *German Yearbook of International Law*, 65 (1985).

—— 'Reform of the Charter of the Organization of American States', 137 *Recueil des Cours, Académie Droit International* 83 (1971–III).

SHELTON, D., 'The Jurisprudence of the Inter-American Court of Human Rights', 10 *American University Journal of International Law and Policy*, 333 (1994).

—— 'Private Violence, Public Wrongs and the Responsibility of States', 13 *Fordham International Law Journal*, 1 (1989–90).

—— 'Judicial Review of State Action by International Courts', 12 *Fordham International Law Journal*, 361 (1988–9).

—— 'Implementation Procedures of the American Convention of Human Rights', 26 *German Yearbook of International Law*, 238 (1983).

—— 'Abortion and the Right to Life in the Inter-American System: The Case of "Baby Boy"', 2 *Human Rights Law Journal*, 309 (1981).

—— 'The Decision of the IACHR of March 27, 1987 in the Case of Roach and Pinkerton: A Note', 8 *Human Rights Law Journal*, 355 (1987).

SUNG, A., 'Freedom of the Press: Costa Rican Journalist Licensing Law Violates the American Convention on Human Rights', 27 *Harvard International Law Journal*, 678 (1986).

VARGAS, M. D., 'Individual Access to the Inter-American Court on Human Rights', 16 *New York University Journal of Internatioal Law and Politics*, 601 (1984).

VASAK, K., 'La Commission Interaméricaine des Droits de l'Homme', 1 *Revue de Droits de l'Homme*, 109 (1968).

VENTURA, M., 'Costa Rica and the Inter-American Court of Human Rights', 4 *Human Rights Law Journal*, 273 (1983).

VIVANCO, J. M., 'Las organizaciones no gubernamentales de derechos humanos', in *Estudios Básicos de Derechos Humanos I*, Cerdas Cruz & Nieto Loaiza, Comp., Instituto Interamericano de Derechos Humanos & Comisión de la Comunidad Europea, San José de Costa Rica, 275 (1994).

VOLIO, F., 'The Inter-American Commision on Human Rights', 30 *American University Law Review*, 70 (1980).

VAN COTT, D. L., 'Prospects for Self-Determination of Indigenous Peoples in Latin America: Questions of Law and Practice', 2 *Global Governance* 43 (1996).

—— 'The Inter-American Human Rights System', in Hannum, H. (ed.), *Guide to International Human Rights Practice*, 2nd edn., University of Pennsylvania Press, Philadelphia, 1992, Chapter 7.

WEINER, R., 'Trying to Make Ends Meet: Reconciling the Law and Practice of Human Rights Amnesties', 26 *Saint Mary's Law Journal*, 857 (1995).

WEISSBRODT, D., 'Execution of Juvenile Offenders by the United States Violates International Human Rights Law', 3 *American University Journal of International Law and Policy* 339 (1988).

WESTON, B., LUKES, R. A. & HNATT, K., 'Regional Human Rights Regimes: A Comparison and Appraisal', 20 *Vanderbilt Journal of Transnational Law*, 585 (1987).

WITTEN, S., 'Human Rights Compliance of Honduras with American Convention Exhaustion of Domestic Legal Remedies, Proof of Disappearance, Proof of Governmental Liability', 83 *American Journal of International Law*, 381 (1989).

WOJCIK, M., 'Using International Human Rights Law to Advance Queer Rights: a Case Study for the American Declaration on the Rights and Duties of Man', 55 *Ohio State Law Journal*, 649 (1994).

WOOD, B., 'Human Rights and the Inter-American System', in Farer, T. (ed.), *The Future of the Inter-American System*, Praeger, NY, 19 (1979).

ZANGHI, C., 'La Convenzione interamericana dei diritti dell'uomo', 25 *Comunità Internazionale*, 266 (1970).

SYMPOSIUM, 'Security of the Person and Security of the State: Human Rights and Claims of National Security: A Symposium', 9 *Yale Journal of World Public Order*, 1 (1982).

SYMPOSIUM, 'Law and Lustration: Righting the Wrongs of the Past. Symposium', 20 *Law and Social Inquiry*, 1 (1995).

PANEL, 'The OAS Charter After 40 Years', 82 *American Society of International Law Proceedings*, 101 (1988).

Appendix I

*Signed in Bogotá in 1948 and amended by the Protocol of Buenos Aires in 1967, by the Protocol of Cartagena de Indias in 1985, by the Protocol of Washington 1992, and by the Protocol of Managua in 1993. In force as of January 29, 1996.

IN THE NAME OF THEIR PEOPLES, THE STATES REPRESENTED AT THE NINTH INTERNATIONAL CONFERENCE OF AMERICAN STATES,

Convinced that the historic mission of America is to offer to man a land of liberty and a favorable environment for the development of his personality and the realization of his just aspirations;

Conscious that that mission has already inspired numerous agreements, whose essential value lies in the desire of the American peoples to live together in peace and, through their mutual understanding and respect for the sovereignty of each one, to provide for the betterment of all, in independence, in equality and under law;

Convinced that representative democracy is an indispensable condition for the stability, peace and development of the region;

Confident that the true significance of American solidarity and good neighborliness can only mean the consolidation on this continent, within the framework of democratic institutions, of a system of individual liberty and social justice based on respect for the essential rights of man;

Persuaded that their welfare and their contribution to the progress and the civilization of the world will increasingly require intensive continental cooperation;

Resolved to persevere in the noble undertaking that humanity has conferred upon the United Nations, whose principles and purposes they solemnly reaffirm;

Convinced that juridical organization is a necessary condition for security and peace founded on moral order and on justice;

and In accordance with Resolution IX of the Inter-American Conference on Problems of War and Peace, held in Mexico City,

HAVE AGREED
upon the following

PART ONE

Chapter I. Nature and Purposes

Article 1

The American States establish by this Charter the international organization that they have developed to achieve an order of peace and justice, to promote their solidarity, to strengthen their collaboration, and to defend their sovereignty, their territorial integrity, and their independence. Within the United Nations, the Organization of American States is a regional agency.

The Organization of American States has no powers other than those expressly conferred upon it by this Charter, none of whose provisions authorizes it to intervene in matters that are within the internal jurisdiction of the Member States.

Article 2

The Organization of American States, in order to put into practice the principles on which it is founded and to fulfill its regional obligations under the Charter of the United Nations, proclaims the following essential purposes:

a. To strengthen the peace and security of the continent.

b. To promote and consolidate representative democracy, with due respect for the principle of nonintervention;

c. To prevent possible causes of difficulties and to ensure the pacific settlement of disputes that may arise among the Member States;

d. To provide for common action on the part of those States in the event of aggression;

e. To seek the solution of political, juridical, and economic problems that may arise among them;

f. To promote, by cooperative action, their economic, social, and cultural development; and

g. To eradicate extreme poverty, which constitutes an obstacle to the full democratic development of the peoples of the hemisphere; and

h. To achieve an effective limitation of conventional weapons that will make it possible to devote the largest amount of resources to the economic and social development of the Member States.

Chapter II. Principles

Article 3

The American States reaffirm the following principles:

a. International law is the standard of conduct of States in their reciprocal relations;

b. International order consists essentially of respect for the personality, sovereignty, and independence of States, and the faithful fulfillment of obligations derived from treaties and other sources of international law;

c. Good faith shall govern the relations between States;

d. The solidarity of the American States and the high aims which are sought through it require the political organization of those States on the basis of the effective exercise of representative democracy;

e. Every State has the right to choose, without external interference, its political, economic, and social system and to organize itself in the way best suited to it, and has the duty to abstain from intervening in the affairs of another State.

Subject to the foregoing, the American States shall cooperate fully among themselves, independently of the nature of their political, economic, and social systems;

f. The elimination of extreme poverty is an essential part of the promotion and consolidation of representative democracy and is the common and shared responsibility of the American States;

g. The American States condemn war of aggression: victory does not give rights.

h. An act of aggression against one American State is an act of aggression against all the other American States;

i. Controversies of an international character arising between two or more American States shall be settled by peaceful procedures;

j. Social justice and social security are bases of lasting peace;

k. Economic cooperation is essential to the common welfare and prosperity of the peoples of the continent;

l. The American States proclaim the fundamental rights of the individual without distinction as to race, nationality, creed, or sex;

m. The spiritual unity of the continent is based on respect for the cultural values of the American countries and requires their close cooperation for the high purposes of civilization;

n. The education of peoples should be directed towards justice, freedom, and peace.

Chapter III. Members

Article 4

All American States that ratify the present Charter are Members of the Organization.

Article 5

Any new political entity that arises from the union of several Member States and that, as such, ratifies the present Charter, shall become a Member of the Organization. The entry of the new political entity into the Organization shall result in the loss of membership of each one of the States which constitute it.

Article 6

Any other independent American State that desires to become a Member of the Organization should so indicate by means of a note addressed to the Secretary General, in which it declares that it is willing to sign and ratify the Charter of the Organization and to accept all the obligations inherent in membership, especially those relating to collective security expressly set forth in Articles 27 and 28 of the Charter.

Article 7

The General Assembly, upon the recommendation of the Permanent Council of the Organization, shall determine whether it is appropriate that the Secretary General be authorized to permit the applicant State to sign the Charter and to accept the deposit of the corresponding instrument of ratification. Both the recommendation of the Permanent Council and the decision of the General Assembly shall require the affirmative vote of two thirds of the Member States.

Article 8

Membership in the Organization shall be confined to independent States of the Hemisphere that were Members of the United Nations as of December 10, 1985, and the nonautonomous territories mentioned in document OEA/Ser. P., AG/doc. 1939/85, of November 5, 1985, when they become independent.

Article 9

A Member of the Organization whose democratically constituted government has been overthrown by force may be suspended from the exercise of the right to participate in the sessions of the General Assembly, the Meeting of Consultation, the Councils of the Organization and the Specialized Conferences as well as in the commissions, working groups and any other bodies established.

    a. The power to suspend shall be exercised only when such diplomatic initiatives undertaken by the Organization for the purpose of promoting the restoration of representative democracy in the affected Member State have been unsuccessful.

    b. The decision to suspend shall be adopted at a special session of the General Assembly by an affirmative vote of two-thirds of the Member States;

    c. The suspension shall take effect immediately following its approval by the General Asembly;

    d. The suspension notwithstanding, the Organization shall endeavor to undertake additional diplomatic initiatives to contribute to the re-establishment of representative democracy in the affected Member State;

    e. The Member which has been subject to suspension shall continue to fulfill its obligations to the Organization;

    f. The General Assembly may lift the suspension by a decision adopted with the approval of two-thirds of the Member States;

    g. The powers referred to in this article shall be exercised in accordance with this Charter.

Chapter IV. Fundamental Rights and Duties of States

Article 10

States are juridically equal, enjoy equal rights and equal capacity to exercise these rights, and have equal duties. The rights of each State depend not upon its power to ensure the exercise thereof, but upon the mere fact of its existence as a person under international law.

Article 11

Every American State has the duty to respect the rights enjoyed by every other State in accordance with international law.

Article 12

The fundamental rights of States may not be impaired in any manner whatsoever.

Article 13

The political existence of the State is independent of recognition by other States. Even before being recognized, the State has the right to defend its integrity and independence, to provide for its preservation and prosperity, and consequently to organize itself as it sees fit, to legislate concerning its interests, to administer its services, and to determine the jurisdiction and competence of its courts. The exercise of these rights is limited only by the exercise of the rights of other States in accordance with international law.

Article 14

Recognition implies that the State granting it accepts the personality of the new State, with all the rights and duties that international law prescribes for the two States.

Article 15

The right of each State to protect itself and to live its own life does not authorize it to commit unjust acts against another State.

Article 16

The jurisdiction of States within the limits of their national territory is exercised equally over all the inhabitants, whether nationals or aliens.

Article 17

Each State has the right to develop its cultural, political, and economic life freely and naturally. In this free development, the State shall respect the rights of the individual and the principles of universal morality.

Article 18

Respect for and the faithful observance of treaties constitute standards for the development of peaceful relations among States. International treaties and agreements should be public.

Article 19

No State or group of States has the right to intervene, directly or indirectly, for any reason whatever, in the internal or external affairs of any other State. The foregoing principle prohibits not only armed force but also any other form of interference or attempted threat against the personality of the State or against its political, economic, and cultural elements.

Article 20

No State may use or encourage the use of coercive measures of an economic or political character in order to force the sovereign will of another State and obtain from it advantages of any kind.

Article 21

The territory of a State is inviolable; it may not be the object, even temporarily, of military occupation or of other measures of force taken by another State, directly or indirectly, on any grounds whatever. No territorial acquisitions or special advantages obtained either by force or by other means of coercion shall be recognized.

Article 22

The American States bind themselves in their international relations not to have recourse to the use of force, except in the case of self-defense in accordance with existing treaties or in fulfillment thereof.

Article 23

Measures adopted for the maintenance of peace and security in accordance with existing treaties do not constitute a violation of the principles set forth in Articles 18 and 20.

Chapter VII. Integral Development

Article 30

The Member States, inspired by the principles of inter-American solidarity and cooperation, pledge themselves to a united effort to ensure international social justice in their relations and integral development for their peoples, as conditions essential to peace and security. Integral development encompasses the economic, social, educational, cultural, scientific, and technological fields through which the goals that each country sets for accomplishing it should be achieved.

Article 31

Inter-American cooperation for integral development is the common and joint responsibility of the Member States, within the framework of the democratic principles and the institutions of the inter-American system. It should include the economic, social, educational, cultural, scientific, and technological fields, support the achievement of national objectives of the Member States, and respect the priorities established by each country in its development plans, without political ties or conditions.

Article 32

Inter-American cooperation for integral development should be continuous and preferably channeled through multilateral organizations, without prejudice to bilateral cooperation between Member States.

The Member States shall contribute to inter-American cooperation for integral development in accordance with their resources and capabilities and in conformity with their laws.

Article 33

Development is a primary responsibility of each country and should constitute an integral and continuous process for the establishment of a more just economic and social order that will make possible and contribute to the fulfillment of the individual.

Article 34

The Member States agree that equality of opportunity, equitable distribution of wealth and income, and the full participation of their peoples in decisions relating to their own development are, among others, basic objectives of integral development. To achieve them, they likewise agree to devote their utmost efforts to accomplishing the following basic goals:

   a. Substantial and self-sustained increase of per capita national product;
   b. Equitable distribution of national income;
   c. Adequate and equitable systems of taxation;
   d. Modernization of rural life and reforms leading to equitable and efficient land-tenure systems, increased agricultural productivity, expanded use of land, diversification of production and improved processing and marketing systems for agricultural products; and the strengthening and expansion of the means to attain these ends;
   e. Accelerated and diversified industrialization, especially of capital and intermediate goods;
   f. Stability of domestic price levels, compatible with sustained economic development and the attainment of social justice;
   g. Fair wages, employment opportunities, and acceptable working conditions for all;
   h. Rapid eradication of illiteracy and expansion of educational opportunities for all;
   i. Protection of man's potential through the extension and application of modern medical science;
   j. Proper nutrition, especially through the acceleration of national efforts to increase the production and availability of food;
   k. Adequate housing for all sectors of the population;
   l. Urban conditions that offer the opportunity for a healthful, productive, and full life;
   m. Promotion of private initiative and investment in harmony with action in the public sector; and
   n. Expansion and diversification of exports.

Article 35

The Member States should refrain from practising policies and adopting actions or measures that have serious adverse effects on the development of other Member States.

Article 36

Transnational enterprises and foreign private investment shall be subject to the legislation of the host countries and to the jurisdiction of their competent courts and to the international treaties and agreements to which said countries are parties, and should conform to the development policies of the recipient countries.

Article 37

The Member States agree to join together in seeking a solution to urgent or critical problems that may arise whenever the economic development or stability of any Member State is seriously affected by conditions that cannot be remedied through the efforts of that State.

Article 38

The Member States shall extend among themselves the benefits of science and technology by encouraging the exchange and utilization of scientific and technical knowledge in accordance with existing treaties and national laws.

Article 39

The Member States, recognizing the close interdependence between foreign trade and economic and social development, should make individual and united efforts to bring about the following:

a. Favorable conditions of access to world markets for the products of the developing countries of the region, particularly through the reduction or elimination, by importing countries, of tariff and nontariff barriers that affect the exports of the Member States of the Organization, except when such barriers are applied in order to diversify the economic structure, to speed up the development of the less-developed Member States, and intensify their process of economic integration, or when they are related to national security or to the needs of economic balance;

b. Continuity in their economic and social development by means of:

i. Improved conditions for trade in basic commodities through international agreements, where appropriate; orderly marketing procedures that avoid the disruption of markets, and other measures designed to promote the expansion of markets and to obtain dependable incomes for producers, adequate and dependable supplies for consumers, and stable prices that are both remunerative to producers and fair to consumers;

ii. Improved international financial cooperation and the adoption of other means for lessening the adverse impact of sharp fluctuations in export earnings experienced by the countries exporting basic commodities;

iii. Diversification of exports and expansion of export opportunities for manufactured and semimanufactured products from the developing countries; and

iv. Conditions conducive to increasing the real export earnings of the Member States, particularly the developing countries of the region, and to increasing their participation in international trade.

Article 40

The Member States reaffirm the principle that when the more developed countries grant concessions in international trade agreements that lower or eliminate tariffs or other barriers to foreign trade so that they benefit the less-developed countries, they should not expect reciprocal concessions from those countries that are incompatible with their economic development, financial, and trade needs.

Article 41

The Member States, in order to accelerate their economic development, regional integration, and the expansion and improvement of the conditions of their commerce, shall promote improvement and coordination of transportation and communication in the developing countries and among the Member States.

Article 42

The Member States recognize that integration of the developing countries of the Hemisphere is one of the objectives of the inter-American system and, therefore, shall orient their efforts and take the necessary measures to accelerate the integration process, with a view to establishing a Latin American common market in the shortest possible time.

Article 43

In order to strengthen and accelerate integration in all its aspects, the Member States agree to give adequate priority to the preparation and carrying out of multinational projects and to their financing, as well as to encourage economic and financial institutions of the inter-American system to continue giving their broadest support to regional integration institutions and programs.

Article 44

The Member States agree that technical and financial cooperation that seeks to promote regional economic integration should be based on the principle of harmonious, balanced, and efficient development, with particular attention to the relatively less-developed countries, so that it may be a decisive factor that will enable them to promote, with their own efforts, the improved development of their infrastructure programs, new lines of production, and export diversification.

Article 45

The Member States, convinced that man can only achieve the full realization of his aspirations within a just social order, along with economic development and true peace, agree to dedicate every effort to the application of the following principles and mechanisms:

    a. All human beings, without distinction as to race, sex, nationality, creed, or social condition, have a right to material well-being and to their spiritual development, under circumstances of liberty, dignity, equality of opportunity, and economic security;

    b. Work is a right and a social duty, it gives dignity to the one who performs it, and it should be performed under conditions, including a system of fair wages, that ensure life, health, and a decent standard of living for the worker and his family, both during his working years and in his old age, or when any circumstance deprives him of the possibility of working;

c. Employers and workers, both rural and urban, have the right to associate themselves freely for the defense and promotion of their interests, including the right to collective bargaining and the workers' right to strike, and recognition of the juridical personality of associations and the protection of their freedom and independence, all in accordance with applicable laws;

d. Fair and efficient systems and procedures for consultation and collaboration among the sectors of production, with due regard for safeguarding the interests of the entire society;

e. The operation of systems of public administration, banking and credit, enterprise, and distribution and sales, in such a way, in harmony with the private sector, as to meet the requirements and interests of the community;

f. The incorporation and increasing participation of the marginal sectors of the population, in both rural and urban areas, in the economic, social, civic, cultural, and political life of the nation, in order to achieve the full integration of the national community, acceleration of the process of social mobility, and the consolidation of the democratic system. The encouragement of all efforts of popular promotion and cooperation that have as their purpose the development and progress of the community;

g. Recognition of the importance of the contribution of organizations such as labor unions, cooperatives, and cultural, professional, business, neighborhood, and community associations to the life of the society and to the development process;

h. Development of an efficient social security policy; and

i. Adequate provision for all persons to have due legal aid in order to secure their rights.

Article 46

The Member States recognize that, in order to facilitate the process of Latin American regional integration, it is necessary to harmonize the social legislation of the developing countries, especially in the labor and social security fields, so that the rights of the workers shall be equally protected, and they agree to make the greatest efforts possible to achieve this goal.

Article 47

The Member States will give primary importance within their development plans to the encouragement of education, science, technology, and culture, oriented toward the overall improvement of the individual, and as a foundation for democracy, social justice, and progress.

Article 48

The Member States will cooperate with one another to meet their educational needs, to promote scientific research, and to encourage technological progress for their integral development. They will consider themselves individually and jointly bound to preserve and enrich the cultural heritage of the American peoples.

Article 49

The Member States will exert the greatest efforts, in accordance with their constitutional processes, to ensure the effective exercise of the right to education, on the following bases:

a. Elementary education, compulsory for children of school age, shall also be offered to all others who can benefit from it. When provided by the State it shall be without charge;

b. Middle-level education shall be extended progressively to as much of the population as possible, with a view to social improvement. It shall be diversified in such a way that it meets the development needs of each country without prejudice to providing a general education; and

c. Higher education shall be available to all, provided that, in order to maintain its high level, the corresponding regulatory or academic standards are met.

Article 50

The Member States will give special attention to the eradication of illiteracy, will strengthen adult and vocational education systems, and will ensure that the benefits of culture will be available to the entire population They will promote the use of all information media to fulfill these aims.

Article 51

The Member States will develop science and technology through educational, research, and technological development activities and information and dissemination programs. They will stimulate activities in the field of technology for the purpose of adapting it to the needs of their integral development. They will organize their cooperation in these fields efficiently and will substantially increase exchange of knowledge, in accordance with national objectives and laws and with treaties in force.

Article 52

The Member States, with due respect for the individuality of each of them, agree to promote cultural exchange as an effective means of consolidating inter-American understanding; and they recognize that regional integration programs should be strengthened by close ties in the fields of education, science, and culture.

PART TWO

Chapter VIII. The Organs

Article 53

The Organization of American States accomplishes its purposes by means of:

a. The General Assembly;
b. The Meeting of Consultation of Ministers of Foreign Affairs;
c. The Councils;

d. The Inter-American Juridical Committee;
e. The Inter-American Commission on Human Rights;
f. The General Secretariat;
g. The Specialized Conferences; and
h. The Specialized Organizations.

There may be established, in addition to those provided for in the Charter and in accordance with the provisions thereof, such subsidiary organs, agencies, and other entities as are considered necessary.

Chapter IX. The General Assembly

Article 54

The General Assembly is the supreme organ of the Organization of American States. It has as its principal powers, in addition to such others as are assigned to it by the Charter, the following:

a. To decide the general action and policy of the Organization, determine the structure and functions of its organs, and consider any matter relating to friendly relations among the American States;

b. To establish measures for coordinating the activities of the organs, agencies, and entities of the Organization among themselves, and such activities with those of the other institutions of the inter-American system;

c. To strengthen and coordinate cooperation with the United Nations and its specialized agencies;

d. To promote collaboration, especially in the economic, social, and cultural fields, with other international organizations whose purposes are similar to those of the Organization of American States;

e. To approve the program-budget of the Organization and determine the quotas of the Member States;

f. To consider the reports of the Meeting of Consultation of Ministers of Foreign Affairs and the observations and recommendations presented by the Permanent Council with regard to the reports that should be presented by the other organs and entities, in accordance with the provisions of Article 90.f, as well as the reports of any organ which may be required by the General Assembly itself;

g. To adopt general standards to govern the operations of the General Secretariat; and

h. To adopt its own rules of procedure and, by a two-thirds vote, its agenda.

The General Assembly shall exercise its powers in accordance with the provisions of the Charter and of other inter-American treaties.

Article 55

The general Assembly snail establish the bases for fixing the quota that each Government is to contribute to the maintenance of the Organization, taking into account the ability to pay of the respective countries and their determination to contribute in an equitable manner. Decisions on budgetary matters require the approval of two thirds of the Member States.

Article 56

All Member States have the right to be represented in the General Assembly. Each State has the right to one vote.

Article 57

The General Assembly shall convene annually during the period determined by the rules of procedure and at a place selected in accordance with the principle of rotation. At each regular session the date and place of the next regular session shall be determined, in accordance with the rules of procedure.

If for any reason the General Assembly cannot be held at the place chosen, it shall meet at the General Secretariat, unless one of the Member States should make a timely offer of a site in its territory, in which case the Permanent Council of the Organization may agree that the General Assembly will meet in that place.

Article 58

In special circumstances and with the approval of two thirds of the Member States, the Permanent Council shall convoke a special session of the General Assembly.

Article 59

Decisions of the General Assembly shall be adopted by the affirmative vote of an absolute majority of the Member States, except in those cases that require a two-thirds vote as provided in the Charter or as may be provided by the General Assembly in its rules of procedure.

Article 60

There shall be a Preparatory Committee of the General Assembly, composed of representatives of all the Member States, which shall:

    a. Prepare the draft agenda of each session of the General Assembly;

    b. Review the proposed program-budget and the draft resolution on quotas, and present to the General Assembly a report thereon containing the recommendations it considers appropriate; and

    c. Carry out such other functions as the General Assembly may assign to it.

The draft agenda and the report shall, in due course, be transmitted to the Governments of the Member States.

Chapter X. The Meeting of Consultation of Ministers of Foreign Affairs

Article 61

The Meeting of Consultation of Ministers of Foreign Affairs shall be held in order to consider problems of an urgent nature and of common interest to the American States, and to serve as the Organ of Consultation.

Article 62

Any Member State may request that a Meeting of Consultation be called. The request shall be addressed to the Permanent Council of the Organization, which shall decide by an absolute majority whether a meeting should be held.

Article 63

The agenda and regulations of the Meeting of Consultation shall be prepared by the Permanent Council of the Organization and submitted to the Member States for consideration.

Article 64

If, for exceptional reasons, a Minister of Foreign Affairs is unable to attend the meeting, he shall be represented by a special delegate.

Article 65

In case of an armed attack on the territory of an American State or within the region of security delimited by the treaty in force, the Chairman of the Permanent Council shall without delay call a meeting of the Council to decide on the convocation of the Meeting of Consultation, without prejudice to the provisions of the Inter-American Treaty of Reciprocal Assistance with regard to the States Parties to that instrument.

Article 66

An Advisory Defense Committee shall be established to advise the Organ of Consultation on problems of military cooperation that may arise in connection with the application of existing special treaties on collective security.

Article 67

The Advisory Defense Committee shall be composed of the highest military authorities of the American States participating in the Meeting of Consultation. Under exceptional circumstances the Governments may appoint substitutes. Each State shall be entitled to one vote.

Article 68

The Advisory Defense Committee shall be convoked under the same conditions as the Organ of Consultation, when the latter deals with matters relating to defense against aggression.

Article 69

The Committee shall also meet when the General Assembly or the Meeting of Consultation or the Governments, by a two-thirds majority of the Member States, assign to it technical studies or reports on specific subjects.

Chapter XI. The Councils of the Organization

Common Provisions

Article 70

The Permanent Council of the Organization and the Inter-American Council for Integral Development are directly responsible to the General Assembly, and each has the authority granted to it in the Charter and other inter-American instruments, as well as the functions assigned to it by the General Assembly and the Meeting of Consultation of Ministers of Foreign Affairs.

Chapter XII. The Permanent Council of the Organization

Article 80

The Permanent Council of the Organization is composed of one representative of each Member State, especially appointed by the respective Government, with the rank of ambassador. Each Government may accredit an acting representative, as well as such alternates and advisers as it considers necessary.

Chapter XV. The Inter-American Commission on Human Rights

Article 106

There shall be an Inter-American Commission on Human Rights, whose principal function shall be to promote the observance and protection of human rights and to serve as a consultative organ of the Organization in these matters.

An inter-American convention on human rights shall determine the structure, competence, and procedure of this Commission, as well as those of other organs responsible for these matters.

Chapter XVI. The General Secretariat

Article 107

The General Secretariat is the central and permanent organ of the Organization of American States. It shall perform the functions assigned to it in the Charter, in other inter-American treaties and agreements, and by the General Assembly, and shall carry out the duties entrusted to it by the General Assembly, the Meeting of Consultation of Ministers of Foreign Affairs, or the Councils.

Article 108

The Secretary General of the Organization shall be elected by the General Assembly for a five-year term and may not be reelected more than once or succeeded by a person of the same nationality. In the event that the office of Secretary General becomes vacant, the Assistant Secretary General shall assume his duties until the General Assembly shall elect a new Secretary General for a full term.

Article 109

The Secretary General shall direct the General Secretariat, be the legal representative thereof, and, notwithstanding the provisions of Article 90.b, be responsible to the General Assembly for the proper fulfillment of the obligations and functions of the General Secretariat.

Article 110

The Secretary General, or his representative, may participate with voice but without vote in all meetings of the Organization.

The Secretary General may bring to the attention of the General Assembly or the Permanent Council any matter which in his opinion might threaten the peace and security of the Hemisphere or the development of the Member States.

The authority to which the preceding paragraph refers shall be exercised in accordance with the present Charter.

Article 111

The General Secretariat shall promote economic, social, juridical, educational, scientific, and cultural relations among all the Member States of the Organization, in keeping with the actions and policies decided upon by the General Assembly and with the pertinent decisions of the Councils.

Article 112

The General Secretariat shall also perform the following functions:

a. Transmit ex officio to the Member States notice of the convocation of the General Assembly, the Meeting of Consultation of Ministers of Foreign Affairs, the Inter-American Council for Integral Development, and the Specialized Conferences;

b. Advise the other organs, when appropriate, in the preparation of agenda and rules of procedure;

c. Prepare the proposed program-budget of the Organization on the basis of programs adopted by the Councils, agencies, and entities whose expenses should be included in the program-budget and, after consultation with the Councils or their permanent committees, submit it to the Preparatory Committee of the General Assembly and then to the Assembly itself;

d. Provide, on a permanent basis, adequate secretariat services for the General Assembly and the other organs, and carry out their directives and assignments. To the extent of its ability, provide services for the other meetings of the Organization;

e. Serve as custodian of the documents and archives of the inter-American Conferences, the General Assembly, the Meetings of Consultation of Ministers of Foreign Affairs, the Councils, and the Specialized Conferences;

f. Serve as depository of inter-American treaties and agreements, as well as of the instruments of ratification thereof;

g. Submit to the General Assembly at each regular session an annual report on the activities of the Organization and its financial condition; and

h. Establish relations of cooperation, in accordance with decisions reached by the General Assembly or the Councils, with the Specialized Organizations as well as other national and international organizations.

Article 113

The Secretary General shall:

a. Establish such offices of the General Secretariat as are necessary to accomplish its purposes: and

b. Determine the number of officers and employees of the General Secretariat. appoint them, regulate their powers and duties, and fix their remuneration.

The Secretary General shall exercise this authority in accordance with such general standards and budgetary provisions as may be established by the General Assembly.

Chapter XXII. Transitory Provisions

Article 145

Until the inter-American convention on human rights, referred to in Chapter XV, enters into force, the present Inter-American Commission on Human Rights shall keep vigilance over the observance of human rights.

Appendix II

Adopted by the Ninth International Conference of American States, Bogotá, Colombia, 1948

WHEREAS:

The American peoples have acknowledged the dignity of the individual, and their national constitutions recognize that juridical and political institutions, which regulate life in human society, have as their principal aim the protection of the essential rights of man and the creation of circumstances that will permit him to achieve spiritual and material progress and attain happiness;

The American States have on repeated occasions recognized that the essential rights of man are not derived from the fact that he is a national of a certain state, but are based upon attributes of his human personality;

The international protection of the rights of man should be the principal guide of an evolving American law;

The affirmation of essential human rights by the American States together with the guarantees given by the internal regimes of the states establish the initial system of protection considered by the American States as being suited to the present social and juridical conditions, not without a recognition on their part that they should increasingly strengthen that system in the international field as conditions become more favorable,

The Ninth International Conference of American States

AGREES

To adopt the following

AMERICAN DECLARATION OF THE RIGHTS AND DUTIES OF MAN

Preamble

All men are born free and equal, in dignity and in rights, and, being endowed by nature with reason and conscience, they should conduct themselves as brothers one to another.

The fulfillment of duty by each individual is a prerequisite to the rights of all. Rights and duties are interrelated in every social and political activity of man. While rights exalt individual liberty, duties express the dignity of that liberty.

Duties of a juridical nature presuppose others of a moral nature which support them in principle and constitute their basis.

Inasmuch as spiritual development is the supreme end of human existence and the highest expression thereof, it is the duty of man to serve that end with all his strength and resources.

Since culture is the highest social and historical expression of that spiritual development, it is the duty of man to preserve, practice and foster culture by every means within his power.

And, since moral conduct constitutes the noblest flowering of culture, it is the duty of every man always to hold it in high respect.

CHAPTER ONE

Rights

Article I. Every human being has the right to life liberty and, the security of his person.

Right to life, liberty and personal security.

Article II. All persons are equal before the law and have the rights and duties established in this Declaration, without distinction as to race, sex, language, creed or any other factor.

Right to equality before law.

Article III. Every person has the right freely to profess a religious faith, and to manifest and practice it both in public and in private .

Right to religious freedom and worship.

Article IV. Every person has the right to freedom of investigation, of opinion, and of the expression and dissemination of ideas, by any medium whatsoever.

Right to freedom of investigation, opinion, expression and dissemination.

Article V. Every person has the right to the protection of the law against abusive attacks upon his honor, his reputation, and his private and family life.

Right to protection of honor, personal reputation, and private and family life.

Article VI. Every person has the right to establish a family, the basic element of society, and to receive protection therefor.

Right to a family and to protection thereof.

Article VII. All women, during pregnancy and the nursing period, and all children have the right to special protection, care and aid.

Right to protection for mothers and children

Article VIII. Every person has the right to fix his residence within the territory of the state of which he is a national, to move about freely within such territory, and not to leave it except by his own will.

Right to residence and movement

Article IX. Every person has the right to the inviolability of his home

Right to inviolability of the home.

Article X. Every person has the right to the inviolability and transmission of his correspondence.

Right to the inviolability and transmission of correspondence.

Article XI. Every person has the right to the preservation of his health through sanitary and social measures relating to food, clothing, housing and medical care, to the extent permitted by public and community resources.

Right to the preservation of health and to well-being.

Article XII. Every person has the right to an education, which should be based on the principles of liberty, morality and human solidarity.

Right to education.

Likewise every person has the right to an education that will prepare him to attain a decent life, to raise his standard of living, and to be a useful member of society.

The right to an education includes the right to equality of opportunity in every case, in accordance with natural talents, merit and the desire to utilize the resources that the state or the community is in a position to provide.

Every person has the right to receive, free, at least a primary education.

Article XIII. Every person has the right to take part in the cultural life of the community, to enjoy the arts, and to participate in the benefits that result from intellectual progress, especially scientific discoveries .

Right to the benefits of culture.

He likewise has the right to the protection of his moral and material interests as regards his inventions or any literary, scientific or artistic works of which he is the author.

Article XIV. Every person has the right to work, under proper conditions, and to follow his vocation freely, insofar as existing conditions of employment permit.

Right to work and to fair remuneration.

Every person who works has the right to receive such remuneration as will, in proportion to his capacity and skill, assure him a standard of living suitable for himself and for his family.

Article XV. Every person has the right to leisure time, to wholesome recreation, and to the opportunity for advantageous use of his free time to his spiritual, cultural and physical benefit.

Right to leisure time and to the use thereof.

Article XVI. Every person has the right to social security which will protect him from the consequences of unemployment, old age, and any disabilities arising from causes beyond his control that make it physically or mentally impossible for him to earn a living.

Right to social security.

Article XVII. Every person has the right to be recognized everywhere as a person having rights and obligations, and to enjoy the basic civil rights.

Right to recognition of juridical personality and civil rights.

Article XVIII. Every person may resort to the courts to ensure respect for his legal rights. There should likewise be available to him a simple, brief procedure whereby the courts will protect him from acts of authority that, to his prejudice, violate any fundamental constitutional rights.

Right to a fair trial.

Article XIX. Every person has the right to the nationality to which he is entitled by law and to change it, if he so wishes, for the nationality of any other country that is willing to grant it to him.

Right to nationality.

Article XX. Every person having legal capacity is entitled to participate in the government of his country, directly or through his representatives, and to take part in popular elections, which shall be by secret ballot, and shall be honest, periodic and free.

Right to vote and to participate in government.

Article XXI. Every person has the right to assemble peaceably with others in a formal public meeting or an informal gathering, in connection with matters of common interest of any nature.

Right of assembly.

Article XXII. Every person has the right to associate with others to

Right of association

promote, exercise and protect his legitimate interests of a political, economic, religious, social, cultural, professional, labor union or other nature.

Article XXIII. Every person has a right to own such private property as meets the essential needs of decent living and helps to maintain the dignity of the individual and of the home.

Right to property.

Article XXIV. Every person has the right to submit respectful petitions to any competent authority, for reasons of either general or private interest, and the right to obtain a prompt decision thereon.

Right of petition.

Article XXV. No person may be deprived of his liberty except in the cases and according to the procedures established by pre-existing law.

Right of protection from arbitrary arrest.

No person may be deprived of liberty for nonfulfillment of obligations of a purely civil character.

Every individual who has been deprived of his liberty has the right to have the legality of his detention ascertained without delay by a court, and the right to be tried without undue delay or, otherwise, to be released. He also has the right to humane treatment during the time he is in custody.

Article XXVI. Every accused person is presumed to be innocent until proved guilty.

Right to due process of law.

Every person accused of an offense has the right to be given an impartial and public hearing, and to be tried by courts previously established in accordance with pre-existing laws, and not to receive cruel, infamous or unusual punishment.

Article XXVII. Every person has the right, in case of pursuit not resulting from ordinary crimes, to seek and receive asylum in foreign territory, in accordance with the laws of each country and with international agreements.

Right of asylum.

Article XXVIII. The rights of man are limited by the rights of others, by the security of all, and by the just demands of the general welfare and the advancement of democracy.

Scope of the rights of man.

CHAPTER TWO

Duties

Article XXIX. It is the duty of the individual so to conduct himself in relation to others that each and every one may fully form and develop his personality.

Duties to society.

Article XXX. It is the duty of every person to aid, support, educate and protect his minor children, and it is the duty of children to honor their parents always and to aid, support and protect them when they need it.

Duties toward children and parents.

Article XXXI. It is the duty of every person to acquire at least an elementary education.

Duty to receive instruction.

Article XXXII. It is the duty of every person to vote in the popular elections of the country of which he is a national, when he is legally capable of doing so.

Duty to vote.

Article XXXIII. It is the duty of every person to obey the law and other legitimate commands of the authorities of his country and those of the country in which he may be.

Duty to obey the law.

Article XXXIV. It is the duty of every able-bodied person to render whatever civil and military service his country may require for its defense and preservation, and, in case of public disaster, to render such services as may be in his power.

It is likewise his duty to hold any public office to which he may be elected by popular vote in the state of which he is a national.

Duty to serve the community and the nation.

Article XXXV. It is the duty of every person to cooperate with the state and

Duties with respect to social security and welfare.

the community with respect to social security and welfare, in accordance with his ability and with existing circumstances.

Article XXXVI. It is the duty of every person to pay the taxes established by law for the support of public services.

Duty to pay taxes.

Article XXXVII. It is the duty of every person to work, as far as his capacity and possibilities permit, in order to obtain the means of livelihood or to benefit his community.

Duty to work.

Article XXXVIII. It is the duty of every person to refrain from taking part in political activities that, according to law, are reserved exclusively to the citizens of the state in which he is an alien.

Duty to refrain from political activities in a foreign country.

Appendix III

AMERICAN CONVENTION ON HUMAN RIGHTS AND PROTOCOLS

Signed at the Inter-American Specialized Conference
on Human Rights, San José, Costa Rica, 22 November 1969

Preamble

The American states signatory to the present Convention,

Reaffirming their intention to consolidate in this hemisphere, within the framework of democratic institutions, a system of personal liberty and social justice based on respect for the essential rights of man;

Recognizing that the essential rights of man are not derived from one's being a national of a certain state, but are based upon attributes of the human personality, and that they therefore justify international protection in the form of a convention reinforcing or complementing the protection provided by the domestic law of the American states;

Considering that these principles have been set forth in the Charter of the Organization of American States, in the American Declaration of the Rights and Duties of Man, and in the Universal Declaration of Human Rights, and that they have been reaffirmed and refined in other international instruments, worldwide as well as regional in scope;

Reiterating that, in accordance with the Universal Declaration of Human Rights, the ideal of free men enjoying freedom from fear and want can be achieved only if conditions are created whereby everyone may enjoy his economic, social, and cultural rights, as well as his civil and political rights; and

Considering that the Third Special Inter-American Conference (Buenos Aires, 1967) approved the incorporation into the Charter of the Organization itself of broader standards with respect to economic, social, and educational rights and resolved that an inter-American convention on human rights should determine the structure, competence, and procedure of the organs responsible for these matters,

Have agreed upon the following:

PART I—STATE OBLIGATIONS AND RIGHTS PROTECTED

Chapter I—General Obligations

Article 1. Obligation to Respect Rights

1. The States Parties to this Convention undertake to respect the rights and freedoms recognized herein and to ensure to all persons subject to their jurisdiction the free and full exercise of those rights and freedoms, without any

discrimination for reasons of race, color, sex, language, religion, political or other opinion, national or social origin, economic status, birth, or any other social condition.

2. For the purposes of this Convention, 'person' means every human being.

Article 2. Domestic Legal Effects

Where the exercise of any of the rights or freedoms referred to in Article 1 is not already ensured by legislative or other provisions, the States Parties undertake to adopt, in accordance with their constitutional processes and the provisions of this Convention, such legislative or other measures as may be necessary to give effect to those rights or freedoms.

Chapter II—Civil and Political Rights

Article 3. Right to Juridical Personality

Every person has the right to recognition as a person before the law.

Article 4. Right to Life

1. Every person has the right to have his life respected. This right shall be protected by law and, in general, from the moment of conception. No one shall be arbitrarily deprived of his life.

2. In countries that have not abolished the death penalty, it may be imposed only for the most serious crimes and pursuant to a final judgment rendered by a competent court and in accordance with a law establishing such punishment, enacted prior to the commission of the crime. The application of such punishment shall not be extended to crimes to which it does not presently apply.

3. The death penalty shall not be reestablished in states that have abolished it.

4. In no case shall capital punishment be inflicted for political offenses or related common crimes.

5. Capital punishment shall not be imposed upon persons who, at the time the crime was committed, were under 18 years of age or over 70 years of age; nor shall it be applied to pregnant women.

6. Every person condemned to death shall have the right to apply for amnesty, pardon, or commutation of sentence, which may be granted in all cases. Capital punishment shall not be imposed while such a petition is pending decision by the competent authority.

Article 5. Right to Humane Treatment

1. Every person has the right to have his physical, mental, and moral integrity respected .

2. No one shall be subjected to torture or to cruel, inhuman, or degrading punishment or treatment. All persons deprived of their liberty shall be treated with respect for the inherent dignity of the human person.

3. Punishment shall not be extended to any person other than the criminal.

4. Accused persons shall, save in exceptional circumstances, be segregated from convicted persons, and shall be subject to separate treatment appropriate to their status as unconvicted persons.

5. Minors while subject to criminal proceedings shall be separated from adults and brought before specialized tribunals, as speedily as possible, so that they may be treated in accordance with their status as minors.

6. Punishments consisting of deprivation of liberty shall have as an essential aim the reform and social readaptation of the prisoners.

Article 6. Freedom from Slavery

1. No one shall be subject to slavery or to involuntary servitude, which are prohibited in all their forms, as are the slave trade and traffic in women.

2. No one shall be required to perform forced or compulsory labor. This provision shall not be interpreted to mean that, in those countries in which the penalty established for certain crimes is deprivation of liberty at forced labor, the carrying out of such a sentence imposed by a competent court is prohibited. Forced labor shall not adversely affect the dignity or the physical or intellectual capacity of the prisoner.

3. For the purposes of this article, the following do not constitute forced or compulsory labor:

   a. work or service normally required of a person imprisoned in execution of a sentence or formal decision passed by the competent judicial authority. Such work or service shall be carried out under the supervision and control of public authorities, and any persons performing such work or service shall not be placed at the disposal of any private party, company, or juridical person;

   b. military service and, in countries in which conscientious objectors are recognized, national service that the law may provide for in lieu of military service;

   c. service exacted in time of danger or calamity that threatens the existence or the well-being of the community; or

   d. work or service that forms part of normal civic obligations.

Article 7. Right to Personal Liberty

1. Every person has the right to personal liberty and security.

2. No one shall be deprived of his physical liberty except for the reasons and under the conditions established beforehand by the constitution of the State Party concerned or by a law established pursuant thereto.

3. No one shall be subject to arbitrary arrest or imprisonment.

4. Anyone who is detained shall be informed of the reasons for his detention and shall be promptly notified of the charge or charges against him.

5. Any person detained shall be brought promptly before a judge or other officer authorized by law to exercise judicial power and shall be entitled to trial within a reasonable time or to be released without prejudice to the continuation of the proceedings. His release may be subject to guarantees to assure his appearance for trial .

6. Anyone who is deprived of his liberty shall be entitled to recourse to a competent court, in order that the court may decide without delay on the lawfulness of his arrest or detention and order his release if the arrest or detention is unlawful. In States Parties whose laws provide that anyone who believes himself

to be threatened with deprivation of his liberty is entitled to recourse to a competent court in order that it may decide on the lawfulness of such threat, this remedy may not be restricted or abolished. The interested party or another person in his behalf is entitled to seek these remedies.

7. No one shall be detained for debt. This principle shall not limit the orders of a competent judicial authority issued for nonfulfillment of duties of support.

Article 8. Right to a Fair Trial

1. Every person has the right to a hearing, with due guarantees and within a reasonable time, by a competent, independent, and impartial tribunal, previously established by law, in the substantiation of any accusation of a criminal nature made against him or for the determination of his rights and obligations of a civil, labor, fiscal, or any other nature.

2. Every person accused of a criminal offense has the right to be presumed innocent so long as his guilt has not been proven according to law. During the proceedings, every person is entitled, with full equality, to the following minimum guarantees:

   a. the right of the accused to be assisted without charge by a translator or interpreter, if he does not understand or does not speak the language of the tribunal or court;
   b. prior notification in detail to the accused of the charges against him;
   c. adequate time and means for the preparation of his defense;
   d. the right of the accused to defend himself personally or to be assisted by legal counsel of his own choosing, and to communicate freely and privately with his counsel;
   e. the inalienable right to be assisted by counsel provided by the state, paid or not as the domestic law provides, if the accused does not defend himself personally or engage his own counsel within the time period established by law;
   f. the right of the defense to examine witnesses present in the court and to obtain the appearance, as witnesses, of experts or other persons who may throw light on the facts;
   g. the right not to be compelled to be a witness against himself or to plead guilty; and
   h. the right to appeal the judgment to a higher court.

3. A confession of guilt by the accused shall be valid only if it is made without coercion of any kind.

4. An accused person acquitted by a nonappealable judgment shall not be subjected to a new trial for the same cause.

5. Criminal proceedings shall be public, except insofar as may be necessary to protect the interests of justice.

Article 9. Freedom from Ex Post Facto Laws

No one shall be convicted of any act or omission that did not constitute a criminal offense, under the applicable law, at the time it was committed. A heavier penalty shall not be imposed than the one that was applicable at the time the criminal offense was committed. If subsequent to the commission of the offense the law provides for the imposition of a lighter punishment, the guilty person shall benefit therefrom.

Article 10. Right to Compensation

Every person has the right to be compensated in accordance with the law in the event he has been sentenced by a final judgment through a miscarriage of justice.

Article 11. Right to Privacy

1. Everyone has the right to have his honor respected and his dignity recognized.

2. No one may be the object of arbitrary or abusive interference with his private life, his family, his home, or his correspondence, or of unlawful attacks on his honor or reputation.

3. Everyone has the right to the protection of the law against such interference or attacks.

Article 12. Freedom of Conscience and Religion

1. Everyone has the right to freedom of conscience and of religion. This right includes freedom to maintain or to change one's religion or beliefs, and freedom to profess or disseminate one's religion or beliefs, either individually or together with others, in public or in private.

2. No one shall be subject to restrictions that might impair his freedom to maintain or to change his religion or beliefs.

3. Freedom to manifest one's religion and beliefs may be subject only to the limitations prescribed by law that are necessary to protect public safety, order, health, or morals, or the rights or freedoms of others.

4. Parents or guardians, as the case may be, have the right to provide for the religious and moral education of their children or wards that is in accord with their own convictions.

Article 13. Freedom of Thought and Expression

1. Everyone has the right to freedom of thought and expression. This right includes freedom to seek, receive, and impart information and ideas of all kinds, regardless of frontiers, either orally, in writing, in print, in the form of art, or through any other medium of one's choice.

2. The exercise of the right provided for in the foregoing paragraph shall not be subject to prior censorship but shall be subject to subsequent imposition of liability, which shall be expressly established by law to the extent necessary to ensure:

a. respect for the rights or reputations of others; or

b. the protection of national security, public order, or public health or morals.

3. The right of expression may not be restricted by indirect methods or means, such as the abuse of government or private controls over newsprint, radio broadcasting frequencies, or equipment used in the dissemination of information, or by any other means tending to impede the communication and circulation of ideas and opinions.

4. Notwithstanding the provisions of paragraph 2 above, public entertainments may be subject by law to prior censorship for the sole purpose of regulating access to them for the moral protection of childhood and adolescence.

5. Any propaganda for war and any advocacy of national, racial, or religious hatred that constitute incitements to lawless violence or to any other similar action against any person or group of persons on any grounds including those of race, color, religion, language, or national origin shall be considered as offenses punishable by law.

Article 14. Right of Reply

1. Anyone injured by inaccurate or offensive statements or ideas disseminated to the public in general by a legally regulated medium of communication has the right to reply or to make a correction using the same communications outlet, under such conditions as the law may establish.

2. The correction or reply shall not in any case remit other legal liabilities that may have been incurred.

3. For the effective protection of honor and reputation, every publisher, and every newspaper, motion picture, radio, and television company shall have a person responsible who is not protected by immunities or special privileges.

Article 15. Right of Assembly

The right of peaceful assembly, without arms, is recognized. No restrictions may be placed on the exercise of this right other than those imposed in conformity with the law and necessary in a democratic society in the interest of national security, public safety or public order, or to protect public health or morals or the rights or freedom of others.

Article 16. Freedom of Association

1. Everyone has the right to associate freely for ideological, religious, political, economic, labor, social, cultural, sports, or other purposes.

2. The exercise of this right shall be subject only to such restrictions established by law as may be necessary in a democratic society, in the interest of national security, public safety or public order, or to protect public health or morals or the rights and freedoms of others.

3. The provisions of this article do not bar the imposition of legal restrictions, including even deprivation of the exercise of the right of association, on members of the armed forces and the police.

Article 17. Rights of the Family

1. The family is the natural and fundamental group unit of society and is entitled to protection by society and the state.

2. The right of men and women of marriageable age to marry and to raise a family shall be recognized, if they meet the conditions required by domestic laws, insofar as such conditions do not affect the principle of nondiscrimination established in this Convention.

3. No marriage shall be entered into without the free and full consent of the intending spouses.

4. The States Parties shall take appropriate steps to ensure the equality of rights and the adequate balancing of responsibilities of the spouses as to marriage, during marriage, and in the event of its dissolution. In case of dissolution, provision shall be made for the necessary protection of any children solely on the basis of their own best interests.

5. The law shall recognize equal rights for children born out of wedlock and those born in wedlock.

Article 18. Right to a Name

Every person has the right to a given name and to the surnames of his parents or that of one of them. The law shall regulate the manner in which this right shall be ensured for all, by the use of assumed names if necessary.

Article 19. Rights of the Child

Every minor child has the right to the measures of protection required by his condition as a minor on the part of his family, society, and the state.

Article 20. Right to Nationality

1. Every person has the right to a nationality.

2. Every person has the right to the nationality of the state in whose territory he was born if he does not have the right to any other nationality.

3. No one shall be arbitrarily deprived of his nationality or of the right to change it.

Article 21. Right to Property

1. Everyone has the right to the use and enjoyment of his property. The law may subordinate such use and enjoyment to the interest of society.

2. No one shall be deprived of his property except upon payment of just compensation, for reasons of public utility or social interest, and in the cases and according to the forms established by law.

3. Usury and any other form of exploitation of man by man shall be prohibited by law.

Article 22. Freedom of Movement and Residence

1. Every person lawfully in the territory of a State Party has the right to move about in it, and to reside in it subject to the provisions of the law.

2. Every person has the right lo leave any country freely, including his own.

3. The exercise of the foregoing rights may be restricted only pursuant to a law to the extent necessary in a democratic society to prevent crime or to protect national security, public safety, public order, public morals, public health, or the rights or freedoms of others.

4. The exercise of the rights recognized in paragraph 1 may also be restricted by law in designated zones for reasons of public interest.

5. No one can be expelled from the territory of the state of which he is a national or be deprived of the right to enter it.

6. An alien lawfully in the territory of a State Party to this Convention may be expelled from it only pursuant to a decision reached in accordance with law.

7. Every person has the right to seek and be granted asylum in a foreign territory, in accordance with the legislation of the state and international conventions, in the event he is being pursued for political offenses or related common crimes.

8. In no case may an alien be deported or returned to a country, regardless of whether or not it is his country of origin, if in that country his right to life or personal freedom is in danger of being violated because of his race, nationality, religion, social status, or political opinions.

9. The collective expulsion of aliens is prohibited.

Article 23. Right to Participate in Government

1. Every citizen shall enjoy the following rights and opportunities:
a. to take part in the conduct of public affairs, directly or through freely chosen representatives;
b. to vote and to be elected in genuine periodic elections, which shall be by universal and equal suffrage and by secret ballot that guarantees the free expression of the will of the voters; and
c. to have access, under general conditions of equality, to the public service of his country.

2. The law may regulate the exercise of the rights and opportunities referred to in the preceding paragraph only on the basis of age, nationality, residence, language, education, civil and mental capacity, or sentencing by a competent court in criminal proceedings.

Article 24. Right to Equal Protection

All persons are equal before the law. Consequently, they are entitled, without discrimination, to equal protection of the law.

Article 25. Right to Judicial Protection

1. Everyone has the right to simple and prompt recourse, or any other effective recourse, to a competent court or tribunal for protection against acts that violate his fundamental rights recognized by the constitution or laws of the state concerned or by this Convention, even though such violation may have been committed by persons acting in the course of their official duties.

2. The States Parties undertake:
a. to ensure that any person claiming such remedy shall have his rights determined by the competent authority provided for by the legal system of the state;
b. to develop the possibilities of judicial remedy; and
c. to ensure that the competent authorities shall enforce such remedies when granted.

Chapter III—Economic, Social, and Cultural Rights

Article 26. Progressive Development

The States Parties undertake to adopt measures, both internally and through international cooperation, especially those of an economic and technical nature, with a view to achieving progressively, by legislation or other appropriate means, the full realization of the rights implicit in the economic, social, educational, scientific, and cultural standards set forth in the Charter of the Organization of American States as amended by the Protocol of Buenos Aires.

Chapter IV—Suspension of Guarantees, Interpretation, and Application

Article 27. Suspension of Guarantees

1. In time of war, public danger, or other emergency that threatens the independence or security of a State Party, it may take measures derogating from its obligations under the present Convention to the extent and for the period of time strictly required by the exigencies of the situation, provided that such measures are not inconsistent with its other obligations under international law and do not involve discrimination on the ground of race, color, sex, language, religion, or social origin.

2. The foregoing provision does not authorize any suspension of the following articles: Article 3 (Right to Juridical Personality), Article 4 (Right to Life), Article 5 (Right to Humane Treatment), Article 6 (Freedom from Slavery), Article 9 (Freedom from *Ex Post Facto* Laws), Article 12 (Freedom of Conscience and Religion), Article 17 (Rights of the Family), Article 18 (Right to a Name), Article 19 (Rights of the Child), Article 20 (Right to Nationality), and Article 23 (Right to Participate in Government), or of the judicial guarantees essential for the protection of such rights.

3. Any State Party availing itself of the right of suspension shall immediately inform the other States Parties, through the Secretary General of the Organization of American States, of the provisions the application of which it has suspended, the reasons that gave rise to the suspension, and the date set for the termination of such suspension.

Article 28. Federal Clause

1. Where a State Party is constituted as a federal state, the national government of such State Party shall implement all the provisions of the Convention over whose subject matter it exercises legislative and judicial jurisdiction.

2. With respect to the provisions over whose subject matter the constituent units of the federal state have jurisdiction, the national government shall immediately take suitable measures, in accordance with its constitution and its laws, to the end that the competent authorities of the constituent units may adopt appropriate provisions for the fulfillment of this Convention.

3. Whenever two or more States Parties agree to form a federation or other type of association, they shall take care that the resulting federal or other compact contains the provisions necessary for continuing and rendering effective the standards of this Convention in the new state that is organized.

Article 29. Restrictions Regarding Interpretation

No provision of this Convention shall be interpreted as:

a. permitting any State Party, group, or person to suppress the enjoyment or exercise of the rights and freedoms recognized in this Convention or to restrict them to a greater extent than is provided for herein;

b. restricting the enjoyment or exercise of any right or freedom recognized by virtue of the laws of any State Party or by virtue of another convention to which one of the said states is a party;

c. precluding other rights or guarantees that are inherent in the human personality or derived from representative democracy as a form of government; or

d. excluding or limiting the effect that the American Declaration of the Rights and Duties of Man and other international acts of the same nature may have.

Article 30. Scope of Restrictions

The restrictions that, pursuant to this Convention, may be placed on the enjoyment or exercise of the rights or freedoms recognized herein may not be applied except in accordance with laws enacted for reasons of general interest and in accordance with the purpose for which such restrictions have been established.

Article 31. Recognition of Other Rights

Other rights and freedoms recognized in accordance with the procedures established in Articles 76 and 77 may be included in the system of protection of this Convention.

Chapter V—Personal Responsibilities

Article 32. Relationship between Duties and Rights

1. Every person has responsibilities to his family, his community, and mankind.

2 The rights of each person are limited by the rights of others, by the security of all, and by the just demands of the general welfare, in a democratic society.

PART II—MEANS OF PROTECTION

Chapter VI—Competent Organs

Article 33

The following organs shall have competence with respect to matters relating to the fulfillment of the commitments made by the States Parties to this Convention:

a. the Inter-American Commission on Human Rights, referred to as 'The Commission;' and

b. the Inter-American Court of Human Rights, referred to as 'The Court.'

Chapter VII—Inter-American Commission on Human Rights

Section 1. Organization

Article 34

The Inter-American Commission on Human Rights shall be composed of seven members, who shall be persons of high moral character and recognized competence in the field of human rights.

Article 35

The Commission shall represent all the member countries of the Organization of American States.

Article 36

1. The members of the Commission shall be elected in a personal capacity by the General Assembly of the Organization from a list of candidates proposed by the governments of the member states.

2. Each of those governments may propose up to three candidates, who may be nationals of the states proposing them or of any other member state of the Organization of American States. When a slate of three is proposed, at least one of the candidates shall be a national of a state other than the one proposing the slate.

Article 37

1. The members of the Commission shall be elected for a term of four years and may be reelected only once, but the terms of three of the members chosen in the first election shall expire at the end of two years. Immediately following that election the General Assembly shall determine the names of those three members by lot.

2. No two nationals of the same state may be members of the Commission.

Article 38

Vacancies that may occur on the Commission for reasons other than the normal expiration of a term shall be filled by the Permanent Council of the Organization in accordance with the provisions of the Statute of the Commission.

Article 39

The Commission shall prepare its Statute, which it shall submit to the General Assembly for approval. It shall establish its own Regulations.

Article 40

Secretariat services for the Commission shall be furnished by the appropriate specialized unit of the General Secretariat of the Organization. This unit shall be provided with the resources required to accomplish the tasks assigned to it by the Commission .

Section 2. Functions

Article 41

The main function of the Commission shall be to promote respect for and defense of human rights. In the exercise of its mandate, it shall have the following functions and powers:

    a. to develop an awareness of human rights among the peoples of America;

    b. to make recommendations to the governments of the member states, when it considers such action advisable, for the adoption of progressive measures in favor of human rights within the framework of their domestic law and Constitutional provisions as well as appropriate measures to further the observance of those rights;

c. to prepare such studies or reports as it considers advisable in the performance of its duties;

d. to request the governments of the member states to supply it with information on the measures adopted by them in matters of human rights;

e. to respond, through the General Secretariat of the Organization of American States, to inquiries made by the member states on matters related to human rights and, within the limits of its possibilities, to provide those states with the advisory services they request;

f. to take action on petitions and other communications pursuant to its authority under the provisions of Articles 44 through 51 of this Convention; and

g. to submit an annual report to the General Assembly of the Organization of American States.

Article 42

The States Parties shall transmit to the Commission a copy of each of the reports and studies that they submit annually to the Executive Committees of the Inter-American Economic and Social Council and the Inter-American Council for Education, Science, and Culture, in their respective fields, so that the Commission may watch over the promotion of the rights implicit in the economic, social, educational, scientific, and cultural standards set forth in the Charter of the Organization of American States as amended by the Protocol of Buenos Aires.

Article 43

The States Parties undertake to provide the Commission with such information as it may request of them as to the manner in which their domestic law ensures the effective application of any provisions of this Convention.

Section 3. Competence

Article 44

Any person or group of persons, or any nongovernmental entity legally recognized in one or more member states of the Organization, may lodge petitions with the Commission containing denunciations or complaints of violation of this Convention by a State Party.

Article 45

1. Any State Party may, when it deposits its instrument of ratification of or adherence to this Convention, or at any later time, declare that it recognizes the competence of the Commission to receive and examine communications in which a State Party alleges that another State Party has committed a violation of a human right set forth in this Convention.

2. Communications presented by virtue of this article may be admitted and examined only if they are presented by a State Party that has made a declaration

recognizing the aforementioned competence of the Commission. The Commission shall not admit any communication against a State Party that has not made such a declaration.

3. A declaration concerning recognition of competence may be made to be valid for an indefinite time, for a specified period, or for a specific case.

4. Declarations shall be deposited with the General Secretariat of the Organization of American States, which shall transmit copies thereof to the member states of that Organization.

Article 46

1. Admission by the Commission of a petition or communication lodged in accordance with Articles 44 or 45 shall be subject to the following requirements:
   a. that the remedies under domestic law have been pursued and exhausted in accordance with generally recognized principles of international law;
   b. that the petition or communication is lodged within a period of six months from the date on which the party alleging violation of his rights was notified of the final judgment;
   c. that the subject of the petition or communication is not pending in another international proceeding for settlement; and
   d. that, in the case of Article 44, the petition contains the name, nationality, profession, domicile, and signature of the person or persons or of the legal representative of the entity lodging the petition.

2. The provisions of paragraphs 1.a and 1.b of this article shall not be applicable when:
   a. the domestic legislation of the state concerned does not afford due process of law for the protection of the right or rights that have allegedly been violated;
   b. the party alleging violation of his rights has been denied access to the remedies under domestic law or has been prevented from exhausting them; or
   c. there has been unwarranted delay in rendering a final judgment under the aforementioned remedies.

Article 47

The Commission shall consider inadmissible any petition or communication submitted under Articles 44 or 45 if:
   a. any of the requirements indicated in Article 46 has not been met;
   b. the petition or communication does not state facts that tend to establish a violation of the rights guaranteed by this Convention;
   c. the statements of the petitioner or of the state indicate that the petition or communication is manifestly groundless or obviously out of order; or
   d. the petition or communication is substantially the same as one previously studied by the Commission or by another international organization.

Section 4. Procedure

Article 48

1. When the Commission receives a petition or communication alleging violation of any of the rights protected by this Convention, it shall proceed as follows:
   a. If it considers the petition or communication admissible, it shall request information from the government of the state indicated as being responsible for the alleged violations and shall furnish that government a transcript of the pertinent portions of the petition or communication. This information shall be submitted within a reasonable period to be determined by the Commission in accordance with the circumstances of each case.
   b. After the information has been received, or after the period established has elapsed and the information has not been received, the Commission shall ascertain whether the grounds for the petition or communication still exist. If they do not, the Commission shall order the record to be closed.
   c. The Commission may also declare the petition or communication inadmissible or out of order on the basis of information or evidence subsequently received.
   d. If the record has not been closed, the Commission shall, with the knowledge of the parties, examine the matter set forth in the petition or communication in order to verify the facts. If necessary and advisable, the Commission shall carry out an investigation, for the effective conduct of which it shall request, and the states concerned shall furnish to it, all necessary facilities.
   e. The Commission may request the states concerned to furnish any pertinent information and, if so requested, shall hear oral statements or receive written statements from the parties concerned.
   f. The Commission shall place itself at the disposal of the parties concerned with a view to reaching a friendly settlement of the matter on the basis of respect for the human rights recognized in this Convention.

2. However, in serious and urgent cases, only the presentation of a petition or communication that fulfills all the formal requirements of admissibility shall be necessary in order for the Commission to conduct an investigation with the prior consent of the state in whose territory a violation has allegedly been committed.

Article 49

If a friendly settlement has been reached in accordance with paragraph 1.f of Article 48, the Commission shall draw up a report, which shall be transmitted to the petitioner and to the States Parties to this Convention, and shall then be communicated to the Secretary General of the Organization of American States for publication. This report shall contain a brief statement of the facts and of the solution reached. If any party in the case so requests, the fullest possible information shall be provided to it.

Article 50

1. If a settlement is not reached, the Commission shall, within the time limit established by its Statute, draw up a report setting forth the facts and stating its

conclusions. If the report, in whole or in part, does not represent the unanimous agreement of the members of the Commission, any member may attach to it a separate opinion. The written and oral statements made by the parties in accordance with paragraph 1.e of Article 48 shall also be attached to the report.

2. The report shall be transmitted to the states concerned, which shall not be at liberty to publish it.

3. In transmitting the report, the Commission may make such proposals and recommendations as it sees fit.

Article 51

1. If, within a period of three months from the date of the transmittal of the report of the Commission to the states concerned, the matter has not either been settled or submitted by the Commission or by the state concerned to the Court and its jurisdiction accepted, the Commission may, by the vote of an absolute majority of its members, set forth its opinion and conclusions concerning the question submitted for its consideration.

2. Where appropriate, the Commission shall make pertinent recommendations and shall prescribe a period within which the state is to take the measures that are incumbent upon it to remedy the situation examined.

3. When the prescribed period has expired, the Commission shall decide by the vote of an absolute majority of its members whether the state has taken adequate measures and whether to publish its report.

Chapter VIII—Inter-American Court of Human Rights

Section 1. Organization

Article 52

1. The Court shall consist of seven judges, nationals of the member states of the Organization, elected in an individual capacity from among jurists of the highest moral authority and of recognized competence in the field of human rights, who possess the qualifications required for the exercise of the highest judicial functions in conformity with the law of the state of which they are nationals or of the state that proposes them as candidates.

2. No two judges may be nationals of the same state.

Article 53

1. The judges of the Court shall be elected by secret ballot by an absolute majority vote of the States Parties to the Convention, in the General Assembly of the Organization, from a panel of candidates proposed by those states.

2. Each of the States Parties may propose up to three candidates, nationals of the state that proposes them or of any other member state of the Organization of American States. When a slate of three is proposed, at least one of the candidates shall be a national of a state other than the one proposing the slate.

Article 54

1. The judges of the Court shall be elected for a term of six years and may be reelected only once. The term of three of the judges chosen in the first election shall expire at the end of three years. Immediately after the election, the names of the three judges shall be determined by lot in the General Assembly.

2. A judge elected to replace a judge whose term has not expired shall complete the term of the latter.

3. The judges shall continue in office until the expiration of their term. However, they shall continue to serve with regard to cases that they have begun to hear and that are still pending, for which purposes they shall not be replaced by the newly elected judges.

Article 55

1. If a judge is a national of any of the States Parties to a case submitted to the Court, he shall retain his right to hear that case.

2. If one of the judges called upon to hear a case should be a national of one of the States Parties to the case, any other State Party in the case may appoint a person of its choice to serve on the Court as an *ad hoc* judge.

3. If among the judges called upon to hear a case none is a national of any of the States Parties to the case, each of the latter may appoint an *ad hoc* judge.

4. An *ad hoc* judge shall possess the qualifications indicated in Article 52.

5. If several States Parties to the Convention should have the same interest in a case, they shall be considered as a single party for purposes of the above provisions. In case of doubt, the Court shall decide.

Article 56

Five judges shall constitute a quorum for the transaction of business by the Court.

Article 57

The Commission shall appear in all cases before the Court.

Article 58

1. The Court shall have its seat at the place determined by the States Parties to the Convention in the General Assembly of the Organization; however, it may convene in the territory of any member state of the Organization of American States when a majority of the Court considers it desirable, and with the prior consent of the state concerned. The seat of the Court may be changed by the States Parties to the Convention in the General Assembly by a two-thirds vote.

2. The Court shall appoint its own Secretary.

3. The Secretary shall have his office at the place where the Court has its seat and shall attend the meetings that the Court may hold away from its seat.

Article 59

The Court shall establish its Secretariat, which shall function under the direction of the Secretary of the Court, in accordance with the administrative standards of the General Secretariat of the Organization in all respects not incompatible with the independence of the Court. The staff of the Court's Secretariat shall be appointed by the Secretary General of the Organization, in consultation with the Secretary of the Court.

Article 60

The Court shall draw up its Statute which it shall submit to the General Assembly for approval. It shall adopt its own Rules of Procedure.

Section 2. Jurisdiction and Functions

Article 61

1. Only the States Parties and the Commission shall have the right to submit a case to the Court.

2. In order for the Court to hear a case, it is necessary that the procedures set forth in Articles 48 and 50 shall have been completed.

Article 62

1. A State Party may, upon depositing its instrument of ratification or adherence to this Convention, or at any subsequent time, declare that it recognizes as binding, *ipso facto*, and not requiring special agreement, the jurisdiction of the Court on all matters relating to the interpretation or application of this Convention.

2. Such declaration may be made unconditionally, on the condition of reciprocity, for a specified period, or for specific cases. It shall be presented to the Secretary General of the Organization, who shall transmit copies thereof to the other member states of the Organization and to the Secretary of the Court.

3. The jurisdiction of the Court shall comprise all cases concerning the interpretation and application of the provisions of this Convention that are submitted to it, provided that the States Parties to the case recognize or have recognized such jurisdiction, whether by special declaration pursuant to the preceding paragraphs, or by a special agreement.

Article 63

1. If the Court finds that there has been a violation of a right or freedom protected by this Convention, the Court shall rule that the injured party be ensured the enjoyment of his right or freedom that was violated. It shall also rule, if appropriate, that the consequences of the measure or situation that constituted the breach of such right or freedom be remedied and that fair compensation be paid to the injured party.

2. In cases of extreme gravity and urgency, and when necessary to avoid irreparable damage to persons, the Court shall adopt such provisional measures as it deems pertinent in matters it has under consideration. With respect to a case not yet submitted to the Court, it may act at the request of the Commission.

Article 64

1. The member states of the Organization may consult the Court regarding the interpretation of this Convention or of other treaties concerning the protection of human rights in the American states. Within their spheres of competence, the organs listed in Chapter X of the Charter of the Organization of American States, as amended by the Protocol of Buenos Aires, may in like manner consult the Court.

2. The Court, at the request of a member state of the Organization, may provide that state with opinions regarding the compatibility of any of its domestic laws with the aforesaid international instruments.

Article 65

To each regular session of the General Assembly of the Organization of American States the Court shall submit, for the Assembly's consideration, a report on its work during the previous year. It shall specify, in particular, the cases in which a state has not complied with its judgments, making any pertinent recommendations.

Section 3. Procedure

Article 66

1. Reasons shall be given for the judgment of the Court.

2. If the judgment does not represent in whole or in part the unanimous opinion of the judges, any judge shall be entitled to have his dissenting or separate opinion attached to the judgment.

Article 67

The judgment of the Court shall be final and not subject to appeal. In case of disagreement as to the meaning or scope of the judgment, the Court shall interpret it at the request of any of the parties, provided the request is made within ninety days from the date of notification of the judgment.

Article 68

1. The States Parties to the Convention undertake to comply with the judgment of the Court in any case to which they are parties.

2. That part of a judgment that stipulates compensatory damages may be executed in the country concerned in accordance with domestic procedure governing the execution of judgments against the state.

Article 69

The parties to the case shall be notified of the judgment of the Court and it shall be transmitted to the States Parties to the Convention.

Chapter IX—Common Provisions

Article 70

1. The judges of the Court and the members of the Commission shall enjoy, from the moment of their election and throughout their term of office, the immunities extended to diplomatic agents in accordance with international law. During the exercise of their official function they shall, in addition, enjoy the diplomatic privileges necessary for the performance of their duties.

2. At no time shall the judges of the Court or the members of the Commission be held liable for any decisions or opinions issued in the exercise of their functions.

Article 71

The position of judge of the Court or member of the Commission is incompatible with any other activity that might affect the independence or impartiality of such judge or member, as determined in the respective statutes.

Article 72

The judges of the Court and the members of the Commission shall receive emoluments and travel allowances in the form and under the conditions set forth in their statutes, with due regard for the importance and independence of their office. Such emoluments and travel allowances shall be determined in the budget of the Organization of American States, which shall also include the expenses of the Court and its Secretariat. To this end, the Court shall draw up its own budget and submit it for approval to the General Assembly through the General Secretariat. The latter may not introduce any changes in it.

Article 73

The General Assembly may, only at the request of the Commission or the Court, as the case may be, determine sanctions to be applied against members of the Commission or judges of the Court when there are justifiable grounds for such action as set forth in the respective statutes. A vote of a two-thirds majority of the member states of the Organization shall be required for a decision in the case of members of the Commission and, in the case of judges of the Court, a two-thirds majority vote of the States Parties to the Convention shall also be required.

PART III—GENERAL AND TRANSITORY PROVISIONS

Chapter X—Signature, Ratification, Reservations, Amendments, Protocols, and Denunciation

Article 74

1. This Convention shall be open for signature and ratification by or adherence of any member state of the Organization of American States.

2. Ratification of or adherence to this Convention shall be made by the deposit of an instrument of ratification or adherence with the General Secretariat of the Organization of American States. As soon as eleven states have deposited their instruments of ratification or adherence, the Convention shall enter into force. With respect to any state that ratifies or adheres thereafter, the Convention shall enter into force on the date of the deposit of its instrument of ratification or adherence.

3. The Secretary General shall inform all member states of the Organization of the entry into force of the Convention.

Article 75

This Convention shall be subject to reservations only in conformity with the provisions of the Vienna Convention on the Law of Treaties signed on May 23, 1969.

Article 76

1. Proposals to amend this Convention may be submitted to the General Assembly for the action it deems appropriate by any State Party directly, and by the Commission or the Court through the Secretary General.

2. Amendments shall enter into force for the States ratifying them on the date when two-thirds of the States Parties to this Convention have deposited their respective instruments of ratification. With respect to the other States Parties, the amendments shall enter into force on the dates on which they deposit their respective instruments of ratification.

Article 77

1. In accordance with Article 31, any State Party and the Commission may submit proposed protocols to this Convention for consideration by the States Parties at the General Assembly with a view to gradually including other rights and freedoms within its system of protection.

2. Each protocol shall determine the manner of its entry into force and shall be applied only among the States Parties to it.

Article 78

1. The States Parties may denounce this Convention at the expiration of a five-year period from the date of its entry into force and by means of notice given one year in advance. Notice of the denunciation shall be addressed to the Secretary General of the Organization, who shall inform the other States Parties.

2. Such a denunciation shall not have the effect of releasing the State Party concerned from the obligations contained in this Convention with respect to any act that may constitute a violation of those obligations and that has been taken by that state prior to the effective date of denunciation.

Chapter XI—Transitory Provisions

Section 1. Inter-American Commission on Human Rights

Article 79

Upon the entry into force of this Convention, the Secretary General shall, in writing, request each member state of the Organization to present, within ninety days, its candidates for membership on the Inter-American Commission on Human Rights. The Secretary General shall prepare a list in alphabetical order of the candidates presented, and transmit it to the member states of the Organization at least thirty days prior to the next session of the General Assembly.

Article 80

The members of the Commission shall be elected by secret ballot of the General Assembly from the list of candidates referred to in Article 79. The candidates who obtain the largest number of votes and an absolute majority of the votes of the representatives of the member states shall be declared elected. Should it become necessary to have several ballots in order to elect all the members of the Commission, the candidates who receive the smallest number of votes shall be eliminated successively, in the manner determined by the General Assembly.

Section 2. Inter-American Court of Human Rights

Article 81

Upon the entry into force of this Convention, the Secretary General shall, in writing, request each State Party to present, within ninety days, its candidates for membership on the Inter-American Court of Human Rights. The Secretary General shall prepare a list in alphabetical order of the candidates presented and transmit it to the States Parties at least thirty days prior to the next session of the General Assembly .

Article 82

The judges of the Court shall be elected from the list of candidates referred to in Article 81, by secret ballot of the States Parties to the Convention in the General Assembly. The candidates who obtain the largest number of votes and an absolute majority of the votes of the representatives of the States Parties shall be declared elected. Should it become necessary to have several ballots in order to elect all the judges of the Court, the candidates who receive the smallest number of votes shall be eliminated successively, in the manner determined by the States Parties.

ADDITIONAL PROTOCOL TO THE AMERICAN CONVENTION ON HUMAN RIGHTS IN THE
AREA OF ECONOMIC, SOCIAL AND CULTURAL RIGHTS
'PROTOCOL OF SAN SALVADOR'

Signed at San Salvador, El Salvador on November 17, 1988, at the eighteenth regular session of the General Assembly

Preamble

The States Parties to the American Convention on Human Rights 'Pact of San José, Costa Rica,'

Reaffirming their intention to consolidate in this hemisphere, within the framework of democratic institutions, a system of personal liberty and social justice based on respect for the essential rights of man;

Recognizing that the essential rights of man are not derived from one's being a national of a certain State, but are based upon attributes of the human person, for which reason they merit international protection in the form of a convention reinforcing or complementing the protection provided by the domestic law of the American States;

Considering the close relationship that exists between economic, social and cultural rights, and civil and political rights, in that the different categories of rights constitute an indivisible whole based on the recognition of the dignity of the human person, for which reason both require permanent protection and promotion if they are to be fully realized, and the violation of some rights in favor of the realization of others can never be justified;

Recognizing the benefits that stem from the promotion and development of cooperation among States and international relations;

Recalling that, in accordance with the Universal Declaration of Human Rights and the American Convention on Human Rights, the ideal of free human beings enjoying freedom from fear and want can only be achieved if conditions are created whereby everyone may enjoy his economic, social and cultural rights as well as his civil and political rights;

Bearing in mind that, although fundamental economic, social and cultural rights have been recognized in earlier international instruments of both world and regional scope, it is essential that those rights be reaffirmed, developed, perfected and protected in order to consolidate in America, on the basis of full respect for the rights of the individual, the democratic representative form of government as well as the right of its peoples to development, self-determination, and the free disposal of their wealth and natural resources; and

Considering that the American Convention on Human Rights provides that draft additional protocols to that Convention may be submitted for consideration to the States Parties, meeting together on the occasion of the General Assembly of the Organization of American States, for the purpose of gradually incorporating other rights and freedoms into the protective system thereof,

Have agreed upon the following Additional Protocol to the American Convention on Human Rights 'Protocol of San Salvador:'

Article 1
Obligation to Adopt Measures

The States Parties to this Additional Protocol to the American Convention on Human Rights undertake to adopt the necessary measures, both domestically and through international cooperation, especially economic and technical, to the extent allowed by their available resources, and taking into account their degree of development, for the purpose of achieving progressively and pursuant to their internal legislations, the full observance of the rights recognized in this Protocol.

Article 2
Obligation to Enact Domestic Legislation

If the exercise of the rights set forth in this Protocol is not already guaranteed by legislative or other provisions, the States Parties undertake to adopt, in accordance with their constitutional processes and the provisions of this Protocol, such legislative or other measures as may be necessary for making those rights a reality.

Article 3
Obligation of nondiscrimination

The State Parties to this Protocol undertake to guarantee the exercise of the rights set forth herein without discrimination of any kind for reasons related to race, color, sex, language, religion, political or other opinions, national or social origin, economic status, birth or any other social condition.

Article 4
Inadmissibility of Restrictions

A right which is recognized or in effect in a State by virtue of its internal legislation or international conventions may not be restricted or curtailed on the pretext that this Protocol does not recognize the right or recognizes it to a lesser degree.

Article 5
Scope of Restrictions and Limitations

The State Parties may establish restrictions and limitations on the enjoyment and exercise of the rights established herein by means of laws promulgated for the purpose of preserving the general welfare in a democratic society only to the extent that they are not incompatible with the purpose and reason underlying those rights.

Article 6
Right to Work

1. Everyone has the right to work, which includes the opportunity to secure the means for living a dignified and decent existence by performing a freely elected or accepted lawful activity.
2. The State Parties undertake to adopt measures that will make the right to

work fully effective, especially with regard to the achievement of full employment, vocational guidance, and the development of technical and vocational training projects, in particular those directed to the disabled. The States Parties also undertake to implement and strengthen programs that help to ensure suitable family care, so that women may enjoy a real opportunity to exercise the right to work.

Article 7
Just, Equitable, and Satisfactory Conditions of Work

The States Parties to this Protocol recognize that the right to work to which the foregoing article refers presupposes that everyone shall enjoy that right under just, equitable, and satisfactory conditions, which the States Parties undertake to guarantee in their internal legislation, particularly with respect to:

a. Remuneration which guarantees, as a minimum, to all workers dignified and decent living conditions for them and their families and fair and equal wages for equal work, without distinction;

b. The right of every worker to follow his vocation and to devote himself to the activity that best fulfills his expectations and to change employment in accordance with the pertinent national regulations;

c. The right of every worker to promotion or upward mobility in his employment, for which purpose account shall be taken of his qualifications, competence, integrity and seniority;

d. Stability of employment, subject to the nature of each industry and occupation and the causes for just separation. In cases of unjustified dismissal the worker shall have the right to indemnity or to reinstatement on the job or any other benefits provided by domestic legislation;

e. Safety and hygiene at work;

f. The prohibition of night work or unhealthy or dangerous working conditions and, in general, of all work which jeopardizes health, safety, or morals, for persons under 18 years of age. As regards minors under the age of 16, the work day shall be subordinated to the provisions regarding compulsory education and in no case shall work constitute an impediment to school attendance or a limitation on benefiting from education received;

g. A reasonable limitation of working hours, both daily and weekly. The days shall be shorter in the case of dangerous or unhealthy work or of night work;

h. Rest, leisure and paid vacations as well as remuneration for national holidays.

Article 8
Trade Union Rights

1. The States Parties shall ensure:

a. The right of workers to organize trade unions and to join the union of their choice for the purpose of protecting and promoting their interests. As an extension of that right, the States Parties shall permit trade unions to establish national federations or confederations, or to affiliate with those that already exist, as well as to form international trade union organizations and to affiliate with that of their choice. The States Parties shall also permit trade unions, federations and confederations to function freely;

b. The right to strike.

2. The exercise of the rights set forth above may be subject only to restrictions established by law, provided that such restrictions are characteristic of a democratic society and necessary for safeguarding public order or for protecting public health or morals or the rights and freedoms of others. Members of the armed forces and the police and of other essential public services shall be subject to limitations and restrictions established by law.

3. No one may be compelled to belong to a trade union.

Article 9
Right to Social Security

1. Everyone shall have the right to social security protecting him from the consequences of old age and of disability which prevents him, physically or mentally, from securing the means for a dignified and decent existence. In the event of the death of a beneficiary, social security benefits shall be applied to his dependents.

2. In the case of persons who are employed, the right to social security shall cover at least medical care and an allowance or retirement benefit in the case of work accidents or occupational disease and, in the case of women, paid maternity leave before and after childbirth.

Article 10
Right to Health

1. Everyone shall have the right to health, understood to mean the enjoyment of the highest level of physical, mental and social well-being.

2. In order to ensure the exercise of the right to health, the States Parties agree to recognize health as a public good and, particularly, to adopt the following measures to ensure that right:

a. Primary health care, that is, essential health care made available to all individuals and families in the community;

b. Extension of the benefits of health services to all individuals subject to the State's jurisdiction;

c. Universal immunisation against the principal infectious diseases;

d. Prevention and treatment of endemic, occupational and other diseases;

e. Education of the population on the prevention and treatment of health problems, and

f. Satisfaction of the health needs of the highest risk groups and of those whose poverty makes them the most vulnerable.

Article 11
Right to a Healthy Environment

1. Everyone shall have the right to live in a healthy environment and to have access to basic public services.

2. The States Parties shall promote the protection, preservation, and improvement of the environment.

Article 12
Right to Food

1. Everyone has the right to adequate nutrition which guarantees the possibility of enjoying the highest level of physical, emotional and intellectual development.

2. In order to promote the exercise of this right and eradicate malnutrition, the States Parties undertake to improve methods of production, supply and distribution of food, and to this end, agree to promote greater international cooperation in support of the relevant national policies.

Article 13
Right to Education

1. Everyone has the right to education.

2. The States Parties to this Protocol agree that education should be directed towards the full development of the human personality and human dignity and should strengthen respect for human rights, ideological pluralism, fundamental freedoms, justice and peace. They further agree that education ought to enable everyone to participate effectively in a democratic and pluralistic society and achieve a decent existence and should foster understanding, tolerance and friendship among all nations and all racial, ethnic or religious groups and promote activities for the maintenance of peace.

3. The States Parties to this Protocol recognize that in order to achieve the full exercise of the right to education:

   a. Primary education should be compulsory and accessible to all without cost;
   b. Secondary education in its different forms, including technical and vocational secondary education, should be made generally available and accessible to all by every appropriate means, and in particular, by the progressive introduction of free education;
   c. Higher education should be made equally accessible to all, on the basis of individual capacity, by every appropriate means, and in particular, by the progressive introduction of free education;
   d. Basic education should be encouraged or intensified as far as possible for those persons who have not received or completed the whole cycle of primary instruction;
   e. Programs of special education should be established for the handicapped, so as to provide special instruction and training to persons with physical disabilities or mental deficiencies.

4. In conformity with the domestic legislation of the States Parties, parents should have the right to select the type of education to be given to their children, provided that it conforms to the principles set forth above.

5. Nothing in this Protocol shall be interpreted as a restriction of the freedom of individuals and entities to establish and direct educational institutions in accordance with the domestic legislation of the States Parties.

Article 14
Right to the Benefits of Culture

  1. The States Parties to this Protocol recognize the right of everyone:
  a. To take part in the cultural and artistic life of the community;
  b. To enjoy the benefits of scientific and technological progress;
  c. To benefit from the protection of moral and material interests deriving from any scientific, literary or artistic production of which he is the author.
  2. The steps to be taken by the States Parties to this Protocol to ensure the full exercise of this right shall include those necessary for the conservation, development and dissemination of science, culture and art.
  3. The States Parties to this Protocol undertake to respect the freedom indispensable for scientific research and creative activity.
  4. The States Parties to this Protocol recognize the benefits to be derived from the encouragement and development of international cooperation and relations in the fields of science, arts and culture, and accordingly agree to foster greater international cooperation in these fields.

Article 15
Right to the Formation and the Protection of Families

  1. The family is the natural and fundamental element of society and ought to be protected by the State, which should see to the improvement of its spiritual and material conditions.
  2. Everyone has the right to form a family, which shall be exercised in accordance with the provisions of the pertinent domestic legislation.
  3. The States Parties hereby undertake to accord adequate protection to the family unit and in particular:
  a. To provide special care and assistance to mothers during a reasonable period before and after childbirth;
  b. To guarantee adequate nutrition for children at the nursing stage and during school attendance years;
  c. To adopt special measures for the protection of adolescents in order to ensure the full development of their physical, intellectual and moral capacities;
  d. To undertake special programs of family training so as to help create a stable and positive environment in which children will receive and develop the values of understanding, solidarity, respect and responsibility.

Article 16
Rights of Children

Every child, whatever his parentage, has the right to the protection that his status as a minor requires from his family, society and the State. Every child has the right to grow under the protection and responsibility of his parents; save in exceptional, judicially-recognized circumstances, a child of young age ought not to be separated from his mother. Every child has the right to free and compulsory education, at least in the elementary phase, and to continue his training at higher levels of the educational system.

Article 17
Protection of the Elderly

Everyone has the right to special protection in old age. With this in view the States Parties agree to take progressively the necessary steps to make this right a reality and, particularly, to:

    a. Provide suitable facilities, as well as food and specialized medical care, for elderly individuals who lack them and are unable to provide them for themselves;

    b. Undertake work programs specifically designed to give the elderly the opportunity to engage in a productive activity suited to their abilities and consistent with their vocations or desires;

    c. Foster the establishment of social organizations aimed at improving the quality of life for the elderly.

Article 18
Protection of the Handicapped

Everyone affected by a diminution of his physical or mental capacities is entitled to receive special attention designed to help him achieve the greatest possible development of his personality. The States Parties agree to adopt such measures as may be necessary for this purpose and, especially, to:

    a. Undertake programs specifically aimed at providing the handicapped with the resources and environment needed for attaining this goal, including work programs consistent with their possibilities and freely accepted by them or their legal representatives, as the case may be;

    b. Provide special training to the families of the handicapped in order to help them solve the problems of coexistence and convert them into active agents in the physical, mental and emotional development of the latter;

    c. Include the consideration of solutions to specific requirements arising from needs of this group as a priority component of their urban development plans;

    d. Encourage the establishment of social groups in which the handicapped can be helped to enjoy a fuller life.

Article 19
Means of Protection

1. Pursuant to the provisions of this article and the corresponding rules to be formulated for this purpose by the General Assembly of the Organization of American States, the States Parties to this Protocol undertake to submit periodic reports on the progressive measures they have taken to ensure due respect for the rights set forth in this Protocol.

2. All reports shall be submitted to the Secretary General of the OAS, who shall transmit them to the Inter-American Economic and Social Council and the Inter-American Council for Education, Science and Culture so that they may examine them in accordance with the provisions of this article. The Secretary General shall send a copy of such reports to the Inter-American Commission on Human Rights.

3. The Secretary General of the Organization of American States shall also transmit to the specialized organizations of the inter-American system of which the States Parties to the present Protocol are members, copies or pertinent portions of the reports submitted, insofar as they relate to matters within the purview of those organizations, as established by their constituent instruments.

4. The specialized organizations of the inter-American system may submit reports to the Inter-American Economic and Social Council and the Inter-American Council for Education, Science and Culture relative to compliance with the provisions of the present Protocol in their fields of activity.

5. The annual reports submitted to the General Assembly by the Inter-American Economic and Social Council and the Inter-American Council for Education, Science and Culture shall contain a summary of the information received from the States Parties to the present Protocol and the specialized organizations concerning the progressive measures adopted in order to ensure respect for the rights acknowledged in the Protocol itself and the general recommendations they consider to be appropriate in this respect.

6. Any instance in which the rights established in paragraph a) of Article 8 and in Article 13 are violated by action directly attributable to a State Party to this Protocol may give rise, through participation of the Inter-American Commission on Human Rights and, when applicable, of the Inter-American Court of Human Rights, to application of the system of individual petitions governed by Article 44 through 51 and 61 through 69 of the American Convention on Human Rights.

7. Without prejudice to the provisions of the preceding paragraph, the Inter-American Commission on Human Rights may formulate such observations and recommendations as it deems pertinent concerning the status of the economic, social and cultural rights established in the present Protocol in all or some of the States Parties, which it may include in its Annual Report to the General Assembly or in a special report, whichever it considers more appropriate.

8. The Councils and the Inter-American Commission on Human Rights, in discharging the functions conferred upon them in this article, shall take into account the progressive nature of the observance of the rights subject to protection by this Protocol .

Article 20
Reservations

The States Parties may, at the time of approval, signature, ratification or accession, make reservations to one or more specific provisions of this Protocol, provided that such reservations are not incompatible with the object and purpose of the Protocol.

Article 21
Signature, Ratification or Accession. Entry into Effect

1. This Protocol shall remain open to signature and ratification or accession by any State Party to the American Convention on Human Rights.

2. Ratification of or accession to this Protocol shall be effected by depositing

an instrument of ratification or accession with the General Secretariat of the Organization of American States.

3. The Protocol shall enter into effect when eleven States have deposited their respective instruments of ratification or accession.

4. The Secretary General shall notify all the member states of the Organization of American States of the entry of the Protocol into effect.

Article 22
Inclusion of other Rights and Expansion of those Recognized

1. Any State Party and the Inter-American Commission on Human Rights may submit for the consideration of the States Parties meeting on the occasion of the General Assembly proposed amendments to include the recognition of other rights or freedoms or to extend or expand rights or freedoms recognized in this Protocol.

2. Such amendments shall enter into effect for the States that ratify them on the date of deposit of the instrument of ratification corresponding to the number representing two thirds of the States Parties to this Protocol. For all other States Parties they shall enter into effect on the date on which they deposit their respective instrument of ratification.

PROTOCOL TO THE AMERICAN CONVENTION ON HUMAN RIGHTS TO ABOLISH THE
DEATH PENALTY
(Approved at Asunción, Paraguay, on June 8, 1990, at the
twentieth regular session of the
General Assembly)

Preamble

THE STATES PARTIES TO THIS PROTOCOL,

CONSIDERING:

That Article 4 of the American Convention on Human Rights recognizes the right to life and restricts the application of the death penalty;

That everyone has the inalienable right to respect for his life, a right that cannot be suspended for any reason;

That the tendency among the American States is to be in favor of abolition of the death penalty;

That application of the death penalty has irrevocable consequences, forecloses the correction of judicial error, and precludes any possibility of changing or rehabilitating those convicted;

That the abolition of the death penalty helps to ensure more effective protection of the right to life;

That an international agreement must be arrived at that will entail a progressive development of the American Convention on Human Rights, and

That States Parties to the American Convention on Human Rights have expressed their intention to adopt an international agreement with a view to consolidating the practice of not applying the death penalty in the Americas.

Have agreed to sign the following Protocol to the American Convention on Human Rights to abolish the death penalty.

Article 1

The States Parties to this Protocol shall not apply the death penalty in their territory to any person subject to their jurisdiction.

Article 2

1. No reservations may be made to this Protocol. However, at the time of ratification or accession, the States Parties to this instrument may declare that they reserve the right to apply the death penalty in wartime in accordance with international law, for extremely serious crimes of a military nature.

2. The State Party making this reservation shall, upon ratification or accession, inform the Secretary General of the Organization of American States of the pertinent provisions of its national legislation applicable in wartime, as referred to in the preceding paragraph.

3. Said State Party shall notify the Secretary General of the Organization of American States of the beginning or end of any state of war in effect in its territory.

Article 3

1. This Protocol shall be open for signature and ratification or accession by any State Party to the American Convention on Human Rights.

2. Ratification of this Protocol or accession thereto shall be made through the deposit of an instrument of ratification or accession with the General Secretariat of the Organization of American States.

Article 4

This Protocol shall enter into force among the States that ratify or accede to it when they deposit their respective instruments of ratification or accession with the General Secretariat of the Organization of American States.

Appendix IV

STATUTE OF THE INTER-AMERICAN COMMISSION ON HUMAN RIGHTS

Approved by the General Assembly of the OAS, Resolution No 447, at its
Ninth Regular Session, held in La Paz, Bolivia, October 1979

I. Nature and Purposes

Article 1

1. The Inter-American Commission on Human Rights is an organ of the
Organization of the American States, created to promote the observance and
defense of human rights and to serve as consultative organ of the Organization in
this matter.
2. For the purposes of the present Statute, human rights are understood to be:
a. The rights set forth in the American Convention on Human Rights, in
relation to the States Parties thereto;
b. The rights set forth in the American Declaration of the Rights and Duties of
Man, in relation to the other member states.

II. Membership and Structure

Article 2

1. The Inter-American Commission on Human Rights shall be composed of
seven members, who shall be persons of high moral character and recognized
competence in the field of human rights.
2. The Commission shall represent all the member states of the Organization.

Article 3

1. The members of the Commission shall be elected in a personal capacity by
the General Assembly of the Organization from a list of candidates proposed by
the governments of the member states.
2. Each government may propose up to three candidates, who may be nationals
of the state proposing them or of any other member state of the Organization.
When a slate of three is proposed, at least one of the candidates shall be a
national of a state other than the proposing state.

Article 4

1. At least six months prior to completion of the terms of office for which the
members of the Commission were elected,[25] the Secretary General shall request,

---

[25] Modified by AG/Res. 1098 (XXI-0/90).

in writing, each member state of the Organization to present its candidates within 90 days .

2. The Secretary General shall prepare a list in alphabetical order of the candidates nominated, and shall transmit it to the member states of the Organization at least thirty days prior to the next General Assembly.

Article 5

The members of the Commission shall be elected by secret ballot of the General Assembly from the list of candidates referred to in Article 4(2). The candidates who obtain the largest number of votes and an absolute majority of the votes of the member states shall be declared elected. Should it become necessary to hold several ballots to elect all the members of the Commission, the candidates who receive the smallest number of votes shall be eliminated successively, in the manner determined by the General Assembly.

Article 6

The members of the Commission shall be elected for a term of four years and may be reelected only once. Their terms of office shall begin on January 1 of the year following the year in which they are elected.

Article 7

No two nationals of the same state may be members of the Commission.

Article 8

1. Membership on the Inter-American Commission on Human Rights is incompatible with engaging in other functions that might affect the independence or impartiality of the member or the dignity or prestige of his post on the Commission.

2. The Commission shall consider any case that may arise regarding incompatibility in accordance with the provisions of the first paragraph of this Article, and in accordance with the procedures provided by its Regulations.

If the Commission decides, by an affirmative vote of a least five of its members, that a case of incompatibility exists, it will submit the case, with its background, to the General Assembly for decision.

3. A declaration of incompatibility by the General Assembly shall be adopted by a majority of two thirds of the member states of the Organization and shall occasion the immediate removal of the member of the Commission from his post, but it shall not invalidate any action in which he may have participated.

Article 9

The duties of the members of the Commission are:

1. Except when justifiably prevented, to attend the regular and special meetings the Commission holds at its permanent headquarters or in any other place to which it may have decided to move temporarily.

2. To serve, except when justifiably prevented, on the special committees which the Commission may form to conduct on-site observations, or to perform any other duties within their ambit.

3. To maintain absolute secrecy about all matters which the Commission deems confidential.

4. To conduct themselves in their public and private life as befits the high moral authority of the office and the importance of the mission entrusted to the Commission.

Article 10

1. If a member commits a serious violation of any of the duties referred to in Article 9, the Commission, on the affirmative vote of five of its members, shall submit the case to the General Assembly of the Organization, which shall decide whether he should be removed from office.

2. The Commission shall hear the member in question before taking its decision.

Article 11

1. When a vacancy occurs for reasons other than the normal completion of a member's term of office, the Chairman of the Commission shall immediately notify the Secretary General of the Organization, who shall in turn inform the member states of the Organization.

2. In order to fill vacancies, each government may propose a candidate within a period of 30 days from the date of receipt of the Secretary General's communication that a vacancy has occurred.

3. The Secretary General shall prepare an alphabetical list of the candidates and shall transmit it to the Permanent Council of the Organization, which shall fill the vacancy.

4. When the term of office is due to expire within six months following the date on which a vacancy occurs, the vacancy shall not be filled.

Article 12

1. In those member states of the Organization that are Parties to the American Convention on Human Rights, the members of the Commission shall enjoy, from the time of their election and throughout their term of office, such immunities as are granted to diplomatic agents under international law. While in office, they shall also enjoy the diplomatic privileges required for the performance of their duties.

2. In those member states of the Organization that are not Parties to the American Convention on Human Rights, the members of the Commission shall enjoy the privileges and immunities pertaining to their posts that are required for them to perform their duties with independence.

3. The system of privileges and immunities of the members of the Commission may be regulated or supplemented by multilateral or bilateral agreements between the Organization and the member states.

Article 13

The members of the Commission shall receive travel allowances and per diem and fees, as appropriate, for their participation in the meetings of the Commission or in other functions which the Commission, in accordance with its Regulations, entrusts to them, individually or collectively. Such travel and per diem allowances and fees shall be included in the budget of the Organization, and their amounts and conditions shall be determined by the General Assembly.

Article 14

1. The Commission shall have a Chairman, a First Vice-Chairman and a Second Vice-Chairman, who shall be elected by an absolute majority of its members for a period of one year; they may be re-elected only once in each four-year period.

2. The Chairman and the two Vice-Chairmen shall be the officers of the Commission, and their functions shall be set forth in the Regulations.

Article 15

The Chairman of the Commission may go to the Commission's headquarters and remain there for such time as may be necessary for the performance of his duties.

III. Headquarters and Meetings

Article 16

1. The headquarters of the Commission shall be in Washington, D.C.

2. The Commission may move to and meet in the territory of any American State when it so decides by an absolute majority of votes, and with the consent, or at the invitation of the government concerned.

3. The Commission shall meet in regular and special sessions, in conformity with the provisions of the Regulations.

Article 17

1. An absolute majority of the members of the Commission shall constitute a quorum.

2. In regard to those States that are Parties to the Convention, decisions shall be taken by an absolute majority vote of the members of the Commission in those cases established by the American Convention on Human Rights and the present Statute. In other cases, an absolute majority of the members present shall be required.

3. In regard to those States that are not Parties to the Convention, decisions shall be taken by an absolute majority vote of the members of the Commission, except in matters of procedure, in which case, the decisions shall be taken by simple majority.

IV. Functions and Powers

Article 18

The Commission shall have the following powers with respect to the member states of the Organization of American States:

a. to develop an awareness of human rights among the peoples of the Americas;
b. to make recommendations to the governments of the states on the adoption of progressive measures in favor of human rights in the framework of their legislation, constitutional provisions and international commitments, as well as appropriate measures to further observance of those rights;
c. to prepare such studies or reports as it considers advisable for the performance of its duties;
d. to request that the governments of the states provide it with reports on measures they adopt in matters of human rights;
e. to respond to inquiries made by any member state through the General Secretariat of the Organization on matters related to human rights in the state and, within its possibilities, to provide those states with the advisory services they request;
f. to submit an annual report to the General Assembly of the Organization, in which due account shall be taken of the legal regime applicable to those States Parties to the American Convention on Human Rights and of that system applicable to those that are not Parties;
g. to conduct on-site observations in a state, with the consent or at the invitation of the government in question; and
h. to submit the program-budget of the Commission to the Secretary General, so that he may present it to the General Assembly.

Article 19

With respect to the States Parties to the American Convention on Human Rights, the Commission shall discharge its duties in conformity with the powers granted under the Convention and in the present Statute, and shall have the following powers in addition to those designated in Article 18:

a. to act on petitions and other communications, pursuant to the provisions of Articles 44 to 51 of the Convention;
b. to appear before the Inter-American Court of Human Rights in cases provided for in the Convention;
c. to request the Inter-American Court of Human Rights to take such provisional measures as it considers appropriate in serious and urgent cases which have not yet been submitted to it for consideration, whenever this becomes necessary to prevent irreparable injury to persons;
d. to consult the Court on the interpretation of the American Convention on Human Rights or of other treaties concerning the protection of human rights in the American states;
e. to submit additional draft protocols to the American Convention on Human Rights to the General Assembly, in order to progressively include other rights and freedoms under the system of protection of the Convention, and
f. to submit to the General Assembly, through the Secretary General, proposed amendments to the American Convention on Human Rights, for such action as the General Assembly deems appropriate.

Article 20

In relation to those member states of the Organization that are not parties to the American Convention on Human Rights, the Commission shall have the following powers, in addition to those designated in Article 18:

　　a. to pay particular attention to the observance of the human rights referred to in Articles I, II, III, IV, XVIII, XXV, and XXVI of the American Declaration of the Rights and Duties of Man;

　　b. to examine communications submitted to it and any other available information, to address the government of any member state not a Party to the Convention for information deemed pertinent by this Commission, and to make recommendations to it, when it finds this appropriate, in order to bring about more effective observance of fundamental human rights; and,

　　c. to verify, as a prior condition to the exercise of the powers granted under subparagraph b. above, whether the domestic legal procedures and remedies of each member state not a Party to the Convention have been duly applied and exhausted.

V. Secretariat

Article 21

　　1. The Secretariat services of the Commission shall be provided by a specialized administrative unit under the direction of an Executive Secretary. This unit shall be provided with the resources and staff required to accomplish the tasks the Commission may assign to it.

　　2. The Executive Secretary, who shall be a person of high moral character and recognized competence in the field of human rights, shall be responsible for the work of the Secretariat and shall assist the Commission in the performance of its duties in accordance with the Regulations.

　　3. The Executive Secretary shall be appointed by the Secretary General of the Organization, in consultation with the Commission. Furthermore, for the Secretary General to be able to remove the Executive Secretary, he shall consult with the Commission and inform its members of the reasons for his decision.

VI. Statute and Regulations

Article 22

　　1. The present Statute may be amended by the General Assembly.

　　2. The Commission shall prepare and adopt its own Regulations, in accordance with the present Statute.

Article 23

　　1. In accordance with the provisions of Articles 44 to 51 of the American Convention on Human Rights, the Regulations of the Commission shall determine the procedure to be followed in cases of petitions or communications alleging violation of any of the rights guaranteed by the Convention, and imputing such violation to any State Party to the Convention.

2. If the friendly settlement referred to in Articles 44-51 of the Convention is not reached, the Commission shall draft, within 180 days, the report required by Article 50 of the Convention.

Article 24

1. The Regulations shall establish the procedure to be followed in cases of communications containing accusations or complaints of violations of human rights imputable to States that are not Parties to the American Convention on Human Rights.

2. The Regulations shall contain, for this purpose, the pertinent rules established in the Statute of the Commission approved by the Council of the Organization in resolutions adopted on May 25 and June 8, 1960, with the modifications and amendments introduced by Resolution XXII of the Second Special Inter-American Conference, and by the Council of the Organization at its meeting held on April 24, 1968, taking into account resolutions CP/RES. 253 (343/78), "Transition from the present Inter-American Commission on Human Rights to the Commission provided for in the American Convention on Human Rights," adopted by the Permanent Council of the Organization on September 20, 1979.

VII. Transitory Provisions

Article 25

Until the Commission adopts its new Regulations, the current Regulations (OEA/Ser.L/VII. 17, doc. 26) shall apply to all the member states of the Organization.

Article 26

1. The present Statute shall enter into effect 30 days after its approval by the General Assembly.

2. The Secretary General shall order immediate publication of the Statute, and shall give it the widest possible distribution.

Appendix V

REGULATIONS OF THE INTER-AMERICAN COMMISSION ON HUMAN RIGHTS

Approved by the Commission at its 660th Meeting, 49th Session, held on April 8, 1980, and modified at its 64th Session, 840th Meeting, held on March 7, 1985, at its 70th Session, 938th Meeting, held on June 29, 1987, at its 90 Session 1282 Meeting, held on September 21, 1995 and at its 92nd Special Session, held on May 3, 1996

TITLE I. ORGANIZATION OF THE COMMISSION

Chapter I. Nature and Composition

Article 1. Nature and Composition

1. The Inter-American Commission on Human Rights is an autonomous entity of the Organization of American States whose principal function is to promote the observance and defense of human rights and to serve as an advisory body to the Organization in this area.

2. The Commission represents all the member states of the Organization.

3. The Commission is composed of seven members elected in their individual capacity by the General Assembly of the Organization who shall be persons of high moral standing and recognized competence in the field of human rights.

Chapter II. Membership

Article 2. Duration of the term of office

1. The members of the Commission shall be elected for four years and may be reselected only once.

2. In the event that new members of the Commission are not elected to replace those completing their term of office, the latter shall continue to serve until the new members are elected.

Article 3. Precedence

The members of the Commission shall follow the Chairman and Vice-Chairmen in order of precedence according to their length of service. When there are two or more members with equal seniority, precedence shall be determined according to age.

Article 4. Incompatibility

1. The position of member of the Inter-American Commission on Human

Rights is incompatible with the exercise of activities which could affect the independence, impartiality, dignity or prestige of membership on the Commission.

2. The Commission, with the affirmative vote of at least five of its members, shall decide if a situation of incompatibility exists.

3. The Commission, prior to taking a decision, shall hear the member who is considered to be in a situation of incompatibility.

4. The decision with respect to the incompatibility, together with all the background information, shall be sent to the General Assembly by means of the Secretary General of the Organization for the purposes set forth in Article 8 (3), of the Commission's Statute.

Article 5. Resignation

In the event that a member resigns, his resignation shall be presented to the Chairman of the Commission who shall notify the Secretary General of the Organization for the appropriate purposes.

Chapter III. Officers

Article 6. Composition and functions

The Commission shall have as its officers a Chairman, a first Vice-Chairman, and a second Vice-Chairman, who shall perform the functions set forth in these regulations.

Article 7. Elections

1. In the election for each of the posts referred to in the preceding article, only members present shall participate.

2. Elections shall be by secret ballot. However, with the unanimous consent of the members present, the Commission may decide on another procedure.

3. The vote of an absolute majority of the members of the Commission shall be required for election to any of the posts referred to in Article 6.

4. Should it be necessary to hold more than one ballot for election to any of these posts, the names receiving the lowest number of votes shall be eliminated successively .

5. Elections shall be held on the first day of the Commission's first session of the new calendar year.

Article 8. Duration of Mandate

1. The board of officers shall hold office for a year and may be reelected only once in every four year period.

2. The mandate of the board of officers extends from the date of their election until the elections held the following year for the new board, pursuant to Article 7, paragraph 5.

3. In case the mandate of the Chairman or any of the Vice-Chairmen expires, the provisions of Article 9, paragraphs 3 and 4 will apply.

Article 9. Resignation, Vacancy and Replacements

1. If the Chairman resigns from his post or ceases to be a member of the Commission, the Commission shall elect a successor to fill the post for the remainder of the term of office at the first meeting held after the date on which it is notified of the resignation or vacancy.

2. The same procedure shall be applied in the event of the resignation of either of the Vice-Chairmen, or if a vacancy occurs.

3. The First Vice-Chairman shall serve as Chairman until the Commission elects a new Chairman under the provisions of paragraph 1 of this article.

4. The First Vice-Chairman shall also replace the Chairman if the latter is temporarily unable to perform his duties. The Second Vice-Chairman shall replace the Chairman in the event of the absence or disability of the First Vice-Chairman, or if that post is vacant.

Article 10. Functions of the Chairman

The Duties of the Chairman shall be:

a. to represent the Commission before all the other organs of the Organization and other institutions;

b. to convoke regular and special meetings of the Commission in accordance with the Statute and these Regulations;

c. to preside over the sessions of the Commission and submit to it, for consideration, all matters appearing on the agenda of the work schedule approved for the corresponding session;

d. to give the floor to the members in the order in which they have requested it;

e. to rule on points of order that may arise during the discussions of the Commission. If any member so requests, the Chairman's ruling shall be submitted to the Commission for its decision;

f. to submit to a vote matters within his competence, in accordance with the pertinent provisions of these Regulations;

g. to promote the work of the Commission and see to compliance with its program-budget;

h. to present a written report to the Commission at the beginning of its regular or special sessions on what he has done during its recesses to carry out the functions assigned to him by the Statute and by these Regulations;

1. to see to compliance with the decisions of the Commission;

j. to attend the meetings of the General Assembly of the Organization and, as an observer, those of the United Nations Commission on Human Rights; further, he may participate in the activities of other entities concerned with protecting and promoting respect for human rights;

k. to go to the headquarters of the Commission and remain there for as long as he considers necessary to carry out his functions;

l. to designate special committees, *ad hoc* committees, and subcommittees composed of several members, to carry out any mandate within his area of competence;

m. to perform any other functions that may be conferred upon him in these Regulations.

Article 11. Delegation of Functions

The Chairman may delegate to one of the Vice-Chairmen or to another member of the Commission the functions specified in Article 10(a), (j), and (m).

Chapter IV. Secretariat

Article 12. Composition[26]

The Secretariat of the Commission shall be composed of an Executive Secretary, two Assistant Executive Secretaries, and the professional, technical, and administrative staff needed to carry out its activities.

Article 13. Functions of the Executive Secretary[27]

1. The functions of the Executive Secretary shall be:
a. to direct, plan, and coordinate the work of the Secretariat;
b. to prepare the draft work schedule for each session in consultation with the Chairman;
c. to provide advisory services to the Chairman and members of the Commission in the performance of their duties;
d. to present a written report to the Commission at the beginning of each session, on the activities of the Secretariat since the preceding session, and on any general matters that may be of interest to the Commission;
e. to implement the decisions entrusted to him by the Commission or by the Chairman.

2. One of the Assistant Executive Secretaries shall replace the Executive Secretary in the event of his absence or disability.

3. The Executive Secretary, the Assistant Executive Secretaries and the staff of the Secretariat must observe strict discretion in all matters that the Commission considers confidential.

Article 14. Functions of the Secretariat

1. The Secretariat shall prepare the draft reports, resolutions, studies and any other papers entrusted to it by the Commission or by the Chairman, and shall see that the summary minutes of the sessions of the Commission and any documents considered by it are distributed among its members.

2. The Secretariat shall receive petitions addressed to the Commission and, when appropriate, shall request the necessary information from the governments concerned and, in general, it shall make the necessary arrangements to initiate any proceedings to which such petitions may give rise.

[26] Article 12 was modified by the Commission during its 90th Session, held on September 11–22, 1 995.

[27] Article 13, paragraph 2 and 3, were modified by the Commission during its 90th Session, held on September 11–22, 1995.

Chapter V. Functioning of the Commission

Article 15. Sessions

1. The Commission shall meet for a period not to exceed a total of eight weeks a year, divided into however many regular meetings the Commission may decide, without prejudice to the fact that it may convoke special sessions at the decision of its Chairman, or at the request of an absolute majority of its members.

2. The sessions of the Commission shall be held at its headquarters. However, by an absolute majority vote of its members, the Commission may decide to meet elsewhere, with the consent of or at the invitation of the government concerned.

3. Any member who because of illness or for any other serious reason is unable to attend all or part of any session or meeting of the Commission, or to fulfill any other functions, must notify the Executive Secretary to this effect as soon as possible, and he shall so inform the Chairman

Article 16. Meetings

1. During the sessions, the Commission shall hold as many meetings as necessary to carry out its activities.

2. The length of the meetings shall be determined by the Commission subject to any changes that, for justifiable reasons, are decided on by the Chairman after consulting with the members of the Commission.

3. The meetings shall be closed unless the Commission decides otherwise.

4. The date and time for the next meeting shall be set at each meeting.

Article 17. Working Groups

1. When the Commission considers it advisable, prior to the beginning of every regular session a working group shall convene to prepare the draft resolutions and other decisions on petitions and communications which are dealt with under Title II, Chapters I, II and III of the present Regulations and which are to be considered by the full Commission during the session. Said Working Group will be composed of three members, designated by the Chairman of the Commission, following a rotation policy, when possible.

2. The Commission, with a vote of the absolute majority of its members, shall determine the formation of other working groups the purpose of which shall be the consideration of specific subjects which will then be considered by the full Commission. Each working group will be made up of no more than three members, who will be designated by the Chairman. As far as possible, these working groups will meet immediately before or after each session for the period of time the Commission determines.

Article 18. Quorum for Meetings

The presence of an absolute majority of the members of the Commission shall be necessary to constitute a quorum.

Article 19. Discussion and Voting[28]

1. The meetings shall conform primarily to the Regulations and secondarily, to the pertinent provisions of the Regulations of the Permanent Council of the Organization of American States.

2. Members of the Commission may not participate in the discussion, investigation, deliberation or decision of a matter submitted to the Commission in the following cases:

   a. if they were nationals of the State which is [the] subject of the Commission's general or specific consideration, or if they were accredited to, or carrying out, a special mission, as diplomatic agents, on behalf of said State.

   b. if previously they have participated in any capacity in a decision concerning the same facts on which the matter is based or have acted as an adviser to, or representative of, any of the parties involved in the decision.

3. When any member thinks that he should abstain from participating in the study or decision of a matter, he shall so inform the Commission, which shall decide if the withdrawal is warranted.

4. Any member may raise the issue of the withdrawal of another member provided that it is based upon reasons formulated in paragraph 2 of this article.

5. Any member who has withdrawn from the case shall not participate in the discussion, investigation, deliberation or decision of the matter even though the reason for the withdrawal has been superseded.

6. During the discussion of a given subject, any member may raise a point of order, which shall be ruled upon immediately by the Chairman or, when appropriate, by the majority of the members present. The discussion may be ended at any time, as long as the members have had the opportunity to express their opinion.

7. Once the discussion has been terminated, and if there is no consensus on the subject submitted to the Commission for deliberation, the Chairman shall put the matter to a vote in the reverse order of precedence among the members.

8. The Chairman shall announce the results of the vote and shall declare (as approved) the proposal that has the majority of votes. In the case of a tie, the Chairman shall decide.

9 Any doubt which may arise as regards the application or interpretation of the present article shall be resolved by the Commission.

Article 20. Special Quorum to take Decisions

1 Decisions shall be taken by an absolute majority vote of the members of the Commission in the following cases:

   a. to elect the executive officers of the Commission;

   b. for matters where such a majority is required under the provisions of the Convention, the Statute or these Regulations;

   c. to adopt a report on the situation of human rights in a specific state;

   d. for any amendment or interpretation on the application of these Regulations.

---

[28] Article 19, paragraph 2.a. was modified by the Commission during its 90th Session, held on September 11–22, 1995.

2. To take decisions regarding other matters, a majority vote of members present shall be sufficient.

Article 21. Explanation of Vote

1. Whether or not members agree with the decisions of the majority, they shall be entitled to present a written explanation of their vote, which shall be included following that decision.

2. If the decision concerns the approval of a report or draft, the explanation of the vote shall be included after that report or draft.

3. When the decision does not appear in a separate document, the explanation of the vote shall be included in the minutes of the meeting, following the decision in question.

Article 22. Minutes of the Meetings

1. Summary minutes shall be taken of each meeting. They shall state the day and time at which it was held, the names of the members present, the matters dealt with, the decisions taken, the names of those voting for and against each decision, and any statement made by a member especially for inclusion in the minutes.

2. The Secretariat shall distribute copies of the summary minutes of each meeting to the members of the Commission, who may present their observations to the Secretariat prior to the meeting at which they are to be approved.

Article 23. Compensation for Special Services

The Commission may assign any of its members, with the approval of an absolute majority, the preparation of a special study or other specific papers to be carried out individually outside the sessions. Such work shall be compensated in accordance with funds available in the budget. The amount of the fees shall be set on the basis of the number of days required for preparation and drafting of the paper.

Article 24. Program-budget

1. The proposed program-budget of the Commission shall be prepared by its Secretariat in consultation with the Chairman and shall be governed by the Organization's current budgetary standards.

2. The Executive Secretary will advise the Commission of said program-budget.

TITLE II. PROCEDURES

Chapter I. General Provisions

Article 25. Official Languages

1. The official languages of the Commission shall be Spanish, French, English and Portuguese. The working languages shall be those decided on by the

Commission every two years, in accordance with the languages spoken by its members.

2. A member of the Commission may allow omission of the interpretation of debates and the preparation of documents in his language.

Article 26. Presentation of Petitions

1. Any person or group of persons or nongovernmental entity legally recognized in one or more of the member states of the Organization may submit petitions to the Commission, in accordance with these Regulations, on one's own behalf or on behalf of third persons, with regard to alleged violations of a human right recognized, as the case may be, in the American Convention on Human Rights or in the American Declaration of the Rights and Duties of Man.

2. The Commission may also, *motu proprio,* take into consideration any available information that it considers pertinent and which might include the necessary factors to begin processing a case which in its opinion fulfills the requirements for the purpose.

Article 27. Form

1. The petition shall be lodged in writing.

2. The petitioner may appoint, in the petition itself, or in another written petition, an attorney or other person to represent him before the Commission.

Article 28. Special Missions

The Commission may designate one or more of its members or staff members of the Secretariat to take specific measures, investigate facts or make the necessary arrangements for the Commission to perform its functions.

Article 29. Precautionary Measures

1. The Commission may, at its own initiative, or at the request of a party, take any action it considers necessary for the discharge of its functions.

2. In urgent cases, when it becomes necessary to avoid irreparable damage to persons, the Commission may request that provisional measures be taken to avoid irreparable damage in cases where the denounced facts are true.

3. If the Commission is not in session, the Chairman, or in his absence, one of the Vice-Chairmen, shall consult with the other members, through the Secretariat, on implementation of the provisions of paragraphs 1 and 2 above. If it is not possible to consult within a reasonable time, the Chairman shall take the decision on behalf of the Commission and shall so inform its members immediately.

4. The request for such measures and their adoption shall not prejudice the final decision.

Article 30. Initial Processing

1. The Secretariat of the Commission shall be responsible for the study and initial processing of petitions lodged before the Commission and that fulfill all the requirements set forth in the Statute and in these Regulations

2. If a petition or communication does not meet the requirements called for in

these Regulations, the Secretariat of the Commission may request the petitioner or his representative to complete it.

3. If the Secretariat has any doubt as to the admissibility of a petition, it shall submit it for consideration to the Commission or to the Chairman during recesses of the Commission.

Chapter II. Petitions and Communications regarding States Parties to the American Convention on Human Rights

Article 31. Condition for Considering the Petition

The Commission shall take into account petitions regarding alleged violations by a state party of human rights defined in the American Convention on Human Rights, only when they fulfill the requirements set forth in that Convention, in the Statute and in these Regulations.

Article 32. Requirements for the Petitions

Petitions addressed to the Commission shall include:
   a. the name, nationality, profession or occupation, postal address, or domicile and signature of the person or persons making the denunciation; or in cases where the petitioner is a nongovernmental entity, its legal domicile or postal address, and the name and signature of its legal representative or representatives;
   b. an account of the act or situation that is denounced, specifying the place and date of the alleged violations and, if possible, the name of the victims of such violations as well as that of any official that might have been appraised of the act or situation that was denounced;
   c. an indication of the state in question which the petitioner considers responsible, by commission or omission, for the violation of a human right recognized in the American Convention on Human Rights in the case of States Parties thereto, even if no specific reference is made to the article alleged to have been violated;
   d. information on whether the remedies under domestic law have been exhausted or whether it has been impossible to do so.

Article 33. Omission of Requirements

Without prejudice to the provisions of Article 26, if the Commission considers that the petition is inadmissible or incomplete, it shall notify the petitioner, whom it shall ask to complete the requirements omitted in the petition.

Article 34. Initial Processing[29]

1. The Commission, acting initially through its Secretariat, shall receive and process petitions lodged with it in accordance with the standards set forth below:
   a. it shall enter the petition in a register especially prepared for that purpose, and the date on which it was received shall be marked on the petition or communication itself;

---

[29] Article 34 was modified incorporating paragraphs 7 a. and b. and 8 by the Commission during its 92nd special session, held from April 29 to May 3, 1996.

b. it shall acknowledge receipt of the petition to the petitioner, indicating that it will be considered in accordance with the Regulations;

c. if it accepts, in principle, the admissibility of the petition, it shall request information from the government of the State in question and include the pertinent parts of the petitions.

2. In serious or urgent cases or when it is believed that the life, personal integrity or health of a person is in imminent danger, the Commission shall request the promptest reply from the government, using for this purpose the means it considers most expeditious.

3. The request for information shall not constitute a prejudgment with regard to the decision the Commission may finally adopt on the admissibility of the petition.

4. In transmitting the pertinent parts of a communication to the government of the State in question, the identity of the petitioner shall be withheld, as shall any other information that could identify him, except when the petitioner expressly authorizes in writing the disclosure of his identity.

5. The Commission shall request the affected government to provide the information requested within 90 days after the date on which the request is sent.

6. The government of the State in question may, with justifiable cause, request a 30 day extension, but in no case shall extensions be granted for more than 180 days after the date on which the first communication is sent to the government of the State concerned.

7. The Commission may, in order to gain a better understanding of the case:

a. Forward to the petitioner or his attorney the documents supplied by the government, requesting petitioner to submit his comments and any opposing evidence he may have within a period of 30 days.

b. Any such comments or evidence as may be received shall be transmitted to the government, with the request that it submit its final arguments within a period of 30 days.

If the Commission authorizes their presentation, the documents under reference shall be designed to emphasize the points separating the parties with respect to the issues set forth and the points accepted by the parties. Repetitions of arguments shall not be admitted.

8. Any additional information received under conditions other than those previously established shall be communicated to the opposing party, and any relevant oral or written presentations shall be made at the hearing referred to in Article 67.

Article 35. Preliminary Questions

The Commission shall proceed to examine the case and decide on the following matters:

a. whether the remedies under domestic law have been exhausted, and it may determine any measures it considers necessary to clarify any remaining doubts;

b. other questions related to the admissibility of the petition or its manifest inadmissibility based upon the record or submission of the parties;

c. whether grounds for the petition exist or subsist, and if not, to order the file closed.

Article 36. Examination by the Commission

The record shall be submitted by the Secretariat to the Commission for consideration at the first session held after the period referred to in Article 34, paragraph 5, if the government has not provided the information on that occasion, or after the periods indicated in paragraphs 7 and 8 have elapsed if the petitioner has not replied or if the government has not submitted its final observations.

Article 37. Exhaustion of Domestic Remedies

1. For a petition to be admitted by the Commission, the remedies under domestic jurisdiction must have been invoked and exhausted in accordance with the general principles of international law.
2. The provisions of the preceding paragraph shall not be applicable when:
   a. the domestic legislation of the State concerned does not afford due process of law for protection of the right or rights that have allegedly been violated;
   b. the party alleging violation of his rights has been denied access to the remedies under domestic law or has been prevented from exhausting them;
   c. there has been unwarranted delay in rendering a final judgment under the aforementioned remedies.
3. When the petitioner contends that he is unable to prove exhaustion as indicated in this Article, it shall be up to the government against which this petition has been lodged to demonstrate to the Commission that the remedies under domestic law have not previously been exhausted, unless it is clearly evident from the background information contained in the petition.

Article 38. Deadline for the Presentation of Petitions

1. The Commission shall refrain from taking up those petitions that are lodged after the six-month period following the date on which the party whose rights have allegedly been violated has been notified of the final ruling in cases where the remedies under domestic law have been exhausted.
2. In the circumstances set forth in Article 37, (2) of these Regulations, the deadline for presentation of a petition to the Commission shall be within a reasonable period of time, in the Commission's judgment, as from the date on which the alleged violation of rights has occurred, considering the circumstances of each specific case.

Article 39. Duplication of Procedures

1. The Commission shall not consider a petition in cases where the subject of the petition:
   a. is pending settlement in another procedure under an international governmental organization of which the State concerned is a member;
   b. essentially duplicates a petition pending or already examined and settled by the Commission or by another international governmental organization of which the state concerned is a member.

2. The Commission shall not refrain from taking up and examining a petition in cases provided for in paragraph 1 when:
  a. the procedure followed before the other organization or agency is one limited to an examination of the general situation on human rights in the state in question and there has been no decision on the specific facts that are the subject of the petition submitted to the Commission, or is one that will not lead to an effective settlement of the violation denounced;
  b. the petitioner before the Commission or a family member is the alleged victim of the violation denounced and the petitioner before the organizations in reference is a third party or a nongovernmental entity having no mandate from the former.

Article 40. Separation and Combination of Cases

1. Any petition that states different facts that concern more than one person, and that could constitute various violations that are unrelated in time and place shall be separated and processed as separate cases, provided the requirements set forth in Article 32 are met.

2. When two petitions deal with the same facts and persons, they shall be combined and processed in a single file.

Article 41. Declaration of Inadmissibility

The Commission shall declare inadmissible any petition when:
  a. any of the requirements set forth in Article 32 of these Regulations has not been met;
  b. when the petition does not state facts that constitute a violation of rights referred to in Article 31 of these Regulations in the case of States Parties to the American Convention on Human Rights;
  c. the petition is manifestly groundless or inadmissible on the basis of the statement by the petitioner himself or the government.

Article 42. Presumption

The facts reported in the petition whose pertinent parts have been transmitted to the government of the State in reference shall be presumed to be true if, during the maximum period set by the Commission under the provisions of Article 34 paragraph 5, the government has not provided the pertinent information, as long as other evidence does not lead to a different conclusion.

Article 43. Hearing

1. If the file has not been closed and in order to verify the facts, the Commission may conduct a hearing following a summons to the parties and proceed to examine the matter set forth in the petition.

2. At that hearing, the Commission may request any pertinent information from the representative of the State in question and shall receive, if so requested, oral or written statements presented by the parties concerned.

Article 44. On-site Investigation

1. If necessary and advisable, the Commission shall carry out an on-site investigation, for the effective conduct of which it shall request, and the States concerned shall furnish to it, all necessary facilities.

2. However, in serious and urgent cases, only the presentation of a petition or communication that fulfills all the formal requirements of admissibility shall be necessary in order for the Commission to conduct an on-site investigation with the prior consent of the State in whose territory a violation has allegedly been committed.

3. Once the investigatory stage has been completed, the case shall be brought for consideration before the Commission, which shall prepare its decision in a period of 180 days.

Article 45. Friendly Settlement

1. At the request of any of the parties, or on its own initiative, the Commission shall place itself at the disposal of the parties concerned, at any stage of the examination of a petition, with a view to reaching a friendly settlement of the matter on the basis of respect for the human rights recognized in the American Convention on Human Rights.

2. In order for the Commission to offer itself as an organ of conciliation for a friendly settlement of the matter it shall be necessary for the positions and allegations of the parties to be sufficiently precise; and in the judgment of the Commission, the nature of the matter must be susceptible to the use of the friendly settlement procedure.

3. The Commission shall accept the proposal to act as an organ of conciliation for a friendly settlement presented by one of the parties if the circumstances described in the above paragraph exist and if the other party to the dispute expressly accepts the procedure.

4. The Commission, upon accepting the role of an organ of conciliation for a friendly settlement shall designate a Special Commission or an individual from among its members. The Special Commission or the member so designated shall inform the Commission within the time period set by the Commission.

5. The Commission shall fix a time for the reception and gathering of evidence, it shall set dates for the holding of hearings, if appropriate, it shall plan an on-site observation, which will be carried out following the receipt of consent of the State to be visited and it shall fix a time for the conclusion of the procedure, which the Commission may extend.

6. If a friendly settlement is reached, the Commission shall prepare a report which shall be transmitted to the parties concerned and referred to the Secretary General of the Organization of American States for publication. This report shall contain a brief statement of the facts and of the solution reached. If any party in the case so requests, it shall be provided with the fullest possible information.

7. In a case where the Commission finds, during the course of processing the matter, that the case, by its very nature, is not susceptible to a friendly settlement; or finds that one of the parties does not consent to the application of this procedure; or does not evidence good will in reaching a friendly settlement based

on the respect for human rights, the Commission, at any stage of the procedure shall declare its role as organ of conciliation for a friendly settlement to have terminated.

Article 46. Preparation of the Report[30]

1. If a friendly settlement is not reached, the Commission shall examine the evidence provided by the government in question and the petitioner, evidence taken from witnesses to the facts or that obtained from documents, records, official publications, or through an on-site investigation.

2. After the evidence has been examined, the Commission shall prepare a report stating the facts and conclusions regarding the case submitted to it for its study.

3. The Commission shall deliberate in private, and all aspects of the discussions shall remain confidential.

Only the members shall participate in them, although the Executive Secretary and the Assistant Executive Secretaries or those acting for them may be present, as well as necessary Secretariat staff, under oath of confidentiality. No one else may be admitted except by special decision of the Commission, and such admission shall require a pledge to treat all deliberations and actions as confidential.

4. Any question put to a vote shall be formulated in precise terms in one of the official languages of the OAS.

The text shall be translated by the Secretariat into the other official languages and distributed prior to the vote at the request of any of the members.

5. The minutes referring to the Commission's deliberations shall restrict themselves to the subject of the debate and the decision approved, as well as the dissenting votes and any statements made for inclusion in the minutes.

6. The reports shall be signed by all members that have participated in the deliberation, and the dissenting and reasoned votes shall be signed by those casting them. However, a report signed by a majority of the members shall be valid.

7. The originals of the reports shall be deposited in the Commission archives. The Executive Secretary shall deliver properly certified copies to the interested government and to the petitioner when appropriate.

Article 47. Proposals and Recommendations[31]

1. In transmitting the report, the Commission may make such proposals and recommendations as it sees fit.

2. If, within a period of three months from the date of the transmittal of the report of the Commission to the States concerned, the matter has not been settled or submitted by the Commission, or by the State concerned, to the Court and its jurisdiction accepted, the Commission may, by the vote of an absolute majority of its members, set forth its opinion and conclusions concerning the question submitted for its consideration.

[30] Article 46 was modified incorporating paragraphs 3, 4, 5, 6 and 7 by the Commission during its 92nd special session held from April 29 to May 3, 1996.
[31] Article 47, paragraph 6, was modified by the Commission during its 90th Session, held on September 11–22, 1995.

3. The Commission may make the pertinent recommendations and prescribe a period within which the government in question must take the measures that are incumbent upon it to remedy the situation examined.

4. If the report does not represent, in its entirety, or, in part, the unanimous opinion of the members of the Commission, any member may add his opinion separately to that report.

5. Any verbal or written statement made by the parties shall also be included in the report.

6. The report shall be transmitted to the interested State, which shall not be authorized to publish it.

Article 48. Publication of the Report

1. When the prescribed period has expired, the Commission shall decide by the vote of an absolute majority of its members whether the State has taken suitable measures and whether to publish its report.

2. That report may be published by including it in the Annual Report to be presented by the Commission to the General Assembly of the Organization or in any other way the Commission may consider suitable.

Article 49. Communications from a Government

1. Communications presented by the government of a State Party to the American Convention on Human Rights, which has accepted the competence of the Commission to receive and examine such communications against other States Parties, shall be transmitted to the State Party in question, whether or not it has accepted the competence of the Commission. Even if it has not accepted such competence, the communication shall be transmitted so that the State can exercise its option under the provisions of Article 45 (3) of the Convention to recognize the Commission's competence in the specific case that is the subject of the communication.

2. Once the State in question has accepted the competence of the Commission to take up the communication of the other State Party, the corresponding procedure shall be governed by the provisions of Chapter II insofar as they may be applicable.

Article 50. Referral of the Case to the Court

1. If a State Party to the Convention has accepted the Court's jurisdiction in accordance with Article 62 of the Convention, the Commission may refer the case to the Court, subsequent to transmittal of the report referred to in Article 46 of these Regulations to the government of the State in question.

2. When it is ruled that the case is to be referred to the Court, the Executive Secretary of the Commission shall immediately notify the Court, the petitioner and the government of the State in question.

3. If the State Party has not accepted the Court's jurisdiction, the Commission may call upon that State to make use of the option referred to in Article 62, paragraph 2 of the Convention to recognize the Court's jurisdiction in the specific case that is the subject of the report.

Chapter III. Petitions Concerning States that are not Parties to the American Convention on Human Rights

Article 51. Receipt of the Petitions

The Commission shall receive and examine any petition that contains a denunciation of alleged violations of the human rights set forth in the American Declaration of the Rights and Duties of Man, concerning the member states of the Organization that are not parties to the American Convention on Human Rights.

Article 52. Applicable Procedure

The procedure applicable to petitions concerning member states of the Organization that are not parties to the American Convention on Human Rights shall be that provided for in the General Provisions included in Chapter I of Title II, in Articles 32 to 43 of these Regulations, and in the articles indicated below.

Article 53. Final Decision[32]

1. In addition to the facts and conclusions, the Commission's final decision shall include any recommendations the Commission deems advisable and a deadline for their implementation.

2. That decision shall be transmitted to the State in question or to the petitioner.

3. If the State does not adopt the measures recommended by the Commission within the deadline referred to in paragraphs 1 or 3, the Commission may publish its decision.

4. The decision referred to in the preceding paragraph may be published in the Annual Report to be presented by the Commission to the General Assembly of the Organization or in any other manner the Commission may see fit.

Article 54. Request for Reconsideration[33]

1. When the State in question or the petitioner, prior to the expiration of the 90 day deadline, invokes new facts or legal arguments which have not been previously considered, it may request a reconsideration of the conclusions or recommendations of the Commission's Report. The Commission shall decide to maintain or modify its decision, fixing a new deadline for compliance, where appropriate.

2. The Commission, if it considers it necessary, may request the State in question or the petitioner, as the case may be, to present any observations for reconsideration.

3. The reconsideration procedure may be utilized only once.

4. The Commission shall consider the request for reconsideration during the first regular session following its presentation.

5. If the State does not adopt the measures recommended by the Commission within the deadline referred to in paragraph 1, the Commission may publish its decision in conformity with Articles 48(2) and 53(4) of the present Regulations.

---

[32] Article 53 was modified by the Commission during its 70th Session, held on June–July 1987.

[33] Article 54 was modified by the Commission during its 70th Session, held on June–July 1987.

Chapter IV. On-Site Observations

Article 55. Designation of the Special Commission

On-site observations shall be carried out in each case by a Special Commission named for that purpose. The number of members of the Special Commission and the designation of its Chairman shall be determined by the Commission. In cases of great urgency, such decisions may be made by the Chairman subject to the approval of the Commission.

Article 56. Disqualification

A member of the Commission who is a national of or who resides in the territory of the State in which the on-site observation is to be carried out shall be disqualified from participating therein.

Article 57. Schedule of Activities

The Special Commission shall organize its own activities. To that end, it may appoint its own members and, after hearing the Executive Secretary, any staff members of the Secretariat or personnel necessary to carry out any activities related to its mission.

Article 58. Necessary Facilities

In extending an invitation for an on-site observation or in giving its consent, the government shall furnish to the Special Commission all necessary facilities for carrying out its mission. In particular, it shall bind itself not to take any reprisals of any kind against any persons or entities cooperating with the Special Commission or providing information or testimony

Article 59. Other Applicable Standards

Without prejudice to the provisions in the preceding article, any on-site observation agreed upon by the Commission shall be carried out in accordance with the following standards:
  a. the Special Commission or any of its members shall be able to interview freely and in private, any persons, groups, entities or institutions, and the government shall grant the pertinent guarantees to all those who provide the Commission with information, testimony or evidence of any kind;
  b. the members of the Special Commission shall be able to travel freely throughout the territory of the country, for which purpose the government shall extend all the corresponding facilities, including the necessary documentation;
  c. the government shall ensure the availability of local means of transportation;
  d. the members of the Special Commission shall have access to the jails and all other detention and interrogation centers and shall be able to interview in private those persons imprisoned or detained;
  e. the government shall provide the Special Commission with any document related to the observance of human rights that it may consider necessary for the presentation of its reports;

f. the Special Commission shall be able to use any method appropriate for collecting, recording or reproducing the information it considers useful;

g. the government shall adopt the security measures necessary to protect the Special Commission;

h. the government shall ensure the availability of appropriate lodging for the members of the Special Commission;

i. the same guarantees and facilities that are set forth here for the members of the Special Commission shall also be extended to the Secretariat staff;

j. any expenses incurred by the Special Committee, any of its members and the Secretariat staff shall be borne by the Organization, subject to the pertinent provisions.

Chapter V. General and Special Reports

Article 60. Preparation of Draft Reports

The Commission shall prepare the general or special draft reports that it considers necessary.

Article 61. Processing and Publication

1. The reports prepared by the Commission shall be transmitted as soon as possible through the General Secretariat of the Organization to the government or pertinent organs of the Organization.

2. Upon adoption of a report by the Commission, the Secretariat shall publish it in the manner determined by the Commission in each instance, except as provided for in Article 47, Paragraph 6, of these Regulations.

Article 62. Report on Human Rights in a State

The preparation of reports on the status of human rights in a specific state shall meet the following standards:

a. after the draft report has been approved by the Commission, it shall be transmitted to the government of the member state in question so that it may make any observations it deems pertinent;

b. the Commission shall indicate to that government the deadline for presentation of its observations;

c. when the Commission receives the observations from the government, it shall study them and, in light thereof, may uphold its report or change it and decide how it is to be published;

d. if no observation has been submitted on expiration of the deadline by the government, the Commission shall publish the report in the manner it deems suitable.

Article 63. Annual Report

The Annual Report presented by the Commission to the General Assembly of the Organization shall include the following:

a. a brief account of the origin, legal basis, structure and purposes of the Commission as well as the status of the American Convention;

b. a summary of the mandates and recommendations conferred upon the Commission by the General Assembly and the other competent organs, and of the status of implementation of such mandates and recommendations;

c. a list of the meetings held during the period covered by the report and of other activities carried out by the Commission to achieve its purposes, objectives, and mandates;

d. a summary of the activities of the Commission carried out in cooperation with other organs of the Organization and with regional or world organisations of the same type, and the results achieved through these activities;

e. a statement on the progress made in attaining the objectives set forth in the American Declaration of the Rights and Duties of Man and the American Convention on Human Rights;

f. a report on the areas in which measures should be taken to improve observance of human rights in accordance with the aforementioned Declaration and Convention;

g. any observations that the Commission considers pertinent with respect to petitions it has received, including those processed in accordance with the Statute and the present Regulations which the Commission decides to publish as reports, resolutions, or recommendations;

h. any general or special report that the Commission considers necessary with regard to the situation of human rights in the member states, noting in such reports the progress achieved and difficulties that have arisen in the effective observance of human rights;

i. any other information, observation, or recommendation that the Commission considers advisable to submit to the General Assembly and any new program that implies additional expense.

Article 64. Economic, Social and Cultural Rights

1. The States Parties shall forward to the Commission copies of the reports and studies referred to in Article 42 of the American Convention on Human Rights on the same date on which they submit them to the pertinent organs.

2. The Commission may request annual reports from the other member states regarding the economic, social, and cultural rights recognized in the American Declaration of the Rights and Duties of Man.

3. Any person, group of persons, or organization may present reports, studies or other information to the Commission on the situation of such rights in all or any of the member states.

4. If the Commission does not receive the information referred to in the preceding paragraphs or considers it inadequate, it may send questionnaires to all or any of the member states, setting a deadline for the reply or it may turn to other available sources of information.

5. Periodically, the Commission may entrust to experts or specialized entities studies on the situation of one or more of the aforementioned rights in a specific country or group of countries.

6. The Commission shall make the pertinent observations and recommendations on the situation of such rights in all or any of the member states and shall

include them in the Annual Report to the General Assembly or in a Special Report, as it considers most appropriate.

7. The recommendations may include the need for economic aid or some other form of cooperation to be provided among the member states, as called for in the Charter of the Organization and in other agreements of the inter-American system.

Chapter VI. Hearing before the Commission

Article 65. Decision to Hold Hearing

On its own initiative, or at the request of the person concerned, the Commission may decide to hold hearings on matters defined by the Statute as within its jurisdiction.

Article 66. Purpose of the Hearings[34]

Hearings may be held in connection with a petition or communication alleging a violation of a right set forth in the American Convention on Human Rights or in the American Declaration on the Rights and Duties of Man or in order to receive information of a general or particular nature related to the situation of human rights in one State or in a group of American states.

Article 67. Hearings on Petitions or Communications[35]

1. Hearings on cases concerning violations of human rights and which the Commission is examining pursuant to the procedures established in Chapters II and III of Title II of these Regulations, will have as their purpose the receipt of testimony oral or written of the parties, relative to the additional information regarding the admissibility of the case, the possibility of applying the friendly settlement procedure, the verification of the facts or the merits of the matter submitted to the Commission for consideration, or as regards any other matter pertinent to the processing of the case.

2. To implement the provisions of the previous article, the Commission may invite the parties to attend a hearing, or one of the parties may request that a hearing be held.

3. If one of the two parties requests a hearing for the purposes indicated above, the Secretariat shall immediately inform the other party of that petition, and when the hearing date is set, shall invite the other party to attend, unless the Commission considers that there are reasons warranting a confidential hearing.

4. The Government shall furnish the appropriate guarantees to all persons attending a hearing or providing the Commission with information, testimony or evidence of any kind during a hearing.

---

[34] Article 66 was modified by the Commission during its 70th Session, held on June–July 1987.
[35] Article 67.

Article 68. Hearings of a General Nature[36]

1. Persons who are interested in presenting testimony or information of a general nature to the Commission shall indicate prior to the meeting, to the Executive Secretary that they wish to appear before the next session of the Commission.

2. In their petition, interested persons shall give their reasons for desiring to appear, a summary of the information they will furnish, and the approximate time required for their testimony.

3. The Executive Secretary shall, in consultation with the Chairman of the Commission, accede to the request for a hearing, unless the information presented by the interested person reveals that the hearing bears no relation to matters within the Commission's competence or if the purpose of the hearing and its circumstances are substantially the same as an earlier one.

4. The Executive Secretary shall, in consultation with the Chairperson of the Commission, draw up a schedule and propose the time and date for the general hearings to be held during the session, and shall submit them to the Commission for approval on the first day of the session.

Article 69. Conduct of Hearings[37]

The Commission shall, in each case, decide which of its members will take part in the hearing.

Article 70. Attendance at Hearings[38]

1. Hearings shall be private, unless the Commission decides that other persons should attend.

2. Hearings called specifically to review a petition shall be held in private, in the presence of the parties or their representatives, unless they agree that the hearing should be public.

TITLE III. RELATIONS WITH THE INTER-AMERICAN COURT OF HUMAN RIGHTS

Chapter I. Delegates, Advisers, Witnesses, and Experts

Article 71. Delegates and Assistants

1. The Commission shall delegate one or more of its members to represent it and participate as delegates in the consideration of any matter before the Inter-American Court of Human Rights.

2. In appointing such delegates, the Commission shall issue any instructions it considers necessary to guide them in the Court's proceedings.

3. When it designates more than one delegate, the Commission shall assign to

---

[36] Article 68 was modified by the Commission during its 70th Session, held on June–July 1987.
[37] Article 69.
[38] Article 70.

one of them the responsibility of settling situations that are not foreseen in the instructions, or of clarifying any doubts raised by a delegate.

4. The delegates may be assisted by any person designated by the Commission. In the discharge of their functions, the advisers shall act in accordance with the instructions of the delegates.

Article 72. Witnesses and Experts

1. The Commission may also request the Court to summon other persons as witnesses or experts.

2. The summoning of such witnesses or experts shall be in accordance with the Regulations of the Court.

Chapter II. Procedure before the Court

Article 73. Presentation of the Case

1. When, in accordance with Article 61 of the American Convention on Human Rights, the Commission decides to bring a case before the Court, it shall submit a request in accordance with the provisions of the Statute and the Regulations of the Court, and specifying:

    a. the parties who will be intervening in the proceedings before the Court;

    b. the date on which the Commission approved its report;

    c. the names and addresses of its delegates;

    d. a summary of the case;

    e. the grounds for requesting a ruling by the Court.

2. The Commissions's request shall be accompanied by certified copies of the items in the file that the Commission or its delegate considers pertinent.

Article 74. Transmittal of other Elements

The Commission shall transmit to the Court, at its request, any other petition, evidence, document, or information concerning the case, with the exception of documents concerning futile attempts to reach a friendly settlement. The transmittal of documents shall in each case be subject to the decision of the Commission, which shall withhold the name and identity of the petitioner.

Article 75. Notification of the Petitioner

When the Commission decides to refer a case to the Court, the Executive Secretary shall immediately notify the petitioner and alleged victim of the Commission's decision and offer him the opportunity of making observations in writing on the request submitted to the Court. The Commission shall decide on the action to be taken with respect to these observations.

Article 76. Provisional Measures

1. In cases of extreme gravity and urgency, and when it becomes necessary to avoid irreparable damage to persons in a matter that has not yet been submitted to the Court for consideration, the Commission may request it to adopt any provisional measures it deems pertinent.

2. When the Commission is not in session, that request may be made by the Chairman, or in his absence by one of the Vice-Chairmen, in order of precedence.

TITLE IV. FINAL PROVISIONS

Article 77. Calendar Computation[39]

All time periods set forth in the present Regulations—in numbers of days—will be understood to be counted as calendar days.

Article 78. Interpretation

Any doubt that might arise with respect to the interpretation of these Regulations shall be resolved by an absolute majority of the members of the Commission.

Article 79. Amendment of the Regulations

The Regulations may be amended by an absolute majority of the members of the Commission.

[39] Article 77 was modified by the Commission during its 64th Session, held on March 7, 1985.

Appendix VI

STATUTE OF THE INTER-AMERICAN COURT OF HUMAN RIGHTS

Approved by the General Assembly of the OAS Resolution No 448, at its
Ninth Regular Session, held in La Paz, Bolivia, October 1979

Chapter I. General Provisions

Article 1. Nature and Legal Organization

The Inter-American Court of Human Rights is an autonomous judicial institution
whose purpose is the application and interpretation of the American Convention
on Human Rights. The Court exercises its functions in accordance with the
provisions of the aforementioned Convention and the present Statute.

Article 2. Jurisdiction

The Court shall exercise adjudicatory and advisory jurisdiction:
    1. Its adjudicatory jurisdiction shall be governed by the provisions of Articles
61, 62 and 63 of the Convention, and
    2. Its advisory jurisdiction shall be governed by the provisions of Article 64 of
the Convention.

Article 3. Seat

    1. The seat of the Court shall be San José, Costa Rica; however, the Court may
convene in any member state of the Organization of American States (OAS)
when a majority of the Court considers it desirable. and with the prior consent of
the State concerned.
    2. The seat of the Court may be changed by a vote of two-thirds of the States
Parties to the Convention, in the OAS General Assembly.

Chapter II. Composition of the Court

Article 4. Composition

    1. The Court shall consist of seven judges, nationals of the member states of
the OAS, elected in an individual capacity from among jurists of the highest moral
authority and of recognized competence in the field of human rights, who possess
the qualifications required for the exercise of the highest judicial functions under
the law of the State of which they are nationals or of the State that proposes them
as candidates.
    2. No two judges may be nationals of the same State.

Article 5. Judicial Terms[38]

1. The judges of the Court shall be elected for a term of six years and may be reelected only once. A judge elected to replace a judge whose term has not expired shall complete that term.

2. The terms of office of the judges shall run from January 1 of the year following that of their election to December 31 of the year in which their terms expire.

3. The judges shall serve until the end of their terms. Nevertheless, they shall continue to hear the cases they have begun to hear and that are still pending, and shall not be replaced by the newly elected judges in the handling of those cases.

Article 6. Election of the Judges—Date

1. Election of judges shall take place, insofar as possible, during the session of the OAS General Assembly immediately prior to the expiration of the term of the outgoing judges.

2. Vacancies on the Court caused by death, permanent disability, resignation or dismissal of judges shall, insofar as possible, be filled at the next session of the OAS General Assembly. However, an election shall not be necessary when a vacancy occurs within six months of the expiration of a term.

3. If necessary in order to preserve a quorum of the Court, the States Parties to the Convention, at a meeting of the OAS Permanent Council, and at the request of the President of the Court, shall appoint one or more interim judges who shall serve until such time as they are replaced by elected judges.

Article 7. Candidates

1. Judges shall be elected by the States Parties to the Convention, at the OAS General Assembly, from a list of candidates nominated by those States.

2. Each State Party may nominate up to three candidates, nationals of the state that proposes them or of any other member state of the OAS.

3. When a slate of three is proposed, at least one of the candidates must be a national of a state other than the nominating state.

Article 8. Election—Preliminary Procedures[39]

1. Six months prior to expiration of the terms to which the judges of the Court were elected, the Secretary General of the OAS shall address a written request to each State Party to the Convention that it nominate its candidates within the next ninety days.

2. The Secretary General of the OAS shall draw up an alphabetical list of the candidates nominated, and shall forward it to the States Parties, if possible, at least thirty days before the next session of the OAS General Assembly.

---

[38] Amended by Resolution 625 (Xll–0/82) of the Twelfth Regular Session of the OAS General Assembly.
[39] Modified by AG/RES. 1098 (XXI-91).

3. In the case of vacancies on the Court, as well as in cases of the death or permanent disability of a candidate, the aforementioned time periods shall be shortened to a period that the Secretary General of the OAS deems reasonable.

Article 9. Voting

1. The judges shall be elected by secret ballot and by an absolute majority of the States Parties to the Convention, from among the candidates referred to in Article 7 of the present Statute.

2. The candidates who obtain the largest number of votes and an absolute majority shall be declared elected. Should several ballots be necessary, those candidates who receive the smallest number of votes shall be eliminated successively, in the manner determined by the States Parties.

Article 10. Ad Hoc Judges

1. If a judge is a national of any of the States Parties to a case submitted to the Court, he shall retain his right to hear that case.

2. If one of the judges called upon to hear a case is a national of one of the States Parties to the case, any other State Party to the case may appoint a person to serve on the Court as an *ad hoc* judge.

3. If among the judges called upon to hear a case, none is a national of the States Parties to the case, each of the latter may appoint an *ad hoc* judge. Should several States have the same interest in the case, they shall be regarded as a single party for purposes of the above provisions. In case of doubt, the Court shall decide.

4. The right of any State to appoint an *ad hoc* judge shall be considered relinquished if the State should fail to do so within thirty days following the written request from the President of the Court.

5. The provisions of Articles 4, 11, 15, 16, 18, 19 and 20 of the present Statute shall apply to *ad hoc* judges.

Article 11. Oath

1. Upon assuming office, each judge shall take the following oath or make the following solemn declaration: 'I swear'—or 'I solemnly declare'—'that I shall exercise my functions as a judge honorably, independently and impartially and that I shall keep secret all deliberations.'

2. The oath shall be administered by the President of the Court and, if possible, in the presence of the other judges.

Chapter III. Structure of the Court

Article 12. Presidency

1. The Court shall elect from among its members a President and Vice-President who shall serve for a period of two years; they may be reelected.

2. The President shall direct the work of the Court, represent it, regulate the disposition of matters brought before the Court, and preside over its sessions.

3. The Vice-President shall take the place of the President in the latter's

temporary absence, or if the office of the President becomes vacant. In the latter case, the Court shall elect a new Vice-President to serve out the term of the previous Vice-President.

4. In the absence of the President and the Vice-President, their duties shall be assumed by other judges, following the order of precedence established in Article 13 of the present Statute.

Article 13. Precedence

1. Elected judges shall take precedence after the President and Vice-President according to their seniority in office.

2. Judges having the same seniority in office shall take precedence according to age.

3. *Ad hoc* and interim judges shall take precedence after the elected judges, according to age. However, if an *ad hoc* or interim judge has previously served as an elected judge, he shall have precedence over any other *ad hoc* or interim judge.

Article 14. Secretariat

1. The Secretariat of the Court shall function under the immediate authority of the Secretary, in accordance with the administrative standards of the OAS General Secretariat, in all matters that are not incompatible with the independence of the Court.

2. The Secretary shall be appointed by the Court. He shall be a full-time employee serving in a position of trust to the Court, shall have his office at the seat of the Court and shall attend any meetings that the Court holds away from its seat.

3. There shall be an Assistant Secretary who shall assist the Secretary in his duties and shall replace him in his temporary absence.

4. The Staff of the Secretariat shall be appointed by the Secretary General of the OAS, in consultation with the Secretary of the Court.

Chapter IV. Rights, Duties and Responsibilities

Article 15. Privileges and Immunities

1. The judges of the Court shall enjoy, from the moment of their election and throughout their term of office, the immunities extended to diplomatic agents under international law. During the exercise of their functions, they shall, in addition, enjoy the diplomatic privileges necessary for the performance of their duties.

2. At no time shall the judges of the Court be held liable for any decisions or opinions issued in the exercise of their functions.

3. The Court itself and its staff shall enjoy the privileges and immunities provided for in the Agreement on Privileges and Immunities of the Organization of American States, of May 15, 1949, *mutatis mutandis,* taking into account the importance and independence of the Court.

4. The provision of paragraphs 1, 2 and 3 of this article shall apply to the States

Parties to the Convention. They shall also apply to such other member states of the OAS as expressly accept them, either in general or for specific cases.

5. The system of privileges and immunities of the judges of the Court and of its staff may be regulated or supplemented by multilateral or bilateral agreements between the Court, the OAS and its member states.

Article 16. Service

1. The judges shall remain at the disposal of the Court, and shall travel to the seat of the Court or to the place where the Court is holding its sessions as often and for as long a time as may be necessary, as established in the Regulations.

2. The President shall render his service on a permanent basis.

Article 17. Emoluments

1. The emoluments of the President and the judges of the Court shall be set in accordance with the obligations and incompatibilities imposed on them by Articles 16 and 18, and bearing in mind the importance and independence of their functions.

2. The *ad hoc* judges shall receive the emoluments established by Regulations, within the limits of the Court's budget.

3. The judges shall also receive per diem and travel allowances, when appropriate.

Article 18. Incompatibilities

1. The position of judge of the Inter-American Court of Human Rights is incompatible with the following positions and activities:
   a. Members or high-ranking officials of the executive branch of government, except for those who hold positions that do not place them under the direct control of the executive branch and those of diplomatic agents who are not Chiefs of Missions to the OAS or to any of its member states;
   b. Officials of international organizations;
   c. Any others that might prevent the judges from discharging their duties, or that might affect their independence or impartiality, or the dignity and prestige of the office.

2. In case of doubt as to incompatibility, the Court shall decide. If the incompatibility is not resolved, the provisions of Article 73 of the Convention and Article 20(2) of the present Statute shall apply.

3. Incompatibilities may lead only to dismissal of the judge and the imposition of applicable liabilities, but shall not invalidate the acts and decisions in which the judge in question participated.

Article 19. Disqualification

1. Judges may not take part in matters in which, in the opinion of the Court, they or members of their family have a direct interest or in which they have previously taken part as agents, counsel or advocates, or as members of a national or international court or an investigatory committee, or in any other capacity.

2. If a judge is disqualified from hearing a case or for some other appropriate

reason considers that he should not take part in a specific matter, he shall advise the President of his disqualification. Should the latter disagree, the Court shall decide.

3. If the President considers that a judge has cause for disqualification or for some other pertinent reason should not take part in a given matter, he shall advise him to that effect. Should the judge in question disagree, the Court shall decide.

4. When one or more judges are disqualified pursuant to this article, the President may request the States Parties to the Convention, in a meeting of the OAS Permanent Council, to appoint interim judges to replace them.

Article 20. Disciplinary Regime

1. In the performance of their duties and at all other times, the judges and staff of the Court shall conduct themselves in a manner that is in keeping with the office of those who perform an international judicial function. They shall be answerable to the Court for their conduct, as well as for any violation, act of negligence or omission committed in the exercise of their functions.

2. The OAS General Assembly shall have disciplinary authority over the judges, but may exercise that authority only at the request of the Court itself, composed for this purpose of the remaining judges. The Court shall inform the General Assembly of the reasons for its request.

3. Disciplinary authority over the Secretary shall lie with the Court, and over the rest of the staff, with the Secretary, who shall exercise that authority with the approval of the President.

4. The Court shall issue disciplinary rules, subject to the administrative regulations of the OAS General Secretariat insofar as they may be applicable in accordance with Article 59 of the Convention.

Article 21. Resignation—Incapacity

1. Any resignation from the Court shall be submitted in writing to the President of the Court. The resignation shall not become effective until the Court has accepted it.

2. The Court shall decide whether a judge is incapable of performing his functions.

3. The President of the Court shall notify the Secretary General of the OAS of the acceptance of a resignation or a determination of incapacity, for appropriate action.

Chapter V. The Workings of the Court

Article 22. Sessions

1. The Court shall hold regular and special sessions.

2. Regular sessions shall be held as determined by the Regulations of the Court.

3. Special sessions shall be convoked by the President or at the request of a majority of the judges.

Article 23. Quorum

1. The quorum for deliberations by the Court shall be five judges.
2. Decisions of the Court shall be taken by a majority vote of the judges present.
3. In the event of a tie, the President shall cast the deciding vote.

Article 24. Hearings, Deliberations, Decisions

1. The hearings shall be public, unless the Court, in exceptional circumstances, decides otherwise.
2. The Court shall deliberate in private. Its deliberations shall remain secret unless the Court decides otherwise.
3. The decisions, judgments and opinions of the Court shall be delivered in public session, and the parties shall be given written notification thereof. In addition the decisions, judgments and opinions shall be published, along with judges' individual votes and opinions and with such other data or background information that the Court may deem appropriate.

Article 25. Rules and Regulations

1. The Court shall draw up its Rules of Procedure.
2. The Rules of Procedure may delegate to the President or to Committees of the Court authority to carry out certain parts of the legal proceedings, with the exception of issuing final rulings or advisory opinions. Rulings or decisions issued by the President or the Committees of the Court that are not purely procedural in nature may be appealed before the full Court.
3. The Court shall also draw up its own Regulations.

Article 26. Budget, Financial System

1. The Court shall draw up its own budget and shall submit it for approval to the General Assembly of the OAS, through the General Secretariat. The latter may not introduce any changes in it.
2. The Court shall administer its own budget.

Chapter VI. Relations with Governments and Organizations

Article 27. Relations with the Host Country, Governments and Organizations

1. The relations of the Court with the host country shall be governed through a headquarters agreement. The seat of the Court shall be international in nature.
2. The relations of the Court with governments, with the OAS and its organs, agencies and entities and with other international governmental organizations involved in promoting and defending human rights shall be governed through special agreements.

Article 28. Relations with the Inter-American Commission on Human Rights

The Inter-American Commission on Human Rights shall appear as a party before the Court in all cases within the adjudicatory jurisdiction of the Court, pursuant to Article 2(1) of the present Statute.

Article 29. Agreements of Cooperation

1. The Court may enter into agreements of cooperation with such nonprofit institutions as law schools, bar associations, courts, academies and educational or research institutions dealing with related disciplines in order to obtain their cooperation and to strengthen and promote the juridical and institutional principles of the Convention in general and of the Court in particular.

2. The Court shall include an account of such agreements and their results in its Annual Report to the OAS General Assembly.

Article 30. Report to the OAS General Assembly

The Court shall submit a report on its work of the previous year to each regular session of the OAS General Assembly. It shall indicate those cases in which a State has failed to comply with the Court's ruling. It may also submit to the OAS General Assembly proposals or recommendations on ways to improve the inter-American system of human rights, insofar as they concern the work of the Court.

Chapter VII. Final Provisions

Article 31. Amendments to the Statute

The present Statute may be amended by the OAS General Assembly, at the initiative of any member state or of the Court itself.

Article 32. Entry into Force

The present Statute shall enter into force on January 1, 1980.

Appendix VII

RULES OF PROCEDURE OF THE INTER-AMERICAN COURT OF HUMAN RIGHTS

Approved by the Court at its XXVI Regular Session held September 9–20, 1996

Preliminary Provisions

Article 1. Purpose

1. These Rules regulate the organization and establish the procedure of the Inter-American Court of Human Rights.

2. The Court may adopt such other Rules as may be necessary to carry out its functions.

3. In the absence of a provision in these Rules or in case of doubt as to their interpretation, the Court shall decide.

Article 2. Definitions

For the purposes of these Rules

a. the term *'agent'* refers to the person designated by a State to represent it before the Court;

b. the expression *'General Assembly'* refers to the General Assembly of the Organization of American States;

c. the term *'Commission'* refers to the Inter-American Commission on Human Rights;

d. the expression *'Permanent Commission'* refers to the Permanent Commission of the Court;

e. The expression *'Permanent Council'* refers to the Permanent Council of the Organization of American States;

f. the term *'Convention'* refers to the American Convention on Human Rights (Pact of San Josè, Costa Rica);

g. the term *'Court'* refers to the Inter-American Court of Human Rights;

h. the expression *'Delegates of the Commission'* refers to the persons designated by the Commission to represent it before the Court;

i. the expression *'original claimant'* refers to the person, group of persons, or nongovernmental entity that instituted the original petition with the Commission, pursuant to Article 44 of the Convention;

j. the term *'day'* shall be understood to be a natural day;

k. the expression *'States Parties'* refers to the States that have ratified or adhered to the Convention;

l. the expression *'Member States'* refers to the States that are members of the Organization of American States;

m. the term *'Statute'* refers to the Statute of the Court, as adopted by the

General Assembly of the Organization of American States on October 31, 1979 (AG/RES. 448[IX–0/79]), as amended;

n. the expression *'report of the Commission'* refers to the report provided for in Article 50 of the Convention;

o. the expression *'judge ad hoc'* refers to any judge appointed in pursuance of Article 55 of the Convention;

p. the expression *'interim judge'* refers to any judge appointed in pursuance of Articles 6(3) and 19(4) of the Statute;

q. the expression *'titular judge'* refers to any judge elected in pursuance of Articles 53 and 54 of the Convention;

r. the term *'month'* shall be understood to be a calendar month;

s. the acronym *'OAS'* refers to the Organization of American States;

t. the expression *'parties to the case'* refers to the parties in a case before the Court;

u. the term *'Secretariat'* refers to the Secretariat of the Court;

v. the term *'Secretary'* refers to the Secretary of the Court;

w. the expression *'Deputy Secretary'* refers to the Deputy Secretary of the Court;

x. the expression *'Secretary General'* refers to the Secretary General of the Organization of American States;

y. the term *'victim'* refers to the person whose rights under the Convention are alleged to have been violated.

TITLE I. ORGANIZATION AND FUNCTIONING OF THE COURT

Chapter I. The Presidency and Vice-Presidency ·

Article 3. Election of the President and Vice-President

1. The President and Vice-President shall be elected by the Court for a period of two years and may be reelected. Their terms shall begin on July 1 of the corresponding year. The election shall be held during the regular session nearest to that date.

2. The elections referred to in this Article shall be by secret ballot of the titular judges present. The judge who wins four or more votes shall be deemed to have been elected. If no candidate receives the required number of votes, a ballot shall take place between the two judges who have received the most votes. In the event of a tie, the judge having precedence in accordance with Article 13 of the Statute shall be deemed to have been elected.

Article 4. Functions of the President

The functions of the President are to:

a. represent the Court;

b. preside over the meetings of the Court and to submit for its consideration the topics appearing on the agenda;

c. direct and promote the work of the Court;

d. rule on points of order that may arise during the meetings of the Court. If any judge so requests, the point of order shall be decided by a majority vote;

e. present a biannual report to the Court on the activities he has carried out as President during that period,

f. exercise such other functions as are conferred upon him by the Statute or these Rules, or entrusted to him by the Court.

2. In specific cases, the President may delegate the representation referred to in paragraph 1(a) of this Article to the Vice-President, to any of the judges or, if necessary, to the Secretary or Deputy Secretary .

3. If the President is a national of one of the parties to a case before the Court, or in special situations in which he considers it appropriate, he shall relinquish the Presidency for that particular case. The same rule shall apply to the Vice-President or to any judge called upon to exercise the functions of President.

Article 5. Functions of the Vice-President

1. The Vice-President shall replace the President in the latter's temporary absence, and shall assume the Presidency when the absence is permanent. In the latter case, the Court shall elect a Vice-President to serve out that term. The same procedure shall be followed if the absence of the Vice-President is permanent.

2. In the absence of the President and the Vice-President, their functions shall be assumed by the other judges in the order of precedence established in Article 13 of the Statute.

Article 6. Commissions

1. The Permanent Commission shall be composed of the President, the Vice-President and any other judges the President deems it appropriate to appoint, according to the needs of the Court. The Permanent Commission shall assist the President in the exercise of his functions.

2. The Court may appoint other commissions for specific matters. In urgent cases, they may be appointed by the President if the Court is not in session.

3. In the performance of their functions, the commissions shall be governed by the provisions of these Rules, as applicable.

Chapter II. The Secretariat

Article 7. Election of the Secretary

1. The Court shall elect its Secretary, who must possess the legal qualifications required for the position, a good command of the working languages of the Court, and the experience necessary for discharging his functions.

2. The Secretary shall be elected for a term of five years and may be re-elected. He may be freely removed at any time if the Court so decides by the vote of not less than four judges. The vote shall be by secret ballot.

3. The Secretary shall be elected in accordance with the provisions of Article 3(2) of these Rules.

Article 8. Deputy Secretary

1. The Deputy Secretary shall be appointed on the proposal of the Secretary of the Court, in the manner prescribed in the Statute. He shall assist the Secretary in the performance of his functions and replace him during his temporary absences.

2. If the Secretary and Deputy Secretary are both unable to perform their functions, the President may appoint an Interim Secretary.

Article 9. Oath

1. The Secretary and Deputy Secretary shall take an oath in the presence of the President.

2. The staff of the Secretariat, including any persons called upon to perform interim or temporary duties, shall, upon assuming their functions, take an oath before the President undertaking to respect the confidential nature of any facts that may come to their attention during their performance of such duties. If the President is not present at the seat of the Court, the Secretary shall administer the oath.

3. All oaths shall be recorded in a document which shall be signed by the person being sworn and by the person administering the oath.

Article 10. Functions of the Secretary

The functions of the Secretary shall be to:
  a. communicate the judgments, advisory opinions, orders and other rulings of the Court;
  b. keep the minutes of the meetings of the Court;
  c. attend all meetings of the Court held at its seat or elsewhere;
  d. deal with the correspondence of the Court;
  e. direct the administration of the Court, pursuant to the instructions of the President;
  f. prepare the draft programs, rules and regulations, and budgets of the Court;
  g. plan direct and coordinate the work of the staff of the Court;
  h. carry out the tasks assigned to him by the Court or the President;
  i. perform any other duties provided for in the Statute and in these Rules.

Chapter III. Functioning of the Court

Article 11. Regular Sessions

The Court shall meet in two regular sessions each year, one during each semester, on the dates decided upon by the Court at the previous session. In exceptional circumstances, the President may change the dates of these sessions after prior consultation with the Court.

Article 12. Special Sessions

Special sessions may be convoked by the President on his own initiative or at the request of a majority of the judges.

Article 13. Quorum

The quorum for the deliberations of the Court shall consist of five judges.

Article 14. Hearings, Deliberations and Decisions

1. Hearings shall be public and shall be held at the seat of the Court. When exceptional circumstances so warrant, the Court may decide to hold a hearing in private or at a different location. The Court shall decide who may attend such hearings. Even in these exceptional circumstances, however, minutes shall be kept in the manner prescribed in Article 42 of these Rules.

2. The Court shall deliberate in private, and its deliberations shall remain secret. Only the judges shall take part in the deliberations, although the Secretary and Deputy Secretary or their substitutes may attend, as well as such other Secretariat staff as may be required. No other persons may be admitted, except by special decision of the Court and after taking an oath.

3. Any question that calls for a vote shall be formulated in precise terms in one of the working languages. At the request of any of the judges, the Secretariat shall translate the text thereof into the other working languages and distribute it prior to the vote.

4. The minutes of the deliberations of the Court shall be limited to a statement of the subject of the discussion and the decisions taken. Dissenting and concurring opinions and declarations made for the record shall also be noted.

Article 15. Decisions and Voting

1. The President shall present, point by point, the matters to be voted upon. Each judge shall vote either in the affirmative or the negative; there shall be no abstentions.

2. The votes shall be cast in inverse order to the order of precedence established in Article 13 of the Statute.

3. The decisions of the Court shall be adopted by a majority of the judges present.

4. In the event of a tie, the President shall have a casting vote.

Article 16. Continuation in Office by the Judges

1. Judges whose terms have expired shall continue to exercise their functions in cases that they have begun to hear and that are still pending. However, in the event of death, resignation or disqualification, the judge in question shall be replaced by the judge who was elected to take his place, if applicable, or by the judge who has precedence among the new judges elected upon expiration of the term of the judge to be replaced.

2. All matters relating to reparations and indemnities, as well as supervision of the implementation of the judgments of this Court, shall be heard by the judges comprising it at that stage of the proceedings, unless a public hearing has already been held. In that event, they shall be heard by the judges who had attended that hearing.

Article 17. Interim Judges

Interim judges shall have the same rights and functions as titular judges, except for such limitations as shall have been expressly established

Article 18. Judges Ad Hoc

1. In a case arising under Article 55(2) and 55(3) of the Convention and Article 10(2) and 10(3) of the Statute, the President, acting through the Secretariat, shall inform the States referred to in those provisions of their right to appoint an judge *ad hoc* within thirty days of notification of the petition.

2. When it appears that two or more States have a common interest, the President shall inform them that they may jointly appoint one judge *ad hoc,* pursuant to Article 10 of the Statute. If those States have not communicated any agreement to the Court within thirty days of the last notification of the petition. each State shall have fifteen days in which to propose a candidate. Thereafter, and if more than one candidate has been nominated, the President shall choose one judge *ad hoc* by lot, and shall communicate the result to the interested parties.

3. Should the interested States fail to exercise their right within the time limits established in the preceding paragraphs, they shall be deemed to have waived that right.

4. The Secretary shall communicate the appointment of judges *ad hoc* to the other parties to the case.

5. A judge *ad hoc* shall take an oath at the first meeting devoted to the consideration of the case for which he has been appointed.

6. Judges *ad hoc* shall receive honoraria on the same terms as titular judges.

Article 19. Disqualification

1. Disqualification of a judge shall be governed by the provisions of Article 19 of the Statute.

2. Motions for disqualification must be filed prior to the first hearing of the case. However, if the grounds therefor were not known at the time, such motions may be submitted to the Court at the first possible opportunity, so that it can rule on the matter immediately.

3. When, for any reason whatsoever, a judge is not present at one of the hearings or at other stages of the proceedings, the Court may decide to disqualify him from continuing to hear the case, taking all the circumstances it deems relevant into account.

TITLE II. PROCEDURE

Chapter I. General Rules

Article 20.Official Languages

1. The official languages of the Court shall be those of the OAS.

2. The working languages shall be those agreed upon by the Court each year.

However, in a specific case. the language of one of the parties may be adopted as a working language provided it is one of the official languages

3. The working languages for each case shall be determined at the start of the proceedings, unless they are the same as those already being employed by the Court.

4. The Court may authorize any person appearing before it to use his own language if he does not have sufficient knowledge of the working languages. In such circumstances, however, the Court shall make the necessary arrangements to ensure that an interpreter is present to translate that testimony into the working languages.

5. The Court shall, in all cases, determine which text is authentic.

Article 21. Representation of the States

1. The States parties to a case shall be represented by an Agent, who may, in turn, be assisted by any persons of his choice.

2. If a State replaces its Agent, it shall so notify the Court, and the replacement shall only take effect once the notification has been received at the seat of the Court.

3. A Deputy Agent may be designated. His actions shall have the same validity as those of the Agent.

4. When appointing its Agent, the State in question shall indicate the address at which all relevant communications shall be deemed to have been officially received.

Article 22. Representation of the Commission

1. The Commission shall be represented by the Delegates it has designated for the purpose. The Delegates may be assisted by any persons of their choice.

2. If the original claimant or the representatives of the victims or of their next of kin are among the persons selected by the Delegates of the Commission to assist them, in accordance with the preceding paragraph, that fact shall be brought to the attention of the Court, which shall, on the proposal of the Commission, authorize their participation in the discussions.

Article 23. Representation of the Victims or their Next of Kin

At the reparations stages, the representatives of the victims or of their next of kin may independently submit their own arguments and evidence.

Article 24. Cooperation of the States

1. The States parties to a case have the obligation to cooperate so as to ensure that all notices, communications or summonses addressed to persons subject to their jurisdiction are duly executed. They shall also expedite compliance with summonses by persons who either reside or are present within their territory.

2. The same rule shall apply to any proceedings that the Court decides to conduct or order on the territory of a State party to a case.

3. When the performance of any of the measures referred to in the preceding paragraphs requires the cooperation of any other State, the President shall request the government in question to provide the requisite assistance.

Article 25. Provisional Measures

1. At any stage of the proceedings involving cases of extreme gravity and urgency and when necessary to avoid irreparable damage to persons, the Court may, at the request of a party or on its own motion, order such provisional measures as it deems pertinent, pursuant to Article 63(2) of the Convention.

2. With respect to matters not yet submitted to it, the Court may act at the request of the Commission.

3. The request may be made to the President, to any judge of the Court, or to the Secretariat, by any means of communication. The recipient of the request shall immediately bring it to the President's attention.

4. If the Court is not sitting. the President, in consultation with the Permanent Commission and, if possible, with the other judges, shall call upon the government concerned to adopt such urgent measures as may be necessary to ensure the effectiveness of any provisional measures subsequently ordered by the Court at its next session.

5. In its Annual Report to the General Assembly, the Court shall include a statement concerning the provisional measures ordered during the period covered by the report. If those measures have not been duly implemented, the Court shall make such recommendations as it deems appropriate.

Article 26. Filing of Briefs

1. The application and the reply thereto, and the communication setting out the preliminary objections and the reply thereto, as well as any other briefs addressed to the Court, may be presented in person, by courier, facsimile, telex, mail or any other method in general use. If they are dispatched by electronic mail, the original documents must be submitted within fifteen days.

2. The President may, in consultation with the Permanent Commission, reject any communication from the parties which he considers patently unreceivable, and shall order that it be returned to the interested party, without further action.

Article 27. Default Procedure

1. When a party fails to appear in or continue with a case, the Court shall, on its own motion, take such measures as may be necessary to complete the consideration of the case.

2. When a party enters a case at a later stage of the proceedings, it shall take up the proceedings at that stage.

Article 28. Joinder of Cases and Proceedings

1. The Court may. at any stage of the proceedings, order the joinder of interrelated cases.

2. The Court may also order the joinder of the written or oral proceedings of several cases, including the introduction of witnesses.

3. After consulting the Agents and the Delegates, the President may direct that the proceedings in two or more cases be conducted simultaneously.

Article 29. Decisions

1. The judgments and interlocutory decisions for discontinuance of a case shall be rendered exclusively by the Court.

2. All other orders shall be rendered by the Court if it is sitting, and by the President if it is not, unless otherwise provided. Decisions of the President that are not purely procedural may be appealed before the Court.

3. Judgments and decisions of the Court may not be contested in any way.

Article 30. Publication of Judgments and Other Decisions

1. The Court shall order the publication of:
a. the judgments and other decisions of the Court; the former shall include only those explanations of votes which fulfill the requirements set forth in Article 55(2) of these Rules;
b. documents from the dossier, except those considered irrelevant or unsuitable for publication;
c. the records of the hearings;
d. any other document that the Court considers suitable for publication.

2. The judgments shall be published in the working languages used in each case. All other documents shall be published in their original language.

3. Documents relating to cases already adjudicated, and deposited with the Secretariat of the Court shall be made accessible to the public, unless the Court decides otherwise.

Article 31. Application of Article 63(1) of the Convention

Application of this provision may be invoked at any stage of the proceedings.

Chapter II. Written Proceedings

Article 32. Institution of the Proceedings

For a case to be referred to the Court under Article 61(1) of the Convention, the application shall be filed with the Secretariat of the Court in each of the working languages. Whereas the filing of an application in only one working language shall not suspend the proceeding, the translations into the other language or languages must be submitted within thirty days.

Article 33. Filing of the Application

The brief containing the application shall indicate:

1. the parties to the case; the purpose of the application; a statement of the facts; the supporting evidence, specifying the facts on which they will bear; the particulars of the witnesses and expert witnesses; the legal arguments, and the conclusions reached.

2. The names of the Agents and Delegates.

If the application is filed by the Commission, it shall be accompanied by the report referred to in Article 50 of the Convention.

Article 34. Preliminary Review of the Application

When, during a preliminary review of the application, the President finds that the basic requirements have not been met, he shall request the Applicant to correct any deficiencies within twenty days.

Article 35. Notification of the Application

1. The Secretary of the Court shall give notice of the application to:
a. The President and the judges of the Court;
b. the respondent State;
c. the Commission, when it is not also the Applicant;
d. the original claimant, if known;
e. the victim or his next of kin, if applicable.

2. The Secretary of the Court shall inform the other States Parties and the Secretary General of the filing of the application.

3. When giving notice, the Secretary shall request that the respondent States designate their Agent, and that the Commission appoint its Delegates, within one month. Until the Delegates are duly appointed, the Commission shall be deemed to be properly represented by its Chairman for all purposes of the case.

Article 36. Preliminary Objections

1. Preliminary objections shall be filed within two months of notification of the application.

2. The document setting out the preliminary objections shall be filed with the Secretariat and shall set out the facts on which the objection is based, the legal arguments, and the conclusions and supporting documents, as well as any evidence which the party filing the objection may wish to produce.

3. The Secretary shall immediately give notice of the preliminary objections to the persons indicated in Article 35(1) above.

4. The presentation of preliminary objections shall not cause the suspension of the proceedings on the merits, nor of the respective time periods or terms.

5. Any parties to the case wishing to submit written briefs on the preliminary objections may do so within thirty days of receipt of the communication.

6. The Court may, if it deems it appropriate, convene a special hearing on the preliminary objections, after which it shall rule on the objections.

Article 37. Answer to the application

The respondent shall answer the application in writing within four months of the notification. The requirements indicated in Article 33 of these Rules shall apply. The Secretary shall communicate the answer to the persons referred to in Article 35(1) above.

Article 38. Other Steps in the Written Proceedings

Once the application has been answered, and before the start of the oral proceedings, the parties may seek the permission of the President to enter additional written pleadings. In such a case, the President, if he sees fit, shall establish the time limits for presentation of the relevant documents.

Chapter III. Oral Proceedings

Article 39. Opening

The President shall announce the date for the opening of the oral proceedings and shall call such hearings as may be necessary.

Article 40. Conduct of the Hearings

The President shall direct the hearings. He shall prescribe the order in which the persons eligible to take part shall be heard, and determine the measures required for the smooth conduct of the hearings.

Article 41. Questions Put During the Hearings

1. The judges may ask all persons appearing before the Court any questions they deem proper.

2. The witnesses, expert witnesses and any other persons the Court decides to hear may, subject to the control of the President, be examined by the persons referred to in Articles 21, 22 and 23 of these Rules.

3. The President is empowered to rule on the relevance of the questions posed and to excuse the person to whom the questions are addressed from replying, unless the Court decides otherwise.

Article 42. Minutes of the Hearings

1. Minutes shall be taken at each hearing and shall contain the following:
a. the names of the judges present;
b. the names of those persons referred to in Articles 21, 22 and 23 of these Rules, who are present at the hearing;
c. the names and other relevant information concerning the witnesses, expert witnesses and other persons appearing at the hearing;
d. statements made expressly for the record by the States parties to the case or by the Commission;
e. the statements of the witnesses, expert witnesses and other persons appearing at the hearing, as well as the questions put to them and the replies thereto;
f. the text of the questions put by the judges and the replies thereto;
g. the text of any decisions rendered by the Court during the hearing.

2. The Agents and Delegates, as well as the witnesses, expert witnesses and other persons appearing at the hearing, shall receive a copy of the relevant parts of the transcript of the hearing to enable them, subject to the control of the Secretary, to correct any substantive errors. The Secretary shall set the time limits for this purpose, in accordance with the instructions of the President.

3. The minutes shall be signed by the President and the Secretary, and the latter shall attest to their accuracy.

4. Copies of the minutes shall be transmitted to the Agents and Delegates.

Chapter IV. Evidence

Article 43. Admission of Evidence

Items of evidence tendered by the parties shall be admissible only if previous notification thereof is contained in the application and in the reply thereto and, where appropriate, in the communication setting out the preliminary objections and in the answer thereto. Should any of the parties allege *force majeure*, serious impediment or the emergence of supervening events as grounds for producing an item of evidence, the Court may, in that particular instance, admit such evidence at a time other than those indicated above, provided that the opposing party is guaranteed the right of defense.

Article 44. Procedure for Taking Evidence

The Court may, at any stage of the proceedings:

1. Obtain, on is own motion, any evidence it considers helpful. In particular, it may hear as a witness, expert witness, or in any other capacity, any person whose evidence, statement or opinion it deems to be relevant.

2. Invite the parties to provide any evidence at their disposal or any explanation or statement that, in its opinion may be useful.

3. Request any entity, office, organ or authority of its choice to obtain information, express an opinion, or deliver a report or pronouncement on any given point. The documents may not be published without the authorization of the Court.

4. Commission one or more of its members to conduct an inquiry, undertake an *in situ* investigation or obtain evidence in some other manner.

Article 45. Cost of Evidence

The party requesting the production of evidence shall defray the cost thereof.

Article 46. Convocation of Witnesses and Expert Witnesses

1. The Court shall determine when the parties are to call their witnesses and expert witnesses whom the Court considers it necessary to hear. They shall be summoned in the manner deemed most suitable by the Court.

2. The summons shall indicate:
a. the name of the witness or expert witness;
b. the facts on which the examination will bear or the object of the expert opinion.

Article 47. Oath or Solemn Declaration by Witnesses and Expert Witnesses

1. After his identity has been established and before giving evidence, every witness shall take an oath or make a solemn declaration as follows:

'I swear'—or 'I solemnly declare'—'upon my honor and conscience that I will speak the truth, the whole truth and nothing but the truth.'

2. After his identity has been established and before performing his task, every expert witness shall take an oath or make a solemn declaration as follows:

'I swear'—or 'I solemnly declare'—'that I will discharge my duty as an expert witness honorably and conscientiously.'

3. The oath shall be taken, or the declaration made, before the Court or President or any of the judges so delegated by the Court.

Article 48. Objections to Witnesses

1. The interested party may object to a witness before he testifies.

2. If the Court considers it necessary, it may nevertheless hear, for purposes of information, a person who is not qualified to be heard as a witness.

3. The Court shall assess the value of the testimony and of the objections by the parties.

Article 49. Objections to an Expert Witness

1. The grounds for disqualification applicable to judges under Article 19(1) of the Statute shall also apply to expert witnesses.

2. Objections shall be presented within fifteen days of notification of the appointment of the expert witness.

3. If the expert witness who has been challenged contests the ground invoked against him, the Court shall rule on the matter. However, when the Court is not in session, the President may, after consultation with the Permanent Commission, order the evidence to be presented. The Court shall be informed thereof and shall rule on the value of the evidence.

4. Should it become necessary to appoint a new expert witness, the Court shall rule on the matter. Nevertheless, if the evidence needs to be heard as a matter of urgency, the President, after Consultation with the Permanent Commission, shall make the appointment and inform the Court accordingly. The Court shall rule on the value of the evidence.

Article 50. Protection of Witnesses and Expert Witnesses

States may neither institute proceedings against witnesses or expert witnesses nor bring illicit pressure to bear on them or on their families on account of declarations or opinions they have delivered before the Court.

Article 51. Failure to Appear or False Evidence

The Court may request that the States apply the sanctions provided for in their domestic legislation against persons who, without good reason, fail to appear or refuse to give evidence or who, in the opinion of the Court, have violated their oath.

Chapter V. Early Termination of the Proceedings

Article 52. Discontinuance

1. When the party that has brought the case notifies the Court of its intention not to proceed with it, the Court shall, after hearing the opinions of the other parties thereto and the representatives of the victims or their next of kin, decide whether to discontinue the hearing and, consequently, to strike the case from its list.

2. If the respondent informs the Court of its acquiescence in the claims of the

party that has brought the case, the Court shall decide, after hearing the opinions of the latter and the representatives of the victims or their next of kin, whether such acquiescence and its juridical effects are acceptable. In that event, the Court shall determine the appropriate reparations and indemnities.

Article 53. Friendly Settlement

When the parties to a case before the Court inform it of the existence of a friendly settlement, compromise, or any other occurrence likely to lead to a settlement of the dispute, the Court may, in that case and after hearing the representatives of the victims or their next of kin, decide to discontinue the hearing and strike the case from its list.

Article 54. Continuation of a Case

The existence of the conditions indicated in the preceding paragraphs notwith-standing the Court may, bearing in mind its responsibiliy to protect human rights, decide to continue the consideration of a case.

Chapter VI. Judgments

Article 55. Contents of the Judgment

1. The judgment shall contain:
   a. the names of the President, the judges who rendered it, and the Secretary and Deputy Secretary.
   b. the identity of the parties and their representatives and, where appropriate, representatives of the victims or their next of kin;
   c. a description of the proceedings;
   d. the facts of the case;
   e. the conclusions of the parties;
   f. the legal arguments;
   g. the ruling on the case;
   h. the decision, if any, in regard to costs;
   i. the result of the voting;
   j. a statement indicating which text is authentic.

2. Any judge who has taken part in the consideration of a case is entitled to append a dissenting or concurring opinion to the judgment. These opinions shall be submitted within a time limit to be fixed by the President, so that the other judges may take cognizance thereof prior to notification of the judgment.

Article 56. Judgment on Reparations

1. When no specific ruling on reparations has been made in the judgment on the merits, the Court shall set the time and determine the procedure for the deferred decision thereon.

2. If the Court is informed that the injured party and the party adjudged to be responsible have reached an agreement in regard to the execution of the judgment on the merits, it shall verify the fairness of the agreement and rule accordingly.

Article 57. Delivery and Communication of the Judgment

1. When a case is ready for a judgment, the Court shall meet in private. A preliminary vote shall be taken, the wording of the judgment approved, and a date fixed for the public hearing at which the parties shall be so notified.

2. The texts, legal arguments and votes shall all remain secret until the parties have been notified of the judgments.

3. Judgments shall be signed by all the judges who participated in the voting and by the Secretary. However, a judgment signed by only a majority of the judges shall be valid.

4. Dissenting or concurring opinions shall be signed by the judges submitting them and by the Secretary.

5. The judgments shall conclude with an order, signed by the President and the Secretary and sealed by the latter, providing for the communication and execution of the judgment.

6. The originals of the judgments shall be deposited in the archives of the Court. The Secretary shall dispatch certified copies to the States parties to the case, the Commission, the President of the Permanent Council, the Secretary General, the representatives of the victims or their next of kin, and any interested persons who request them.

7. The Secretary shall transmit the judgment to all the States Parties.

Article 58. Request for Interpretation

1. The request for interpretation, referred to in Article 67 of the Convention, may be made in connection with judgments on the merits or on reparations and shall be filed with the Secretariat. It shall state with precision the issues relating to the meaning or scope of the judgment of which the interpretation is requested.

2. The Secretary shall transmit the request for interpretation to the States that are parties to the case and to the Commission, as appropriate, and shall invite them to submit any written comments they deem relevant, within a time limit established by the President.

3. When considering a request for interpretation, the Court shall be composed, whenever possible of the same judges who delivered the judgment of which the interpretation is being sought. However, in the event of death, resignation or disqualification, the judge in question shall be replaced pursuant to Article 16 of these Rules.

4. A request for interpretation shall not suspend the effect of the judgment.

5. The Court shall determine the procedure to be followed and shall render its decision in the form of a judgment.

TITLE III. ADVISORY OPINIONS

Article 59. Interpretation of the Convention

1. Requests for an advisory opinion under Article 64(1) of the Convention shall state with precision the specific questions on which the opinion of the Court is being sought.

2. Requests for an advisory opinion submitted by a Member State or by the Commission shall, in addition, identify the provisions to be interpreted, the considerations giving rise to the request, and the names and addresses of the Agent or the Delegates.

3. If the advisory opinion is sought by an OAS organ other than the Commission, the request shall also specify further to the information listed in the preceding paragraph, how it relates to the sphere of competence of the organ in question.

Article 60. Interpretation of Other Treaties

1. If the interpretation requested refers to other treaties for the protection of human rights in the American states, as provided for in Article 64(1) of the Convention, the request shall indicate the name of, and parties to, the treaty, the specific questions on which the opinion of the Court is being sought, and the considerations giving rise to the request.

2. If the request is submitted by one of the organs of the OAS, it shall also indicate how the subject of the request falls within the sphere of competence of the organ in question.

Article 61. Interpretation of Domestic Laws

1. A request for an advisory opinion presented pursuant to Article 64(2) of the Convention shall indicate the following:
   a. the provisions of domestic law and of the Convention or of other treaties concerning the protection of human rights to which the request relates;
   b. the specific questions on which the opinion of the Court is being sought;
   c. the name and address of the applicant's Agent.

2. Copies of the domestic laws referred to in the request shall accompany the application.

Article 62. Procedure

1. On receipt of a request for an advisory opinion, the Secretary shall transmit copies thereof to all the Member States, the Commission, the Secretary General, and the OAS organs within whose spheres of competence the subject of the request falls, as appropriate.

2. The President shall establish the time limits for the filing of written comments by the interested parties.

3. The President may invite or authorize any interested party to submit a written opinion on the issues covered by the request. If the request is governed by Article 64(2) of the Convention, he may do so after prior consultation with the Agent.

4. At the conclusion of the written proceedings, the Court shall decide whether there should be oral proceedings and shall fix the date for such a hearing, unless it delegates the latter task to the President. Prior consultation with the Agent is required in cases governed by Article 64(2) of the Convention.

Article 63. Application by Analogy

The Court shall apply the provisions of Title II of these Rules to advisory proceedings, to the extent that it deems them to be compatible.

Article 64. Delivery and Content of Advisory Opinions

1. The delivery of advisory opinions shall be governed by Article 57 of these Rules.
2. Advisory opinions shall contain:
   a. the name of the President, the judges who rendered the opinion, and the Secretary and Deputy Secretary;
   b. the issues presented to the Court;
   c. a description of the various steps in the proceedings;
   d. the legal arguments;
   e. the opinion of the Court;
   f. a statement indicating which text is authentic.
3. Any judge who has taken part in the delivery of an advisory opinion is entitled to append a dissenting or concurring opinion to the opinion of the Court. These opinions shall be submitted within a time limit to be fixed by the President, so that the other judges can take cognizance thereof before the advisory opinion is rendered. They shall be published in accordance with Article 30(1)(a) of these Rules.
4. Advisory opinions may be delivered in public.

TITLE IV. FINAL AND TRANSITORY PROVISIONS

Article 65. Amendments to the Rules of Procedure

These Rules of Procedure may be amended by the decision of an absolute majority of the titular judges of the Court. Upon their entry into force, they shall abrogate the previous Rules of Procedure.

Article 66. Entry into Force

These Rules of Procedure, the Spanish and English versions of which are equally authentic, shall enter into force on January 1, 1997.

Appendix VIII

Signed at San José, Costa Rica, 22 November 1969, at the
Inter-American Specialized Conference on Human Rights

ENTRY INTO FORCE: 18 July 1978, in accordance with Article 74.2 of the Con-
vention
DEPOSITORY: OAS General Secretariat (Original instrument and
ratifications)
TEXT: *OAS. Treaty Series*, Nº 36.
UN REGISTRATION: 27 August 1979, Nº 17955

Country	Date of Signature	Date of Ratification	Date of Acceptance of the Jurisdiction of the Court
Argentina	2/2/84	5/9/84*	5/9/84*
Barbados	20/6/78	27/11/82*	
Bolivia	22/11/69	19/7/79	27/7/83*
Brazil	22/11/69	25/9/92*	
Chile	22/11/69	21/8/90*	21/8/90
Colombia	22/11/69	31/7/73	21/6/85*
Costa Rica	22/11/69	8/4/70	2/7/80
Dominica	22/11/69	3/6/93*	
Dominican Republic	7/9/77*	19/4/78	
Ecuador	22/11/69	28/12/77	24/7/84
El Salvador	22/11/69	23/6/78*	6/6/95*
Grenada	14/7/78	18/7/78	
Guatemala	22/11/69	25/5/78*	9/3/87*
Haiti	22/11/69	27/9/77	
Honduras	22/11/69	8/9/77	9/9/81*
Jamaica	16/9/77	7/8/78	
Mexico	22/11/69	3/4/82*	
Nicaragua	22/11/69	25/9/79	12/2/91*
Panama	22/11/69	22/6/78	3/5/90
Paraguay	22/11/69	24/8/89	11/3/93*
Peru	27/7/77	28/7/78	21/1/81

Suriname	22/11/69	12/11/87	12/11/87*
Trinidad and			
Tobago	22/11/69	28/5/91*	28/5/91
United States	1/6/77		
Uruguay	22/11/69*	19/4/85*	19/4/85*
Venezuela	22/11/69	9/8/77*	24/6/81

*indicates a reservation or statement at this date. Text of these is given below.

RESERVATIONS OR DECLARATIONS AT TIME OF SIGNATURE OR RATIFICATION

Uruguay

(Reservation made at the time of signature)

Article 80.2 of the Constitution of Uruguay provides that a person's citizenship is suspended if the person is 'under indictment on a criminal charge which may result in a penitentiary sentence'. Such a restriction on the exercise of the rights recognized in Article 23 of the Convention is not envisaged among the circumstances provided for in Article 23, paragraph 2, for which reason the Delegation of Uruguay expresses a reservation on this matter.

Dominican Republic

(Declaration made at the time of signature)

The Dominican Republic, upon signing the American Convention on Human Rights, aspires that the principle pertaining to the abolition of the death penalty shall become purely and simply that, with general application throughout the states of the American region, and likewise maintains the observations and comments made on the aforementioned Draft Convention which it distributed to the delegations to the Council of the Organization of American States on 20 June 1969.

Venezuela

(Reservation and declaration made at the time of ratification)

Article 60, paragraph 5 of the Constitution of the Republic of Venezuela establishes that: No one may be convicted in a criminal trial without first having been personally notified of the charges and heard in the manner prescribed by law. Persons accused of an offense against the *res publica* may be tried *in absentia*, with the guarantees and in the manner prescribed by law. Such a possibility is not provided for in Article 8, paragraph 1 of the Convention, and for this reason Venezuela formulates the corresponding reservations, and,

   DECLARES: That, in accordance with the provisions of Article 45, paragraph I of the Convention, the Government of the Republic of Venezuela recognizes the competence of the Inter-American Commission on Human Rights to receive and examine communications in which a State Party alleges that another State Party has committed violations of human rights set forth in that Convention, in the terms stipulated in paragraph 2 of that article. This recognition of competence is made for an indefinite period of time.

The instrument of ratification was received at the General Secretariat of the OAS on 9 August 1977 with a reservation and a declaration. The notification procedure of the reservation was taken in conformity with the Vienna Convention on the Law of Treaties signed on 23 May 1969.

Guatemala

(Reservation made at the time of ratification)

The Government of the Republic of Guatemala ratifies the American Convention on Human Rights, signed at San José, Costa Rica, on 22 November 1969, with a reservation as to Article 4, paragraph 4 thereof, since the Constitution of the Republic of Guatemala, in its Article 54, only excludes the application of the death penalty to political crimes, but not to common crimes related to political crimes.

The instrument of ratification was received at the General Secretariat of the OAS on 25 May 1978 with a reservation. The notification procedure of the reservation was taken in conformity with the Vienna Convention on the Law of Treaties signed on 23 May 1969.

Withdrawal of Guatemala's reservations

The Government of Guatemala, by Government Agreement No 281-86, dated 20 May 1986, has withdrawn the above-mentioned reservation, which was included in its instrument of ratification dated 27 April 1978, considering that it is no longer supported by the Constitution in the light of the new legal system in force. The withdrawal of the reservation will become effective as of 12 August 1986, in conformity with Article 22 of the Vienna Convention on the Law of Treaties of 1969, in application of Article 75 of the American Convention on Human Rights.

El Salvador

(Declaration and reservations made at the time of ratification)

The present Convention is ratified, its provisions being interpreted to mean that the Inter-American Court of Human Rights shall have jurisdiction to hear any case that can be submitted to it, either by the Inter-American Commission on Human Rights or by any state party, provided that the State of El Salvador, as a party to the case, recognizes or has recognized such jurisdiction, by any of the means and under the arrangements indicated in the Convention.

The American Convention on Human Rights, known as the 'Pact of San José, Costa Rica', signed at San José, Costa Rica, on 22 November 1969, composed of a preamble and eighty-two articles, approved by the Executive Branch in the Field of Foreign Affairs by Agreement 405, dated June 14 of the current year, is hereby ratified, with the reservation that such ratification is understood without prejudice to those provisions of the Convention that might be in conflict with express precepts of the Political Constitution of the Republic.

The instrument of ratification was received at the General Secretariat of the

OAS on 23 June 1978 with a reservation and a declaration. The notification procedure of the reservation was taken in conformity with the Vienna Convention on the Law of Treaties signed on 23 May 1969.

Jamaica

Recognition of Competence

The instrument of ratification, dated 19 July 1978, states, in conformity with Article 45, paragraph 1 of the Convention, that the Government of Jamaica recognizes the competence of the Inter-American Commission on Human Rights to receive and examine communications in which a State Party alleges that another State Party has committed a violation of a human right set forth in this Convention.

Mexico

(Declarations and reservation made at the time of ratification)

The instrument of accession was received at the General Secretariat of the OAS on 24 March 1981, with two interpretative declarations and one reservation. Notification of the reservation submitted was given in conformity with the provisions of the Vienna Convention on the Law of Treaties, signed on 23 May 1969. The twelve-month period from the notification of said reservation expired on 2 April 1982, without any objection being raised to the reservation.

The texts of the interpretative declarations and the reservation are the following:

Interpretative Declarations

With respect to Article 4, paragraph 1, the Government of Mexico considers that the expression 'in general' does not constitute an obligation to adopt, or keep in force, legislation to protect life 'from the moment of conception', since this matter falls within the domain reserved to the States.

Furthermore, the Government of Mexico believes that the limitation established by the Mexican Constitution to the effect that all public acts of religious worship must be performed inside places of public worship, conforms to the limitations set forth in Article 12, paragraph 3.

Reservation

The Government of Mexico makes express reservation to Article 23, paragraph 2, since the Mexican Constitution provides, in Article 130, that ministers of denominations shall not have an active or passive vote, nor the right to associate for political purposes.

Barbados

(Reservations made at the time of ratification)

The instrument of ratification was received at the General Secretariat of the OAS on 5 November 1981, with reservations. Notification of the reservations submitted was given in conformity with the Vienna Convention on the Law of Treaties, signed on 23 May 1969. The twelve-month period from the notification of said reservations expired on 26 November 1982, without any objection being raised to the reservations.

The text of the reservations with respect to Articles 4(4), 4(5) and 8(2)(e), is the following:

In respect of 4(4) the Criminal Code of Barbados provides for death by hanging as a penalty for murder and treason. The Government is at present reviewing the whole matter of the death penalty which is only rarely inflicted but wishes to enter a reservation on this point in as much as treason in certain circumstances might be regarded as a political offence and falling within the terms of section 4(4).

In respect of 4(5) while the youth or old age of an offender may be matters which the Privy Council, the highest Court of Appeal, might take into account in considering whether the sentence of death should be carried out, persons of 16 years and over, or over 70 years of age, may be executed under Barbadian law.

In respect of 8(2)(e) Barbadian law does not provide, as a minimum guarantee in criminal proceeding, any inalienable right to be assisted by counsel provided by the state. Legal aid is provided for certain scheduled offences such as homicide and rape.

Argentina

(Reservation and interpretative declarations made at the time of ratification)

The instrument of ratification was received at the General Secretariat of the OAS on 5 September 1984 with a reservation and interpretative declarations. The notification procedure of the reservation was taken in conformity with the Vienna Convention on the Law of Treaties signed on 23 May 1969.

The texts of the above-mentioned reservation and of the interpretative declarations are the following:

Reservation

Article 21 is subject to the following reservation: 'The Argentine Government establishes that questions relating to the Government's economic policy shall not be subject to review by an international tribunal. Neither shall it consider reviewable anything the national courts may determine to be matters of "public utility" and "social interest", nor anything they may understand to be "fair compensation".'

Interpretative Statements

Article 5, paragraph 3, shall be interpreted to mean that a punishment shall not be applied to any person other than the criminal, that is, that there shall be no vicarious criminal punishment.

Article 7, paragraph 7, shall be interpreted to mean that the prohibition against 'detention for debt' does not involve prohibiting the state from basing punishment on default of certain debts, when the punishment is not imposed for default itself but rather for a prior independent, illegal, punishable act.

Article 10 shall be interpreted to mean that the 'miscarriage of justice' has been established by a national court.

Uruguay

(Reservation made at the time of ratification)

With the reservation made at the time of signature. Notification of this reservation was given in conformity with the Vienna Convention on the Law of Treaties, signed on 23 May 1969.

Chile

(Reservations made at the time of ratification)

a. The Government of Chile declares that it recognizes, for an indefinite period of time and on the condition of reciprocity, the competence of the Inter-American Commission on Human Rights to receive and examine communications in which a State Party alleges that another State Party has committed a violation of the human rights established in the American Convention on Human Rights, as provided for in Article 45 of the Convention.

b. The Government of Chile declares that it recognizes as legally binding the obligatory jurisdiction of the Inter-American Court of Human Rights in cases dealing with the interpretation and application of this Convention pursuant to Article 62.

On formulating said declarations, the Government of Chile notes that the recognition of jurisdiction it has accepted refers to situations occurring subsequent to the date of deposit of this instrument of ratification, or, in any event, to circumstances which arose after March 11, 1990. Likewise the Government of Chile, on accepting the competence of the Inter-American Commission and the Inter-American Court of Human Rights declares that these organs, in applying Article 21(2) of the Convention, shall refrain from judgments concerning the concept of public use or social interest cited in cases involving the expropriation of an individual's property.

Trinidad and Tobago

(Reservations made at the time of accession)

1. As regards Article 4(5) of the Convention the Government of The Republic of Trinidad and Tobago makes reservation in that under the laws of Trinidad and Tobago there is no prohibition against the carrying out a sentence of death on a person over seventy (70) years of age.

2. As regards Article 62 of the Convention, the Government of the Republic of Trinidad and Tobago recognizes the compulsory jurisdiction of the Inter-American Court of Human Rights as stated in said article only to such extent that recognition is consistent with the relevant sections of the Constitution of the Republic of Trinidad and Tobago; and provided that any judgment of the Court does not infringe, create or abolish any existing rights or duties of any private citizen.

Brazil

(Interpretative declaration made at the time of adhesion)

The Government of Brazil understands that Articles 43 and 48, (d) do not include the automatic right of on site visits and inspections by the Inter-American Commission on Human Rights, which will depend on the express consent of the State.

Dominica

(Reservations at the time of ratification)

1) Article 5. This should not be read as prohibiting corporal punishment administered in accordance with the Corporal Punishment Act of Dominica or the Juvenile Offenders Punishment Act.

2) Article 4.4. Reservation is made in respect of the words 'or related common crimes'.

3) Article 8.21 (e). This Article shall not apply in respect of Dominica.

4) Article 21.2. This must be interpreted in the light of the provisions of the Constitution of Dominica and is not to be deemed to extend or limit the rights declared in the Constitution.

5) Article 27.1. This must also be read in the light of our Constitution and is not to be deemed to extend or limit the rights declared by the Constitution.

6) Article 62. The Commonwealth of Dominica does not recognize the jurisdiction of the Court.

THE FOLLOWING COUNTRIES MADE STATEMENTS AT THE TIME OF ACCEPTING
THE JURISDICTION OF THE COURT

Honduras

Recognition of Competence:

On 9 September 1981, presented at the General Secretariat of the OAS, an instrument recognizing the jurisdiction of the Inter-American Court of Human Rights in accordance with Article 62 of the Convention.

Bolivia

Recognition of Competence

On July 27, 1993 the instrument of recognition of the competence of the Inter-American Court of Human Rights was deposited with the OAS General Secretariat, in accordance with Article 62 of the American Convention on Human Rights, with the following declaration:

I. The constitutional Government of the Republic, in accordance with Article 59, paragraph 12 of the Political Constitution of the State, by law No. 1430 of February 11, provided for adoption and ratification of the American Convention on Human Rights 'Pact of San José de Costa Rica', signed in San José, Costa Rica, on November 22, 1969 and also provided for recognition of the competence of the Inter-American Court of Human Rights, in accordance with Articles 45 and 62 of the Convention.

II. In exercise of the powers conferred upon it by Article 96, paragraph 2 of the Political Constitution of the State, this Instrument of Ratification of the American Convention on Human Rights 'Pact of San José' is issued along with the recognition of the jurisdiction and competence of the Inter-American Court of Human Rights as unconditionally binding by law for an indefinite period, in accordance with Article 62 of the Convention.

Argentine

Recognition of Competence

In the instrument of ratification dated 14 August 1984 and deposited with the General Secretariat of the OAS on 5 September 1984, the Government of Argentina recognizes the competence of the Inter-American Commission on Human Rights and of the jurisdiction of the Inter-American Court of Human Rights. This recognition is for an indeterminate period and on condition of reciprocity on all cases related to the interpretation or application of the Convention cited, with the partial reservation and bearing in mind the interpretative statements contained in the Instrument of Ratification.

Uruguay

Recognition of Competence

In the instrument of ratification dated 26 March 1985 and deposited with the General Secretariat of the OAS on 19 April 1985, the Government of the Oriental Republic of Uruguay declares that it recognizes the competence of the Inter-American Commission on Human Rights for an indefinite period and of the Inter-American Court of Human Rights on all matters relating to the interpretation or application of this Convention, on the condition of reciprocity, in accordance with Articles 45.3 and 62.2 of the Convention.

Colombia

Recognition of Competence

On 21 June 1985 presented an instrument of acceptance by which recognizes the competence of the Inter-American Commission on Human Rights for an indefinite time, on the condition of strict reciprocity and nonretroactivity, for cases involving the interpretation or application of the Convention, and reserves the right to withdraw its recognition of competence should it deem this advisable. The same instrument recognizes the jurisdiction of the Inter-American Court of Human Rights, for an indefinite time, on the condition of reciprocity and nonretroactivity, for cases involving the interpretation or application of the Convention, and reserves the right to withdraw its recognition of competence should it deem this advisable.

Guatemala

Recognition of Competence

On 9 March 1987, presented at the General Secretariat of the OAS, the Government Agreement N° 123-87, dated 20 February 1987, of the Republic of Guatemala, by which it recognizes the jurisdiction of the Inter-American Court of Human Rights, in the following terms:

'(Article 1) To declare that it recognizes as binding, *ipso facto,* and not requiring special agreement, the jurisdiction of the Inter-American Court of Human Rights on all matters relating to the interpretation or application of the American Convention on Human Rights.'

'(Article 2) To accept the competence of the Inter-American Court of Human Rights for an indefinite period of time, such competence being general in nature, under terms of reciprocity and with the reservation that cases in which the competence of the Court is recognized are exclusively those that shall have taken place after the date that this declaration is presented to the Secretary General of the Organization of American States.'

Suriname

Recognition of Competence

On 12 November 1987, presented at the General Secretariat of the OAS, an instrument recognizing the jurisdiction of the Inter-American Court of Human Rights in accordance with Article 62 of the Convention.

Nicaragua

Recognition of Competence

On February 12, 1991, presented at the General Secretariat of the OAS, an instrument dated January 15, 1991, by which the Government of Nicaragua declares:

I. The Government of Nicaragua recognizes as binding as of right with no special convention the competence of the Inter-American Court of Human Rights in all cases involving interpretation and application of the Inter-American Convention on Human Rights, 'Pact of San José, Costa Rica', by virtue of Article 62(1) thereof.

II. The foregoing notwithstanding, the Government of Nicaragua states for the record that its acceptance of the competence of the Inter-American Court of Human Rights is given for an indefinite period, is general in character and grounded in reciprocity, and is subject to the reservation that this recognition of competence applies only to cases arising solely out of events subsequent to, and out of acts which began to be committed after, the date of deposit of this declaration with the Secretary General of the Organization of American States.

Paraguay

Recognition of Competence

On March 11, 1993, Paraguay presented to the General Secretariat of the OAS an instrument recognizing the jurisdiction of the Inter-American Court of Human

Rights, 'for an indefinite period of time and which should be interpreted in accordance with the principles of International Law in the sense that this recognition refers expressly to acts that occurred after the deposit of this instrument and only for cases in which there exists reciprocity'.

El Salvador

Recognition of competence

I. The Government of El Salvador declares as binding, *ipso facto,* and not requiring special agreement, the jurisdiction of the Inter-American Court on Human Rights, pursuant to the provisions of Article 62 of the American Convention on Human Rights or 'Pact of San José'.

II. The Government of El Salvador, in recognizing that jurisdiction, notes that its acceptance applies to an undetermined period, under the condition of reciprocity and with the reservation that the cases for which the jurisdiction is recognized comprise solely and exclusively legal events or acts that are subsequent, or legal events or acts whose start of execution were subsequent, to the deposit of this Declaration of Acceptance, and reserves the right to nullify the jurisdiction at whatever moment it considers opportune.

III. The Government of El Salvador recognizes the jurisdiction of the Court insofar as this recognition is compatible with the provisions of the Constitution of the Republic of El Salvador.

ADDITIONAL PROTOCOL TO THE AMERICAN CONVENTION ON HUMAN RIGHTS IN THE AREA OF ECONOMIC, SOCIAL AND CULTURAL RIGHTS 'PROTOCOL OF SAN SALVADOR'

Signed at San Salvador, El Salvador on November 17, 1988, at the eighteenth regular session of the General Assembly

ENTRY INTO FORCE: When eleven States have deposit their respective instruments of ratification or accession. Not in force.

DEPOSITORY: OAS General Secretariat (Original instrument and ratifications).

TEXT: *OAS. Treaty Series*, No. 69.

SIGNATORY COUNTRIES		*DEPOSIT OF RATIFICATION*
Argentina	17 November 1988	
Brazil	8 August 1996	21 August 1996
Bolivia	17 November 1988	
Costa Rica	17 November 1988	
Dominican Republic	17 November 1988	
Ecuador	17 November 1988	25 March 1993
El Salvador	17 November 1988	6 June 1995

Guatemala	17 November 1988	
Haiti	17 November 1988	
Mexico	16 April 1996	16 April 1996
Nicaragua	17 November 1988	
Panama	17 November 1988	18 February 1993
Paraguay	26 August 1996	
Peru	17 November 1988	4 June 1995
Suriname	17 November 1988	10 July 1990
Uruguay	2 April 1996	2 April 1996
Venezuela	27 January 1989	

PROTOCOL TO THE
AMERICAN CONVENTION ON HUMAN RIGHTS
TO ABOLISH THE DEATH PENALTY

Approved at Asunción, Paraguay, on June 8, 1990, at the
twentieth regular session of the
General Assembly

ENTRY INTO FORCE: August 28, 1991
DEPOSITORY: OAS General Secretariat (Original instrument and
ratifications).
TEXT: *OAS, Treaty Series*, No. 73

SIGNATORY COUNTRIES		*DEPOSIT OF RATIFICATION*
Brazil	6 June 1994	13 August 1996
Costa Rica	28 August 1991	
Ecuador	27 August 1990	
Nicaragua	30 August 1990	
Panama	26 November 1990	28 August 1991
Uruguay	2 October 1990	4 April 1994
Venezuela	25 September 1990	6 October 1993

INTER-AMERICAN CONVENTION TO PREVENT AND PUNISH TORTURE

Signed at Cartagena de India, Colombia, 9 December 1985, at the 15th Regular Session of the OAS General Assembly

ENTRY INTO FORCE: 28 February 1987, in accordance with Article 22 of the Convention

DEPOSITORY: OAS General Secretariat (Original instrument and ratifications).

TEXT: *OAS, Treaty Series*, No. 67

SIGNATORY COUNTRIES	RATIFICATIONS
Argentina	31 March 1989
Bolivia	
Brazil	20 July 1989
Chile	30 September 1988
Colombia	
Costa Rica	
Dominican Rep	29 January 1987
Ecuador	
El Salvador	9 December 1994
Guatemala	29 January 1987
Haiti	
Honduras	
Mexico	22 June 1987
Nicaragua	
Panama	28 August 1991
Paraguay	9 March 1990
Peru	28 March 1991
Suriname	12 November 1987
Uruguay	11 November 1992
Venezuela	26 August 1991

INTER-AMERICAN CONVENTION ON THE FORCED DISAPPEARANCE OF PERSONS

Approved at Belem do Para, Brazil, on June 9, 1994, by the 24th Regular Session
of the General Assembly

ENTRY INTO FORCE: 29 March 1996
DEPOSITORY: OAS General Secretariat (Original instrument and
                     ratifications).
TEXT: 3 IHRR 226 (1996)

SIGNATORY COUNTRIES	*RATIFICATIONS*
Argentina	28 February 1996
Bolivia	
Brazil	
Chile	
Colombia	
Costa Rica	2 June 1996
Guatemala	
Honduras	
Nicaragua	
Panama	28 February 1996
Paraguay	
Uruguay	2 April 1996
Venezuela	

INTER-AMERICAN CONVENTION ON THE PREVENTION, PUNISHMENT AND ERADICATION OF VIOLENCE AGAINST WOMEN

Adopted by acclamation at Belem do Para, Brazil, on 9 June 1994 by the 24th
Regular ession of the General Assembly

ENTRY INTO FORCE: 5 March 1995
DEPOSITORY: OAS General Secretariat (Original instrument and
                     ratifications).
TEXT: 3 IHRR 232 (1996)

SIGNATORY COUNTRIES	*RATIFICATIONS*
Argentina	
Bahamas	16 May 1995
Barbados	16 May 1995
Bolivia	5 December 1994

Brazil	27 November 1995
Chile	
Costa Rica	12 July 1995
Dominica	6 June 1995
Dominican Rep	7 March 1996
Ecuador	15 September 1995
El Salvador	26 January 1996
Guatemala	4 April 1995
Guyana	28 February 1996
Honduras	12 July 1995
Mexico	
Nicaragua	12 December 1995
Panama	12 July 1995
Paraguay	18 October 1995
Peru	4 June 1996
St Kitts and Nevis	12 June 1995
St Lucia	4 April 1995
St Vincent	31 May 1996
Trinidad and Tobago	8 May 1996
Uruguay	2 April 1996
Venezuela	3 February 1995

Appendix IX

ANNUAL REPORTS OF THE INTER-AMERICAN COMMISSION ON HUMAN RIGHTS

Annual Report of 1970, OEA/Ser.L/V/25, doc.9, rev. (1971).
—— *Annual Report of 1971,* OEA/Ser.L/V/27, doc.11, rev. (1972).
—— *Annual Report of 1972,* OEA/Ser.L/V/29, doc.41, rev.2 (1973).
—— *Annual Report of 1973,* OEA/Ser.L/V/32, doc.3, rev.2 (1974).
—— *Annual Report of 1974,* OEA/Ser.L/V/34, doc.31, rev.1 (1974).
—— *Annual Report of 1975,* OEA/Ser.L/V/37, doc.20, rev.1 (1976).
—— *Annual Report of 1976,* OEA/Ser.L/V/40, doc.5, corr.1 (1977).
—— *Annual Report of 1977,* OEA/Ser.L/V/43, doc.21, rev. 1 (1978) .
—— *Annual Report of 1978,* OEA/Ser.L/V/47, doc.13, rev.1 (1979).
—— *Annual Report of 1979-1980,* OEA/Ser.L/V/50, doc.13, rev.1 (1980).
—— *Annual Report of 1980-1981,* OEA/Ser.L/V/54, doc.9, rev.1 (1981).
—— *Annual Report of 1981-1982,* OEA/Ser.L/V/57, doc.6, rev.1 (1982).
—— *Annual Report of 1982-1983,* OEA/Ser.L/V/61, doc.22, rev.l (1983).
—— *Annual Report of 1983-1984,* OEA/Ser.L/V/63, doc.l0 (1984).
—— *Annual Report of 1984-1985,* OEA/Ser.L/V/66, doc.10, rev.1 (1985).
—— *Annual Report of 1985-1986,* OEA/Ser.L/V/68, doc.8, rev.1 (1986).
—— *Annual Report of 1986-1987,* OEA/Ser.L/V/II.71, doc.9, rev.1 (1987).
—— *Annual Report of 1987-1988,* OEA/Ser.L/V/II.74, doc.10, rev.2 (1988).
—— *Annual Report of 1988-1989,* OEA/Ser.L/V/II.76, doc.10 (1989).
—— *Annual Report of 1989-1990,* OEA/Ser.L/V/II.77, doc.7, rev.1, (1990).
—— *Annual Report of 1990-1991,* OEA/Ser.L/V/II.79, doc.12, rev.1 (1991).
—— *Annual Report of 1991,* OEA/Ser.L/V/II.81, doc.6, rev.1 (1992).
—— *Annual Report of 1992-1993,* OEA/Ser.L/V/II.83 (1993).
—— *Annual Report of 1994,* OEA/Ser.L/V/II.85, (1995).
—— *Annual Report of 1995,* OEA/Ser.L/V/II.91, doc. 7, rev. (1996).
—— *Annual Report of 1996,* OEA/Ser.L/V/II.95, doc. 7, rev. (1997).

DECISIONS ISSUED BY THE INTER-AMERICAN COURT OF HUMAN RIGHTS

1. Contentious Cases

In the Matter of Viviana Gallardo et al (Costa Rica)

I/A Court H.R., *In the Matter of Viviana Gallardo et al,* No. G 101/81 Series A&B.
2 *HRLJ* 328.

Velásquez Rodríguez Case (Honduras)

I/A Court of H.R., *Velásquez Rodríguez, Preliminary Objections,* Judgment of 26 June 1987, Series C No.l.

I/A Court H.R., *Velásquez Rodríguez,* Judgment of 29 July 1988, Series C No.4, 9 *HRLJ* 212.

I/A Court H.R., *Three Cases v. Honduras: Velásquez Rodríguez, Fairén Garbi y Solís Corrales, Godinez Cruz,* Order of 15 January 1988, 9 *HRLJ* 104.

I/A Court H.R., *Velásquez Rodríguez, Compensatory Damages,* Judgment of 21 July 1989, Series C No.7, 11 *HRLJ* 127.

I/A Court H.R., *Velásquez Rodríguez, Interpretation of the Judgment of Compensatory Damages.* Judgment of 17 August 1990, Series C No.9, 12 *HRLJ* 14.

I/A Court H.R., *Velásquez Rodríguez,* Order of the Court of 10 September 1996.

Fairén Garbi and Solís Corrales Case (Honduras)

I/A Court of H.R. *Fairén Garbi and Solís Corrales. Preliminary Objections* Judgment of 26 June 1987, Series C No.2.

I/A Court of H.R., *Fairén Garbi and Solís Corrales.* Judgment of 15 March 1989, Series C No.6.

Godínez Cruz Case (Honduras)

I/A Court H.R., *Godínez Cruz, Preliminary Objections,* Judgment of 26 June 1987, Series C No.3.

I/A Court H.R., *Godínez Cruz,* Judgment of 20 January 1989, Series C No.5.

I/A Court H.R., *Godínez Cruz, Compensatory Damages*, Judgment of 21 July 1989, Series C No.8.

I/A Court H.R., *Godínez Cruz, Interpretation of the Judgment of Compensatory Damages*, Judgment of 17 August 1990, Series C No.10.

I/A Court H.R., *Godínez Cruz*, Order of 10 September 1996.

Aloeboetoe et al. Case (Suriname)

I/A Court H.R., *Aloeboetoe et al.,* Judgment of 4 December 1991, Series C No. 11, 13 *HRLJ* 140, 1 IHRR Vol 2 208.

I/A Court H.R., *Aloeboetoe et al,* Order of 7 July 1992.

I/A Court H.R., *Aloeboetoe et al, Reparations (Article 63.1 of the American Convention* on Human Rights) Judgment of 10 September 1993, Series C No. 15, 14 *HRLJ* 413.

Gangaram Panday Case (Suriname)

I/A Court H.R., *Gangaram Panday, Preliminary Objections,* Judgment of 4 July 1991, Series C No.12.

I/A Court H.R., *Gangaram Panday,* Order of the Court of 7 July 1992.

I/A Court H.R., *Gangaram Panday,* Judgment of 21 January 1994, Series C No.16, 15 *HRLJ* 168, 2 IHRR 360.

Neira Alegría et al. Case (Peru)

I/A Court H.R., *Neira Alegría et al. Preliminary Objections,* Judgment of 11 December 1991, Series C No. 13, 13 *HRLJ* 146.

I/A Court H.R., *Neira Alegría et al.,* Order of 29 June 1992, 13 *HRLJ* 407.

I/A Court H.R., *Neira Alegría et al.,* Order of 30 June 1992.

I/A Court H.R., *Neira Alegría et al.,* Order of 3 July 1992, 14 *HRLJ* 19.

I/A Court H.R., *Neira Alegría et al.,* Judgment of 19 January 1995, Series C No. 20 16 *HRLJ* 403, 3 IHRR 362.

I/A Court H.R., *Neira Alegría et al., Reparations,* Judgment of 19 September 1996.

Cayara Case (Peru)

I/A Court H.R., *Cayara Case, Preliminary Objections,* Judgment of 3 February 1993. Series C No.14, 14 *HRLJ* 159, 1–1 IHRR 175.

Caballero Delgado and Santana Case (Colombia)

I/A Court H.R., *Caballero Delgado and Santana Case, Preliminary Objections,* Judgment of 21 January 1994, Series C No.17, 15 *HRLJ* 176, 2 IHRR 393.

I/A Court H.R., *Caballero Delgado and Santana Case, Provisional Measures Requested by the Inter-American Commission on Human Rights in the Matter of Colombia,* Decision of 7 December 1994.

I/A Court H.R., *Caballero Delgado and Santana Case, Merits,* Judgment of 8 December 1995, Series C No.21, 17 *HRLJ* 24, 3 IHRR 548.

Jean Paul Genie Lacayo Case (Nicaragua)

I/A Court H.R., *Jean Paul Genie Lacayo Case, Preliminary Objections,* Judgment of 27 January 1995, Series C No. 14, 16, *HRLJ* 414, 3 IHRR 384.

I/A Court H.R., *Jean Paul Genie Lacayo Case,* Order of 8 July 1996, Annual Report 1997, 157.

'El Amparo' Case (Venezuela)

I/A Court H.R., *'El Amparo' Case,* Judgment of 18 January 1995, Series C No.19, 16 *HRLJ* 149, 3 IHRR 349.

I/A Court H.R., *'El Amparo' Case,* Order of 17 May 1995, 3 IHRR 396.

I/A Court H.R., *'El Amparo' Case,* Order of 21 September 1995.

I/A Court H.R., *'El Amparo' Case, Reparations,* Judgment of 14 September 1996, Annual Report 1997, 159.

Maqueda Case (Argentina)

I/A Court H.R., *Maqueda Case,* Resolution of 18 January 1995, Series C No.18, 16 *HRLJ* 151, 3 IHRR 355.

Castillo Páez Case (Peru)

I/A Court H.R., *Castillo Páez Case, Preliminary Objections,* Judgment of 25 January 1996.

I/A Court H.R., *Castillo Páez Case*, Decision of 10 September 1996, Annual Report 1997, 217.

Loayza Tamayo Case (Peru)

I/A Court H.R., *Loayza Tamayo Case, Preliminary Objections,* Judgment of 31 January 1996, Annual Report 1997, 59.

I/A Court H.R., *Loayza Tamayo ,* Order of 27 June 1996, Annual Report 1997, 111.

I/A Court H.R. *Loayza Tamayo, Provisional Measures in the Matter of Peru,* Order of 2 July 1996, Annual Report 1997, 119.

I/A Court H.R., *Loayza Tamayo, Provisional Measures in the Matter of Peru,* Order of 13 September 1996.

Paniagua Morales et al. (Guatemala)

I/A Court H.R., *Paniagua Morales et al.,* Order of 11 September 1995, 3 IHRR 544.

I/A Court H.R., *Paniagua Morales et al., Preliminary Objections,* Judgment of 25 January 1996, Annual Report 1997, 29.

Garrido and Baigorria Case (Argentina)

I/A Court H.R., *Garrido and Baigorria Case, Merits,* Judgment of 2 February 1996, Annual Report 1997, 75.

Blake Case (Guatemala)

I/A Court H.R., *Blake Case,* Order of 22 September 1995, 3 IHRR 539.

I/A Court H.R., *Blake Case, Preliminary Objections,* Judgment of 2 July 1996, Annual Report 1997, 97.

Suárez Rosero Case (Ecuador)

I/A Court H.R., *Suárez Rosero Case, Provisional Measures in the Matter of Ecuador,* Order of 28 June 1996, Annual Report 1997, 151.

2. Provisional Measures

I/A Court H.R., *Bustíos and Rojas Case, Provisional Measures Requested by the Inter-American Commission on Human Rights Regarding Peru,* Resolution of 8 August 1990, 11 *HRLJ* 257.

I/A Court H.R., *Chunimá Case, Provisional Measures Requested by the Inter-American Commission on Human Rights Regarding, Guatemala,* Resolution of 15 July 1991.

I/A Court H.R., *Carlos Chipoco Case, Provisional Measures Requested by the Inter-American Commission on Human Rights Regarding Peru,* Decision of 27 January 1993.

I/A Court *H.R., Peruvian Prisons Case, Provisional Measures Requested by the Inter-American Commission on Human Rights Regarding Peru,* Decision of 27 January 1993.

I/A Court H.R., *Reggiardo-Tolosa, Provisional Measures Requested by the Inter-*

American Commission on Human Rights in the Matter of the Republic of Argentina, Resolution of 19 January 1994, 2 IHRR 411.

I/A Court H.R., *Colotenango, Provisional Measures Requested by the Inter-American Commission on Human Rights in the Matter of Guatemala,* Resolution of 22 June 1994, 2 IHRR 414.

I/A Court H.R., *Colotenango, Provisional Measures Requested by the Inter-American Commission on Human Rights in the Matter of Guatemala,* Resolution of 1 December 1994, 2 IHRR 421.

I/A Court H.R., *Colotenango, Provisional Measures Requested by the Inter-American Commission on Human Rights in the Matter of Guatemala,* Order of 18 May 1995, 3 IHRR 405.

I/A Court H.R., *Carpio Nicolle Case, Provisional Measures Requested by the Inter-American Commission on Human Rights in the Matter of Guatemala,* Order of 19 September l995.

I/A Court H.R., *Colotenango Case, Provisional Measures Requested by the Inter-American Commission on Human Rights in the Matter of Guatemala;* Order of 17 February 1996, Annual Report 1997, 83.

I/A Court H.R., *Carpio Nicolle Case, Provisional Measures Requested by the Inter-American Commission on Human Rights in the Matter of Guatemala;* Order of 1 February, 1996, Annual Report 1997, 87.

I/A Court H.R., *Alemán Lacayo Case, Provisional Measures Requested by the Inter-American Commission on Human Rights in the Matter of Nicaragua,* Order of 2 February 1996.

I/A Court H.R., *Vogt Case, Provisional Measures Requested by the Inter-American Commission on Human Rights in the Matter of Guatemala,* Order of 27 June 1996, Annual Report 1997, 127.

I/A Court H.R., *Serech and Saquic Case, Provisional Measures Requested by the Inter-American Commission on Human Rights in the Matter of Guatemala,* Order of 28 June 1996, Annual Report 1997, 137.

I/A Court H.R., *Colotenango Case, Provisional Measures Requested by the Inter-American Commission on Human Rights in the Matter of Guatemala,* Order of 10 September 1996, Annual Report 1997, 197.

I/A Court H.R*., Carpio Nicolle Case, Provisional Measures Requested by the Inter-American Commission on Human Rights in the Matter of Guatemala*, Order of 10 September 1996, Annual Report 1997, 201.

3. Advisory Opinions

I/A Court H.R. *'Other Treaties' Subject to the Advisory Jurisdiction of the Court (Article 64 of the American Convention on Human Rights),* Advisory Opinion OC-1/82 of 24 September 1982, Series A & B No.1. 22 ILM 51, 3 *HRLJ* 140.

I/A Court H.R., *The Effect of Reservations on the Entry into Force of the American Convention on Human Rights (Arts 74 and 75),* Advisory Opinion OC-2/82 of 24 September 1982, Series A & B No.2, 22 ILM 37, 3 *HRLJ* 153.

I/A Court H.R., *Restrictions to the Death Penalty (Arts 4(2) and 4(4) American Convention Human Rights),* Advisory Opinion OC-3/83 of 8 September 1983, Series A & B No.3. 23 ILM 320, 4 *HRLJ* 339.

I/A Court H.R., *Proposed Amendments to the Naturalization Provisions of the Political Constitution of Costa Rica,* Advisory Opinion OC-4/84 of 19 January 1984, Series A & B No.4 5 *HRLJ* 161.

I/A Court H.R., *Compulsory Membership in an Association Prescribed by Law for the Practice of Journalism (Arts 13 and 29 American Convention on Human Rights),* Advisory Opinion OC-5/85 of 13 November 1985, Series A No.5 25 ILM 123, 7 *HRLJ* 74.

I/A Court H.R., *The Word "Laws" in Article 30 of the American Convention on Human Rights,* Advisory Opinion OC-6/86 of 9 May 1986, Series A No.6 7 *HRLJ* 231.

I/A Court H.R., *Enforceability of the Right to Reply or Correction (Arts 14(1), 1(1) and 2 of the American Convention on Human Rights),* Advisory Opinion OC-7/85 29 August 1986, Series A No. 7 7 *HRLJ* 238.

I/A Court *H.R., Habeas Corpus in Emergency Situations (Arts 27(2), 25(1) and 7(6) American Convention on Human Rights),* Advisory Opinion OC-8/87 of 30 January 1987, Series A No. 8 27 ILM 512, 9 *HRLJ* 94.

I/A Court H.R., *Judicial Guarantees in State of Emergency (Arts 27(2), 25 and 8 American Convention on Human Rights),* Advisory Opinion OC-9/87 of 6 October 1987, Series A No. 9 9 *HRLJ* 204.

I/A Court H.R., *Interpretation of the American Declaration on the Rights and Duties of man within the Framework of Article 64 of the American Convention on Human Rights,* Advisory Opinion OC-10/89 of 14 July 1989, Series A No.10 29 ILM 379, 11 *HRLJ* 118.

I/A Court H.R., *Exceptions to the Exhaustion of Domestic Remedies (Art. 46(1)(a) and 46(2)(b) American Convention on Human Rights),* Advisory Opinion OC-11/90 of 10 August 1990. Series A No. 11 12 *HRLJ* 20.

I/A Court H.R., *Compatibility of Draft Legislation with Article 8(2) of the American Convention on Human Rights,* Advisory Opinion OC-12/91 of 6 December 1991, Series A No.12 13 *HRLJ* 149.

I/A Court H.R., *Certain Attributes of the Inter-American Commission on Human Rights (Arts. 41, 42, 46, 47, 50 and 51 of the American Convention),* Advisory Opinion OC-13/93 of 16 July 1993, Series A No.13 14 *HRLJ* 252, 1–2 IHRR 197.

I/A Court H.R., *International Responsibility for the Promulgation and Enforcement of Laws in Violation of the Convention (Arts. 1 and 2 of the American Convention on Human Rights),* Advisory Opinion OC-14/94, of December 1994. Series A No.14 16 *HRLJ* 9, 2 IHRR 380.

Index